PENGUIN ACADEMICS

CIVILIZATION IN THE WEST

Combined Volume

MARK KISHLANSKY
Harvard University

PATRICK GEARY
University of California, Los Angeles

PATRICIA O'BRIEN
University of California, Los Angeles

Longman

Boston Columbus Indianapolis New York San Francisco Upper Saddle River
Amsterdam Cape Town Dubai London Madrid Milan Munich Paris Montreal Toronto
Delhi Mexico City Sao Paulo Sydney Hong Kong Seoul Singapore Taipei Tokyo

Editorial Director: Leah Jewell
Acquisitions Editor: Charles Cavaliere
Editorial Assistant: Lauren Aylward
Director of Marketing: Brandy Dawson
Senior Marketing Manager: Maureen Prado
   Roberts
Marketing Assistant: Marissa O'Brien
Senior Managing Editor: Ann Marie McCarthy
Project Manager: Debra Wechsler
Senior Operations Supervisor: Nick Sklitsis
Operations Specialist: Christina Amato
Senior Art Director: Jayne Conte
Art Director: Mirella Signoretto
Text and Cover Designer: Karen Salzbach
Manager, Rights and Permissions: Zina Arabia
Manager, Visual Research: Beth Brenzel

Manager, Cover Visual Research & Permissions:
   Karen Sanatar
Image Permission Coordinator: Nancy Seise
Cover Art: Paolo Uccello, "The Battle of San
   Romano", 1438-40. Tempera on wood panel,
   appx. 6' x 10'7" (1.83 x 3.23 m). National
   Gallery, London. Reproduced by courtesy of
   the Trustees. © National Gallery, London
Media Director: Brian Hyland
Lead Media Project Manager: Sarah Kinney
Supplements Editor: Emsal Hasan
Full-Service Project Management: Elm Street
   Publishing Services
Printer/Binder: R. R. Donnelley/Harrisonburg
Cover Printer: R. R. Donnelley/Harrisonburg
Text Font: 9.75/13 NexusMix-Regular

Credits and acknowledgments borrowed from other sources and reproduced, with permission, in this textbook appear beginning on page C-1.

Library of Congress Cataloging-in-Publication Data

Kishlansky, Mark A.
   Civilization in the West / Mark Kishlansky, Patrick Geary, Patricia O'Brien.
      p. cm.—(Penguin academics)
   Includes bibliographical references and index.
   ISBN 978-0-205-66473-3 (single volume edition)
      1. Civilization, Western—Textbooks.   2. Europe—Civilization—Textbooks.   I. Geary, Patrick J.
II. O'Brien, Patricia.   III. Title.
   CB245.K546 2010
   909'.09821—dc22

                                                                      2009034110

                                                        10 9 8 7 6 5 4 3 2 1

Longman
is an imprint of

www.pearsonhighered.com

Combined Volume
ISBN 13: 978-0-205-66473-3
ISBN 10:   0-205-66473-3

Examination Copy
ISBN 13: 978-0-205-67517-3
ISBN 10:   0-205-67517-4

brief contents

contents

maps

chronologies, genealogies, and figures

When we set out to write *Civilization in the West*, we tried to write, first of all, a book that students would *want* to read. Throughout many years of planning, writing, revising, rewriting, and numerous meetings together, this was our constant overriding concern. Would the text work across the variety of Western civilization courses, with the different levels and formats that make up this fundamental course? We also solicited the reactions of scores of reviewers to this single question: "Would students *want* to read these chapters?" Whenever we received a resounding "No!" we began again—not just rewriting, but rethinking how to present material that might be complex in argument or detail or that might simply seem too remote to engage the contemporary student. Though all three of us were putting in long hours in front of computers, we quickly learned that we were engaged in a teaching rather than a writing exercise. And though the work was demanding, it was not unrewarding. We enjoyed writing this book, and we wanted students to enjoy reading it. We have been gratified to learn that our book successfully accomplished our objectives. It stimulated student interest and motivated students to want to learn about European history. *Civilization in the West* was successful beyond our expectations.

The text was so well received, in fact, that we decided to publish this alternative, brief version: *Civilization in the West, Penguin Academics*. In an era of rapidly changing educational materials, alternative formats and models should be available. We believe that students and general readers alike will enjoy a conveniently sized book that offers them a coherent, well-told story. In this edition of the brief text, we have enlarged and added detail to many of the maps so that they are easier to see and use. We have also added a new feature, "Map Discovery," that teaches students how to think critically about maps.

Approach

The approach used in *Civilization in the West, Penguin Academics*, upholds and confirms a number of decisions made early in the writing of *Civilization in the West*. First, this brief, alternative version is, like the full-length text, a mainstream text in which most of our energies have been focused on developing a solid, readable narrative of Western civilization that integrates coverage of women and minorities into the discussion. We highlight personalities while identifying trends. We spotlight social history, both in sections of chapters and in separate chapters, while maintaining a firm grip on political developments.

Neither *Civilization in the West, Penguin Academics* nor *Civilization in the West* is meant to be an encyclopedia of Western civilization. Information is not included in a chapter unless it fits within the themes of that chapter. In both the full-length and brief versions of this text, we are committed to integrating the history of ordinary men and women into our narrative. We believe that isolated sections placed at the end of chapters that deal with the experiences of women or minority groups in a particular era profoundly distort historical experience. We call this technique "caboosing," and whenever we found ourselves segregating women or families or the masses, we stepped back and asked how we might recast our treatment of historical events to account for a diversity of actors. How did ordinary men, women, and children affect the course of world historical events? How did world historical events affect the fabric of daily life for men, women, and children from all walks of life? We also tried to rethink critical historical problems of civilization as gendered phenomena.

We take the same approach to the coverage of central and eastern Europe that we did to women and minorities. Even before the epochal events of the late 1980s and early 1990s that returned this region to the forefront of international attention, we realized that many textbooks treated the Slavic world as marginal to the history of Western civilization. Therefore, we worked to integrate more of the history of eastern Europe into our text than is found in most others and to do so in a way that presented these regions, their cultures, and their institutions as integral rather than peripheral to Western civilization.

Features

In *Civilization in the West, Penguin Academics*, we wanted to present features that would have the most immediate and positive impact on our readers and fulfill our goal of involving students in learning.

"Discovering Western Civilization Online" encourages students to explore the study of Western civilization beyond the confines of a textbook. These end-of-chapter Website resources link students to enriching documents, images, and cultural sites. They have been updated for this edition.

Changes in the New Edition

In *Civilization in the West, Penguin Academics*, we have made several changes to the book's content and coverage:

Revised and Improved Map Program

When teachers of Western civilization courses are surveyed, no single area of need is cited more often than that of geographical knowledge. Most students simply have no mental image of Europe, no familiarity with those geophysical features that are a fundamental part of the geopolitical realities of Western history. We realized that maps, carefully planned and skillfully executed, would be an important component of our text. In this edition, we have revised the entire map program, improving the look of the maps and increasing the sizes of many of them for easier readability. The great number of maps throughout the text, the specially designed "Map Discovery" feature, and the ancillary programs of map transparencies and workbook exercises combine to provide the strongest possible program for teaching historical geography.

Map Discovery

"Map Discovery," which appears two to three times per chapter, offers specially designed maps with supporting caption information and questions designed to engage students in analyzing the map data and making larger connections to chapter discussions. We have found that focusing students' attention on the details of a map and asking them to consider why that information is important is an effective way to strengthen critical thinking skills, as well as to expand geographical knowledge.

Acknowledgments

We want to thank the many conscientious historians who gave generously of their time and knowledge to review our manuscript. We would like to thank the reviewers of the previous editions of *Civilization in the West*, as well as those of the current edition. Their valuable critiques and suggestions have contributed greatly to the final product. We are grateful to the following:

Daniel F. Callahan, *University of Delaware*; Michael Clinton, *Gwynedd-Mercy College*; Bob Cole, *Utah State University*; Gary P. Cox, *Gordon College*; Peter L. de Rosa, *Bridgewater State College*; Frank Lee Earley, *Arapahoe Community College*; Steven Fanning, *University of Illinois at Chicago*; Patrick Foley, *Tarrant County College*; Charlotte M. Gradie, *Sacred Heart University*; Richard Grossman, *Northeastern Illinois University*; David Halamy, *Cypress College*; Gary J. Johnson, *University of Southern Maine*; Cynthia Jones, *University of Missouri at Kansas City*; John Kemp, *Truckee Meadows Community College*; Janilyn Kocher, *Richland Community College*; Lisa M. Lane, *MiraCosta College*; Oscar Lansen, *University of North Carolina at Charlotte*; Michael R. Lynn, *Agnes Scott College*; Mark S. Malaszczyk, *St. John's University*; John M. McCulloh, *Kansas State University*; David B. Mock, *Tallahassee Community College*; Don Mohr, Emeritus, *University of Alaska, Anchorage*; Martha G. Newman, *University of Texas at Austin*; Lisa Pace-Hardy, *Jefferson Davis Community College*; Marlette Rebhorn, *Austin Community College*; Steven G. Reinhardt, *University of Texas at Arlington*; Kimberly Reiter, *Stetson University*; Robert Rockwell, *Mt. San Jacinto College*; Maryloy Ruud, *University of West Florida*; Jose M. Sanchez, *St. Louis University*; Erwin Sicher, *Southwestern Adventist College*; Ruth Suyama, *Los Angeles Mission College*; David Tengwall, *Anne Arundel*

Community College; Janet M. C. Walmsley, *George Mason University*; John E. Weakland, *Ball State University*, and Rick Whisonant, *York Technical College*.

Our special thanks go to our colleagues at Marquette University for their longstanding support, valuable comments, and assistance on this edition's design: Lance Grahn, Lezlie Knox, Timothy G. McMahon, and Alan P. Singer.

We also acknowledge the assistance of the many reviewers of *Civilization in the West* whose comments have been invaluable in the development of *Civilization in the West, Penguin Academics*:

Joseph Aieta, III, *Lasell College*; Ken Albala, *University of the Pacific*; Patricia Ali, *Morris College*; Gerald D. Anderson, *North Dakota State University*; Jean K. Berger, *University of Wisconsin, Fox Valley*; Susan Carrafiello, *Wright State University*; Andrew Donson, *University of Massachusetts, Amherst*; Frederick Dotolo, *St. John Fisher College*; Janusz Duzinkiewicz, *Purdue University*; Brian Elsesser, *St. Louis University*; Bryan Ganaway, *University of Illinois*; David Graf, *University of Miami*; Benjamin Hett, *Hunter College*; Mark M. Hull, *St. Louis University*; Barbara Klemm, *Broward Community College*; Lawrence Langer, *University of Connecticut*; Elise Moentmann, *University of Portland*; Alisa Plant, *Tulane University*; Salvador Rivera, *State University of New York*; Thomas Robisheaux, *Duke University*; Ilicia Sprey, *Saint Joseph's College*; George S. Vascik, *Miami University, Hamilton*; Vance Youmans, *Spokane Falls Community College*; Achilles Aavraamides, *Iowa State University*; Meredith L. Adams, *Southwest Missouri State University*; Arthur H. Auten, *University of Hartford*; Suzanne Balch-Lindsay, *Eastern New Mexico University*; Sharon Bannister, *University of Findlay*; John W. Barker, *University of Wisconsin*; Patrick Bass, *Mount Union College*; William H. Beik, *Northern Illinois University*; Patrice Berger, *University of Nebraska*; Lenard R. Berlanstein, *University of Virginia*; Raymond Birn, *University of Oregon*; Donna Bohanan, *Auburn University*; Werner Braatz, *University of Wisconsin, Oshkosh*; Thomas A. Brady, Jr., *University of Oregon*; Anthony M. Brescia, *Nassau Community College*; Elaine G. Breslaw, *Morgan State University*; Ronald S. Brockway, *Regis University*; April Brooks, *South Dakota State University*; Daniel Patrick Brown, *Moorpark College*; Ronald A. Brown, *Charles County Community College*; Blaine T. Browne, *Broward Community College*; Kathleen S. Carter, *High Point University*; Robert Carver, *University of Missouri, Rolla*; Edward J. Champlin, *Princeton University*; Stephanie Evans Christelow, *Western Washington University*; Sister Dorita Clifford, BVM, *University of San Francisco*; Gary B. Cohen, *University of Oklahoma*; Jan M. Copes, *Cleveland State University*; John J. Contreni, *Purdue University*; Tim Crain, *University of Wisconsin, Stout*; Norman Delaney, *Del Mar College*; Samuel E. Dicks, *Emporia State University*; Frederick Dumin, *Washington State University*; Laird Easton, *California State University, Chico*; Dianne E. Farrell, *Moorhead State University*; Margot C. Finn, *Emory University*; Allan W. Fletcher, *Boise State University*; Luci Fortunato De Lisle, *Bridgewater State College*; Elizabeth L. Furdell, *University of North Florida*; Thomas W. Gallant, *University of Florida*; Frank Garosi, *California State University, Sacramento*; Lorne E. Glaim, *Pacific Union College*; Joseph J. Godson, *Hudson Valley Community College*; Sue Helder Goliber, *Mount St. Mary's*

College; Manuel G. Gonzales, *Diablo Valley College*; Louis Haas, *Duquesne University*; Eric Haines, *Bellevue Community College*; Paul Halliday, *University of Virginia*; Margaretta S. Handke, *Mankato State University*; David A. Harnett, *University of San Francisco*; Paul B. Harvey, Jr., *Pennsylvania State University*; Neil Heyman, *San Diego State University*; Daniel W. Hollis, *Jacksonville State University*; Kenneth G. Holum, *University of Maryland*; Patricia Howe, *University of St. Thomas*; David Hudson, *California State University, Fresno*; Charles Ingrao, *Purdue University*; George F. Jewsbury, *Oklahoma State University*; Donald G. Jones, *University of Central Arkansas*; William R. Jones, *University of New Hampshire*; Richard W. Kaeuper, *University of Rochester*; David Kaiser, *Carnegie-Mellon University*; Jeff Kaufmann, *Muscatine Community College*; Carolyn Kay, *Trent University*; William R. Keylor, *Boston University*; Joseph Kicklighter, *Auburn University*; Charles L. Killinger, III, *Valencia Community College*; Alan M. Kirshner, *Ohlone College*; Charlene Kiser, *Milligan College*; Alexandra Korros, *Xavier University*; Cynthia Kosso, *Northern Arizona University*; Lara Kriegel, *Florida International University*; Lisa M. Lane, *MiraCosta College*; David C. Large, *Montana State University*; Catherine Lawrence, *Messiah College*; Bryan LeBeau, *Creighton University*; Robert B. Luehrs, *Fort Hays State University*; Donna J. Maier, *University of Northern Iowa*; Margaret Malamud, *New Mexico State University*; Roberta T. Manning, *Boston College*; Lyle McAlister, *University of Florida*; Therese M. McBride, *College of the Holy Cross*; David K. McQuilkin, *Bridgewater College*; Victor V. Minasian, *College of Marin*; David B. Mock, *Tallahassee Community College*; Robert Moeller, *University of California, Irvine*; R. Scott Moore, *University of Dayton*; Ann E. Moyer, *University of Pennsylvania*; Pierce C. Mullen, *Montana State University*; John A. Nichols, *Slippery Rock University*; Thomas F. X. Noble, *University of Virginia*; J. Ronald Oakley, *Davidson County Community College*; Bruce K. O'Brien, *Mary Washington College*; Dennis H. O'Brien, *West Virginia University*; Maura O'Connor, *University of Cincinnati*; Richard A. Oehling, *Assumption College*; James H. Overfield, *University of Vermont*; Catherine Patterson, *University of Houston*; Sue Patrick, *University of Wisconsin, Barron County*; Peter C. Piccillo, *Rhode Island College*; Peter O'M. Pierson, *Santa Clara University*; Theophilus Prousis, *University of North Florida*; Marlette Rebhorn, *Austin Community College*; Jack B. Ridley, *University of Missouri, Rolla*; Constance M. Rousseau, *Providence College*; Thomas J. Runyan, *Cleveland State University*; John P. Ryan, *Kansas City Community College*; Geraldine Ryder, *Ocean County College*; Joanne Schneider, *Rhode Island College*; Steven Schroeder, *Indiana University of Pennsylvania*; Steven C. Seyer, *Lehigh County Community College*; Lixin Shao, *University of Minnesota, Duluth*; George H. Shriver, *Georgia Southern University*; Ellen J. Skinner, *Pace University*; Bonnie Smith, *University of Rochester*; Patrick Smith, *Broward Community College*; James Smither, *Grand Valley State University*; Sherill Spaar, *East Central University*; Charles R. Sullivan, *University of Dallas*; Peter N. Stearns, *Carnegie-Mellon University*; Saulius Suziedelis, *Millersville University*; Darryl B. Sycher, *Columbus State Community College*; Roger Tate, *Somerset Community College*; Janet A. Thompson, *Tallahassee Community College*; Anne-Marie Thornton,

Bilkent University; Donna L. Van Raaphorst, Cuyahoga Community College; James Vanstone, John Abbot College; Steven Vincent, North Carolina State University; Richard A. Voeltz, Cameron University; Faith Wallis, McGill University; Sydney Watts, University of Richmond; Eric Weissman, Golden West College; Christine White, Pennsylvania State University; William Harry Zee, Gloucester County College.

Each author also received invaluable assistance and encouragement from many colleagues, friends, and family members over the years of research, reflection, writing, and revising that went into the making of this text:

Mark Kishlansky thanks Ann Adams, Robert Bartlett, Ray Birn, David Buisseret, Ted Cook, Frank Conaway, Constantine Fasolt, James Hankins, Katherine Haskins, Richard Hellie, Matthew Kishlansky, Donna Marder, Mary Beth Rose, Victor Stater, Jeanne Thiel, and the staffs of the Joseph Regenstein Library, the Newberry Library, and the Widener and Lamont Libraries at Harvard.

Patrick Geary thanks Mary, Catherine, and Anne Geary for their patience, support, and encouragement. He also thanks Anne Picard, Dale Schofield, Hans Hummer, and Richard Mowrer for their able assistance throughout the project.

Patricia O'Brien thanks Christopher Reed for his loving support; Tristan Reed for his intellectual engagement; and Erin and Devin Reed for "keeping me in touch with the contemporary world."

MARK KISHLANSKY

PATRICK GEARY

PATRICIA O'BRIEN

Ancillary Instructional Materials

The ancillary instructional materials that accompany Civilization in the West, Penguin Academics are designed to reinforce and enliven the richness of the past and inspire students with the excitement of studying the history of Western civilization.

Primary Source: Documents in Western Civilization DVD.   This DVD-ROM offers a rich collection of textual and visual—many never before available to a wide audience—and serves as an indispensable tool for working with sources. Extensively developed with the guidance of historians and teachers, Primary Source: Documents in Western Civilization includes over 800 sources in Western civilization history—from cave art, to text documents, to satellite images of Earth from space. All sources are accompanied by headnotes and focus questions and are searchable by topic, region, or theme. In addition, a built-in tutorial guides students through the process of working with documents. The DVD can be bundled with Civilization in the West, Penguin Academics, at no charge. Please contact your Pearson Arts and Sciences representative for ordering information. (ISBN 0-13-134407-2)

An abridged two-volume print version of Primary Source: Documents in Western Civilization is also available:

Primary Sources in Western Civilization, Volume 1: To 1700, 2/e (ISBN 0-13-175583-8)
Primary Sources in Western Civilization, Volume 2: Since 1400, 2/e (ISBN 0-13-175584-6)

Please contact your Pearson Arts and Sciences representative for ordering information.

Lives and Legacies: Biographies in Western Civilization, Second Edition. Extensively revised, *Lives and Legacies* includes brief, focused biographies of 60 individuals whose lives provide insight into the key developments of Western civilization. Each biography includes an introduction, prereading questions, and suggestions for additional reading. (Volume 1: ISBN 0-205-64915-7); (Volume 2: ISBN 0-205-64914-9)

 Titles from the renowned **Penguin Classics** series can be bundled with *Civilization in the West, Penguin Academics,* for a nominal charge. Please contact your Pearson Arts and Sciences sales representative for details.

The Prentice Hall Atlas of Western Civilization, Second Edition. (ISBN 0-13-604246-5) Produced in collaboration with Dorling Kindersley, the leader in cartographic publishing, the updated second edition of *The Prentice Hall Atlas of Western Civilization* applies the most innovative cartographic techniques to present Western civilization in all of its complexity and diversity. Copies of the atlas can be bundled with *Civilization in the West, Penguin Academics,* for a nominal charge. Contact your Pearson Arts and Sciences sales representative for details.

A Guide to Your History Course: What Every Student Needs to Know. (ISBN 0-13-185087-3) Written by Vincent A. Clark, this concise, spiral-bound guidebook orients students to the issues and problems they will face in the history classroom. Available at a discount when bundled with *Civilization in the West, Penguin Academics.*

A Short Guide to Writing about History, Seventh Edition. (ISBN 0-205-67370-8) Written by Richard Marius, late of Harvard University, and Melvin E. Page, Eastern Tennessee State University, this engaging and practical text helps students get beyond merely compiling dates and facts. Covering both brief essays and the documented resource paper, the text explores the writing and researching processes, identifies different modes of historical writing, including argument, and concludes with guidelines for improving style.

Library of World Biography Series Series Editor Peter N. Stearns. Concise and incisive, each interpretive biography in the Library of World Biography Series focuses on a person whose actions and ideas either significantly influenced world events or whose life reflects important themes and developments in world history. Contract your local Pearson representative for details.

mysearchlab Pearson's MySearchLab™ is the easiest way for students to start a research assignment or paper. Complete with extensive help on the research process and four databases of credible and reliable source material, MySearchLab™ helps students quickly and efficiently make the most of their research time. (www.mysearchlab.com)

MARK KISHLANSKY is Frank B. Baird, Jr., Professor of English and European History and has served as the Associate Dean of the Faculty at Harvard University. He was educated at the State University of New York at Stony Brook, where he first studied history, and at Brown University, where he received his Ph.D. in 1977. For 16 years, he taught at the University of Chicago and was a member of the staff that taught Western Civilization. Currently, he lectures on the History of Western Civilization at Harvard. Professor Kishlansky is a specialist on seventeenth-century English political history and has written, among other works, *A Monarchy Transformed*; *The Rise of the New Model Army*; and *Parliamentary Selection: Social and Political Choice in Early Modern England*. From 1984 to 1991, he was editor of the *Journal of British Studies* and is presently the general editor of *History Compass*, the first online history journal. He is also the general editor for Pearson Custom Publishing's source and interpretations databases, which provide custom book supplements for Western Civilization courses.

PATRICK GEARY holds a Ph.D. in Medieval Studies from Yale University and has broad experience in interdisciplinary approaches to European history and civilization. He has served as President of the Medieval Academy of America, as the director of the Medieval Institute at the University of Notre Dame, as well as director for the Center for Medieval and Renaissance Studies at the University of California, Los Angeles, where he is currently Distinguished Professor of History. He has also held positions at the University of Florida and Princeton University and has taught at the École des Hautes Études en Sciences Sociales in Paris, the Central European University in Budapest, and the University of Vienna. His many publications include *Readings in Medieval History*; *Before France and Germany: The Creation and Transformation of the Merovingian World*; *Phantoms of Remembrance: Memory and Oblivion at the End of the First Millennium*; *The Myth of Nations: The Medieval Origins of Europe*; and *Women at the Beginning: Origin Myths from the Amazons to the Virgin Mary*.

PATRICIA O'BRIEN is a specialist in modern French cultural and social history and received her Ph.D. from Columbia University. She has held appointments at Yale University, the University of California–Irvine, the University of California–Riverside, the École des Hautes Études en Sciences Sociales in Paris, and the University of California–Los Angeles. Between 1995 and 1999, Professor O'Brien worked to foster collaborative interdisciplinary research in the humanities as director of the University of California Humanities Research Institute. Since 2004, she has served as Executive Dean of the College of Letters and Science at UCLA. Professor O'Brien has published widely on the history of French crime and punishment, cultural theory, urban history, and gender issues. Representative publications include *The Promise of Punishment: Prisons in Nineteenth-Century France*; "The Kleptomania Diagnosis: Bourgeois Women and Theft in Late Nineteenth-Century France" in *Expanding the Past: A Reader in Social History*; and "Michel Foucault's History of Culture" in *The New Cultural History*, edited by Lynn Hunt. Professor O'Brien's commitment to this textbook grew out of her own teaching experiences in large, introductory Western civilization courses. She has benefited from the contributions of her students and fellow instructors in her approach to the study of Western civilization in the modern period.

CIVILIZATION IN THE WEST

Combined Volume

The Idea of Western Civilization

THE WEST IS AN IDEA. IT IS NOT VISIBLE FROM SPACE. AN ASTRONAUT viewing the blue-and-white terrestrial sphere can make out the forms of Africa, bounded by the Atlantic, the Indian Ocean, the Red Sea, and the Mediterranean. Australia, the Americas, and even Antarctica are distinct patches of blue-green in the darker waters that surround them. But nothing comparable separates Asia from Europe, East from West. Viewed from 100 miles up, the West itself is invisible. Although astronauts can see the great Eurasian landmass curving around the Northern Hemisphere, the Ural Mountains—the theoretical boundary between East and West— appear faint from space. Certainly they are less impressive than the towering Himalayas, the Alps, or even the Caucasus. People, not geology, determined that the Urals should be the arbitrary boundary between Europe and Asia.

Even this determination took centuries. Originally, Europe was a name that referred only to central Greece. Gradually, Greeks extended it to include the whole Greek mainland and then the landmass to the north. Later, Roman explorers and soldiers carried Europe north and west to its modern boundaries. Asia too grew with time. Initially, Asia was only that small portion of what is today Turkey inland from the Aegean Sea. Gradually, as Greek explorers came to know of lands farther east, north, and south, they expanded their understanding of Asia to include everything east of the Don River to the north and of the Red Sea to the south.

Western civilization is as much an idea as the West itself. Under the right conditions, astronauts can see the Great Wall of China snaking its way from the edge of the Himalayas to the Yellow Sea. No comparable physical legacy of the West is so massive that its details can be discerned from space. Nor are Western achievements rooted forever in one corner of the world. What we call Western civilization belongs to no particular place. Its location has changed since the origins of civilization; that is, the cultural and social traditions characteristic of the *civitas*, or city. "Western" cities appeared first outside the "West," in the Tigris and Euphrates river basins in present-day Iraq and Iran, a region that we today call the Middle East. These areas have never lost their urban traditions, but in time, other cities in North Africa, Greece, and Italy adapted and expanded this heritage.

Until the sixteenth century C.E., the western end of the Eurasian landmass was the crucible in which disparate cultural and intellectual traditions of the Near East, the Mediterranean, and northern and western Europe were smelted into a new and powerful alloy. Then "the West" expanded by establishing colonies overseas and by giving rise to the "settler societies" of the Americas, Australia and New Zealand, and South Africa.

Western technology for harnessing nature, Western forms of economic and political organization, Western styles of art and music are—for good or ill—dominant influences in world civilization. Japan is a leading power in the Western traditions of capitalist commerce and technology. China, the most populous country in the world, adheres to Marxist socialist principles—a European political tradition. Millions of people in Africa, Asia, and the Americas follow the religions of Islam and Christianity, both of which developed from Judaism in the cradle of Western civilization.

Many of today's most pressing problems are also part of the legacy of the Western tradition. The remnants of European colonialism have left deep hostilities throughout the world. The integration of developing nations into the world economy keeps much of humanity in a seemingly hopeless cycle of poverty as the wealth of poor countries goes to pay interest on loans from Europe and America. Hatred of Western civilization is a central, ideological tenet that inspired terrorist attacks on symbols of American economic and military strength on September 11, 2001, and that continues to fuel anti-Western terrorism around the world. The West itself faces a crisis. Impoverished citizens of former colonies flock to Europe and North America seeking a better life but instead often find poverty, hostility, and racism. Finally, the advances of Western civilization endanger our very existence. Technology pollutes the world's air, water, and soil, and nuclear weapons threaten the destruction of all civilization. Yet these are the same advances that allow us to lengthen life expectancy, harness the forces of nature, and conquer disease. It is the same technology that allows us to view our world from outer space.

How did we get here? In this book we attempt to answer that question. The history of Western civilization is not simply the triumphal story of progress, the creation of a better world. Even in areas in which we can see development, such as technology, communications, and social complexity, change is not always for the better. However, it would be equally inaccurate to view Western civilization as a progressive decline from a mythical golden age of the human race. The roughly 300 generations since the origins of civilization have bequeathed a rich and contradictory legacy to the present. Inherited political and social institutions, cultural forms, and religious and philosophical traditions form the framework within which the future must be created. The past does not determine the future, but it is the raw material from which the future will be made. To use this legacy properly, we must first understand it, not because the past is the key to the future, but because understanding yesterday frees us to create tomorrow.

CHAPTER

The First Civilizations

Before Civilization

The first humanlike creatures whose remains have been discovered date from as long as five million years ago. These creatures, neither fully ape nor human, survived for over four million years.

Varieties of the modern species of humans, *Homo sapiens* ("thinking human"), appeared well over 100,000 years ago and spread across the Eurasian landmass and Africa. The earliest *Homo sapiens* in Europe, the *Neanderthal*, differed little from us today. They spread throughout much of Africa, Europe, and Asia during the last great ice age. To survive in the harsh tundra landscape, they developed a cultural system that enabled them to modify their environment. Customs such as the burial of their dead with food offerings indicate that Neanderthals may have developed a belief in an afterlife. DNA studies suggest that Neanderthals are not directly related to modern humans. Their subspecies appears to have been a dead end.

No one knows why or how the Neanderthals were replaced by our sub-species, *Homo sapiens sapiens* ("thinking thinking human"), around 40,000 years ago. Whatever the reason and whatever the process—extinction, evolution, or extermination—this last arrival on the human scene was universally successful. All humans today belong to this same subspecies. Differences in skin color, type of hair, and build are minor variations on the same theme. The identification of races, while selectively based on some of these physical variations, is, like civilization itself, a fact not of biology but of culture.

Early *Homo sapiens sapiens* lived in small kin groups of 20 or 30, following game and seeking shelter in tents, lean-tos, and caves. People of the **Paleolithic era** or Old Stone Age (ca. 600,000–10,000 B.C.E.) worked together for hunting and defense and apparently formed emotional bonds that were based on more than sex or economic necessity.

Chronology

BEFORE CIVILIZATION

ca. 100,000 B.C.E.	*Homo sapiens*
ca. 40,000 B.C.E.	*Homo sapiens sapiens*
ca. 35,000–10,000 B.C.E.	Late Paleolithic era (Old Stone Age)
ca. 8000–6500 B.C.E.	Neolithic era (New Stone Age)
ca. 3500 B.C.E.	Civilization begins

The Dominance of Culture

During the upper or late Paleolithic era (ca. 35,000–10,000 B.C.E.), **culture**, meaning everything about humans that is not inherited biologically, was increasingly deter-minant in human life. Paleolithic people were not on an endless and all-consuming quest to provide for the necessities of life. They spent less time on such things than we do today. Therefore, they were able to find time to develop speech, religion, and artistic expression. Wall paintings, small clay and stone figurines of female figures (which may reflect concerns about fertility), and finely decorated stone and bone tools indicate not just artistic ability but also abstract and symbolic thought.

The end of the glacial era marked the beginning of the Mesolithic, or Middle Stone Age (ca. 10,000–8000 B.C.E.). This period occurred at different times in different places as the climate grew milder, vast expanses of glaciers melted, and sea levels rose. Mesolithic peoples began the gradual domestication of plants and animals and sometimes formed settled communities. They developed the bow and arrow and pottery, and they made use of small flints (microliths) and fishhooks.

Paintings: A Cultural Record. An amazing continuous record of the civilizing of the West is found in the arid wastes of Africa's Sahara Desert. At Tassili-n-Ajjer in modern Algeria, succeeding generations of inhabitants left over 4,000 paintings on cliff and cave walls that date from about 6000 B.C.E. until the time of Jesus. Like a pictorial time line, these paintings show the gradual transformations of human culture.

The earliest cave paintings were produced by people who, like the inhabitants of Europe and the Near East, lived by hunting game and gathering edible plants, nuts, and fruit.

Sedentarization. Sometime around 5000 B.C.E., the artists at Tassili-n-Ajjer began to include images of domesticated cattle and harnesslike equipment in their paintings. Such depictions give evidence of the arrival in North Africa of two of the most profound transformations in human history: sedentarization, that is, the adoption of a fixed dwelling place, and the agricultural revolution. These fundamental changes in human culture began independently around the world and continued for roughly 5,000 years. They appeared first around 10,000 B.C.E. in the Near East, then elsewhere in Asia around 8000 B.C.E. By 5000 B.C.E., the domestication of plants and animals was under way in Africa and what is today Mexico.

Around 10,000 B.C.E., many hunter-gatherers living along the coastal plains of what is today Syria and Israel and in the valleys and the hill country near the Zagros Mountains between modern Iran and Iraq began to develop specialized strategies that led, by accident, to a transformation in human culture. Rather than constantly traveling in search of food, people living near the Mediterranean coast stayed put and exploited the various seasonal sources of food, fish, wild grains, fruits, and game. Such a sedentary existence was easier on the very young and the very old, and consequently infant mortality dropped and life expectancy rose.

Social Organization, Agriculture, and Religion

No one really knows why settlement led to agriculture. As population growth put pressure on the local food supply, gathering activities demanded more formal coordination and organization and led to the development of political leadership. In any case, people no longer simply looked for favored species of plants and animals where they occurred naturally. Now they introduced these species into other locations and favored them at the expense of plant and animal species that were not deemed useful. Agriculture had begun.

Control of Nature. The ability to domesticate goats, sheep, pigs, and cattle and to cultivate barley, wheat, and vegetables changed human communities from passive harvesters of nature to active partners with it. These peoples of the **Neolithic era**, or New Stone Age (ca. 8000–6500 B.C.E.), organized sizable villages. Jericho, which

In this cave painting in northern Africa, animal magic evokes help from the spirit world in ensuring the prosperity of the cattle herd. A similar ceremony is still performed by members of the Fulani tribes in the Sahel, on the southern fringe of the Sahara.

had been settled before the agricultural revolution, grew into a fortified town complete with ditch, stone walls, and towers and sheltered perhaps 2,000 inhabitants. Çatal Hüyük in southern Turkey may have been even larger.

The really revolutionary aspect of agriculture was not simply that it ensured settled communities a food supply. The true innovation was that agriculture was portable. For the first time, rather than looking for a place that provided them with the necessities of life, humans could carry with them what they needed to make a site inhabitable. This portability also meant the rapid spread of agriculture throughout the region.

Religion. Agricultural societies brought changes in the form and organization of formal religious cults. In larger communities the bonds of kinship that had united small hunter-gatherer bands were being supplemented by religious organization, which helped to control and regulate social behavior. The nature of this religion is a matter of speculation. Images of a female deity, interpreted as a guardian of animals, suggest the religious importance of women and fertility.

Mesopotamia: Between the Two Rivers

Need drove the inhabitants of Mesopotamia—a name that means "between the rivers"—to create a civilization; nature itself offered little for human comfort or prosperity. The upland regions of the north receive most of the rainfall, but the soil is thin and poor. In the south the soil is fertile, but rainfall is almost nonexistent. There, the twin rivers provide life-giving water but also bring destructive floods that usually arrive at harvest time. Therefore, agriculture is impossible without irrigation. But irrigation systems, if not properly maintained, deposit harsh alkaline chemicals on the soil, gradually reducing its fertility. In addition, Mesopotamia's only natural resource is clay. It has no metals, no workable stone, no valuable minerals of use to ancient people. These very obstacles pressed the people to cooperative, innovative, and organized measures for survival. Survival in the region required planning and the mobilization of labor, which was possible only through centralization.

Until around 3500 B.C.E., the inhabitants of the lower Tigris and Euphrates lived in scattered villages and small towns. Then the population of the region, which was known as Sumer, began to increase rapidly. Small settlements became increasingly common; then towns such as Eridu and Uruk in what is now Iraq began to grow rapidly. These towns developed in part because of the need to concentrate and organize population in order to carry on the extensive irrigation systems necessary to support Mesopotamian agriculture. These towns soon spread their control out to the surrounding cultivated areas, incorporating the smaller towns and villages of the region. They also fortified themselves against the hostile intentions of their neighbors.

As population growth increased pressure on the region's food supply, cities supplemented their resources by raiding their more prosperous neighbors. Victims sought protection within the ramparts of the settlements that had grown up around religious centers. As a result, the populations of the towns rose along with their towering temples, largely at the expense of the countryside. Between about 3500 and 3000 B.C.E., the population of Uruk quadrupled, from 10,000 to 40,000. Other Mesopotamian cities, notably Umma, Eridu, Lagash, and Ur, developed along the same general lines as they concentrated water supplies within their districts with artificial canals and dikes. At the same time, the number of smaller towns and villages in the vicinity decreased rapidly. The city had become the dominant force in the organization of economy and society, and the growth of the Sumerian cities established a precedent that would continue throughout history.

The Ramparts of Uruk

Cities did more than simply concentrate population. Within the walls of the city, men and women developed new technologies and new social and political structures. They created cultural traditions such as writing and literature. The pride of the first city dwellers is captured in a passage from the *Epic of Gilgamesh*, the earliest known great heroic poem, which was composed sometime before 2000 B.C.E. In the poem, the hero Gilgamesh boasts of the mighty walls he had built to encircle his city, Uruk:

> Go up and walk on the ramparts of Uruk
> Inspect the base terrace, examine the brickwork:
> Is not its brickwork of burnt brick?
> Did not the Seven Sages lay its foundations?

Gilgamesh was justifiably proud of his city. In his day (ca. 2700 B.C.E.), these walls were marvels of military engineering; even now their ruins remain a tribute to his age. Archaeologists have uncovered the remains of the ramparts of Uruk, which stretched over five miles and were protected by some 900 semicircular tow-

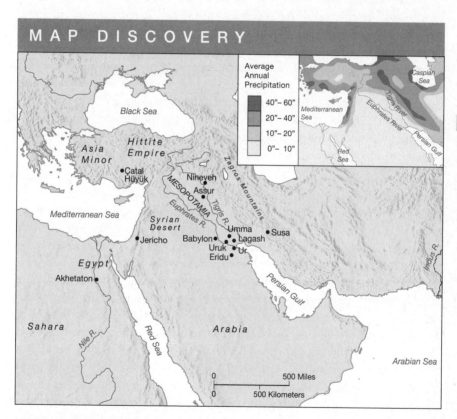

MAP DISCOVERY

THE ANCIENT WORLD

Notice the locations of the earliest civilizations. What geographical similarities can you see between the Nile Valley and the valleys of the Tigris and Euphrates rivers that might have encouraged the appearance of complex civilizations? How dependent on rainfall were the agricultures that supported these civilizations? What problems do river valleys pose to settlement that civilization might solve?

ers. These massive protective walls enclosed about two square miles of houses, palaces, workshops, and temples. Uruk may with reason be called the first true city in the history of Western civilization.

Urban Life. Within Uruk's walls the peculiar circumstances of urban life changed the traditional social structure of Mesopotamia. In Neolithic times, social and economic differences within society had been minimal. Urban immigration increased the power, wealth, and status of two groups. In the first group were the religious authorities who were responsible for the temples. The second consisted of the emerging military and administrative elites, such as Gilgamesh, who were responsible for the construction and protection of the cities. These two groups probably encouraged much of the migration to the cities.

Whether they lived inside the city or on the farmland it controlled, Mesopotamians formed a highly stratified society that shared unequally in the benefits of civilization. Slaves, who did most of the unskilled labor within the city, were the primary victims of civilization. Most were prisoners of war, but some were people forced by debt to sell themselves or their children. Most of the remaining rural people were peasants who were little more than slaves. Better off were soldiers, merchants, and workers and artisans who served the temple or palace. At the next level were land-owning free persons. Above all of these were the priests responsible for temple services and the rulers. Rulers included the *ensi*, or city ruler, and the *lugal*, or king, the earthly representative of the gods. Kings were powerful and feared.

Women's Status. Urban life also redefined the role and status of women, who in the Neolithic period had enjoyed roughly the same roles and status as men. In cities, women tended to exercise private authority over children and servants within the household, while men controlled the household and dealt in the wider world. This change in roles resulted in part from the economic basis of the first civilization. Southern Mesopotamia has no sources of metal or stone. To acquire these precious commodities, trade networks were extended into Syria, the Arabian Peninsula, and even India. The primary commodities that Mesopotamians produced for trade were textiles, and these were produced largely by women captured in wars with neighboring city-states. Some historians suggest that the disproportionate numbers of low-status women in Mesopotamian cities affected the status of women in general. Although women could own property and even appear as heads of households, by roughly 1500 B.C.E. the pattern of patriarchal households predominated. Throughout Western history, while individual women might at times exercise great power, they did so largely in the private sphere.

Tools: Technology and Writing

Changes in society brought changes in technology. The need to feed, clothe, protect, and govern growing urban populations led to major technological and conceptual discoveries. Canals and systems of dikes partially harnessed water supplies. Farmers began to work their fields with improved plows and to haul their produce to town, first on sleds and ultimately on carts. These land-transport devices, along with sailing ships, made it possible not only to produce greater agricultural surplus but also to move this surplus to distant markets. Artisans used a refined potter's wheel to produce ceramic vessels of great beauty. Government officials and private individuals began to use cylinder seals, small stone cylinders engraved with a pattern, to mark ownership. Metalworkers fashioned gold and silver into valuable items of adornment and prestige. They also began to cast bronze, an alloy of copper and tin, which came into use for tools and weapons about 3000 B.C.E.

Pictograms. Perhaps the greatest invention of early cities was writing. As early as 7000 B.C.E., small clay or stone tokens with distinctive shapes or markings were being used to keep track of animals, goods, and fruits in inventories and bartering. By 3500 B.C.E., government and temple administrators were using simplified drawings— today termed **pictograms**—that were derived from these tokens to assist them in keeping records of their transactions.

Cuneiform. In time, these pictograms developed into a true system of writing called **cuneiform** (from the Latin *cuneus*, "wedge") after the wedge shape of the characters. Finally, scribes took a radical step. Rather than simply using pictograms to indicate single objects, they began to use cuneiform characters to represent concepts. Ultimately, pictograms came to represent sounds divorced from any particular meaning.

The implications of the development of cuneiform writing were revolutionary. Since symbols were liberated from meaning, they could be used to record any language. Writing soon allowed those who had mastered it to achieve greater centralization and control of government, to communicate over enormous distances, to preserve and transmit information, and to express religious and cultural beliefs. Writing reinforced memory, consolidating and expanding the achievements of the first civilization and transmitting them to the future.

Gods and Mortals in Mesopotamia

A world of many cities, Mesopotamia was also a world of many gods, and Mesopotamian cities bore the imprint of the cult of their gods.

Mesopotamian Divinities. The gods were like the people who worshipped them. They lived in a replica of human society, and each god had a particular responsibility. Every object and element from the sky to the brick or the plow had its own active god. The gods had the physical appearance and personalities of humans as well as human virtues and vices. Greater gods such as Nanna and Ufu were the protectors of Ur and Sippar. Others, such as Inanna, or Ishtar, the goddess of love, fertility, and wars, and her husband Dumuzi, were worshiped throughout Mesopotamia. Finally, at the top of the pantheon were the gods of the sky, the air, and the rivers.

Temples and Rituals. Mesopotamians believed that the role of mortals was to serve the gods and to feed them through sacrifice. By around 2500 B.C.E., although military lords and kings had gained political power, the temples still controlled a major portion of economic resources. They owned vast estates where peasants cultivated crops and tended flocks to support the priests, scribes, artisans, laborers, farmers, teamsters, smiths, and weavers who operated these complex religious centers. A **ziggurat**, or tiered tower, dedicated to the god stood near many temples.

Although Mesopotamians looked to hundreds of personal divinities for assistance, they did not attempt to establish personal relationships with their great gods. However, since they assumed that the gods lived in a structured world that operated rationally, they believed that mortals could deal with the gods and enlist their aid by following the right rituals. Rites centered on the worship of idols.

Through the proper rituals a person could buy the god's protection and favor. Still, mortal life was harsh, and the gods offered little solace in coping with the great issues of human existence. This attitude is powerfully presented in the *Epic of Gilgamesh*, which, while not an accurate picture of Mesopotamian religion, does convey much of the values of this civilization. In this popular legend, Gilgamesh, king of Uruk, civilizes the wild man Enkidu, who was sent by the gods to temper

The Standard of Ur, made of shells, lapis lazuli, and limestone, was found at Ur. In the top panel, known as *War,* soldiers and horse-drawn chariots return victorious from battle. In the lower panel *Peace,* the king celebrates the victory, captives are paraded before him, and the conquered people bring him tribute.

the king's harshness. Gilgamesh and Enkidu become friends and undertake a series of adventures. However, even their great feats cannot overcome death. Enkidu displeases the gods and dies. Gilgamesh then sets out to find the magic plant of eternal life with which to return his friend from the somber underworld. On his journey he meets Ut-napishtim, the Mesopotamian Noah, who recounts the story of the Great Flood and tells Gilgamesh where to find the plant. Gilgamesh follows Ut-napishtim's advice and is successful but loses the plant on his journey home. The message is that only the gods are immortal, and the human afterlife is at best a shadowy and mournful existence.

Sargon and Mesopotamian Expansion

The temple was one center of the city; the palace was the other. As representative of the city's god, the king was the ruler and highest judge. He was responsible for the construction and maintenance of religious buildings and the complex system of canals that maintained the precarious balance between swamp and arid steppe. Finally, he commanded the army, defending his community against its neighbors and leading his forces against rival cities.

Competition and War. The cultural and economic developments of early Mesopotamia occurred within the context of almost constant warfare. From around 3000 B.C.E. until 2300 B.C.E. the rulers of Ur, Lagash, Uruk, and Umma fought among themselves for control of Sumer, their name for the southern region of Mesopotamia. The population was a mixture of Sumerians and Semites, peoples who spoke Semitic languages related to modern Arabic or Hebrew, all jealously protective of their cities and gods and eager to extend their domination over their weaker neighbors.

The Akkadian Empire. The extraordinary developments in this small corner of the Middle East might have remained isolated phenomena were it not for Sargon (ca. 2334–2279 B.C.E.), king of Akkad and the most important figure in Mesopotamian history. During his long reign of 55 years, Sargon built on the conquests and confederacies of the past to unite, transform, and expand Mesopotamian civilization. In his youth he was the cupbearer to the king of Kish, another Sumerian city. Sargon overthrew his master and conquered Uruk, Ur, Lagash, and Umma. Then, he extended his military operations east across the Tigris, west along the Euphrates, and north into modern Syria, thus creating the first great multiethnic empire state in the West.

The Akkadian state—so named by contemporary historians for Sargon's capital at Akkad—consisted of a vast and heterogeneous collection of city-states and territories. Sargon attempted to rule it by transforming the traditions of royal government. Rather than eradicating the traditions of conquered cities, he allowed them to maintain their own institutions but replaced many of their autonomous ruling aristocracies with his own functionaries. He was thus the first in a long tradition of Near Eastern rulers who sought to unite his disparate conquests into a true state.

Sargon did more than just conquer cities. Although a Semite, he spread the achievements of Sumerian civilization throughout his vast state.

The Akkadian state proved as ephemeral as Sargon's accomplishments were lasting. All Mesopotamian states tended to undergo a cycle of rising rapidly under a gifted military commander and then beginning to crumble under the internal stresses of dynastic disputes and regional assertions of autonomy. Thus weakened, they could then be conquered by other expanding states. First Ur, under its Sumerian king and first law codifier, Shulgi (2094–2047 B.C.E.), and then Amoritic Babylonia, under its great ruler, Hammurabi (1792–1750 B.C.E.), assumed dominance in the land between the rivers. From about 2000 B.C.E. on, the political and economic centers of Mesopotamia were in Babylonia and in Assyria, the region to the north at the foot of the Zagros Mountains.

Hammurabi and the Old Babylonian Empire

In the tradition of Sargon, Hammurabi expanded his state through arms and diplomacy. He expanded his power south as far as Uruk and north to Assyria. In the tradition of Shulgi, he promulgated an important body of law, known as the Code of Hammurabi.

Law and Society. As the favored agent of the gods, the king had responsibility for regulating all aspects of Babylonian life. Therefore, Hammurabi's code offers a view of many aspects of Babylonian life, though always from the perspective of the royal law. The code lists offenses and prescribes penalties, which vary according to the social status of the victim and the perpetrator. Hammurabi's code thus creates a picture of a prosperous society composed of three legally defined social strata: a well-to-do elite, the mass of the population, and slaves. Each group had its own rights and obligations in proportion to its status.

Much of the code sought to protect women and children from arbitrary and unfair treatment. Husbands ruled their households but did not have unlimited authority over their wives. Women could initiate their own court cases, practice various trades, and even hold public positions. The wife's father gave her a dowry over which she had full control. Some elite women personally controlled great wealth.

The Code of Hammurabi was less a royal attempt to restructure Babylonian society than an effort to reorganize, consolidate, and preserve previous laws in order to maintain the established social and economic order.

Mathematics. Law was not the only area in which the Old Babylonian kingdom began an important tradition. To handle the economics of business and government administration, Babylonians developed the most sophisticated mathematical system known before the fifteenth century C.E. Although Babylonian mathematicians were not interested primarily in theoretical problems and were seldom given to abstraction, their technical proficiency indicates the advanced level of sophistication with which Hammurabi's contemporaries could tackle the problems of living in a complex society.

For all its achievements, Hammurabi's state was no more successful than those of his predecessors at defending itself against internal conflicts or external enemies. Despite his efforts, the traditional organization that he inherited from his Sumerian and Akkadian predecessors could not ensure orderly administration of a far-flung collection of cities. Hammurabi's son lost over half of his father's kingdom to internal revolts. Weakened by internal dissension, the kingdom fell to a new and potent force in Western history: the Hittites.

Chronology

BETWEEN THE TWO RIVERS

ca. 3500 B.C.E.	Pictograms appear
ca. 3000–2316 B.C.E.	War for control of Sumer
ca. 2700 B.C.E.	Gilgamesh
ca. 2334–2279 B.C.E.	Sargon
1792–1750 B.C.E.	Hammurabi
ca. 1600 B.C.E.	Hittites destroy Old Babylonian state
ca. 1286 B.C.E.	Battle of Kadesh

The Hittite Empire. The Hittite state emerged in Anatolia in the shadow of Mesopotamian civilization. The Hittite court reflected Mesopotamian influence in its art and religion and in its adaptation and use of cuneiform script. Unlike the Sumerians, the Semitic nomads, the Akkadians, and the Babylonians, the Hittites were an Indo-European people. Their language was part of the linguistic family that includes most modern European languages as well as Persian, Greek, Latin, and Sanskrit. From their capital of Hattushash (modern Bogazköy in Turkey), they established a centralized state based on agriculture and trade in the metals mined from the ore-rich mountains of Anatolia and exported to Mesopotamia. The Hittites were among the earliest people to succeed in smelting iron.

Perfecting the light horse-drawn war chariot, the Hittites expanded into northern Mesopotamia and along the Syrian coast. They were able to destroy the Babylonian state around 1600 B.C.E. The Hittite Empire was the chief political and cultural force in western Asia from about 1400 to 1200 B.C.E. Its gradual expansion south along the coast was checked at the battle of Kadesh about 1286 B.C.E., when Hittite forces encountered the army of an even greater and more ancient power: the Egypt of Ramses II.

The Gift of the Nile

Like that of the Tigris and Euphrates valleys, the rich soil of the Nile Valley can support a dense population. There, however, the similarities end. Unlike the Mesopotamian floodplain, the Nile floodplain required little effort to make the land productive. Each year, the river flooded at exactly the right time to irrigate crops and to deposit a layer of rich, fertile silt. Egypt knew only two environments: the fertile Nile Valley and the vast wastes of the Sahara Desert surrounding it. This inhospitable and largely uninhabitable region limited Egypt's contact with outside influences. Thus while trade, communication, and violent conquest characterized Mesopotamian civilization, Egypt knew self-sufficiency, an inward focus in culture and society, and stability. In its art, political structure, society, and religion, the Egyptian universe was static. Nothing was ever expected to change.

The earliest sedentary communities in the Nile Valley appeared on the western margin of the Nile Delta around 4000 B.C.E. Farther south, in Upper Egypt, similar communities developed somewhat later but achieved an earlier political unity and a higher level of culture. By around 3200 B.C.E., Upper Egypt was in contact with Mesopotamia and had apparently borrowed something of that region's artistic and architectural traditions. During the same period, Upper Egypt developed a pictographic script.

These cultural achievements coincided with the political centralization of Upper Egypt under a series of kings. Probably around 3150 B.C.E., King Narmer or one of his predecessors in Upper Egypt expanded control over the fragmented south, uniting Upper and Lower Egypt and establishing a capital at Memphis on the border between these two regions. For over 2,500 years, the Nile Valley, from the first cataract to the Mediterranean, enjoyed the most stable civilization the Western world has ever known.

Tending the Cattle of God

Historians divide the vast sweep of Egyptian history into 31 dynasties, regrouped in turn into four periods of political centralization: pre- and early dynastic Egypt (ca. 3150–2770 B.C.E.), the Old Kingdom (ca. 2770–2200 B.C.E.), the Middle Kingdom (ca. 2050–1786 B.C.E.), and the New Kingdom (ca. 1560–1087 B.C.E.). The time gaps between kingdoms were periods of disruption and political confusion termed intermediate periods. While minor changes in social, political, and cultural life certainly occurred during these centuries, the changes were less significant than the astonishing stability and continuity of the civilization that developed along the banks of the Nile.

God-Kings. Divine kingship was the cornerstone of Egyptian life. Initially, the king was the incarnation of Horus, a sky and falcon god. Later, the king was identified with the sun-god Ra (subsequently known as Amen-Re, the great god), as well as with Osiris, the god of the dead. As divine incarnation, the king was obliged

ANCIENT EGYPT. The thin strip of rich land bordering the Nile saw the development of an extraordinary civilization that endured for more than 2,000 years.

above all to care for his people. It was he who ensured the annual flooding of the Nile, which brought water to the parched land. His commands preserved **maat**, the ideal state of the universe and society, a condition of harmony and justice. In the poetry of the Old Kingdom, the king was the divine herdsman; the people were the cattle of god.

Unlike the rulers in Mesopotamia, the kings of the Old Kingdom were not warriors but divine administrators. Protected by the Sahara, Egypt had few external enemies and no standing army. A vast bureaucracy of literate court officials and provincial administrators assisted the god-king. They wielded wide authority as religious leaders, judicial officers, and, when necessary, military leaders. A host of subordinate overseers, scribes, metalworkers, stonemasons, artisans, and tax collectors rounded out the royal administration. At the local level, governors administered provinces called *nomes*, the basic units of Egyptian local government.

Gender and Bureaucracy. Women of ancient Egypt were more independent and involved in public life than those of Mesopotamia. Egyptian women owned property, conducted their own business, entered legal contracts, and brought lawsuits. They shared in the economic and professional life of the country at every level except one: Women were apparently excluded from formal education. The professional bureaucracy was open only to those who could read and write. As a result, the primary route to public power was closed to women, and the bureaucratic machinery remained firmly in the hands of men.

The role of this bureaucracy was to administer estates, collect taxes, and channel revenues and labor toward vast public works projects, which focused on the king.

The Pyramids. During the Old and Middle Kingdoms, great pyramid temple-tomb complexes more imposing than the Great House were built for the kings who ruled from the splendor of a Per-ao or "great house," from which comes the Hebrew term for the Egyptian king, pharaoh. Within the temples, priests and servants performed rituals to serve the dead kings just as they had served the kings when they were alive. Even death did not disrupt the continuity that was so vital to Egyptian civilization. The cults of dead kings reinforced the monarchy, since veneration of past rulers meant veneration of the reigning king's ancestors.

Building and equipping the pyramids focused and transformed Egypt's material and human resources. Artisans had to be trained, engineering and transportation problems had to be solved, quarrying and stoneworking techniques had to be perfected, and laborers had to be recruited. In the Old Kingdom, whose population has been estimated at perhaps 1.5 million, more than 70,000 workers at a time were employed in building these great temple-tombs. The pyramids were constructed by peasants working when the Nile was in flood and they could not till the soil. Although actual construction was seasonal, the work was unending. No sooner was one complex completed than the next was begun.

Feeding the masses of laborers absorbed most of the country's agricultural surplus. Equipping the temples and pyramids provided a constant demand for the highest-quality luxury goods, since royal tombs and temples were furnished as luxuriously as palaces. Thus the construction and maintenance of these vast complexes focused the organization and production of Egypt's economy and government.

Democratization of the Afterlife

In the Old Kingdom, future life was available through the king. The graves of thousands of his attendants and servants surrounded his temple. All the wealth, labor, and expertise of the kingdom thus flowed into these temples, reinforcing the position of the king. Like the tip of a pyramid, the king was the summit, supported by all of society.

Decline of Royal Power. Gradually, however, the absolute power of the king declined. The increasing demands for consumption by the court and the cults forced agricultural expansion into areas where returns were poor, thus decreasing the flow of wealth. As bureaucrats increased their efforts to supply the voracious needs of living and dead kings and their attendants, they neglected the maintenance of the economic system that supplied those needs. The royal government was not protecting society; the "cattle of god" were not being well tended. Finally, tax-exempt religious foundations, established to ensure the perpetual cult of the dead, received donations of vast amounts of property, and their power came to rival the king's. This removed an ever greater amount of the country's wealth from the control of the king and his agents. Thus the wealth and power of the Egyptian kings declined at roughly the time that Sargon was expanding his Akkadian state in Mesopotamia. By around 2200 B.C.E., Egyptian royal authority collapsed entirely, leaving political and religious power in the hands of provincial governors.

The Middle Kingdom. After almost 200 years of fragmentation, the governors of Thebes in Upper Egypt reestablished centralized royal traditions, but with a difference. Kings continued to build vast temples, but they did not resume the tremendous investments in pyramid complexes on the scale of the Old Kingdom. The bureaucracy was opened to all men, even sons of peasants, who could master the complex pictographic writing. Private temple-tombs proliferated and with them new pious foundations. These promised eternal care by which anyone with sufficient wealth could enjoy a comfortable afterlife.

The memory of the Old Kingdom's shortcomings introduced a new ethical perspective that was expressed in the literature written by the elite. For the first time, the elite voiced the concern that justice might not always be served and that the innocent might suffer at the hands of royal agents.

The Hyksos. The greater access to power and privilege in the Middle Kingdom benefited foreigners as well as Egyptians. Assimilated Semites rose to important administrative positions. By around 1600 B.C.E., when the Hittite armies were destroying the state of Hammurabi's successors, large bands of Semites had settled in the eastern Delta, setting the stage for the first foreign conquest of Egypt. A series of kings referred to by Egyptian sources as "rulers of foreign lands," or Hyksos, overran the country and ruled the Nile Valley as far south as

Memphis. These foreigners adopted the traditions of Egyptian kingship and continued the tradition of divine rule.

The Hyksos kings introduced their military technology and organization into Egypt. In particular, they brought with them the light horse-drawn war chariot. This mobile fighting platform transformed Egyptian military tactics. These innovations remained even after the Hyksos were expelled by Ahmose I (1552–1527 B.C.E.), the Theban founder of the Eighteenth Dynasty, with whose reign the New Kingdom began.

The Egyptian Empire

Ahmose did not stop with the liberation of Egypt. He forged an empire. He and his successors used their newfound military might to extend the frontiers of Egypt south up the Nile beyond the fourth cataract and well into Nubia. To the east they absorbed the caravan routes to the Red Sea, from which they were able to send ships to Punt (probably modern Somalia), the source of the myrrh and frankincense that were needed for funeral and religious rituals. Most important was the Egyptian expansion into Canaan. Here Egyptian chariots crushed their foes as kings pressed on as far as the Euphrates. Thutmose I (1506–1494 B.C.E.) proclaimed, "I have made the boundaries of Egypt as far as that which the sun encircles."

This painted limestone head of Hatshepsut was originally from a statue depicting the pharaoh as the god Osiris. Hatshepsut was one of at least four women who ruled as pharaoh and her representations may have been influenced by those of her predecessors. Other statues show her in typically female dress, but as her reign progressed representations of her emphasized her role as pharaoh wearing the nemes or striped headcloth, the uraeus or cobra head, the kilt or shendyt, and the traditional false beard. This is especially true in these Osirian statues, that emphasize her assimilation with the god.

In spite of the efforts of Thutmose and his successors, the Egyptian Empire was never as grand as its kings proclaimed. Many of the northern expeditions were raids rather than conquests. Still, the expanded political frontiers meant increased trade and unprecedented interaction with the rest of the ancient world.

Religious and Royal Consolidation Under Akhenaten

Religion was both the heart of royal power and its only limiting force. Although the king was the embodiment of the religious tradition he was also bound by that tradition as it was interpreted by an ancient and powerful system of priesthoods, pious foundations, and cults. The intimate relationship between royal absolutism and religious cult culminated in the reign of Amenhotep IV (1364–1347 B.C.E.), the most controversial and enigmatic ruler of the New Kingdom, who challenged the very basis of royal religious control. In a calculated break with over a thousand years of Egyptian religious custom, Amenhotep attempted to abolish the cult of Amen-Re along with all of the other traditional gods, their priesthoods, and their festivals. In their place he promoted a new divinity, the sun-disk god Aten. Amenhotep moved his capital from Thebes to a new temple city, Akhetaton, near modern Tel al-'Amarna, and changed his own name to Akhenaten ("It pleases Aten").

Akhenaten has been called the first monotheist, a reformer who sought to revitalize a religion that had decayed into superstition and magic. Yet his monotheism was not complete. The god Aten shared divine status with Akhenaten himself. Akhenaten attacked other cults, especially that of Amen-Re, to consolidate royal power and to replace the old priesthoods with his own family members and supporters.

A New Aesthetic. In attempting to reestablish royal divinity, Akhenaten temporarily transformed the aesthetics of Egyptian court life. Traditional archaic language gave way to the everyday speech of the fourteenth century B.C.E. Wall paintings and statues showed people in the clothing that they actually wore rather than in stylized parade dress. This new naturalism rendered the king at once more human and more divine. It differentiated him from the long line of preceding kings, emphasizing his uniqueness and his royal power.

The strength of royal power was so great that during his reign, Akhenaten could command acceptance of his radical break with Egyptian tradition. However, his ambitious plan did not long survive his death. His innovations annoyed the Egyptian elite, while his abolition of established festivals alienated the masses. His son-in-law, Tutankhamen (1347–1337 B.C.E.), the son of Akhenaten's predecessor, was a child when he became king upon Akhenaten's death. Under the influence of his court advisers, probably inherited from his father's reign, he restored the ancient religious traditions and abandoned the new capital of Akhetaton for his father's palace at Thebes.

The Hittites. Return to the old ways meant return to the old problems. Powerful pious foundations controlled fully 10 percent of the population. Dynastic continuity ended after Tutankhamen, and a new military dynasty seized the throne. These internal problems provided an opportunity for the growing Hittite state in Asia Minor to expand south at the expense of Egypt. Ramses II (1289–1224 B.C.E.) checked the Hittite expansion at the battle of Kadesh, but the battle was actually a draw. Eventually, Ramses and the Hittite king Hattusilis III signed a peace treaty whose terms included nonaggression and mutual defense.

The mutual standoff at Kadesh did not long precede the disintegration of both Egypt and the Hittite state. Within a century, states large and small along the Mediterranean coast from Anatolia to the Delta and from the Aegean Sea in the west to the Zagros Mountains in the east collapsed or were destroyed in what seems to have been a general crisis of the civilized world. The various raiders, sometimes erroneously called the "Sea Peoples," who struck Egypt, Syria, the Hittite state, and elsewhere, were not the primary cause of the crisis. It was rather internal political, economic, and social strains within both Egypt and the Hittite state that provided the opportunity for various groups—including Anatolians, Greeks, Israelites, and others—to raid the ancient centers of civilization. In the ensuing confusion, the small Semitic kingdoms of Syria and Canaan developed a precarious independence in the shadow of the great powers.

Chronology

THE GIFT OF THE NILE

ca. 3150–2770 B.C.E.	Predynastic and early dynastic Egypt
ca. 2770–2200 B.C.E.	Old Kingdom
ca. 2600 B.C.E.	Pyramid of Khufu
ca. 2050–1786 B.C.E.	Middle Kingdom
ca. 1560–1087 B.C.E.	New Kingdom
1552–1527 B.C.E.	Ahmose I
1506–1494 B.C.E.	Thutmose I
1494–1490 B.C.E.	Thutmose II
1490–1468 B.C.E.	Hatshepsut
1364–1347 B.C.E.	Amenhotep IV (Akhenaten)
1347–1337 B.C.E.	Tutankhamen
1289–1224 B.C.E.	Ramses II

Between Two Worlds

City-based civilization was an endangered species throughout antiquity. Just beyond the well-tilled fields of Mesopotamia and the fertile delta of the Nile lay the world of the Semitic tribes of seminomadic shepherds and traders. Of course, not all Semites were nonurban. Many had formed part of the heterogeneous population of the Sumerian world. But the majority of Semitic peoples continued to live a life that was radically different from that of the people of the floodplain civilizations. From these, one small group, the Hebrews, emerged to establish a religious and cultural tradition that was unique in antiquity.

The Hebrew Alternative

Sometime after 2000 B.C.E., small Semitic bands under the leadership of patriarchal chieftains spread into what is today Syria, Lebanon, Israel, and Palestine. These bands crisscrossed the Fertile Crescent, searching for pasture for their flocks. Semitic Aramaeans and Chaldeans brought with them not only their flocks and families, but Mesopotamian culture as well.

Mesopotamian Origins. Hebrew history records such Mesopotamian traditions as the story of the flood (Genesis 6–10), legal traditions strongly reminiscent of those of Hammurabi, and the worship of the gods on high places. Stories such as that of the Tower of Babel (Genesis 11) and the garden of Eden (Genesis 2–4) likewise have a Mesopotamian flavor, but with a difference. For these wandering shepherds, urban culture was a curse. In the Hebrew Bible (the Christian Old Testament) the first city was built by Cain, the first murderer. The Tower of Babel, probably a ziggurat, was a symbol not of human achievement but of human pride.

At least some of these wandering Aramaeans, among them the biblical patriarch Abraham, rejected the gods of Mesopotamia. Religion among these nomadic groups focused on the specific divinity of the clan. In the case of Abraham, this was the god El. Abraham and his successors were not monotheists. They did not deny the existence of other gods. They simply believed that they had a personal pact with their own god.

In its social organization and cultural traditions, Abraham's clan was no different from its neighbors. These independent clans were ruled by a senior male. Women, whether wives, concubines, or slaves, were treated as distinctly inferior, virtually as property.

Egypt and Exodus. Some of Abraham's descendants must have joined the steady migration from Canaan into Egypt that took place during the Middle Kingdom and the Hyksos period. Although they were initially well treated, after the expulsion of the Hyksos in the sixteenth century B.C.E., many of the Semitic settlers in Egypt were reduced to slavery. Around the thirteenth century B.C.E., a small band of Semitic slaves numbering fewer than 1,000 left Egypt for Sinai and Canaan under the leadership of Moses. The memory of this departure, known as the Exodus, became the formative experience of the descendants of those who had taken part and those who later joined them. Moses, a Semite who carried an Egyptian name and who, according to tradition, had been raised in the royal court, was the founder of the Israelite people.

During the years that they spent wandering in the desert and then slowly conquering Canaan, the Israelites forged a new identity and a new faith. From the

A relief on a basalt obelisk (ca. 830 B.C.E.) depicts Jehu, a king of Israel, making obeisance to the Assyrian monarch Shalmaneser III. This is the oldest identified portrait of an Israelite.

Midianites of the Sinai Peninsula, they adopted the god Yahweh as their own. Although composed of various Semitic and even Egyptian groups, the Israelites adopted the oral traditions of the clan of Abraham and identified his god, El, with Yahweh. They interpreted their extraordinary escape from Egypt as evidence of a covenant with this god, a treaty similar to those concluded between the Hittite kings and their dependents. Yahweh was to be the Israelites' exclusive god; they were to make no alliances with any others. They were to preserve peace among themselves, and they were obligated to serve Yahweh with arms. This covenant was embodied in the law of Moses. Inspired by their new identity and their new religion, the Israelites swept into Canaan. Taking advantage of the vacuum of power left by the Hittite-Egyptian standoff following the battle of Kadesh, they destroyed or captured the cities of the region. In some cases, the local population welcomed the Israelites and their religion. In other places, the indigenous people were slaughtered down to the last man, woman, and child.

A King Like All the Nations

During its first centuries, Israel was a loosely organized confederation of tribes whose only focal point was the religious shrine at Shiloh. This shrine, in contrast with the temples of other ancient peoples, housed no idols, only a chest, known as the Ark of the Covenant, which contained the law of Moses and mementos of the Exodus. In times of danger, temporary leaders would lead united tribal armies. The power of these leaders, who were called judges in the Hebrew Bible, rested solely on their personal leadership qualities. This charisma indicated that the spirit of Yahweh was with the leader. Yahweh alone was the ruler of the people.

By the eleventh century B.C.E., this disorganized political tradition placed the Israelites at a disadvantage in fighting their neighbors. The Philistines, who dominated the Canaanite seacoast and had expanded inland, posed the greatest threat. By 1050 B.C.E., the Philistines had defeated the Israelites, captured the Ark of the Covenant, and occupied most of their territory. To consolidate their forces, the Israelite religious leaders reluctantly established a kingdom. Its first king was Saul, and its second was David.

David (ca. 1000–962 B.C.E.) and his son and successor, Solomon (ca. 961–922 B.C.E.), brought the kingdom of Israel to its peak of power, prestige, and territorial expansion. David defeated and expelled the Philistines, subdued Israel's other enemies, and created a united state that included all of Canaan from the desert to the sea. He established Jerusalem as the political and religious capital. Solomon went still further, building a magnificent temple complex to house the Ark of the Covenant and to serve as Israel's national shrine. David and Solomon restructured Israel from a tribal to a monarchical society. The old tribal structure remained only as a religious tradition.

The cost of this transformation was high. The kingdom under David and especially under Solomon grew more tyrannical as it grew more powerful. Solomon behaved like any other king of his time. He contracted marriage alliances with neighboring princes and allowed his wives to practice their own cults. He demanded extraordinary taxes and services from his people to pay for his lavish building projects. When he was unable to pay his Phoenician creditors for supplies and workers, he deported Israelites to work as slaves in Phoenician mines.

THE KINGDOMS OF ISRAEL AND JUDAH. From its greatest extent under Solomon, the Kingdom of Israel split into rival northern and southern kingdoms and then progressively lost ground against Assyria and Babylon.

Exile

Not surprisingly, the united kingdom did not survive Solomon's death. The northern region broke off to become the Kingdom of Israel with its capital in Shechem. The south, the Kingdom of Judah, continued the tradition of David from his capital of Jerusalem. These small, weak kingdoms did not long maintain their independence. Beginning in the ninth century B.C.E., a new Mesopotamian power, the Assyrians, began a campaign of conquest and unprecedented brutality throughout the Near East. In 722 B.C.E., the Assyrians destroyed the Kingdom of Israel and deported thousands of its people to upper Mesopotamia. In 586 B.C.E., the Kingdom of Judah was conquered by Assyria's destroyers, the New Babylonian Empire under King Nebuchadnezzar II (604–562 B.C.E.). The temple of Solomon was destroyed, Jerusalem was burned, and Judah's elite were deported to Babylon.

The Babylonian captivity ended some 50 years later when the Persians, who had conquered Babylonia, allowed the people of Judah to return to their homeland. Those who returned did so with a new understanding of themselves and their covenant with Yahweh, who was now seen as not just one god among many but as the one universal God. This new understanding was central to the development of Judaism.

The fundamental figures in this transformation were Ezra and Nehemiah (fifth and fourth centuries B.C.E.), who were particularly concerned with keeping Judaism uncontaminated by other religious and cultural influences. They condemned those who had remained in Judaea and who had intermarried with foreigners during the exile. Only the exiles who had remained faithful to Yahweh and who had avoided foreign marriages could be the true interpreters of the **Torah**, or law. This ideal of separatism and national purity came to characterize the Jewish religion in the post-exilic period.

Among its leaders were the Pharisees, a group of zealous adherents to the Torah, who produced a body of oral law termed the **Mishnah**, or second law, by which the law of Moses was to be interpreted and safeguarded. In subsequent centuries this oral law, along with its interpretation, developed into the Talmud, which did not assume its final form until almost a thousand years after the Babylonian exile. Pharisees believed in resurrection and in spirits such as angels and devils. They also believed that a messiah, or savior, would arise as a new David to reestablish Israel's political independence. Among the priestly elite, the hope for a Davidic messiah was seen as more universal: A priestly messiah would arise and bring about the kingdom of glory. Some Jews actively sought political liberation from the Persians and their successors. Others were more intent on preserving ritual and social purity until the coming of the messiah. Still others, such as the Essenes, withdrew into isolated communities to await the fulfillment of the prophecies.

Nineveh and Babylon

The Assyrian state that destroyed Israel accomplished what no other power had ever achieved. It tied together the floodplain civilizations of Mesopotamia and Egypt. But the Assyrian state was not just larger than the nation-states that had preceded it; it differed in nature as well as in size. The nation-states of Akkadia, Babylonia, the Hittites, and even the Egyptian Empire were essentially diverse collections of city-states. The Assyrian Empire was an integrated state in which conquered regions were reorganized and remade along the model of the central government. By the middle of the seventh century B.C.E., the Assyrian Empire stretched from the headwaters of the Tigris and Euphrates rivers to the Persian Gulf, along the coast from Syria to beyond the Nile Delta, and up the Nile to Thebes.

The Assyrian Empire

The Assyrian plain north of Babylonia had long been the site of a small Mesopotamian state. Early expansion soon gave rise to internal revolt and external threats. However, revolt paved the way for the ascension of Tiglath-pileser III (746–727 B.C.E.), the greatest empire builder of Mesopotamia since Sargon. In the sense that the Assyrians not only conquered but created an administrative system by which to rule, theirs was the first true empire, and as such, it served as a model for Persia, Macedonia, and Rome.

From his palace at Nineveh, Tiglath-pileser combined all of the traditional elements of Mesopotamian statecraft with a new religious ideology and social system to create the framework for a lasting multiethnic imperial system. The heart of Tiglath-pileser's program was the most modern army the world had ever seen. In place of traditional armies of peasants and slaves supplied by great aristocrats, he raised professional armies from the conquered lands of the empire and placed them under the command of Assyrian generals. The Assyrian army was also the first to make massive use of iron weapons, which were superior to the bronze swords and shields of their enemies.

In addition to the professional army, Tiglath-pileser created the most developed military-religious ideology of any ancient people. Kings had long been agents of the gods, but Ashur, the god of the Assyrians, had but one command: Enlarge the empire! Thus warfare was the mission and duty of all.

Tiglath-pileser restructured his empire, both at home in Assyria and abroad, so that revolts of the sort that had nearly destroyed it would be less likely. Within Assyria he increased the number of administrative districts, thus decreasing the strength of each, which reduced the likelihood of successful rebellions launched by dissatisfied governors. Outside Assyria proper, the king liquidated traditional leaders whenever possible and appointed Assyrian governors or at least assigned loyal overseers to protect his interests. To shatter regional identities, which could lead to separatist movements, Tiglath-pileser deported and resettled conquered peoples on a massive scale. Finally, in the tradition of his Assyrian predecessors, Tiglath-pileser and his successors maintained control of conquered peoples through a policy of unprecedented cruelty and brutality. One ruler, for example, boasted of once having flayed an enemy's chiefs and used their skins to cover a great pillar that he erected at their city gate and on which he impaled his victims.

The New Babylonian Empire

Ironically, while the imperial military and administrative system created by the Assyrians became in time the blueprint for future empires, its very ferocity led to its downfall. The hatred inspired by such brutality led to the destruction of the Assyrian Empire at the hands of a coalition of its subjects. In what is today Iran, Indo-European tribes coalesced around the Median dynasty. Egypt shook off its Assyrian lords under the leadership of the pharaoh Psamtik I (664–610 B.C.E.). In Babylon, which had always proven difficult for the Assyrians to control, a new Aramaean dynasty began to oppose Assyrian rule. In 612 B.C.E., the Medes and Babylonians joined forces to attack and destroy Nineveh.

However, the lessons that the Assyrians taught the world were not forgotten by the Babylonians, who modeled their imperial system on that of their predecessors. Administration of the New Babylonian Empire, which extended roughly over the length of the Tigris and extended west into Syria and Canaan, owed much to Assyrian tradition. The Code of Hammurabi once more formed the fundamental basis for justice. Babylonian kings restored and enriched temples to the Babylonian gods, and temple lands, administered by priests appointed by the king, played an important role in Babylonian economy and culture. Babylonian priests, using the mathematical methods developed during the Old Kingdom, made important advances in mathematical astronomy. Under King Nebuchadnezzar II, the city of Babylon reached its zenith, covering some 500 acres and containing a population of over 100,000, more than twice the population of Uruk at its height. The city walls, later counted among the seven wonders of the world by the Greeks, were so wide that two chariots could ride abreast on them. Yet this magnificent fortification was never tested. In 539 B.C.E., a Persian army under King Cyrus II (ca. 585–ca. 529 B.C.E.), who had ousted the Median dynasty in 550 B.C.E., slipped into the city through the Euphrates riverbed at low water and took the city by surprise.

SUMMARY

Before Civilization   Evolving from earlier humanlike creatures, *Homo sapiens sapiens* emerged around 40,000 years ago. Early *Homo sapiens sapiens* lived in small kin groups of 20 or 30 hunter-gatherers. During the upper or late Paleolithic era (ca. 35,000–10,000 B.C.E.), culture was increasingly determinant in human life. Around 10,000 B.C.E., two profound transformations began: sedentarization and the agricultural revolution. These twin revolutions brought with them dramatic developments in social and political organization, settlement patterns, religion, and the relationship between humans and nature.

Mesopotamia: Between the Two Rivers   The harsh conditions of Mesopotamia drove its inhabitants to create civilization. Early Mesopotamian civilization was city-oriented and dominated by religious, military, and administrative elites. Cities were centers of Mesopotamian religion. The power of Mesopotamian civilization was multiplied many times over by technological innovation, particularly the invention of writing. Sargon's Akkadian state was the first great multiethnic empire in the West, spreading Sumerian civilization as it expanded. The collapse of the Akkadian state made room for new powers to rise. Hammurabi followed in the tradition of Sargon and Shulgi, expanding the Babylonian state and creating a codified body of law.

The Gift of the Nile   Conditions in the Nile Valley helped create an extraordinarily stable civilization in Egypt. Historians divide Egyptian history into four periods of political centralization: pre- and early dynastic Egypt (ca. 3150–2770 B.C.E.), the Old Kingdom (ca. 2770–2200 B.C.E.), the Middle Kingdom (ca. 2050–1786 B.C.E.), and the New Kingdom (ca. 1560–1087 B.C.E.). Egyptian kings were seen as gods whose primary responsibility was the care of their people. The transition from the Old Kingdom to the Middle Kingdom was marked by increased power for elites at the expense of the king. Weakness in the Middle Kingdom allowed for domination by the Hyksos which, in turn, gave way to the New Kingdom, a period of expansion and empire building. Competition between the Egyptian and Hittite empires for regional dominance ended in a draw and the signing of a peace treaty.

Between Two Worlds   Hebrew society and culture were rooted in Mesopotamian traditions. The early Hebrews did not deny the existence of other gods, but believed that they had a special covenant with their god. Led by Moses, the founder of the Israelite people, the Israelites forged a new identity and faith out of their experience of the exodus from Egypt. The conquest of Canaan and pressure from regional rivals led to the establishment of the Kingdom of Israel. After King Solomon's death, the kingdom split into the kingdom of Israel and the kingdom of Judah. These two kingdoms quickly succumbed to the domination of more powerful neighbors. The kingdom of Judah was destroyed and its elites were sent into exile in Babylon. The experience of exile proved to be another transforming moment in the history of Judaism.

Nineveh and Babylon   The Assyrian state tied together the floodplain civilizations of Mesopotamia and Egypt. It differed dramatically from its predecessors in that it was an integrated state in which conquered regions were reorganized and remade along the model of the central government. Assyrian power rested on a professional military, the governing of conquered territories by Assyrian officials, the deportation and resettlement of conquered peoples, and the use of terror. The hatred the Assyrians inspired led to the creation of a Mede and Babylonian coalition that destroyed the Assyrian Empire. The fall of the Assyrians was followed by the rise of the New Babylonian Empire which, in turn, fell to a new power, the Persians.

QUESTIONS FOR REVIEW

1. What cultural developments allowed people to secure food, organize society, and overcome hostile environments before the rise of the first cities?
2. How did urbanization, the invention of writing, and political centralization first develop in the resource-poor area between the Tigris and Euphrates rivers?
3. How did the differing geographic conditions of Mesopotamia and Egypt shape the development of civilization in each?
4. What was the Hebrew people's covenant with Yahweh, and how did this help make a society quite different from the societies around it?
5. What political, religious, and military innovations made the Assyrian Empire more vast and powerful than any previously seen?

Early Greece, 2500–500 B.C.E.

Greece in the Bronze Age to 700 B.C.E.

Unlike the rich floodplains of Mesopotamia and Egypt, Greece is a stark world of mountains and sea. The rugged terrain of Greece, only 10 percent of which is flat, and the scores of islands that dot the Aegean and Ionian seas favor the development of small, self-contained agricultural societies. The Greek climate is uncertain, constantly threatening Greek farmers with failure. Rainfall varies enormously from year to year, and arid summers alternate with cool, wet winters. Wheat, barley, and beans were the staples of Greek life. Greek farmers struggled to produce the Mediterranean triad of grains, olives, and wine, which first began to dominate agriculture around 3000 B.C.E. Constant fluctuations in climate and weather from region to region helped to break down the geographical isolation by forcing insular communities to build contacts with a wider world in order to survive.

Islands of Peace

Since the late nineteenth century, archaeologists have discerned three fairly distinct late Bronze Age cultures—the Cycladic, the Minoan, and the Mycenaean—that flourished in the Mediterranean before the end of the twelfth century B.C.E.

The Cyclades. The first culture appeared on the Cyclades, the rugged islands strewn across the bottom of the Aegean from the Greek mainland to the coast of Asia Minor. As early as 2500 B.C.E., artisans in small settlements on the islands of Naxos and Melos developed a high level of metallurgical and artistic skill. Cycladic society was not concentrated into towns, nor, apparently, was it particularly warlike. Many of the largest Cycladic settlements were unfortified. Cycladic religion, to judge from fragments of large clay statues of female figures found in a temple on the island of Ceos, focused on female deities, perhaps fertility goddesses.

This early Bronze Age society slowly faded, but not before influencing its neighbors, especially Crete, the large Mediterranean island to the south. There, beginning around 2500 B.C.E., a sophisticated centralized civilization developed that was termed Minoan after the legendary King Minos of Crete.

Minoan Crete. Minoan civilization developed on the island of Crete. Crete's location between the civilizations of the Fertile Crescent, Egypt, and the barbarian worlds of the north and west made the island a natural point of exchange and amalgamation of cultures. Still, during the Golden Age of Crete, roughly between 2000 and 1550 B.C.E., the island developed its unique traditions.

Great palace complexes were constructed at Knossos, Phaistos, Hagia Triada, and elsewhere on the island. Palace bureaucrats, using a unique form of syllabic writing known as Linear A, controlled agricultural production and distribution as well as the work of skilled artisans in their surrounding areas.

Chronology

GREECE IN THE BRONZE AGE

ca. 2500 B.C.E.	Beginning of Minoan civilization in Crete
ca. 2000–1500 B.C.E.	Golden Age of Crete
ca. 1600 B.C.E.	Beginning of Mycenaean civilization in Greece
ca. 1450 B.C.E.	Cretan cities, except Knossos, destroyed
ca. 1375 B.C.E.	Knossos destroyed
ca. 1200–700 B.C.E.	Greek Dark Age
ca. 1200 B.C.E.	Mycenaean sites in Greece destroyed; Knossos destroyed again
ca. 1100–1000 B.C.E.	Writing disappears from Greece

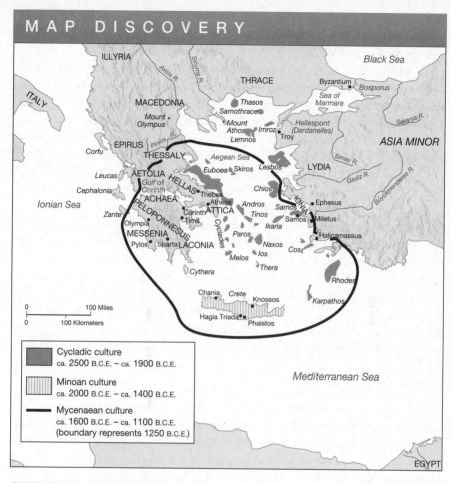

GREECE IN THE BRONZE AGE

What geographical characteristics distinguished Cycladic, Minoan, and Mycenaean civilizations? Given its location, what older civilizations might have exerted a major influence on the civilization of Crete?

Cretan Society and Religion. Like other ancient civilizations, Minoan Crete was strongly stratified. The vast peasantry paid a heavy tribute in olive oil and other produce. Tribute or taxes flowed to local and regional palaces and ultimately to Knossos, which stood at the pinnacle of a four-tiered network uniting the island. To some extent, the palace elites redistributed this wealth back down the system through their patterns of consumption.

Though the system may have been exploitive, it was not militaristic. None of the palaces or towns of Crete was fortified. Nor was the cult of the ruler particularly emphasized. A key to this unique social tone may be Cretan religion and, with it, the unusually high status of women. Although male gods received veneration, Cretans particularly worshipped female deities. Chief among the female deities was the mother goddess, who was the source of good and evil.

Although Minoan society was not clearly matriarchal, it nevertheless differed considerably from the floodplain civilizations of the Near East and the societies that were developing on the mainland. At least until the fourteenth century B.C.E., both men and women seem to have played important roles in religious and public life and together built a structured society without the need for vast armies or warrior kings.

Around 1450 B.C.E., a wave of destruction engulfed all of the Cretan cities except Knossos, which was finally annihilated around 1375 B.C.E. The causes of this catastrophe continue to inspire historical debate. Some argue that a natural disaster such as an earthquake or the eruption of a powerful volcano on Thera was responsible for the destruction. More likely, given the martial traditions of the continent and their total absence on Crete, the destruction was the work of mainland Greeks taking control of Knossos and other Minoan centers. Around this same time, true warrior graves equipped with weapons and armor begin to appear on Crete and at Knossos for the first time. Following this violent conquest, only Knossos and Phaistos were rebuilt, presumably by Greek lords who had eliminated the other political centers on the island. Knossos was ravaged again around 1200 B.C.E.

Mainland of War

The contrast between the vulnerable islands and the violent Greek mainland was particularly marked. Around 1600 B.C.E., a new and powerful warrior civilization arose on the Peloponnesus at Mycenae. This entire civilization, which encompassed not only the mainland but also parts of the coast of Asia Minor, is called **Mycenaean**, although there is no evidence that the city of Mycenae actually ruled all of Greece.

The Mycenaeans quickly adopted artisanal and architectural techniques from neighboring cultures, especially from the Hittites and from Crete, and incorporated these techniques into a distinctive tradition of their own. Unlike the open Cretan palaces and towns, Mycenaean palaces were strongly walled fortresses. From these palaces, Mycenaean kings and their staffs controlled the collection of taxes and tribute as well as the production of bronze and woolen cloth and governed maritime trade. Palace administrators adopted the Linear A script of Crete, transforming it to write their own language, a Greek dialect, in a writing known as **Linear B**, which appears to have been used almost exclusively for record keeping in palaces.

The Dark Age

Mycenaean domination did not last for long. Around 1200 B.C.E., many of the mainland and island fortresses and cities were sacked and totally destroyed. In some areas, such as Pylos, the population fell to roughly 10 percent of what it had

Female divinity from Knossos, ca. 1600 B.C.E. This extraordinary statuette, which has recently been judged by some scholars as a modern fake or at least a composite of modern and ancient parts, draws on traditions that link snakes as symbols of the underworld and sources of wisdom, as well as birds of prey such as that balanced on the head of this divinity. The place of such divinities in Minoan civilization, if it is indeed from Knossos, is uncertain.

been previously. Centralized government, literacy, urban life—civilization itself—disappeared from Greece for over 400 years.

No single invasion or natural disaster destroyed Mycenaean Greece. It self-destructed. Its disintegration was part of the widespread crisis affecting the eastern Mediterranean in the twelfth century B.C.E. The pyramid of Mycenaean lordship, built by small military elites commanding maritime commercial networks, was always threatened with collapse. Overpopulation, the fragility of the agrarian base, the risks of overspecialization in cash crops such as grain in Messenia and sheep raising in Crete, and rivalry among states—all made Mycenaean culture vulnerable. The disintegration of the Hittite Empire and the near-collapse of the Egyptian Empire disrupted Mediterranean commerce, exacerbating hostilities among Greek states.

As internal warfare raged, the delicate structures of elite lordship disappeared in the mutual sackings and destructions of the palace fortresses. With the collapse of the administrative and political system on which Mycenaean civilization was built, the tiny elite that had ruled it vanished as well. From roughly

1200 until 800 B.C.E., the Aegean world entered what is generally termed the Dark Age, a confused period about which little is known, during which Greece returned to a more primitive level of culture and society.

A New Material Culture. In the wake of the Mycenaean collapse, bands of northerners moved slowly into the Peloponnesus while other Greeks migrated out from the mainland to the islands and the coast of Asia Minor. As these tribal groups merged with the indigenous populations, they gave certain regions distinctive dialectic and cultural characteristics. Thus, the Dorians settled in much of the Peloponnesus, Crete, and southwest Asia Minor. Ionians made Attica, Euboea, and the Aegean islands their home; a mixed group called Aeolians began to migrate to central and northwest Asia Minor. As a result, from the eleventh century B.C.E., both shores of the Aegean became part of a Greek-speaking world. Still later, Greeks established colonies in what is today southern Ukraine, Italy, North Africa, Spain, and France. Throughout its history, Greece was less a geographical than a cultural designation.

Everywhere in this world, between roughly 1100 and 1000 B.C.E., architecture and urban traditions declined, and writing disappeared along with the elites for whose exclusive benefit these achievements had served. The Greece of this Dark Age was much poorer, more rural, and more simply organized. It was also a society of ironworkers. Iron began to replace bronze as the most common metal for ornaments, tools, and weapons. At first this was a simple necessity. The collapse of long-distance trade deprived Greeks of access to tin and copper, the essential ingredients of bronze. Gradually, however, the quality of iron tools and weapons began to improve as smiths learned to work hot iron into a primitive steel.

What little is known of this period must be gleaned from archaeology and from the *Iliad* and the *Odyssey*, Homer's two great epic poems that were written down around 750 B.C.E., near the end of the Dark Age. The archaeological record is bleak. Pictorial representation of humans and animals almost disappears. Luxury goods and most imports are gone from tombs. Pottery made at the beginning of the Dark Age shows little innovation, crudely imitating forms of Mycenaean production.

Gradually, beginning in the eleventh century B.C.E., things began to change a bit. New geometric forms of decoration began to appear on pottery. New types of iron pins, weapons, and decorations appeared that owed little or nothing to the Mycenaean tradition. Cultural changes accompanied these material changes. Around the middle of the eleventh century B.C.E., Greeks in some locations stopped burying their dead and began to practice cremation. Whatever the meaning of these changes, they signaled something new on the shores of the Aegean.

The Evidence of Homer. The two epic poems—the *Iliad* and the *Odyssey*—hint at this something new. Traditionally ascribed to Homer, these epics were actually the work of oral bards or performers who composed as they chanted. Although the Homeric poems explicitly harken back to the Mycenaean Age, much of the description of life, society, and culture actually reflects Dark Age

A golden funeral mask (ca.1500 B.C.E.) found in the royal tombs of Mycenae. The mask is one of four masks excavated along with engraved swords and daggers as well as other weapons and, silver and gold drinking cups and horns, at Mycenae by Heinrich Schliemann in the nineteenth century. The artistry shows the influence of Minoan art in Mycenae. Although these objects are at least three centuries older than the period to which the Trojan War is attributed, Schliemann sought to publicize his work by claiming that this was likeness of Agamemnon, the king of Mycenae in the Homeric epics.

conditions. Thus Homer's heroes were petty kings, chieftains, and nobles, whose positions rested on their wealth, measured in land and flocks, on personal prowess, on networks of kin and allies, and on military followings. The Homeric hero Odysseus is typical of these Dark Age chieftains. In the *Iliad* and the *Odyssey* he is king of Ithaca, a small island on the west coast of Greece. He retained command of his men only as long as he could lead them to victory in the raids against their neighbors.

When present, the king was judge, gift giver, lawgiver, and commander. Absent, no legal or governmental institutions preserved his authority. Instead, the nobility, lesser warriors who were constantly at odds with the king, sought to take his place. In the *Odyssey*, only their mutual rivalry saves Odysseus's wife, Penelope, from being forced to marry one of these haughty aristocrats who were eager to replace the king. Odysseus's son Telemachus summoned the assembly of the people to listen to his complaints against the noble suitors of his mother. Thus the people were not entirely excluded from public life; but this does not mean that they were particularly effective. The assembly listened to both sides and did nothing. Still, a time was coming when changes in society would give hitherto unimagined power to the silent farmers and herdsmen of the Dark Age.

From the Bronze Age civilizations, speakers of Greek had inherited distant memories of an original, highly organized urban civilization grafted onto the rural, aristocratic warrior society of the Dark Ages. Most important, this common dimly recollected past gave all Greek-speaking inhabitants of the Mediterranean world common myths, values, and identity.

MAP DISCOVERY

GREEK CITIES AND COLONIES OF THE ARCHAIC AGE

Where are the areas of Greek settlement and major colonies in the Archaic Age? What does the location of Greek settlements tell us about the relationship between Greek culture and geography? What regions of Europe and the Near East lacked Greek colonies? Why?

Archaic Greece, 700–500 B.C.E.

Between roughly 800 and 500 B.C.E., extraordinary changes took place in the Greek world. The descendants of the farmers and herdsmen of Homer's Dark Age brought about a revolution in political organization, artistic traditions, intellectual values, and social structures. In a burst of creativity forged in conflict and competition, they invented politics, abstract thought, and the individual. Greeks of the Archaic Age (ca. 700–500 B.C.E.) set the agenda for the rest of Western history.

The first sign of radical change in Greece was a major increase in population in the eighth century B.C.E. The consequences were enormous. First, population increase meant more villages and towns, greater communication among them, and thus the more rapid circulation of ideas and skills. Second, the rising population placed impossible demands on the agricultural system of much of Greece. Third, it led to greater division of labor and, with an increasingly diverse population, to fundamental changes in political systems. The old structure of loosely organized tribes and chieftains became inadequate to deal with the more complex nature of the new society.

The multiplicity of political and social forms developing in the Archaic Age set the framework within which the first flowering of Greek culture developed.

Economic and political transformations laid the basis for intellectual advance by creating a broad class with the prosperity to enjoy sufficient leisure for thought and creative activity. Finally, maritime relations brought people and ideas from around the Greek world together, cross-fertilizing artists and intellectuals in a way never before seen in the West.

Ethnos and Polis

In general, two forms of political organization developed in response to the population explosion of the eighth century B.C.E. On the mainland and in much of the western Peloponnesus, people continued to live in large territorial units called *ethne* (sing. *ethnos*). In each **ethnos**, people lived in villages and small towns scattered across a wide region. Common customs and a common religion focusing on a central religious sanctuary united them. The ethnos was governed by an elite, or **oligarchy** (meaning "rule by the few"), made up of major landowners who met from time to time in one or another town within the region. This form of government, which had its roots in the Dark Ages, continued to exist throughout the classical period.

A much more innovative form of political organization, which developed on the shores of the Aegean and on the islands, was the **polis** (pl. *poleis*), or city-state. Initially, *polis* meant simply "citadel." Villages clustered around these fortifications, which were both protective structures and cult centers for specific deities. These high, fortified sites—*acropolis* means "high citadel"—were sacred to specific gods. In addition to protection, the polis offered a marketplace, or *agora*, where farmers and artisans could trade and conduct business. The rapid population growth of the eighth century B.C.E. led to the fusion of these villages and the formation of real towns. Each town was independent, each was ruled by a monarchy or an oligarchy, and each controlled the surrounding region, the inhabitants of which were on an equal footing with the townspeople. At times of political or military crisis, the rulers might summon an assembly of the free males of the community to the agora to participate in or to witness the decision-making process. In the following centuries these city-states became the center for that most dramatic Greek experiment in government: democracy.

Technology of Writing and Warfare

The general model of the polis may have been borrowed from the eastern Mediterranean Phoenicians, the merchant society that was responsible for much of the contact Greeks of the eighth century B.C.E. had with the surrounding world. The Phoenicians were certainly the source of an equally important innovation that appeared in Greece at the same time: the reintroduction of writing. Sometime in the eighth century B.C.E., Greeks adopted the Phoenician writing system. But unlike the abandoned Mycenaean script, the purpose of the new writing system was not primarily central administrative record keeping. From the start, this writing system was intended for private, personal use and was available to virtually anyone.

Within the polis, political power was not the monopoly of the aristocracy. The gradual expansion of the politically active population resulted largely from the demands of warfare. In the Dark Age, warfare had been dominated by heavily armed, mounted aristocrats who engaged their equals in single combat. In the Archaic Age, such individual combat between aristocratic warriors gave way to battles that were decided by the use of well-disciplined ranks of infantrymen called *phalange* (sing. **phalanx**). Although few Greeks could afford costly weapons, armor, and horses, between 25 and 40 percent of the landowners could provide the shields, lances, and bronze armor needed by the infantrymen, or **hoplites**.

The democratization of war led gradually to the democratization of political life. Those who brought victory in the phalanx were unwilling to accept total domination by the aristocracy in the agora. The rapid growth of the urban population, the increasing impoverishment of the rural peasantry, and the rise of a new class of wealthy merchant commoners were all challenges that traditional forms of government failed to meet. Everywhere, traditional aristocratic rule was being undermined, and cities searched for ways to resolve this social conflict. No one solution emerged, and one of the outstanding achievements of archaic Greece was the almost limitless variety of political forms elaborated in its city-states.

Colonists and Tyrants

Colonization and tyranny were two intertwined results of the political and social turmoil of the seventh century B.C.E. Population growth, changes in economy, and opposition to aristocratic power led Greeks to seek change externally through emigration and internally through political restructuring.

A Corinthian vase showing hoplites marching into battle.

Late in the eleventh century B.C.E., Greeks had begun to migrate to new homes on the islands and along the coast of Asia Minor, in search of commercial advantages or a better life.

Beginning around 750 B.C.E., a new form of colonization began in the western Mediterranean. The impetus for this expansion was not primarily trade, but rather the need to reduce population pressure at home. The colonists were not always volunteers. At Thera, for example, young men were chosen by lot to colonize Cyrene. The penalty for refusing to participate was death and confiscation of property. Usually, colonists were only single males, the most volatile portion of the community. Colonies were thus a safety valve to release the pressures of population growth and political friction. Although colonies remained attached culturally to their mother cities, they were politically independent. The men who settled them were warriors as well as farmers or traders and carved out their new cities at the expense of the local population.

Colonization relieved some of the population pressure on Greek communities, but it did not solve the problem of political conflict. As opposition to entrenched aristocracies grew, new leaders opposed to aristocratic rule seized power. These rulers were known as **tyrants**, a term that originally meant the same as king. In the course of the later sixth century B.C.E., "tyrant" came to designate those who had achieved supreme power without benefit of official position. Often, this rise to power came through popularity with hoplite armies.

However, the term tyrant did not carry the negative connotation associated with it today. Tyrants weakened the power of entrenched aristocratic groups, promoted the prosperity of their supporters by protecting farmers and encouraging trade, undertook public works projects, founded colonies, and entered into marriage alliances with rulers of other cities, which provided some external peace. Although they stood outside the traditional organs of government, tyrants were frequently content to govern through them, leaving magistracies and offices intact but ensuring that through elections these offices were filled with the tyrant's supporters. Thus at Corinth, Mytilene, Athens, and elsewhere, tyrants preserved and even strengthened constitutional structures as a hedge against the return to power of aristocratic factions.

The great weakness of tyrannies was that they depended for their success on the individual qualities of the ruler. Tyrants tended to pass their powers on to their sons, and as tyrannies became hereditary, cities came to resent incompetent or excessively cruel successors. As popular tyranny gave way to harsh and arbitrary rule, opposition brought on civil war and the deposition or abdication of the tyrant. Gradually, "tyranny" acquired the meaning it bears today, and new forms of government emerged.

Gender and Power

Military, political, and cultural life in the city-states became more democratic, but this democratization did not extend to women. Greek attitudes toward gender roles and sexuality were rigid. Except in a few cities and in certain religious cults, women played no public role in the life of the community. They remained firmly under male control throughout their lives, passing from the authority of their fathers to that of their husbands. For the most part, friendship existed only between members of the same sex, and this friendship was often intensely sexual. Bisexuality was the norm in Greek society, although neither Greek homosexuality nor heterosexuality was the same as in modern society. Rather, they coexisted and formed parts of a sexuality of domination by those considered superior in age, rank, or sex over others. Mature men took young boys as their lovers, helped to educate them, and inspired them by word and deed to grow into ideal warriors and citizens.

Those women who were in public life were mostly slaves, frequently prostitutes. Many female slaves were acquired by collecting and raising female infants who had been abandoned. Greek society did not condemn or even question abandonment of infants, prostitution, or sexual exploitation of women and slave boys. These practices formed part of the complex and varied social systems of the developing city-states.

Gods and Mortals

Greeks and their gods enjoyed an ambivalent, almost irreverent relationship. On the one hand, Greeks made regular offerings to the gods, pleaded with them for help, and gave them thanks for assistance. On the other, the gods were thoroughly human, sharing in an exaggerated manner not only human strengths and virtues but also weaknesses and vices.

Greeks offered sacrifices to the gods on altars, which were raised everywhere—in homes, in fields, in sacred groves. No group had the sort of monopoly on the cult of the gods that Mesopotamian and Egyptian priests enjoyed. Unlike the temples of other societies, Greek temples were houses of the gods, not centers of ritual. These temples reflected the wealth and patriotism of the city. They stood as monuments to the human community rather than to the divine.

On special occasions, festivals were celebrated at sanctuaries, honoring the gods of the city with processions, athletic contests, and feasts. Some of these celebrations drew participants from all of the Greek world. The two greatest pan-Hellenic (meaning "all Greek," from *Hellas*, the Greek word for Greece) sanctuaries were Olympia and Delphi. Because both were remote from centers of political power, they were insulated from interstate rivalry and provided neutral ground on which hostile neighbors could meet in peace.

Beginning in 776 B.C.E., every four years, wars and conflicts were temporarily suspended while athletes from the whole Greek world met at Olympia to participate in contests in honor of Zeus. Olympic victors were treated as national heroes.

Delphi, the site of the shrine of Apollo, god of music, archery, medicine, and prophecy, was the second pan-Hellenic cult center. Delphi's fame lay in its oracle, or spokeswoman, for the god Apollo. From the eighth century B.C.E., before undertaking any important decision such as establishing a colony, beginning a war, or even contracting a marriage, individuals and representatives of distant cities traveled to Delphi to ask Apollo's advice or to seek purification from the guilt attached to shedding the blood of others and reconciliation with their fellow citizens.

Though gods were petitioned, placated, and pampered, they were not privileged or protected. Unlike the awe-inspiring gods of the Mesopotamians and Egyptians, the traditional Greek gods, inherited from the Dark Age, were represented in ways that showed them as all too human, vicious, and frequently ridiculous. The Greek gods were immortal, superhuman in strength, and able to interfere in human affairs. But in all things they reflected the values and weaknesses of the Greek mortals, who could bargain with them, placate them, and even trick them.

Religious cults were not under the exclusive control of any priesthood or political group. Therefore there were no official versions of stories of gods and goddesses. No one group or sacred site enjoyed a monopoly on access to the gods. Like literacy and government, the gods belonged to all.

Myth and Reason

The glue holding together the individual and frequently hostile Greek poleis and the ethne scattered throughout the Mediterranean was their common stock of myths. Stories of gods and heroes, told and retold, were fashioned into *mythoi* (myths, literally, "formulated speech"), which explained and described the world both as it was and as it should be. Myths were told about every city, shrine, river, mountain, and island. Myths explained the origins of cities, festivals, the world itself. Such stories were more than simply fanciful explanations of how things came to be. Myths sanctioned and supported the authority of social, political, and religious traditions and provided a means of reasoning about the world.

Chronology

ARCHAIC GREECE

ca. 780–720 B.C.E.	Population increase in Greece
776 B.C.E.	First Olympic Games held
ca. 750–700 B.C.E.	Greeks develop writing system based on Phoenician model; Greeks begin colonizing western Mediterranean
ca. 700–500 B.C.E.	Archaic Age of Greece
ca. 700 B.C.E.	First stone temples appear in Greece
ca. 650 B.C.E.	Cypselus breaks rule of Bacchiads in Corinth; rules city as tyrant
594 B.C.E.	Solon elected chief archon of Athens; institutes social and political reforms
586 B.C.E.	Death of Periander ends tyrants' rule in Corinth
499 B.C.E.	Ionian cities revolt

Art and the Individual

Archaic Greeks borrowed from everywhere and transformed all that they borrowed. Just as they adopted and adapted the Phoenician alphabet and Mesopotamian science, they took Near Eastern and Egyptian painting and sculpture and made them their own. During the Dark Age, the Mycenaean traditions of art had entirely disappeared. Pottery showed only geometric decorations; sculpture was unknown. Gradually, from the ninth century B.C.E., stylized human and animal figures, lions, griffins, and other strange beasts began to appear within the tightly composed geometric patterns. By the eighth century B.C.E., such exotic subjects had given way to the Greek passion for human images taken from their own myths and legends. As the popularity of these mythic and heroic scenes increased, so too did the artists' technical competence. Greek artists competed with one another to overcome technical problems of perspective and foreshortening. From the sixth century B.C.E., many of the finest examples were signed. Such masterpieces celebrated not only the heroes of the past but also the artist as individual and as the interpreter of culture no less original than the poet.

Greek sculpture underwent a similar dramatic development. The earliest and most common subject of archaic sculpture was the standing male nude, or **kouros** figure, which was in wide demand as a grave monument, dedication to a

The Calf-Bearer was commissioned for the temple of Athena ca. 570 B.C.E., which was destroyed by the Persians in 480 B.C.E. when they captured Athens and burned the Acropolis. This archaic statue clearly shows its affinity to the archaic kouros, particularly in the way that the figure steps forward in a tradition that has its origins in Egyptian sculpture. However here one sees a slight adjustment of the weight to the left leg, suggesting genuine movement, as well as the position of the arms and the animal's legs, all suggesting a move toward a more naturalistic depiction of the human and animal forms.

god, or even a cult statue of male deity. In Egypt, Greeks of the seventh century B.C.E. had seen colossal statues and had learned to work stone. The rigidly formulaic position of the kouros followed Egyptian tradition and left little room for creativity. Thus sculptors sought to give their statues originality and individuality, not as representations of individuals, but as the creations of the individual sculptor. To this end, they experimented with increasingly natural molding of limbs and body and began signing their works. Thus, as in vase painting, Greek sculpture reflected the importance of the individual, not in its subject matter, but in its creator.

The real challenges in sculpture came in the portrayal of narrative in decorations on monuments, primarily temples. Unlike kouroi, which were usually private commissions intended to adorn the tombs of aristocrats, these public buildings were constructed as expressions of civic pride and were accessible to everyone. Here the creativity and dynamism of Greek cities could be paralleled in stone. Figures such as the Calf-Bearer (ca. 590 B.C.E.) from the Athenian acropolis are daring in the complexity of composition and the delicacy of execution. (See photo on p. 44.) These are statues that tell stories. In the Calf-Bearer, a master farmer carries a calf to be sacrificed to Athena. The two gentle heads and the cross formed by the farmer's hands and the calf's legs are individual traits without precedent in ancient art. Although formally intended for religious purposes, these figures serve not only the gods and the aristocratic elite, but the whole community.

A Tale of Three Cities

The political, social, and cultural transformations that occurred in the Archaic Age took different forms across the Greek world. No community or city-state was typical of Greece. The best way to understand the diversity of Archaic Greece is to examine three very different cities that by the end of the sixth century B.C.E. had become leading centers of Greek civilization. Corinth, Sparta, and Athens present something of the spectrum of political, cultural, and social models of the Hellenic world.

Wealthy Corinth

Corinth owed its prosperity to its privileged site, dominating both a rich coastal plain and the narrow isthmus connecting the Peloponnesus to the mainland. In the eighth century B.C.E., as Greeks turned their attention to the west, Corinthians led the way. Corinthian trade led to colonization, and settlers from Corinth founded Syracuse and other cities in Sicily and Italy, which served as markets for Corinthian products. Even more important to Corinthian prosperity was its role in the transport of other cities' products from east to west. By carrying goods across the isthmus and loading them onto other ships, merchants could avoid the long, dangerous passage around the Peloponnesus.

Social Tensions. The precise details of early Corinthian government are uncertain. Still, it appears that in Corinth, as in many other cities, a tyranny replaced a ruling clan, and in time this tyranny ended with an oligarchic government. Until the middle of the seventh century B.C.E., Corinth and its wealth were ruled in typical Dark Age fashion by an aristocratic clan known as the Bacchiads. Corinth began its rise under this aristocratic rule, and individual Bacchiads led colonizing expeditions to Italy and Sicily. However, the increasing pressures of population growth, rapidly expanding wealth, and dramatic changes in the economy produced social tensions that the traditional aristocratic rulers were unable to handle. As in cities throughout the Greek world, these tensions led to the creation of a new order.

The early history of Corinth is obscure, but apparently around 650 B.C.E. a revolution led by a dissident Bacchiad named Cypselus (ca. 657–627 B.C.E.) and supported by non-Bacchiad aristocrats and other Corinthians broke the Bacchiads' grip on the city. The revolution led to the establishment of Cypselus as tyrant. Cypselus and his son Periander (ca. 627–586 B.C.E.) seem to have been generally popular with most Corinthians.

Corinth Under Its Tyrants. In Corinth, as in many other cities, the tyrants restructured taxes, relying primarily on customs duties, which were less of a burden on the peasantry. Around 600 B.C.E., Periander began construction of a causeway across the isthmus on which ships could be hauled from the Aegean to the western Mediterranean. This causeway eventually became a major source of Corinth's wealth. Periander attacked conspicuous consumption on the part of the aristocracy. He introduced laws against idleness and put thousands of Corinthians to work in extensive building programs. He erected temples and sent colonists to Italy. Under his leadership, the Corinthian fleet developed into the most powerful naval force in the Adriatic and Aegean seas. Under its tyrants, Corinth led the Greek world in the production of black figure pottery, which spread throughout the Mediterranean.

The tyrants also laid the foundation for broader political participation. Cypselus divided the population into eight tribes, based not on traditional ethnic divisions, but on arbitrary groupings by region. All of Corinth was divided into three large regions. The population of each region was distributed among each of the eight tribes. This assignment prevented the emergence of political factions based on regional disputes. Ten representatives from each tribe formed a council of 80 men. Under the tyrants this council was largely advisory and provided a connection between the autocratic rulers and the citizens.

In Corinth, as elsewhere, the strength or weakness of tyranny rested on the abilities and personality of individual tyrants. Cypselus had been a beloved liberator. His son Periander, in spite of his accomplishments, was remembered for his cruelty and violence. Shortly after Periander's death in 586 B.C.E., a revolt killed his successor, and tyranny in Corinth ended.

Oligarchy. The new government continued the tribal and council system established by Cypselus. From the sixth century B.C.E. until its conquest by Macedonia in 338 B.C.E., Corinth was ruled by an oligarchy. Although an assembly of the *demos,* or adult males, met occasionally, actual government was in the hands of eight deliberators, or *probouloi,* and nine other men from each tribe who together formed the council of eighty. The oligarchs who made up the council avoided the kind of exclusive and arbitrary tendencies that had destroyed both the Bacchiads and the tyrants. They were remarkably successful in maintaining popular support among the citizens and provided a reliable and effective government.

Martial Sparta

At the beginning of the eighth century B.C.E., the Peloponnesus around Sparta and Laconia faced circumstances similar to those of Corinth and other Greek communities. Population growth, increasing disparity between rich and poor, and an expanding economy created powerful tensions. The Spartan solution was a rigid two-tiered social structure. By the end of the Archaic Age, a small, homogeneous class of warriors called *homoioi* ("those alike"), or equals, ruled a vast population of state serfs, or *helots.* The two classes lived in mutual fear and mistrust. Spartans controlled the helots through terror and ritual murder. The helots in turn were in the philosopher Aristotle's words, "an enemy constantly waiting for the disasters of the Spartans."

Messenia. War was the center of Spartan life, and war lay at the origin of the Spartans' extraordinary social and political organization. In the eighth century B.C.E., the Spartans conquered the fertile region of Messenia and compelled the vanquished Messenians to turn over one-half of their harvests. The spoils were not divided equally but went to increase the wealth of the aristocracy, thus creating resentment among the less privileged. Early in the seventh century B.C.E., the Spartans attempted a similar campaign to take the plain of Thyreatis from the city of Argos. This time they were not so fortunate; they were defeated, and resentment of the ordinary warriors toward their aristocratic leaders flared into open conflict. The Messenians seized on this time as a moment to revolt, and for a time, Sparta was forced to fight at home and abroad for its very existence. In many cities, such crises gave rise to tyrants. In Sparta, the crisis led to radical political and social reforms that transformed the polis into a unique military system.

Reforms of Lycurgus. The Spartans attributed these reforms to the legendary lawgiver Lycurgus (seventh century B.C.E.). Whether or not Lycurgus ever existed and was responsible for all of the reforms, they saved the city and ended its internal tensions at the expense of abandoning the mainstream of Greek development. Traditionally, Greeks had placed personal honor above communal concerns. During the crisis of the second Messenian war, Spartans of all social ranks were urged to look not to individual interest but to **eunomia**, good order and obedience to the laws, which alone could unite Spartans and bring victory. United, the Spartans crushed the Messenians. In return for obedience, poor citizens received equality before the law and benefited from a land distribution that relieved their poverty. Conquered land, especially that in Messenia, was divided and distributed to Spartan warriors. However, the Spartan warriors were not expected to work the land themselves. Instead, the state reduced the defeated Messenians to the status of helots and assigned them to individual Spartans. While this system did not erase all economic inequalities among the Spartans (aristocrats continued to hold more land than others), it did decrease some of the disparity. It also provided a minimum source of wealth for all Spartan citizens and allowed them to devote themselves to full-time military service.

This land reform was coupled with a political reform that incorporated elements of monarchy, oligarchy, and democracy. The state was governed by two hereditary kings, probably representing different groups that had formed the Spartan polis earlier, and a council of elders, the *gerousia*. In peacetime, the authority of the two royal families was limited to familial and religious affairs. In war, they commanded the army and held the power of life and death.

In theory at least, the central institution of Spartan government was the gerousia, which was composed of 30 men at least 60 years of age and included the two kings. The gerousia directed all political activity, especially foreign affairs, and served as high court. Members were elected for life by the assembly, or *apella*, which was composed of all equals over the age of 30 and approved decisions of the gerousia. However, this approval, made by acclamation, could easily be manipulated, as could the course of debate within the gerousia itself. Wealth, cunning, and patronage were more important than its formal structures in the direction of the Spartan state.

Actual administration was in the hands of five magistrates, termed *ephors*, whose powers were extremely broad. They presided over joint sessions of the gerousia and apella. They held supreme authority over the kings during wartime, acted as judges for noncitizens, and controlled the *krypteia*, or secret police. The krypteia were a band of youths who practiced state terrorism as part of their rite of passage to the status of equal. On the orders of the ephors, the krypteia assassinated, intrigued, and arrested powerful people and terrorized helots. Service in this corps was considered a necessary part of a youth's education.

Social Control. The key to the success of Sparta's political reform was an even more radical social reform that placed everyone under the direct supervision and service of the state from birth until death. Although admiring aristocratic visitors often exaggerated their accounts of Spartan life, the main outlines are clear enough.

Eunomia was the sole guiding principle, and service to the state came before family, social class, and every other duty or occupation.

Spartan equals were made, not born. True, only a man born of free Spartan parents could hope to become an equal, but birth alone was no guarantee of admission to this select body, or even of the right to live. Public officials examined infants and decided whether they were sufficiently strong to be allowed to live or should be exposed on a hillside to die. From birth until age seven, a boy lived with his mother; he then entered the state education system, or *agoge*, living in barracks with his contemporaries and enduring 13 years of rigorous military training. At age 12, training with swords and spears became more intense, as did the rigors of the lifestyle.

Much of the actual education of the youths was entrusted to older, accomplished warriors, who selected boys as their homosexual lovers. The lover served as tutor and role model, and in time the two became a fighting team. At age 20, Spartan youths were enrolled in the krypteia. Each was sent out into the countryside with nothing but a cloak and a knife, forbidden to return until he had killed a helot.

If a youth survived the rigors of his training until age 30, he could at last be incorporated into the rank of equals, provided that he could pass the last obstacle. He had to be able to furnish a sufficient amount of food from his own lands for the communal dining group to which he would be assigned. This food might come from inherited property or, if he had proved himself an outstanding warrior, from the state. Those who passed this final qualification became full members of the assembly, but they continued to live with the other warriors. Men could marry at age 20, but family life in the usual sense was nonexistent. A man could not live with his wife until age 30 because he was bound to the barracks.

Although their training was not as rigorous as that of males, Spartan women were given an education and allowed a sphere of activity unknown elsewhere in Greece. Girls, like boys, were trained in athletic competition and, like boys, competed naked in wrestling, footraces, and spear throwing. This training was based not on a belief in the equality of the sexes but simply on the desire to improve the physical stamina and childbearing abilities of Spartan women. Women were able to own land and to participate widely in business and agricultural affairs; since men were entirely involved in military pursuits, women were expected to look after economic and household affairs.

Few Lacedaemonians (as Spartans were also called) ever became equals. Not only were there far more helots than Spartans, but many free citizens of their local communities in the region, termed *perioikoi*, or peripherals, were not allowed into the agoge. Others were unable to endure the harsh life, and still others lacked the property qualifications to supply their share of the communal meals. For all the trappings of egalitarianism, equality in Sparta was the privilege of a tiny minority.

The total dedication to military life was reinforced by a deliberate rejection of other activities. From the time of the second Messenian war, Sparta withdrew from the mainstream of Greek civilization. Equals could not engage in crafts, trade, or any other forms of economic activity. Because Sparta banned silver and gold coinage, it could not participate in the growing commercial network of the Greek world. The role of Sparta in the economic, architectural, and cultural life of Greece was negligible after the seventh century B.C.E. Militarily, Sparta cast a long shadow across the Peloponnesus and beyond, but the number of equals was always too small to allow Sparta both to create a vast empire and to maintain control over the helots at home. Instead, Sparta created a network of alliances and nonaggression pacts with oligarchic neighbors. In time, this network came to be known as the Peloponnesian League.

Democratic Athens

Athens did not enjoy the advantages of a strategic site such as that of Corinth, nor was it surrounded by rich plains like Sparta. However, what Homer called the "goodly citadel of Athens" was one of the few Mycenaean cities to have escaped destruction at the start of the Dark Age. Gradually, Athens united the whole surrounding region of Attica into a single polis, by far the largest in the Greek world. Well into the seventh century B.C.E., Athens followed the general pattern of the polis seen in Corinth and Sparta. Like other Dark Age communities, Athens was ruled by aristocratic clans, particularly the Alcmaeonids. Only the members of these clans could participate in the *areopagus,* or council, which they entered after serving a year as one of the nine *archons,* or magistrates, elected yearly. Until the seventh century B.C.E., Athens escaped the social pressures brought on by population growth and economic prosperity that led to civil strife, colonialism, and tyranny elsewhere. This was due largely to its relative abundance of arable land and its commercial prosperity based on the export of grain.

Social Tensions. By the late seventh century B.C.E., however, Athens began to suffer from the same class conflict that had shaken other cities. Sometime around 630 B.C.E., an aristocrat named Cylon attempted to seize power as tyrant. His attempt failed, but when he was murdered by one of the Alcmaeonids, popular revulsion drove the Alcmaeonids from the city. A decade of strife ensued as aristocratic clans, wealthy merchants, and farmers fought for control of the city. Violence between groups and families threatened to tear the community apart.

Reforms of Solon. In 621 B.C.E., the Athenians granted a judge, Draco, extraordinary powers to revise and systematize traditional laws concerning vengeance and homicide. His restructuring of procedures for limiting vengeance and preventing bloodshed was harsh enough to add the term "draconian" to Western legal vocabulary. Still, these measures did nothing to solve the central problems of political control. Finally, in 594 B.C.E., an Athenian merchant who was respected by both aristocrats and commoners was elected chief archon and charged with reforming the city's government. Solon (ca. 630–ca. 560 B.C.E.) based his reform on the ideal of eunomia, as had the Spartans, but he followed a very different path to secure good order.

In Sparta, Lycurgus had begun with a radical redistribution of land. In Athens, Solon began with the less extreme measure of eliminating debt bondage. Athenians who had been forced into slavery or into sharecropping because of their debts were restored to freedom. A law forbade mortgaging free men and women as security for debts. Athenians might be poor, but they would be free. This free peasantry formed the basis of Athenian society throughout its history.

Solon also reorganized the rest of the social hierarchy and broke the aristocracy's exclusive control of the areopagus by dividing the society into four classes based on wealth rather than birth and opening the archonship to the top two classes. He further weakened the areopagus by establishing a council of 400 members drawn from all four classes, to which citizens could appeal decisions of the magistrates.

Solon's efforts to resolve Athens's social tensions did not entirely succeed. His laws were more humane than those of Draco, but Solon himself did not consider his new constitution perfect, only practical. Resistance from the still powerful aristocracy prompted some Athenians to urge Solon to assume the powers of a tyrant to force through his reforms. He refused, but after his death, Peisistratus (d. 527 B.C.E.), an aristocrat who was strongly supported by the peasants against his own class, hired a mercenary force to seize control of the city. After two abortive attempts, Peisistratus ruled as tyrant from 545 B.C.E. until his death.

Athenian Tyranny. Peisistratus and later his son Hippias (d. 490 B.C.E.), who succeeded him until 510 B.C.E., ruled through Solon's constitution but took care to ensure that the archons who were elected each year were their agents. Thus they strengthened the constitution even while they further weakened the aristocracy.

Peisistratus and Hippias drew their support from the *demos,* or people at large, rather than from an aristocratic faction. They claimed divine justification for their rule and made a great show of devotion to the Athenian gods. Peisistratus promoted annual festivals and, in so doing, began the great tradition of Athenian literature. The tyrants also directed a series of popular nationalistic public works programs that beautified the city, increased national pride, and provided work for the poor. They rebuilt the temple of Athena on the acropolis, for which the statue of the Calf-Bearer was commissioned. These internal measures were accompanied

An Athenian silver coin called a *tetradrachm*, dating from the fifth century B.C.E. The owl is the symbol of the goddess Athena. As Athenian wealth and power developed, its coinage became one of the most widely used currencies in the Mediterranean for exchange, even in cities hostile to Athens and the Delian League.

by support for commerce and export, particularly of grain. Soon, Athens was challenging Corinth as the leading commercial power and was trading in grain as far away as the Black Sea.

Peisistratus was firm. His son Hippias was harsh. Still, even Hippias enjoyed the support of the majority of the citizens of both popular and aristocratic factions. Only after the assassination of his younger brother did Hippias become sufficiently oppressive to drive his opponents into exile. Some of these exiles obtained the assistance of Sparta and returned to overthrow Hippias in 510 B.C.E. Hippias's defeat ended the tyrants' rule in Athens and won for Sparta an undeserved reputation as the opponent of all tyranny.

Athenian Democracy. Following the expulsion of Hippias, some aristocrats attempted to return to the "good old days" of aristocratic rule. However, Athenians had been accustomed to Solon's constitution for more than 80 years and were unwilling to give it up. Moreover, the tyrants had created a fierce sense of nationalistic pride among all ranks of Athenians, and few were willing to turn over government to the hands of only a few. When the aristocrats made their bid to recover power, their primary opponent, Cleisthenes (ca. 570–ca. 507 B.C.E.), a descendant of the Alcmaeonids, made the demos his faction and pushed through a final constitutional reform that became the basis for Athenian **democracy**.

The essence of Cleisthenes' reform lay in his reorganization of the major political units by which members of the council were selected. Previously, each citizen had belonged to one of four tribes, which were further broken down into 12 brotherhoods, or *phratries*, which were administrative and religious units. In a manner similar to that of Cypselus in Corinth, Cleisthenes reshuffled these phratries into 30 territorial units comprising urban, inland, or coastal regions. These 30 units in turn were grouped into 10 tribes, each consisting of one unit from each of the urban, inland, and coastal regions. The tribes elected the members of the council, military commanders, jurors, and magistrates. As in Corinth, this reorganization destroyed the traditional kin-based social and political pattern and integrated people of differing social, economic, and regional backgrounds. Aristocrats, merchants, and poor farmers had to work together to find common ground for political action, both regionally and nationally. With this new integrated democracy and its strong sense of nationalism, Athens emerged from the Archaic Age as the leading city of the Hellenic world.

The Coming of Persia and the End of the Archaic Age

By the end of the sixth century B.C.E., the products of Greek experimentation were evident throughout the Mediterranean. Still, these achievements were the product of small, independent, and relatively weak communities on the fringe of the civilized world.

In the second half of the sixth century B.C.E., all this changed. The Persian Empire, under its dynamic king Cyrus II, began a process of conquest and expansion west into Asia Minor, absorbing the kingdom of Lydia and conquering Ionia on the coast of Asia Minor. The Persians placed tyrants loyal to Cyrus to rule over these Greek communities, and for a few decades these centers of Greek culture and thought accepted foreign control. In 499 B.C.E., the passion for democracy, which had swept much of mainland Greece, reached Ionia. Cities such as Miletus, Ephesus, Chios, and Samos revolted, expelled their Persian-appointed tyrants, established democracies, and sent ambassadors to the mainland to seek assistance. Eretria and Athens, two mainland cities with Ionian roots, responded, sending ships and men to aid the Ionian rebels. Athenian interests were more than simple solidarity with their Ionian cousins. Athens depended on grain from the Black Sea region and believed its direct interests to lie with the area. The success of the revolt was short lived. The puny Greek cities were dealing with the largest empire the West had yet known. By 500 B.C.E., the Persian Empire included Asia Minor, Mesopotamia, Palestine, and Egypt, uniting all peoples from the Caucasus to the Sudan.

THE PERSIAN EMPIRE, CA. 500 B.C.E.

Examine the extent of the Persian Empire. Which ancient civilizations that you have studied so far were incorporated into the Persian Empire? What effects on cultural and economic exchange can you imagine to have resulted from this territorial conquest?

The giant Persian Empire responded slowly, but with force, to the Greek revolt. King Darius I (522–486 B.C.E.) gathered a vast international force from throughout his empire and set about recapturing the rebellious cities. The war lasted five years and ended in a Persian victory. By 494 B.C.E., the Persians had retaken the cities of the coast and nearby islands. In the cities that were deemed most responsible for the revolt, the population was herded together, the boys were castrated and made into royal eunuchs, the girls were sent to Darius's court, the remainder of the population was sold into slavery, and the towns were burned to the ground. Once the rebels had been disposed of, Darius set out to punish their supporters on the mainland, Eretria and Athens. With the same meticulous planning and deliberate pace, the Persian king turned his vast armies toward the Greek mainland.

SUMMARY

Greece in the Bronze Age to 800 B.C.E.   The challenges of Greek geography and climate favored the development of small, self-contained agricultural societies. The two most important late Bronze Age cultures in Greece were the Minoan and the Mycenaean. Minoan Crete was a strongly stratified civilization centered on great palace complexes. The society was not militaristic, a fact that may have contributed to its downfall. In contrast, warriors were at the heart of Mycenaean civilization. Between 1600 B.C.E. and 1200 B.C.E., the Mycenaeans dominated Greece. Their demise was followed by the Greek Dark Age, a period of violence and instability.

Archaic Greece, 800–500 B.C.E.   Between roughly 800 and 500 B.C.E., the Greeks carried out a revolution in political organization, artistic traditions, intellectual values, and social structures. A dramatic rise in population was key to these changes. Two new forms of political organization developed: the ethnos and the polis. Ethne were large territorial units with scattered populations ruled by an oligarchy. Poleis were independent city-states that controlled their surrounding regions. Colonization and tyranny were two intertwined results of political and social turmoil in the seventh century B.C.E. Public life was the almost exclusive preserve of men. Greek gods had all the virtues and vices of human beings. Greek religion was not monopolized by any particular social group. Greek art celebrated the originality of the individual artist.

A Tale of Three Cities   Corinth, Sparta, and Athens present the spectrum of political, cultural, and social models of the Hellenic world. Corinth's was built on trade and colonization. At its height, Corinth was governed by an oligarchy that was remarkably successful in maintaining popular support among the citizens and provided a reliable and effective government. In Sparta, social and economic tensions gave rise to a military government. The individual was subservient to the state and all aspects of life were subject to rigid social control. As was the case with many other Greek city-states, aristocratic rule in Athens gave way to series of tyrants. In Athens, however, tyranny was not replaced by oligarchy, as it was in Corinth, but by democracy.

The Coming of Persia and the End of the Archaic Age   In the second half of the sixth century B.C.E., the Persian Empire, under Cyrus II, began a process of conquest and expansion west into Asia Minor, conquering the Greek communities along the Ionian coast. In 499 B.C.E. a number of these communities revolted, prompting Eretria and Athens to come to their aid. The Persians crushed the Greek revolt and retook the coastal cities. This accomplished, they turned to the task of punishing the rebels' supporters on the Greek mainland.

QUESTIONS FOR REVIEW

1. What social and geographic factors shaped Greek culture in the age of the *Iliad* and the *Odyssey*?
2. What social forces spurred colonization, and what impact did colonization have on Archaic Greek civilization?
3. What do the gods, myths, and art of the Greek people reveal about their lives?
4. How did the Corinthian, Spartan, and Athenian cultures differ, and why did these city-states evolve in such different directions?

Classical and Hellenistic Greece, 500–100 B.C.E.

War and Politics in the Fifth Century B.C.E.

The vast Persian army moving west in 490 B.C.E. threatened the fruits of three centuries of Greek political, social, and cultural experimentation. The shared ideal of freedom within community and the common bond of language and culture seemed no basis on which to build an effective resistance to the great Persian Empire. Moreover, Darius I was not marching against the Greeks as such. Few Greek states other than Athens had supported the Ionians against their Persian conquerors. Many Greeks saw the Persians as potential allies or even rulers who were preferable to their more powerful Greek neighbors and to rivals within their own states. Particular interest, rather than patriotism or love of freedom, determined which cities opposed the Persian march. In the end, only Eretria, a badly divided Athens, and the small town of Plataea were prepared to refuse the Persian king's demand for gifts of earth and water, the traditional symbols of submission.

The Persian Wars

Initially, the Persian campaign followed the pattern established in Ionia. In the autumn of 490 B.C.E., Darius quickly destroyed the city of Eretria and carried off its population in captivity. The victorious Persian forces then landed at the Bay of Marathon. The total Athenian force was no more than half that of its enemies, but the Greeks were better armed and commanded the hills facing the Marathon plain on which the Persian troops had massed. The Athenians also benefited from the leadership of Miltiades (ca. 544–489 B.C.E.), an experienced soldier who had served Darius and who knew the Persian's strengths and weaknesses. For more than a week, the two armies faced each other in a battle of nerves. When the battle was finally joined, it was all over in a few hours. Six thousand Persians lay dead, while fewer than 200 Athenians were buried in the heroes' grave that still marks the Marathon plain.

The almost miraculous victory at Marathon had three enormous consequences for Athens and for Greece in general. First, it established the superiority of the hoplite phalanx as the finest infantry formation in the Mediterranean world. Second, Greeks expanded this belief in military superiority to a faith in the general superiority of Greeks over the "barbarians" (those who spoke other languages). Finally, by proving the value of the citizen army, the victory of the Athenians solidified and enhanced the democratic reforms of Cleisthenes.

Common citizens were determined that the victory won by the hoplite phalanx at Marathon should not be lost to an aristocratic faction at home. To guard against this danger, the Athenian assembly began to practice **ostracism**, a ten-year exile without loss of property, which was imposed on those who threatened to undermine the constitution of Cleisthenes. At the same time, Athenians also began to select their chief officers not simply by direct election but by lot. This practice prevented any individual from rising to power by creating a powerful faction. Themistocles (ca. 528–426 B.C.E.), the son of a noble father and a non-Greek mother, took the lead in using the tools of ostracism and selection by lot to hold the aristocratic factions at bay.

Thermopylae and Salamis

Occupied by problems elsewhere in their vast empire and by the unexpected death of Darius I in 486 B.C.E., the Persians paid little attention to Greece for six years. After Darius's death, his son Xerxes (486–465 B.C.E.) began to amass foodstuffs, weapons, and armies for a land assault on his Greek enemies. Though some Greek states more or less willingly allied themselves with the Persians, the others met in Sparta in 481 B.C.E. to plan resistance. The allies agreed that the Spartans would take command of the combined land and sea forces.

Although larger than those mustered by Athens against Darius, the Greek forces were puny compared with Xerxes' infantry and 1,000 light and highly maneuverable Ionian and Phoenician ships. The Spartan commanders sought a strategic point at which the numerical superiority of the Persian forces would be neutralized. The choice fell on the narrow pass of Thermopylae and the adjacent Euboean strait.

At Thermopylae, the Greeks held firm for days against wave after wave of assaulting troops. Finally, Greek allies of the Persians showed them a narrow mountain track by which they were able to attack the Greek position from the rear. Seeing that all was lost, the Spartan king Leonidas (490–480 B.C.E.) sent most of his allies home, leaving him and his 300 Spartan equals to face certain death.

While the Persian troops were blocked at Thermopylae, their fleet was being battered by fierce storms in the Euboean straits and harassed by the heavier

THE PERSIAN WARS. Greeks fought on both sides in the Persian Wars, while many others remained neutral.

Greek ships. Here, the Greeks learned that in close quarters they could stand up to Xerxes' Phoenician navy. This lesson proved vital a short time later. While the Persian army burned Athens and occupied Attica, Themistocles lured Xerxes' fleet into the narrow strait between Salamis and the mainland. There, the slower Greek vessels bottled up the larger and vastly more numerous enemy ships and cut them to pieces.

After Salamis, Xerxes lost his appetite for fighting Greeks. Without his fleet he could not supply a vast army far from home in hostile territory. Leaving a force to do what damage it could, he led the bulk of his army back to Persia. Soon the Athenians were taking the offensive, liberating the Ionian cities of Asia Minor and, in the process, laying the foundations of an Athenian empire that was every bit as threatening to their neighbors as that of Xerxes.

The Athenian Empire

Sparta, not Athens, should have emerged as the leader of the Greek world after 479 B.C.E. However, the constant threat of a helot revolt and the desire of the members of Sparta's Peloponnesian League to go their separate ways left Sparta too preoccupied with internal problems to fill the power vacuum left by the Persian defeat.

Athens, on the other hand, was only too ready to take the lead in bringing the war home to the Persians. With Sparta out of the picture, the Athenian fleet was the best hope of liberating the Aegean from Persians and pirates.

The Delian League. Athens accepted control in 478 B.C.E. of what historians have come to call the **Delian League**, after the island of Delos, a religious center that housed the league's treasury. Athens and some of the states with navies provided ships; others contributed annual payments to the league. Initially, the league pursued the war against the Persians, driving them back along the Aegean and the Black seas. At the same time, Athens hurriedly rebuilt its defensive fortifications, a move that Sparta and other states correctly interpreted as directed more against them than against the Persians.

Athens's domination of the Delian League ensured its prosperity. Attica, with its fragile agriculture, depended on Black Sea wheat, and the league kept these regions under Athenian control. Since Athens received not only cash "contributions" from league members but also half of the spoils taken in battle, the state's public coffers were filled. The new riches made possible the reconstruction of the city, which had been burned by the Persians, into the most magnificent city of Greece.

The league was too vital to Athenian prosperity to stand and fall with the Persian threat. Discouraged by a number of setbacks, the Athenian Callias, acting for the league, apparently concluded a peace treaty with Persia in 449 B.C.E., making the alliance no longer necessary. For a brief moment it appeared that the Delian

League might disband. But it was too late. The league had become an empire, and Athens's allies were its subjects.

Athenian Imperialism. The Athenian Empire was an economic, judicial, religious, and political union that was held together by military might. Athens controlled the flow of grain through the Hellespont to the Aegean, ensuring its own supply and heavily taxing cargoes to other cities. Athens controlled the law courts of member cities and used them to repress anti-Athenian groups. Rich and poor Athenian citizens alike acquired territory throughout the empire. Control over this empire depended on the Athenian fleet to enforce cooperation. Athenian garrisons were established in each city, and "democratic" puppet governments ruled according to the wishes of the garrison commanders. Revolt, resignation from the league, or refusal to pay the annual tribute resulted in brutal suppression. Persian tyranny had hardly been worse than Athenian imperialism.

Private and Public Life in Athens

During the second half of the fifth century B.C.E., Athens was a vital, crowded capital that drew merchants, artisans, and laborers from throughout the Greek world. At its height, the total population of Athens and surrounding Attica numbered perhaps 350,000, although probably fewer than 60,000 were citizens—adult males qualified to own land and participate in Athenian politics. Over one-quarter of the total population were slaves.

Greek slaves were not distinguished by race, ethnicity, or physical appearance. Slaves were as much the property of their owners as land, houses, cattle, and sheep were. Many masters treated their slaves well, but they were under no obligation to do so, and beatings, sexual exploitation, tattooing, starvation, and shackling were all too common.

Metics. Roughly half of Athens's free population were foreigners—*metoikoi*, or **metics**. The number of metics increased after the middle of the fifth century B.C.E.—both because of the flood of foreigners into the empire's capital and because Athenian citizenship was restricted to persons with two parents who were of citizen families. Metics could not own land in Attica, nor could they participate directly in politics. They were required to have a citizen protector and to pay a small annual tax. Otherwise, they were free to engage in every form of activity.

Women. More than half of those born into citizen families were entirely excluded from public life. These were the women who controlled and directed the vital sphere of the Athenian home, but who were considered citizens only for purposes of marriage, transfer of property, and procreation. From birth to death, every

On this fifth-century B.C.E. Athenian vase women are depicted making preparations for a wedding. Vases depicting wedding preparations and wedding scenes were a valued part of a woman's possessions, recalling the day that she passed from the authority of her father to that of her husband. Athenian red-figure pottery, in which the figure itself is outlined in paint but after firing remains unpainted, unlike the relief lines and the background, was extremely popular throughout the Mediterranean and beyond.

female citizen lived under the protection of a male guardian, either a close relative such as a father or brother, or a husband or son. Women spent almost their entire lives in the inner recesses of the home.

An honorable Athenian woman stayed at home and managed her husband's household. Only the poorest citizens sent their wives and daughters to work in the marketplace or the fields. For women, even the most casual contact with other men without permission was strictly forbidden.

Freedom in Community. The male citizens of fifth-century B.C.E. Athens were free to an extent previously unknown in the world. But Athenian freedom was freedom *in* community, not freedom *from* community. The essence of their freedom lay in their participation in public life, especially self-government, which was their passion. This participation was always within a complex network of familial, social, and religious connections and obligations. Each person belonged to a number of groups: a deme, a tribe, a family, various religious associations, and occupational groups. Each of these communities placed different and even contradictory demands on its members. The impossibility of satisfying all of these demands, of responding to the special interests of each, forced citizens to make hard choices, to set priorities, and to balance conflicting obligations. This process of selection was the essence of Athenian freedom, a freedom that, unlike that of the modern world, was based not on individualism but on a multitude of collectivities. The sum of these overlapping groupings was Athenian society, in which friends and opponents alike were united.

Unity did not imply equality. Even in fifth-century B.C.E. Athens, not all Athenians were socially or economically equal. The aristocracy was still strong, and most of the popular leaders of the century came from the ranks of old wealth and influence. Still, sovereignty lay not with these aristocrats but with the demos—the people.

In theory, the adult male citizens of Athens were its sovereigns. Since the time of Solon, they had formed the **ekklesia**, or assembly. They also made up the large juries, always composed of several hundred citizens, who decided legal cases less on law than on the political merits of the case and the quality of the orators who pleaded for each side. Such large bodies were too unwieldy to deal with the daily tasks of government. Therefore, control of these tasks fell to the council, or *boule*, composed of 500 members selected by lot by the tribes; the magistrates, who were also chosen by lot; and ten military commanders or generals, the only major office-holders who were elected rather than chosen at random.

Demagogues. Paradoxically, the resolute determination of Athenian democrats to prevent individuals from acquiring too much power helped to create a series of extraconstitutional power brokers. Since most offices were filled by lot and turned over frequently, real political leadership came not from officeholders but from generals and from popular leaders. These so-called demagogues, while at times holding high office, exercised their power through their speaking skills, informal networks, and knowledge of how to get things done. Governing an empire demanded skill, energy, and experience, but Athenian democracy was formally run by amateurs. Small wonder that the city's public life was dominated by these popular leaders.

Pericles and Athens

For 30 years, one individual dominated Athenian public life: the general Pericles (ca. 495–429 B.C.E.), a great orator and successful military commander who led Athens during the decades of its greatest glory. Athens's system of radical democracy reached its zenith under his leadership, even while Athens's imperial program drew it into a long and fatal war against Sparta, the only state powerful enough to resist it.

Pericles never ruled Athens. As a general he could only carry out the orders of the ekklesia and the boule, and as a citizen he could only attempt to persuade his fellows. Still, he was largely responsible for the extension of Athenian democracy to all free citizens. Under his influence, Athens abolished the last property requirements for officeholding. He convinced the state to pay those who served on juries, thus making it possible for even the poorest citizens to participate in this important part of Athenian government. But he was also responsible for a restriction of citizenship to those whose mothers and fathers had both been Athenians. Such a law would have denied citizenship to many of the most illustrious Athenians of the sixth century B.C.E., including his own ancestors. The law also prevented citizens of Athens's subject states from developing a real stake in the fate of the empire.

Pericles believed that the Athenian Empire had to be preserved at all costs. This policy ultimately drew Athens into deadly conflict with Sparta. The first clash between the two rival powers came around 460 B.C.E. at Megara, which lay between the Peloponnesus and Attica. The Athenians emerged victorious, checking Sparta and absorbing Megara, Aegina, and Boeotia. However, in 446 B.C.E. Megara and Boeotia rebelled, and Sparta invaded the disputed region. Unable to face this new threat at home after the disastrous loss abroad, in 445 B.C.E. the Athenians, under the leadership of Pericles, concluded a peace treaty with Sparta whereby Athens abandoned all of its continental possessions. The treaty was meant to last for 30 years, but it held for only 14.

The two great powers were eager to preserve the peace, but the whole Greek world was a tinderbox ready to burst into flame. The spark came from an unexpected direction. In 435 B.C.E., Corinth and its colony Corcyra on the Adriatic Sea came to blows, and Corcyra sought the assistance of Athens. The Athenians agreed to a defensive alliance with Corcyra and assisted it in defeating its enemy. This assistance infuriated Corinth, an ally of Sparta, and in 432 B.C.E., the Corinthians convinced the Spartans that Athens's imperial ambitions were insatiable. The next year, Sparta invaded Attica, and the Peloponnesian War, which would destroy both great powers, had begun.

The Peloponnesian War

The Peloponnesian War was actually a series of wars and rebellions. Athens and Sparta waged two devastating ten-year wars, from 431 B.C.E. to 421 B.C.E. and then again from 414 B.C.E. to 404 B.C.E. At the same time, cities in each alliance took advantage of the wars to revolt against the great powers, eliciting terrible vengeance from both Athens and Sparta. Within many of the Greek city-states, oligarchs and democrats waged bloody civil wars for control of their governments. Moreover, between 415 and 413 B.C.E., Athens attempted to expand its empire in Sicily, an attempt that ended in disaster. Before it was over, the Peloponnesian War had become an international war, with Persia entering the fray on the side of Sparta. In the end, there were no real victors, only victims.

The Archidamian War. The first phase of the war, called the Archidamian War after the Spartan king Archidamus (431–427 B.C.E.), was indecisive. Sparta pillaged

Black Sea

THRACE

Amphipolis
422 B.C.E.

MACEDON

Aegospotami
405 B.C.E.

EPIRUS

THESSALY

Hellespont

Ionian Sea

PERSIAN EMPIRE
(allied with Sparta,
413 B.C.E.)

BOEOTIA   EUBOEA

ACHAEA   ATTICA   *Aegean Sea*
        Megara ● ●Athens
Peloponnesus
        ●Aegina

IONIA

LACONIA
        ●Delos
Pylos
425 B.C.E.   ●Sparta

Mediterranean Sea

Delos

CRETE

Major battles

Delian League

Sparta and its allies

Neutral states

0   100 Miles

0   100 Kilometers

THE DELIAN LEAGUE AND THE PELOPONNESIAN WAR

When Athens turned the Delian League into its own empire, the resulting war pitted the Attica city-state against the combined forces of Sparta and Persia. Examine the extent of the Delian League, Sparta and its allies, and the neutral states. Why would Sparta and its allies feel threatened strategically and economically by the Delian League? Why was an alliance with Persia a vital part of Spartan strategy? What threats faced those states that remained neutral?

Attica but could not breach the great wall or starve Athens. In 430 B.C.E., the Spartans received unexpected help in the form of plague, which ravaged Athens for five years. By the time it ended in 426 B.C.E., as much as one-third of the Athenian population had died, including Pericles. Still Athens held out, establishing bases encircling the Peloponnesus and urging Spartan helots and allies to revolt.

At Pylos in 425 B.C.E., the Athenian generals Cleon and Demosthenes captured a major force of Spartan equals. The Spartans offset this defeat by capturing the city of Amphipolis on the northern Aegean. The defeated Athenian commander, Thucydides (d. ca. 401 B.C.E.), was exiled for his failure and retired to Spartan territory to write his great history of the war. Exhausted by a decade of death and destruction, the two sides contracted peace in 421 B.C.E. Although Athens was victorious in that its empire was intact, the peace changed nothing, and tensions festered for five years.

Alcibiades and the Sicilian Expedition. After the peace of 421 B.C.E., Pericles' kinsman Alcibiades (ca. 450–404 B.C.E.) came to dominate the demos. In 415 B.C.E., he urged Athens to expand its empire westward by attacking Syracuse, the most prosperous Greek city of Sicily, which had largely escaped the devastation of the Archidamian War. The expedition went poorly, and Alcibiades, accused at home of having profaned one of the most important Athenian religious cults, was ordered home. Instead, he fled to Sparta, where he began to assist the Spartans against Athens. The Sicilian expedition ended in disaster. Athens lost over 200 ships and 50,000 men. At the same time, Sparta resumed the war, this time with naval support provided by Persia.

Suddenly, Athens was fighting for its life. Alcibiades soon abandoned Sparta for Persia and convinced the Athenians that if they would abandon their democracy for an oligarchy, Persia would withdraw its support of Sparta. In 411 B.C.E., the desperate Athenian assembly established a brutal, antidemocratic oligarchy, but when the war continued, Athens, amid bitter factionalism, reestablished its democracy. The Persian king renewed his support for Sparta, sending his son Cyrus (ca. 424–401 B.C.E.) to coordinate the war against Athens. Under the Spartan general Lysander (d. 395 B.C.E.), Sparta and its allies finally closed in on Athens. Lysander captured the Athenian fleet in the Hellespont, destroyed it, and severed Athens's vital grain supply. Within months, Athens was entirely cut off from the outside world and starving. In 404 B.C.E., Sparta accepted Athens's unconditional surrender. Athens's fortifications came down, its empire vanished, and its fleet, except for a mere 12 ships, dissolved.

The Peloponnesian War showed not only the limitations of Athenian democracy but the potential brutality of oligarchy as well. More ominously, it demonstrated the catastrophic effects of disunity and rivalry among Greek cities of the Mediterranean.

Athenian Culture in the Hellenic Age

Most of what we today call Greek is actually Athenian. Throughout the Hellenic age (the fifth and early fourth centuries B.C.E., as distinct from the Hellenistic period of roughly the later fourth through second centuries B.C.E.), the turbulent issues of democracy and oligarchy, war and peace, hard choices and conflicting obligations found expression in Athenian culture even as the glory of the Athenian Empire was manifested in art and architecture.

The Examined Life

A primary characteristic of Athenian culture was its critical and rational nature. Secure in their identity and protected by the openness of their radical democracy, Athenians began to examine the past and present and to question the foundations of traditional values. From this climate of inquiry emerged the traditions of moral philosophy and its cousin, history.

The Ionian interest in natural philosophy, the explanation of the universe in rational terms, continued throughout the fifth century B.C.E. But philosophers began also to turn their attention to the human world, in particular to the powers and limitations of the individual's mind and the individual's relationship with society.

The Sophists. In the political world of fifth-century B.C.E. Athens, rhetoric, the art of persuasion, was particularly important because it was the key to political influence. Teachers called **sophists** ("wise people") traveled throughout Greece, offering to provide an advanced education for a fee. Although the sophistic tradition later gained a negative reputation, teachers such as Gorgias (ca. 485–ca. 380 B.C.E.) and Protagoras (ca. 490–421 B.C.E.) trained young men not only in the art of rhetoric but also in logic.

Socrates. The teacher Socrates (ca. 470–399 B.C.E.) was considered by many of his contemporaries as but one more sophist, but he himself reacted against what he saw as the amoral and superficial nature of sophistic education. He was interested in the search for moral self-enlightenment. Socrates' method infuriated his contemporaries. He would approach individuals who had reputations for wisdom or skill and then, through a series of disarmingly simple questions, force them to defend their beliefs. The inevitable result was that in their own words the outstanding sophists, politicians, and poets of the day demonstrated the inadequacy of the foundations of their beliefs.

Since Socrates refused to commit any of his teaching to writing, we know of him only from the conflicting reports of his former students and opponents. One thing is certain, however: While demanding that every aspect of life be investigated, Socrates never doubted the moral legitimacy of the Athenian state.

This bust of Socrates, a Roman copy of a Greek original, portrays him with the traditional beard of a philosopher. Also portrayed is his lack of physical beauty. In Plato's dialogue *Theaetetus*, Plato even playfully boasts of his looks, saying that his flared nostrils improved his sense of smell and his bulging eyes helped his vision, while his discussion partner suggests that Socrates's outsized lips were perhaps better for kissing and his large mouth helped him eat. The point of such characterizations was that this physically ugly man had the most beautiful mind.

Condemned to death in 399 B.C.E. on the trumped-up charges of corrupting the morals of the Athenian youth and introducing strange gods, he declined the opportunity to escape into exile. Rather than reject Athens and its laws, he drank the fatal potion of hemlock given him by the executioner.

Understanding the Past

The philosophical interest in human choices and social constraints found echo in the historical writing of the age. In particular, two writers established the spectrum of how to understand the past.

Herodotus. Herodotus (ca. 484–420 B.C.E.), the first historian, was one of the many foreigners who found in Athens the intellectual climate and audience he needed to write an account of the Persian wars of the preceding generation. His book of inquiries, or *historia*, into the origins and events of the conflict between Greeks and Persians is the first true history.

As Herodotus explained in his introduction, his purpose in writing was first to preserve the memory of the past by recording the achievements of both Greeks and eastern non-Greeks and second to show how the two came into conflict. It was this concern to explain, to go beyond mere storytelling, that earned Herodotus the designation "father of history."

Thucydides. The story of the Peloponnesian War was recorded by a different sort of historian, one who focused more narrowly on the Greek world and on political power. Thucydides had been an Athenian general and a major actor in the first part of the Peloponnesian War until his exile in 425 B.C.E. He began his account at the very outbreak of the conflict, thus writing a contemporary record of the war rather than a history of it.

For Thucydides, the central subject was human society in action. He viewed the Greek states as acting out of rational self-interest. His favorite device for showing the development of such policies was the political set speech in which two opposing leaders attempt to persuade their fellow citizens on the proper course of action.

Still, morality is always just below the surface of Thucydides' narrative. Even as he unflinchingly chronicles the collapse of morality and social order in the face of political expediency, he recognizes that this process will destroy his beloved Athens. In the later, unfinished chapters (Thucydides died shortly after Athens's final defeat), the Peloponnesian War takes on the characteristics of a tragedy. Here Thucydides, the ultimate political historian, shows the deep influence of the dominant literary tradition of his day: Greek drama.

Athenian Drama

Since the time of its introduction by Peisistratus in the middle of the sixth century B.C.E., drama had become popular, not only in Athens but throughout the Greek world. Plays formed part of the annual feast of Dionysus and dealt with mythic subject matter largely taken from the *Iliad* and the *Odyssey*. Three types of plays honored the Dionysian festival. Tragedies dealt with great men who failed because of flaws in their natures. Comedies were more directly topical and political. They parodied real Athenians, often by name, and amused even while making serious points in defense of democracy. Somewhere between tragedies and comedies, satyr plays remained closest to the Dionysian cult. In them, lecherous drunken satyrs, mythical half-man, half-goat creatures, interact with gods and men as they roam in search of Dionysus.

Aeschylus. Only a handful of the hundreds of Greek plays written in the fifth century B.C.E. survive. The first of the great Athenian tragedians whose plays we know is Aeschylus (525–456 B.C.E.). His one surviving trilogy, the *Oresteia*, traces the fate of the family of Agamemnon, the Greek commander at Troy. The three plays of the trilogy explore the chain of violent acts, vengeance, and conflicting obligations that ultimately must be settled by rational yet divinely sanctioned law.

Sophocles. Aeschylus's younger contemporary Sophocles (496–406 B.C.E.), the most successful of the fifth century B.C.E. tragedians, sought in his mature plays to express human character. He shows how humans make decisions and carry them out, constrained by their pasts, their weaknesses, and their vices, but free nonetheless. Sophocles' message is endurance, acceptance of human responsibility and, at the same time, of the ways of the gods, who overrule people's plans.

Euripides. Compared with Aeschylus and Sophocles, Euripides (485–406 B.C.E.) was far more original and daring in his subject matter and treatment of human emotions. His female characters were often wronged and seldom accepted their lot. His plays abound in plot twists and unexpected, violent outbursts. Passion, not reason, rules Euripides' world. His characters are less reconciled to their fates and less ready to accept the traditional gods.

Greek Comedy. Neither passion nor reason but politics rules the world of Greek comedy. Rather than the timelessness of the human condition, Athenian comic playwrights focused their biting satire on the political and social issues of the moment. Particularly, the comic genius Aristophanes (ca. 450–ca. 388 B.C.E.) used wit, imagination, vulgarity, and great poetic sensitivity to attack everything that offended him in his city. In his plays, he mocks and ridicules statesmen, philosophers, rival playwrights, and even the gods. Yet Aristophanes was a deeply patriotic Athenian, dedicated to the democratic system and to the cause of peace. Through the sharp satire and absurd plots of his plays, Aristophanes communicates his sympathy for ordinary people, who must match wits with the charlatans and pompous frauds who attempt to dominate Athens's public life.

Art and the Human Image

The humanity in Greek drama found its parallel in art. In sculpture, we see development toward balance and realism contained within an ideal of human form. The finest bronzes and marbles of the fifth century B.C.E. show freestanding figures whose natural vigor and force, even when they are engaged in strenuous exertion, are balanced by the placidity of their faces and their lack of emotion. The tradition established by the Athenian sculptor Phidias (ca. 500–ca. 430 B.C.E.) sought a naturalism in the portrayal of the human figure, which remained ideal rather than individual.

The greatest sculptural program of the fifth century B.C.E. was that produced for the Athenian acropolis. The reconstruction of the acropolis, which had been destroyed by the Persians, was the culmination of Athenian art. The result was the greatest complex of buildings in the ancient world.

The intellectual and artistic accomplishments of Athens were as enduring as its empire proved ephemeral. Writers and artists alike focused their creative energies on human existence, seeking a proper proportion, order, and meaning, a blend of the practical and ideal, which Athens's political leaders lacked.

From City-States to Macedonian Empire, 404–323 B.C.E.

The Peloponnesian War touched every aspect of Greek life. The war brought changes to the social and political structures of Greece by creating an enduring bitterness between the elites and the populace and a distrust of both democracy and traditional oligarchy. The mutual exhaustion of Athens and Sparta left a vacuum of power in the Aegean. Finally, the war raised fundamental questions about the nature of politics and society throughout the Greek world.

Politics After the Peloponnesian War

Over the decades-long struggle, the conduct of war and the nature of politics had changed, bringing new problems for victor and vanquished alike.

Spartan Imperialism. Victory left Sparta no more capable of assuming leadership in 404 B.C.E. than it had been in 478 B.C.E. Years of war had reduced the population of equals to fewer than 3,000. The Spartans proved to be extremely unpopular imperialists.

The brutality of Spartan rule sparked opposition throughout the Greek world, shattering the fragile peace created by Athens's defeat. For over 70 years, the Greek world boiled in constant warfare. Mutual distrust, fear of any city that seemed about to establish a position of clear superiority, and the machinations of the Persian Empire to keep Greeks fighting each other produced a constantly shifting series of alliances.

Thebes. Persia turned against its former ally when, in 401 B.C.E., Sparta supported an unsuccessful attempt by Cyrus to unseat his brother Artaxerxes II. Soon the unlikely and unstable alliance of Athens, Corinth, Argos, Thebes, and Euboea, financed by Persia, entered a series of vicious wars against Sparta. The first round ended in Spartan victory, due to the shifting role of Persia, whose primary interest was the continued disunity of the Greeks. By 377 B.C.E., however, Athens had reorganized its league and, with Thebes as an ally, was able to break Spartan sea power. The decline of Sparta left a power vacuum that was soon filled by Thebes.

Theban hegemony was short-lived. Before long, the same process of greed, envy, and distrust that had devastated the other Greek powers destroyed Thebes. By the 330s B.C.E., all of the Greek states had proven themselves incapable of creating stable political units larger than their immediate polis.

Philosophy and the Polis

The failure of Greek political forms, oligarchy and democracy alike, profoundly affected Athenian philosophers. Plato (ca. 428–347 B.C.E.), an aristocratic student of Socrates, grew up during the Peloponnesian War and had witnessed the collapse of the empire, the brutality of the Thirty Tyrants, the execution of Socrates, and the revival of the democracy and its imperialistic ambitions. From these experiences he developed a hatred for Athenian democracy and a profound distrust of ordinary people's ability to tell right from wrong.

Platonic Forms. Plato argued that true knowledge is impossible as long as it focuses on the constantly changing, imperfect world of everyday experience. Human beings can have real knowledge only of that which is eternal, perfect, and beyond the experience of the senses, the realm of what Plato called the **Forms**. Plato believed that when one judged individuals or actions to be true or good or beautiful, one did so not because those individuals or actions were truly virtuous, but because one recognized that they participated in some way in the Idea or Form of truth or goodness or beauty.

According to Plato, the evils of the world, in particular the vices and failures of government and society, result from ignorance of the truth. Most people live as though chained in a cave in which all they can see are the shadows cast by a fire on the walls. In their ignorance they mistake these flickering, imperfect images for reality. Their proper ruler must be a philosopher, one who is not deceived by the shadows. The philosopher's task is to break their chains and turn them toward the source of the light so that they can see the world as it really is.

Aristotelian Empiricism. Plato's idealist view (in the sense of the Ideas or Forms) of knowledge dominated much of ancient philosophy. However, his greatest student, Aristotle (384–322 B.C.E.), rejected this view in favor of **empiricism**, a philosophy rooted in observation of the natural world. Systematic investigation and explanation characterize Aristotle's vast work, and his interests ranged from biology to statecraft to the most abstract philosophy. In each field he employed essentially the same method. He observed as many individual examples of the topic as possible and from these specific observations extracted general theories.

In human affairs, Aristotle recommended moderation. Unlike Plato, he did not regard any particular form of government as ideal. Rather, he concluded that the type of government ultimately mattered less than the balance between narrow oligarchy and radical democracy. Moderation was the key to stability and justice. Yet, during the very years that Aristotle was teaching, the vacuum created by the failure of the Greek city-states was being filled by the growing Macedonian monarchy that finally ended a century of Greek warfare and, with it, the independence of the Greek city-states.

The Rise of Macedon

The polis had never been the only form of the Greek state. Alongside the city-states of Athens, Corinth, Syracuse, and Sparta were more decentralized ethne ruled by traditional hereditary chieftains and monarchs. Macedonia, in the northeast of the mainland, was one such ethnos. Macedonia had long served as a buffer between the barbarians to the north and the Greek mainland, and its tough farmers and pastoralists were geared to constant warfare. As Athens, Sparta, and Thebes fought each other to mutual exhaustion, Macedonia under King Philip II (359–336 B.C.E.) moved into the resulting power vacuum.

A Roman copy of a Greek statue of Aristotle. Already in his own lifetime at least one portrait of Aristotle was in existence and his student Alexander the Great commissioned others of him. Ancient authors described him as thin with short hair and a mocking expression on his face. In the Roman world, statues and busts of Aristotle were very popular in gardens, whether or not the owners had actually read the philosopher, which probably accounts for the survival of this and other similar statues.

After some early military successes against northern barbarians, Philip, a skillful politician and outstanding military strategist, turned his attention to the south and relentlessly swallowed up one Greek state after another. In 338 B.C.E., Philip achieved a final victory at Chaeronea and established a new league, the League of Corinth. However, unlike all those that had preceded it, this league was no confederation of sovereign states. It was an empire ruled by a king and supported by wealthy citizens whose cooperation Philip rewarded well. This new model of government, a monarchy drawing its support from a wealthy elite, became a fixture of the Mediterranean world for over 2,000 years.

No sooner had Philip subdued Greece than he announced a campaign against Persia. Before he could begin, however, he was cut down by an assassin's knife, leaving his 20-year-old son, Alexander (336–323 B.C.E.), to lead the expedition. Within 13 years, Alexander had conquered the world.

The Empire of Alexander the Great

In 334 B.C.E., the first year of his campaign, Alexander captured the Greek cities of Asia Minor. Then he continued east. Two months later, he defeated the Persian king Darius III at Issus and then headed south toward the Mediterranean coast and Egypt. After his victories there, he turned again to the north and entered Mesopotamia. At Gaugamela in 331 B.C.E., he defeated Darius a second, decisive time. Shortly afterward, Darius was murdered by the remnants of his followers.

Alexander captured the Persian capital of Persepolis with its vast treasure and became the undisputed ruler of the vast empire.

The conquest of Persia was not enough. Alexander pushed on, intending to conquer the whole world. His armies marched eastward, subduing the rebellious Asian provinces of Bactria and Sogdiana. He negotiated the Khyber Pass from what is now Afghanistan into the Punjab, crossed the Indus River, and defeated the local Indian king. Everywhere he went, he reorganized or founded cities, entrusting them to loyal Macedonians and other Greeks and settling them with veterans of his campaigns, and then pushed on toward the unknown. On the banks of the Hyphasis River in what is now Pakistan, his Macedonian warriors finally halted. Worn out by years of bloody conquest and exhausting travel, they refused to go farther. Furious but impotent, Alexander led his troops back to Persepolis in 324 B.C.E.

Binding Together an Empire

Alexander is remembered as a greater conqueror than ruler, but his plans for his reign, had he lived to complete them, might have won him equal fame. He recognized that only by merging local and Greek peoples and traditions could he forge a lasting empire. Whether his program of cultural and social amalgamation could have succeeded is a moot point. In 323 B.C.E., less than two years after his return from India, he died at Babylon at the age of 32.

MAP DISCOVERY

THE EMPIRE OF ALEXANDER THE GREAT

Compare the empire of Alexander with the map of the ancient world (p. 9). How do you account for the specific areas Alexander chose to conquer? Based on information presented in this chapter, what lasting effects remained in this region?

The empire did not outlive the emperor. Vicious fighting soon broke out among his generals and his kin. The various units of the empire broke apart into separate kingdoms and autonomous cities in which each ruler attempted to continue the political and cultural tradition of Alexander in a smaller sphere. By 275 B.C.E., three large kingdoms dominated Alexander's former domain. The most stable was Egypt, which Ptolemy I (323–285 B.C.E.), one of Alexander's closest followers, acquired on Alexander's death and which he and his descendants ruled until Cleopatra VII (51–30 B.C.E.) was defeated by the Roman Octavian in 31 B.C.E. In the east, the Macedonian general Seleucus (246–226 B.C.E.) captured Babylon in 312 B.C.E., and he and his descendants ruled a vast kingdom reaching from what is today western Turkey to Afghanistan. However, whittled away over time by its neighbors, the Seleucid kingdom gradually shrank to a small region of northern Syria before it fell to Rome in 64 B.C.E. After 50 years of conflict, Antigonus Gonatas (276–239 B.C.E.), the grandson of another of Alexander's commanders, secured Macedon and Greece. His Antigonid successors ruled the kingdom until it fell to the Romans in 168 B.C.E.

Alexander's conquests brought Greek traditions of urban organization to a wide area, replacing indigenous ruling elites with Hellenized dynasties. But Alexander's successors never integrated this Greek culture and the more ancient indigenous cultures of their subjects. This failure proved fatal for the Hellenistic kingdoms.

Chronology

CLASSICAL GREECE

525–456 B.C.E.	Aeschylus
ca. 500–ca. 430 B.C.E.	Phidias
496–406 B.C.E.	Sophocles
490 B.C.E.	Battle of Marathon
485–406 B.C.E.	Euripides
ca. 484–ca. 420 B.C.E.	Herodotus
480 B.C.E.	Battles of Thermopylae and Salamis
478 B.C.E	Athens assumes control of Delian League
ca. 470–399 B.C.E.	Socrates
ca. 460–430 B.C.E.	Pericles dominates Athens
ca. 450–ca. 388 B.C.E.	Aristophanes
431–421; 414–404 B.C.E.	Peloponnesian War
ca. 428–347 B.C.E.	Plato
384–322 B.C.E.	Aristotle
384–322 B.C.E.	Demosthenes
338 B.C.E.	Philip of Macedon defeats Athens
336–323 B.C.E.	Reign of Alexander the Great

The Hellenistic World

Although vastly different in geography, language, and custom, the Hellenistic king-doms (so called to distinguish them from the Hellenic civilization of the fifth and early fourth centuries B.C.E.) shared two common traditions. First, great portions of the Hellenistic world, from Asia Minor to Bactria and south to Egypt, had been united at various times by the Assyrian and Persian empires. During these periods they had absorbed much of Mesopotamian civilization, in particular the adminis-trative traditions begun by the Assyrian Tiglath-pileser. Therefore, the Hellenistic kings ruled kingdoms that were already accustomed to centralized government.

Hellenistic monarchs remained Greek and lavished their attentions on the newly created Greek cities, which absorbed vast amounts of the kingdom's wealth. Nonetheless, these cities and their particular form of Greek culture were the second unifying factor in the Hellenistic world. In the tradition of Alexander himself, the Ptolemys, Seleucids, and Antigonids cultivated Greek urban culture and recruited Greeks for their most important positions of responsibility. The new Greek cities became the centers of political control, economic consumption, and cultural diffu-sion throughout the Hellenistic world.

Urban Life and Culture

The Hellenistic kingdoms lived in a perpetual state of warfare with one another. Kings needed Greek soldiers, merchants, and administrators and competed with their rivals in offering Greeks all the comforts of home. These Greeks were drawn from throughout the Greek-speaking world, and in time a universal Greek dialect, *koine*, became the common language of culture and business. Hellenistic cities were Greek in physical organization, constitution, and language.

For all their Greek culture, Hellenistic cities differed fundamentally from Greek cities and colonies of the past. Not only were they far larger than any earlier Greek cities, they were never politically sovereign. The regional kings maintained firm control over the cities, even while working to attract Greeks from the main-land and the islands to them.

At the same time, Hellenistic cities were much less closed than were the tradi-tional poleis of the Hellenic world. In the new cities of the east, Greeks from all over were welcomed as soldiers and administrators regardless of their city of ori-gin. By the second century B.C.E., Greeks no longer identified themselves by their city of origin but as "Hellenes," that is, Greeks. Native elites could also become Greeks by adopting Greek language and culture.

Women in Public Life

The great social and geographical mobility that was possible in the new cities extended to women as well as men. No longer important simply as transmitters of citizenship, women began to assume a greater role in the family, in the economy,

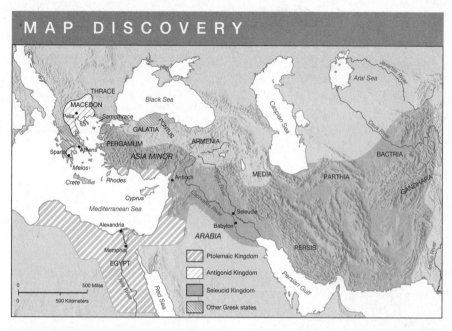

THE HELLENISTIC KINGDOMS

Consider the locations of the Hellenistic kingdoms carved out of Alexander's empire by his generals. From what you have read in previous chapters, which indigenous cultures do you think might have most influenced the Ptolemaic and Seleucid Kingdoms? Where would you expect to find Greek culture most important?

---

and in public life. Marriage contracts, particularly in Ptolemaic Egypt, emphasized the theoretical equality of husband and wife. Since women could control their own property, many engaged in business, and some became wealthy and influential.

Just as monarchs competed with one another in creating Greek cities, they vied in making their cities centers of Greek culture. Socially ambitious and newly wealthy citizens supported poets, philosophers, and artists and endowed gymnasia and libraries.

Alexandria

The most vibrant center of this rich complex of social change and culture was Alexandria in Egypt. Alexander the Great had founded it after having himself crowned pharaoh in the ancient capital of Memphis in 331 B.C.E. After Alexander's death, Ptolemy I made it not only his political and commercial center but the cultural center for Greek art, science, and scholarship for the whole world. In time, the library at Alexandria housed half a million book-rolls, including all of the great classics of Greek literature.

The *Nike,* or Winged Victory, is an outstanding example of third century Hellenistic sculpture. It was found in fragments on the island of Samothrace in the Aegean Sea in 1863 and originally formed part of the Samothrace temple complex. The statue depicted the goddess descending from the sky to the victorious naval fleet. The head and arms were never discovered although portions of the right hand have been discovered. The depiction of movement and the dynamic and naturalistic draping of the figure's torso make it one of the greatest Hellenistic works to have survived to the present. The statue is now in the Louvre in Paris.

Hellenistic Literature

Hellenistic writers developed new forms of literature, including the romance, which often recounted imaginary adventures of Alexander the Great, and the pastoral poem, which the Sicilian Theocritus (ca. 310–250 B.C.E.) developed out of popular shepherd songs. The Athenian playwright Menander's (342–292 B.C.E.) gift was for comedy, but it was a new type of comedy quite removed from the politically biting and often vulgar humor of Aristophanes. Menander wrote with great poetic skill and artistry some 100 wildly complicated, good-natured plays. More than any other ancient poet or playwright, he drew a sympathetic image of ordinary men and women.

Architecture and Art

Political rivalry also encouraged architectural and artistic rivalry, as kings competed for the most magnificent Hellenistic cities.

Freestanding statues and magnificent murals and mosaics adorned the public squares, temples, and private homes of Hellenistic cities. While artists continued the traditions of the Hellenic age, they displayed more freedom in portraying tension and restlessness as well as individuality in the human form.

Hellenistic Philosophy

Philosophy, too, flourished in the Hellenistic world, but in directions different from those initiated by Plato and Aristotle, who both were deeply committed to political involvement in the free polis. The new philosophies appealed to the rootless Greeks of the Hellenistic east, who were no longer tied by bonds of religion or patriotism to any community.

Cynics. The Cynic tradition was established by Antisthenes (ca. 445–ca. 365 B.C.E.), a pupil of Socrates, and Diogenes of Sinope (d. ca. 320 B.C.E.). The **Cynics** taught that excessive attachment to the things of this world was the source of evil and unhappiness and that an individual achieved freedom by renouncing material things, society, and pleasures. The Cynics believed that the more one had, the more one was vulnerable to the whims of fortune.

Epicureans. Like the Cynics, the **Epicureans** sought freedom, but from pain rather than from the conventions of ordinary life. Epicurus (341–270 B.C.E.) and his disciples have often been attacked for their emphasis on pleasure. But, for the Epicureans, the real goal was to reduce desires to those that were simple and attainable. Therefore, Epicureans urged retirement from politics, retreat from public competition, and concentration instead on friendship and private enjoyment. For Epicurus, reason properly applied illuminated how best to pursue pleasure.

Stoics. **Stoics** also followed nature, but rather than leading them to retire from public life, it led them to greater participation in it. Stoics believed that just as the universe is a system in which stars and planets move according to fixed laws, so too was human society ordered and unified. As the founder of Stoicism, Zeno (ca. 335–ca. 263 B.C.E.), expressed it, "All men should regard themselves as members of one city and people, having one life and order." According to the Stoics, every person had a role in the divinely ordered universe, and all roles were of equal value. True happiness consisted in freely accepting one's role, whatever it was, while unhappiness and evil resulted from attempting to reject one's place in the divine plan.

Mathematics and Science

Particularly for mathematics, astronomy, and engineering, the Hellenistic period was a golden age. Ptolemaic Egypt became the center of mathematical studies. Euclid (ca. 300 B.C.E.), whose *Elements* was the fundamental textbook of geometry until the twentieth century, worked there, as did his student Apollonius of Perga (ca. 262–ca. 190 B.C.E.), whose work on conic sections is one of the greatest monuments of geometry. Both Apollonius and his teacher were as influential for their method as for their conclusions. Their treatises follow rigorous logical proofs of mathematical theorems, which established the form of mathematical reasoning to the present day. Archimedes of Syracuse (ca. 287–212 B.C.E.) corresponded with the Egyptian mathematicians and made additional contributions to geometry, such as the calculation of the approximate value of pi, as well as to mechanics, arithmetic, and engineering.

Mathematical Astronomy. Many mathematicians, such as Archimedes and Apollonius, were also mathematical astronomers, and the application of their mathematical skills to the exact data collected by earlier Babylonian and Egyptian empirical astronomers greatly increased the understanding of the heavens and the earth. Archimedes devised a means of measuring the diameter of the sun, and Eratosthenes of Cyrene (ca. 276–194 B.C.E.) calculated the circumference of the earth to within 200 miles.

Medicine. Like astronomy, Hellenistic medicine combined theory and observation. In Alexandria, Herophilus of Chalcedon (ca. 270 B.C.E.) and Erasistratus of Ceos (ca. 260 B.C.E.) conducted important studies in human anatomy. Through his studies, Herophilus recognized the brain as the center of the nervous system and was able to distinguish accurately between motor and sensory nerves. He also produced the first accurate descriptions of such organs as the eye, brain, liver, and salivary glands.

Cultural Resistance. For all of their vitality, the Hellenistic cities remained parasites on the local societies. No real efforts were made to merge the two and to develop a new civilization. Some ambitious members of the indigenous elites tried to adopt the customs of the Greeks; others plotted insurrection.

In time, the Hellenistic kingdoms' inability to bridge the gap between Greek and indigenous populations proved fatal. In the east, the non-Greek kingdom of Parthia replaced the Seleucids in much of the old Persian Empire. In the west, continuing hostility between kingdoms and within kingdoms prepared the way for their progressive absorption by the new power to the west: Rome.

SUMMARY

War and Politics in the Fifth Century B.C.E. Greek victories over the Persians had important consequences for the Greeks in general, and the Athenians in particular. Athens moved further toward democracy, at the same time as it built an empire. The Athenian Empire was an economic, judicial, religious, and political union that was held together by military might. Only male citizens were full participants in Athenian democracy. Slaves, metics, and women were excluded. Pericles was the most successful of the Athenian demagogues. The Peloponnesian War pitted Athens against Sparta, with Sparta emerging as the eventual victor.

Athenian Culture in the Hellenic Age   A primary characteristic of Athenian culture was its critical and rational nature. The tensions, conflicts, and choices that shaped Athenian politics and society were reflected in art, philosophy, history, and drama. Writers and artists alike focused their creative energies on human existence, seeking proper proportion, order, and meaning.

From City-States to Macedonian Empire, 404–323 B.C.E.   The mutual exhaustion of Athens and Sparta after the Peloponnesian War left a vacuum of power in the Aegean. The war raised fundamental questions about the nature of politics and society throughout the Greek world. Plato's philosophy was one response to the post-war world. Macedonia under King Philip II (359–336 B.C.E.) took advantage of the weakness of Athens, Sparta, and Thebes. Philip's son, Alexander (336–323 B.C.E.), led a campaign against Persia that ended with the conquest of a vast empire. After Alexander's death, his empire broke into a number of kingdoms.

The Hellenistic World   The Hellenistic kingdoms were shaped by both Mesopotamian and Greek civilization. Greeks played a key part in Hellenistic urban life, but Hellenistic cities were very different than Greek poleis. Women experienced greater social and geographical mobility. Writers developed new literary forms. Philosophers turned inward to answer questions about the relationships among the individual, society, and the natural world. Greek cities made little effort to truly merge with local societies.

QUESTIONS FOR REVIEW

1. Why did Athens become Greece's greatest power in the wake of the Persian wars?
2. What social concerns and cultural accomplishments were expressed in Greek philosophy, drama, and art?
3. What does the Peloponnesian War reveal about weaknesses and divisions in Greek culture?
4. What factors explain Alexander the Great's success in expanding his empire?
5. What changes did Greek culture experience as it was carried eastward with the creation of the Hellenistic kingdoms?

Early Rome and the Roman Republic, 800–146 B.C.E.

The Western Mediterranean to 509 B.C.E.

Civilization came late to the western Mediterranean, carried in the ships of Greeks and Phoenicians. While the great floodplain civilizations of Mesopotamia and Egypt and the Greek communities of the eastern Mediterranean were developing sophisticated systems of urban life and political organization, western Europe and Africa knew only the scattered villages of simple farmers and pastoralists. The West was rich in metals, however, and an indigenous Bronze Age culture developed slowly between 1500 and 1000 B.C.E., spreading widely north of the Alps and south into Italy and Spain.

Sometime around the year 1000 B.C.E., a new, distinctive iron-using civilization first appeared in northern Italy. No one knows whether these **Villanovans**, so called for a major archaeological discovery of this civilization at Villanova near Bologna, were new arrivals in Italy or simply the descendants of previous inhabitants. However, around this same time, small groups of people did begin to infiltrate Italy from the east and the north, occupying the mountainous terrain of the Apennines and pushing the indigenous society westward. These new arrivals shared no common organization or identity, but all spoke related Indo-European languages that we call *Italic*, including Latin. These newcomers were warriors. By 800 B.C.E. they were in firm control of the mountainous region of central Italy and threatened the coastal societies of the west and south.

Carthage: The Merchants of Baal

Also around 800 B.C.E., Phoenicians arrived in the West from the regions of Tyre, Sidon, and Byblos. They established a series of bases along the route to and from Spain on the coast and on the islands of Corsica, Sicily, Ibiza, and Motya in the Mediterranean and at Utica and Carthage on the coast of North Africa. Gradually Carthage established itself as the center of an expanding Phoenician presence in the western Mediterranean.

The city was perfectly situated to profit from both the land and the sea. Its excellent double harbor made it an ideal port where ships could lie at rest, protected from storms as well as from enemies by a narrow 70-foot entrance to the sea that could be closed with iron chains. The city was equally protected on land, situated on a narrow isthmus and surrounded by massive walls. As long as Carthage controlled the sea, its commercial center was secure from any enemies.

By the middle of the sixth century B.C.E., Carthage was the center of a real empire. But in contrast with the Athenian Empire of the following century, Carthage was much more successful at integrating other cities and peoples into its mercenary military and thus sharing the burden of warfare. This multiethnic empire endured for three centuries, proving far more stable than any of those created by the Greeks.

Although superficially similar to many Greek cities, the Punic (from *Puni* or *Poeni*, the Roman name for the Carthaginians) state differed profoundly in the relationship between citizen and state. Ordinary citizens had little involvement and, apparently, little interest in government, and officials consistently came from among the wealthy and powerful merchant aristocracy. According to Aristotle, however, the aristocracy treated the rest of the population generously, sharing with it the profits of its commercial and imperial wealth. Thus the class pressures that created the Greek tyrants never emerged in Carthage.

Stable, prosperous, and devout, Carthage was the master of the western Mediterranean. But its dominion was not undisputed. From the sixth century B.C.E., the Punic Empire felt the pressure of ambitious Greek cities that were eager to gain a share of the West's riches.

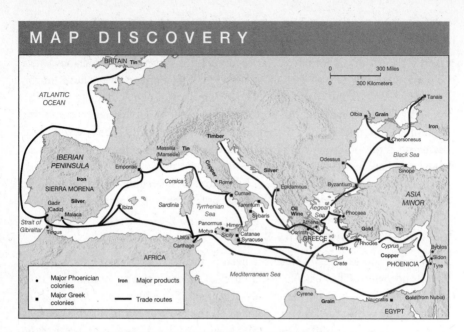

MAP DISCOVERY

GREEK AND PHOENICIAN COLONIES AND TRADE

Note the location of the major Phoenician and Greek colonies and the extent of the trade routes to and from these colonies. Where, if at all, did Greek and Phoenician colonies come into close proximity and competition? Did the two systems compete for the same trade goods?

The Western Greeks

The Greek arrival in the west was the result of a much more complex process than the trading policy of the Phoenicians. As we saw in Chapter 2, toward the end of the Dark Age, commerce, overpopulation, and civic tension sent Greek colonists out in all directions. In the eighth century B.C.E., Crete, Rhodes, Corinth, Argos, Chalcis, Eretria, and Naxos all established colonies in Sicily and southern Italy.

In the seventh century B.C.E., Syracuse became the greatest city of Sicily and one of the most prosperous cities of the Greek world. Greek colonies spread slowly up the boot of Italy, known as Greater Greece, in pursuit of trade and arable land. By the last quarter of the seventh century B.C.E., the autonomous Greek colonies began to encroach on the Carthaginian empire's sphere of influence.

Both commercial rivalry and open warfare characterized the relationship between Greeks and Phoenicians in the western Mediterranean. In the course of the sixth century B.C.E., Greeks in Sicily attempted to expel the Phoenicians from the island. In the fifth century B.C.E., Syracuse, under its tyrant Gelon (ca. 540–478 B.C.E.), threatened both Punic and Greek cities on the island. In an attempt to defend its colonies, in 480 B.C.E. Carthage launched an enormous force to support Gelon's Greek enemies. The attack took place, probably not coincidentally, at the same moment that Xerxes invaded Greece. At the battle of Himera—fought, we are told, on the same day as the battle of Salamis—the Syracusans soundly defeated the Carthaginians.

Gelon's victory at Himera ushered in a period of prosperity and cultural achievement in Sicily. This prosperity continued after the elimination of the tyranny in midcentury, and in 415 B.C.E., Syracuse was able to withstand Athens's attempt at conquest. (See Chapter 3, p. 65.)

A far more serious threat appeared in 410 B.C.E., when a new Carthaginian army arrived in Sicily seeking revenge. The Carthaginians rapidly captured and destroyed Himera, extending the boundaries of Punic Sicily. This invasion initiated a century of inconclusive conflict between Syracuse and Carthage.

Early on in their struggle with the Sicilian Greeks, the Carthaginians found allies in the third major civilization of the West. These were the Etruscans, who in the seventh century B.C.E. dominated the western part of central Italy, known as Etruria.

Italy's First Civilization

Etruscan civilization was the first great civilization to emerge in Italy. The **Etruscans** have long been regarded as a people whose origins, language, and customs are shrouded in mystery. However, in recent years, while some DNA evidence suggests affinities with Asia Minor, archaeologists have demonstrated that Etruscan culture developed in western Italy out of indigenous tradition long present in Italy. This tradition shares much with Eastern civilizations, such as the importance of underworld gods, fertility cults, and the high status of women.

Etruscan civilization coalesced slowly in Etruria over the course of the seventh century B.C.E. from diverse groups sharing a similar cultural and linguistic tradition. In the mid-sixth century B.C.E., in the face of Greek pressure from the south, 12 of these groups united in a religious and military confederation. Over the next 100 years, the confederation expanded north into the Po Valley and south to Campania. Cities, each initially ruled by a king, were the centers of Etruscan civilization, and everywhere the Etruscans spread, they either improved on existing towns or founded new ones. The Etruscan confederation remained loose and never developed into a centralized empire. Etruscan kings assumed power in conquered towns, but between the sixth and fifth centuries B.C.E., Etruscan kingship gave way to oligarchic governments, much as Greek monarchies had a bit earlier. In the place of kings, aristocratic assemblies selected magistrates, often paired together or combined into "colleges" to prevent individuals from seizing power. These republican institutions provided the foundation for later Roman republican government.

An Archaic Society. The remnants of an ancient civilization, the Etruscans retained throughout their history social and cultural traditions that had long since vanished elsewhere in the Mediterranean. Society was divided sharply into two classes, lords and servants. The lords' wealth was based on the rich agricultural regions of Etruria where grain grew in abundance and on the equally rich deposits of copper and iron. The vast majority of the population were actual slaves, working the lands and mines of the aristocracy.

The aristocrats were aggressive and imaginative landowners. They developed hydraulic systems for draining marshes, produced a wine that was famous throughout the Mediterranean, and put their slaves to work in mines and in smelting. Still, they were largely absentee landlords, spending much of their time in the towns that characterized Etruscan civilization. These cities, with their massive walls, enclosed populations of as many as 20,000.

The most striking aspect of Etruscan life to Greek contemporaries and to later Romans was the elevated status of Etruscan women. As in the much earlier Minoan civilization, women played an active, public role in society. Unlike honorable Greek women, Etruscan women took part in banquets, attended and even occasionally presided over dances, concerts, and sporting events, and were active in political life. Greeks such as Aristotle regarded the public behavior of Etruscan women as lewd. When a king died, his successor had to be designated and consecrated by the Etruscan queen to establish his legitimacy. To later Romans, this practice was shocking.

Etruscan Dominance. While the Etruscans were consolidating their hegemony in western Italy, they were at the same time establishing their maritime power. From the seventh to the fifth centuries B.C.E., Etruscans controlled the Italian coast of the Tyrrhenian Sea as well as Sardinia. Attempts to extend farther south into Greek southern Italy and toward the Greek colonies on the modern French coast brought the Etruscans and the Greeks into inevitable conflict.

Common hostility toward the Greeks as well as complementary economic interests soon brought the Etruscans into alliances with Carthage. Toward the end of the sixth century B.C.E., Etruscan cities including Rome signed a series of pacts with Carthage that created military alliances against the Phocaeans and Syracuse. Etruscan fleets were victorious over the Phocaeans, driving them from Corsica, but they were no match for Syracuse. In 474 B.C.E., shortly after the battle of Himera, the Syracusan fleet destroyed that of the Etruscans off Cumae.

Cumae marked the beginning of Etruscan decline. Through the fifth century B.C.E., Etruscan cities lost control of the sea to the Greeks. Around the same time, Celts from north of the Alps invaded and conquered the Po Valley. And to the south, Etruscans saw their inland territories progressively slipping into the hands of their former subjects, the Romans, who had begun to acquire the commercial, political, and military expertise that would drive their long rise to dominance.

On the Etruscan sarcophagus of Larthia Scianti, a matron reclines as at a banquet. Etruscan scarcophagi, usually made of terracotta, frequently depicted the dead, often husband and wife, together reclining on a couch. Much of our knowledge of the first Italian civilization comes from the elaborate paintings and statuary found in Etruscan cemeteries. Nothing is know of Larthia Scianti, however women in Etruscan society exercised a more public and political role than did the Roman matrons who followed them.

From City to Empire, 509–146 B.C.E.

What manner of people were these Romans who, from obscure origins, came to rule an empire? Their own answer would have been simple: They were farmers and soldiers, simple people accustomed to simple, straightforward actions. Throughout their long history, Romans liked to refer to the clear-cut models provided by their semilegendary predecessors. These were myths, but they were important myths to Romans, who preferred concrete models to abstract principles.

Later Romans liked to imagine the history of their city as one predestined by the gods for greatness. Some liked to trace the origins of Rome to Romulus and Remus, twin sons of the war god Mars and a Latin princess. Other Romans, having absorbed the Homeric traditions of Greece, taught that the founder of Rome was Aeneas, son of the goddess of love, Aphrodite, and the Trojan Anchises, who had wandered west after the fall of Troy. All agreed that Rome had been ruled by kings, who underwent a steady decline in ability and morals until the last, Tarquin the Proud, was expelled by outraged Latins. These legends tell much about the attitudes and values of later Romans. They tell nothing about the actual origins of the city or its rise to greatness.

Latin Rome

Civilization in Italy meant Etruria to the north and Greater Greece to the south. In between lay Latium, a marshy region punctuated by hills on which a sparse population could find protection from disease and enemies.

The Alban Hills south of the Tiber were a center of Latin population. Sometime in the eighth century B.C.E., roughly 40 Latin villages formed a loose confederation, the Alban League, for military and religious purposes. Not long afterward, in the face of an expanding Etruscan confederation from the north and Sabine penetration from the east, the Albans established a village on the steep Palatine hill to the north. This Alban village, called Roma Quadrata, was soon joined by other Latin and Sabine settlements on nearby hills. By the end of the eighth century B.C.E., seven Latin villages along the route from the Tiber to Alba had formed a league for mutual defense and shared religious cults.

Early Roman society was composed of households; clans, or *gentes;* and village councils, or *curiae* (sing. *curia*). The male head of each household, the **paterfamilias**, had the power of life and death over its members and was responsible for the proper worship of the spirits of the family's ancestors, on whom continued prosperity depended.

Male members of village families formed councils, which were essentially religious organizations but also provided a forum for public discussion. These curiae tended to be dominated by gentes, but all males could participate, including those who belonged to the *plebians* or **plebs**, that is, families that were not organized into gentes. Later, the leaders of the gentes called themselves **patricians** ("descendants of fathers") and claimed superiority to the plebs, or common people.

Important plebeian and patrician families increased their power through a system of clientage, which remained a fundamental aspect of social and political organization throughout Roman history. Clients were free men who depended on the protection of a more powerful individual or family and who owed various services, including political support, in return for this protection.

Villages themselves grouped together for military and voting purposes into ethnic *tribus,* or tribes, each composed of a number of curiae. Each curia supplied a contingent of infantry, and each tribe cooperated to supply a unit of horsemen to the Roman army.

Assemblies of all members of the curiae expressed approval of major decisions, especially declaration of war and the selection of new kings, and thus played a real if limited political role. More powerful although less formal was the role of the Senate (assembly of elders), which was composed of heads of families. The Senate's power derived from the individual importance of its members and from its role in selecting a candidate for king, who was then presented to the assembly of the curiae for approval.

Kings served as religious leaders, the primary means of communication between gods and humans. Through the early Latin period, royal power remained fundamentally religious and limited by the Senate, curiae, gentes, and families.

The seven villages that made up primitive Rome developed independently of their Etruscan and Greek neighbors. This independent course of development changed in the middle of the seventh century B.C.E., when the Etruscans overwhelmed Latium and absorbed it into their civilization. Under its Etruscan kings, Rome first entered civilization.

Etruscan Rome

The Etruscans introduced in Latium, especially in Rome, their political, religious, and economic traditions. Etruscan city organization partially replaced Latin tribal structures. Etruscan kings and magistrates ruled Latin towns, increasing the power of traditional Latin kingship. The kings not only were religious leaders, but also led the army, served as judges, and held supreme political power. As Latium became an integral part of the Etruscan world, the Tiber became an important commercial route. For the first time, Rome began to enter the wider orbit of Mediterranean civilization.

Urban Growth. As Rome's importance grew, so did its size. Etruscan engineers drained the marshes into a great canal flowing to the Tiber, thus opening the lowlands between the hills to settlement. This in turn allowed them to create and pave the Forum. The Etruscans constructed a series of vast fortifications encircling the town. Under Etruscan influence, the fortified Capitoline hill, which served much like a Greek acropolis, became the cult center with the erection of the temple to Jupiter, the supreme god; Juno, his consort; and Minerva, an Etruscan goddess of craftwork who was similar to Athena. In its architecture, religion, commerce, and culture, Latin Rome was deeply indebted to its Etruscan conquerors.

As important as the physical and cultural changes brought by the Etruscans was their reorganization of the society. As in Greece, this restructuring was tied to changes in the military. Weakening the traditional Latin social units, the king divided Roman society into two groups: property owners and others. Landowners who were wealthy enough to provide armed military service were organized into five classes and ranked according to the quality of their arms and hence their wealth. Each class was further divided into military units called *centuries*. Members of these centuries constituted the centuriate assembly, which replaced the older curial assemblies for such vital decisions as the election of magistrates and the declaration of war.

The constitution and operation of this centuriate assembly ensured control by the most conservative forces within the society. Small centuries of wealthy well-armed cavalrymen and fully armed warriors outnumbered the more modestly equipped but more numerous centuries. Likewise, men over the age of 47, although in a minority, controlled over half the centuries in each class. Since votes were counted not by individuals but by centuries, this ensured within the assembly the domination of the rich over the poor, the older over the younger. The remainder of the society was the *infra classem* (literally "under class"), who owned no property and were thus excluded from military and political activity.

With this military and political reorganization came a reconstruction of the tribal system. Servius Tullius abolished the old tribal organization in favor of geographically organized tribes into which newcomers could easily be incorporated. Henceforth, while the family remained powerful, involvement in public life was based on property and geography.

Class Divisions. While the old tribal units and curiae declined, divisions between the patricians and the plebeians grew more distinct. During the monarchy, the patricians came to compose an upper stratum of wealthy nobles. Although partially protected by the kings, the plebeians, whether rich or poor, were pressed into a second-class status and denied access to political power.

The transformations brought about by the Etruscan kings became an enduring part of Rome. The Etruscans themselves did not. Around the traditionally reported date of 509 B.C.E. the Roman patricians expelled the last Etruscan king, Tarquin the Proud, and established a republic.

Rome and Italy

Just as in Rome, monarchy was giving way to oligarchic republics across Etruria in the sixth century B.C.E. Rome was hardly exceptional. However, the establishment of the Roman republic coincided roughly with the beginning of the Etruscan decline, allowing Rome to assert itself and to develop its Latin and Etruscan traditions in unique ways.

The Early Republic. The patrician oligarchy had engineered the end of the monarchy, and patricians dominated the offices and institutions of the new republic at the expense of the plebs, who, in losing the king, lost their only defender. Governmental institutions of the early republic developed within this context of patrician supremacy.

Characteristic of republican institutions was that at every level, power was shared by two or more equals who were elected for fixed terms. Replacing the king were the two *consuls*, each elected by the assembly for a one-year term. Initially, only the consuls held the **imperium**, the supreme power to command, to execute the law, and to impose the death penalty. Only in moments of grave crisis might a consul, with the approval of the Senate, name a single **dictator** with extraordinary absolute power for a very brief period, never more than six months. In time, other magistracies developed to perform specialized functions. *Praetors*, who in time also exercised the imperium, administered justice and defended the city in the absence of the consuls. *Quaestors* controlled finances. *Censors* assigned individuals their places in society, determined the amount of their taxes, filled vacancies in the Senate, and negotiated contracts for public construction projects. A variety of military commanders directed wars against neighboring cities and peoples under the imperium of the consuls. In all their actions these officeholders consulted with each other and with the Senate, which was composed of roughly 300 powerful former magistrates. The centuriate assembly functioned as the legislative organ of the state, but it continued to be dominated by the oldest and wealthiest members of society.

Patricians, Plebs, and Public Law. During the early republic, wealthy patricians, aided by their clients, monopolized the Senate and the magistracies. Patricians also controlled the priesthoods, positions which they held for life. With political and religious power came economic power. The poorer plebs in particular found themselves sinking into debt to wealthy patricians, losing their property, and with it the basis for military service and political participation.

The plebs began to organize in response to patrician control. On several occasions in the first half of the fifth century B.C.E., the whole plebeian order withdrew a short distance from the city, refusing to return or to serve in the military until conflicts with the patricians were resolved. In time, the plebs created their own assembly, the Council of the Plebs, which enacted laws that were binding on all plebeians. This council founded its own temples and elected magistrates called *tribunes,* whose persons were declared sacred to the gods. This conflict between the plebeians and the patricians, known as the Struggle of Orders, threatened to tear Roman society apart just as pressure from hostile neighbors placed Rome on the defensive.

Political Expansion. Roman preeminence in Latium had ended with the expulsion of the last king. The Etruscan town of Veii just north of the Tiber began periodic attacks against Rome. To the south, the Volscians had begun to expand northward into the Litis and Trerus valleys. This military pressure from the outside forced the patricians to seek a compromise with the plebeians. One of the first victories won by the plebs around 450 B.C.E. was the codification of basic Roman law, the Law of the Twelve Tables, which recognized the basic rights of all free citizens. The new law was posted publicly so that all could have access to it. Around the same time, the state began to absorb the plebeian political and religious organizations intact. Gradually, priesthoods, magistracies, and thus the Senate were opened to plebeians. In 287 B.C.E., as the result of a final secession of the plebs, the decisions of the plebeian assembly became binding on all citizens, patrician and plebeian alike.

Bitter differences at home did not prevent patricians and plebs from presenting a united front against their enemies abroad. By the beginning of the fourth century B.C.E., the united patrician-plebeian state was expanding its rule both northward and southward. Roman legions, commanded by patricians but formed of the whole spectrum of property-owning Romans, reestablished Roman preeminence in Latium and then began a series of wars that brought most of Italy under Roman control. In 396 B.C.E., Roman forces captured and destroyed Veii and shortly afterward conquered the rest of southern Etruria. In the south, Roman and Latin forces turned back the Volscians. By 295 B.C.E., Rome had secured its rule as far north as the Po Valley. In the south, Roman infantry and persistence proved the equal of professional Greek armies. Rome won a war of attrition against a series of Hellenistic commanders. By 265 B.C.E., Rome had absorbed the Hellenistic cities of the south.

Roman conquest benefited patrician and plebeian alike. While the patricians acquired wealth and power, the plebeians received a prize of equal value: land. After the capture of Veii, for example, the poor of Rome received shares of the conquered land. Since landowning was a prerequisite for military service, this distribution created still more peasant soldiers for further expeditions. Still, while the constant supply of new land did much to diffuse the tensions between orders, it did not actually resolve them. Into the late third century B.C.E., debt and landlessness remained major problems, creating tensions in Roman society. Probably not more than half of the citizen population owned land by 200 B.C.E.

Incorporating the Conquered. The Roman manner of treating conquered populations, radically different from anything seen before, also contributed to Rome's success. In war, no one could match the Roman legions for ruthless, thorough destruction. Yet no conquerors had ever shown themselves so generous in victory. After Rome crushed the Latin revolt of 338 B.C.E., virtually all of the Latins were incorporated into the Roman citizenry. Later colonies founded outside of Latium were given the same status as Latin cities. Other, more distant conquered peoples were considered allies and were required to provide troops but no tribute to Rome. In time, they too might become citizens.

The implications of these measures were revolutionary. By extending citizenship to conquered neighbors and by offering the future possibility to allies, Rome tied their fate to its own. Rather than potentially subversive subjects, conquered populations became strong supporters. Thus, in contrast to the Hellenistic cities of the east, where Greeks jealously guarded their status from the indigenous population, Rome's colonies acted as magnets, drawing local populations into the Roman cultural and political orbit. Finally, in all of its wars of conquest, Rome claimed a moral mandate. Romans went to great lengths to demonstrate that theirs were just wars, basing their claims on alleged acts of aggression by their enemies, on the appeal to Rome by its allies, and, increasingly, by presenting themselves as the preservers and defenders of Greek traditions of freedom. Both these political and propagandistic measures proved successful. Between 265 and 91 B.C.E. few serious revolts shook the peace and security of Italy south of the Po.

By 264 B.C.E., all of Italy was united under Roman hegemony. Roman expansion finally brought Rome into conflict with the great Mediterranean power of the west: Carthage.

Rome and the Mediterranean

Since its earliest days, Rome had allied itself with Carthage against the Greek cities of Italy. The zones of interest of the two cities had been quite separate. However, once Rome had conquered the Greek cities to the south, it became enmeshed in the affairs of neighboring Sicily, a region with well-established Carthaginian interests. There, in 265 B.C.E., a group of Italian mercenary pirates in Messina, threatened by Syracuse, requested Roman assistance. The Senate refused, but the plebeian assembly, eager for booty, exercised its newly won right to legislate for the republic and accepted. Shortly afterward, the Romans invaded Sicily, and Syracuse turned to its old enemy, Carthage, for assistance. The First Punic War had begun.

The First Punic War. This war, which lasted from 265 to 241 B.C.E., was a costly, brutal, and drawn-out affair that Rome won by dint of persistence and methodical calculation rather than strategic brilliance. Rome invaded and concluded an alliance with Syracuse in 263 B.C.E. The Romans won impressive initial victories but still could not deliver a knockout blow in either Sicily or North Africa for over 20 years. Finally, in 241 B.C.E., Rome forced the Carthaginian commander, Hamilcar Barca (ca. 270–229 B.C.E.), to surrender simply because the Romans could afford to build one more fleet than he. Carthage paid a huge indemnity and abandoned Sicily. Syracuse and Messina became allies of Rome. In a break with tradition, Rome obligated the rest of Sicily to pay a true tribute in the form of a tithe (one-tenth) of their crops. Shortly after that, Rome helped itself to Sardinia as well, from which it again demanded tribute, not simply troops. Rome had established an empire.

During the next two decades, Roman legions defeated the Ligurians on the northwest coast, the Celtic Gauls south of the Alps, and the Illyrians along the Adriatic coast. At the same time, Carthage fought a bitter battle against its own mercenary armies, which it had been unable to pay off after its defeat. Carthage then began the systematic creation of an empire in Spain. Trade between Carthage and Rome reached the highest level in history, but trade did not create friendship—only a wary peace. On both sides, powerful leaders saw the treaty of 241 B.C.E. as just a pause in a fight to the death.

Securing Western Hegemony. After the death of Hamilcar, Carthaginian successes in Spain, led by Hamilcar's son-in-law Hasdrubal (d. 221 B.C.E.) and his son Hannibal (247–183 B.C.E.), finally provoked Rome to war in 218 B.C.E. As soon as this Second Punic War had begun, Hannibal began an epic march north out of Spain, along the Mediterranean coast, and across the Alps. In spite of great hardships he was able to transport over 23,000 troops and approximately 18 war elephants into the plains of northern Italy.

Hannibal's brilliant generalship brought victory after victory to the Carthaginian forces. In the first engagement, on the Trebia River in the Po Valley, the Romans lost 20,000 men, two-thirds of their army. Carthaginian success encouraged the Gauls to join the fight against the Romans. Initially, Italian, Etruscan, and Greek allies remained loyal, but after Rome's catastrophic defeats at Lake Trasimene in Etruria in 217 B.C.E. and especially at Cannae in 216 B.C.E., a number of Italian colonies and allies, namely the cities of Capua and Syracuse, went over to the enemy. In the east, Philip V of Macedon (238–179 B.C.E.) made a treaty with Carthage in the hope of taking Illyria (today the coast of Croatia) from a defeated Rome.

MAP DISCOVERY

THE PUNIC WARS

What accidents of geography and political expansion made war between Rome and Carthage almost inevitable? What advantages might Hannibal have seen in taking the route he did to attack Rome? What were the long-term effects of Hannibal's route for the inhabitants of the Iberian Peninsula and Gaul? What parts of Carthage's African Empire might have been most attractive to Roman conquerors?

Three things, however, saved the Roman state. First, while some important allies and colonies defected, the majority held firm. Rome's traditions of sharing the fruits of victory with its allies, extending the rights of Roman citizenship, and protecting central and southern Italy against its enemies proved stronger than the appeals of Hannibal. Although he was victorious time and again, without local support Hannibal could not hold the terrain and cities he won.

The second reason for Rome's survival was the tremendous social solidarity that all classes and factions of its population showed during these desperate years. In spite of the internal tensions between patricians and plebeians, their ultimate dedication to Rome never faltered. Much of this loyalty was due to the Roman system of strong family and patronage ties. Kinsmen and clients answered the call of their patriarchs and patrons to bounce back repeatedly from defeat. Roman farmer-soldiers stood firm.

The third reason for Rome's ultimate success was Publius Cornelius Scipio (236–184 B.C.E.), also known as Scipio the Elder, a commander who was able to force Hannibal from Italy. Scipio, who earned the title Africanus for his victory, accomplished this not by attacking Hannibal directly, but by taking the war home to the enemy, first in Spain and then in Africa. In 210 B.C.E., Scipio arrived in Spain and rapidly captured the city of Cartagena (New Carthage). Within four years he destroyed Punic power in Spain. Riding the crest of popular enthusiasm at home, he raised a new army and in 204 B.C.E. sailed for Africa. His victories there drew Hannibal home, where at Zama in 202 B.C.E. the Roman commander destroyed the Carthaginian army. Zama put an end to both the Second Punic War and Carthaginian political power. Saddled with a huge indemnity and forced to abandon all of its territories and colonies to Rome, Carthage was reduced to a small portion of the North African coast. It had, in effect, become a Roman subject.

The Final Destruction. Still, this humiliating defeat was not enough for Rome. While some Roman senators favored allowing Carthage to survive as a means of keeping the Roman plebs under senatorial control, others demanded destruction. Chief among them was the censor Marcus Porcius Cato, known as Cato the Elder (234–149 B.C.E.), who ended every speech with "Carthage must be destroyed." Ultimately, trumped-up reasons were found to renew the war in 149 B.C.E. In contrast to the desperate, hard-fought campaigns of the Second Punic War, the Third was an unevenly matched slaughter. In 146 B.C.E., Scipio Aemilianus (184–129 B.C.E.), or Scipio the Younger, the adopted grandson of Scipio the Elder, overwhelmed Carthage and sold its few survivors into slavery. As a symbolic act of final destruction, he then had the site razed, plowed, and cursed. Carthage's fertile hinterland became the property of wealthy Roman senators.

Expansion into the Hellenistic East. In the same year that Carthage was destroyed, Roman armies destroyed Corinth, a second great center of Mediterranean commerce. This victory marked the culmination of Roman imperialist expansion eastward into the Greek and Hellenistic world, which had begun with the conquest of Illyria. This expansion was not simply the result of Roman imperialist ambitions. The Hellenistic states, in their constant warring and bickering, had drawn Rome into their conflicts against their neighbors. Greek states asked the Roman Senate to arbitrate their disputes. Pergamum requested military assistance against Macedonia. Appealing to Rome's claims as "liberator," cities pressed the Senate to preserve their freedom in the face of aggressive expansion by their more powerful neighbors.

Roman intentions may not have been conquest, but Roman intervention upset the balance of power in the Hellenistic world. The price of Roman arbitration, intervention, and protection was loss of independence. Gradually, the Roman shadow fell over the eastern Mediterranean.

The treaty that Philip V of Macedon concluded with Carthage during the Second Punic War provided an initial excuse for war, one that was seized on more eagerly by the plebeian assembly than by the Senate. Shortly after its victory at Zama, Rome provoked Philip to war and then easily defeated him in 197 B.C.E., proclaiming the freedom of the Greek cities and withdrawing from Greece. In 189 B.C.E., the Seleucid Antiochus III (223–187 B.C.E.) of Syria suffered the same fate, and Rome declared the Greek cities in Asia Minor that he had controlled free. The Greeks venerated the Roman commander, Titus Quinctius Flamininus (228–174 B.C.E.), as a god—the first Roman to be accorded this eastern honor.

In reality, the control of the freed cities lay in the hands of local oligarchs who were favorable to Rome. In 179 B.C.E., Philip's son Perseus (179–168 B.C.E.) attempted to stir up democratic opposition to Rome within the cities. This time, Rome responded more forcefully. The Macedonian kingdom was divided into four republics governed by their own senates and magistrates selected from among the local aristocrats. In Epirus, 70 cities were destroyed, and 150,000 people were sold into slavery.

The final episode of Rome's expansionist drama unfolded during the Third Punic War. When Rome resumed its war with Carthage in 149 B.C.E., several Greek cities attempted once more to assert their autonomy from the hated oligarchies established by Rome. Retribution was swift. Roman legions crushed the rebel forces, and, as an example to all, Corinth was razed and its population was enslaved.

In the west, in northern Italy, Spain, and Africa, Roman conquest had been direct and complete. Tribal structures had been replaced by Roman provinces governed by former magistrates or proconsuls. In the east, Rome preferred to work through the existing political hierarchies. Still, Rome cultivated its image as protector of Greek liberties against the Macedonian and Seleucid monarchies and preferred indirect control to annexation. Its power was no less real for being indirect.

By 146 B.C.E., the Roman republic controlled the whole rim of the Mediterranean from Rhodes in the east across Greece, Dalmatia, Italy, southern Gaul, Spain, and North Africa. Even Syria and Egypt, although nominally independent, had to bow before Roman will. Through perseverance and determination, Rome had risen from obscurity to become the greatest power the West had ever known. The republic had endured great adversity. It would not survive prosperity.

THE ROMAN REPUBLIC

509 B.C.E.	Expulsion of last Etruscan king; beginning of Roman Republic
ca. 450 B.C.E.	Law of the Twelve Tables
396 B.C.E.	Rome conquers southern Etruria
295 B.C.E.	Rome extends rule north to Po Valley
265–241 B.C.E.	First Punic War
264 B.C.E.	All of Italy under Roman control
218–202 B.C.E.	Second Punic War
149–146 B.C.E.	Third Punic War; Carthage is destroyed

Republican Civilization

Territorial conquest, the influx of unprecedented riches, and exposure to sophisticated Hellenistic civilization ultimately overwhelmed earlier Roman civilization. This civilization had been created by stubborn farmers and soldiers who valued authority, simplicity, and piety above all else. This unique culture was the source of strength that led Rome to greatness, but its limitations prevented the republic from resolving its internal social tensions and the external problems caused by the burden of empire.

One of a series of Roman mosaics illustrating tasks appropriate to the months of the year. Here two laborers are using an olive press with a horizontal screw for the December olive pressing.

Farmers and Soldiers

The ideal Roman farmer was not the great estate owner of the Greek world, but the smallholder, the dirt farmer of central Italy. Typical farm families, with holdings of perhaps as little as 10 acres, raised grain, beans, and hogs for their own consumption. In addition, they cultivated vineyards and olive groves for cash crops. But the most important crop of Roman farms was citizens. "From farmers come the bravest men and the sturdiest soldiers," wrote Cato the Elder. Nor was the ideal Roman soldier the gallant cavalryman but rather the solid foot soldier. Cavalry—composed of wealthy citizens who made up the elite **equestrian** order—and especially allies provided reconnaissance and protected Roman flanks. The main fighting force, however, was the infantry. Sometime in the early republic the Greek phalanx was transformed into the Roman legion, a flexible unit composed of 30 companies of 120 men each, armed with javelins and short swords.

These solid, methodical troops, the backbone of the republican armies that conquered the Mediterranean, were among the victims of that conquest. The pressures of constant international warfare were destroying the farmer-soldiers whom the traditionalists loved to praise. When the Roman sphere of interest had been confined to central Italy, farmers could do their planting in spring, serve in the army during the summer months, and return home to care for their farms in time for harvest. When Rome's wars became international expeditions lasting for years, many soldiers, unable to work their lands while doing military service, had to mortgage their farms in order to support their families. When they returned, they often found that during their prolonged absences they had lost their farms to wealthy aristocratic moneylenders. While aristocrats amassed vast landed estates worked by imported slaves, ordinary Romans and Italians lacked even a family farm capable of supporting themselves and their families. Without land they and their sons were excluded from further military service and sank into the growing mass of desperately poor, disfranchised citizens.

The Roman Family

In Roman tradition, the paterfamilias was the master of the family—which in theory included his wife, children, and slaves—over whom he exercised the power of life and death. This authority lasted as long as he lived. Only at his death did his sons, even if they were long grown and married, achieve legal and financial independence. The family was the basic unit of society, of the state.

Although not kept in seclusion as in Greece, Roman women theoretically never exercised independent power in this male-dominated world. Before marriage, a Roman girl was subject to the authority of her father. When she married, her father traditionally transferred legal guardianship to her husband, thus severing her bonds to paternal family. A husband could divorce his wife at will, returning her and her dowry to her father. However, wives did exercise real though informal authority within the family. Part of this authority came from their role in the moral education of their children and the direction of the household. Part also came from their control over their dowries.

Paternal authority over children was absolute. Not all children born into a marriage became members of the family. The Law of the Twelve Tables allowed defective children to be killed for the good of the family. Newborn infants were laid on the ground before the father, who decided whether the child should be raised. If there were too many mouths to feed or the child was simply unwanted, the father could command that the infant be killed or abandoned. Abandoned children might be adopted by childless couples.

Nor were all sons born into Roman families. Romans made use of adoption for many purposes. Families without heirs could adopt children. Powerful political and military figures might adopt promising young men as their political heirs. These adopted sons held the same legal rights as the father's natural offspring and thus were integral members of his family.

Slaves, too, were members of the family. On the one hand, slaves were property without personal rights. On the other, they might live and work alongside the free members of the family, worship the family gods, and enjoy the protection and endure the authority of the paterfamilias.

Social Effects of Expansion

In the wake of imperial conquests, the Roman family and its environment began to change in ways that were disturbing to many of the oligarchy. Some women, perhaps in imitation of their more liberated Hellenistic sisters, began to take a more active role in public life. One example is Cornelia, a daughter of Scipio Africanus. After her husband's death in 154 B.C.E., she refused to remarry, devoting herself instead to raising her children, administering their inheritance, and directing their political careers.

Some married women, too, escaped the authority of their husbands. Fewer and fewer fathers transferred authority over their daughters to their husbands. Instead, daughters remained under their father's authority as long as he lived. This meant that on the father's death, they became independent persons, able to manage their own affairs without their husbands' consent or interference. Although some historians believe that sentimental bonds of affection may have increased between many husbands and wives and parents and children as legal bonds loosened, it also meant that the wife's relationship to her children was weakened. Roman mothers had never been legally related to their children. Wives and mothers were not fully part of their husbands' families. Their brother's families, not their own children, were their natural heirs. Just as adoption created political bonds, marriage to daughters sealed alliances between men. However, when these alliances fell apart or more advantageous ones presented themselves, fathers could force their daughters to divorce their husbands and to marry someone else. Divorce became increasingly common in the second century B.C.E. More and more, wives were temporary visitors in their husbands' homes.

Roman Religion

Romans worshipped many gods, the more the better. Every aspect of daily life and work was the responsibility of individual powers, or *numina*. Every man had his *genius* or personal *numen*, just as every woman had her *juno*. Each family had its household powers, the *lares familiares*, whose proper worship was the responsibility of the paterfamilias. These family spirits exercised a binding power, a *religio*, on the Romans, and the pious Roman householder recognized these claims and undertook the *officia*, or duties, to which the spirits were entitled. These basic attitudes of religion, piety, and office lay at the heart of Roman reverence for order and authority. They extended to other traditional Roman and Latin gods such as Jupiter, the supreme god; Juno, his wife; Mars, the god of war; and the two-faced Janus, spirit of gates and new beginnings.

Outside the household, worship of the gods and the reading of the future in the entrails of sacrificed animals, the flight of birds, or changes in weather were the responsibilities of colleges of priests. Roman priests did not, as did those in the Near East, form a special caste but rather were important members of the elite who held priesthoods in addition to other public offices. Religion was less a matter of personal relationship with the gods than a public, civic activity that bound society together. State-supported cults with their colleges of priests, Etruscan- and Greek-style temples, and elaborate ceremonies were integral parts of the Roman state and society. The world of the gods reflected that of mortals. As the Roman mortal world expanded, so did the divine. Romans were quick to identify foreign gods with their own. Thus Zeus became Jupiter, Hera became Juno, and Aphrodite became Venus.

Still, the elasticity of Roman religion could stretch just so far. With the empire came not only the cults of Zeus, Apollo, and Aphrodite to Rome but that of Dionysus as well. Unlike the formal public cults of the other Greek deities, which were firmly in the control of authorities, that of Dionysus was largely outside state control. Women, in the tradition of the maenads, controlled much of the ecstatic and overtly sexual rituals associated with the god. Following the Second Punic War, the cult of Dionysus, known in Latin as Bacchus, spread rapidly in Italy. At its secret rites, or *Bacchanalia*, men and women were rumored to engage in every kind of sexual act.

In 186 B.C.E., the Senate decreed the cult of Bacchus a conspiracy and ordered an inquiry. The consul Spurius Postumius Albinus, acting on the false testimony of a former prostitute, began a brutal persecution. Rituals were banned, priests and adherents were arrested, and rewards were offered to informants, who provided lurid and fanciful accounts of what had taken place at the Bacchanalia. Hundreds of people were imprisoned, and greater numbers were executed. The Senate ordered all shrines to Bacchus destroyed and Bacchanalia banned throughout Italy. Perhaps more than any other episode, the suppression of the Bacchic cult showed the oligarchy's fear of the changes sweeping Roman civilization.

Republican Letters

As Rome absorbed foreign gods, it also absorbed foreign letters. From the Etruscans the Romans adopted and adapted the alphabet, the one in which most Western languages are written to this day. However, before the third century B.C.E., apart from extravagant funerary eulogies carefully preserved within families, Romans had no apparent interest in writing or literature as such. The birth of Latin letters began with Rome's exposure to Greek civilization.

Greek Historians of Rome. Early in the third century B.C.E., Greek authors had begun to pay attention to expanding Rome. The first serious Greek historian to focus on this new Western power was Timaeus (ca. 356–ca. 260 B.C.E.), who spent most of his productive life in Athens. There he wrote a history of Rome up to the Pyrrhic war, interviewing Roman and Greek witnesses to gain an understanding of this Italian city that had defeated a Hellenistic army. Polybius (ca. 200–ca. 118 B.C.E.), the greatest of the Greek historians to record Rome's rise to power, wrote a history that is both the culmination of the traditions of Greek historiography and its transformation, since it centers on the rise of a non-Greek power to rule "almost the whole inhabited world."

The Origins of Latin Literature. At the same time that Greeks began to take Rome seriously, Romans themselves became interested in Greece, in particular in the international Hellenistic culture of the eastern Mediterranean. The earliest Latin literary works were clearly adaptations if not translations of Hellenistic genres and texts. Already in 240 B.C.E., plays in the Greek tradition were said to have been performed in Rome. The earliest extant literary works, ironically for the sober image of the Roman farmer-soldier, are the plays of Plautus (ca. 254–184 B.C.E.) and Terence (186–159 B.C.E.), lightly adapted translations of Hellenistic comedies.

The Crisis of Roman Virtue

Rome's rise to world power within less than a century profoundly affected every aspect of republican life. Magistrates operating far from senatorial control in conquered provinces exercised power and found opportunities for enrichment never before seen. Successful commanders, honored and even deified by Eastern cities, felt the temptation to ignore the strict requirements of senatorial accountability. Provincial commanders enriched themselves through extortion, collusion with dishonest government contractors and tax collectors, and wholesale bribe-taking. Ordinary citizens, aware of such abuses, felt increasingly threatened by the wealthy and powerful.

In the second century B.C.E., Romans found themselves in a dilemma as the old and the new exerted equal pressures. These tensions led to almost a century of bitter civil strife and ultimately to the disintegration of the republic. The complex interaction of these tensions can best be seen in the life of one man, Marcus Porcius Cato.

Cato the Elder is often presented as the preserver of the old traditions, in contrast to Scipio Aemilianus, destroyer of Carthage and proponent of Hellenism in the Roman world. But if the division between old and new, between Cato and Scipio, had been so clear-cut, the dilemma of republican Rome would not have been so great. As it was, Cato reflected in himself this contradictory clash of values. Like the two-faced god Janus, whom he invoked in all his undertakings, Cato was the stern censor, the guardian and proponent of traditional Roman virtue, as well as the new Roman of shrewd business acumen, influence, and power unimaginable to the simple farmers he professed to admire.

Cato was born in the Latin town of Tusculum in 234 B.C.E. and grew to maturity on a family estate in Sabine territory. He came of age just at the start of the Second Punic War and distinguished himself in campaigns against Hannibal in Italy and Syracuse in Sicily. In between campaigns he became even more famous for his eloquence in pleading legal cases. His talents and energy brought him to the attention of powerful members of the senatorial aristocracy, under whose patronage he came to Rome. There he began to rise through the offices of military tribune, quaestor, and ultimately consul and censor.

This first-generation senator became the spokesman for the traditional values of Rome, for severity and simplicity, for honesty and frugality in private and public life. Cato ridiculed Greek philosophy and education, and he glorified his own simple farm life, the care he took in the management of his estates and of his extended *familia*, and his working in his fields side by side with his slaves.

Actually, Cato, as much as anyone else, was deeply involved in the rapid changes brought about by the empire. He may have worked along with his slaves, but as soon as they grew old, he sold them to the state to avoid having to support them, something no conscientious paterfamilias would ever have done. Although he led the battle to prevent senators from participating in commerce, he was perhaps the first of that body to diversify his holdings and investments. Although he avoided conspicuous

A memorial sculpture of Cato the Elder and his wife. Cato defended the ancient Roman traditions even as he himself was deeply influenced by the changes sweeping Rome. His married life was but one example of this: his treatment of his wives differed little from that of his slaves. After the death of his first wife, Licinia, he used a slave for sexual pleasure until his married son showed his disapproval. Cato immediately asked one of his clients, a former secretary for his daughter, Salonia, whom he promptly married. The sculpture represents him with Salonia.

consumption himself, as consul and censor he was responsible for many of the sumptuous building projects in Rome through which ordinary Romans first experienced the luxuries of the Hellenistic world. While scorning Greek culture, he worked bits of Greek authors even into his attacks on Greek civilization.

Cato was neither duplicitous nor hypocritical. He was simply typical. Many senators agreed with him that the old values were slipping away and, with them, the foundation of the republic. Many feared that personal ambition was undermining the power of the oligarchy. Yet these same people could not resist exploiting the changed circumstances for their own benefit.

SUMMARY

The Western Mediterranean to 509 B.C.E.   Civilization came to the western Mediterranean through Greek and Phoenician expansion. The Phoenicians established bases on the route to and from Spain, including a base at Carthage on the coast of North Africa. By the middle of the sixth century B.C.E., Carthage was the center of a stable and prosperous empire. In the eighth and seventh centuries B.C.E., the Greeks colonized Sicily and parts of Italy. Greek expansion led to conflict with Carthage. The Etruscans laid the foundations of Roman society and government.

From City to Empire, 509–146 B.C.E.   Early Roman society was composed of households headed by a paterfamilias. Over time, Roman society divided into plebians and patricians. Roman political institutions evolved from family and village networks. Etruscan and Latin traditions merged in Rome. Around 509 B.C.E., Roman patricians expelled the last Etruscan king and established a republic, an event that led to greater concentration of power in the hands of the patricians. Roman expansion contributed to social tension. In this context, the plebeians won a series of political victories. The Romans were remarkably successful at incorporating conquered peoples into their society. The Punic Wars with Carthage marked a turning point in the history of the Republic. By 146 B.C.E., the Roman republic controlled the whole rim of the Mediterranean.

Republican Civilization   The Roman ideal was the small farmer. Such people were the backbone of the Roman army. Ironically, Roman military success and expansion concentrated land and wealth in the hands of elites, at the expense of small farmers. The Roman family was centered on the almost unlimited power of the male head of the household, the paterfamilias. Roman expansion created perceived threats to traditional familial order. The Romans worshiped many gods. Religion was less a matter of personal relationship with the gods than a public, civic activity that bound society together. The birth of Latin letters began with Rome's exposure to Greek civilization.

The Crisis of Roman Virtue Rome's rise to world power within less than a century profoundly affected every aspect of republican life. The life of Marcus Porcius Cato epitomizes the tension between tradition and change in the late Republic. Like many others of his generation, Cato feared change at the same time as he exploited it for his own benefit.

QUESTIONS FOR REVIEW

1. Why might the Greeks have been surprised by certain characteristics of Carthaginian and Etruscan society?
2. What social, political, and military practices made possible the expansion of Rome from a collection of villages into a power that ultimately destroyed Carthage in the Punic Wars?
3. How were family and household life organized in the domus of the Roman Republic?
4. Why were Romans like Cato the Elder concerned by the changes that accompanied the expansion of Roman international power?

CHAPTER 5

Imperial Rome, 146 B.C.E.–192 C.E.

chapter outline

The Price of Empire, 146–121 B.C.E.

The End of the Republic

The Augustan Age and the *Pax Romana*

Religions from the East

The Culture of Antonine Rome

The Price of Empire, 146–121 B.C.E.

Roman victory defeated the republic. The creation of a Mediterranean empire brought in its wake a century of revolutionary change before new and stable social, cultural, and political forms were achieved in the Roman world.

Winners and Losers

Rome had emerged victorious in the Punic and Macedonian wars, but the real winners were the members of the oligarchy, the **optimates** (the "best"), as they called themselves, whose wealth and power had grown beyond all imagining. These optimates included roughly 300 senators and magistrates, most of whom

105

had inherited wealth, political connections, and long-established clientages. Since military command and government of the empire were entrusted to magistrates who were answerable only to the Senate of which they were members, the empire was essentially their private domain.

But new circumstances created new opportunities for many others. Italian merchants, slave traders, entrepreneurs, and bankers, many of lowly origin, poured into the cities of the East in the wake of the Roman legions. These newly enriched Romans constituted a second elite and formed themselves into a separate order, that of the *equites,* or equestrians, who were distinguished by their wealth and honorific military service on horseback but were connected with the old military elite. Since the Senate did not create a government bureaucracy to administer the empire, equestrian tax, farmers became essential to provincial government. Companies of these *publicans,* or tax collectors, purchased the right to collect rents on public land, tribute, and customs duties from provincials. Whatever they collected beyond the amount contracted for by Roman officials was theirs to keep.

The losers in the wars included the vanquished who were sold into slavery by the tens of thousands; the provincials who bore the Roman yoke; the Italian allies who had done so much for the Romans; and even the citizen farmers, small shopkeepers, and free artisans of the republic. All four groups suffered from the effects of empire, and over the next century, all resorted to violence against the optimates.

Roman slaves sifting grain. Roman victories in the Punic and Macedonian wars brought a huge influx of slaves from the conquered lands. Slaves were pressed into service on the estates and plantations of wealthy landowners.

Slave Revolts. The slaves revolted first. Thousands of them, captured in battle or taken after victory, flooded the Italian and Sicilian estates of the wealthy. Estimates vary, but in the first century B.C.E. the slave population of Italy was probably around two million, fully one-third of the total population. This vastly expanded slave world overwhelmed the traditional role of slaves within the Roman familia. Rural slaves on absentee estates enjoyed none of the protections afforded traditional Roman servants. Cato sold off his slaves when they reached old age; others simply worked them to death. Many slaves, born free citizens of Hellenistic states, found such treatment unbearable. Slaves rose up against their masters in Sicily in 135 B.C.E. and again a generation later and in southern Italy between 104 and 101 B.C.E. The most serious slave revolt occurred in Italy between 74 and 71 B.C.E. Gladiators—professional slave fighters trained for Roman amusement—revolted in Capua. Under the competent leadership of the Thracian gladiator Spartacus, over 100,000 slaves took up arms against Rome. Ultimately, eight legions, more troops than had met Hannibal at Zama, were needed to put down the revolt.

Provincial Revolts. Revolts profoundly disturbed the Roman state, all the more because it was not just slaves who revolted. In many cases, poor free peasants and disgruntled provincials rose up against Rome. The most significant provincial re-volt was that of Aristonicus, the illegitimate half-brother of Attalus III (ca. 138–133 B.C.E.) of Pergamum, a Roman client state. Attalus had left his kingdom to Rome at his death. In an attempt to assert his right to the kingdom, Aristonicus armed slaves and peasants and attacked the Roman garrisons. The hellenized cities of Asia Minor remained loyal to Rome, but this provincial uprising, the first of many over the centuries, lasted more than three years, from 133 to 130 B.C.E.

Revolts by slaves and provincials were disturbing enough. Revolts by Rome's Italian allies were much more serious. After the Second Punic War, these allies, on whose loyalty Rome had depended for survival, found themselves badly treated and exploited. Government officials used state power to undermine the position of the Italian elites. At the same time, Roman aristocrats used their economic power to drive the Italic peasants from their land, replacing them with slaves. A serious revolt took place between 91 and 89 B.C.E. after the Senate blocked an attempt to ex-tend citizenship to the allies. During this so-called Social War (from *socii*, the Latin word for allies), almost all the Italian allies rose against Rome. These revolts dif-fered from those in the provinces in that the Italian elites as well as the masses aligned themselves against the Roman oligarchy. Even some ordinary Roman citi-zens joined the rebel forces against the powerful elite.

Optimates and Populares

The despair that could lead ordinary Roman citizens to armed rebellion grew from the social and economic consequences of conquests. While aristocrats amassed vast landed estates worked by cheap slaves, ordinary Romans often lacked even a family farm capable of supporting them and their families. Many found their way to Rome, where they swelled the ranks of the unemployed, crowded into shoddily constructed tenements, and lived off the public subsidies.

In the face of the oligarchy's unwillingness to deal with the problem, the tribune Tiberius Gracchus (ca. 163–133 B.C.E.) in 133 B.C.E. attempted to introduce a land-reform program that would return citizens to agriculture. Gracchus was the first of the **populares**, political leaders appealing to the masses.

Tiberius Gracchus. During the previous century, great amounts of public land had illegally come into private hands. With the support of reform-minded aristocrats and commoners, Gracchus proposed a law that would limit the amount of public land an individual could hold to about 312 acres. He also proposed a commission to distribute to landless peasants the land recovered by the state as a result of the law. Because many senators who illegally held vast amounts of public land strongly opposed the measure, it faced certain failure in the Senate. Gracchus therefore took it to the plebeian assembly, where it was assured support from the rural poor. The law passed, but Gracchus's maneuvering lost him many of his aristocratic supporters, who feared that a popular democracy led by a demagogue was replacing the senatorial oligarchy.

Also in 133 B.C.E., Gracchus introduced another bill that called for the royal treasury of the kingdom of Pergamum, bequeathed to Rome by Attalus III, to be used to help citizens receiving land to purchase livestock and equipment. These laws, which challenged the Senate's traditional control over finance and foreign affairs, angered the conservative elite; but as long as Gracchus held office, he was protected from any sort of attack by the traditional immunity accorded to tribunes. It was no secret, however, that the Senate planned to prosecute him as soon as his one-year term expired. To escape this fate, he appealed to the assembly to reelect him for an unprecedented second consecutive term. To his opponents this appeal smacked of an attempt to make himself sole ruler, a democratic tyrant on the Greek model. A group of senators and their clients, led by one of Gracchus's own cousins, broke into the assembly meeting at which the election was to take place and murdered the tribune and 300 of his supporters.

Gaius Gracchus. The optimates in the Senate could eliminate Tiberius Gracchus, but they could not so easily eliminate the movement he had led. In 123 B.C.E., his younger brother, Gaius Sempronius Gracchus (153–121 B.C.E.), became tribune. During his two one-year terms he initiated an even broader and more radical reform program. Tiberius had been concerned only about poor citizens. Gaius attempted to broaden the citizenry and to shift the balance of power away from the Senate.

In the short run, Gaius's program was a failure. In 121 B.C.E., he was not reelected for a third term and thus lost the immunity of the tribunate. Recalling his brother's fate, he armed his supporters. Once more the Senate acted, ordering the consul to take whatever measures he deemed necessary. Gaius and some 3,000 of his supporters died.

The deaths of Tiberius and Gaius Gracchus marked a new beginning in Roman politics. Not since the end of the monarchy had a political conflict been decided with personal violence. The whole episode provided a model for future attempts at reform. Reformers would look not to the Senate or the aristocracy but to the people, from whom they would draw their political power. The experience of the Gracchi also provided a model for repression of other reform programs: violence.

The End of the Republic

With the Gracchi dead and the core of their reforms dismantled, the Senate appeared victorious against all challengers. In reality, Rome had solved neither the problem of internal conflict between rich and poor nor that of how to govern its enormous empire. The apparent calm ended when revolts in Africa and Italy exposed the fragility of the Senate's control and ushered in an ever-increasing spiral of violence and civil war.

The Crisis of Government

In 112 B.C.E., the Senate declared war against Jugurtha (ca. 160–104 B.C.E.), a North African client state king, who, in his war against a rival, had killed some Roman merchants in the Numidian city of Cirta. The war dragged on for five years amid accusations of corruption, incompetence, and treason. Finally, in 107 B.C.E., the people elected as consul Gaius Marius (157–86 B.C.E.), a "new man" who had risen through the tribunate, and entrusted to him the conduct of the war. To raise an army, Marius ignored property qualifications and enlisted many impoverished Romans, arming them at public expense. Although recruiting of landless citizens had probably taken place before, no one had done it in such an overt and massive manner. Marius quickly defeated Jugurtha in 106 B.C.E.

In the following year, Celtic and Germanic barbarians crossed the Alps into Italy. Although technically disqualified from further terms, Marius was elected consul five times between 104 and 100 B.C.E. to meet the threat. During this period he continued to recruit soldiers from among the poor and, on his own authority, extended citizenship to allies. To his impoverished soldiers, Marius promised land, but after his victory in 101 B.C.E., the Senate refused to give farms to veterans. As a result, Marius's armies naturally shifted their allegiance away from the Roman state and to their popular commander. Soon this pattern of loyalty became the norm. Politicians forged close bonds with the soldiers of their armies. Individual commanders, not the state or the Senate, ensured that their recruits received their pay, shared in the spoils of victory, and obtained land on their retirement. In turn, the soldiers became fanatically devoted to their commanders. Republican armies had become personal armies, potent tools in the hands of ambitious politicians.

The Civil Wars. The outbreak of the Social War in 91 B.C.E. marked the first use of these armies in civil war. Both Marius and the consul Lucius Cornelius Sulla (138–78 B.C.E.) raised armies to fight the Italians, who were pacified only after Roman citizenship was extended to all Italians in 89 B.C.E. The next year, Mithridates VI (120–63 B.C.E.), the king of Pontus, took advantage of the Roman preoccupation in Italy to invade the province of Asia. As soon as the Italian threat receded, Sulla, as the representative of the optimates, raised an army to fight Mithridates. Marius, as leader of the populares who favored reform, attempted to have Sulla relieved of command. Sulla marched on Rome, initiating a bloody civil war. In the course of this war, Rome was occupied three times, once by Marius and twice by Sulla. Each commander ordered mass executions of his opponents and confiscated their property, which he then distributed to his supporters.

Ultimately, Sulla emerged victorious and ruled as dictator from 82 to 79 B.C.E., using this time to shore up senatorial power. In 79 B.C.E., his reforms in place, Sulla stepped down to allow a return to oligarchic republican rule. Although his changes bought a decade of peace, they did not solve the fundamental problems dividing optimates and populares. If anything, his rule had proved that the only real political option was a dictatorship by a powerful individual with his own army.

Republican Crisis. Marcus Tullius Cicero (106–43 B.C.E.) reflected the strengths and weaknesses of the republican tradition in the first century B.C.E. Like Cato in an earlier age, he was a "new man," the son of a wealthy equestrian who provided his children with the best possible education both in Rome and in Athens and Rhodes. After returning to Rome, Cicero quickly earned a reputation for his skills as a courtroom orator.

Cicero identified firmly with the elite, hoping that the republic could be saved through the harmonious cooperation of the equestrian and senatorial orders. In 63 B.C.E., Cicero was elected consul, the first "new man" to hold the office in over 30 years. The real threat to the existence of the republic was posed by the ambitions of powerful military commanders: Pompey (106–48 B.C.E.), Crassus (ca. 115–53 B.C.E.), and Julius Caesar (100–44 B.C.E.).

Pompey and Crassus, both protégés of Sulla, rose rapidly and unconstitutionally through a series of special proconsular commands by judicious use of fraud, violence, and corruption. Pompey first won public acclaim by commanding a victorious army in Africa and Spain. On his return to Rome in 70 B.C.E., he united with Crassus, who had won popularity for suppressing the Spartacus rebellion. Together, they worked to dismantle the Sullan constitution to the benefit of the populares. In return, Pompey received an extraordinary command over all of the coasts of the Mediterranean, in theory to suppress piracy but actually to give him control over all of the provinces of the empire. When, in 66 B.C.E., King Mithridates of Pontus again attacked Greece,

Pompey assumed command of the provinces of Asia. His army not only destroyed Mithridates but continued on and conquered Armenia, Syria, and Palestine.

While Pompey was extending the frontiers of the empire to the Euphrates, Crassus, whose wealth was legendary, was consolidating his power. He allied himself with Julius Caesar, a young, well-connected orator from one of Rome's most ancient patrician families, who nevertheless promoted the cause of the populares. The Senate feared the ambitious and ruthless Crassus. It was to block the election of Crassus's candidate Catiline (Lucius Sergius Catilina, ca. 108–62 B.C.E.) to the consulate in 63 B.C.E. that the Senate elected Cicero instead. Catiline soon joined a conspiracy of Sullan veterans and populares, but Cicero quickly uncovered and suppressed the conspiracy and ordered Catiline's execution.

The First Triumvirate. When Pompey returned from Asia in triumph in 62 B.C.E., he expected to find Italy convulsed with the Catiline revolt and in need of a military savior in the tradition of Sulla. Instead, thanks to Cicero's quick action, all was in order. Although he never forgave Cicero for stealing his glory, Pompey disbanded his army and returned to private life, asking only that the Senate approve his organization of the territories he had conquered and grant land to his veterans. The Senate refused. In response, Pompey formed an uneasy alliance with Crassus and Caesar. This alliance was known as the **First Triumvirate**, from the Latin for "three men." Caesar was elected consul in 59 B.C.E. and the following year received command of the province of Cisalpine Gaul in northern Italy.

Pompey and Crassus may have thought that this command would remove the ambitious young man from the political spotlight. Instead, Caesar used his province as a staging ground for the conquest of a vast area of western Europe to the mouth of the Rhine. In 53 B.C.E., Crassus died leading an army in Syria, leaving Pompey and the popular young Caesar to dispute supreme power. As word of Caesar's military successes increased his popularity at Rome, it also increased Pompey's suspicion of his younger associate. Finally, in 49 B.C.E., Pompey's supporters in the Senate relieved Caesar of his command and ordered him to return to Italy.

Return he did, but not as commanded. Rather than leave his army, as ordered, on the far side of the Rubicon River, which marked the boundary between his province of Cisalpine Gaul and Italy, Caesar marched on Rome at the head of his legions. This meant civil war, a vicious bloodletting that convulsed the whole Mediterranean world. In 48 B.C.E., Caesar defeated Pompey in northern Greece. Pompey was assassinated shortly afterward in Egypt. Still, the wars went on between Pompey's supporters and Caesar until 45 B.C.E., when, with all his enemies defeated, Caesar returned to Rome.

The Second Triumvirate. In Rome, unlike Sulla, Caesar showed his opponents clemency as he sought to heal the wounds of war and to undertake an unprecedented series of reforms.

Still, Caesar made no pretense of returning Rome to republican government. In early 44 B.C.E., although serving that year as consul together with his general

MAP DISCOVERY

THE CAREER OF JULIUS CAESAR

Examine the extent of the Roman Empire in ca. 49 B.C.E. and the movement of Julius Caesar's military campaigns. How vital was Gaul to the Roman Empire before Caesar's campaigns? Based on the locations of Caesar's campaigns during the civil war, what can you assume about the center of power of his enemies? What geographical considerations might have led Pompey to seek an alliance with Egypt's Cleopatra?

Mark Antony (ca. 81–30 B.C.E.), Caesar had himself declared perpetual dictator. This move was too much for some 60 die-hard republican senators. On 15 March, a group led by two enemies whom Caesar had pardoned, Cassius Longinus and Marcus Junius Brutus, assassinated him as he entered the Senate chamber.

Cicero rejoiced when he heard of the assassination, clear evidence of his political naïveté. The republic was dead long before Caesar died, and the assassination simply returned Rome to civil war, a war that destroyed Cicero himself. Antony, Marcus Lepidus (d. 12 B.C.E.), another of Caesar's generals, and Caesar's grandnephew and adopted son Octavian (63 B.C.E.–14 C.E.), who took the name of his great uncle, soon formed the **Second Triumvirate** to destroy Caesar's enemies. After a bloody purge of senatorial and equestrian opponents, including Cicero, Antony and Octavian set out after Cassius and Brutus, who had fled into Macedonia. At Philippi in 42 B.C.E., Octavian and Antony defeated the armies of the two assassins (or, as they called themselves, liberators), who preferred suicide to capture.

After the defeat of the last republicans at Philippi, the members of the Second Triumvirate began to look suspiciously at one another. Antony took command of the east, protecting the provinces of Asia Minor and the Levant from the Parthians and bleeding them dry in the process. Lepidus received Africa, and Octavian was left to deal with the problems of Italy and the west.

Initially, Octavian had cut a weak and unimposing figure. He was only 18 when he was named adopted son and heir in Caesar's will. Still, he had the magic of Caesar's name with which to inspire the army, he had a visceral instinct for politics and publicity, and he combined these with an absolute determination to succeed at all costs. Aided by more competent and experienced commanders, notably Marcus Agrippa (ca. 63–12 B.C.E.) and Gaius Maecenas (ca. 70–8 B.C.E.), he began to consolidate his power at the expense of his two colleagues. Lepidus was forced out of his position and allowed to retire in obscurity, retaining only the honorific title of pontifex maximus.

Antony, to meet his ever-growing demand for cash, became dependent on the Ptolemaic ruler of Egypt, the clever and competent Cleopatra. For her part, Cleopatra manipulated Antony in order to maintain the integrity and independence of her kingdom. Octavian seized the opportunity to portray Antony as a traitor to Rome, a weakling controlled by an Oriental woman who planned to move the capital of the empire to Alexandria. Antony's supporters replied with propaganda of their own, pointing to Octavian's humble parentage and his lack of military ability. The final break came in 32 B.C.E. Antony, for all his military might, could not attack Italy as long as the despised Cleopatra was with him. Nor could he abandon her without losing her financial support. Instead, he tried to lure Octavian to a showdown in Greece. His plan misfired. Agrippa forced him into a naval battle off Actium in 31 B.C.E. in which Antony was soundly defeated. He and his Egyptian queen committed suicide, and Octavian ruled supreme in the Roman Empire.

A Life Worth Leading

Mere survival was a difficult and elusive goal through the last decades of the republic. Still, some members of the elite sought more. They tried to make sense of the turmoil around them and formulate a philosophy of life and a model of personal conduct. By now, the members of Rome's elite were in full command of Greek literature and philosophy, which they studied and adapted to their needs, creating a distinctive Latin cultural tradition. The most prominent figure in the late republic is Cicero, who combined his active life as lawyer and politician with an abiding devotion to Stoic philosophy. In the Stoics' belief in divine providence, morality, and duty to one's allotted role in the universe, Cicero found a rational basis for his deeply committed public life. For Cicero, humans and gods were bound together in a world governed not simply by might but by justice. The universe, while perhaps not fully intelligible, was nonetheless rational, and reason had to be the basis for society and its laws.

These same concerns for virtue are evident in the writings of the great historians of the late republic, Sallust (86–ca. 34 B.C.E.) and Livy (59 B.C.E.–17 C.E.). For Sallust, as well as for his younger contemporary, Livy, the chaos of civil war was the direct result of moral corruption and decline that followed the successes of the empire. For Sallust, the moral failing was largely that of the Senate and its members, who trampled the plebs in their quest for power and personal glory. Livy, who was much more conservative, condemned plebeian demagogues as well as power-hungry senators.

A different kind of morality dominated the work of Lucretius (ca. 100–55 B.C.E.), the greatest poet of the late republic. Just as Cicero had molded Stoicism into a Roman civic philosophy, Lucretius presented Epicurean materialist philosophy as a Roman alternative to the hunger for power, wealth, and glory. In his great poem *On the Nature of Things*, Lucretius presented the Epicurean's thoroughly physical understanding of the universe. He wrote that "a rational, proportional enjoyment of life is all that matters. Sorrow and anxiety come from but an ignorant emotionalism."

Emotion was precisely the goal of another poetic tradition of the late republic, that of the *neoteric* or new-style poets, especially Catullus (ca. 84–ca. 54 B.C.E.). Avoiding politics and moralistic philosophy, these poets created short, striking lyric poems that, although inspired by Hellenistic poetry, combine polished craftsmanship with a direct realism that is without precedent. One of the most striking differences between such Latin poetry and its Greek antecedents is the reality and individuality of the persons and relationships expressed.

The same interest in the individual affected the way artists of the late republic borrowed from Greek art. Hellenistic artists concentrated on the ideal, but Romans cherished the individual. The result was portraiture that caught the personality of the individual's face, even while portraying him or her as one of a type.

Chronology

THE END OF THE REPUBLIC

135–81 B.C.E.	Revolts against the republic
133–121 B.C.E.	Gracchi reform programs
107 B.C.E.	Gaius Marius elected consul
91–82 B.C.E.	Social War and Civil War (Marius vs. Sulla)
82–79 B.C.E.	Sulla rules as dictator
79–27 B.C.E.	Era of civil wars
63 B.C.E.	Cicero elected consul; First Triumvirate (Pompey, Crassus, Caesar)
59 B.C.E.	Caesar elected consul
45 B.C.E.	Caesar defeats Pompey's forces
44 B.C.E.	Caesar is assassinated; Second Triumvirate (Mark Antony, Lepidus, Octavian)
42 B.C.E.	Octavian and Mark Antony defeat Cassius and Brutus at Philippi
31 B.C.E.	Octavian defeats Mark Antony and Cleopatra at Actium
27 B.C.E.	Octavian is declared Augustus

The Augustan Age and the *Pax Romana*

It took Octavian two years after his victory at Actium in 31 B.C.E. to eliminate remaining pockets of resistance and to work out a system to reconcile his rule with Roman constitutional traditions while not surrendering any of his power. That power rested on three factors: his immense wealth, which he used to secure support; his vast following among the surviving elites as well as among the populares; and his total command of the army. It also rested on the exhaustion of the Roman people, who were eager, after decades of civil strife, to return to peace and stability. Remembering the fate of Julius Caesar, however, Octavian had no intention of rekindling opposition by establishing an overt monarchy. Instead, in 27 B.C.E. he returned the republic from his own charge to the Senate and the people of Rome. In turn the Senate decreed him the title of Augustus, meaning "exalted."

This meant that Augustus, as Octavian was now called, continued to rule no less strongly than before, but he did so not through any autocratic office or title—he preferred to be called simply the "first citizen," or **princeps**—but by preserving the form of the traditional Roman magistracies. For four years he rested his authority on consecutive terms as consul, and after 23 B.C.E. he held a life position as tribune. The Senate granted him proconsular command of the provinces of Gaul, Spain, Syria, and Egypt, the major sources of imperial wealth and the locations of more than three-quarters of the Roman army. Later, the Senate declared his *imperium*, or command, of these "imperial" provinces superior to that of any governors of other provinces.

The Senate's formalities deceived no one. Augustus's power was absolute. However, by choosing not to exercise it in an absolutist manner, he forged a new constitutional system that worked well for himself and his successors. By the end of his reign, few living persons could remember the days of the republic, and fewer still mourned its passing. Under Augustus and his successors the empire enjoyed two centuries of stability and peace, the **Pax Romana**, or "Roman Peace."

The Empire Renewed

Cicero had sought in vain a concord of the orders, a settlement of the social and political frictions of the empire through the voluntary efforts of a public-minded oligarchy. What could not happen voluntarily, Augustus imposed from above, reforming the Roman state, society, and culture.

The Senate. Key to Augustus's program of renewal was the Senate, which he made, if not a partner, then a useful subordinate in his reform. He gradually reduced the number of senators, which had grown to over 1,000, back down to 600. At the same time, he made membership hereditary, although he continued to appoint individuals of personal integrity, ability, and wealth to the body.

Augustus also shared with the Senate the governance of the empire, although again not on an equal footing. The Senate remained a creature of the emperor, seldom asserting itself even when asked to do so by Augustus or his successors and competing within its own ranks to see who could be first to do the emperor's bidding.

The Equites. Augustus undertook an even more fundamental reform of the equites, the wealthy businessmen, bankers, and tax collectors who had vied with the senatorial aristocracy since the reforms of Tiberius Gracchus. After Actium, many equites found themselves proscribed—sentenced to death or banishment—and had their property confiscated. Augustus began to rebuild their ranks by enrolling a new generation of successful merchants and speculators who became the foundation of his administration. The equestrian order was open at both ends. Freedmen and soldiers who acquired sufficient wealth moved into the order, and the most successful and accomplished equestrians were promoted into the Senate.

The Army. The land crisis had provoked much of the unrest in the late republic, and after Actium, Augustus had to satisfy the needs of the loyal soldiers of his 60 legions. Drawing on his immense wealth, acquired largely from the estates of his proscripted enemies, he pensioned off 32 legions, sending them to colonies that he purchased for them throughout the empire. The remaining 28 legions became a permanent professional army stationed in imperial provinces. Augustus established a small elite unit, the praetorian guard, in and around Rome as his personal military force. Initially, the praetorians protected the emperors; in later reigns, they would make them.

These measures created a permanent solution to the problem of the citizen-soldier of the later republic. Veteran colonies—all built as model Roman towns with their central forum, baths, temples, arenas, and theaters as well as their outlying villas and farms—helped to romanize the far provinces of the empire. These colonies, unlike the independent colonies of Greece in an earlier age, remained an integral part of the Roman state. Thus romanization and political integration went hand in hand, uniting through peaceful means an empire that had first been acquired by arms. Likewise, ambitious provincials, through service as auxiliaries and later as citizens, acquired a stake in the destiny of Rome.

Not every citizen, of course, could find prosperity in military service and a comfortable retirement. The problems of urban poverty in Rome continued to grow. By the time of Augustus, the capital city had reached a population of perhaps 600,000 people. The emperors, their power as tribunes making them protectors of the poor, provided over 150,000 resident citizens with a basic dole of wheat brought from Egypt. The emperors also built aqueducts to provide water to the city. In addition, they constructed vast public recreation centers.

These included both the sumptuous baths, which were combination bathing facilities, health clubs, and brothels, and arenas such as the Colosseum, where 50,000 spectators could watch gladiatorial displays, and the Circus Maximus, where a quarter of the city's population could gather at once to watch chariot races. Such mass gatherings replaced the plebeian assemblies of the republic as the occasions on which the populace could express its will. Few emperors were foolish enough to ignore the wishes that the crowd roared out in the Circus.

Divine Augustus. Augustus's renewal of Rome rested on a religious reform. He restored numerous temples and revived ancient Roman cults. He established a series of public religious festivals, reformed priesthoods, and encouraged citizens to participate in the traditional cults of Rome. His goals in all these religious reforms were twofold. After decades of public authority controlled by violence and naked aggression, he was determined to restore the traditions of Roman piety, morality, sacred order, and faith in relationship between the gods and Roman destiny. An equally important goal was Augustus's promotion of his own cult. His adoptive father, Julius Caesar, had been deified after his death,

This idealized marble portrait statue of the emperor Augustus addressing his army was found in the villa of Livia, wife of Augustus, at Prima Porta in Rome. The carvings on his breastplate recall the moment in 20 B.C. when Augustus was able to recover the military standards lost to the Parthians by Mark Anthony and Crassius. Since Augustus accomplished this through diplomacy rather than war, the event commemorates the establishment of the Pax Augusta.

and Augustus benefited from this association with a divine ancestor. His own genius, or guiding spirit, received special devotion in temples throughout the west dedicated to "Rome and Augustus." In the east, he was worshiped as a living god. In this manner, the emperor became identical with the state, and the state religion was closely akin to emperor worship. After his death, Augustus and virtually all of the emperors after him were worshiped as official deities in Rome itself.

Closely related to his fostering of traditional cults was Augustus's attempt to restore traditional Roman virtues, especially within the family. Like the reformers of the late republic, he believed that the declining power of the paterfamilias was at the root of much that was wrong with Rome. To reverse the trend and to restore the declining population of free Italians, Augustus encouraged marriage, procreation, and the firm control of husbands over wives.

Poetry and Patronage. Augustus actively patronized those writers who shared his conservative religious and ethical values and who might be expected to glorify the princeps, and he used his power to censor and silence writers whom he considered immoral. Chief among the favored were the poets Virgil (70–19 B.C.E.) and Horace (65–8 B.C.E.). Through their poetry in praise of the emperor, these poets conferred immortality on Augustus.

The finest of the poets who felt the heavy hand of Augustus's disfavor was Ovid (43 B.C.E.–17 C.E.), the great Latin poet of erotic love. In *Art of Love* and *Amores* he cheerfully preached the art of seduction and adultery. He delighted in poking irreverent fun at everything from the sanctity of Roman marriage to the serious business of warfare. By 8 C.E., Augustus had had enough. He exiled the witty poet to Tomis, a miserable frontier post on the Black Sea.

Augustus's Successors

The problem of succession occupied Augustus throughout much of his long reign and was never satisfactorily solved. Since the princeps was not a specific office, but a combination of offices and honors held together by military might and religious aura, formal dynastic succession was impossible. Instead, Augustus attempted to select a blood relative as successor, include him in his reign, and have him voted the various offices and dignities that constituted his own position.

Unfortunately, Augustus outlived all of his first choices. Augustus's final choice, his stepson Tiberius (14–37 C.E.), proved to be a gloomy and unpopular successor but nevertheless was a competent ruler under whom the machinery of the empire functioned smoothly. The continued orderly functioning of the empire even under the subsequent members of Augustus's family—the mad Gaius, also known as Caligula (37–41), the bookish but competent Claudius (41–54), and initially under Nero (54–68)—is a tribute to the soundness of Augustus's constitutional

THE ROMAN EMPIRE, 14 AND 117 C.E.

Examine the extent of the Roman Empire in 14 C.E. and in 117 C.E. What civilizations and empires that you previously have studied were incorporated into the Roman Empire by 14 C.E.? By 117 C.E.? Which regions had never before been part of ancient civilizations? What natural geographical features defined the boundaries of the empire in the west, north, south, and east?

changes and the vested interest that the descendants of Augustus's military and aristocratic supporters had in them.

Nero was more than even they could bear, however. Profligate, vicious, and paranoid, Nero divided his time between murdering his relatives and associates—including his mother, his aunt, his wife, his tutors, and eventually his most capable generals—and squandering his vast wealth on mad attempts to gain recognition as a great poet, actor, singer, and athlete. Finally, in 68 C.E., the exasperated commanders in Gaul, Spain, and Africa revolted. Once more, war swept the empire. Nero slit his own throat, and in the next year, the "Year of the Four Emperors," four men in quick succession won the office, only to lose their lives just as quickly. Finally, in 70 C.E., Vespasian (69–79 C.E.), the son of a "new man," who had risen through the ranks to the command in Egypt, secured the principate and restored order.

The emperors of the Flavian dynasty, Vespasian and his sons and successors Titus (79–81) and Domitian (81–96), were stern and unpretentious provincials who restored the authority and dignity of their office, although they also did away with most of the trappings of republican legitimacy that Augustus and his immediate successors had used. They solidified the administrative system, returned the legions to their fairly permanent posts, and opened the highest reaches of power to provincial elites as never before. After the Flavian emperors, the Antonines (96–193)—especially Trajan (98–117), Hadrian (117–138), and Antoninus Pius (138–161)—ruled for what has been termed "the period in the history of the world during which the human race was most happy and prosperous."

Breaking the Peace. Not all was peaceful in this period, however. Trajan initiated a new and final expansion of the imperial frontiers. Between 101 and 106 he conquered Dacia (modern Romania). He resumed war with the Parthians, conquering the provinces of Armenia and Mesopotamia by 116. During the second century the Palestinian Jews revolted in 115–117 and again in 132–135. The emperor Hadrian put down this second revolt and expelled the surviving Jews from Judaea. Along both the eastern and western frontiers, legions had to contend with sporadic border incidents. Within the borders, however, a system of Roman military camps, towns, and rural states constituted a remarkably heterogeneous and prosperous civilization.

Chronology

THE ROMAN EMPIRE

Julio-Claudian Period, 27 B.C.E.–68 C.E.	Augustus (27 B.C.E.–14 C.E.)
	Tiberius (14–37 C.E.)
	Caligula (37–41)
	Claudius (41–54)
	Nero (54–68)
Year of the Four Emperors, 69 C.E.	
Flavian Period, 69–96	Vespasian (69–79)
	Titus (79–81)
	Domitian (81–96)
Antonine Period, 96–192	Trajan (98–117)
	Hadrian (117–138)
	Antoninus Pius (138–161)
	Marcus Aurelius (161–180)
	Commodus (180–192)

Administering the Empire. The imperial government of this vast empire was as oppressive as it was primitive. Taxes, rents, forced labor service, military levies and requisitions, and outright extortion weighed heavily on its subjects. To a considerable extent, the inhabitants of the empire continued to be governed by the indigenous elites whose cooperation Rome won by giving them broad autonomy. In return for their participation in Roman rule, these elites received Roman citizenship, a prize that carried prestige, legal protection, and the promise of further advancement in the Roman world.

In those imperial provinces that were controlled directly by the emperor, the army was much more in evidence, and the professional legions were the ultimate argument of imperial tax collectors and imperial representatives, or *procurators.* Moreover, as the turmoil of the Year of the Four Emperors amply demonstrated, the military was the ultimate foundation of imperial rule itself. Still, soldiers were as much farmers as fighters. Legions usually remained in the same location for years, and veterans' colonies sprang up around military camps.

Finally, much of the governing of the empire was done by the vast households of the Roman elite, particularly that of the princeps. Freedmen and slaves from the emperor's household often governed vast regions, oversaw imperial estates, and managed imperial factories and mines. The descendants of the old Roman nobility might look down their noses at imperial freedmen, but they obeyed their orders.

The empire worked because it rewarded those who worked with it and left alone those who paid their taxes and kept quiet. As provincials were drawn into the Roman system, they were also drawn into the world of Roman culture. Proper education in Latin and Greek, the ability to hold one's own in philosophical discussion, and the absorption of Roman ways, including styles of dress, recreation, and religious cults, all were essential for ambitious provincials. Thus, in the course of the first century C.E., the disparate portions of the empire competed, not to free themselves from the Roman yoke, but to become Roman themselves.

Religions from the East

The same openness that permitted the spread of Latin letters and Roman baths to distant Gaul and the shores of the Black Sea provided paths of dissemination for other, distinctly un-Roman religious traditions. For many in the empire, the traditional rituals offered to the household gods and the state cults of Jupiter, Mars, and the other official deities were insufficient foci of religious devotion. Many educated members of the elite were actually vaguely monotheistic. Many others in the empire sought personal, emotional bonds with the divine world.

As noted in Chapter 4, in the second century B.C.E. the Roman world had been caught up in the emotional cult of Dionysus, an ecstatic, personal, and liberating religion entirely unlike the official Roman cults. Again in the first century C.E., so-called **mystery cults**—that is, religions promising immediate personal contact with a deity that would bring immortality—spread throughout the empire. The cult of the Egyptian goddess Isis spread throughout the Hellenistic world and to Rome in the republican period. From Persia came the cult of Mithras, the ancient Indo-Iranian god of light and truth, who, as bringer of victory, found special favor with Roman soldiers and merchants eager for success in this life and immortality beyond the grave. Generally, Rome tolerated these alien cults as long as they could be assimilated into, or at least reconciled in some way with, the cult of the Roman gods and the genius of the emperor.

Jewish Resistance

With one religious group this assimilation was impossible. The Jews of Palestine had long refused any accommodation with the polytheistic cults of the Hellenistic kingdoms or with Rome. Roman conquerors and emperors, aware of the problems of their Hellenistic predecessors, went to considerable lengths to avoid antagonizing this small and unusual group of people. When Pompey seized Jerusalem in 63 B.C.E., he was careful not to interfere in Jewish religion and even left Judaea under the control of the Jewish high priest. Later, Judaea was made into a client kingdom under the puppet Herod. Jews were allowed to maintain their monotheistic cult and were excused from making sacrifices to the Roman gods.

Still, the Jewish community remained deeply divided about its relationship with the wider world and with Rome. At one end of the spectrum were the Sadducees, a party composed largely of members of priestly families, who enjoyed considerable influence with their foreign rulers. They were staunch defenders of the ancient Jewish law, or Torah, but not to the exclusion of other later religious and legal traditions.

At the other end of the spectrum were the Hasidim (not to be confused with the modern Hasidic movement), those who rejected all compromise with Hellenistic culture and collaboration with foreign powers. Many expected the arrival of a messiah, a liberator who would destroy the Romans and reestablish the kingdom of David. One party within the Hasidim were the Pharisees, who practiced strict dietary rules and rituals to maintain the separation of Jews and Gentiles (literally, "the peoples," that is, all non-Jews). The Pharisees accepted the writings of the Hebrew prophets along with the Torah and abided by a still larger body of orally transmitted law, the "tradition of the elders."

For all their insistence on purity and separation from other peoples, the Pharisees did not advocate violent revolt against Rome. They preferred to await divine intervention. Another group of Hasidim, the Zealots, were less willing to wait. After 6 C.E., when Judaea, Samaria, and Idumaea were annexed and combined into the province of Judaea and administered by imperial procurators, the Zealots began to organize sporadic armed resistance to Roman rule. As ever, armed resistance was met with violent suppression. Throughout the first century C.E., clashes between Roman troops and Zealot revolutionaries grew more frequent and more widespread.

The Origins of Christianity

The already complex landscape of the Jewish religious world became further complicated by the brief career of Joshua ben Joseph (ca. 6 B.C.E.–30 C.E.), known to history as Jesus of Nazareth and to his followers as Jesus the Messiah or the Christ. Jesus came from Galilee, an area known as a Zealot stronghold. However, while Jesus preached the imminent coming of the kingdom, he did so in an entirely nonpolitical manner. He was, like many popular religious leaders, a miracle worker. When people flocked around him to see his wonders, he preached a message of peace and love of God and neighbor. His teachings were entirely within the Jewish tradition. However, while many contemporary religious leaders announced the imminent coming of the Messiah, Jesus' closest followers, the apostles and disciples, began to think that Jesus himself was the Messiah and expected him to restore the kingdom of Israel.

For roughly three years, Jesus preached in Judaea and Galilee, drawing large, excited crowds. Many of his followers pressed him to lead a revolt against Roman authority and reestablish the kingdom of David, even though he insisted that the kingdom he would establish was not of this world. Other Jews saw his claims as blasphemy and his assertion that he was the king of Jews, even if a heavenly one, as a threat to the status quo. Jesus became more and more a figure of controversy, a catalyst for violence. Ultimately, the Roman procurator, Pontius Pilate, decided that Jesus posed a threat to law and order. Pilate, like other Roman magistrates, had no interest in the internal religious affairs of the Jews. However, he was troubled by anyone who had the potential for causing political disturbances, no matter how unintentional. Pilate ordered Jesus scourged and put to death by crucifixion, a common Roman form of execution for slaves, pirates, thieves, and noncitizen troublemakers.

Spreading the Faith. The cruel death of Jesus ended the popular agitation he had stirred up, but it did not deter his closest followers. They soon announced that three days after his death, he had risen and had appeared to them numerous times during the following few weeks. They took this resurrection as proof of his claims to be the Messiah and confirmation of his promise of eternal life to those who believed in him. Soon a small group of his followers, led by Peter

A Roman tombstone inscribed with some of the earliest examples of Christian symbols. The anchor represents hope, while the fish recall Jesus' words, "I will make you fishers of men."

(d. ca. 64 C.E.), formed another Jewish sect—preaching and praying daily in the temple. New members were initiated into this sect, which soon became known as Christianity—through baptism, a purification rite in which the initiate was submerged briefly in flowing water. They also shared a ritual meal in which bread and wine were distributed to members. Otherwise, they remained entirely within the Jewish religious and cultural tradition, and hellenized Jews and pagans who wanted to join the sect had to observe strict Jewish law and custom.

Christianity spread beyond its origin as a Jewish sect because of the work of one man, Paul of Tarsus (ca. 5–ca. 67 C.E.). Although Paul was an observant Jew, he was part of the wider cosmopolitan world of the empire and from birth enjoyed the privileges of Roman citizenship. He saw Christianity as a separate tradition, completing and perfecting Judaism but intended for the whole world.

Paul set out to spread his message, crisscrossing Asia Minor and Greece and even traveling to Rome. Wherever he went, Paul won converts and established churches, called *ecclesiae*, or assemblies. Paul's teachings, while firmly rooted in the Jewish historical tradition, were radically new. God had created the human race, he taught, in the image of God and destined it for eternal life. However, by the deliberate sin of the first humans, Adam and Eve, humans had lost eternal life and introduced evil and death into the world. Even then, God did not abandon his people but began, through the Jews, to prepare for their eventual redemption. That salvation was accomplished by Jesus, the son of God, through his faith, a free and unmerited gift of God to his elect. Through faith, the Christian ritual of baptism, and participation in the church, men and women could share in the salvation offered by God, Paul said.

How many conversions resulted from Paul's theological message and how many resulted from the miracles he and the other disciples were believed to have worked will never be known, but another factor certainly played a part in the success of conversions. That was the courage Christians showed in the face of persecution.

Even Rome's elasticity and tolerance of new religions could be stretched only so far. The Christians' stubborn refusal to acknowledge the existence of the other gods and to participate in the cult of the genius of the emperor was intolerable. Christianity was an aggressive and successful cult, attracting followers throughout the empire. It was viewed not as religion, but as subversion. Beginning during Nero's reign, Roman officials sporadically rounded up Christians, destroyed their sacred scriptures, and executed those who refused to sacrifice to the imperial genius. But instead of decreasing the cult's appeal, persecution only aided it. For those who believed that death was birth into a new and better life, martyrdom was a reward, not a penalty. The strength of their convictions convinced others of the truth of their religion.

Christian Institutions. As the number of Christians increased in the face of persecution, the organization and teaching of this new faith began to evolve. A hierarchy developed within the various communities that Paul and the other apostles established. The leader of each community was the bishop who was assisted by **presbyters** (priests), deacons, and deaconesses.

Christian teaching focused on the Gospels, accounts of Jesus' life written toward the end of the first century; letters, or Epistles; and narratives and visionary writings by his early disciples and their immediate successors. In their preaching, bishops connected these texts to the tradition of Jewish Scriptures, explaining that the life of Jesus was the completion and fulfillment of the Jewish tradition. Over centuries, certain Gospels and Epistles and one book of revelation came to be regarded as authoritative and, together with the version of Jewish Scripture that was in use in Greek-speaking Jewish communities, constituted the Christian Bible. In the second and third centuries, the Christian message began to be challenged. Even within the Christian community, different groups held different views. Monatists argued that Christians were obligated to fast and abstain from marriage until the second coming. Dualist **Gnostics** interpreted the Christian message as a secret wisdom, or *gnosis*, which, combined with baptism, freed men and women from their fates.

Bishops defended the faith and determined what was correct. By the end of the first century, episcopal (from the Greek word for bishop) authority was understood to derive from the bishops' status as successors of the apostles. Gradually, the exalted position of the bishop and his assistants led to a distinction between the clergy and the laity, the rank and file of Christians. At the same time, women, who had played central roles in Jesus' ministry, were excluded from positions of authority within the clergy. In this process, the Christian community came to resemble closely the Roman patriarchal household, a resemblance that increased the appeal of the new sect to nonbelievers.

The Culture of Antonine Rome

The Romans themselves took little interest in natural science. However, they supported Greek science pursued in the East, particularly in Alexandria, where centuries of Greek mathematics, astronomy, and geography came to fruition in the work of Claudius Ptolemaeus (ca. 85–ca.165 C.E.), usually known as Ptolemy. Ptolemy was a cartographer and geographer, but his greatest work was as a mathematician and astronomer.

Building on the work of Hipparchus, Ptolemy developed a complex model for the universe that could explain the apparent motion of the sun, moon, and planets. Ptolemy's theory, which placed the earth in the center of the universe, remained the accepted model of the solar system for the next 1,400 years.

Romans themselves, however, were more interested in how humans should lead their lives than in how the planets moved. Rome's greatest historian, Cornelius Tacitus (ca. 56–ca. 120), recorded the history of the first century of the empire. His picture of Germanic and British societies served as a warning to Rome against excessive self-confidence and laxity.

Tacitus's contemporaries, Plutarch (ca. 46–after 119) and Suetonius (ca. 69–after 122), were biographers rather than historians. Plutarch, who wrote in Greek, composed *Parallel Lives,* a series of character studies in which he compared an eminent Greek with an eminent Roman. Suetonius also wrote biographies, using anecdotes to portray character.

In the later second century, Romans in general preferred the study and writing of philosophy, particularly Stoicism, over history. The most influential Stoic philosopher of the century was Epictetus (ca. 55–135), a former slave who taught that people could be free by the control of their will and the cultivation of inner peace. Like the early Stoics, Epictetus taught the universal brotherhood of humankind and the identity of nature and divine providence.

The philosophy of Epictetus found its most eager pupil in an emperor. Marcus Aurelius (161–180) reigned during a period when the stresses afflicting the empire were beginning to show in a much more alarming manner. Once more, the Parthians attacked the eastern frontier, while in Britain and Germany, barbarians struck across the borders. In 166, a confederation of barbarians known as the Marcomanni crossed the Danube and raided as far south as northern Italy. A plague, brought west by troops returning from the Parthian front, ravaged the entire empire. Aurelius spent virtually the whole of his reign on the Danubian frontier, repelling the barbarians and shoring up the empire's defenses.

This fifteenth-century Latin translation of Ptolemy's *Almagest* presents his model for the motion of the outer planets, Mars, Jupiter, and Saturn. The complicated cycles and epicycles are necessary to explain the motion of these planets while keeping the Earth at the center of the universe.

Throughout his reign, Aurelius found consolation in the Stoic philosophy of Epictetus. In his soldier's tent at night he composed his *Meditations*, a volume of philosophical musings. Like the slave, the emperor sought freedom from the burden of his office in his will and in the proper understanding of his role in the divine order.

However, his Stoic philosophy did not serve the empire well. For all his emphasis on understanding, Aurelius badly misjudged his son Commodus (180–192), who succeeded him. Commodus, whose chief interest was in being a gladiator, saw himself as the incarnation of Heracles and appeared in public clad as a gladiator and as consul. As Commodus sank into insanity, Rome was once more convulsed by purges and proscriptions. Commodus's assassination in 192 did not end the violence. The *Pax Romana* was over.

SUMMARY

The Price of Empire   The creation of an empire brought a century of revolutionary change before new and stable social, cultural, and political norms were established. The optimates, members of the ruling oligarchy, gained the most from Roman conquest. Slaves and provincials revolted against Roman rule. Reformers such as Tiberius and Gaius Gracchus appealed to the people for political support, prompting a violent backlash from the optimates.

The End of the Republic Revolts in Africa and Italy exposed the fragility of the Senate's control and ushered in an ever-increasing spiral of violence and civil war. Marius and Sulla battled for control of the military, and thus Rome, setting a pattern for future events. Pompey, Crassus, and Caesar ruled Rome as the First Triumvirate. Competition among the three men ended with Caesar's triumph. Caesar's assassination led to a new round of civil wars, from which Caesar's adopted son Augustus emerged as the undisputed ruler of Rome. Roman writers, artists, and philosophers struggled to find meaning in the turbulent events of their time.

The Augustan Age and the *Pax Romana* The reign of Augustus saw political, social, military, and religious reform. Under his rule, artists who celebrated the empire and his reign were rewarded with imperial patronage. The continued orderly functioning of the empire under the rule of subsequent members of his family is a tribute to the soundness of Augustus's constitutional changes and the vested interest that the descendants of Augustus's military and aristocratic supporters had in them. The suicide of Nero (54–68) ushered in a period of chaos that was followed by two new dynasties: first the Flavians and then the Antonines.

Religions from the East In the first century C.E. many Romans were attracted to so-called mystery cults, religions promising personal contact with a deity. The Jews of Palestine had a range of responses to Roman rule. Jesus lived and taught in this complex political and religious context. After his death, Christianity spread beyond its origins as a Jewish sect as the result of the efforts of Paul of Tarsus. Christians developed institutions to meet their religious and social needs. The Christian community came to resemble closely the Roman patriarchal household.

The Culture of Antonine Rome Greeks living under Roman rule took the lead in the natural sciences. Roman thinkers focused on questions of how humans should live their lives. In the later second century, many Romans, including the emperor Marcus Aurelius, were drawn to Stoicism.

QUESTIONS FOR REVIEW

1. How were rifts in Roman society widened by Rome's expansion into an empire?
2. In what ways were the life and thought of Cicero indicative of an age characterized by civil conflict and the collapse of republican traditions?

3. How was religious reform an important part of Augustus's efforts to restore stability to Roman society?
4. What did the Flavian and Antonine emperors do to keep Rome's vast empire intact and in relative peace?
5. How did Paul of Tarsus transform the teachings of Jesus of Nazareth from an outgrowth of Judaism into a separate spiritual tradition?

The Transformation of the Classical World, 192–500

The Crisis of the Third Century

From the reign of Septimius Severus (193–211) to the time of Diocletian (284–305), both internal and external challenges shook the Roman Empire. The empire survived, but its social, political, and economic structures were radically transformed.

Sheer size was a fundamental problem for the empire. Haphazard expansion in many regions—to the north and west, for instance—overextended the frontiers. The labor and resources needed to maintain this vast territory strained the economic system of the empire.

The economic system itself was part of the reason for this strain on resources. For all of its commercial networks, the economy of the empire remained tied to agriculture. To the aristocrats of the ancient world, agriculture was the only honorable source of wealth. The goal of the successful merchant was to liquidate his commercial assets, buy estates, and rise into the leisured landholding elite. As a result, liquid capital for either investment or taxation was always scarce.

The lack of sophistication seen in commercial and industrial business practice characterized the financial system of the empire as well. Government had always been conducted on the cheap. The tax system of the empire had never been very efficient at tapping into the real wealth of the aristocracy. Each individual city made its own collective assessments. Individuals eager to win the gratitude of their local communities were expected to provide essential services from their own pockets. Even with the vast wealth of the empire at its disposal, the government never developed a system of public debt—that is, a policy of borrowing against future revenues. As a result, the only way to solve short-term cash-flow problems was to debase the coinage by using more copper and less silver. This practice became epidemic in the third century, when the price of a bushel of wheat rose over 200 percent.

The failure of the empire to develop a stable political base complicated its economic problems. In times of emergency, imperial control relied on the personal presence and command of the emperor. As the empire grew, it became impossible for this presence to be felt everywhere. Moreover, the empire never developed either a regular system of imperial succession or an adequate power base. Control of the army, which was the ultimate source of imperial power, was possible only as long as the emperor could lead his armies to victory.

Enrich the Army and Scorn the Rest

Through much of the late second and third centuries, emperors failed dismally to lead their armies to victory. When the emperors selected by the distant Roman Senate failed to win victory, frontline armies unhesitatingly raised their own commanders to the imperial office. These commanders set about restructuring the empire in favor of the army. They opened important administrative posts to soldiers, expanded the army's size, raised military pay, initiated expensive building programs in frontier settlements, and in general introduced authoritarian military discipline throughout society. To finance these costly measures, the new military government confiscated senatorial wealth, introduced new forms of taxation, and increasingly debased the coinage.

The Rise of the Military. With their first rise in real income, soldiers in the provinces could improve their standard of living while in service and buy their way into provincial elites on retirement. Free-spending soldiers and imperial extravagance helped the bleak settlements on the edges of military camps grow into prosperous cities with all the comforts of the older parts of the empire. For the first time, capable soldiers could hope to rise to the highest levels of public power, regardless of their birth.

Economic Disaster. Soon, however, the military control of the empire turned into a nightmare even for the provinces and their armies. Exercising their newly discovered power, armies raised and then destroyed pretender after pretender, offering support to whichever imperial candidate promised them the greatest riches. The army's incessant demands for higher pay led emperors to lower the amount of silver in the coins with which the soldiers were paid, leading to ever-escalating inflation. Such drastic inflation wrecked the economic stability of the empire and spurred the army on to greater and more impossible demands for raises. Emperors who could not meet the demands were killed by their troops.

External Threats. The crisis of the third century did not result only from economic and political instability within the empire. Rome's internal crises coincided with an increase of attacks from outside the empire.

The greatest danger to Rome came from the west. There, along the Rhine, various Germanic tribes known collectively as the Franks and the Alemanni began raiding expeditions into the empire. Along the lower Danube and in southern Ukraine, the Gothic confederation raided the Balkans and harassed Roman shipping on the Black Sea.

This cameo was made to the order of Shapur I after the capture of Valerian during the great battle near Antioch in 260. The symbolic scene has Shapur seizing Valerian simply by grasping his hand.

An Empire on the Defensive

The central administration of the empire simply could not deal effectively with the numerous barbarian attacks. Left on their own, regional provincial commanders at times even headed separatist movements. Provincial aristocrats who despaired of receiving any help from distant Rome often supported these pretenders.

Political and military instability had devastating effects on the lives of ordinary people. Citizenship had been extended to virtually all free inhabitants of the empire in 212, but that right was a formality given simply to enlarge the tax base, since only citizens paid inheritance taxes. Society became sharply divided into the privileged **honestiores**—senators, municipal gentry, and the military—and the increasingly burdened **humiliores**—everyone else. The humiliores suffered the most from the tax increases because, unlike the honestiores, they could neither bribe their way out of them nor intimidate tax collectors with private armies. They were also frequent targets of extortion by the military and of violence perpetrated by bandits.

Slave and peasant bandits, rustlers, and even pirates played an ambivalent role in society. Often they terrorized the countryside, descending from the hills to attack villages or travelers. However, at times they also protected peasants from greedy tax collectors and military commanders. In Gaul and Spain, peasants and local leaders organized armed resistance movements, termed *Bacaudae*, to withstand the exorbitant demands of tax collectors. In the first centuries of the empire, bandits operated primarily in peripheral areas that had been recently and poorly subjugated to Roman rule. In the late second and third centuries they became an increasing problem in Italy itself.

The Barbarian Menace

Compounding the internal violence that threatened to destroy the Roman Empire were the external attacks of the Germanic barbarians. These attacks reflected changes within the Germanic world as profound as those within the empire. Between the second and fifth centuries, the Germanic world was transformed from a mosaic of small, decentralized, agricultural tribes into a number of powerful military tribal confederations capable of challenging Rome itself.

Germanic Society. The Germanic peoples typically inhabited small villages organized into patriarchal households, which were integrated into clans, which in turn composed tribes. For the most part, clans governed themselves and, except in war, tribal leaders had little authority over their followers. In the second century, many tribes had kings, but they were religious rather than political leaders.

Germanic communities lived by farming, but cattle raising and especially warfare carried the highest social prestige. Men measured their status by the number of cattle they owned and by their martial ability. Women took care of agricultural chores and household duties. Like the number of cattle, the number of wives showed a man's social position. Polygyny was common among chiefs.

Warfare defined social groupings, and warriors dominated public life. Only within the clan was fighting inappropriate. But rival clans within the same tribe dealt with one another brutally. Conflict took the form of the feud, and each act of aggression was repaid in kind. If an individual within a clan had a grievance with an individual within another clan, all his kinsmen were obliged to assist him. Thus a single incident could result in a continuous escalation of acts of revenge.

Feuding and Peacemaking. Clans in other tribes were fair game for raiding, looting, and conquering. Individuals, clans, and tribes built their wealth and reputations on warfare. The more successful a tribe was in warfare, the more clans it attracted and the greater its position became in the barbarian world.

The practice of feuding, especially within the tribe, had enormous costs. Families were decimated, and strong warriors who were needed to defend the tribe from outside attack faced constant danger from members of their own tribe. Tribal leaders attempted to reduce hostilities by establishing payments called **wergeld** in place of the blood vengeance demanded in reparation for crimes.

Tribes also attempted to reinforce unity through religious cults involving shared myths of common ancestry and rituals intended to underline group cohesion. When not fighting, Germanic warriors spent much of their time drinking beer together at the table of their war leader. Communal beer drinking was a way of uniting potentially hostile neighbors.

Warrior Bands. In contrast to the familial structure of barbarian society stood another warrior group that cut across kindred and even tribal units. This was the warrior band, called in Latin the *comitatus*. Some young warriors formed personal bonds with particularly able leaders and pledged them absolute loyalty. In return, the leaders were obligated to lead their warriors to victory and to share with them the spoils of war. Successful warrior leaders might draw sufficient numbers of followers and conquer so many other groups that in time the band would become a new tribe.

Roman Influence in the Barbarian World

Intratribal and intertribal violence produced a rough equilibrium of power and wealth as long as small Germanic tribes lived in isolation. The presence of the Roman Empire, felt both directly and indirectly in the barbarian world, upset this equilibrium. Unintentionally, Rome itself helped to transform the Germanic tribes into the major threat to the imperial system.

The Lure of Roman Culture. The attraction of Roman luxury goods and the Romans' efforts to establish friendly Germanic buffer zones along the borders drew even distant tribes into the Roman imperial system. Across the barbarian world, tribal leaders and comitatus leaders sought the prestige that Roman goods brought them. Roman provincial commanders encouraged these leaders to enter into commercial arrangements with the Romans. This outside source of wealth greatly increased economic disparity within Germanic society. In addition, some leaders made treaties with Rome, thus receiving the advantage of Roman support, which other tribal leaders lacked. In return for payments of gold and foodstuffs, chieftains of these "federated" tribes agreed to oppose tribes that were hostile to Rome and to prevent young hotheads of their own tribes from raiding across the frontier. Some chiefs supplied warriors for the Roman army. Others even led their comitatus into Roman service. Such "imperial Germans" moved back and forth between the Roman and barbarian worlds, using each as a foundation for increased power in the other and obscuring the cultural and political differences between the two.

The West Germanic Revolution. The effects of contact between barbarians and Romans reached far and wide throughout the empire and beyond the frontier. Along the Rhine and Danube the result was the so-called West Germanic Revolution. To survive in a time of constant warfare, tribes had to become armies. The armies needed a united and effective leadership. Among most of the western Germanic peoples, the tradition of the older tribal king was abandoned. A new kind of nonroyal chieftain emerged as the war leader of the people and as the representative of the war god Woden. In the later second and third centuries, the turmoil resulted in the formation of new tribes and tribal confederations: the Marcomanni, the Alemanni, and the Franks. By the end of the second century, this internal barbarian transformation spilled over into the empire in the form of the Marcomannian wars and the Saxon, Frankish, and Alemannic incursions into the western provinces.

The Gothic Confederation. Around the same time, along the Oder and Vistula rivers to the north, a group later known as the Goths began their slow consolidation around a royal family. The Goths were unique in that their kings exercised more military authority than was usual for a Germanic tribe.

Between the second and fourth centuries, the bearers of this Gothic royal tradition began to filter to the south and east, ultimately transferring their model of barbarian organization to the area of present-day Kiev in southern Ukraine. This move was not so much a physical migration of thousands of people across Europe as the gradual confederation under Gothic leadership of various Germanic, Scythian, and other peoples living around the Black Sea. By the early third century, this Gothic confederation was strong enough to challenge Roman supremacy in the region. These first Gothic wars in the east were even more devastating than the later wars in the west.

The Empire Restored

By the last decades of the third century, the empire seemed in danger of crumbling under combined internal and external pressure. That it did not was largely due to the efforts of the soldier-emperor Aurelian (270–275), who was able to repulse the barbarians, restore the unity of the empire, and then set about stabilizing the internal imperial structure.

Diocletian, the God-Emperor

Diocletian (284–305), a Dalmatian soldier who had risen through the ranks to become emperor, completed the process of stabilization and reorganization of the imperial system begun by Aurelian. The result was a regime that in some ways increased imperial power and in other ways simply did away with the pretenses that had previously masked the emperor's true position.

No longer was the emperor *princeps*, or "first citizen." Now he was *dominus*, or "lord," the term of respect used by slaves in addressing their masters. He also assumed the title of *Iovius*, or Jupiter, thus claiming divine status, and demanded adoration as a living god. Diocletian recognized that the empire was too large and complex for one man to rule. To solve the problem, he divided the empire into eastern and western parts, each part to be ruled by both an augustus and a junior emperor, or caesar. Diocletian was augustus in the east, supported by his caesar, Galerian. In the west, the rulers were the augustus Maximian and his caesar, Constantius.

The Tetrarchy. In theory, this **tetrarchy**, or rule by four, provided for regular succession. The caesars, who were married to daughters of the augusti, were to succeed them. Although from time to time subsequent emperors would rule alone, Diocletian's innovation proved successful and enduring.

In addition to this constitutional reform, Diocletian enacted or consolidated a series of measures to improve the functioning of the imperial administration. He reorganized and expanded the army, approximately doubled the number of provinces, separated their military and civil administration, and greatly increased the number of bureaucrats to administer them. He attempted to stem runaway inflation by increasing the amount of silver in coins and fixing maximum prices and wages throughout the empire. He restructured the imperial tax system, basing it on payments in goods and produce in order to distribute the burden more equitably among all citizens and to avoid problems of currency debasement.

A Militarized Society. The pillar of Diocletian's success was his victorious military machine. He was effective because, like the barbarian chieftains who had turned their tribes into armies, he militarized society and led this military society to victory. Like Diocletian himself, his soldiers were drawn from provincial marginal regions.

MAP DISCOVERY

Diocletian's empire

■ Where Aurelius Gaius served

THE EMPIRE UNDER DIOCLETIAN

This map shows the extent of the empire in 305, at the end of Diocletian's reign. Compared with the map on page 119, what portions of the empire had been lost or abandoned during his reign? Why? What geographical challenges did the empire's size pose to the emperor? Note where Aurelius Gaius served. What were the troubles and disturbances that influenced his itinerary?

They showed tremendous devotion to their god-emperor. For Diocletian and his soldiers, the periphery of the empire had become its center; the center was increasingly marginal to the program of the empire.

Fiscal Reform. Some aspects of Diocletian's program, such as the improvement of the civil administration and the military, were successful. Others, such as the reform of silver currency and wage and price controls, were dismal failures. One effect of the fiscal reforms was to bind **coloni**, or hereditary tenant farmers, to their lands, since they were forbidden to leave the villages where they were registered to pay their taxes. In this practice lay the origins of European serfdom. Another effect was the gradual destruction of the local city councils, since their members, the **decurions**, were held personally responsible for the payment of local assessments whether or not they could be collected from the other inhabitants. In time, this led to the dissolution of local civil government.

All of these measures were designed to marshal the entire population in the monumental task of preserving *Romanitas*. Central to this task was the proper reverential attitude toward the divine emperors who directed it. One group seemed stubbornly opposed to this heroic effort: the Christians. In 298, an incident occurred that seemed to confirm their subversive attitude. At a sacrifice in the presence of Diocletian, the Roman priests were unable to obtain the desired favorable omens; they attributed their failure to the presence of Christians, who were crossing themselves to ward off demons. Such blasphemous conduct—it might be compared, for instance, to desecrating the flag at a modern public assembly—led to the launching of the Great Persecution, which formally began in 303 and lasted sporadically until 313. It resulted in the death of hundreds of Christians who refused to sacrifice to the pagan gods.

Constantine, the Emperor of God

In 305, in the midst of the Great Persecution, Diocletian and his co-augustus Maximian took the extraordinary step of abdicating in favor of their caesars, Galerian and Constantius. This abdication was intended to provide for an orderly succession. Instead, the sons of Constantius and Maximian, Constantine (306–337) and Maxentius (306–312), drawing on the prejudice of the increasingly barbarian armies toward hereditary succession, set about wrecking the tetrarchy. In so doing, they plunged the empire once more into civil war as they fought over the western half of the empire.

Victory and Conversion. Victory in the west came to Constantine in 312, when he defeated and killed Maxentius in a battle at the Milvian Bridge outside Rome. Constantine attributed his victory to a vision telling him to paint symbols on the shields of his soldiers. For pagans, this symbol was the solar emblem of the cult of the Unconquered Sun. For Christians, it was the Chi-Rho, formed from the first two letters of the Greek word for Christ. The next year, in Milan, Constantine rescinded the persecution of Christians and granted Christian clergy the same privileges that pagan priests enjoyed. Constantine himself was not baptized until near death, a common practice in antiquity. However, during his reign, Christianity grew from a persecuted minority to the most favored cult in the empire.

Constantinople. Almost as important as Constantine's conversion to Christianity was his decision to establish his capital in Byzantium, a city founded by Greek colonists on the narrow neck of water connecting the Black Sea to the Mediterranean. Later it was known as Constantinople, the city of Constantine. For the next 11 centuries, Constantinople served as the heart of the Roman and then the Byzantine world. From his new city, Constantine began to transform the empire into a Christian state and Christianity into a Roman state religion.

The Triumph of Christianity

While paganism was being disestablished, Christianity was rapidly becoming the established religion. The effects of Constantine's conversion on the empire and on Christianity were enormous. Constantine made large financial contributions to Christian communities to repay them for their losses during persecutions. He erected rich churches on the model of Roman basilicas, or administrative buildings, and converted temples into Christian places of worship. He gave bishops the authority to act as magistrates within the Christian community. Once the particular subjects of persecution, bishops became favored courtiers. Constantine attempted to make himself the de facto head of the Church. Constantine and his successors, with the brief exception of his nephew Julian (r. 361–363), sought to use the cult of the one God to strengthen their control over the empire.

Emperor and Church. After Constantine's death in 337, emperors began restricting paganism. In 341, pagan sacrifice was banned, and by 355 the temples had been closed and the death penalty for sacrificing to pagan gods had been decreed, although not enforced.

Imperial control over Christianity was strong, but not total. One of the most powerful Christian successors to Constantine, Theodosius I (347–395), met his match in Ambrose (339–397), the bishop of Milan. In 390, the emperor, angered by riots in the Greek city of Thessalonica, ordered a general massacre of the population. Ambrose dared to excommunicate, or ban, the emperor from his church in Milan until Theodosius did public penance for that brutal act. Eventually, the emperor acquiesced, acknowledging that even he was subject to the rule of God as interpreted by the bishops.

Conversion. Although imperial support was essential to the spread of Christianity in the fourth century, other factors encouraged conversion as well. Christian miracles, particularly that of exorcism, or the casting out of demons, won many converts.

Over the course of the fourth century, the number of Christians rose from 5 to 30 million. Imperial support, miracles, and preaching could not, by themselves, account for this phenomenal growth. Physical coercion played a large part. The story was told that in one town, on imperial command, all of the local temples were destroyed and "a great number" of leading pagans who refused conversion were tortured to death. The remaining pagan population converted. Conversion—by whatever method—also suited the emperors, who saw a unified cult as an essential means of bolstering their position.

This mosaic found under St. Peter's Basilica in Rome is believed by many to be the earliest representation of Jesus, while others see it as Helios, the sun-god. The catacombs were underground passages near Rome used by the early Christians as cemeteries, for funeral and memorial services, and as places of refuge during times of persecution.

Imperial Christianity

The religion to which Constantine converted had matured institutionally and intellectually since its origins as a reform movement within Judaism. By the late third century, Christian communities existed throughout the empire, each headed by a bishop who was considered divinely guided and answerable only to his flock and to God. In the west, the bishop of Rome, termed the pope, had acquired the position of first among equals. However, the Church as a whole was divided on fundamental questions of belief, and the growing importance of Christianity in the Roman Empire added to the gravity of these divisions.

Divinity, Humanity, and Salvation

Jesus, the savior or Christ, was at the heart of Christian belief, but individual Christian communities interpreted the nature of Christ differently as they attempted to reconcile their faith with the intellectual traditions of late antiquity. Christian Scriptures spoke of the Father, the Son, and the Spirit. Yahweh was generally accepted as the Father and Christ as the Son; the Spirit was understood to be the continuing presence of God sent by Jesus after his resurrection and ascension.

Christology. Generally, Christians saw God as a Trinity, at once one and three. But the relationship among the three was a source of endless debate, particularly for

Greek-speaking Christians attempting to reconcile their faith with the Neoplatonic ideas of successive emanations from God to creation, which were incorporated into the Christian understanding of the Trinity. Was Christ just a man, chosen by God as a divine instrument, or was he God? If he was God, had he simply appeared to be human? These were not trivial or academic questions for Christians, since the possibility of salvation depended on their answers. Throughout the eastern half of the empire, ordinary people were ready to fight not only with words, but even with weapons to defend their positions.

Throughout the so-called **Christological controversies**—which began in the early third century and continued through the fifth—two extremes presented Christ as either entirely human or entirely God, with centrists attempting to hold a middle ground. At one extreme were the Monarchians, who emphasized the oneness of God by arguing that the three represented three activities although God possessed only one substance, and the Gnostics, who argued that Jesus had only appeared to be human but in reality was only divine. At the other extreme were the **Arians**, who explained that Jesus was a man and not divine.

MAP DISCOVERY

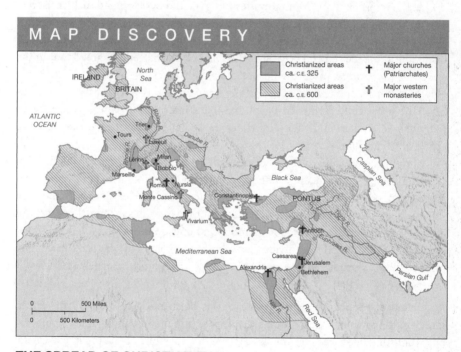

Christianized areas ca. c.e. 325

Christianized areas ca. c.e. 600

† Major churches (Patriarchates)

☩ Major western monasteries

THE SPREAD OF CHRISTIANITY

Examine the regions in which Christianity first became established. What is distinctive about the areas Christianized in the first three centuries of Christendom? What major differences can you detect between Christian centers in the eastern and western portions of the Roman Empire? To what extent did Christianity exist outside the empire by 600?

Origen of Alexandria. The first Christian intellectual to undertake a systematic exposition of the Trinity was the great Alexandrine theologian Origen (185–254). In all of his teachings, Origen moved Christian teaching from a literal to a symbolic understanding of Scripture and gave it a sound philosophical foundation by synthesizing the Neoplatonic tradition with Christianity. His trinitarian teachings insisted on the co-eternality of the Son with the Father, but, drawing as he did on Neoplatonic ideas of emanations, he seemed to subordinate the Son to the Father and to make the Spirit a creation of the Son. In the generations following Origen, the controversy continued, particularly between those who taught the equality of the persons of the Trinity and those who, like the Alexandrine theologian Arius (ca. 250–336), insisted that Jesus was not equal to God the Father but was a lesser divinity created by God. By the time of Constantine, the issue of whether or not Jesus was one with God threatened to destroy the unity of Christianity. To settle the controversy, the emperor commanded the bishops of the entire Church to assemble at Nicaea in 325. At the emperor's urging, the council condemned the teachings of Arius and adopted the term *homousion*, "of one being," to describe the equality of the Father and the Son.

At the other extreme, Monophysites in Egypt and Syria argued that Christ had only one nature—the divine. A century after Nicaea, another council was held at Chalcedon in 451 to resolve the issue. Following the recommendation of the bishop of Rome, Pope Leo I (440–461), the bishops at Chalcedon agreed that in the one God there were three divine persons: the Father, the Son, and the Spirit. However, the second person of the Trinity, the Son, had two natures: one fully human, the other fully divine. In Egypt and Palestine the decree was greeted with outrage. Mobs of monks and laity rioted in the streets to oppose the "unclean synod of Chalcedon."

Although a western bishop had provided the formula for Chalcedon, Latin Christians were not as deeply concerned with the Christological debates as were the easterners. For westerners, the great question was less the nature of God than the mechanism of salvation and the role of humans in the salvational process. An attempt to answer this and other key doctrinal questions was provided by a man who, more than any other individual, would set the course of western Christianity and political philosophy for the next thousand years: Augustine of Hippo.

Augustine of Hippo. Augustine (354–430) was born into a well-off North African family in the town of Tagaste. In his *Confessions*, the first psychological autobiography, Augustine describes how his skills in rhetoric took him to the provincial capital of Carthage and then on to Rome and finally Milan, the western imperial residence, where he gained fame as one of the foremost rhetoricians of the empire.

While in Milan, Augustine came into contact with kinds of people he had never encountered in Africa, particularly Neoplatonists and Christians. The most important of these was Ambrose, bishop of Milan. The encounter with a spiritual philosophy and a Christianity that was compatible with it profoundly changed the young professor. After a period of agonized searching, Augustine converted to the new religion. Abandoning his Italian life, he returned to the North African town of Hippo to found a monastery where he could devote himself to reading the Scriptures.

Augustine spent the remainder of his life as bishop of this small provincial town, but his reputation as spokesperson for the Christian tradition spread throughout the empire. As a professor of rhetoric he had become an expert in debate, and much of his episcopal career was spent in refuting opponents within the Church as well as dealing with traditional pagans who blamed the problems of the empire on the new religion.

In responding to these attacks, Augustine elaborated a new Christian understanding of human society and the individual's relationship to God, which dominated Western thought for the next 15 centuries. He rejected elitist attempts to identify the true Church with any earthly community. Likewise, he rejected the claim of pagans that the Roman tradition was the embodiment of true virtue. Instead, he argued that the true members of God's elect necessarily coexisted in the world with sinners. No earthly community, not even the empire or the visible Church, was the true "city of God." Earthly society participated in the true Church, the city of God, through the sacraments and did so quite apart from the individual worthiness of the recipients or even of the ministers of these rites. Belief that the presence of sinners within the Church blocked the plan of salvation or that responsibility for salvation lay with the individual was to deny the omnipotence of God.

According to Augustine, salvation was free, a gift not earned by virtuous lives but freely granted by God to the elect. In this way, Augustine argued for a distinction between the visible Christian empire and the Christian community.

The Call of the Desert

At the same time that intellectuals like Augustine were attempting to explain Christian doctrine, less intellectual but equally determined men and women were searching for a different way of living Christ's message. This was the hermit, monk, or recluse, who taught less by his or her words than by his or her life, a life that was often so unusual that even the most ignorant and worldly citizen of the late empire could recognize in it the power of God. Beneath the apparent eccentricity, however, lay a fundamental principle: the radical rejection of society's values in favor of absolute dedication to God's.

Shortly after the death of Origen in 254, another Egyptian was undertaking a different path to enduring fame. Anthony (ca. 250–355), a well-to-do peasant, heard the same biblical text that later converted Augustine: "Go, sell all you have and give to the poor and follow me." This straightforward peasant did exactly what the text commanded. He disposed of all his goods and left his village for the Egyptian desert. There, for the next 70 years, he sought to follow Christ in a life of constant self-mortification and prayer.

This dropout from civilization deeply touched his fellow Christians, many of whom were disturbed by the abrupt transformation of their religion from persecuted minority to privileged majority. Over the next few centuries, thousands rejected the worldliness of civilization and the easy life of the average Christian to lead a monastic life in the wildernesses of the empire.

Monastic Communities

Monasticism took two forms: communal organization and solitary life. Pachomius (ca. 290–346) and Basil the Great (ca. 329–379) in the east and Benedict of Nursia (ca. 480–547) in the west perfected the communal life. Faced with the impossibility of surviving in a harsh environment without cooperation, Egyptian monks banded together into small monastic towns. As many as 2,000 monks lived in these monasteries. They placed themselves under the control of the abbot, who served as spiritual guide and administrator of the community. These men and women sought spiritual perfection through physical self-mortification and through the subordination of their own wills to that of the abbot. Monks drank no wine, ate no meat, used no oil. They spent their days in prayer and work. During the fourth century, this monastic tradition spread east to Bethlehem, Jerusalem, Caesarea, and Constantinople and west to Rome, Milan, Trier, Marseille, and Tours. In the following centuries, it reached beyond the borders of the empire when Egyptian-style monasticism was introduced into Ireland.

In the Greek-speaking world, the definitive form of the monastic community was provided by Basil the Great. Basil had visited the monasteries of Egypt, Palestine, and Syria before founding his own monastery at Pontus near his family estate at Annesi in present-day Turkey. Although he did not write a specific rule for the governance of his monastery, his collection of commentaries and spiritual advice to his followers outlined a form of monastic life in which a day of agriculture, craft work, and care for the sick and the poor was organized within an ordered progression of liturgical prayer. His emphasis on communal life rather than on heroic acts of individual asceticism provided the model for eastern monasticism from his day to the present.

Unlike Anthony of Egypt, Basil was a brilliant and well-educated intellectual who frequently left his monastery to throw himself into the ecclesiastical politics of the empire. By the end of his life, Basil had become bishop of Caesarea. Eastern monastic communities continued this active involvement in political and secular affairs. Monasteries provided the early religious training for most religious leaders. Monks and abbots often involved themselves wholeheartedly in the politics of the empire.

In the west, Benedict of Nursia was as influential in structuring communal religious life as Basil was in the east. In time, Benedict became abbot of a small community of monks at Monte Cassino, between Rome and Naples. The rule that he drafted for the governance of his community, while drawn largely from earlier monastic rules circulating in Italy, became the definitive statement of western monasticism. Benedict's rule encouraged moderation and flexibility while emphasizing a life of poverty, chastity, and obedience to an elected abbot. Monks were required to perform some physical labor, and the monastery was intended to be a self-sufficient community. However, the real task of the monk was the continuous praise of God. This consisted of gathering at regular intervals through the day and night for communal prayer. Although Benedict lived and died in obscurity, within two and a half centuries his rule became the universal rule for western monasticism.

Western monasteries, too, provided their share of bishops, but unlike those in the east, western monks remained more isolated from population centers and from direct involvement in public affairs. However, western monasteries were not peripheral to western society and religion. Rather, these rustic communities were centers of religious and economic activity as well as education and learning in the largely rural west. They remained under the authority of the local bishops, who were usually drawn from the lay aristocracy of the empire in the west. Also, western monasteries depended on the political and economic support that they received from lay patrons.

Solitaries and Hermits

Although Anthony had begun as a hermit, he and most Egyptian monks eventually settled into communal lives. Elsewhere, particularly in the desert of Syria, the model of the monk remained the individual hermit. The Syrian desert, unlike that of Egypt, was particularly suitable for such an ascetic life. Here, the desert was milder, an individual could find food in wild roots and water in rain pools, and villages were never too far off. Moreover, the life of the wandering hermit was closely connected to traditional seminomadic lifestyles in the Fertile Crescent. But the Christian hermits who appeared across Syria in late antiquity were unlikely to be mistaken for the familiar Bedouin nomads. The Christian hermits were wild men and women who came down from the mountainsides and galvanized the attention of their contemporaries by their lifestyles.

Such people of God, rejecting civilized life in the most overt and radical ways, nevertheless met very real social and cultural needs of the population. Their lack of ties to human society made them the perfect arbitrators in the constant disputes that threatened to disrupt village life. They were individuals of power, whose perceived ability to cast out demons and work miracles made them ideal community patrons at a time when traditional power brokers of the village were being lured away to imperial service or provincial cities. The greatest of these holy people received as visitors not only local peasants but also emperors and empresses, who eagerly sought their advice.

Unlike the eastern monks, the Syrian hermits of the fourth and fifth centuries had few parallels in the west. Hermits did inhabit the caves and forests of Italy and Gaul, and pious women found solitude as recluses even in the center of Rome. But

A gold plaque from a sixth-century Syrian reliquary. The subject is Simeon Stylites on his pillar; the snake represents the vanquished devil. Clients could consult the holy man by climbing up the ladder on the left.

these westerners did not establish themselves either as independent sources of religious power or as political power brokers. Their monasticism remained a personal religious commitment. When one Roman woman was asked why she remained shut up in her cell, she replied, "I am on a journey." When asked where she was going, she answered simply, "To God."

Chronology

IMPERIAL REFORM AND IMPERIAL CHRISTIANITY

284–305	Reign of Diocletian; establishment of the tetrarchy
303–313	Great Persecution of Christians
305	Abdication of Diocletian
306–312	Civil War
312	Victory of Constantine in civil war; Constantine converts to Christianity; establishment of Byzantium as Constantine's capital
325	Council of Nicaea
337	Official restrictions on paganism
341	Pagan sacrifice banned
355	Temples closed and death penalty established for sacrificing to pagan gods
480	Death of Julius Nepos, last legitimate emperor in the west

A Parting of the Ways

Those who remained in "the world" at the end of the fourth century could hardly take so serene a view of life. Christians and pagans might differ in their explanations for the ills that had befallen the empire, but none could deny their severity. The vulnerability of the Constantinian system became clear shortly after 376, when the Huns, a nomadic horse-riding people from central Asia, swept into the Black Sea region and threw the entire barbarian world once more into chaos. The Huns quickly destroyed the Gothic confederation and absorbed many of the peoples who had constituted the Goths. Others sought protection in the empire. The Visigoths, as they came to be known, were the largest of these groups, and their fate illustrated how precarious existence could be for all the inhabitants of the imperial frontier.

Driven from their lands and thus from their food supply, the Visigoths turned to the empire for assistance. But the Roman authorities treated them as brutally as had the Huns, forcing some to sell their children into slavery in return for morsels of dog flesh. In despair, the Visigoths rose up against the Romans, and against all odds, their desperate rebellion succeeded. They annihilated an imperial army at Adrianople in 378, and the emperor Valens himself was killed. His successor, Theodosius (379–395), was forced to allow the Visigoths to settle along the Danube and to be governed by their own leaders even though they lived within the boundaries of the empire.

Theodosius's treaty with the Visigoths set an ominous precedent. Never before had a barbarian people been allowed to settle as a political unit within the empire. Within a few years the Visigoths were again on the move, traveling across the Balkans into Italy under the command of their chieftain Alaric (ca. 370–410). In 410, they captured Rome and sacked it for three days, an event that sent shock waves throughout the entire empire. The symbolic effect of the Visigoths' victory far exceeded the amount of real damage, which was relatively light. Only after Alaric's death did the Visigoths leave Italy, ultimately settling in Spain and southern Gaul with the emperor's approval.

The Barbarization of the West

Rome did not fall. It was transformed. Romans participated in and even encouraged this transformation. Roman accommodation of the Visigoths set the pattern for subsequent settlement of barbarians in the western half of the empire. By this time, barbarians made up the bulk of the imperial army, and commanders were frequently themselves barbarians. However, these barbarian troops had been integrated into existing Roman military structures. In the late fourth and fifth centuries, emperors accepted whole barbarian peoples as integral parts of the Roman army and settled them within the empire.

The Visigoths were not the only powerful barbarian people to challenge the empire. The Vandals, who had entered the empire in 406, crossed over into Africa, the richest region of the western empire, and quickly conquered it. Avowed enemies of the empire, the Vandals used their base in North Africa to raid the European coastline and attack Roman shipping. In 455, they sacked Rome much more thoroughly than had the Goths 45 years earlier.

Another threat appeared in the 430s, when the Huns, formerly Roman allies, invaded the empire under their charismatic leader Attila (ca. 406–453). Although defeated in Gaul by a combined army of barbarians under the command of the Roman general Flavius Aetius in 451, they turned toward Italy and penetrated as far as Rome. There, they were stopped not by the rapidly disintegrating imperial forces but by the bishop of Rome, Pope Leo I, who met Attila before the city's gates. What transpired between the two is not known, but Attila's subsequent withdrawal from Italy vastly increased the prestige of the papacy. Now popes not only were successors of Saint Peter and bishops of the principal city of the west, but were replacing the emperor as protector of the city. The foundation of the political power of the papacy was established.

The confederation of the Huns collapsed after the death of Attila in 453, but imperial power did not revive in Italy. A series of incompetent emperors were pushed aside by barbarian generals who assumed power on the peninsula and sought recognition from Zeno, the emperor in the east. However, after the death in 480 of the last legitimate western emperor, Julius Nepos, Zeno conferred the title of patrician on the Ostrogothic king Theodoric. In 489, Theodoric invaded Italy with imperial blessing and established himself as ruler of Italy.

In Gaul, between the Seine and the Loire, the Roman general Flavius Aetius and, after his death, the general Syagrius continued to represent some imperial presence. But the armies that Aetius and Syagrius commanded consisted entirely of barbarians—particularly Visigoths and Franks—and they represented the interests of local aristocratic factions rather than those of Constantinople. So thoroughly barbarized had these last Roman commanders become in their military command and political control that the barbarians referred to Syagrius as "king of the Romans." Ultimately, in 486, Syagrius was defeated and replaced by the Frank Clovis, son of Syagrius's military commander Childeric, probably with the blessing of the emperor.

Britain met a similar fate. Abandoned by the Roman legions around 407, the Romano-Celtic population in this province concluded a treaty with bands of Saxons and Angles to protect Britain from other barbarian raiders. As had happened elsewhere in the empire, the barbarians came as federated troops and stayed as rulers. Gradually, during the fifth century, Germanic warrior groups conquered much of the island. The Anglo-Saxons pushed the native inhabitants to the west and the north. There, as the Cornish and the Welsh (in Anglo-Saxon, *Welsh* means simply "enemy"), they preserved the Christian religion but largely lost their other Roman traditions.

The New Barbarian Kingdoms

The establishment of barbarian kingdoms within the Roman world meant the end of the western empire as a political entity. However, the emperors in the east and west continued to pretend that all these barbarian peoples, with the exception of the Vandals, were Roman troops commanded by loyal Roman officers who happened to be of barbarian origin. The emperors gave the barbarian kings or war leaders official status within the empire as Roman generals or patricians and occasionally granted them portions of abandoned lands or existing estates. Local Roman elites considered these leaders rude and uncultured barbarians who nevertheless could be made to serve these elites' own interests more easily than better educated imperial bureaucrats.

As a result, the aristocracy of the west, the *maiores,* viewed the decay of the civil government without dismay. This decay was due largely to the poverty of the imperial treasury. In the fifth century, the entire public revenues of the west amounted to little more than the annual incomes of a few wealthy private aristocrats. Managing to escape both taxation and the jurisdiction of public officials, these individuals carved out for themselves vast estates, which they and their families controlled with private armies and which they governed as virtually autonomous lordships. Ordinary freemen, pressed by the remnants of imperial taxation and by barbarians, were forced into accepting the protection and hence control offered by aristocrats, who thereby came to control whole villages and districts.

The primary source of friction between barbarians and provincial elites was religion. Many Goths had converted to Christianity around the time that the Huns had destroyed the Gothic confederation. However, they had chosen the Arian form of Christianity to appease the Arian emperors Constantius and Valens. But the Goths and most other barbarian peoples held to their Arian form of faith long after it had been abandoned in the empire. Therefore, wherever the barbarians settled, they were met with distrust and hostility from the orthodox clergy. In southern Gaul and Italy, this hostility created serious difficulties because during the fifth century bishops had assumed many of the traditional duties and powers held by provincial Roman administrators.

Although during the fifth century the western aristocracy had largely given up on the civil administration, these wealthy landowners increasingly identified with the episcopacy. In Gaul, bishops were regularly selected from members of the greatest Gallo-Roman senatorial families, establishing veritable episcopal dynasties. In Italy and Spain, too, bishops were drawn from the landed aristocracy. These bishops, most of whom were elected after long years of outstanding secular leadership, served as the primary protectors and administrators of their communities, filling the vacuum left by the erosion of other civil offices. They, more than either local civil officials or the Bacaudae, were successful in representing the community before imperial tax collectors or barbarian chieftains.

Thus, in spite of the creation of the barbarian kingdoms, cultural and political leadership at the local level remained firmly in the hands of the aristocracy. Aristocratic bishops, rather than hermits, monopolized the role of mediators of divine power just as their lay brothers, in cooperation with barbarian military leaders, monopolized the role of mediators of secular power.

MAP DISCOVERY

BARBARIAN MIGRATIONS AND INVASIONS

Study these maps of barbarian migrations and invasions. Who were Rome's western neighbors in the fourth century? What effects did the Huns have on barbarian migrations? From these maps, how might you explain the relative stability of the eastern or Byzantine Empire in the sixth century compared with the western?

Barbarian military leaders needed local ties by which to govern the large indigenous populations over whom they ruled. They found cooperation with these aristocrats to be both necessary and advantageous. Thus, while individual landowners might have suffered in the transition from Roman to barbarian rule, for the most part this transition took place with less disturbance of the local social or political scene than was once thought. During the fifth century, the imperial presence simply faded away as barbarian kings came to rule in the name of the emperor. After 480, the emperor resided exclusively in the east. The last western emperors disappeared without serious opposition either from western aristocrats or from their eastern colleagues.

The Hellenization of the East

The eastern half of the empire, in contrast to the west, managed to survive and even to prosper in the fifth and sixth centuries. In the east, beginning in 400, the trends toward militarization and barbarization of the administration were reversed, the strength of the imperial government was reaffirmed, and the vitality and integrity of the empire were restored.

Several reasons account for the contrast between east and west. First, the east had always been more urbanized and civilized than the west. It had an old tradition of civil control that antedated the Roman Empire itself. When the decay of Roman traditions allowed regionalism and tribalism to arise in the west, the same decay brought in the east a return to Hellenistic traditions. Second, the east had never developed the tradition of public poverty and private wealth that was characteristic of the west. In the east, tax revenues continued to support an administrative apparatus, which remained in the hands of civilians rather than barbarian military commanders. Moreover, the local aristocracies in the eastern provinces never achieved the wealth and independence of their western counterparts. Finally, Christian bishops, frequently divided over doctrinal issues, never managed to monopolize either sacred power, which was shared by itinerant holy men and monks, or secular power, which was wielded by imperial agents. Thus, under the firm direction of its emperors, especially Theodosius and later Zeno, the eastern empire not only survived but prepared for a new expansionist phase under the emperor Justinian.

SUMMARY

The Crisis of the Third Century   The crisis of the third century had territorial, economic, political, and military roots. The Roman army became the arbiter of political power. Political and military instability had devastating effects on the lives of ordinary people. Rome faced increasingly serious external threats from Germanic tribes. Rome itself helped transform small and isolated tribes into a major threat to the imperial system.

The Empire Restored   Diocletian carried out a series of military, political, and economic reforms that helped stabilize the empire. The key to Diocletian's success was his militarization of Roman society. Constantine converted to Christianity, established a new capital at Byzantium, and began to transform the empire into a Christian state. Imperial control over Christianity was strong, but not total. Imperial support, Christian miracles, and raw coercion all contributed to the spread of Christianity.

Imperial Christianity   By the late third century, Christian communities existed throughout the empire, each headed by a bishop. The Church as a whole was divided on fundamental questions of belief. In the east, debate centered on the divinity of Christ. In the west, the issue of the role of humans in salvation was paramount. Hermits, monks, and recluses sought escape from the worldly life of the empire. Monasticism took two forms: communal organization and solitary life. Pachomius and Basil the Great in the east and Benedict of Nursia in the west created influential models of the communal life.

A Parting of the Ways   New barbarian threats destabilized the empire. The Visigoths were allowed to settle as a political unit within the empire, setting a dangerous precedent. Rome was transformed by its encounters with barbarians, a transformation that Romans participated in and even encouraged. The establishment of barbarian kingdoms within the Roman world meant the end of the western empire as a political entity. In the west, cultural and political leadership at the local level remained firmly in the hands of the aristocracy. In the east, beginning in 400, the trends toward militarization and barbarization of the administration were reversed, the strength of the imperial government was reaffirmed, and the vitality and integrity of the empire were restored.

QUESTIONS FOR REVIEW

1. How did increasing contact between Roman civilization and the Germanic barbarians transform both?
2. How did Constantine's adoption of Christianity and the movement of his capital to Byzantium contribute to the decline of the western empire?
3. How did different views of the divinity of Christ and the means of salvation divide early Christians?
4. What was the attraction of monasticism, and why did it take so many different forms?
5. What were the differences in politics and culture in the eastern and western portions of the empire by the end of the fifth century C.E.?

CHAPTER 7

The Classical Legacy in the East: Byzantium and Islam

The Byzantines

At the end of the fifth century C.E., the eastern empire of Theodosius and Zeno had escaped the fate that its western counterpart had suffered at the hands of the Germanic peoples. Still, the long-term survival of the eastern empire seemed far from certain.

Little unified the empire of Constantinople. The population of the capital split into two rival political factions, whose violent conflicts often threatened the stability of the government. When these two factions joined forces with the army, they were powerful enough to create or destroy emperors. Beyond Constantinople, the empire's population consisted of the more or less hellenized peoples of Asia

Minor, Armenians, Slavs, Arabs, Syrians, Egyptian Copts, and others. Unlike western Europe, the east was still a world of cities. But the importance of these urban centers began to decline in favor of the rural peasant world.

Finally, the eastern empire was more divided than unified by its Christianity. Rivalry among the great cities of Antioch, Alexandria, Jerusalem, Rome, and Constantinople was expressed in the competition among their bishops, or patriarchs. By the time of Justinian (527–565), emperors were obsessed with maintaining absolute authority and imposing uniformity on their empire.

Justinian and the Creation of the Byzantine State

Although Justinian's goals were essentially conservative, his attempts to return to the past and restore the territory, power, and prestige of the ancient Roman Empire created a new world. With the assistance of his dynamic wife Theodora, his great generals Belisarius and Narses, his brilliant jurist Tribonian, his scientists Anthemius of Tralles and Isidorus of Miletus, and his brutally efficient administrator and tax collector John of Cappadocia, he remade the empire.

Spurred on by Theodora, in 532 Justinian checked the power of the factions by brutally suppressing a riot that left 30,000 dead in the capital city. Belisarius and

A mosaic from the church of San Vitale in Ravenna. The emperor Justinian, along with secular and ecclesiastical officials, is shown bringing an offering to the church. The halo around his head signifies the sacred nature of the imperial office.

Narses recaptured North Africa from the Vandals, Italy from the Ostrogoths, and part of Spain from the Visigoths, restoring for one last moment some of the geographical unity of the empire of Augustus and Constantine. Tribonian revised and organized the existing codes of Roman law into the *Justinian Code*, a great monument of western jurisprudence that remains today the foundation of most of Europe's legal systems. Anthemius and Isidorus combined their knowledge of mathematics, geometry, kinetics, and physics to build the Church of the Holy Wisdom (Hagia Sophia) in Constantinople, one of the largest and most innovative churches ever constructed. Less well appreciated were the achievements of John of Cappadocia, who was able to squeeze the empire's population for the taxes to pay for these conquests, reforms, and building projects.

Ultimately, Justinian's spectacular achievements came at too high a price. He left his successors an empire that had been virtually bankrupted by the costs of his wars and his building projects, was bitterly divided by his attempts to settle religious controversies, and was poorly protected on its eastern border, where the Sassanid Empire was a constant threat. Most of Italy and Spain soon returned to barbarian control. In 602, the Sassanid emperor Chosroes II (d. 628) invaded the empire, capturing Egypt, Palestine, and Syria and threatening Constantinople itself. In a series of desperate campaigns, the emperor Heraclius (610–641) turned back the tide and crushed the Sassanids, but it was too late. A new power, Islam, had emerged in the deserts of Arabia. This new power was to challenge and ultimately absorb both the Sassanids and much of the eastern Roman Empire. As a result, the east became increasingly less Roman and more Greek—or, specifically, more *Byzantine*, a term derived from the original name of Constantinople, Byzantium.

For over 700 years, the Byzantine Empire played a major role in Western history. From the seventh through tenth centuries, when most of Europe was too weak and disorganized to defend itself against the expansion of Islam, the Byzantines stood as the bulwark of Christianity. When organized government had virtually disappeared in the west, the Byzantine Empire provided a model of a centralized bureaucratic state ruled according to principles of Roman law. When, beginning in the fourteenth century, western Europeans began once more to appreciate the heritage of Greek and Roman art and literature, they turned to Constantinople. Perhaps most important, when urban civilization had all but disappeared from the rest of Europe, Greeks and Latins could still look "to The City," *eis ten polin*, or, as the Turks pronounced it, Istanbul.

Emperors and Individuals

The classic age of Byzantine society, roughly from the eighth through the tenth centuries, has been described as "individualism without freedom." Individuals and small family groups stood as isolated units in a society characterized, until the mid-eleventh century, by the direct relationship between an all-powerful emperor and citizens of all ranks.

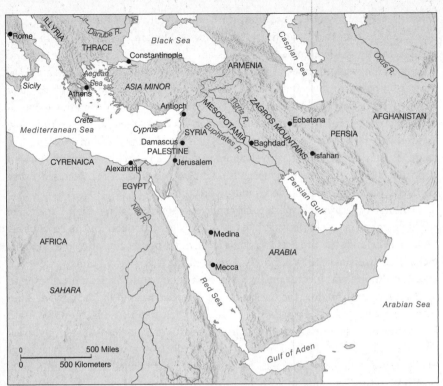

THE EASTERN MEDITERRANEAN. The Arabian Peninsula was peripheral to the Roman and Persian empires until the seventh century when the new Islamic faith suddenly emerged from Arabia to overwhelm its more ancient neighboring empires.

Governing Byzantium. In part, this individualism resulted from the Byzantine form of government. The Byzantine state was, in theory and often in fact, an autocracy. Since the time of Diocletian, all members of society were subjects of the emperor, who alone was the source of law. Although in theory the emperor was elected by the Senate, army, and people of Constantinople, emperors generally selected their own successors and had them crowned in their own lifetimes.

Thus the traditional corporate bodies of the Roman Empire wasted away or became window dressing for the imperial cult. The Senate gradually ceased to play any autonomous role, and its powers were officially abolished in the ninth century.

The factions, which in the sixth century had the power to make or break emperors, met the same fate. From autonomous political groups, they too gradually became no more than participants in imperial ceremonies.

Bureaucracy and Army. Although the emperor was the source of all authority, the actual administration of the empire was carried out by a vast bureaucracy composed of military and civilian officers. The empire was divided into roughly 25 provinces, or *themes*. The soldiers in each theme were also farmers, rather than

MAP DISCOVERY

BYZANTINE EMPIRE UNDER JUSTINIAN

Examine the boundaries of the Byzantine Empire under Justinian. Why would Justinian have been particularly eager to recover the areas that he reconquered? What problems were posed by the conquest of the Ostrogoths that were not present in the conquest of the Vandals?

full-time warriors. Each soldier received a small farm by which to support himself and his family. When a soldier retired or died, his farm and his military obligation passed to his eldest son. These farmer-soldiers were the backbone of both the imperial military and the economic system. They not only formed a regular, native, locally based army, but they also kept much of Byzantine agriculture in the hands of small free peasants rather than great aristocrats. The themes were governed by military commanders, or **strategoi**, who presided over both civilian and military bureaucrats.

In contrast to the military command of the themes, the central administration, which focused on the emperor and the imperial family, was wholly civil. The most important positions at court were occupied by eunuchs, castrated men who offered a number of advantages to imperial administration. Because they could not have descendants, there was no danger that they would attempt to turn their offices into hereditary positions or that they would plot and scheme on behalf of their children. Moreover, since the sacred nature of the emperor required physical perfection, eunuchs could not aspire to replace their masters on the throne. Finally, although at times their influence with the emperor made them immensely powerful, eunuchs were feared and despised by the general population. Therefore, they had little likelihood of building autonomous power bases outside of imperial favor.

Families and Villages

A godlike emperor and a centralized bureaucracy left little room for the development of the hierarchies of private patronage, lordship, and group action that were characteristic of western Europe. In the Byzantine Empire, aristocrat and peasant were equal in their political powerlessness. Therefore, Byzantine society tended to be organized at the lowest level, that of the nuclear family.

Rural Life. The countryside, which was the backbone of Byzantine prosperity into the eleventh century, was also a world with limited horizontal and vertical social bonds. Villages were the basic elements in the imperial system. The village court handled local affairs and tax assessments, but it in turn dealt directly with the imperial bureaucracy. Most peasants, whether they were landowners, peasant soldiers, or renters, survived on the labor of their own family and perhaps one or two slaves. Large cooperative undertakings, as in Islamic lands, and the use of communal equipment, as became the rule in the west, were unknown.

Urban Life. Constantinople was ideally situated to develop into the greatest commercial center of the west, at its height boasting a population of over one million. Because of Constantinople's strategic location on the Bosporus, that slim ribbon of water uniting the Black and Mediterranean seas, all of the products of the empire and those of the Slavic, Latin, and Islamic worlds, as well as Oriental goods arriving overland from central Asia, had to pass through the city.

The empire's cities were centers for the manufacture of luxury goods that were in demand throughout the Islamic and Christian worlds. Imperial workshops in Constantinople and closely regulated workshops in Corinth and Thebes produced fine silks, brocades, carpets, and other luxury products that were marketed throughout the Mediterranean.

A Foretaste of Heaven

The cultural cement that bound emperor and subjects together was **Orthodox Christianity**. The Islamic capture of Alexandria, Jerusalem, and Antioch had removed the centers of regional religious particularism from the empire. The barbarian domination of Italy had isolated Rome and reduced its influence. These two processes left Constantinople as the only remaining patriarchate in the empire and thus the undisputed center of Orthodox Christianity.

In theory, patriarchs were elected; in reality, emperors appointed them. Patriarchs in turn controlled the various levels of the Church hierarchy. This ecclesiastical structure reflected and reinforced the organization of the state bureaucracy.

The essence of Orthodox religion was the liturgy, or ceremonies, of the Church, which provided, it was said, a foretaste of heaven. Adoration of God and veneration of the emperor went hand in hand as the cornerstone of imperial propaganda.

THE BYZANTINE EMPIRE IN 814. By the ninth century, the empire had lost all its territories but Asia Minor, Greece, the boot of Italy, and the islands of Sardinia and Sicily.

Iconoclasm

The one aspect of religious life that was not entirely under imperial control was monasticism. Monasteries were often wealthy and powerful. Moreover, their religious appeal, often based on the possession of miracle-working religious images, or **icons,** posed an independent source of religious authority that was at odds with the imperial centralization of all aspects of Byzantine life.

In this manuscript illustration, an icon is being destroyed while priests try to persuade Leo V to abandon his iconoclast policies.

Beginning with Emperor Leo III, the Isaurian (717–741), the military emperors who had driven back Islam sought to curtail the independence of monastic culture and particularly the cult of icons that was an integral part of it. These emperors and their supporters, termed **iconoclasts** (literally, "breakers of images"), objected to the mediating role of sacred images in worship. Monasteries, with their miracle-working icons, became particular targets of imperial persecution. The defenders of icons—**iconodules**, or image venerators—were imprisoned, tortured, and even executed. Most bishops, the army, and much of the non-European population of the empire supported the iconoclast emperors, but monks, the lesser clergy, and the majority of the populace, particularly women, violently resisted the destruction of their beloved images.

For more than a century, the iconoclast dispute raged. Finally, in 843, the Empress Theodora (842–858), who ruled during the minority of her son, ended the persecution and restored image veneration. Monasteries reopened and regained much of their former wealth and prestige.

The iconoclastic struggle deeply affected Byzantium's relations with the west. The popes considered the iconoclast emperors heretics and looked increasingly to the Frankish Carolingian family for support against them and the Lombards of Italy. In this manner, the Franks first entered Italian politics and began, with papal support, to establish themselves as a rival imperial power in the west.

The Rise of Islam

Arabs lived on the fringes of the Byzantine and Sassanid empires. Trade routes had carried people from the Fertile Crescent and Egypt across northern Arabia for centuries. By the sixth century C.E., Arabic-speaking peoples from the Arabian Peninsula had spread through the Syrian Desert as far north as the Euphrates.

Within both the Byzantine and Sassanid empires the distinction between Arab and non-Arab populations was blurred. Except for the Arabic language and a hazy idea of common Arabic kinship, nothing differentiated Arabs from their neighbors.

This was dramatically changed by an obscure merchant in the Arabian city of Mecca, who embarked on a career that would transform the world. Through faith, Muhammad (ca. 570–632) united the tribes of the Arabian Peninsula and propelled them an unprecedented mission of conquest. Just as their faith combined elements of traditional Arab worship with Christianity and Judaism, the Arabian conquerors and their subject populations created a vital civilization from a mix of Arabian, Roman, Hellenistic, and Sassanid traditions.

Arabia Before the Prophet

Southern Arabia, with relatively abundant rainfall and fertile soils, was an agricultural region long governed by monarchs. During the fifth century C.E., the kings of the Yemen had extended their influence north over the Bedouin tribes of central Arabia in order to control and protect the caravan trade between north and south. In the late sixth century, however, Ethiopian and then Persian conquerors destroyed the Arabian kingdom of the Yemen and absorbed it into their empires. The result was a power vacuum that left central Arabia and its trade routes across the deserts in confusion.

Bedouin Society. Arabic Bedouins roamed the Arabian peninsula in search of pasturage for their flocks. Theirs was a life of independence, simplicity, and danger.

Although they acknowledged membership in various tribes, the Bedouin's real allegiance was to much narrower circles of lineages and tenting groups. Tribal chieftains, called *sheikhs*, chosen from ruling families, had no coercive power, either to right wrongs or to limit feuds. They served only as arbitrators and executors of tribal consensus.

The individual was unimportant in Bedouin society. Private land ownership was unknown, and flocks and herds were often held in common by kindred. Weapons, ornaments, women, and livestock could be acquired through exchange at the market towns around desert oases. More commonly, these goods and women were taken in raids against other tribes, caravans, and settlements or by exacting payments from weaker neighbors in return for protection.

Some of the Arabs of the more settled south, as well as inhabitants of towns along caravan routes, were Christian or Jewish. As farmers or merchants, these groups were looked down upon by the nomadic Bedouin, most of whom remained pagan. Although they recognized some important gods and even a high god usually called Allah, Bedouin worshiped local tribal deities, who were often thought of as inhabiting a sacred stone or spring.

Harams. Rivalry and feuding among tribes could be set aside at a mutually accepted neutral site, which might grow up around a religious sanctuary, or *haram*. Here, enemies could meet under truce to settle differences under the direction of the holy man or his descendants. Merchant communities sprang up within the safety of these sites, since the sanctuary gave them and their goods protection from their neighbors.

Mecca was just such a sanctuary, around whose sacred black rock, or Ka'bah, a holy man named Qusayy established himself and his tribe, the Quraysh, as its guardians sometime early in the sixth century. During the early seventh century, when increased hostilities between the Byzantine and Sassanid empires severed the direct trading links between the empires, the Quraysh network became the leading commercial organization in northern Arabia. Still, its effectiveness remained tied to the religious importance of Mecca and the Ka'bah. When Muhammad, a descendant of Qusayy, began to preach his monotheistic message, he was seen as a threat to the survival of his tribe and his city.

Muhammad, Prophet of God

A member of a lesser branch of the Quraysh, Muhammad was an orphan raised by relatives. At about age 20, he became the business manager for Khadijah, a wealthy widow whom he later married. This marriage gave him financial security among the middle ranks of Meccan merchants. In his thirties, he began to devote an increasing amount of time to meditation, retiring to the barren, arid mountains outside the city. There, in the month of Ramadan in the year 610, he reported a vision of a man who told him: "O Muhammad! Thou art the Messenger of God."

Preaching Islam. Within a year he began preaching openly. His early teachings stressed the absolute unity of God, the evils of idolatry, and the threat of divine judgment. Further revelations to Muhammad were copied word for word in what came to be the Qur'an, or Koran. These messages offered Arabs a faith founded on a book. In their eyes, this faith was both within the tradition of the Christianity and Judaism of their neighbors and superior to them. The Qur'an was the final revelation and Muhammad the last and greatest prophet.

Muslims believe that Allah's revelation emphasized, above all, his power and transcendence and that the duty of humans is worship. The prayers of Islam, in contrast with those of Christianity and Judaism, are essentially prayers of praise, seldom prayers of petition. Muslims regard the whole Qur'an as the exact and complete revelation of God. It is the complete guide for secular and religious life, the fundamental law of conduct for Islamic society. Muslims are not followers of Muhammad but of the God of Abraham and Jesus, who chose to make the final and complete revelation of his power and his judgment through the Prophet.

Initially, such revelations of divine power and judgment neither greatly bothered nor influenced Mecca's merchant elite. But soon Muhammad began to insist that those who did not accept Allah as the only God were damned, as were those who continued to venerate the sorts of idols on which Mecca's prosperity was founded. With this proclamation, toleration gave way to hostility. Muhammad and his followers were ostracized and even persecuted.

The Hijra. Around 620, some residents of Medina, a smaller trading community populated by rival pagan, Jewish, and Islamic clans and racked by internal political dissension, approached the Prophet and invited him to govern the community in order to end the factional squabbles. Rejected at home, he answered their call. On 24 September 622, Muhammad and one supporter secretly made their way from Mecca to Medina. This short journey of less than 300 miles, known as the **Hijra**, was destined to change the world.

The Triumph of Islam

The Hijra marked the Prophet's shift from preaching to action. He organized his followers from Mecca and Medina into the **Umma**, a community that transcended the old bonds of tribe and clan. He set about turning Medina into a haram like Mecca, with himself as founding holy man and the Umma as his new family. But this was not to be a haram or indeed a family like any other. Muhammad was not merely a sheikh whose authority rested on consensus. He was God's messenger, and his authority was absolute. His goal was to extend this authority far beyond his adopted town of Medina to Mecca and ultimately to the whole Arab world.

First, he gained firm control of Medina at the expense of its Jewish clans. When these clans failed to embrace his teachings, the Prophet expelled them in the name of political and religious unity. Those who were not expelled were executed.

Return to Mecca. In 629, Muhammad and 10,000 warriors marched on Mecca and captured the city in a swift and largely bloodless campaign.

During the three years between Muhammad's triumphant return to Mecca and his death, Islam moved steadily toward becoming the major force in the Arabian Peninsula. The Umma became a sort of supertribe, open to all individuals who would accept Allah and his Prophet. The invitation was extended to women as well as to men.

Women in Early Islam. Islam brought a transformation of the rights of women in Arabian society. This did not mean that they achieved equality with men any more than they did in any premodern civilization, east or west.

Islam did, however, forbid female infanticide, a common practice in pre-Islamic society. Brides, not their fathers or other male relatives, received the dowry from their husbands, thus making marriage more a partnership than a sale. Islamic women acquired inheritance and property rights and had protection against mistreatment in marriage. Although they remained second-class in status, at least women had a status, recognized and protected within the Umma.

An Arabian Faith. The attractions of Islam in this world included both economic prosperity and the opportunity to continue a lifestyle of raiding and warfare in the name of Allah. Muhammad won over the leaders of the Quraysh by making Mecca the sacred city of Islam and by retaining the Ka'bah, cleansed of idols, as the center of Islamic pilgrimage.

Muhammad's message spread to other tribes through diplomatic and, occasionally, military means. The divisive nature of Bedouin society contributed to his success. Frequently, factions within other tribes turned to Muhammad for mediation and support against their rivals. In return for his assistance, petitioners accepted his religious message. Since the Qur'an commanded Muslims to destroy idol worship, conversion provided the occasion for holy wars (**jihads**) of conquest and profitable raids against their still-pagan neighbors. Converts showed their piety by sending part of their spoils as alms to Medina.

The Spread of Islam

Muhammad died in the summer of 632 after a short illness, leaving no successor and no directions concerning the leadership of the Umma. Immediately, his closest and most influential followers selected Abu Bakr (632–634), the fourth convert to Islam, to be **caliph**, or successor of the Prophet. Abu Bakr and, after his death two years later, the caliph 'Umar (634–644) faced formidable obstacles. Within the Umma, tensions between the early Medina followers of the Prophet and the Meccan elite were beginning to surface. A more critical problem was that the tribes that had accepted the Prophet's leadership believed that his death freed them from their treaty obligations.

To prevent the collapse of the Umma, Abu Bakr launched a war of reconversion. Purely by chance, this war developed into wars of conquest that reached far beyond the Arab world. Commanded by Khalid ibn al-Walid (d. 642), the greatest early Islamic general, Muslim forces defeated tribe after tribe and brought them back into the Umma. But long-term survival demanded expansion. Since Muslims were forbidden to raid fellow believers and raids were an integral part of Bedouin life, the only way to keep recently converted Bedouin in line was to lead them on military expeditions against non-Muslims. Under Abu Bakr, Muslim expansion covered all of Arabia. Under 'Umar, Islam conquered Iran, Iraq, Syria, and Egypt.

Muslim expansion was facilitated by protracted fighting between the Byzantine and Sassanid empires as well as internal divisions within the Byzantine world. By 650, the great Sassanid Empire had disappeared, and the Byzantine Empire had lost Egypt, Syria, Mesopotamia, Palestine, portions of Asia Minor, and much of North Africa.

MAP DISCOVERY

THE SPREAD OF ISLAM

Consider the geographical extent of the Islamic conquest. What trading and cultural networks were united by the spread of Islam? How did the geography of the Islamic world differ from that of its Roman and Sassanid predecessors? What may have prevented Islam's spread through Asia Minor and up the Iberian peninsula?

Authority and Government in Islam

Conquering the world for Islam proved easier than governing it. What had begun as a religious movement within Arabian society had created a vast multinational empire in which Arabs were a tiny minority. Within the first decades following the Prophet's death, two models of governance emerged, models that continue to dominate Islamic politics to the present.

The Umma. The first model was that of pre-Islamic tribal authority. The Umma could be considered a supertribe, governed by leaders whose authority came from their secular power as leaders of the superior military and economic elements within the community. This model appealed particularly to the Quraysh and local tribal leaders who had exercised authority before Muhammad. The second model was that of the authority exercised by the Prophet. In this model, the Umma was more than a supertribe, and its unity and purity had to be preserved by a religiously sanctioned rule exercised by a member of the Prophet's own family. This model was preferred by many of the more recent converts to Islam, especially the poor.

Regardless of their disagreements on the basis of political authority, both groups adopted the administrative systems of their conquered lands. Byzantine and Sassanid bureaucracy and government, only slightly adjusted, became the models for government in the Islamic world until the twentieth century.

Likewise, the Muslims left intact the social structures and economic systems of the empires they conquered. Lands remained in the hands of their previous owners. Only state property or, in the Sassanid Empire, that of the Zoroastrian priesthood became common property of the Muslim community.

The Last Orthodox Caliphs. The division of the spoils of conquest badly divided the Umma and precipitated the first crisis in the caliphate. Under 'Umar, two groups received most of the spoils of the conquests. First were the earliest followers of the Prophet, who received a disproportionate share of revenues. Second were the conquerors themselves, who were often recent converts from tribes on the fringes of Arabia. After 'Umar's death, his successor 'Uthman (d. 656), a member of the powerful Umayya clan of Mecca, attempted to consolidate control over Islam by Quraysh elite. The result was rebellion, both within Arabia and in Egypt. Abandoned at home and abroad, 'Uthman was finally murdered as he sat reading the Qur'an in his home.

In spite of 'Uthman's unpopularity, his murder sent shock waves throughout the Umma. The fate of his successor, Muhammad's beloved son-in-law and nephew 'Ali (656–661), had an even more serious effect on the future of Islam. Although chosen as fourth caliph, 'Ali was immediately charged with complicity in 'Uthman's murder and was strongly opposed by the Umayyad commander of Syria. To protect himself, 'Ali moved the caliphate from Arabia to Iraq, but in 661, 'Ali was murdered by supporters of his Umayyad rivals. Still, the memory of the "last orthodox caliph" remained alive in the Islamic world, especially in Iraq and Iran. Centuries later, a tradition developed in Baghdad that legitimate leadership of Islam could come only from the house of 'Ali. Adherents to this belief developed into a political and religious sect known as Shia Islam. Although frequently persecuted as heretical by the majority of Muslims, **Shiites** remain a potent minority within the Islamic world today.

Umayyad and 'Abbasid Caliphates

The immediate effect of 'Ali's death, however, was the triumph of the old Quraysh and in particular the Umayyads, who established at Damascus in Syria a caliphate that lasted a century. The Umayyads made no attempt to base their rule on spiritual authority. Instead, they ruled as secular leaders, attempting to unite the Islamic Empire through an appeal to Arab unity.

Umayyad Caliphate. The Umayyads extended the Islamic Empire to its farthest reaches. In the north, armies from Syria marched into Anatolia and were stopped only in 677 by the Byzantine fleet before Constantinople itself. In the east, Umayyad armies pressed as far as the Syr Darya River on the edge of the Chinese Tang Empire. In the south and southwest, the general Tariq ibn Ziyad (d. ca. 720) conquered the Mediterranean coast of Africa and in 711 crossed over the strait near the Rock of Gibraltar (the name comes from the Arabic *jabal Tariq*, "Tariq's mountain") and quickly conquered virtually the entire Iberian peninsula.

The Umayyad caliphate's external success in conquering failed to extend to its dealings with the internal tensions of the Umma. The Umayyads could not build a stable empire on the twin foundations of a tiny Arabian elite and a purely secular government taken over from their Byzantine predecessors.

The 'Abbasid Revolution. Growing numbers of devout Muslims—Arabs and non-Arabs alike—were convinced that leadership had to be primarily spiritual and that this spiritual mandate was the exclusive right of the family of the Prophet. Ultimately, a coalition of dissatisfied Persian Muslims and Arabian religious reformers united under the black banners of the descendants of Muhammad's paternal uncle, 'Abbas (566–ca. 653). In 750, this group overthrew the Umayyads everywhere but in Spain and established a new caliphate in favor of the 'Abbasids.

With the fall of the Umayyad caliphate, Arabs lost control of Islam forever. The 'Abbasids attempted to govern the empire according to religious principles. These were found in the Qur'an and in the **sunnah**, or practices established by the Prophet and preserved first orally and then in the **hadith**, or traditions, which were somewhat comparable to the Christian Gospels. This new empire was to be a universal Muslim commonwealth in which Arabs had no privileged position.

The institutional foundations of the new caliphate, however, like those of the Umayyads, remained firmly in the ancient empires they had conquered. The great caliph Mansur (754–775) moved the capital from Damascus to Baghdad, an acknowledgment of the crucial role of Iraqi and Iranian military and economic strength. The 'Abbasids constructed an autocratic imperial system on the model of their Persian predecessors. With firm control of the military, increasingly composed of slave armies known as mamluks, the 'Abbasids governed the Islamic Empire at its zenith.

Division and Revolt. Ultimately, however, the 'Abbasids were no more successful than the Umayyads in maintaining authority over the whole Muslim world. By the tenth century, local military commanders, termed **emirs**, took control of provincial governments in many areas while preserving the fiction that they were appointed by the 'Abbasid caliphs. The majority of Muslims accepted this situation as a necessary compromise. In contrast to the Shiites, who continued to look for a leader from the family of 'Ali, the **Sunnis**, as they came to be known, remain to the present the majority group of Muslims. The Sunnis had no fixed theory of government or succession to the caliphate. Instead, they accepted the events of history in a practical manner, secure in the truth of the hadith: "My umma will never agree upon an error."

In the west, the 'Abbasids could not maintain even a facade of unity. The Shiites launched sporadic revolts and separatist movements. The most successful was that of 'Ubayd Allah the Fatimid (d. 934), who claimed to be the descendant of 'Ali and rightful leader of Islam. By the middle of the eleventh century, the Fatimid caliphate controlled all of North Africa, Sicily, Syria, and western Arabia. In Umayyad Spain, although the Muslim population remained firmly Sunni, the powerful emir 'Abd ar-Rahman III (891–961) in 929 also took the title of caliph, thus making his position religious as well as secular. Everywhere, the political and religious unity of Islam was being torn apart.

The Turks. The arrival in all three caliphates of Muslim peoples who were not yet integrated into the civilization of the Mediterranean world accelerated this disintegration. From the east, Seljuk Turks, long used as slave troops, entered Iraq and in 1055 conquered Baghdad. Within a decade they had conquered Iran, Syria, and Palestine as well. Around the same time, Moroccan Berbers conquered much of North Africa and Spain, while Bedouin raided freely in what are today Libya and Tunisia. These invasions by Muslims from the fringes of the Islamic commonwealth had catastrophic effects on the Islamic world. The Turks, unaccustomed to commerce and to the administrative traditions of the caliphate, divided their empire among their war leaders, displacing traditional landowners and disrupting commerce. The North African Berbers and Bedouin destroyed the agricultural and commercial systems that had survived successive Vandal, Byzantine, and Arabian invasions.

Islamic Civilization

The Islamic conquest of the seventh century brought peace to Iraq and Iran after generations of struggle and set the stage for a major agricultural recovery. In the tradition of their Persian predecessors, the caliphs organized vast irrigation systems, which made Mesopotamia the richest agricultural region west of China.

By uniting the Mediterranean world with Arabia and India, the 'Abbasid Empire created the greatest trade network that had ever been seen. Muslim merchants met in bustling ports on the Persian Gulf and the Red Sea to trade goods from China, India, Africa, and Europe.

The marketplace for ideas was as active as that for merchandise. Within a few generations, descendants of Bedouin established themselves in the great cities of the ancient Near East and absorbed the traditions of Persian, Roman, and Hellenistic civilization. While 'Abassid political unity was falling apart, this new civilization was reaching its first great synthesis.

Science and Faith. Islamic intellectuals synthesized and expanded Greek, Persian, and Indian traditions of astronomy and mathematics and sought to find the proper balance between science and faith. Because of the need to establish hours for prayer, Islamic scholars were particularly interested in practical aspects of astronomy and devices for determining time such as the astrolabe, which allows one to determine the time of day or night as well as to determine the exact time of sunrise and sunset and to solve various astronomical problems.

Abu Ja'far Muhammad ibn Musa Al-Khwarizimi (790–850), known as the father of algebra, developed the solution to quadratic equations and wrote treatises that remained fundamental in the East and the West well into the Renaissance. Muslim intellectuals also introduced the so-called Arabic numerals from India and by the tenth century had perfected the use of decimal fractions.

Medicine was perhaps the area in which Muslims made the greatest contributions in both theory and practice. Charity is fundamental to Islam, and across the Islamic world hospitals were established where the sick could be cared for without

This miniature shows scholars at the Taqf ad Din Observatory in Istanbul. Various scientists are using astrolabes, instruments used to observe and calculate the position of heavenly bodies, as well as various clocks, an armillary sphere or model of the heavens, and a spherical map, and instruments developed or perfected by generations of Muslim scientists.

cost. Al-Razi (864–930), an Iranian physician who became the head of the hospital in Baghdad, wrote a comprehensive medical encyclopedia that became a standard text, East and West. The Persian physician Ibn Sina (980–1037), known in the West as Avicenna, was the first to recognize the contagious nature of tuberculosis, the value of anesthetics, and the effectiveness of experimenting with new drugs on animals before administering them to humans.

Islamic intellectuals also applied ancient learning to questions of Islamic faith. Legal scholars concerned with the authenticity of hadith used Greek rationalist methods to distinguish genuine from spurious traditions. Religious mystics called Sufis blended Neoplatonic and Muslim traditions to create new forms of religious devotion.

Philosophy. Although Islamic scientists were professional physicians, astronomers, or lawyers, most were also deeply concerned with abstract philosophical questions, particularly those raised by the works of Plato and Aristotle, which had been translated into Arabic. Many sought to reconcile Islam with that philosophical heritage in the same manner that Origen and Augustine had done for Christianity. The Cordoban philosopher Ibn Rushd (1126–1198), called Averroës in the west, taught an authentic Aristotelian philosophy stripped of Neoplatonic mystical trappings. His commentaries on Aristotle were enormously influential even outside the Islamic world. For Christian philosophers of the thirteenth century, Averroës was known simply as "the Commentator."

Christian Invasion. At the same time that Muslim thought and culture were at their most creative, Islam faced invasion from a new and unaccustomed quarter: Constantinople. In the tenth and early eleventh centuries, the Byzantines pressed the local rulers of northern Syria and Iraq in a series of raids, which reached as far as the border of Palestine. At the end of the eleventh century, western Europeans, encouraged and supported by the Byzantines, captured Jerusalem and established a Western-style kingdom in Palestine that survived for over a century. Once more, Constantinople was a power in the Mediterranean world.

The Byzantine Apogee and Decline, 1000–1453

During the tenth and eleventh centuries, Byzantium dominated the Mediterranean world for the last time. Imperial armies under the Macedonian dynasty (867–1059) began to recover some lands that had been lost to Islam during the previous two centuries.

The conquests of the Macedonian dynasty laid the foundation for a short-lived economic prosperity and cultural renaissance. Conquered lands, particularly Anatolia, brought new agricultural wealth. Security of the sea fostered a resurgence of commerce, and customs duties enriched the imperial treasury. New wealth financed the flourishing of Byzantine art and literature.

The Disintegration of the Empire

In all domains, however, the successes of the Macedonian emperors set the stage for serious problems. Rapid military expansion and economic growth allowed new elites to establish themselves as autonomous powers and to position themselves between the imperial administration and the people. The constant demand for troops always exceeded the supply of traditional salaried soldiers. In the eleventh century, emperors began to grant imperial estates to great magnates in return for military service. These grants, termed *pronoia*, often included immunity from imperial taxation and the right to certain administrative activities traditionally carried out by the central government. The practice created in effect a largely independent, landed military aristocracy that stood between the peasantry and the imperial government. This policy weakened the centralized state and reduced its income from taxes.

Internal Conflict. As generals became dissatisfied with the civilian central administration, they began to turn their armies against the emperors, launching over 30 revolts in as many years. To defend itself against both the Muslims without and the generals within, the central government, composed of intellectuals, eunuchs, and urban aristocrats, had to spend vast sums on mercenary armies. These armies, composed largely of Armenians, Germans, and Normans, soon began to plunder the empire they were hired to protect. Further danger came from other, independent Normans who, under their commander Robert Guiscard (ca. 1015–1085), conquered Byzantine Bari and southern Italy and then Muslim Sicily. Soon Guiscard was threatening the empire itself. The hostility between aristocracy and imperial administration largely destroyed the tradition of civilian government.

Under increasing pressure from local magnates on the one hand and desperate imperial tax collectors on the other, villages began to make deals with powerful patrons who would represent them in return for the surrender of their independence. Through the eleventh and twelfth centuries, the Byzantine peasantry passed from the condition of individualism without freedom to that of collectivism without freedom. Through the same process, landlords and patrons acquired the means to exercise a political role, which ended the state's monopoly on public power.

Commercial Threats. At the same time that civil war and external pressure were destroying the provincial administration, Byzantine disdain for commerce was weakening the empire's ability to control its income from customs duties. Initially, the willingness to turn over commerce to Italians and others posed few problems. However, in the tenth and eleventh centuries, merchants of Amalfi, Bari, and then Venice came to dominate Byzantine commerce. Venetian merchant fleets could double as a powerful navy in times of need, and by the eleventh century the Venetians were the permanent military and commercial power in the Mediterranean. When Robert Guiscard and his Normans threatened the empire, the emperors had to turn to the Venetians for protection and were forced to cede them major economic privileges. The Venetians acquired the right to maintain important self-governing communities in major ports throughout the empire and were allowed to pay lower tariffs than the Byzantines paid.

In 1071, the year that Robert Guiscard captured the last Byzantine city in Italy, the empire suffered an even more disastrous defeat in the east. At Manzikert in Anatolia, the emperor Romanus IV (1067–1071) and his unreliable mercenary army fell to the Seljuk Turks, who captured Romanus. The defeat at Manzikert sealed the fate of the empire. Anatolia was lost, and the gradual erosion of the empire in both the west and the east had begun.

The Conquests of Constantinople and Baghdad

At the end of the eleventh century the Comnenian dynasty (1081–1185) briefly halted the political and economic chaos of the empire. Rather than fighting the tendency of the centralized state to devolve into a decentralized aristocratic one, Alexius I Comnenus (1081–1118) tied the aristocracy to his family, thus making it an instrument of imperial government. In the short run the process was successful. Still, by the late twelfth century the empire was a vulnerable second-rate power caught between Latin Europe and Islam.

Initially, the Christian west was a more deadly threat than the Islamic east. In the eleventh century, after more than 500 years of economic and political weakness, western Europe was beginning to reach parity with Byzantium.

Chronology

THE BYZANTINE EMPIRE AND THE RISE OF ISLAM

527–565	Reign of Justinian
610	Muhammad's vision
662	The Hijra, Muhammad's journey from Mecca to Medina
726–787	First phase of iconoclast dispute
732	Muslim advance halted by Franks
750	'Abbasids overthrow Umayyads; take control of Muslim world
802–884	Second phase of iconoclast dispute
843	Empress Theodora ends iconoclast persecution; restores image veneration
867–1059	Macedonian dynasty rules Byzantine Empire; begins recovering lands from Muslims
1054	Schism splits churches of Rome and Constantinople
1071	Robert Guiscard captures Sicily and southern Italy; Battle of Manzikert; Seljuk Turks defeat Byzantines
1099	First Crusade establishes Latin kingdom in Jerusalem
1221	Genghis Khan leads Mongol army into Persia
1453	Constantinople falls to Ottomans

Dangers from the West. The military threat from the west was paralleled by a religious one. In the centuries that Rome had been largely cut off from Constantinople, Western Christianity had developed a number of rituals and beliefs that differed from Orthodox practice. This parting of the ways had already appeared during the iconoclastic controversies of the eighth and ninth centuries. In the eleventh, it was directed by an independent and self-assertive papacy in Rome, which claimed supreme authority throughout Christendom.

Disagreements between the patriarchs of Constantinople and the popes of Rome prevented cooperation between the two Christian worlds and led to further deterioration of relationships between Greeks and Latins. These disagreements came to a head in 1054, when the papal representative, or legate, Cardinal Humbert (ca. 1000–1061) met with the patriarch of Constantinople, Michael Cerularius (ca. 1000–1059), to negotiate ecclesiastical control over southern Italy and Sicily. Humbert was arrogant and demanding, Michael Cerularius haughty and uncompromising. Acting beyond his authority, Humbert excommunicated the patriarch and all his followers. The patriarch responded in kind, excommunicating Humbert and all connected with him. This formal excommunication was lifted in the 1960s, but the split between the churches of Rome and Constantinople continues to the present.

Excommunication was probably the least of the dangers the Byzantines faced from the west. The full fury of the often ignorant, greedy, and violent Western society reached the empire when, after the defeat at Manzikert, the emperor Alexius called on Western Christians for support against the Muslims. To his horror, adventurers of every sort, eager to conquer land and wealth in the name of the cross of Jesus, flooded the empire. Even while recognizing that the crusaders were uncouth and barbarous, the Byzantines had to admit that the Latins were effective. Despite enormous hardships, the First Crusade was able to take advantage of division in the Muslim world to conquer Palestine and establish a Latin kingdom in Jerusalem in 1099.

The Sack of Constantinople. The crusaders' initial victories and the growth of Latin wealth and power created in Constantinople a temporary enthusiasm for western European styles and customs. The Byzantines soon realized, however, that the Latin kingdom posed a threat not only to Islam but to them as well. While crusaders threatened Byzantine territories, Venetian merchants imposed a stranglehold on Byzantine trade. When emperors granted other Italian towns concessions equal to those of the Venetians, they found that they had simply amplified their problems. Anti-Latin sentiment reached the boiling point in 1183. In the riots that broke out in that year, Italians and other westerners in Constantinople were murdered, and their goods were seized. Just 21 years later, in 1204, a wayward crusade, egged on by Venice, turned aside from its planned expedition to Palestine to capture a bigger prize: Constantinople. After pillaging the city for three days, the westerners established one of their own as emperor and installed a Venetian as patriarch.

The Byzantines did manage to hold onto a portion of their empire centering on Nicaea, and before long the Latins fell to bickering among themselves. In 1261, the ruler of Nicaea, Michael Palaeologus (ca. 1224–1282), recaptured Constantinople with the assistance of the Genoese and had himself crowned emperor in the Hagia Sophia. Still, the empire was fatally shattered, its disintegration into autonomous lordships complete. The restored empire consisted of little more than the district around Constantinople, Thessalonica, and the Peloponnesus. Bulgarians and Serbs had expanded far into the Greek mainland. Most of the rich Anatolian regions had been lost to the Turks, and commercial revenues were in the hands of the Genoese allies. The restored empire's survival for almost 200 years was due less to its own prerogative than to the internal problems of the Islamic world.

THE OTTOMAN EMPIRE, CA. 1450. By the mid-fifteenth century the Ottoman Empire had absorbed virtually all of the Byzantine Empire.

Eastern Conquests. The caliphs of Baghdad, like the emperors of Constantinople, succumbed to invaders from the barbarous fringes of their empire. In 1221, the Mongol prince Temujin (ca. 1162–1227), better known to history as Genghis Khan ("Universal Ruler"), led his conquering army into Persia from central Asia. From there, a portion of the Mongols went north, invading Russia in 1237 and dividing it into small principalities ruled by Slavic princes under Mongol control. In 1258, a Mongol army captured Baghdad and executed the last 'Abbasid caliph, ending a 500-year tradition. The Mongol armies then moved westward, shattering the Seljuk principalities in Iraq, Anatolia, and Syria and turning back only before the fierce resistance of the Egyptian Mamluks.

From the ruins of the Seljuk kingdom arose a variety of small Turkish principalities, or emirates. After the collapse of the Mongol Empire, one of these, the Ottoman, began to expand at the expense of both the weakened Byzantine Empire and the Mongol-Seljuk Empire. In the next centuries, the Ottomans expanded east, south, and west. Around 1350, they crossed into the Balkans as Byzantine allies but soon took over the region for themselves. By 1450, the Ottoman stranglehold on Constantinople was complete. The final scene of the conquest, long delayed but inevitable, occurred three years later.

SUMMARY

The Byzantines   In the face of numerous divisive forces, Byzantine emperors were obsessed with maintaining absolute authority and imposing uniformity on their empire. Justinian's achievements came at a high price, and many of his gains were quickly lost. Despite setbacks, the Byzantine Empire played a key role in preserving important elements of ancient civilization for future generations in the west. Although the emperor was the source of all authority, the actual administration of the empire was carried out by a vast bureaucracy composed of military and civilian officers. Villages were the basic elements in the imperial system. Constantinople was a great commercial center and Byzantine cities were centers for the manufacture of luxury goods. The cultural cement that bound emperor and subjects together was Orthodox Christianity. The iconoclast dispute revealed deep fissures within Byzantine society.

The Rise of Islam   Through faith, Muhammad (ca. 570–632) united the tribes of the Arabian Peninsula and propelled them on an unprecedented mission of conquest. In 610 Muhammad had a vision that convinced him he was God's messenger. His early teachings stressed the absolute unity of God, the evils of idolatry, and the threat of divine judgment. Muhammad's preaching upset Mecca's elite and he was forced to move to Medina. In Medina, Muhammad set about creating the Umma, a community that transcended the old bonds of tribe and clan. In 629, Muhammad and his followers captured Mecca and quickly became a major force in the Arabian Peninsula. Muhammad's message spread to other tribes through diplomatic and, occasionally, military means. After Muhammad's death, his successors conquered a vast empire. Conquering the world for Islam proved easier than governing it. The Umayyads attempted to unite the Islamic Empire through an appeal to Arab unity. In 750, the 'Abbasids overthrew the Umayyads everywhere but in Spain, but did not hold on to a unified empire for long. The arrival of the Seljuk Turks accelerated the disintegration of the Islamic Empire. Islamic thinkers made important contributions in science, medicine, mathematics, literature, and philosophy.

The Byzantine Apogee and Decline, 1000–1453 During the tenth and eleventh centuries, Byzantium dominated the Mediterranean world for the last time. The conquests of the Macedonian dynasty laid the foundation for a short-lived economic prosperity and cultural renaissance. The creation of an independent, landed military elite, internal conflicts, and challengers to Constantinople's commercial power all undermined the empire. In 1204 western crusaders pillaged Constantinople. In 1453, the Ottoman Turks conquered Constantinople, ending the Byzantine Empire forever.

QUESTIONS FOR REVIEW

1. In what ways was Byzantine society characterized by individualism without freedom?
2. How and why did Muhammad both break from tribal and clan traditions and build upon them in creating Islam?
3. How did conflicts within Islam after Muhammad's death divide it spiritually but also contribute to Islam's expansion across Africa and Spain?
4. How did the rapid expansion of Byzantium under the Macedonian dynasty contribute to the empire's slow collapse?

The West in the Early Middle Ages, 500–900

The Making of the Barbarian Kingdoms, 500–750

The existence of a united empire had long been but a dream. In the year 500, Emperor Anastasius I (491–518) could delude himself that he ruled the whole empire of Augustus, Diocletian, and Constantine, both east and west. In the west, the governor who ruled Italy had sworn that he "rejoiced to live under Roman law, which we are prepared to defend by arms." The king of the once troublesome Vandals had concluded a marriage alliance with the Italian governor and seemed ready to accept Roman statecraft. Beyond the Alps, a Roman officer called a *patrician* ruled the regions of the upper Rhone, and a consul controlled Gaul. In Aquitaine and Spain, legitimate, recognized officers of the empire ruled both Romans and barbarians. What need was there to speak of the end of the empire in the West?

This imperial unity was more illusionary than real. The Italian governor was the Ostrogothic king Theodoric the Great (493–526), whose Roman title meant less than his Ostrogothic army. The patrician was the Burgundian king Gondebaud (480–516). The Roman officer in Aquitaine and Spain was the Visigothic king Alaric II (485–507), and the Gallic consul was the Frankish king Clovis (482–511). Each of these rulers courted imperial titles and recognition, but none regarded Anastasius as his sovereign.

Italy: From Ostrogoths to Lombards

In the early sixth century, all of the Germanic peoples who were settled within the old Roman Empire acknowledged the Goths as the most successful of the "blond-haired peoples," as the Romans called the barbarians. The Ostrogoths had created an Italian kingdom in which Romans and barbarians lived side by side. The Visigoths ruled Spain and southern Gaul by combining traditions of Roman law and barbarian military might. Yet neither Gothic kingdom endured for more than two centuries.

The Ostrogothic Kingdom. Theodoric the Ostrogoth was the most cultivated, capable, and sophisticated barbarian ruler. He was also the most powerful. Burgundians, Visigoths, and Alemanni looked to him for leadership and protection. Even Clovis, the ambitious Frankish king, usually bowed to his wishes. Theodoric had spent his teenage years as a pampered hostage in Constantinople. There, he had learned to understand and admire Roman ways. Later, after he had conquered Italy

A gold solidus coin bears a portrait of Theodoric. His left hand holds a globe on which stands a personification of victory. The inscription reads "King Theodoric," but the absence of a robe and diadem shows that he was not considered the equal of the emperor.

at the head of his Gothic army, he established a dual government, which respected both the remains of Roman civil administration and Gothic military organization.

Religion as well as government divided Italy's population. The Ostrogoths were Arians; the majority of the Romans were orthodox Christians. Initially, Theodoric made no effort to interfere with the religion of his subjects. This religious toleration attracted into his government outstanding Roman intellectuals and statesmen. Following Theodoric's death in 526, internal conflict over the succession paved the way for a protracted and devastating invasion by the Byzantines, who destroyed not only the Ostrogothic kingdom but also much of what remained of Roman Italy.

Italy was simply too close to Constantinople and too important for the ambitious Emperor Justinian I (527–565) to ignore. Encouraged by his easy victory over the Vandals, he sent an army into Italy, where he anticipated an easy reconquest of the peninsula. Instead, he got almost 20 years of vicious warfare. Not only were the Goths more formidable foes than he had expected, but when Roman tax collectors arrived with the Roman armies, Justinian found that the Italian people did not greet their "liberators" with open arms. In addition, in the midst of the

MAP DISCOVERY

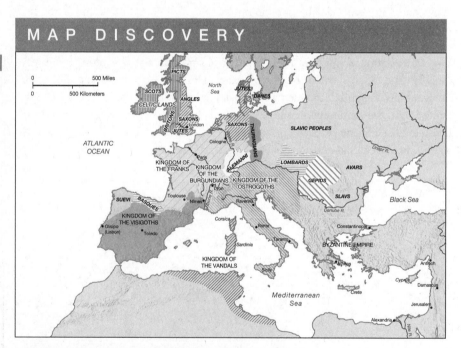

THE BARBARIAN KINGDOMS, CA. 526

Examine the locations of barbarian kingdoms in the sixth century. What strategic geographical advantages did the Ostrogothic kingdom hold that allowed Theodoric the Great to play a dominant role in the West? How did the relative isolation of the kingdom of the Franks aid its future development? Which barbarian kingdoms were in a position to absorb the most Roman traditions? Which the least?

reconquest a new and terrible disease appeared throughout the Mediterranean world. The plague cut down as much as one-third of Europe's population in the next two centuries.

Lombard Conquest. The destruction of Italy by war and disease paved the way for its conquest by the Lombards. In 568, the whole Lombard people left the Carpathian basin to their neighbors, the Avars, and invaded the exhausted and war-torn Italian peninsula. By the end of the sixth century, the Ostrogoths had disappeared, and the Byzantines retained only the heel and toe of the boot of Italy and a narrow strip stretching from Ravenna to Rome. The Byzantine presence in Rome was weak, and by default the popes, especially Gregory the Great (590–604), became the defenders and governors of the city. Gregory organized the resistance to the Lombards, fed the population during famines, and comforted them through the dark years of plague and warfare. A vigorous political as well as spiritual leader, he laid the foundations of the medieval papacy.

The Lombards largely eliminated the Roman tax system under which Italians had long suffered. In the sphere of religion, many of the Lombards initially were Arians, but in the early seventh century the Lombard kings and their followers accepted orthodox Christianity. This conversion paved the way for the unification of society.

Visigothic Spain: Intolerance and Destruction

Rather than accepting a divided society as did the Ostrogoths or merging into an orthodox Roman culture as did the Lombards, the Visigoths of Gaul and Spain sought to unify the indigenous population of their kingdom through law and religion. Roman law deeply influenced Visigothic law codes and formed an enduring legal heritage to the West. Religious unity was a more difficult goal. The king's repeated attempts to force conversion to Arianism failed and created tension and mistrust. This mistrust proved fatal. In 507, Gallo-Roman aristocrats supported the Frankish king Clovis in his successful conquest of the Visigothic kingdom of Toulouse. Defeat drove the Visigoths deeper into Spain, where they gradually forged a unified kingdom based on Roman administrative tradition and Visigothic kingship.

The long-sought religious unity was finally achieved when King Recared (586–601) and the Gothic aristocracy embraced orthodox Christianity. This conversion further blurred the differences between Visigoths and Roman provincials in the kingdom. It also initiated an unprecedented use of the Church and its ideology to strengthen the monarchy.

Still, the Visigoths continued to distrust anyone who was different, and their suspicion focused especially on the considerable Jewish population, which had lived in Spain since the *Diaspora*, or dispersion, in the first century of the Roman Empire. Almost immediately after Recared's conversion, he and his successors began to enact a series of anti-Jewish measures, culminating in 613 with the command that all Jews accept baptism or leave the kingdom. Although this mandate was never fully carried out, the virulence of the persecution of the Jews grew through the seventh century. At the same time, rivalry within the aristocracy weakened the kingdom and left it vulnerable to attack from without. In 711, Muslims from North Africa invaded and quickly conquered the Visigothic kingdom. While some remnants of the Visigoths held on in small kingdoms in the northwest, most of the population quickly came to terms with their new masters. Jews rejoiced in the religious toleration brought by Islam, and many members of the Christian elite converted to Islam and retained their positions of authority under the new regime.

The Anglo-Saxons: From Pagan Conquerors to Christian Missionaries

The motley collection of Saxons, Angles, Jutes, Frisians, Suebians, and others who came to Britain as federated troops and stayed on as rulers did not coalesce into a united kingdom until almost the eleventh century. Instead, these Germanic warriors carved out small kingdoms for themselves, enslaving the romanized Britons or driving them into Wales. Although independent, these little kingdoms (their number varied from five to as many as eleven at different times) maintained some sort of identity as a group. The king of the dominant kingdom enjoyed some deference from his fellow rulers. Other kings looked to him as first among equals and sought his advice and influence in their dealings with one another. Unlike the Goths, none of these peoples had previously been integrated into the Roman world. Rather than fusing Roman and Germanic traditions, they eradicated the former. Urban life disappeared and, with it, the Roman traditions of administration, taxation, and culture.

In their place developed a world whose central values were honor and glory, whose primary occupation was fighting, and whose economic system was based on plunder and the open-handed distribution of riches. These invaders were not, like the Goths, just a military elite. They also included free farmers who partly replaced and partly absorbed romanized British peasantry, introducing their language, agricultural techniques, social organization, and folkloric traditions to the southeastern part of the island. These ordinary settlers, much more than the kings and aristocrats, were responsible for the gradual transformation of Britain into England, the land of the Angles.

The Anglo-Saxons were pagans, and although Christianity survived, the relationship between conquered and conquerors did not provide a climate conducive to conversion. Christianity came instead from without. The conversion of England resulted from a two-part effort. The first originated in Ireland, the most western society of Europe and the one in which Celtic traditions had survived little changed for over 1,000 years. In the fifth century, merchants and missionaries introduced an eastern monastic form of Christianity to Ireland, which adapted easily to the rural tribal organization of Irish society. Around 565, the Irish monk Columba (521–597) established a monastery on the island of Iona off the coast of Scotland. From there, wandering Irish monks began to convert northern Britain.

The second effort at Christianizing Britain began with Pope Gregory the Great. In 596, he sent the missionary Augustine (known as Augustine of Canterbury to distinguish him from the bishop of Hippo) to attempt to convert the English. Augustine laid the foundations for a hierarchical, bishop-centered church based on the Roman model. In time, the pagan king Ethelbert and much of his southwest kingdom of Kent accepted Christianity, and the pope named Augustine archbishop of Canterbury.

As Irish missionaries spread south from Iona and Roman missionaries moved north from Canterbury, their efforts created in England two opposing forms of orthodox Christianity. One was Roman, episcopal, and hierarchical. The other was Celtic, monastic, and decentralized. The Roman and Celtic churches agreed on basic doctrines. However, each had its own calendar of religious feasts and its own rituals. King Oswy of Northumbria (d. 670) called an episcopal meeting, or **synod**, in 664 at Whitby to settle the issue. After hearing arguments from both sides, Oswy accepted the customs of the Roman Church, thus allying himself and ultimately all of Anglo-Saxon England with the centralized, hierarchical form of Christianity, which could be used to strengthen his monarchy.

The elaborate helmet of a seventh-century Anglo-Saxon king, recovered from his ship burial at Sutton Hoo on the southeast coast of England, shows the wealth and culture of these rulers. The king was buried in a ship some 90 feet long with benches for 40 oarsmen. Although the body had totally disappeared over the centuries, the burial chamber held, in addition to this unique helmet with historiated die-struck bronze panels, a magnificent sword with gold and garnet cloissoné pommel, a set of spears, gold shoulder clasps, probably the remains of a magnificent roman-style leather armor, and many other objects of Eastern Mediterranean, Anglo-Saxon, Frankish, and Scandinavian origins.

During the century and a half following the Synod of Whitby, Anglo-Saxon Christian civilization blossomed. Contact with the Continent and especially with Rome increased. The monasteries of Monkwearmouth and Jarrow became centers of learning, culminating in the writings of Bede (673–735), the greatest scholar of his century. His history of the English church and people is the finest historical work of the early Middle Ages.

By the eighth century, England itself had begun to send Christian missionaries to the Continent to convert their still-pagan Germanic cousins. Until the late eighth and ninth centuries, when the Germanic Vikings began to attack Anglo-Saxon settlements, England furnished the Continent with many of its leading thinkers and scholars.

The Franks: An Enduring Legacy

In the fourth century, various small Germanic tribes along the Rhine coalesced into a loose confederation known as the Franks. A significant group of them, the Salians, made the mistake of attacking Roman garrisons and were totally defeated. The Romans resettled the Salians in a largely abandoned region of what is now Belgium and Holland. There, they formed a buffer to protect Roman colonists from other Germanic tribes and provided a ready supply of recruits for the Roman army. During the fourth and fifth centuries, these Salian Franks and their neighbors assumed an increasingly important role in the military defense of Gaul and began to spread out of their "reservation" into more settled parts of the province. Although many high-ranking Roman officers of the fourth century were Franks, most were neither conquerors nor members of the military elite. Rather, they were soldier-farmers who settled beside the local Roman peoples they protected.

In 486, Clovis, leader of the Salian Franks and commander of the barbarized Roman army, staged a successful coup (possibly with the approval of the Byzantine emperor), defeating and killing Syagrius, the last Roman commander in the West. Although Clovis ruled the Franks as king, he worked closely with the existing Gallo-Roman aristocracy as he consolidated his control over various Frankish factions and over portions of Gaul and Germany that were held by other barbarian kingdoms. Clovis's early conversion to orthodox Christianity helped to ensure the effectiveness of this Gallo-Roman cooperation. Clovis converted, hoping that God would give him victory over his enemies and that his new faith would win the support of the Roman aristocracy in Gaul. The king's baptism convinced many of his subjects to convert as well and paved the way for the assimilation of Franks and Romans into a new society. This Frankish society became the model for European social and political organization for over 1,000 years.

The mix of Frankish warriors and Roman aristocrats spread rapidly across western Europe. Clovis and his successors absorbed the Visigothic kingdom of

Toulouse, the Thuringians, and the kingdom of the Burgundians and expanded Frankish hegemony through modern Bavaria and south of the Alps into northern Italy. Unlike other barbarian kingdoms such as those of the Huns or Ostrogoths, which evaporated almost as soon as their great founders died, the Frankish synthesis was enduring. Although the dynasty established by Clovis, called the Merovingian after a legendary ancestor, lasted only until the mid-eighth century, the Frankish kingdom was the direct ancestor of both France and Germany.

After Clovis's death in 511, his kingdom was divided among his four sons. For the next 200 years, the heart of the Frankish kingdom, the region between the Rhine and Loire rivers, was often divided into the kingdoms of Neustria, Burgundy, and Austrasia, each ruled by a Merovingian king. The outlying regions of Aquitaine and Provence to the south and Alemania, Thuringia, and Bavaria to the east were governed by Frankish dukes appointed by the kings. Still, the Frankish world was never as divided as Anglo-Saxon England. In the early eighth century, a unified Frankish kingdom reemerged as the dominant force in Europe.

Living in the New Europe

The substitution of Germanic kings for imperial officials made few obvious differences in the lives of most inhabitants of Italy, Gaul, and Spain. The vast majority of Europeans were poor farmers whose lives centered on their villages and fields. Nevertheless, fundamental if imperceptible changes were transforming daily life at every level of society. The slaves and semifree peasants of Rome gradually began to form new kinds of social groups and to practice new forms of agriculture as they merged with the Germanic warrior-peasants. Elite Gallo-Roman landowners came to terms with their Frankish conquerors, and these two groups began to coalesce into a single unified aristocracy. In the same way that Germanic and Roman society began to merge, Germanic and Roman traditions of governance united between the sixth and eighth centuries to create a powerful new kind of medieval kingdom.

Creating the European Peasantry

Three fundamental changes transformed rural society during the early Middle Ages. First, Roman slavery virtually disappeared. Second, the household emerged as the primary unit of social and economic organization. Third, Christianity spread throughout the rural world. Economics, not ethics, destroyed Roman slavery. In the kind of slavery that was typical of the Roman world, large gangs of slaves were housed in dormitories and directed in large-scale operations by overseers. This form of slavery demanded a highly organized form of estate management and could be quite costly, since slaves had to be fed and housed year-round. Since slaves did not always reproduce at a rate sufficient to replace themselves, the supply had to be replenished from elsewhere. However, as the empire ceased to expand, the supply of fresh captives dwindled. As cities shrank, many markets for agricultural produce disappeared, making market-oriented large-scale agriculture less profitable. Furthermore, the Germanic societies that settled in the West had no tradition of gang slavery.

As a result, from the sixth through the ninth centuries, owners abandoned the practice of keeping gangs of slaves in favor of the less complicated practice of establishing slave families on individual plots of land. The slaves and their descendants cultivated these plots, made annual payments to their owners, and also cultivated the undivided portions of the estate, the fruits of which went directly to the owner. Thus slaves became something akin to sharecroppers. Gradually, they began to intermarry with hereditary tenant farmers and others who, though nominally free, found themselves in an economic situation much like that of slaves. By the ninth century, the distinction between slaves who had acquired traditional rights to their farms, or **manses**, and free peasants who held and worked manses belonging to others was blurred. By the tenth and eleventh centuries, peasant farmers throughout much of Europe were subject to the private justice of their landlords, no matter whether their ancestors had been slave or free. Although not slaves in the classical sense, the peasantry had fused into a homogeneous unfree population.

Rural Households

The division of estates into separate peasant holdings contributed to the second fundamental transformation of European peasant society: the formation of the household. Neither the Roman tradition of slave agriculture nor the Germanic tradition of clan organization had encouraged the household as the basic unit of society. Now individual slaves and their spouses were placed on manses, which they and their children were expected to cultivate. The household had become the basic unit of Western economy.

The household was more than an economic unit, however. It was also the first level of government. The head of the household, whether slave or free, male or female—women, particularly widows, were often heads of households—exercised authority over its other members. This authority made the householder a link in the chain of the social order, which stretched from the peasant hovel to the royal court.

Peasant life centered on the house, the village, and the field. Peasant houses often consisted simply of two or three rooms in which dwelt both the human and animal members of the household. The rhythm of peasant life was tied to the agricultural cycle, which had changed little since antiquity. Although women and men worked together on the harvest, peasants normally divided labor into male and female tasks. Husbands and sons worked in the fields. Wives and daughters tended chickens, prepared the dark bread that was the staple of their diet, spun, and wove.

Peasant culture, like peasant society, experienced a fundamental transformation during the early Middle Ages: the peasantry became Christian. The spread of Christianity throughout the rural world began in earnest in the sixth century, when bishops and monks began to replace the peasant's traditional agrarian cults with Christian feasts, rituals, and beliefs.

Christianity penetrated more deeply into rural society with the systematic establishment of parishes, or rural churches. By the ninth century, this parish system began to cover Europe. Bishops founded parish churches in the villages of large estates, and owners were obligated to set aside one-tenth of the produce of their estates for the maintenance of the parish church. The priests who staffed these churches came from the local peasantry and received a basic education in Latin and in Christian ritual from their predecessors and from their bishops. The continuing presence of priests in each village had a profound effect on the daily lives of Europe's peasants.

Creating the European Aristocracy

At the same time that a homogeneous peasantry was emerging from the blend of slaves and free farmers, a homogeneous aristocracy was evolving out of the mix of Germanic and Roman traditions. In Germanic society, the elite had owed its position to a combination of inherited status and wealth, perpetuated through military command. Families who produced great military commanders were thought to have a special war-luck granted by the gods. The war-luck bestowed on men and women of these families a near-sacred legitimacy. This legitimacy made the aristocrats largely independent of their kings. In times of war, kings might command, but otherwise, the extent to which they could be said to govern aristocrats was minimal.

The Roman aristocracy was also based on inheritance, but of land rather than leadership. During the third and fourth centuries, Roman aristocrats' control of land extended over the people who worked that land. At the same time, great landowners were able to free themselves from provincial government. Like their Germanic counterparts, Roman aristocrats acquired a sacred legitimacy, but within the Christian tradition. They monopolized the office of bishop and became identified with the sacred and political traditions associated with the Church.

In Spain and Italy, the religious differences separating Arians and orthodox Christians impeded the fusion of the Germanic and Roman aristocracies. In Gaul, the conversion of Clovis and his people facilitated the rapid blending of the two worlds. North of the Loire River, where the bulk of the Franks had settled, Roman aristocrats soon became Franks. By the mid-sixth century, the descendants of Bishop Remigius of Reims, who had baptized Clovis, had Frankish names and considered themselves Franks. Still, the Roman aristocratic tradition of great landholders became an integral part of the identity of the Frankish elite.

In the late sixth century, this northern Frankish aristocracy found its own religious identity and legitimacy in the Irish monasticism introduced by Saint Columbanus (543–615) and other wandering monks. Irish monks worked closely with the Frankish aristocrats, who encouraged them to build monasteries on their estates. Eventually, these monasteries amassed huge landholdings and became major economic and political centers headed by aristocrats who abandoned secular life for the cloister.

South of the Loire River, conditions were decidedly different. Here, Irish monasticism was less important than episcopal office. The few Frankish and Gothic families who had settled in the south were rapidly absorbed into the Gallo-Roman aristocracy, which drew its prestige from control of local religious and secular power. Latin speech and Roman culture distinguished these "Romans," regardless of their ancestry.

Aristocratic Lifestyle

Aristocratic life was similar whether north or south of the Loire, in Anglo-Saxon England, Visigothic Spain, or Lombard Italy. Aristocratic family structures were loosely knit clans that traced descent from important ancestors through either the male or the female line. Clans jealously guarded their autonomy against rival clans and from royal authority.

Feasting and Fighting. The aristocratic lifestyle focused on feasting, hospitality, and the male activities of hunting and warfare. In southern Europe, great nobles lived in spacious villas, often surrounded by solid stone fortifications, an inheritance of Roman traditions. In the north, Frankish and Anglo-Saxon nobles lived in great wooden halls, richly decorated but lacking fortifications. During the fall and winter, aristocratic men spent much of their time hunting deer and wild boar in their forests. In March, as soon as the snows of winter had begun to melt and roads had become passable, aristocrats gathered their retainers, who had enjoyed their winter hospitality, and marched to war. The enemy varied. It might be rival families with whom feuds were nursed for generations. It might be raiding parties from a neighboring region. Or the warriors might join a royal expedition led by the king and directed against a rival kingdom. Whoever the enemy was, warfare brought the promise of booty and glory.

Women in Aristocratic Society. Within this aristocratic society, women played a wider and more active role than had been the case in either Roman or barbarian antiquity. In part, women's new role was due to the influence of Christianity, which recognized the distinct—though always inferior—rights of women, fought against the barbarian tradition of allowing chieftains numerous wives, and acknowledged women's right to lead a cloistered religious life. In addition, the combination of Germanic and Roman familial traditions permitted women to participate in court proceedings, to inherit and dispose of property, and, if widowed, to serve as tutors and guardians for their minor children. Finally, the long absence of men at the hunt, at the royal court, or on military expeditions left wives in charge of the domestic scene for months or years at a time. The religious life in particular opened to aristocratic women possibilities of autonomy and authority that had previously been unknown in the West.

Governing Europe

The combination in the early Middle Ages of the extremes of centralized Roman power and fragmented barbarian organization produced a wide variety of governmental systems. At one end of the spectrum were the politically fragmented Celtic and Slavic societies. At the other end were the Frankish kingdoms, in which descendants of Clovis, drawing on the twin heritages of Roman institutions and Frankish tradition, attempted not simply to reign but to rule.

Kings and Aristocrats. Rulers and aristocrats both needed and feared each other. Kings had emerged out of the Germanic aristocracy and could rule only in cooperation with aristocrats. Aristocrats were concerned primarily with maintaining and expanding their own spheres of control and independence. They perceived royal authority as a threat. Still, they needed kings. Strong kings brought victory against external foes and thus maintained the flow of booty to the aristocracy. Aristocrats in turn redistributed the spoils of war among their followers to preserve the bonds of warrior society. Thus, under capable kings, aristocrats were ready to cooperate, not as subjects but as partners.

As the successors of Germanic war leaders and late Roman generals, kings were primarily military commanders. During campaigns and at the annual **Marchfield**, when the free warriors assembled, the king was all-powerful. At those times he could cut down his enemies with impunity. At other times the king's role was strictly limited. His direct authority extended only over the members of his household and his personal warrior band.

Royal Justice. The king's role in administering justice was similarly ambivalent. He was not the source of law, which was held to be simply the customs of the past, nor was he responsible for enforcing this customary law. Enforcement was the duty of individuals and families. Only if they wanted did they bring their grievances to the king or his agents for arbitration or judgment. However, even though they could not formally legislate, kings effectively molded law and legal procedure by collecting, selecting, clarifying, and publishing customary laws.

As heirs of Roman governmental tradition, kings sought to incorporate these traditions into their roles. By absorbing the remains of local administration and taxation, kings acquired nascent governmental systems. Through the use of written documents, Roman scribes expanded royal authority beyond the king's household and personal following. Tax collectors continued to fill royal coffers with duties collected in markets and ports.

Finally, by assuming the role of protector of the Church, kings acquired the support of educated and experienced ecclesiastical advisers and the right to intervene in disputes involving clergy and laity. Further, as defenders of the Church, kings could claim a responsibility for the preservation of peace and the administration of justice—two fundamental Christian (but also Roman) tasks.

Royal Administration. Early medieval kings had no fixed capitals from which they governed. Instead, they were constantly on the move, supervising their kingdoms and consuming the produce of their estates. Since kings could not be everywhere at once, they were represented locally by aristocrats who enjoyed royal favor. In the Frankish world these favorites were called *counts,* and their districts were called *counties.* In England, royal representatives were termed *ealdormen,* and their regions were known as *shires.* Whether counts or ealdormen, these representatives were military commanders and judicial officers drawn from aristocratic families close to the king. Under competent and effective kings, partnership with these aristocratic families worked well. Under less competent rulers and during the reigns of minors, these families often managed to turn their districts into hereditary, almost autonomous regions.

The Carolingian Achievement

The Merovingian dynasty initiated by Clovis presided over the synthesis of Roman and Germanic society. It was left to the Carolingians who followed to forge a new Europe. In the seventh century, members of the new aristocracy were able to take advantage of royal minorities and dynastic rivalries to make themselves into virtual rulers of their small territories. By the end of the century, the kings had become little more than symbolic figures in the Frankish kingdoms. The real power was held by regional strongmen called *dukes.* The most successful of these aristocratic factions was that led by Charles Martel (ca. 688–741) and his heirs, known as the Carolingians.

Charles Martel. This family had risen to prominence in the seventh century by controlling the office of mayor of the palace in Austrasia, the highest court official who advised the king as spokesman for the aristocracy. The Carolingians increased their influence by marrying their sons to daughters of other aristocratic families. In the late seventh century, they extended their control to include Neustria and Burgundy as well as Austrasia. By the second quarter of the eighth century, Charles Martel, while not king, was the acknowledged ruler of the Frankish kingdom.

Charles Martel was ruthless, ambitious, and successful. He crushed rivals in his own family, subdued competing dukes, and united the Frankish realm. He was successful in part because he molded the Frankish cavalry into the most effective military force of the time. His mounted, heavily armored warriors were extremely effective but very costly. He financed them with property confiscated from his enemies. In return for oaths of absolute fidelity, he gave his followers, or **vassals**, estates, which they held as long as they served him faithfully. With this new army he practiced a scorched-earth policy against his opponents that left vast areas of Provence and Aquitaine desolate for decades.

Charles Martel looked beyond military power to the control of religious and cultural institutions. He supported Anglo-Saxon missionaries such as Boniface (ca. 680–755), who were trying to introduce on the Continent the Roman form of Christianity they knew in England. This hierarchical style of Christianity served Carolingian interests in centralization, especially since Charles appointed his loyal supporters as bishops and abbots. Missionaries and Frankish armies worked hand in hand to consolidate Carolingian rule.

The ecclesiastical policy that proved most crucial to later Carolingians was Charles's support of the Roman papacy. Charles caught the attention of Pope Gregory III (731–741) in 732, after a battle near Tours in which Charles defeated a Muslim force that was attempting to continue the northward expansion of Islam. A few years later, when the pope needed protection from the Lombards to maintain his central Italian territories, he sought and obtained help from the Frankish leader.

Pippin III. The alliance with the papacy solidified during the lifetime of Charles's son Pippin (ca. 714–768). Pippin inherited his father's power, but since he was not of the royal Merovingian family, he had no right to the title of king. No Frankish tradition provided a precedent by which a rival family might displace the Merovingians. Pippin turned instead to the pope, seeking legitimacy in religious authority. In a carefully orchestrated exchange between Pippin and Pope Zacharias (741–752), the latter declared that the individual who exercised the power of king ought also to have the title. Following this declaration the last Merovingian was deposed, and in 751 a representative of the pope anointed Pippin king of the Franks.

The alliance between the new dynasty and the papacy marked the first union of royal legitimacy and ecclesiastical sanction in European history. The new Frankish kingship led Europe into the first political, social, and cultural restructuring of the West since the end of the Roman Empire.

Charlemagne and the Renewal of the West

Pippin's son Charlemagne was the heir of the political, religious, and social revolutions begun by his grandfather and father. As the leader of a powerful, united

This bronze equestrian statue of a king dates from the ninth century. The rider wears the typical Frankish attire of hose, tunic, and long riding cloak. The subject is often identified as Charlemagne or his grandson Charles the Bold. The Carolingians admired Roman bronze equestrian statues. The most famous was the statue of Marcus Aurelius, mistaken for a statue of Constantine the Great, which stood outside of the pope's Lateran palace (now in the museum on the Capitoline Hill). Charlemagne was particularly impressed with an equestrian statue of Theoderic which stood in Ravenna and brought it to his palace complex in Aachen. This now lost bronze may well be the model for the much smaller Carolingian statue.

Frankish kingdom for over 40 years, Charlemagne changed the West more profoundly than anyone since Augustus.

Almost every spring, Charlemagne assembled his Frankish armies and led them against internal or external enemies. In wars of aggression his armies were invincible. Not only were they better armed and mounted, but their ability to transport men and matériel great distances was unmatched.

War booty fueled Charlemagne's renewal of European culture. As a Christian king, he considered it his duty to reform the spiritual life of his kingdom and to bring it into line with his concept of the divinely willed order. To achieve this goal, he needed a dedicated and educated clergy. Most of the native clergy were poorly educated and indifferent in their observance of the rules of religious life. Charlemagne set about creating a reformed, educated clergy.

The Carolingian Renaissance

Charlemagne recruited leading intellectuals from England, Spain, Ireland, and Italy to the royal court to lead a thorough educational program. The architect of his cultural reform, Alcuin of York (ca. 732–804), directed a school for young lay and ecclesiastical aristocrats in the king's palace and encouraged the king to finance a wide variety of educational programs. Charlemagne supported schools in great monasteries such as Fulda and St. Gall for the training of young clerics and laymen. These schools needed books. Charlemagne's educational reformers

Legend:
- Charlemagne's empire at his accession, 768
- Territories added before his death in 814
- Tributary states
- Kingdom boundaries

CHARLEMAGNE'S EMPIRE, 814

Compare the empire of Charlemagne with that of Hadrian (p. 119). How similar are they? How does Charlemagne's Frankish Empire compare geographically with the Byzantine Empire in 814 (p. 159)? What new barbarian peoples now appear on the peripheries of the empire?

scoured Italy for fading copies of works by Virgil, Horace, and Tacitus with the same determination with which his builders hunted antique marbles and columns for his chapel. Alcuin and others corrected and copied classical texts that had been corrupted by generations of haphazard transmission. Caroline **minuscule**, the new style of handwriting that was developed to preserve these texts, was so clear and readable that during the Renaissance, humanists adopted it as their standard script.

The reformers of this era laid the necessary foundation for what has been called the **Carolingian Renaissance.** Their successors in the ninth century built on this foundation to make creative contributions in theology, philosophy, and historiography and to some extent in literature. The pursuit of learning was not a purely clerical affair. In the later ninth century, great aristocrats were highly literate and collected their own personal libraries. Count Everard of Friuli, who died in 866, left an estate that included over 50 books, among them works by Augustine, histories, saints' lives, and seven law books. Elite women participated fully in the Carolingian Renaissance. One example is the noblewoman Dhuoda, who composed a manual of instruction for her son.

Educational reform went hand in hand with reform of ecclesiastical institutions. Charlemagne and his son Louis the Pious (814–840) worked to establish the Benedictine rule as the norm for monastic life and to reform the parish clergy. The goal was a purified and organized clergy performing its essential role of celebrating Christian ritual and praying for the Frankish king. At the same time, the monasteries were to provide competent clerics to serve the royal administration at every level. These reforms were expensive. The fiscal reorganization of ecclesiastical institutions was as far-reaching as their cultural reform. For the first time, Frankish synods or councils made *tithing* mandatory, specifying that one-tenth of all agricultural harvests was to go to the maintenance of church buildings, support of the clergy, and care of the poor. Monasteries flourished.

Carolingian Government

Charlemagne recognized that conquest alone could not unify his enormous kingdom with its vast differences in languages, laws, customs, and peoples. The glue that held it together was loyalty to him and to the Roman Church. He appointed as counts throughout Europe members of the great Frankish families who had been loyal to his family for generations. In addition to supervising the royal estates in their counties, each spring these counts led the local military contingent, which included all the free men of the county. Counts also presided over local courts, which exercised jurisdiction over the free persons of the county. The king maintained his control over the counts by sending teams of emissaries, or **missi dominici**, composed of bishops and counts, to examine the state of each county.

Charlemagne recognized that while his representatives might be drawn from Frankish families, he could not impose Frankish legal and cultural traditions on all his subjects. The only universal system that might unify the kingdom was Roman Christianity. Unity of religious practices, directed by the reformed and educated clergy, would provide spiritual unity. Furthermore, since the clergy could also participate in the administration of the kingdom, they could guarantee administrative unity as well. Carolingian monarchs did not intend the enriched and reformed Church to be independent of royal authority; rather, it was to be an integral part of the Carolingian system of government. However, at least some of the educated clerics and lay aristocrats who participated in the system formed a clear political ideology based on Augustinian concepts of Christian government. They attempted to educate Charlemagne and his successors to the duties of a king: maintaining peace and providing justice.

Carolingian government was no modern bureaucracy or state system. It was a mobile palace that included the royal household and ecclesiastical and secular aristocrats. The laymen and clerics who served the king were tied to him by personal oaths of loyalty rather than by any sense of dedication to a state or nation.

Still, the attempts at governmental organization were far more sophisticated than anything that the West had seen for four centuries or would see again for another four.

The size of Charlemagne's empire approached that of the old Roman Empire in the West. Only Britain, southern Italy, and parts of Spain remained outside Frankish control. With the reunification of most of the West and the creative adaptation of Roman traditions of culture and government, it is not surprising that Charlemagne's advisers began to compare his empire to that of Constantine. This comparison was accentuated by Charlemagne's conquest of Lombard Italy and his protection of Pope Leo III—a role traditionally played by the Byzantine emperors. By the end of the eighth century, the throne in Constantinople was held by a woman. Irene (752–802) was powerful and capable, but Western male leaders considered her unfit by reason of her sex for such an office. All these factors finally converged in one of the most momentous events in Western political history: Charlemagne's imperial coronation on Christmas Day in the year 800.

Historians debate the precise meaning of this event, particularly since Charlemagne was said to have remarked afterward that he would never have entered St. Peter's Basilica in Rome had he known what was going to happen. Presumably, he meant that he wanted to be proclaimed emperor by his Frankish people rather than by the pope, since this is how he had his son Louis the Pious acclaimed emperor in 813. Nevertheless, the imperial coronation of 800 subsequently took on great significance. Louis attempted to make his imperial title the sole basis for his rule, and for the next thousand years, Germanic kings traveled to Rome to receive the imperial diadem and title from the pope. In so doing, they inadvertently strengthened papal claims to enthrone—and at times to dethrone—emperors.

Carolingian Art

The same creative adaptation of the classical heritage that gave birth to a new Western empire produced a new Western art. The artistic traditions of the barbarian world consisted almost entirely of the decoration of small, portable objects such as weapons, jewelry, and, after conversion, manuscripts. Barbarian art was essentially nonrepresentational and consisted primarily of elaborate interlaced geometric forms of great sophistication.

For Charlemagne and his reformers, such abstract art was doubly inappropriate. Not only was it too distant from the Roman heritage that they were trying to emulate, but it could not be used for instruction or propaganda. Therefore, Charlemagne invited Italian and Byzantine artists and artisans to his kingdom to teach a form of representational art that would decorate as well as educate. However, these southern traditions were no more slavishly followed by northern artists than were Roman political traditions wholly taken over by Charlemagne's

An example of the animal style common in the Celtic-Germanic art of the early Middle Ages, this wooden dragon head is the terminal of a post from a seventh-century Scandinavian ship. Dragon heads decorated not only the prows of ships but house gables, sleds, wagons, and even bedposts. The intricate interlaced geometric patterns on the head appear also in stone carvings and in complex manuscript illuminations, a tradition particularly developed in Ireland and the British Isles.

government. The synthesis of Mediterranean and northern artistic traditions produced a dynamic plastic style of representation in which figures seem intensely alive and active. These figures, which appear in manuscript illuminations, ivories, and bas-reliefs, are often arranged in narrative cycles that engage the mind as well as the eye.

Chronology

THE CAROLINGIANS AND THE PAPACY

ca. 680–755	Boniface, Anglo-Saxon missionary to the Continent; supported by Charles Martel
ca. 688–741	Charles Martel, acknowledged ruler of the Frankish kingdom
731–741	Papacy of Gregory III; began alliance between papacy and the Carolingians
732	Battle of Tours
ca. 714–768	Pippin III; strengthens Carolingian alliance with the papacy
751	Representative of the papacy anoints Pippin king of the Franks
768–814	Reign of Charlemagne; establishes Carolingian Empire; patron of the Carolingian Renaissance
800	Charlemagne crowned emperor by Pope Leo III
814–840	Reign of Charlemagne's son, Louis the Pious
843	Lothair, Louis the German, and Charles the Bald divide the kingdom

After the Carolingians: From Empire to Lordships

Alien, dynamic, and potentially threatening neighbors surrounded the Carolingian kingdom. To the west was Anglo-Saxon England; to the east were the Slavic and Byzantine worlds. Scandinavia lay to the north, and Al-Andalus threatened to the south. In the later ninth and tenth centuries, the Frankish kingdom collapsed, owing in part to the actions of these neighbors but primarily to the kingdom's own internal weaknesses.

Charlemagne, despite his imperial title, had remained dependent on his traditional power base, the Frankish aristocracy. For them, learned concepts of imperial renovation meant little. They wanted wealth and power. Under Charlemagne, the empire's prosperity and relative internal peace had resulted largely from continued successful expansion at the expense of neighbors. Its economy had been based on plunder and the redistribution of war booty among the aristocracy and wealthy churches. As wars of conquest under Charlemagne gave place to defensive actions against Magyars, Vikings, and Saracens, the supply of wealth dried up. Aristocratic supporters were rewarded with estates within the empire and thus became enormously wealthy and powerful.

Disintegration of the Empire

Competition among Charlemagne's descendants as well as grants to the aristocracy weakened central authority. Charlemagne had bequeathed a united empire to his son Louis the Pious (814–840). Louis's three sons, in contrast, fought one another over their inheritance, and in 843 they divided the empire among them. The eldest son, Lothair (840–855), who inherited his father's imperial title, received an unwieldy middle portion that stretched from the Rhine south through Italy. Louis the German (840–876) received the eastern portions of the empire. The youngest son, Charles the Bald (840–877), was allotted the western portions. In time, the western kingdom became France, and the eastern kingdom became the core of Germany. The middle kingdom, which included modern Holland, Belgium, Luxembourg, Lorraine (or Lotharingia, from "Lothair"), Switzerland, and northern Italy, remained a disputed region into the twentieth century.

The disintegration of the empire meant much more than its division among Charlemagne's heirs. In no region were his successors able to provide the degree of peace and public control that he had established. The Frankish armies, designed for wars of aggression, were too clumsy and slow to deal with the lightning raids of Northmen, Magyars, and Saracens. The constant need to please aristocratic supporters made it impossible for kings to prevent aristocrats from absorbing free peasants and churches into their economic and political spheres. Increasingly, these magnates were able to transform the offices of count and bishop into inherited familial positions. They also determined who would reign in their kingdoms and sought kings who posed no threat to themselves.

MAP DISCOVERY

THE DIVISION OF CHARLEMAGNE'S EMPIRE

Consider how Charlemagne's grandsons divided his empire. What major symbolic locations remained in the kingdom of Emperor Lothair? Do the kingdoms of Kings Charles and Louis appear more culturally and ethnically homogeneous than that of their brother? Into what states would their two kingdoms eventually develop?

Most aristocrats saw this greater autonomy as their just due. Only dukes, counts, and other local lords could organize resistance to internal and external foes at the local level. They needed both economic means and political authority to provide protection and maintain peace. These resources could be acquired only at the expense of royal power. Therefore, during the late ninth and tenth centuries, much of Europe found its equilibrium at the local level as public powers, judicial courts, and military authority became the private possession of wealthy families.

Emergence of France and Germany

Ultimately, new royal families emerged from among these local leaders. The family of the counts of Paris, for example, gained enormous prestige from the fact that they had led the successful defense of the city against the Vikings from 885 to 886. For a time they alternated with Carolingians as kings of the West Franks. After the ascension of Hugh Capet in 987, they entirely replaced the Carolingians.

In a similar manner, the eastern German kingdom, which was divided into five great duchies, began to elect non-Carolingians as kings. In 919, the dukes of this region elected as their king Duke Henry of Saxony (919–936), who had proven his abilities fighting the Danes and Magyars. Henry's son, Otto the Great (936–973), proved to be a strong ruler who subdued the other dukes and definitively crushed the Magyars. In 962, Otto was crowned emperor by Pope John XII (955–964), thus reviving the empire of Charlemagne, though only in its eastern half. However, the dukes of this eastern kingdom chafed constantly at the strong control the Ottonians attempted to exercise at their expense. Although the empire Otto reestablished endured until 1806, he and his successors never matched the political or cultural achievements of the Carolingians.

By the tenth century, the early medieval kingdoms, based on inherited Roman notions of universal states and barbarian traditions of charismatic military leadership, had all ended in failure. After the demise of the Carolingian Empire, the West began to find stability at a more local but also more permanent level. However, the local nature of Western society did not mean that the Roman and Carolingian traditions were forgotten. Carolingian religious reform, classical learning, and political ideology were preserved in the following centuries.

Cluny

Church reform took on a new life in 909 with the foundation of the monastery of Cluny in eastern France. Cluniac monks, drawn from the lesser aristocracy, were God's shock troops, fighting evil with their prayers with the same vigor that their secular cousins fought the enemy with their swords. Cluny, inspired by the monastic program of Louis the Pious and granted immunity from secular interference, became the center of an extraordinary expansion of Benedictine monasticism throughout the West.

The revival of classical learning that was begun in Carolingian schools, although hampered by the new wave of invasions that began in the latter ninth century, continued in centers such as St. Gall, Auxerre, and Corvey. During the late ninth and tenth centuries, Western Christian civilization spread to the north and east. By the year 1000, Scandinavia, Poland, Bohemia, and even Hungary had become Christian kingdoms with national churches whose bishops were approved by the pope. Among the aristocracy, just as all restraints on this warrior elite seemed to have been thrown off, a gradual process of transformation of their material and mental world began. Encouraged by Cluniac monasticism and by episcopal exhortations, nobles began to consider limiting their violence against one another and placing it instead in the service of Christendom.

SUMMARY

The Making of the Barbarian Kingdoms, 500–750 The independent power of barbarian kingdoms undercut the illusion of imperial unity in the West. The destruction of Italy by war and disease paved the way for the Lombards to overthrow the Ostrogoths. The Visigoths of Gaul and Spain sought to unify the indigenous population of their kingdom through law and religion. The Anglo-Saxons established a number of small kingdoms in Britain. Conversion to Christianity in Britain came from the outside. Clovis, leader of the Salian Franks, worked closely with the Gallo-Roman aristocracy to establish his control over parts of Gaul and Germany. In the early eighth century, a unified Frankish kingdom reemerged as the dominant force in Europe.

Living in the New Europe Three fundamental changes transformed rural society during the early Middle Ages. First, Roman slavery virtually disappeared. Second, the household emerged as the primary unit of social and economic organization. Third, Christianity spread throughout the rural world. At the same time that a homogeneous peasantry was emerging from the blend of slaves and free farmers, a homogeneous aristocracy was evolving out of the mix of Germanic and Roman traditions. The combination in the early Middle Ages of the extremes of centralized Roman power and fragmented barbarian organization produced a wide variety of governmental systems.

The Carolingian Achievement Charles Martel laid the foundations of Carolingian power and initiated a crucial alliance between the Carolingians and the Roman papacy. This alliance was solidified during the reign of Charles's son, Pippin III. Pippin's son Charlemagne ruled over a united Frankish kingdom for over 40 years, introducing profound change in the West. His power was fueled by unceasing conquest. The fruits of conquest funded his renewal of European culture, a renewal that came to be known as the Carolingian Renaissance. Charlemagne used loyalty to himself and to the Roman Church to unify his domain. Charlemagne's imperial coronation by the pope set an important precedent. The same creative adaptation of the classical heritage that gave birth to a new Western empire produced a new Western art.

After the Carolingians: From Empire to Lordships As wars of conquest under Charlemagne gave place to defensive actions against Magyars, Vikings, and Saracens, aristocrats demanded independent wealth and power in exchange for loyalty. Three of Charlemagne's grandsons divided his empire in 843. In all three regions, centralized control declined. The rise of local leaders led to the emergence of new regional powers in France and Germany. Cluniac monks played an important role in shaping the cultural development of the European aristocracy.

QUESTIONS FOR REVIEW

1. What social and political forces encouraged division within the various Gothic, Anglo-Saxon, and Frankish kingdoms?
2. How did the household and the parish provide new units for organizing European society?
3. How did the aristocracy evolve out of Germanic and Roman traditions, and how was the aristocracy both a support and a threat to the kingdoms of the early Middle Ages?
4. What were Charlemagne's achievements?
5. Why did Charlemagne's empire not outlive him for long?

The High Middle Ages, 900–1300

The Countryside

Between the years 1000 and 1300, Europe's population almost doubled, from approximately 38 million to 74 million. Various reasons have been proposed for this growth: less warfare and raiding, the decline of slavery, gradually improving agricultural techniques and equipment, and possibly a slowly improving climate.

During the tenth century, the great forests that had covered most of Europe began to be cut back as population spread out from the islands of cultivation.

The Peasantry: Serfs and Freemen

The peasants who engaged in the opening of this internal frontier were the descendants of the slaves, unfree farmers, and petty free persons of the early Middle Ages. Across much of northwestern Europe, in particular in France in the eleventh century, the various gradations in status disappeared, and the peasantry formed a homogeneous social category loosely described as **serfs**. Although they were not slaves in a legal sense, their degraded status, their limited or nonexistent access to public courts of law, and their enormous dependency on their lords left them in a situation similar to that of the Carolingian slaves settled on individual farmsteads in the ninth century. Each year, peasants paid their lords certain fixed portions of their meager harvests. In addition, they had to work a certain number of days on the **demesne**, or reserve of the lord, the produce of which went directly to him for his use or sale. Finally, they were required to make ritual payments symbolizing their subordination.

Most peasants led lives of constant insecurity. They were poorly housed, clothed, and fed; subject to the constant scrutiny of their lords; and defenseless against natural or human-made disasters.

Peasants' houses were clustered in villages on manors or large estates. In some parts of Europe, this was the result of their lord's desire to keep a close eye on his labor supply. Beginning in the tenth century in central Italy and elsewhere, lords forced peasants to abandon isolated farmsteads and traditional villages and to move into small, fortified settlements. In these new villages, peasants were obligated to have disputes settled in the lord's court, to grind their grain in the lord's mill, and to bake their bread in the lord's oven—all primary sources of revenue for the lord.

Each morning men went out to their fields, which surrounded the village. In some villages, each peasant householder held thin strips of widely scattered land, while pasturage and woodland were exploited in common. Such an open-field system allotted all peasant households a portion of all the different sorts of land. In other villages, each household tended a unified parcel of land. Such closed fields generally corresponded with greater divergences in wealth within the village and encouraged more independence.

Agricultural Innovation. Agricultural technology gradually changed the ways that peasants worked their land and the amount of food they could produce. Instead of a light plowshare that simply cut a furrow, a heavier plow with a moldboard—a curved iron plate attached above the plowshare to lift and turn the soil, depositing it to one side of the furrow—spread across Europe. It increased production in the heavy-soil areas north of the Alps and in bottom lands.

With the introduction of new technology for plowing came new systems of crop rotation. Traditionally, farmers divided their land into two parts, one planted, the other plowed (usually twice) but allowed to remain fallow. Around the eighth century, some peasants began to introduce a **three-field system**: One-third of the land was planted in autumn with wheat or rye, one-third remained fallow, and one-third was planted in spring with barley, rye, or a leguminous crop such as beans or peas that added nutrients to the soil. As this innovation became standard after the year 1000, the result was a greatly increased yield, a minimal increase in labor, and an improved diet.

While the men worked the fields, women took charge of the domestic tasks. These included carding wool, spinning, weaving, caring for the family's vegetable garden, bearing and raising children, and brewing the thick, souplike beer that was a primary source of carbohydrates in the peasant diet. During harvest, women worked in the fields alongside the men.

Beer, black bread, beans, cabbage, onions, and cheese made up the typical peasant diet. Meat was a rarity and usually came from pigs. Inadequate agricultural methods and inefficient storage systems left the peasantry in constant threat of famine.

Negotiating Freedom. The expansion of arable land offered new hope and opportunities to peasants. Population growth, as rapid as it was between the tenth and twelfth centuries, did not keep up with the increasing demand for laborers in newly settled areas of Europe. Lords were often willing to make special arrangements with groups of peasants to encourage them to bring new land under cultivation. From the beginning of the twelfth century, peasant villages acquired from their lord the privilege to deal with him and his representatives collectively rather than individually. Villages purchased the right to control petty courts and to limit fines imposed by the lord's representative. Peasants acquired protection from arbitrary demands for labor and extraordinary taxes.

These good times did not last forever. Gradually, during the late twelfth and thirteenth centuries, the labor market stagnated. As a result, lay and ecclesiastical lords found that they could profit more by hiring cheap laborers than by demanding customary services and payments from their serfs. They also found that their serfs were willing to pay for increasing privileges.

In purchasing a wide variety of privileges, peasants were, in effect, purchasing their freedom. This free peasantry benefited the emerging states of western Europe, since kings and towns could extend their legal and fiscal jurisdictions over these persons and their lands at the expense of the nobility. By the fourteenth century, serfs were a rarity in many parts of western Europe.

Even as western serfs were acquiring a fragile freedom, the free peasants in much of eastern Europe and Spain were losing it. In much of the Slavic world, through the eleventh century, peasants lived in large, roughly territorial communes of free families. Gradually, however, princes, churches, and aristocrats began to build great landed estates. By the thirteenth century—under the influences of Western and Byzantine models and of the Mongols, who dominated much of the Slavic world from 1240—lords began to acquire political and economic control over the peasantry. In all of these regions the decline of the free peasantry accompanied the decline of public authority to the benefit of independent nobles. The aristocracy rose on the backs of the peasantry.

The Aristocracy: Warriors and Heiresses

Beginning in the late tenth century, writers of legal documents began to use an old term in a novel manner to designate certain powerful free persons who belonged neither to the old aristocracy nor to the peasantry. The term was *miles*, which in classical Latin meant "soldier." As it was used in the Middle Ages, we would translate it as "knight." The knightly function gradually came to entail a certain status and lifestyle.

The center of the knightly lifestyle was northern France. From there the ideals of knighthood, or **chivalry**, spread out across Europe, influencing aristocrats as far east as Byzantium. The essence of this lifestyle was fighting. Through warfare this aristocracy had maintained or acquired its freedom, and through warfare it justified its privileges.

The origins of this small elite (probably nowhere more than 2 percent of the population) were diverse. Many of its members were descended from the old aristocracy of the Carolingian age. Such noble families, proud of their independence and ancestry, maintained their position through complex kin networks, mutual defense pacts with other nobles, and control of castles, from which they could dominate the surrounding countryside.

Aristocratic Education. For the sons of such nobles, preparation for a life of warfare began early, often in the entourage of a maternal uncle or a powerful lord. Boys learned to ride, to handle heavy swords and shields, to manage a lance on horseback, and to swing an ax with deadly accuracy. They also learned lessons about honor, pride, and family tradition. The culmination of this education for English and French nobles came in a ceremony of knighting. An adolescent of age 16 to 18 received a sword from an older, experienced warrior. No longer a "boy," he now became a "youth," ready to enter the world of fighting for which he had trained.

A youth was a noble who had been knighted but who had not married or acquired land either through inheritance or as a reward from a lord for service and thus had not yet established his own "house." He led the life of a warrior. This was an extraordinarily dangerous lifestyle, and many youths did not survive to the next stage in a knight's life, that of acquiring land, wife, honor, and his own following of youths.

The period between childhood and maturity was as dangerous for noblewomen as for men. Marriage was the primary form of alliance between noble houses, and the production of children was essential to the continued prosperity of the family. Therefore, the daughters of the nobility were generally brought up for marriage and procreation. They were usually married at around age 16 and then were expected to produce as many children as possible. Many noblewomen died in childbirth, often literally exhausted by frequent successive births.

In this martial society, the official political and economic status of women declined considerably. Because they were considered unable to participate in warfare, in northern Europe women were also frequently excluded from inheritance, estate management, courts, and public deliberations.

Still, the most powerful women were widows who had borne sons and who could play a major part in raising them. Such women, experienced in management by years of directing the households of their husbands, well connected by

A knight receives a token from a lady in this image from a manuscript from ca. 1300 that contains the works of more than 100 German courtly love poets. The ideals of chivalry and courtly love glorified women in literature and song, but in real life the subordinate status of women reflected the values of a martial society.

kinship, and experienced in court intrigue from years of attending assemblies in the company of their husbands and sons, could often hold their own with their male counterparts. Their support and alliances were actively sought by aristocrats, kings, and churches.

Land and Loyalty. The noble lifestyle required wealth, and wealth meant land. The nobility was essentially a society of heirs who had inherited not only land but also the serfs who worked their manors. Lesser nobles acquired additional property from great nobles and from ecclesiastical institutions in return for binding contracts of mutual assistance. This tradition was at least as old as the Carolingians, who granted their followers land in return for military service. In later centuries, counts and lesser lords continued this tradition, exchanging land for support. Individual knights became **vassals** of lay or ecclesiastical magnates, swearing fealty or loyalty to the lord and promising to defend and aid him. In return, the lord swore to protect his vassal and granted him a means of support by which the vassal could maintain himself while serving his lord. Usually, this grant, termed a **fief**, was a parcel of productive land and the serfs and privileges attached to it, which the vassal and his heirs could hold as long as they provided the designated service to the lord.

Individual lords often had considerable numbers of vassals, who might also be the vassals of other lay and secular lords. The networks formed vital social and political structures. Individuals often held fiefs from, and owed service to, more than one lord, and not all of the individuals in a given county or duchy owed their primary obligation to the count or duke. Likewise, often most of a noble's land was owned outright rather than held in fief, thus making the feudal bond less central to his status. As a result, these bonds—anachronistically called **feudalism** by French lawyers of the sixteenth and seventeenth centuries—constituted just one more element of a social system tied together by kinship, regional alliances, personal bonds of fealty, and the surviving elements of Carolingian administration inherited by counts and dukes. In much of Europe, the society of the eleventh and twelfth centuries was one of intensely local autonomous powers in which public order and political authority were spread as widely as ever in European history.

The Church: Saints and Monks

Most medieval people, whether peasants or lords, lived in a world of face-to-face encounters, a world in which abstract creeds counted for little. In this world, religion meant primarily action, and the essential religious actions were the liturgical celebrations performed by the clergy. Although many of the parish priests had received only rudimentary instruction from their predecessors and had minimal knowledge of Latin and theology, such intellectual shortcomings were not important. Ordinary lay people just wanted priests who would not extort them by selling the sacraments, would not seduce their wives and daughters, and would remain in the village to perform the rituals necessary to keep the supernatural powers well disposed toward the community.

The most important of these supernatural powers was not some distant divinity but the saints—local, personal, even idiosyncratic persons. During their lives, saintly men and women had shown that they enjoyed God's special favor. After their deaths they continued to be the link between the divine and earthly spheres. Through their bodies, preserved as relics in the monasteries of Europe, they continued to live among mortals even while participating in the heavenly court. Thus they could be approached and won over through offerings, bribes, oaths, and rituals of supplication and submission. Some saints attracted national or even international pilgrimages. As the recipients of gifts to the saints, monastic communities became wealthy and powerful.

Monastic Culture. In addition to orchestrating the cult of saints, monasteries also took responsibility for the cult of the ordinary dead. In particular, monastic communities commemorated and prayed for members of noble families who, through donations of land, had become especially associated with the monastic community. Across Europe, noble families founded monasteries on their own lands or invited famous abbots to reorganize existing monasteries.

Monasteries were communities that specialized in prayer and therein found their social justification. They were also enormously rich and powerful. The monastery of Cluny, in saving souls through prayer, became the first international organization of monastic centers, with abbeys and dependent communities, called priories, throughout Europe. The abbots of Cluny were among the most powerful and influential people of the eleventh and twelfth centuries, considered to be the equals of kings, popes, and emperors. To remain in form for the strenuous liturgical commemoration of living and dead patrons, Cluniac monks largely abandoned the tradition of manual work, leaving such mundane activities to their thousands of serfs and lay agents.

Monastic Reform. The Cluniac monks' comparative luxury and concentration on liturgy to the neglect of other spiritual activities led some monastic reformers to call for a return to simplicity, separation from the rest of society, and a deeper internal spirituality. Chief among these groups were the Cistercians, who, under the dynamic leadership of Bernard of Clairvaux (1090–1153), spread their rigorous ascetic form of monasticism from England to the Vienna woods. The Cistercians built monasteries in the wilderness and discouraged the kinds of close ties with secular society that the Cluniacs had established.

The rural Church not only served the lay population but worked to transform it. Although monks and bishops were spiritual warriors, most abhorred bloodshed among Christians and sought to limit the violence of aristocratic life. This attitude combined altruistic and selfish motives, since Church property was often the focus of aristocratic greed. The decline of public power and the rise of aristocratic autonomy and violence were particularly marked in southern France. There, beginning in the tenth century, churchmen organized the Peace of God and the Truce of God, movements that attempted to protect peasants, merchants, and clerics from aristocratic violence and to limit the times when warfare was allowed. During the eleventh century, the goals of warfare were shifted from attacks against other Christians to the defense of Christian society. This redirection produced the **Crusades**, religious wars of conquest authorized by popes and directed against Europe's non-Christian neighbors.

Crusaders: Soldiers of God

The Crusades left a complex and troubling legacy in world civilization. Between 1096 and 1272, waves of zealous and adventuresome European Christians set out to do battle with the Muslims. The First Crusade originated in 1095, when Pope Urban II (1088–1099), hoping to direct noble violence away from Christendom, urged Western knights to use their arms to free the Holy Land from Muslim occupation. In return, he promised to absolve them from all of the punishment due for their sins in this life or the next. After terrible hardships, the crusaders succeeded in taking Jerusalem in 1099 and established a Latin Kingdom in Palestine. For over two centuries, bands of Western warriors went on armed pilgrimages to defend this precarious kingdom. The Second Crusade (1145–1149) ended in defeat and disaster at the hands of Seljuk Turks in Asia Minor. In 1187, the Muslim commander Saladin recaptured Jerusalem, causing Emperor Frederick Barbarossa and the kings

Religious Divisions of Europe, ca. 1096

- Latin Christianity
- Greek (Eastern) Orthodox Christianity
- Islam

0   400 Miles

0   400 Kilometers

THE CRUSADES

Examine the religious divisions of Europe and the major crusade routes. What different geographical and political obstacles did crusaders face depending on whether they traveled by land or by water? How did the divisions of Christianity and Islam affect the course of the Crusades?

of France and England, Philip II Augustus and Richard the Lion-Hearted, to embark on the Third Crusade (1187–1192). This crusade also failed, but Richard signed a peace treaty with Saladin. Five subsequent crusades accomplished little.

The Idea of the Crusades

Although military failures, the Crusades appealed particularly to younger sons and knights who hoped to acquire in the East the status that constricting lineages denied them in the West. Other such holy wars were directed against the Muslims in Spain, the Slavs in eastern Europe, and even heretics and political opponents in France and Italy.

The Crusades were brutal and vicious, but crusaders themselves were motivated by a combination of religious conviction—most knew that they would probably not survive these wars—and the hope of material gain. Doubts about the spiritual significance of such wars contributed to their decline. So, too, did the rise of centralized monarchies, whose rulers usually viewed the Crusades as wasteful and futile. The age of the Crusades passed with the age of the independent warrior aristocracy.

Medieval Towns

To the traditional rural mind, towns seemed somehow immoral. Nobles disdained urban society for its lack of respect for aristocracy and its disinterest in their cult of violence. Still, as rude warriors were transformed into courtly nobles, these nobles were drawn to urban luxuries and became indebted to urban moneylenders to maintain their "gracious" lifestyles. For many peasants, towns were refuges from the hopelessness of their normal lives.

Italian Cities

Urban life had never ceased in Italy, which had maintained its urban traditions and ties with the Mediterranean world since antiquity.

The coastal cities of Amalfi, Bari, Genoa, and especially Venice had continued to play important roles in commerce both with the Byzantines and with the new Muslim societies. With nothing of their own to trade but perhaps salt and, in Venice, glass, these cities acted as go-betweens for the transport of eastern spices, silks, and ivories, which they exchanged for Western iron, slaves, timber, grain, and oil. To protect their merchant ships, Italian coastal cities developed their own fleets, and by the eleventh century they were major military forces in the Mediterranean.

Merchants and Capitalists. As the merchants of the Italian towns penetrated the markets at the western end of the great overland spice routes connecting China, India, and central Asia with the Mediterranean, they established permanent merchant colonies in the East. When expedient, they did not hesitate to use military force to win concessions.

By the thirteenth century, Italian merchants had spread far beyond the Mediterranean. The great merchant banking houses of Venice, Florence, and Genoa had established offices around the Mediterranean and Black seas; south along the Atlantic coast of Morocco; east into Armenia and Persia; west to London, Bruges, and Ghent; and north to Scandinavia. Some individual merchants, the Venetian Marco Polo (1254–1324), for example, traded as far east as China and even entered the service of the Great Khan.

These international commercial operations required more sophisticated systems of commercial law and credit. Italian merchants responded by developing double-entry bookkeeping, limited-liability partnership, commercial insurance, and international letters of exchange. Complex commercial affairs also required a system of credit and interest-bearing loans, an idea that was abhorrent to traditional rural societies. Churchmen condemned borrowing and lending at credit, but bankers found ways of hiding interest payments in contracts, thus allowing lender and seller to participate in the growing world of credit-based transactions.

Underlying the expanding commercial developments was a basic change: a new mentality that considered commerce an honorable occupation. By the twelfth century, wealthy citizens, whether descended from successful merchants or from landed aristocrats, were indifferently termed magnates. The rest of the town's population were called *populars*. The difference between the two was essentially economic.

Communal Government. In the eleventh and early twelfth centuries, many Italian towns bought off or expelled their traditional lords such as counts and bishops, thus allowing the magnates and populars of these cities to create their own governing institutions or communes. Within many towns the magnates formed their own corporation—the society of knights—to protect their privileged position. Families of nobles and magnates, whose cultural values were similar to those of the rural aristocracy, competed with each other for honor and power. Feuds fought out between noble families and their vassals in city streets were frequent events in Italian towns.

Opposing the magnates were popular corporations—the society of the people—which sought to rein in the violent and independent-minded nobles. Each of these popular organizations, dominated by the prominent leaders of craft and trade associations, had its own elected officers and its own military, headed by a "captain of the people," who might command as many as 1,000 troops against the magnates.

To maintain civic life in spite of these conflicts, cities established complex systems of government in which officers were selected by series of elections and lotteries designed to prevent any one faction from seizing control. Sovereignty lay with the *arengo*, or assembly, which included all adult male citizens. Except in very small communes this body was too large to function efficiently, so most communes selected a series of working councils. Generally, executive authority was vested in consuls, whose numbers varied widely and who were chosen from various factions and classes. When these consuls proved unable to overcome the partisan politics of the factions, many towns turned to hiring *podestas*, nonpolitical professional city managers from outside the community. These were normally magnates from other communes who had received legal educations and who served for relatively short periods.

Northern Towns

Merchant and manufacturing towns also developed along the Baltic and North seas and the English Channel. Scandinavian fish and timber, Baltic grain, English wool, and Flemish cloth circulated by sea around Scandinavia, Lithuania, northern Germany, Flanders, and England, linking them in a common economic network.

In the eleventh century, Flanders, lacking the land for large-scale sheep grazing and facing a growing population, began to specialize in the production of high-quality cloth made from English wool. At the same time, England, which experienced an economic and population decline following the Norman Conquest, began to export the greater part of its wool to Flanders to be worked. By the late eleventh century, the production of wool cloth began to develop from a cottage

MAP DISCOVERY

MEDIEVAL TRADE NETWORKS

Examine the major trade routes of the High Middle Ages. What commodities and products were plentiful in Europe but scarce in the eastern Mediterranean? What regions were the major wool producers? The major cloth producers? How might silks from the East have arrived in London?

occupation into Europe's first major industry. Now manufacture was concentrated in towns, and men replaced women at the looms. Furthermore, production was closely regulated and controlled by a small group of extremely wealthy merchant-drapiers (cloth makers).

Concentration of capital, specialization of labor, and increase of urban population created vibrant, exciting cities that were essentially composed of three social orders. At the top were wealthy patricians, the merchant-drapiers. Through their control of raw materials, equipment, capital, and distribution the merchant-drapiers controlled the cloth trade and thus the economic and political life of the Flemish wool towns. Through their closed associations, or **guilds**, they controlled production and set standards, prices, and wages. They also controlled communal government by monopolizing urban councils.

At the bottom of urban society were the unskilled and semiskilled artisans. These poorly paid workers led an existence that was more precarious than that of most peasants.

Between the patricians and the workers stood the masters, the skilled craftsmen who controlled the day-to-day production of cloth and lesser crafts. They organized

The complex process of spinning, weaving, dying, and marketing woolen cloth gave rise to complex social and economic structures while bringing great wealth to Flemish cities. In this fifteenth-century manuscript illumination, an elite master dyer supervises the work of his laborers. The rise of the woolen industry created new urban elites as well as the first European proletarians.

into guilds to protect themselves from competition. The masters often leased their looms or other equipment from the merchant-drapiers and received from them raw materials and wages to be distributed to their workers.

The Fairs of Champagne

Tying together the northern and southern commercial worlds were the great fairs of Champagne. Six times during the year, the towns of Champagne hosted trade fairs, allowing merchants from north and south to meet, bargain, and trade under the protection of the local counts.

Northern merchants offered cloth. From Italy came merchants of great Italian trading companies to purchase northern cloth for resale throughout the Mediterranean. Southern merchants brought silks, sugar, salt, alum (a chemical that was essential in cloth manufacture), and, most important, spices to trade at the fairs.

These great international exchanges connected the financial and marketing centers of the south with the manufacturing and trading communities of the north, tying the northern world to the south more effectively than had any system since the political institutions of the Roman Empire.

Scholasticism and Urban Intellectual Life

The urban world of the twelfth and thirteenth centuries created forms of religious and cultural expression particularly suited to it. The cathedral schools shifted away from monastic education to an education aimed more at participation in the affairs of the world. Young men were taught the essential urban skills of writing, computation, and law.

The Medieval University. In the late eleventh and early twelfth centuries, the pace of urban intellectual life quickened. The combination of population growth, improved agricultural productivity, political stability, and educational interest culminated in what has been called the renaissance of the twelfth century. Bologna and Paris became the undisputed centers of the new educational movements. Bologna specialized in the study of law, while Paris became the leader in the study of liberal arts and theology. Students at Bologna organized a **universitas**, or guild of students, the first true university.

In the early twelfth century, students from across Europe flocked to Paris to study with the greatest and most original intellect of the century, Peter Abelard (1079–1142). Abelard's intellectual method combined the tools of legal analysis perfected in Bologna with Aristotelian logic and laid the foundation of what has been called the **Scholastic method**. Logical reasoning, Abelard believed, could be applied to all problems, even those concerning the mysteries of faith.

This illustration from a fourteenth-century manuscript shows Henry of Germany delivering a lecture to university students in Bologna.

The intellectual ferment Abelard began in Paris continued long after him. By 1200, education had become so important in the city that the universitas, or corporation of professors, was granted a charter by King Philip Augustus, who guaranteed its rights and immunities from the control of the city.

Students at the University of Paris began their studies at around age 14 or 15 in the faculty of arts. After approximately six years, they received a bachelor of arts degree, which was a prerequisite to enter the higher faculties of theology, medicine, or law. After additional years of reading and commenting on specific texts under the supervision of a master, they received the title of master of arts, which gave them the license to teach anywhere within Christian Europe.

The intellectual life of the universities through the thirteenth and fourteenth centuries was dominated by Aristotelian thought. The introduction of the works of Aristotle into the West between 1150 and 1250 created an intellectual crisis every bit as profound as that of the Newtonian revolution of the seventeenth century or the Einsteinian revolution of the twentieth. For centuries, Western thinkers had depended on the Christianized Neoplatonic philosophy of Origen and Augustine. Aristotle was known in the West only through his basic logical treatises, which in the twelfth century, thanks in large part to the work of Peter Abelard, had become the foundation of intellectual work. Logic, or dialectic, was seen as the universal key to knowledge, and the university system was based on its rigorous application to traditional texts of law, philosophy, and Scripture.

The Aristotelian Challenge. Beginning in the late twelfth century, Christian and Jewish scholars began translating Aristotle's treatises on natural philosophy, ethics, and metaphysics into Latin. Suddenly, Christian intellectuals who had already accepted the Aristotelian method were brought face to face with Aristotle's conclusions: a world without an active, conscious God, a world in which everything from the functioning of the mind to the nature of matter could be understood without reference to a divine creator.

As the full impact of Aristotelian philosophy began to reach churchmen and scholars, reactions varied from condemnation to whole-hearted acceptance. To many, it appeared that there were two irreconcilable kinds of truth, one knowable through divine revelation and the other through human reason.

One Parisian scholar who refused to accept the dichotomy of faith and reason was Thomas Aquinas (1225–1274), a professor of theology and the most brilliant intellect of the High Middle Ages. Aquinas refused to accept the possibility that human reason, which was a gift from God, led necessarily to contradictions with divine revelation. Properly applied, the principles of Aristotelian philosophy could not lead to error, Aquinas argued. However, human reason unaided by revelation could not always lead to certain conclusions. Questions about such matters as the nature of God, creation, and the human soul could not be resolved by reason alone. In developing his thesis, Aquinas recast Christian doctrine and philosophy, replacing their Neoplatonic foundation with an Aristotelian base. Although not universally accepted in the thirteenth century, Aquinas's synthesis came to dominate Christian intellectual life for centuries.

Preaching and Poverty. Aquinas was a member of a new religious order, the Dominicans, who along with the Franciscans appeared in response to the social and cultural needs of the new urbanized, monetized European culture. Lay persons and clerics alike were concerned with the growing wealth of ecclesiastical institutions, and across southern Europe especially, individual reformers attacked the wealthy lifestyles of monks and secular clergy as un-Christian.

Torn between their own involvement in a commercial world and an inherited Christian-Roman tradition that looked on commerce and capital as degrading, reformers called for a return to what they imagined to have been the life of the primitive Church, one that emphasized both individual and collective poverty. Although many reformers were condemned as heretics and were sporadically persecuted, the reform movement continued to grow and threatened to destroy the unity of Western Christendom.

The people who preserved the Church's unity aimed at reforming the Church from within. Francis of Assisi (1182–1226), the son of a prosperous Italian merchant, rejected his luxurious life in favor of one of radical poverty and service to others. Convinced of the importance of obedience, Francis asked Pope Innocent III to approve the way of life he had chosen for himself and his followers. The pope granted his wish, and the Order of Friars Minor, or Franciscans, grew by thousands, drawing members from as far away as England and Hungary.

An altarpiece by Bonaventura Berlinghieri depicting Saint Francis of Assisi painted less than a decade after the saint's death in 1226. The frontal position of the main figure, the way that his feet seem to float rather than to stand firmly on the ground, and the gold-leaf background all point to the Byzantine tradition of icon painting still important in Italy in the thirteenth century. Francis is shown with the stigmata—symbolic marks that represent the wounds Christ received on the cross. He is flanked by two angels, and around him are six scenes from his life. The image of Francis with the signs of Christ's passion in his hands and feet became essential elements in the depiction of this new type of saint who urged imitation of the life of Jesus, both in his poverty and in his suffering.

Francis insisted that his followers observe strict poverty, both individually and collectively. The order could not own property, nor could its members even touch money. They were expected to beg for their food as they traveled from town to town, preaching, performing manual labor, and serving the poor. Francis did not approve of women followers leading such a life but insisted that they pursue radical poverty within cloistered convents that were often within the walls of towns.

The order of friars founded by Dominic (1170–1221) also adopted a rule of strict poverty, but their primary focus was on preaching. This order emphasized intellectual activity and higher education and spoke out against heresies. Thus the Dominicans too gravitated toward the cities of western Europe and especially toward its great universities.

The Invention of the State

The disintegration of the Carolingian Empire in the tenth century left political power fragmented among a wide variety of political entities. In general, these were of two types. The first, the papacy and the empire, were elective traditional structures that claimed universal sovereignty over the Christian world, based on a sacred view of political power. The second, largely hereditary and less extravagant in their religious and political pretensions, were the limited kingdoms that arose within the old Carolingian world or on its borders.

The Universal States: Empire and Papacy

The Frankish world east of the Rhine River had been less affected than the kingdom of the West Franks by the onslaught of Vikings, Magyars, and Saracens. The eastern Frankish kingdom, a loose confederacy of five duchies—Saxony, Lorraine, Franconia, Swabia, and Bavaria—had preserved much of the Carolingian religious, cultural, and institutional traditions. In 919, Duke Henry I of Saxony (919–936) was elected king, and his son Otto I (936–973) laid the foundation for the revival of the empire. Otto inflicted a devastating defeat on the Magyars in 955. In 951, Otto invaded and conquered Lombardy. Eleven years later, he entered Rome, where he was crowned emperor by the pope.

The Medieval Empire. Otto, known to history as "the Great," established the main outlines of German imperial policy for the next 300 years. This policy included conflict with the German aristocracy, reliance on bishops and abbots as imperial agents, and preoccupation with Italy. His successors, both in his own Saxon dynasty (919–1024) and in the succeeding dynasties, the Salians (1024–1125) and the Staufens (1138–1254), continued this tradition. Magnates elected the German kings, who were then consecrated as emperors by the pope. Royal fathers were generally able to bring about the election of their sons, but magnates continued to exercise real power in royal elections. The magnates' ability to expand their own power and autonomy at the expense of their Slavic neighbors to the east also contributed to the weakness of the German monarchy.

To counter such aristocratic power, emperors looked to the Church both for the development of the religious cult of the emperor as "the Anointed of the Lord" and as a source of military and political support. Like the Carolingians, the Saxon and Salian emperors needed a purified, reformed Church that was free of local aristocratic control to serve the interests of the emperor. This imperial church was the cornerstone of the empire.

The laymen on whom the emperor could rely, particularly from the eleventh century, were trusted household serfs whom the emperors used as their agents. Despised by the freeborn nobility, they tended at first to be loyal supporters of the emperor. In the twelfth century, they adopted the chivalric ideals of their aristocratic neighbors and took advantage of conflicts between emperor and pope to acquire autonomy. As old noble families died out, ministerial families replaced them as a new hereditary aristocracy.

Otto the Great had entered Italy to secure his southern flank. His successors became embroiled in Italian affairs until, in the thirteenth century, they abandoned Germany altogether. As the emperors were drawn further into papal and Italian politics, frequently with disastrous results, Germany became merely a source of men and matériel with which to fight the Lombard towns and the pope. From the eleventh through the thirteenth centuries, emperors granted German princes autonomy in return for their support.

The Papacy. The early successes of this imperial program created the seeds of its own destruction. Imperial efforts to reform the Church resulted in a second, competing claimant to universal authority: the papacy. In the later tenth and early eleventh centuries, emperors had intervened in papal elections, deposed and replaced corrupt popes, and worked to ensure that bishops and abbots would be educated, competent churchmen. The most impressive reformer was Leo IX (1049–1054). Leo condemned simony, the practice of buying Church offices, and fostered monastic reforms such as that of Cluny. He also encouraged the efforts of a group of young reformers drawn from across Europe.

Investiture and Reform. In the next decades these new, more radical reformers began to advocate a widespread renewal of the Christian world, led not by emperors but by popes. These reformers pursued an ambitious set of goals. They sought to reform the morals of the clergy and in particular to eliminate married priests. They tried to free churches and monasteries from lay control both by forbidding lay men and women from owning churches and monasteries and by eliminating simony. They particularly condemned **lay investiture**, the practice by which kings and emperors appointed bishops and invested them with the

THE EMPIRE OF OTTO THE GREAT, CA. 963. The Ottonian Empire included not only Germany, but also Slavic lands to the east and disputed regions such as Lorraine to the west.

symbols of their office. Finally, they insisted that the pope, not the emperor, was the supreme representative of God on earth and as such had the right to exercise a universal sovereignty.

Every aspect of the reform movement met with strong opposition throughout Europe. Emperor Henry IV (1056–1106) clashed head-on with Pope Gregory VII (1073–1085) over the emperor's right to appoint and to install or invest bishops in their offices.

In the end, the conflict weakened both the empire and the papacy. In 1075, the emperor Henry IV, supported by many German bishops, attempted to depose Gregory. In return, Gregory excommunicated and deposed Henry, freed the German nobility from their obligations to him, and encouraged them to rebel. As anti-imperial strength grew, Henry took a desperate gamble. Crossing the Alps in the dead of winter in 1077, he arrived before the castle of Canossa in northern Italy, where Gregory was staying. Dressed as a humble penitent, Henry stood in the snow, asking the pope for forgiveness and reconciliation. As a priest, the pope could not refuse, and he lifted the excommunication. Once more in power, Henry resumed appointing bishops. In 1080, Gregory again excommunicated and deposed Henry, but this time the majority of the German nobles and bishops remained loyal to the emperor, and Henry marched on Rome. Deserted by most of his clergy, Gregory fled to southern Italy and died in Salerno in 1085.

Henry did not long enjoy his victory. Gregory's successors rekindled the opposition to Henry and even convinced Henry's own son to join in the revolt. The conflict ended only in 1122, when Emperor Henry V (1106–1125) and Pope Calixtus II (1119–1124) reached an agreement known as the Concordat of Worms, which differentiated between the royal and spiritual spheres of authority and allowed the emperors a limited role in episcopal election and investiture. This compromise changed the nature of royal rule in the empire, weakening the emperors and contributing to the long-term decline of royal government in Germany.

The decline that began with the investiture controversy continued as emperors abandoned political power north of the Alps to pursue their ambitions in Italy. Frederick I Barbarossa (1152–1190) gained the support of the German princes for his largely futile efforts in northern Italy by granting them extraordinary privileges. His successors continued his policy of focusing on Italy with no better success. In 1230, Frederick II (1215–1250) conceded to each German prince sovereign rights in his own territory. From the thirteenth to the nineteenth centuries, these princes ruled their territories as independent states, leaving the office of emperor a hollow title.

The investiture controversy ultimately compromised the authority of the pope as well as that of the emperor. First, the series of compromises beginning with the Concordat of Worms established the potent Western idea of separate spheres of authority for secular and religious government. Second, although in the short run popes were able to exercise enormous political influence, from the thirteenth century they were increasingly unable to make good their claims to absolute authority.

The Pinnacle of Papal Power. During the pontificate of Innocent III (1198–1216), the papacy reached the height of its power. Innocent made and deposed emperors, excommunicated kings, summoned a crusade against heretics in the south of France, and placed whole countries such as England and France under interdict, that is, the suspension of all religious services, when rulers dared to contradict him. Still, he found time to support Francis of Assisi and Dominic and, in 1215, to call the Fourth Lateran Council, which culminated the reforms of the past century.

During the thirteenth century, the papacy continued to perfect its legal system and its control over clergy throughout Europe. However, politically the popes were unable to assert their claims to universal supremacy. This was true both in Italy, where the communes in the north and the kingdom of Naples in the south resisted direct papal control, and in the emerging kingdoms north of the Alps, where monarchs successfully intervened in Church affairs. The old claims of papal authority rang increasingly hollow.

Chronology

PROMINENT POPES AND RELIGIOUS FIGURES OF THE HIGH MIDDLE AGES

1049–1054*	Pope Leo IX
1073–1085	Pope Gregory VII
1088–1099	Pope Urban II
1098–1179	Hildegard of Bingen
1119–1124	Pope Calixtus II
1170–1221	Saint Dominic
1182–1226	Saint Francis of Assisi
1198–1216	Pope Innocent III
1225–1274	Saint Thomas Aquinas
1294–1303	Pope Boniface VIII

*Dates for popes are dates of reign.

The Nation-States: France and England

The claims of kings were much more modest than those of emperors or popes. Kings laid claim to a limited territory; they were only one of many representatives of God on earth; and finally, they were far from absolute rulers. During the tenth and eleventh centuries, the powers of justice, coinage, taxation, and military command, once considered public, had been usurped by aristocrats and nobles. Kings needed the support of these magnates, and often—as in the case of France—these dukes and counts were wealthier and more powerful than the kings. Still, between the tenth and fourteenth centuries, some monarchies, especially those of France and England, developed into powerful, centralized, and vigorous kingdoms. In the process they gave birth to what has become the modern state.

France: Biology, Bureaucracy, and Sanctity. In 987, when Hugh Capet was elected king of the West Franks, no one suspected that his successors would become the most powerful rulers of Europe. The dukes of Normandy, descendants of Vikings whose settlement had been recognized by Frankish kings, ruled their duchy with an authority of which the kings could only dream. Less than a century later, Duke William of Normandy expanded his power even more by conquering England. In the twelfth century, the English kings ruled the Angevin Empire, a vast collection of hereditary lands on both sides of the English Channel. Other nobles, such as the counts of Flanders and the counts of Poitou, also seemed more impressive than the house of Hugh Capet. Nevertheless, under Hugh's successors, the kingdom of France became the most powerful monarchy in Europe and the center of European learning, architecture, and art.

The medieval French monarchy owed its creation in large part to biology and bureaucracy. Between 987 and 1314, every royal descendant of Hugh Capet (after whom the dynasty was called the Capetian) left a male heir—an extraordinary record for a medieval family. By simply outlasting the families of their great barons, the Capetian kings were able to absorb lands when other families became extinct.

The Capetians' long run of biological luck, combined with the practice of having a son crowned during his father's lifetime and thus being firmly established before his father's death, was only part of the explanation for the Capetian success. The Capetians also wisely used their position as consecrated sovereigns to build a power base in the Ile de France (the region around Paris) and among the bishops and abbots of the kingdom and then to insist on their feudal rights as the lords of the great dukes and counts of France. It was this foundation that Louis VII's son Philip II (1180–1223) used to create the French monarchy.

Philip II was known to posterity as Augustus, or the aggrandizer, because through his ruthless political intrigue and brilliant organizational sense he more than doubled the territory he controlled and more than quadrupled the revenue of the French crown. Philip's greatest coup, however, was the confiscation of all the continental possessions of the English King John (1199–1216), the son of Henry II of England and Eleanor of Aquitaine. Although John was sovereign in England, as lord of Normandy, Anjou, Maine, and Touraine, he was technically a vassal of King Philip. When John married the fiancée of one of his continental vassals, the outraged vassal appealed to Philip in his capacity as John's lord. Philip summoned

John to appear before the royal court, and when he refused to do so, Philip ordered him to surrender all of his continental fiefs. This meant war, and one by one, John's continental possessions fell to the French king.

To govern these vast regions, Philip needed an effective administrative system. Using members of families from the old royal demesne, he set up administrative officials called *baillis* and *seneschals*, nonfeudal salaried agents who collected his revenues and represented his interests. The baillis in particular, who were drawn from commoner families and often had received their education at the University of Paris, were the foundation of the French bureaucracy, which grew in strength and importance through the thirteenth century. By governing the regions of France according to local traditions but always with an eye to the king's interest, these bureaucrats did more than anyone else to create a stable, enduring political system.

Philip's grandson Louis IX (1226–1270) fine-tuned this administrative machine and, through his own piety, endowed it with the aura of sanctity. Generous, brave, and capable, Louis took seriously his obligation to provide justice for the poor and protection for the weak. The goodwill and devotion that Louis won from his subjects were a precious heritage that benefited his successors for centuries.

The growth of royal power transformed the traditional role of the aristocracy. As the power and wealth of the French kings increased, the ability of the nobles to maintain their independence decreased. Royal judges undermined lords' control over the peasantry. Royal revenues enabled kings to hire warriors rather than relying on traditional feudal levies. At the same time, the increasing expenses of the noble lifestyle forced all but the wealthiest aristocrats to look for sources of income beyond their traditional estates. Increasingly, they found this in royal service. Thus, in the thirteenth century the nobility began to lose some of its independence to the state.

England: Conquest, Accounting, and Cooperation. A very different path brought the English monarchy to a level of power similar to that of the French by the end of the thirteenth century. While France was made by a family and its bureaucracy, the kingdom that was originally forged by Alfred and his descendants was transformed by the successors of William the Conqueror.

When King Edward the Confessor (1042–1066) died, three claimants disputed the succession. Anglo-Saxon sources insist that Edward and his nobles had chosen Earl Harold Godwinson (ca. 1022–1066) over Duke William of Normandy and the Norwegian king Harold III (1045–1066). Harold of Norway and William sailed for England. Harold Godwinson defeated the Norwegian's army and killed the king, but he met his end shortly afterward on the bloody field of Hastings, and William the Conqueror secured the throne.

William's England was a small, insular kingdom that had been united by Viking raids little more than a century before. Hostile Celtic societies bordered it to the north and west. Still, it had important strengths. First, the king of the English was not simply a feudal lord, a first among equals—he was a sovereign. Second, Anglo-Saxon government had been participatory, with the freemen of each shire taking part in court sessions and sharing the responsibilities of government. Finally, the king had agents, or *reeves*, in each shire (shire reeves, or sheriffs) who were responsible for representing the king's interests, presiding over the local court, and collecting royal taxes and incomes.

This ability to raise money was the most important aspect of the English kingship for William the Conqueror and his immediate successors. England was seen primarily as a source of revenue. To tap this wealth, the Norman kings transformed rather than abolished Anglo-Saxon governmental traditions, adding Norman feudal bonds and administrative control to Anglo-Saxon kingship.

William preserved English government while replacing Anglo-Saxon officers with his continental vassals, chiefly Normans and Flemings. He rewarded his supporters with land confiscated from the defeated Anglo-Saxons, but he was careful to give out land only in fief. In contrast to continental practice, in which many lords owned vast estates outright, in England all land was held directly or indirectly by the king. Because he wanted to know the extent of his new kingdom and its wealth, William ordered a comprehensive survey of all royal rights. The recorded account, known as the Domesday Book, was the most extensive investigation of economic rights since the Merovingians abandoned the late Roman tax rolls.

William and his successors needed an efficient system of controlling England when they were away. To that end, they developed the royal court, an institution inherited from their Anglo-Saxon predecessors, into an efficient system of fiscal and administrative supervision. The most important innovation was the use of a large checkerboard, or exchequer, which functioned like a primitive computer to audit the returns of their sheriffs. Annual payments were recorded on long rolls of parchment called pipe rolls, the first continuous accounting system in Europe. These improved accounting methods produced the most efficient and prosperous royal administration in Europe.

In the first half of the twelfth century, almost two decades of warfare over the succession greatly weakened royal authority, but Henry II (1154–1189) reestablished central power by reasserting his authority over the nobility and through his legal reforms. Using his continental wealth and armies, he brought the English barons into line, destroyed private castles, and reasserted his rights to traditional royal incomes. He strengthened royal courts by expanding royal jurisdiction at the expense of Church tribunals and of the courts of feudal lords.

Henry's efforts to control the clergy led to one of the epic clashes of the investiture struggle. The archbishop of Canterbury, Thomas à Becket (ca. 1118–1170), although a personal friend of Henry, refused to accept the king's claim to jurisdiction over clergy. For six years, Becket lived in exile on the Continent and infuriated Henry by his stubborn adherence to the letter of Church law. He was allowed to return to England in 1170, but that same year he was struck down in his own cathedral by four knights eager for royal favor. The king did penance but, unlike the German emperors, ultimately preserved royal authority over the English Church.

Henry's program to assert royal courts over local and feudal ones was even more successful, laying the foundation for a system of uniform judicial procedures throughout the kingdom: the common law. Henry's legal system simplified and cut through the complex tangle of local and feudal jurisdictions concerning land law.

Henry's son John may have made the greatest contribution to the development of the English state by losing Normandy and most of his other continental lands. Loss of these territories forced English kings to concentrate on ruling England, not on their continental territories. Moreover, John's financial difficulties, brought about by his unsuccessful wars to recover his continental holdings, led him to such extremes of fiscal extortion that his barons, prelates, and the townspeople of London revolted. In June 1215, he was forced to accept the "great charter of liberties," or **Magna Carta**, a conservative feudal document demanding that he respect the rights of his vassals and of the burghers of London. The great significance of the document was its acknowledgment that the king was not above the law.

John and his weak, ineffective son Henry III (1216–1272), although ably served by royal judges, were forced by their failures to cede considerable influence to the great barons of the realm. Henry's son Edward I (1272–1307), a strong and effective king who conquered Wales, defended the remaining continental possessions against France, and expanded the common law, found that he could turn baronial involvement in government to his own advantage. By summoning his barons, bishops, and representatives of the towns and shires to participate in a "parley," or "parliament," he could raise more funds for his wars. Like similar Spanish, Hungarian, and German assemblies of the thirteenth century, these assemblies were occasions to consult, to present royal programs, and to extract extraordinary taxes for specific projects. They were also opportunities for those who were summoned to petition the king for redress of grievances. However, since the growing wealth of the towns and countryside made their financial support essential, these groups came to anticipate that they had a right to be consulted and to consent to taxation.

Through a system of royal courts and justices employing local juries and a tradition of representative parliaments, this forced self-government, coupled with an exacting system of accounting, increased the power of the English monarchy. By 1300, France, with its powerful royal bureaucracy, and England, with its courts and accountants, were the most powerful states in the West.

SUMMARY

The Countryside   Between 1000 and 1300, Europe's population almost doubled. Across much of northwestern Europe in the eleventh century, the peasantry formed a homogeneous social category loosely described as serfs. Agricultural technology gradually changed the ways that peasants worked their land and the amount of food they could produce. Changing conditions in western Europe led to a transition from serfdom to free labor. At the same time, free peasants in eastern Europe and Spain lost their freedom. The essence of the aristocratic lifestyle was fighting. In this martial society, the official political and economic status of women declined considerably. Vassals pledged loyalty to lords in exchange for land. Clergy met the religious needs of both commoners and elites. Monasteries often served the interests of aristocrats. Monastic reformers called for a more stringent separation of the clergy from secular society. The church both served the lay population and worked to transform it. The Crusades were a military failure.

Medieval Towns   Italian towns served as commercial links between East and West. Italian merchants developed sophisticated systems of commercial law and credit. In the eleventh and early twelfth centuries, many Italian towns created their own governing institutions or communes. Merchant and manufacturing towns also developed along the Baltic and North seas and the English Channel. The textile industry linked England and Flanders. Tying together the northern and southern commercial worlds were the great fairs of Champagne. The towns and cities of the twelfth and thirteenth centuries gave rise to new forms of religious and cultural expression, including the medieval university. The introduction of the works of Aristotle into the West between 1150 and 1250 created an intellectual crisis. The Franciscans and Dominicans responded to the needs of a changing Europe.

The Invention of the State   Otto I laid the foundation of the Holy Roman Empire. The policies of Otto and his successors were characterized by conflict with the German aristocracy, reliance on clergy as imperial agents, and preoccupation with Italy. The pope emerged as a challenger to the emperor for the claim of universal authority. Church reformers stressed the authority of the clergy over secular rulers. The investiture controversy pitted the papacy against the empire. The papacy reached the pinnacle of its power during the pontificate of Innocent III. Biology and bureaucracy helped the Capetians build the medieval French monarchy. The growth of royal power transformed the traditional role of the French aristocracy. The Norman kings of England transformed rather than abolished Anglo-Saxon governmental traditions. Henry II increased central power by asserting his authority over the nobility and through his legal reforms. Under Henry's son John, England lost most of its continental territories and John was forced to accept the Magna Carta. The reign of Edward I saw the emergence of the English parliament.

QUESTIONS FOR REVIEW

1. How did the different social roles of peasants, knights, and clergymen interact and complement each other?
2. In what ways did life in the urban world pose a threat to the values and priorities of aristocrats and churchmen?
3. How were the pope and the Holy Roman Emperor both dependent on each other and in conflict?
4. Why would Europe's medieval kings ultimately be more successful than the Holy Roman Emperor or the papacy in establishing strong, centralized states?

The Later Middle Ages, 1300–1500

Politics as a Family Affair

In the fourteenth and fifteenth centuries, politics centered on the ambitions of great families. Everywhere, family politics threatened the fragile institutional developments of the thirteenth century. Aristocrats competed for personal power and used public office, military command, and taxing power for private ends. What mattered was neither territorial boundaries nor political divisions but marriage alliances, kinship, and dynastic ambitions.

The Struggle for Central Europe

Five ambitious families competed for dominance in the empire: the Luxembourgs, the Wittelsbachs, the Habsburgs, the Premysls, and the house of Anjou. The protracted wars and maneuvers that these families conducted for dominance in the empire resembled nothing so much as the competition that had taken place three centuries earlier for dominance in feudal France.

Eastern Expansion. For over a century, not only great princes but also monks, adventurers, and simple peasants streamed into the kingdoms and principalities of eastern Europe. Since the early thirteenth century, the Teutonic orders had used the sword to spread Christianity along the Baltic coast. The pagan inhabitants of these regions had to choose between conversion and expulsion. When they fled, their fields were turned over to land-hungry German peasants.

By the fifteenth century, religious and secular German lords had established a new agrarian economy, modeled on western European estates, in regions that were previously unoccupied or sparsely settled by the indigenous Slavic peoples. This economy specialized in the cultivation of grain for export to the west.

Central European Kingdoms. Farther south, the Christian kingdoms of Poland, Bohemia, and Hungary beckoned different sorts of westerners. Newly opened silver and copper mines in Bohemia, Silesia, southern Poland, and Hungarian Transylvania needed skilled miners, smelters, and artisans. Many were recruited from the overpopulated regions of western Germany.

The wealth of eastern Europe, its abundant land, and its relative freedom attracted both peasants and merchants. The promise of profitable marriages with eastern royalty drew ambitious aristocrats. Continually menaced by one another and by the aggressive German aristocracy to the west, the royal families of Poland, Hungary, and Bohemia were eager to make marriage alliances with powerful aristocratic families from farther afield. Nobles of the eastern European kingdoms were pleased to confirm the election of such outsiders. The elections prevented powerful German nobles from claiming succession to the Bohemian, Hungarian, and Polish thrones. At the same time, the families of the western European aristocracy did not have sufficiently strong local power bases to challenge the autonomy of the eastern nobility.

Charles IV (1347–1378) was typical of these restless dynasts. His grandfather, Emperor Henry VII (1308–1313), had arranged for his son John of Luxembourg to marry Elizabeth (d. 1330), the Premysl heiress of Bohemia, and thus acquire the Bohemian crown in 1310. By mastering the intricate politics of the decaying Holy Roman Empire, John arranged the deposition of the Wittelsbach emperor Louis IV (1314–1347) and secured the election of Charles as king of the Romans, that is, heir of the empire, in 1346. The following year the Bohemian crown passed to Charles.

As king of Bohemia, Charles worked to make Prague a cultural center by combining French and Czech traditions. He imported artisans, architects, and artists to transform and beautify his capital. In 1348, he founded a university in Prague, the first in the empire, modeled on the University of Paris. Keenly interested in history, Charles provided court historians with the sources necessary to write their histories of the Bohemian kingdom.

MAP DISCOVERY

CENTRAL AND EASTERN EUROPE, CA. 1378

Examine this complex map of rival dynasties in fourteenth-century Europe. How do you explain the discontinuous territorial holdings of these great competing families? To what extent could the regions of the Holy Roman Empire be considered a state in 1378? Based on the text discussion, where might the Habsburgs be expected to extend and consolidate their power in the east?

The effects of Charles's cultural policies were far-reaching—but in directions he never anticipated. His interests in Czech culture and religious reform bore unexpected fruit during the reign of his son Sigismund, king of Germany (1410–1437), Bohemia (1419–1437), and Hungary (1387–1437) and Holy Roman Emperor (1433–1437). During Sigismund's reign, Czech religious and political reformers came into open conflict with the powerful German-speaking minority at the University of Prague. Led by the theologian Jan Hus (ca. 1372–1415), this reform movement ultimately challenged the authority of the Roman Church and became the direct predecessor of the great Reformation of the sixteenth century.

Even while building up his beloved city of Prague, Charles was dismantling the Holy Roman Empire. In 1356, he issued the **Golden Bull**, an edict that officially recognized what had long been the reality, namely, that the various German princes and kings were autonomous rulers. The bull also established the procedure by which future emperors would be elected. Thereafter, the emperor was chosen by seven great princes of the empire without the consultation or interference of

GENEALOGY
THE FRENCH AND ENGLISH SUCCESSIONS

The French Succession   The English Succession

Charles of Valois

Philip IV, the Fair
1285–1314

Edward I
1272–1307

Philip VI
1328–1350

Louis X
1314–1316

Philip V
1316–1322

Charles IV
1322–1328

Isabella   *m.*   Edward II
1307–1327

John II
1350–1364

Edward III
1327–1377

Charles V, the Wise
1364–1380

Edward
The Black Prince

John of Gaunt
Duke of Lancaster

Edmund
Duke of York

Charles VI, the Mad
1380–1422

Richard II
1377–1399

Henry IV
1399–1413

Charles VII
1422–1461

Henry V
1413–1422

Henry VI
1422–1461

the pope. The procedure made disputed elections less likely, but it acknowledged that the office itself was less significant.

The same process that sapped the power of the emperor also reduced the significance of the princes. The empire fragmented into a number of large kingdoms, duchies, free towns, and sovereign bishoprics in the west. The inhabitants of these territories, often ruled by foreigners who had inherited sovereign powers through marriage, organized themselves into estates—political units of knights, burghers, and clergy—to present a united front in dealing with their prince. The princes, in turn, did not enjoy any universally recognized right to rule and were forced to negotiate with their estates for any powers they actually enjoyed.

A Hundred Years of War

The political map of western Europe was no less a patchwork quilt of family holdings than was the empire. In the Iberian Peninsula, power struggles and futile wars engaged the three Christian monarchies of Castile, Aragon, and Portugal. Only with the marriage of Ferdinand of Aragon and Isabella of Castile in 1469 did something like a unified Spain begin to emerge from this world of family rivalries.

Similar struggles threatened to overwhelm the feudal monarchies of France and England in the fourteenth and fifteenth centuries. In both kingdoms, weakening economic climates and demographic catastrophe exacerbated dynastic crises and fierce competition.

Three long-simmering disputes triggered the series of campaigns collectively termed the **Hundred Years' War**. The first issue was conflicting rights in Gascony in southern France. Since the mid-thirteenth century, the kings of England had held Gascony as a fief of the French king. Neither monarchy was content with this arrangement, and for the next 75 years, kings quarreled constantly over sovereignty in the region.

The second point of contention was the close relationship between England and the Flemish cloth towns, which were the primary customers for English wool. Early in the fourteenth century, Flemish artisans rose up in a series of bloody revolts against the aristocratic cloth dealers who had long monopolized power. The count of Flanders and the French king supported the wealthy merchants; the English sided with the artisans.

The third dispute concerned the royal succession in France. Charles IV (1322–1328), the son of Philip IV, the Fair, died without an heir. The closest descendant of a French king was the grandson of Philip the Fair, King Edward III of England (1327–1377). However, Edward was the son of Philip's daughter Isabella. The French aristocracy, which did not want an English king to inherit the throne and unite the two kingdoms, pretended that according to ancient Frankish law, the crown could not pass through a woman. Instead, they preferred to give the crown to a cousin of the late king, Philip VI (1328–1350), who became the first of the Valois kings of France. At first, the English voiced no objection to Philip's accession, but in 1337, when the dispute over Gascony again flared up and Philip attempted to confiscate the region from his English "vassal" Edward III, the English king declared war on Philip. Edward's stated goal was not only to recover Gascony but also to claim the crown of his maternal grandfather.

Chivalry and Warfare. Though territorial and dynastic rivalries were the triggers that set off the war, its deeper cause was chivalry. The elites of Europe were both inspired by and trapped in a code of conduct that required them not only to maintain their honor by violence but also to cultivate violence to increase that honor. For a ruler like Edward, obsessed with knightly glory, war with France was the ideal way to win honor and fame.

In spite of his chivalric ideals, Edward was practical when it came to organizing and financing his campaigns. Philip shared Edward's ideals but lacked his rival's practicality and self-assurance. Philip surrounded himself with aristocratic advisers who formed the most brilliant court of Europe, dispensing the royal treasure to his favorites, and dreaming of leading a great crusade to free the Holy Land. However, as the first French king in centuries who was elected rather than born into the right of succession, he treated the magnates from whose ranks he had come with excessive deference. He hesitated to press them for funds and deferred to them on matters of policy even while missing opportunities to raise other revenue from towns and merchants. Finally, although a competent warrior, Philip was no match in strategy or tactics for his English cousin.

Still, the sheer size and wealth of France should have made it the favorite in any war with England. Its population of roughly 16 million made it by far the largest and most densely populated kingdom in Europe. It was a major producer of cereal, wines, and cloth. The Flemish cloth towns, subdued by Philip in 1328, were the most industrialized area of Europe. England, by contrast, was a small, sparsely populated kingdom of under 5 million, and its economy was much less tied into international trade.

At the start of the war, Philip could rely on an income roughly three to five times greater than that of Edward. His greater income was matched by greater expenses, however, and he had no easy way to raise extraordinary funds for war. In contrast, the English king could use Parliament as an efficient source of war subsidies. Edward could also extract great sums from taxes on England's wool exports.

War was expensive. In spite of chivalrous ideals, nobles no longer fought as vassals of the king but as highly paid mercenaries. The nature of this service differed greatly on the two sides of the Channel. In France, the tactics and personnel had changed little since the twelfth century. The core of any army was the body of heavily armored nobles who rode into battle with their lords, supported by lightly armored knights. Behind them marched infantrymen recruited from towns and armed with pikes. Although the French also hired mercenary Italian crossbowmen, the nobles despised them and never used them effectively.

In contrast, centuries of fighting against Welsh and Scottish enemies had sharpened the English armies and their tactics. The great nobles continued to serve as heavily armored horsemen, but professional companies of foot soldiers raised by individual knights made up the bulk of the army. These professional companies consisted largely of pikemen and, most important, longbowmen. Although it was not as accurate as the crossbow, the English longbow had a greater range. Moreover, when massed archers fired volleys of arrows into enemy ranks, they proved extremely effective against enemy pikemen and even lightly armored cavalry.

English Successes. The first real test of the two armies came at the Battle of Crécy in 1346. When an overwhelmingly superior French force advanced against the English army, the English massed their archers on a hill and rained arrows down on the French cavalry, which attacked in a glorious but suicidal manner. The English victory was total. Strangely enough, the French learned nothing from the debacle. In 1356, Philip's successor John II (1350–1364) rashly attacked an English army at Poitiers and was captured. In 1415, the French blundered in a different way at Agincourt. This time, most of the heavily armored French knights dismounted and attempted to charge the elevated English position across a muddy field. Barely able to walk and unable to rise if they fell, all were captured. Out of fear that his numerically inferior army would be overwhelmed if the French recovered their breath, the English king ordered over 1,500 French nobles and 3,000 ordinary soldiers killed. English losses were fewer than 100.

Pitched battles were not the worst defeats for the French. More devastating were the constant raiding and systematic destruction of the French countryside by the English companies.

Raiding and pillaging continued for decades, even during long truces between the French and English kings. The French kings were powerless to prevent such destruction, just as they were unable to defeat the enemy in open battle. Since the kings were incapable of protecting their subjects or winning in battle, the "silken thread binding together the kingdom of France," as one observer put it, began to unravel, and the kingdom that had been so painstakingly constructed by the Capetian monarchs began to fall apart. Not only did the English make significant territorial conquests, but the French nobles began behaving much like those in the Holy Roman Empire, carving out autonomous lordships. Whole regions of the kingdom slipped entirely from royal authority. Duke Philip the Good of Burgundy (1396–1467) allied himself with England against France and profited from the war to form a far-flung lordship that included Flanders, Brabant, Luxembourg, and Hainaut. By the time of his death, he was the most powerful ruler in Europe. Much of the so-called Hundred Years' War was actually a French civil war.

During this century of war, the French economy suffered even more than the French state. Trade routes were broken, and commerce declined as credit disappeared. Politically and economically, France seemed doomed.

The battle of Agincourt (1415) was one of the great battles of the Hundred Years' War. The heavily armored French cavalry met defeat at the hands of a much smaller force of disciplined English pikemen and longbowmen.

Joan of Arc and the Salvation of France. Salvation came at the hands of a simple peasant girl from the county of Champagne. By 1429, the English and their Burgundian allies held virtually all of northern France, including Paris. Now they were besieging Orléans, the key to the south. The heir to the French throne, the dauphin, was the weak-willed and uncrowned Charles VII (1422–1461). To him came Joan of Arc (1412–1431), an illiterate but deeply religious girl who bore an incredible message of hope. She claimed to have heard the voices of saints ordering her to save Orléans and have the dauphin crowned according to tradition at Reims.

Eventually convinced of her sincerity, if not of her ability, Charles allowed her to accompany a relief force to Orléans. The French army, its spirit buoyed by the belief that Joan's simple faith was the work of God, defeated the English and ended the siege. This victory led to others, and on 16 July 1429, Charles was crowned king at Reims.

After the coronation, Joan's luck began to fade. She failed to take Paris, and in 1431 she was captured by the Burgundians, who sold her to the English. Eager to get rid of the troublesome girl, the English had her tried as a heretic. Charles made no move to save her, even though she had saved his kingdom. She was burned at the stake in Rouen on 30 May 1431.

Despite Joan's inglorious end, the tide had turned. The French pushed the English back toward the coast. In the final major battle of the war, fought at Formigny in 1450, the French used a new and telling weapon to defeat the English: gunpowder. Rather than charging the English directly, as they had done so often before, they mounted cannon and pounded the English to bits. Gunpowder completed the destruction of the chivalric traditions of warfare begun by archers and pikemen. By 1452, English continental holdings had been reduced to the town of Calais. The continental warfare of more than a century was over.

The English Wars of the Roses. Though war on the Continent had ended, warfare in England was just beginning. In some ways, the English monarchy had suffered even more from the Hundred Years' War than had the French. At the outset, English royal administration had been more advanced than that of the French. The system of royal agents, courts, and parliaments had created the expectation that the king could preserve peace and provide justice at home while waging successful and profitable wars abroad. As the decades dragged on without a decisive victory, the king came to rely on the aristocracy, enlisting its financial assistance by granting these magnates greater power at home.

War created powerful and autonomous aristocratic families with their own armies. Under a series of weak kings these families fought among themselves. Ultimately, they took sides in a civil war to determine the royal succession. For 30 years, from 1455 to 1485, supporters of the house of York, whose badge was the white rose, fought the rival house of Lancaster, whose symbol was the red rose. The English Wars of the Roses, as the conflict came to be called, finally ended in 1485, when Henry Tudor of the Lancastrian faction defeated his opponents. He inaugurated a new era as Henry VII (1485–1509), the first king of the Tudor dynasty.

Life and Death in the Later Middle Ages

By the end of the thirteenth century, population growth in the West had strained available resources to the breaking point. All arable land was under cultivation, and even marginal moorland, rocky mountainsides, and plains were being pressed into service to feed a growing population. At the same time, kings and nobles demanded ever-higher taxes and rents to finance their wars and extravagant lifestyles. The result was a precarious balance in which a late frost, a bad harvest, or hungry mercenaries could mean disaster. Population began to decline slowly around 1300, and the downturn became catastrophic within 50 years. Between 1300 and 1450, Europe's population fell by more than 30 percent. It did not recover until the seventeenth century.

Dancing with Death

Between 1315 and 1317, the first great famine of the fourteenth century, triggered by crop failures and war, struck Europe. People died by the thousands. Urban workers, because they were chronically undernourished, were particularly hard hit. Although this was the greatest famine in medieval memory, it was not the last. Disease accompanied famine. Crowded and filthy towns, opposing armies with their massed troops, and overpopulated countrysides provided fertile ground for the spread of infectious disease. Moreover, the greatly expanded trade routes of the thirteenth and fourteenth centuries, which carried goods and grain between East and West, also provided highways for deadly microbes.

Between 1347 and 1352, from one-third to one-half of Europe's population died from a virulent combination of bubonic, septicemic, and pneumonic plagues, known to history as the **Black Death**. The disease, carried by the fleas of infected rats, traveled the caravan routes from central Asia. It arrived in Messina, Sicily, aboard a merchant vessel in October 1347. From there the Black Death spread up the boot of Italy and then into southern France, England, and Spain. By 1349, it had reached northern Germany, Portugal, and Ireland. The following year the Low Countries, Scotland, Scandinavia, and Russia fell victim.

Plague was all the more terrifying because its cause, its manner of transmission, and its cure were totally unknown until the end of the nineteenth century. Preachers saw the plague as divine punishment for sin. Ordinary people frequently accused Jews of causing it by poisoning drinking water. The medical faculty of Paris announced that it was the result of the conjunction of the planets Saturn, Jupiter, and Mars, which caused a corruption of the surrounding air.

Responses to the plague were equally varied. In many German towns, terrified Christian citizens looked for outside scapegoats and slaughtered the Jewish community. Cities, aware of the risk of infection although ignorant of its process, closed their gates and turned away outsiders. Individuals with means fled to country houses or locked themselves in their homes to avoid contact with others. Nothing worked. As devastating as the first outbreak of the plague was, its aftershocks were even more catastrophic. Once established in Europe, the disease continued to return roughly once each generation. The last outbreak of the plague in Europe was the 1771 epidemic in Moscow that killed 60,000.

Although no solid statistics exist from the fourteenth century, the plague certainly killed more people than all of the wars and famines of the century. It was the greatest disaster ever to befall Europe. The Black Death touched every aspect of life, hastening a process of social, economic, and cultural transformation that was already under way. The initial outbreak shattered social and economic structures. Fields were abandoned, workplaces stood idle, international trade was suspended. Traditional bonds of kinship, village, and even religion were broken by the horrors of death, flight, and failed expectations.

MAP DISCOVERY

Spread of the Black Death

- 1346
- 1347
- 1348
- 1349
- 1350
- 1351 and later

← General route of the Black Death

✷ ┈┈ Revolts

0 — 500 Miles
0 — 500 Kilometers

North Sea
Stockholm
Moscow
Baltic Sea
Peasant's Rebellion 1381
London
Lübeck
Gdansk
Jacquerie 1358
Cologne
Brunswick
Peasant's Revolt 1524-1525
Kiev
Paris
Prague
Krakow
From Central Asia
Upper Austria 1626
Bordeaux
Lyon
Venice
Genoa
Catalonia 1395
Marseille
Corsica
Clompi Revolt (Florence) 1378
Caffa
Barcelona
Black Sea
Valencia
Rome
Constantinople
Seville
Naples
Sardinia
Sicily
Tunis
Messina
Mediterranean Sea
Alexandria
Cairo

SPREAD OF THE BLACK DEATH AND PEASANT REVOLTS

How closely did the spread of the Black Death follow the medieval trade networks shown in the map on p. 210? What was the general direction and average annual speed of the disease's spread? Was the Black Death only a disaster to western Europe? Note the locations of peasant revolts. Based on the chapter discussion, what similarities and differences existed among the groups that revolted in the later Middle Ages? Was there a relationship between the devastation of the plague and the outbreak of revolts?

A page from the fourteenth-century psalter and prayer book of Bonne of Luxembourg, duchess of Normandy. The three figures of the dead shown here contrast with three living figures on the facing page of the psalter to illustrate a moral fable.

Across Europe, moralists reported a general lapse in traditional ethics, a breakdown in the moral codes. The most troubling aspect of this breakdown was what one defender of the old order termed "the plague of insurrection" that spread across Europe. This plague was brought on by the dimming of the hopes held by the survivors of the Black Death.

The Plague of Insurrection

Initially, even this darkest cloud had a silver lining. Lucky survivors of the plague soon found other reasons to rejoice. Property owners, when they finished burying their dead, discovered that they were far richer in land and goods. At the other end of the social spectrum, the plague had eliminated the labor surplus. Peasants were suddenly in great demand. For a time, at least, they were able to negotiate substantially higher wages and an improved relationship with landlords.

These hopes were short lived. The rise in expectations produced by the redistribution of wealth and the labor shortage created new tensions. Landlords sought laws forcing peasants to accept pre-plague wages and tightened their control over serfs to prevent them from fleeing to cities or other lords. At the same time, governments attempted to benefit from laborers' greater prosperity by imposing new taxes. In cities, where the plague had been particularly devastating, the demographic decline sharply lowered demand for goods and thus lowered the need for manufacturing and production of all kinds. Like rural landowners, master craftsmen sought legislation to protect their incomes. New laws reduced production by restricting access to trades and increased masters' control over the surviving urban laborers. Social mobility, once a characteristic of urban life, slowed to a halt. Membership in guilds became hereditary, and young apprentices and journeymen had little hope of ever rising to the level of independent master craftsmen.

These new tensions led to violence when kings added their demands for new war taxes to the landlords' and masters' attempts to erase the peasants' and workers' recent gains. The first revolts took place in France, where peasants and townspeople, disgusted with the incompetence of the nobility in their conduct of the war against England, feared that their new wealth would be stolen from them by corrupt and incompetent aristocrats.

The Jacquerie. In 1358, to ransom King John II from the English, the French government attempted to increase taxes on the peasantry. At the same time, local nobles increased their rents and demands. Peasants in the area of Beauvais, north of Paris, fearing that they would lose their modest gains of the previous ten years, rebelled against their landlords. The revolt—known as the **Jacquerie** for the archetypical French peasant, Jacques Bonnehomme—was a spontaneous outburst directed against the nobility, whom the peasants saw as responsible for all their ills. Without real leadership or program, peasants attacked as many nobles as they could find, killing men, women, and children and burning their homes and castles. Because the Church largely supported the power structure, the uprising was also strongly anticlerical. Churches were burned, and priests were killed. Success bred further attacks, and the disorganized army of peasants began to march south toward Paris, killing, looting, and burning everything associated with the despised nobility.

In the midst of this peasant revolt, Etienne Marcel (ca. 1316–1358), a wealthy Parisian cloth merchant, led an uprising of Parisian merchants, which sought to take control of royal finances and force fiscal reforms on the dauphin, the future Charles V. Although initially the rebels were primarily members of the merchant and guild elite, Marcel soon enlisted the support of the radical townspeople against the aristocracy. He even made overtures to the leaders of the Jacquerie to join forces. For a brief time it appeared that the aristocratic order in France might succumb. However, in the end, peasant and merchant rebels were no match for professional armies. The Jacquerie met its end at Meaux, outside Paris, where an aristocratic force cut the peasants to pieces. Survivors were systematically hunted down and hanged or burned alive. The Parisian revolt met a similar fate. Aristocratic armies surrounded the city and cut off its food supply. Marcel was assassinated, and the dauphin Charles regained the city.

The English Peasants' Revolt and Urban Uprisings. The French revolts set the pattern for similar uprisings across Europe. Rebels were usually relatively prosperous peasants or townspeople whose economic situations were threatened by aristocratic attempts to turn back the clock to the period before the Black Death. For example, in 1381, English peasants, reacting to new and hated taxes, rose in a less violent but more coordinated revolt known as the Great Rebellion. These outbursts indicated not necessarily the desperation of Europe's peasantry, but the new belief that they could change their lives for the better through united action.

Urban artisans imitated the example of their rural cousins. The town rebels were generally independent artisans and small tradesmen who wanted to break the control of the powerful guilds. In spite of the brutal suppression and ultimate failure of popular revolts, they became permanent if intermittent features on the European social landscape.

Living and Dying in Medieval Towns

Population decline, war, and class conflict in France and the Low Countries fatally weakened the vitality of the commercial and manufacturing system of northwestern Europe. These same events reduced the market for Italian goods and undermined the economic strength of the great Italian cities. Events outside of Europe also led to the decline of Italian economic power. In the course of the fourteenth and fifteenth centuries, the Mongol Khanates gradually lost power or were absorbed into local traditions. The disintegration of the Mongol Empire and the rise of new, aggressive kingdoms caused disruptions of the Silk Route and Italian trade with China and India. Soon, Europeans would begin to look for alternative routes to the east.

Economic Shifts. The setbacks of the Italians worked to the advantage of German towns in the disintegrating empire. Along the Baltic Sea, in Scandinavia, and in northern Germany, towns such as Lübeck, Lüneburg, Visby, Bremen, and Cologne formed a commercial and political alliance to control northern trade. During the second half of the fourteenth century this **Hanseatic League**—the word *hansa* means "company"—monopolized the northern grain trade and forced Denmark to grant its members exclusive rights to export Scandinavian fish throughout Europe. Hanseatic merchants established colonies from Novgorod to London to Bruges and even Venice. They carried dried and salted fish to Prague and supplied grain from Riga to England and France.

English towns also profited from the decline of Flanders and France. The population decline of the fourteenth century led many English landowners to switch from traditional farming to sheep raising, since pasturing sheep required few workers and promised cash profits. While surviving peasants were driven off the land and forced to beg for a living, lords produced more wool than ever before. However, instead of exporting the wool to Flanders to be made into cloth, the English began to make cloth themselves. Protected by high tariffs on imports and low duties on exports, England had become a major exporter of finished cloth by the middle of the fifteenth century.

Addressing Poverty and Crime. The combination of economic depression, plague, and rural crisis deepened the misery of the growing population of urban poor. Medieval towns responded by developing new means of public assistance and social control.

Traditionally, charity, whether by individuals or organizations, had been a religious act that focused more on the soul of the giver than on the life of the recipient. Hospitals, for example, were all-purpose religious institutions providing lodging for pilgrims, the elderly, and the ill. By the fourteenth century, such pious institutions had become inadequate to deal with the increasing numbers of poor and ill. Towns began to assume control over a centralized system of public assistance. Although men and women who had taken religious vows staffed these institutions, city governments contributed to their budgets and oversaw their finances. Cities also attempted to rationalize the distribution of charity according to need and merit. Antwerp, for example, established a centralized relief service, which distributed badges to those deemed worthy of public assistance. Only people who wore the badges could receive food.

Breaking on the wheel was a particularly gruesome punishment inflicted on condemned criminals during the later Middle Ages. The criminal's broken limbs are threaded through the spokes of the wheel and tied with ropes. The mocking executioner holding leftover rope stands at the right. To the left are three seemingly sympathetic spectators.

One consequence of poverty was increased crime, which led to repressive measures and harsh punishments. During the later Middle Ages, gruesome forms of mutilation and execution became common for a long list of offenses. Petty larceny was punished with whipping, cutting off ears or thumbs, branding, or expulsion. In some towns, robbery of an amount over three pence was punished with death. Death by hanging might be replaced by more savage punishments. Drowning, boiling, burning, and burial alive, a particularly common punishment for women, were frequently used methods of execution. The frequency of such punishments increased with their severity.

THE LATER MIDDLE AGES, 1300–1500

240

The Spirit of the Later Middle Ages

In spite of the constant presence of death, Europeans of the later Middle Ages celebrated life with vigor, creativity, and a growing sense of individuality and independence. During the fourteenth century, the Church failed to provide unified leadership. The institutional division of the Church was paralleled by divisions over how to lead the proper Christian life. Many devout Christians developed independent lifestyles that were intended to bring them closer to God without reliance on the Church hierarchy. Some elaborated beliefs that the church branded as heresy. Others called into question the philosophical bases of theological speculation that had developed since the time of Abelard and Aquinas. Finally, the increasing pluralism of European culture gave rise to new literary traditions that both celebrated and criticized the medieval legacy of Christianity, chivalry, and social order.

The Crisis of the Papacy

In 1305, the College of Cardinals elected as pope the bishop of Bordeaux. The new pope, who took the name Clement V (1305–1314), was close to Philip IV of France. Clement took up residence not in Rome but in the papal city of Avignon on the east bank of the Rhone River. Technically, Avignon was a papal estate within the Holy Roman Empire. Actually, with France just across the river, the pope at Avignon was under French control.

The Avignon Papacy. For the next 70 years, French popes and French cardinals ruled the Church. The traditional enemies of France as well as religious reformers who expected leadership from the papacy looked on this situation with disgust.

The popes of Avignon were more successful in achieving their financial goals than in winning political power. Although they attempted to follow an independent course in international affairs, their French orientation eroded their influence in European politics, especially in the Holy Roman Empire.

Frustrated politically, the Avignon popes concentrated on perfecting the legal and fiscal system of the Church and were enormously successful in concentrating the vast financial and legal power of the Church in the papal office. From the papal court, or *curia*, they created a vast and efficient central bureaucracy whose primary role was to increase papal revenues.

Revenues came from two main sources. The less lucrative but ultimately more critical source was the sale of **indulgences**. The Church claimed that the purchase of a papal indulgence could reduce the buyer's time in purgatory or be used to assist the souls of family members already in purgatory. Papal "pardoners" working on commission used high-pressure sales pitches to sell indulgences across Europe.

The second and major source of papal income was the sale of Church offices, or *benefices*. Popes claimed the right to appoint bishops and abbots to all benefices and to collect a hefty tax for the appointment. Papal appointees often acquired numerous offices and viewed them merely as sources of income, leaving pastoral duties, when they were performed at all, to hired local clergy.

The Great Schism. In 1377, Pope Gregory XI (1370–1378) returned from Avignon to Rome but died almost immediately on arrival. Thousands of Italians, afraid that the cardinals would elect another Frenchman, surrounded the church where they were meeting and demanded an Italian pope. The terrified cardinals elected an Italian, who took the name Urban VI (1378–1389). Once elected, Urban attempted to reform the curia, but he did so in a most undiplomatic way, insulting the cardinals and threatening to appoint enough non-French bishops to their number to end French control of the curia. The cardinals soon left Rome and announced that because the election had been made under duress, it was invalid and Urban should resign. When he refused, they held a second election and chose a Frenchman, Clement VII (1378–1394), who took up residence in Avignon. The Church now had two heads, both with reasonable claims to the office.

The chaos created by this so-called **Great Schism** divided Western Christendom. In every diocese, when a bishop died, his successor had to be appointed by the pope. But by which pope? To whom did taxes go? Who received the income from the sale of indulgences or benefices? Did appeals in the Church courts go to Rome or to Avignon? More significantly, since each pope excommunicated the supporters of his opponent, everyone in the West was under a sentence of excommunication. Could anyone be saved?

Nothing in Church law or tradition offered a solution to this crisis. Nor did unilateral efforts to settle the crisis succeed. France twice invaded Italy in an attempt to eliminate Urban but failed both times. When Urban and Clement died, cardinals on both sides elected successors. By the end of the fourteenth century, France and the empire were exasperated with their popes, and even the cardinals were determined to end the stalemate.

Conciliarism. Church lawyers argued that only a general council could end the schism. Both popes opposed **conciliarism** because it suggested that an assembly of the Church rather than the pope held supreme authority. However, in 1408, cardinals from both sides summoned a council in the Italian city of Pisa. The council deposed both rivals and elected a new pope. But this solution only made matters worse, since neither pope accepted the council's decision. Europe now had to contend with not two but three popes, each claiming to be the true successor of Saint Peter.

Six years later, the Council of Constance managed a final solution. There, under the patronage of the emperor-elect Sigismund (1410–1437), cardinals, bishops, abbots, and theologians from across Europe met to resolve the crisis. Their goal was not only to settle the schism but also to reform the Church to prevent a recurrence of such a scandal. The participants at Constance hoped to restructure the Church as a limited monarchy in which the powers of the pope would be controlled through frequent councils. The Pisan and Avignon popes were deposed. The Roman pope, abandoned by all of his supporters, abdicated. Before doing so, however, he formally convoked the council to preserve the tradition that a general council had to be called by the pope. Finally, the council elected as pope an Italian cardinal who was not aligned with any of the claimants. The election of the cardinal, who took the name of Martin V (1417–1431), ended the schism.

The relief at the end of the Great Schism could not hide the very real problems left by over a century of papal weakness. The prestige of the papacy had been permanently compromised. Everywhere, the Church had become more national in character. The conciliarist demand for control of the Church, which had ended the schism, lessened the power of the pope. Moreover, during the century between Boniface VIII and Martin V, new religious movements had taken root across Europe, movements that the political creatures who had occupied the papal office could neither understand nor control. The disintegration of the Church loomed ever closer as pious individuals turned away from the organized Church and sought divine help in personal piety, mysticism, or even magic.

Discerning the Spirit of God

When Joan of Arc first appeared before the dauphin in 1429, he feared that she was a witch. Only a physical examination by matrons, which determined that she was a virgin, persuaded him otherwise—witches were believed to have had intercourse with the devil. Everyone in the late Middle Ages was familiar with witches, saints, and heretics. Distinguishing among them was often a matter of perspective.

Witchcraft. Accusations of witchcraft were relatively rare in the Middle Ages. The age of witch hunts occurred later, in the sixteenth and seventeenth centuries. During the Middle Ages, magic was believed to exist in a wide variety of forms, but its definition was fluid, and its practitioners were not always considered evil. Only at the end of the fifteenth century, with the publication of the *Witches' Hammer*, a handbook for inquisitors, did the European witch craze begin in earnest. Earlier, authorities feared more those people who sought their own pacts not with the devil but with God.

Lay Piety. Even as Europeans were losing respect for the institutional Church, people everywhere were seeking closer and more intimate relationships with God.

Distrusting the formal institutions of the Church, lay persons and clerics turned to private devotions and to mysticism to achieve union with the divine.

In the fourteenth and fifteenth centuries, a great many pious lay men and women chose to live together to strive for spiritual perfection without entering established religious orders. The Brethren of the Common Life in the Rhineland and Low Countries dedicated themselves to preaching, charity, and a pious life.

Christians of the later Middle Ages sought to imitate Christ and venerated the Eucharist, or communion wafer, which the Church taught was the actual body of Jesus. Male mystics focused on imitating Jesus in his poverty, his suffering, and his humility. Women developed their own form of piety, which focused not on wealth and power but on spiritual nourishment, particularly as provided by the Eucharist. For women mystics, radical fasting became preparation for the reception of the Eucharist, which was often described in highly emotional and erotic terms.

Heresy and Revolt

Only a thin line separated the saint's heroic search for union with God from the heretic's identification with God. Members of the sect were hunted down, and many were burned as heretics. The specter of the Inquisition, the ecclesiastical court system that was charged with ferreting out heretics, hung over all such communities.

John Wycliffe. When unorthodox Christians were protected by secular lords, the ecclesiastical courts were powerless. This was the case with John Wycliffe (ca. 1330–1384), an Oxford theologian who attacked the doctrinal and political bases of the Church. He taught that the value of the sacraments depended on the worthiness of the priest administering them, that Jesus was present in the Eucharist only in spirit, that indulgences were useless, and that salvation depended on divine predestination rather than individual merit. Normally, these teachings would have led him to the stake. But he had also attacked the Church's right to wealth and luxury, an idea whose political implications pleased the English monarchy and nobility. Only under Henry V (1413–1422) were Wycliffe's followers, known as Lollards, vigorously suppressed by the state. Before this condemnation took place, however, Wycliffe's teachings reached the kingdom of Bohemia through the marriage of Charles IV's daughter Anne of Bohemia to the English king Richard II. Anne took with her to England a number of Bohemian clerics, some of whom studied at Oxford and absorbed Wycliffe's political and religious teachings, which they then took back to Bohemia.

Jan Hus. In Prague, some of Wycliffe's less radical teachings took root among the theology faculty of the new university, where the leading proponent of Wycliffe's teachings was Jan Hus (1373–1415), an immensely popular young master and preacher. Although Hus rejected Wycliffe's ideas about the priesthood and the sacraments, he and other Czech preachers attacked indulgences and demanded a reform of Church liturgy and morals. They grafted these religious demands onto an attack on German dominance of the Bohemian kingdom. These attacks outraged both the Pisan pope John XXIII (1410–1415) and the Bohemian king Wenceslas IV (1378–1419), who favored the German faction. The pope excommunicated Hus, and the king expelled the Czech faculty from the university. Hus was convinced that he was no heretic and that a fair hearing would clear him. He therefore agreed to travel to the Council of Constance under promise of safe conduct from the emperor-elect Sigismund to defend his position. There, he was tried on a charge of heresy, convicted, and burned at the stake.

News of Hus's execution touched off a revolt in Bohemia. Unlike the peasant revolts of the past, however, this revolt had broad popular support throughout all levels of Czech society. Peasants, nobles, and townspeople saw the attack on Hus and his followers as an attack on Czech independence and national interest by a Church and an empire controlled by Germans. Soon a radical faction known as the Taborites was demanding the abolition of private property and the institution of a communal state. Although moderate **Hussites** and Bohemian Catholics combined to defeat the radicals in 1434, most of Bohemia remained Hussite through the fifteenth century. The sixteenth-century reformer Martin Luther declared himself a follower of Jan Hus.

Religious Persecution in Spain

Through the thirteenth century, even as kings of England and France expelled Jews from their kingdoms and as they were subjected to sporadic pogroms and massacres in Germany, Jews and Muslims were tolerated on the Iberian Penninsula. This fragile existence was shattered in the fourteenth and fifteenth centuries. The causes were complex: a declining economy, political unrest, Christian triumphalism as the reconquest moved into its last stages, and nascent nationalism all increased intercultural tensions. In 1391, mendicant friars inflamed Aragon with preaching against Jews and caused widespread violent attacks. Thereafter, in towns across Spain Christians rose up in arms against their Jewish neighbors in riots animated both by a hatred of Jews and a protest against the king. Thousands died and thousands more were forced to convert.

The Muslim population fared no better. In the fifteenth century, Muslims faced conversion or expulsion, first to Granada and, after that last Muslim principality fell in 1492, to North Africa. Those who resisted were hunted down, their villages destroyed, and their populations dispersed.

William of Ockham and the Spirit of Truth

As in other areas of life in the later Middle Ages, intellectuals questioned the basic suppositions of their predecessors, directing intellectual activity away from general speculations and toward particular, observable reality.

The person primarily responsible for this new intellectual climate was the English Franciscan William of Ockham (ca. 1300–1349). Excommunicated for his defense of radical poverty, Ockham joined the imperialist cause at the court of Emperor

Louis IV. Imperial power, he argued, derived not from the pope but from the people. He believed that people should be free to determine their own form of government and to elect rulers. They should be able to make their choice directly, as in the election of the emperor by electors who represent the people, or implicitly, through continuing forms of government. In either case, Ockham believed, government should be entirely secular and neither popes nor bishops nor priests should have any role. Ockham went still further. He denied the absolute authority of the pope, even in spiritual matters. Rather, Ockham argued, parishes, religious orders, and monasteries should send representatives to regional synods, which in turn would elect representatives to general councils. Ockham's ideas on Church governance offered the one hope for a solution to the Great Schism that erupted shortly after his death. The Council of Constance, which ended the schism, was the fruit of Ockham's political theory.

As radical as Ockham's political ideas were, his philosophical outlook was even more extreme and exerted a more direct and lasting influence. The Christian Aristotelianism that developed in the thirteenth century had depended on the validity of general concepts called universals, which could be analyzed through the use of logic. Aquinas and others who studied the eternity of the world, the existence of God, the nature of the soul, and other philosophical questions believed that people could reach general truths by abstracting universals from particular, individual cases. Ockham argued that universals were merely names, no more than convenient tags for discussing individual things. He stated that universals had no connection with reality and could not be used to reason from particular observations to general truths. This radical **nominalism** (from the Latin *nomen*, "name") thus denied that human reason could aspire to certain truth. For Ockham and his followers, philosophical speculation was essentially a logical, linguistic exercise, not a way to certain knowledge.

Just as Ockham's political theory dominated the later fourteenth century, his nominalist philosophy won over the philosophical faculties of Europe. Since he had discredited the value of Aristotelian logic to increase knowledge, the result was, on the one hand, a decline in abstract speculation and, on the other, a greater interest in scientific observation of individual phenomena. In the next generation, Parisian professors, trained in the tradition of Ockham, laid the foundation for scientific studies of motion and the universe that led to the scientific discoveries of the sixteenth and seventeenth centuries.

Vernacular Literature and the Individual

Just as the religious and philosophical concerns of the later Middle Ages developed within national frameworks and criticized accepted authority from the perspective of individual experience, so too did the vernacular (as opposed to Latin) literatures of the age begin to explore the place of the individual within an increasingly complex society. Across Europe, authors reviewed the traditional values of society with a critical eye, reworking and transforming traditional literary genres into statements both personal and profound.

Italy. In Italy, a trio of Tuscan poets, Dante Alighieri (1265–1321), Petrarch (1304–1374), and Boccaccio (1313–1375), not only made Italian a literary language but composed in it some of the greatest literature of all time. Dante, the first and greatest of the three, wrote the *Divine Comedy* during the last years of his life.

The *Divine Comedy* is a view of the whole Christian universe, populated with people from antiquity and from Dante's own day. The poem is both a sophisticated summary of philosophical and theological thought at the beginning of the fourteenth century and an astute political commentary on his times. The poet sets this vision within a three-part poetic journey through hell (*Inferno*), purgatory (*Purgatorio*), and heaven (*Paradiso*). The *Divine Comedy* is Dante's personal summary of all that is good and bad in medieval culture and politics.

England. Dante had set his great poem within a vision of the other world. Emerging English literature was more firmly rooted in contemporary society. William Langland (ca. 1330–1395) and Geoffrey Chaucer (ca. 1343–1400) both presented images of their social milieu. In *Piers Plowman*, Langland presents society from the perspective of the peasantry. Chaucer's work, *The Canterbury Tales,* is much more sophisticated and wide-ranging, weaving together the whole spectrum of late medieval literature and life.

Chaucer placed his tales in the mouths of a group of 30 pilgrims traveling to the tomb of Thomas à Becket at Canterbury. The tales that they tell are drawn from folklore, Italian literature, the lives of the saints, courtly romance, and religious sermons. However, Chaucer played with the tales and their genres in the retelling. In his mastery of the whole heritage of medieval culture and his independent use of this heritage, Chaucer proved himself the greatest English writer before Shakespeare.

Chronology

THE LATER MIDDLE AGES, 1300–1500

1305–1377	Babylonian Captivity (Avignon papacy)
1337–1452	Hundred Years' War
1347–1352	Black Death spreads throughout Europe
1358	Jacquerie revolt of French peasants; Etienne Marcel leads revolt of Parisian merchants
1378–1417	Great Schism divides Christianity
1381	Great Rebellion of English peasants
1409–1410	Council of Pisa
1414–1417	Council of Constance ends Great Schism
1415	Jan Hus executed
1431	Death of Joan of Arc
1455–1485	English Wars of the Roses

France. Much of Italian and English literature drew material and inspiration from French, which continued into the fifteenth century to be the language of courtly romance, projecting an unreal world of allegory and nostalgia for a glorious if imaginary past. Popular literature, which developed largely in the towns, often dealt with courtly themes but with a critical and more realistic eye.

In this literary world an extraordinary woman, who was widowed at 25, was able to earn a living for herself and her family with her pen. As a successful woman of letters, Christine de Pisan (1364–ca. 1430) fought the stereotypical medieval image of women as weak, sexually aggressive temptresses. With wit and reason, she argued that women could be virtuous and showed the fallacies of traditional antifeminist preaching, poetry, and belief. Christine's life and writing epitomized the new possibilities and new interests of the fifteenth century. They included an acute sense of individuality, a willingness to look for truth not in the clichés of the past but in actual experience, and a readiness to defend one's views with tenacity. Although an heir of the medieval world, Christine, like her contemporaries, already embodied the attitudes of a new age.

That new age was reflected in a second tradition in fifteenth-century France, that of realist poetry. Around 1453, just as the English troops were enduring a final battering from the French artillery, Duke Charles of Orléans (1394–1465) organized a poetry contest. Each contestant was to write a ballad that began with the contradictory line "I die of thirst beside the fountain." The duke, himself an outstanding poet, wrote an entry that embodied the traditional courtly themes of love and fortune.

An unexpected and very different entry came from the duke's prison. The prisoner-poet, François Villon (1432–ca. 1464), was a child of the Paris streets, an impoverished student, a barroom brawler, a killer, and a thief. He was also the greatest realist poet of the Middle Ages, and his poetry won him release from prison. His entry read:

> I die of thirst beside the fountain,
> Hot as fire, my teeth clattering,
> At home I am in an alien land;
> I shudder beside a glowing brazier,
> Naked as a worm, gloriously dressed,
> I laugh and cry and wait without hope,
> I take comfort and sad despair,
> I rejoice and have no joy,
> Powerful, I have no force and no strength,
> Well received, I am expelled by all.

The duke focused on the sufferings of love, the thief on the physical sufferings of the downtrodden. The two poets represent the contradictory tendencies of literature in the later Middle Ages. The themes and ideas that were expressed ranged from the polished, traditional values of the aristocracy trying to maintain the ideals of chivalry in a new and changed world to the views of ordinary people, by turns reverent or sarcastic, joyful or despondent.

SUMMARY

Politics as a Family Affair   In the fourteenth and fifteenth centuries, politics centered on the ambitions of great families. This was particularly the case in central Europe, where five families competed for control of the Holy Roman Empire. Emperor Charles IV helped spark cultural renewal in central Europe. His Golden Bull contributed to political disintegration of the empire. Dynastic issues played a central role in the Hundred Years' War. Early English successes gave way to eventual French victory. The monarchies of both France and England were damaged by the war. Civil war in England followed defeat in France, with the Tudor family emerging triumphant.

Life and Death in the Later Middle Ages   Famine and disease decimated the population of Europe. Between 1347 and 1352, the Black Death killed between one-third and one-half of Europe's population. Responses to the plague varied widely. Social disruption followed demographic collapse. Peasants and townspeople fought to hold onto gains made in the aftermath of the plague. Events in Europe and abroad contributed to a decline in Italian economic power. The Hanseatic League dominated the Baltic trade. Towns employed new measures to address poverty and crime.

The Spirit of the Later Middle Ages   The papacy declined in the fourteenth century. During the Avignon papacy, French popes concentrated the financial and legal power of the Church in the papal office. The Great Schism resulted in a divided Christendom and weakened the papacy. Belief in witchcraft was widespread in the Middle Ages, but witchcraft trials were rare. Disgust with the formal institutions of the Church stimulated a turn to private devotion, mysticism, and sometimes heresy. John Wycliffe and Jan Hus led important challenges to the Church. The persecution of Jews and Muslims in Spain grew out of religious and political anxieties. William of Ockham challenged the Aristotelian foundations of medieval scholarship. The vernacular literatures of the later Middle Ages explored the place of the individual within a complex society.

QUESTIONS FOR REVIEW

1. What social and political forces prevented both the Holy Roman Emperors and the French kings from uniting the lands they ruled?
2. How did disease transform social relations in fourteenth-century Europe?
3. Why did a division in the papacy mean both political chaos and spiritual fear for Europeans?
4. How did the vernacular literature of Dante, Chaucer, and Christine de Pisan represent a departure from previous literary traditions?

The Italian Renaissance

Renaissance Society

What was the Renaissance? A French word for an Italian phenomenon, *renaissance* literally means "rebirth." The word captures both the emphasis on humanity that characterized Renaissance thinking and the renewed fascination with the classical world. But the Renaissance was an age rather than an event. There is no moment at which the Middle Ages ended. Late medieval society was artistically creative, socially well developed, and economically diverse. Yet eventually, the pace of change accelerated, and it is best to think of the Renaissance as an era of rapid transitions. Encompassing the two centuries between 1350 and 1550, it passed through three distinct phases. The first, from 1350 to 1400, was characterized by a declining population, the uncovering of classical texts, and experimentation in a variety of art forms. The second phase, from 1400 to 1500, was distinguished by the creation of a set of cultural values and artistic and literary achievements that defined Renaissance style. The large Italian city-states developed stable and coherent forms of government and the warfare between them gradually ended. In the final period, from 1500 to 1550, invasions from France and Spain transformed Italian political life, and the ideas and techniques of Italian writers and artists radiated to all points of the Continent.

Cities and Countryside

The Italian peninsula differed sharply from other areas of Europe in the extent to which it was urban. By the late Middle Ages, nearly one in four Italians lived in a town, in contrast to one in ten elsewhere. Not even the plague did much to change this ratio. By 1500, seven of the ten largest cities in the West were in Italy. Naples, Venice, and Milan, each with a population of more than 100,000, led the rest. But it was the numerous smaller towns, with populations nearer to 1,000, that gave the Italian peninsula its urban character. Cities dominated their regions economically, politically, and culturally and served as convenient centers of judicial and ecclesiastical power. The diversified activities of their inhabitants created vast concentrations of wealth, and Italy was the banking capital of the world.

Although cities may have dominated Renaissance Italy, by present standards they were small in both area and population. A person could walk across fifteenth-century Florence in less than half an hour. In 1427, its population was 37,000, only half its pre-plague size.

Urban populations were organized far differently than rural ones. On the farms the central distinctions involved ownership of land. Some farmers owned their estates outright and left them intact to their heirs. Others were involved in a sharecropping system by which absentee owners of land supplied working capital in return for half of the farm's produce. A great gulf in wealth separated owners from sharecroppers. Those who owned their land normally lived with surplus; those who sharecropped always lived on the margin of subsistence.

In the city, however, distinctions were based first on occupation, which largely corresponded to social position and wealth. Cities began as markets, and the privilege to participate in the market defined citizens. City governments provided protection for consumers and producers by creating monopolies through which standards for craftsmanship were maintained and profits for craftsmen were guaranteed. These monopolies were called guilds or companies. Each large city had its own hierarchy of guilds. At the top were the important manufacturing groups—clothiers, metalworkers, and the like. Just below them were bankers, merchants, and the administrators of civic and Church holdings. At the bottom were grocers, masons, and other skilled workers. Roughly speaking, all of those within the guild structure, from bottom to top, lived comfortably. Yet the majority of urban inhabitants were not members of guilds. Many managed to eke out a living as wage laborers; many more were simply destitute. As a group, these poor people constituted as much as half of the entire population. Most depended on civic and private charity for their very survival.

LARGEST CITIES IN WESTERN EUROPE, CA. 1500

Examine the locations of western Europe's largest cities at the beginning of the sixteenth century. Where were these cities concentrated? What was the least urbanized part of Europe? Based on this information, why do you suppose the Mediterranean Sea was considered the center of Europe? What was distinctive about the Holy Roman Empire?

The disparities between rich and poor were overwhelming. The concentration of wealth in the hands of an ever-narrowing group of families and favored guilds characterized every large city. In Florence, for example, 10 percent of the families controlled 90 percent of the wealth, with an even more extreme concentration at the top.

Production and Consumption

The concentration of wealth and the way in which it was used defined the Renaissance economy. Economic life is bound up in the relationship between supply and demand. The late medieval economy, despite the development of international banking and long-distance trade, was still an economy of primary producers: Between 70 and 90 percent of Europe's population was involved in subsistence agriculture. Even in Italy, which contained the greatest concentration of urban areas in the world, agriculture predominated. The manufacture of clothing was the only other significant economic activity. Most of what was produced was for local consumption rather than for the marketplace. Even in good times, more than 80 percent of the population lived at subsistence level with food, clothing, and shelter their only expenses. Therefore, when we discuss the market economy of the Renaissance, we are discussing the circumstances of the few rather than the many.

The defining characteristic of the early Renaissance economy was population change. Recurring waves of plague kept population levels low for more than a century. This dramatic reduction in population depressed economic growth. The general economy did not revive until the sustained population increase toward the end of the fifteenth century. Until then, in both agriculture and manufacturing, supply outstripped demand.

On the farms, surviving farmers occupied the best land and enlarged their holdings. In the shops, finished products outnumbered the consumers who survived the epidemics. Overproduction meant lower prices for basic commodities, and the decline in population meant higher wages for labor. At the lowest levels of society, survivors found it easier to earn their living and even to create a surplus than had their parents. For a time the lot of the masses improved.

But for investors, such economic conditions meant that neither agriculture nor cloth making was particularly attractive. In such circumstances, consumption was more attractive than investment, but it was not merely the perceived shortage of profitable investment opportunities that brought on the increase in conspicuous consumption during the fifteenth century. In the psychological atmosphere created by unpredictable, swift, and deadly epidemics, luxurious living seemed an appropriate response. Moreover, although tax rates increased, houses and personal property normally remained exempt, making luxury goods attractive investments. For these reasons the production and consumption of luxuries soared.

The Experience of Life

Luxury helped to improve a life that for rich and poor alike was short and uncertain. Renaissance children who survived infancy found their lives governed by parentage and by gender. In parentage, the great divide was between those who lived with surplus and those who lived at subsistence. The first category encompassed the wealthiest bankers and merchants down to those who owned their own farms or engaged in small urban crafts. The vast majority of urban and rural dwellers were members of the second category. About the children of the poor we know very little, other than that their survival was unlikely. Eldest sons were favored; younger daughters were disadvantaged. In poor families, however, this favoritism meant little more than early apprenticeship to day labor in the city or farm labor in the countryside. Girls were frequently sent out as domestic servants far from the family home.

Childhood. Children of the wealthy had better chances for survival than did children of the poor. For the better off, childhood might begin with "milk parents," in the home of the family of a wet nurse who would breast-feed the baby through infancy.

Only the very wealthy could afford a live-in wet nurse, which would increase the child's chances of survival. Again, daughters were more likely to be sent far from home and least likely to have their nursing supervised.

During the period between weaning and apprenticeship, Renaissance children lived with their families. Sons could expect to be apprenticed to a trade, probably between the ages of 10 and 13. Most, of course, learned the crafts of their fathers, but not necessarily in their father's shop. Sons inherited the family business and its most important possessions—tools of the trade or beasts of labor for the farm.

Marriage and the Family. Expectations for daughters centered on their chances of marriage. For a girl, dowry was everything. If a girl's father could provide a handsome one, her future was secure; if not, the alternatives were a convent, which would take a small bequest, or a match lower down the social scale, where the quality of life deteriorated rapidly. Daughters of poor families entered domestic service in order to have a dowry provided by their masters. The dowry was taken to the household of the husband. There, the couple resided until they established their own separate family. If the husband died, it was to his parental household that the widow returned.

Women married in late adolescence, usually around the age of 20. Among the wealthy, marriages were perceived as familial alliances and business transactions rather than love matches. The dowry was an investment on which fathers expected a return, and while the bride might have some choice, it was severely limited. Compatibility was not a central feature in matchmaking. Husbands were, on the average, ten years older than their wives and likely to leave them widows.

Men married later—near the age of 25 on the farms, nearer 30 in the cities because of the cost of setting up in trade or on the land. Late marriage meant long supervision under the watchful eye of father or master, an extended period between adolescence and adulthood. Many men, even with families, never succeeded in setting up separately from their fathers or older brothers.

Men came of age at 30 but were thought to be old by 50. Thus for men, marriage and parenthood took place in middle age rather than in youth. Valued all their lives more highly than their sisters, male heads of households were the source of all power in their domiciles, in their shops, and in the state. They were responsible for overseeing every aspect of the upbringing of their children. But their wives were essential partners who governed domestic life. Women labored not only at the hearth, but in the fields and shops as well. Their economic contribution to the well-being of the family was critical, both in the dowry they brought at marriage and in the labor they contributed to the household. If their wives died, men with young children remarried quickly.

In most cases, death came suddenly. Epidemic diseases, of which plague was the most virulent, struck with fearful regularity. They struck harder at the young—children and adolescents, who were the majority of the population—and hardest in the summer months, when other viruses and bacteria weakened the population.

Starvation was rare, less because of food shortage than because the seriously under-nourished were more likely to succumb to disease than to famine. In urban areas, the government would intervene to provide grain from public storehouses at times of extreme shortage; in the countryside, large landholders commonly exercised the same function.

The Quality of Life

Although life may have been difficult during the Renaissance, it was not unfulfilling. Despite constant toil and frequent hardship, people of the Renaissance had reason to believe that their lives were better than those of their ancestors and that their children's lives would be better still. On the most basic level, health improved and, for those who survived plague, life expectancy increased owing to the relative surplus of grain throughout the fifteenth century and the wider variety of foods consumed. This diversification of diet resulted from improvements in transportation and communication, which brought more goods and services to a growing number of towns in the chain that linked the regional centers to the rural countryside.

The towns and cities also introduced a new sense of social and political cohesiveness. The city was something to which people belonged. In urban areas, they could join social groups of their own choosing and develop networks of support that were not possible in rural environments. Blood relations remained the primary social group. Kin were the most likely source of aid in times of need, and charity began at home. Kin groups extended well beyond the immediate family, with both cousins and in-laws laying claim to the privileges of blood. The urban family could also depend on the connections of neighborhood. In some Italian cities, wealth or occupation determined housing patterns. In others, like Florence, rich and poor lived side by side and identified themselves with their small administrative unit and with their local church. Thus they could participate in relationships with others both above and below them in social scale. From their superiors they gained connections that helped their families; from their inferiors they gained devoted clients.

As in the Middle Ages, the Church remained the spatial, spiritual, and social center of people's lives. Though Renaissance society became more worldly in outlook, this worldliness took place within the context of an absorbing devotional life. The Church provided explanations for both the mysterious and the mundane. The clergy performed the rituals of baptism, marriage, and burial that measured the passage of life. Religious symbols also adorned the flags of militia troops, the emblems of guilds, and the regalia of the city itself. The Church preserved holy relics that were venerated for their power to protect the city or to endow it with particular skills and resources. Through its holy days, as much as through its rituals, the Church helped to channel leisure activities into community celebrations.

A growing sense of civic pride and individual accomplishment were underlying characteristics of the Italian Renaissance, enhanced by the development of social cohesion and community solidarity that both Church and city-state fostered. The Renaissance was not an event whose causes were the result of the efforts of the few or whose consequences were limited to the privileged. In fact, the Renaissance was not an event at all. Family values that permitted early apprenticeships in surrogate households and emphasized the continuity of crafts from one generation to the next made possible the skilled artists of the Renaissance cities. The stress on the production of luxury goods placed higher value on individual skills and therefore on excellence in workmanship. Church and state sought to express social values through representational art. One of the chief purposes of wall murals was to instruct the unlettered in religion, to help them visualize the central episodes in Christian history. The grandiose architecture and statuary that adorned central places were designed to enhance civic pride and communicate the protective power of public institutions.

Renaissance Art

In every age, artistic achievement represents a combination of individual talent and predominant social ideals. Artists may be at the leading edge of the society in which they live, but it is the spirit of that society that they capture in word or song or image. Artistic disciplines also have their own technical development. Individually, Renaissance artists were attempting to solve problems about perspective and three-dimensionality that had defeated their predecessors. But the particular techniques or experiments that interested them owed as much to the social context as they did to the artistic one. For example, the urban character of Italian government led to the need for civic architecture, public buildings on a grand scale. The celebration of individual achievement led to the explosive growth of portraiture. Not surprisingly, major technological breakthroughs were achieved in both areas.

This relationship between artist and social context was especially important in the Renaissance, when artists were closely tied to the crafts and trades of urban society and to the demands of clients who commissioned their work. Although it was the elite who patronized art, it was skilled tradespeople who produced it. Artists normally followed the pattern of any craftsman: An apprenticeship begun as a teenager and a long period of training and work in a master's shop. This form of education gave the aspiring artist a practical bent and a keen appreciation for the business side of art. Studios were identified with particular styles and competed for commissions from clients, especially the Church. Wealthy individuals commissioned art as investments, as marks of personal distinction, and as displays of public piety.

The survival of so many Renaissance masterpieces allows us to reconstruct the stages by which the remarkable artistic achievements of this era took place. Although advances were made in a variety of fields during the Renaissance, the three outstanding areas were architecture, sculpture, and painting. Few Renaissance artists confined themselves to one area of artistic expression, and many created works of enduring beauty in more than one medium.

An Architect, a Sculptor, and a Painter

The century that culminated in Michelangelo's extraordinary achievements began with the work of three Florentine masters who deeply influenced one another's development: Brunelleschi (1377–1446), Donatello (1386–1466), and Masaccio (1401–1428). In the Renaissance, the dominant artistic discipline was architecture. Buildings were the most expensive investment patrons could make, and the technical knowledge necessary for their successful construction was immense. By 1400, the Gothic style of building had dominated western Europe for over two centuries. Its characteristic pointed arches, vaulted ceilings, and slender spires had simplified building by removing the heavy walls that were formerly thought necessary to support great structures. Gothic construction permitted greater height, a characteristic that was especially desirable in cathedrals, which stretched toward the heavens.

It was Brunelleschi who decisively challenged the principles of Gothic architecture by recombining its basic elements with those of classical structures. Basing his designs on geometric principles, Brunelleschi reintroduced planes and spheres as dominant motifs. His greatest work was the dome on the cathedral in Florence, begun in 1420. Brunelleschi is generally credited with having been the first Renaissance artist to have understood and made use of perspective, though it was immediately put to more dramatic effect in sculpture and painting.

In sculpture, the survival of Roman and Hellenistic pieces, mostly bold and muscular torsos, conveyed the direct influence of classical art. Donatello translated these classical styles into more naturalistic forms. Donatello revived the free-standing statue, which demanded greater attention to human anatomy because it was viewed from many angles. He also led the revival of the equestrian statue, sculpting the Venetian captain-general Gattamelata for a public square in Padua. This enormous bronze horse and rider (1445–1450) relied on the standpoint of the viewer to achieve its overpowering effect. This use of **linear perspective** is also seen in Donatello's breathtaking altar scenes of the miracles of Saint Anthony in Padua, which resemble nothing so much as a canvas cast in bronze.

These altar scenes evince the unmistakable influence of the paintings of Masaccio. His frescoes in the Brancacci Chapel in Florence were studied and sketched by all of the great artists of the next generation, who unreservedly praised his naturalism. What most claim the attention of the modern viewer are Masaccio's shading of light and shadow and his brilliant use of linear perspective to create the illusion that a flat surface has three dimensions.

Renaissance Style

By the middle of the fifteenth century, a recognizable Renaissance style had triumphed. The outstanding architect of this period was Leon Battista Alberti (1404–1472), whose treatise *On Building* (1452) remained the most influential work on the subject until the eighteenth century. Alberti consecrated the geometric principles laid down by Brunelleschi and infused them with a humanist spirit. He

Donatello's bronze statue *Judith Slaying Holofernes* symbolized the Florentines' love of liberty and hatred of tyranny.

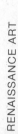

revived the classical dictum that a building, like a body, should have an even number of supports and, like a head, an odd number of openings. This furthered precise geometric calculations in scale and design.

No sculptor challenged the preeminence of Donatello for another 50 years, but in painting there were many contenders for the garlands worn by Masaccio. The first was Piero della Francesca (ca. 1420–1492), who broke new ground in his concern for the visual unity of his paintings. Another challenger was Sandro Botticelli (1445–1510), whose classical themes, sensitive portraits, and bright colors set him apart from the line of Florentine painters with whom he studied.

This concern with beauty and personality is also seen in the paintings of Leonardo da Vinci (1452–1519), whose creative genius embodied the Renaissance ideal of the "universal man." Leonardo's achievements in scientific, technical, and artistic endeavors read like a list of all of the subjects known during the Renaissance. His detailed anatomical drawings and the method he devised for rendering them, his botanical observations, and his engineering inventions (including models for a tank and an airplane) testify to his unrestrained curiosity. His paintings reveal a continuation of the scientific application of mathematics to matters of proportion and perspective.

From Brunelleschi to Alberti, from Masaccio to Leonardo da Vinci, Renaissance artists placed a unique stamp upon visual culture. By reviving classical themes, geometric principles, and a spirit of human vitality, they broke decisively from the dominant medieval traditions. Art became a source of individual and collective pride, produced by masters, but consumed by all. Cities and wealthy patrons commissioned great works of art for public display. New buildings rose everywhere, adorned with the statues and murals that still stand as a testimony to generations of artists.

Michelangelo

The artistic achievements of the Renaissance culminated in the creative outpourings of Michelangelo Buonarroti (1475–1564). Uncharacteristically, he came from a family of standing in Florentine society. At the age of 14, over the opposition of his father, he was apprenticed to a leading painter and spent his spare time in Florentine churches, copying the works of Masaccio, among others.

In 1490, Michelangelo gained a place in the household of Lorenzo de Medici. He claimed to have taught himself sculpturing during this two-year period, a remarkable feat considering the skills required. In the Medici household he came into contact with leading Neoplatonists, who taught that humankind was on an ascending journey of perfectibility toward God. These ideas can be seen as one source of the heroic concept of humanity that Michelangelo brought to his work.

In 1496, Michelangelo moved to Rome, where his abilities as a sculptor brought him to the attention of Jacopo Galli, a banker. Galli commissioned a classical work for himself and procured another for a French cardinal, which became the *Pietà.* The *Pietà* created a sensation in Rome, and by the time Michelangelo returned to Florence in 1501, at the age of 26, he was already acknowledged as one of the great sculptors of his day. He was immediately commissioned to work on an enormous block of marble that had been quarried nearly a half-century before and had defeated the talents of a series of carvers. He worked continuously for three years on his *David* (1501–1504), a piece that completed the union between classical and Renaissance styles.

Though Michelangelo always believed himself to be primarily a sculptor, his next outstanding work was in the field of painting. In 1508, Pope Julius II summoned Michelangelo to Rome and commissioned him to decorate the ceiling of the small ceremonial chapel that had been built next to the new papal residence. Michelangelo's plan was to portray, in an extended narrative, human creation and those Old Testament events that foreshadowed the birth of the Savior. His representations were simple and compelling: The fingers of God and Adam nearly touching, Eve with one leg still emerging from Adam's side, and the half-human snake in the temptation are all majestically evocative.

The *Pietà*, the *David*, and the paintings of the Sistine Chapel were the work of youth. Michelangelo's crowning achievement, the building of Saint Peter's basilica in Rome, was the work of age. The base work of Saint Peter's had already been laid, and drawings for its completion had been made 30 years earlier by Donato Bramante. Michelangelo altered these plans in an effort to bring more light into the church and to provide a more majestic facade outside. His main contribution, however, was the design of the great dome, which centered the interior of the church on Saint Peter's grave. More than the height, it is the harmony of Michelangelo's design that creates the sense of the building thrusting upward like a Gothic cathedral of old. Michelangelo did not live to see the dome of Saint Peter's completed.

Renaissance art served Renaissance society, reflecting both its concrete achievements and its visionary ideals. This art was a synthesis of old and new, building on classical models, particularly in sculpture and architecture, but adding newly discovered techniques and skills. But Renaissance artists did more than construct and adorn buildings or celebrate and beautify spiritual life. Inevitably, their work expressed the ideals and aspirations of the society in which they lived—the new emphasis on learning and knowledge, on the here and now rather than the hereafter, and, most important, on humanity and its capacity for growth and perfection.

Renaissance Ideals

Renaissance thought went hand in glove with Renaissance art. Scholars and philosophers searched the works of the ancients to find the principles on which to build a better life. They scoured monastic libraries for forgotten manuscripts, discovering, among other things, Greek poetry, history, the works of Homer and Plato, and Aristotle's *Poetics*. Their rigorous application of scholarly procedures for the collection and collation of these texts was one of the most important contributions of the Renaissance intellectuals who came to be known as **humanists.** Although humanism was by no means antireligious, it was thoroughly secular in outlook.

Humanists celebrated worldly achievements. Pico della Mirandola's *Oration on the Dignity of Man* (1486) is the best known of a multitude of Renaissance writings influenced by the discovery of the works of Plato. Pico believed that people could perfect their existence on earth because God had endowed humans with the capacity to determine their own fate. This emphasis on human potential found expression in the celebration of human achievement.

Thus humanists studied and taught the humanities, the skills of disciplines such as **philology**, the art of language, and **rhetoric**, the art of expression. Though they were mostly lay people, humanists applied their learning to both religious and secular studies. Their interest in human achievement and human potential must be set beside their religious beliefs. As Petrarch stated quite succinctly, "Christ is my God; Cicero is the prince of the language I use."

Humanists and the Liberal Arts

The most important achievements of humanist scholars centered on ancient texts. It was the humanists' goal to discover as much as had survived from the ancient world and to provide texts of classical authors that were as full and accurate as possible.

The creation of Adam and Eve, a detail from Michelangelo's frescoes on the ceiling of the Sistine Chapel. The Sistine frescoes had become obscured by dirt and layers of varnish and glue applied at various times over the years. In the 1980s, they were cleaned to reveal their original colors.

Studying the Classical World. Although much was already known of the Latin classics, few of the central works of ancient Greece had been recovered. Humanists preserved this heritage by reviving the study of the Greek language and by translating Greek authors into Latin. After the fall of Constantinople in 1453, Italy became the center for Greek studies as Byzantine scholars fled the Ottoman conquerors. Humanists also introduced historical methods in studying texts, establishing principles for determining which of many manuscript copies of an ancient text was the oldest, the most accurate, and the least corrupted by their copyists. The humanist emphasis on the humanistic disciplines fostered new educational ideals. Along with the study of theology, logic, and natural philosophy, which had dominated the medieval university, humanist scholars stressed the importance of grammar, rhetoric, moral philosophy, and history. They believed that the study of these "liberal arts" should be undertaken for its own sake. This gave a powerful boost to the ideal of the perfectibility of the individual that appeared in so many other aspects of Renaissance culture.

Humanists furthered the secularization of Renaissance society through their emphasis on the study of the classical world. The rediscovery of Latin texts during the late Middle Ages spurred interest in all things ancient.

Philology and Lorenzo Valla. The study of the origins of words, their meaning, and their proper grammatical usage may seem an unusual foundation for one of the most vital of all European intellectual movements. But philology was, in fact, the humanists' chief concern. This can best be illustrated by the work of Lorenzo Valla (1407–1457). Valla entered the service of Alfonso I, king of Naples, and applied his humanistic training to affairs of state. The kingdom of Naples bordered on the Papal States, and its kings were in continual conflict with the papacy. The pope asserted the right to withhold recognition of the king, a right that was based on the jurisdictional authority supposedly ceded to the papacy by the Emperor Constantine in the fourth century—the so-called Donation of Constantine. Applying historical and philological critiques to the text of the Donation, Valla proved beyond doubt that the Donation was a forgery and papal claims based on it were without merit.

Civic Humanism. Valla's career demonstrates the impact of humanist values on practical affairs. Although humanists were scholars, they made no distinction between an active and a contemplative life. A life of scholarship was a life of public service. This **civic humanism** is best expressed in the writings of Leon Battista Alberti (1404–1472), whose treatise *On the Family* (1443) is a classic study of the new urban values, especially prudence and thrift. Alberti extolled the virtues of "the fatherland, the public good, and the benefit of all citizens."

Alberti's own life might have served as a model for the most influential of all Renaissance tracts, Castiglione's *The Courtier* (1528). Baldesar Castiglione (1478–1529) directed his lessons to the public life of the aspiring elite. It was his purpose to prescribe the characteristics that would make the ideal courtier, who was as much made as born. Castiglione's perfect courtier was an amalgam of all that the elite of Renaissance society held dear. He was to be educated as a scholar, he was to be occupied as a soldier, and he was to serve his state as an adviser.

Renaissance Science

As the spirit of the Renaissance looked back to the classical world and ahead to the achievements that would come from the adaptation of ancient wisdom, so Renaissance scientific inquiry was focused in two directions. The first was text-based knowledge derived from recovered works mainly from classical Greece; the second was experiment-based knowledge achieved through observation.

The biological sciences were given new life by the recovery of the writings of Hippocrates and Galen. Medicine became a subject for learned inquiry and the medical school at Padua was considered the greatest in Europe. The work of Hippocrates concerned diagnosing common diseases and attempting to find treatments. Galen's studies of the human body, rediscovered, formed the basis for a new interest in anatomy and led to experiments in human dissection. Such experimentation improved knowledge of anatomy, which led to advances in setting broken bones and treating injuries.

While the life sciences were advanced through attention to ancient texts, engineering developed through the experiences of Renaissance craftsmen and artists who were attempting to solve practical problems of proportion, stability, and height in the buildings, bridges, and ultimately domes that they built. Most of the important advances in engineering were actually made in the service of military ventures. Leonardo da Vinci attempted to apply a theory of mechanics to Renaissance warfare, and he made drawings for the creation of war machines such as tanks and flying machines such as airplanes. But he was expert in building working models of machines, in advising princes on their fortifications, and suggesting improvements in the art of gunnery. All his contributions were made by experimentation rather than through text-based learning. Wherever he went, Leonardo built workshops to construct models and kept careful notebooks of the results of his trials. This spirit of experimentation would ultimately lead to the birth of a recognizably scientific method in the next century.

Machiavelli and Politics

At the same time that Castiglione was drafting a blueprint for the idealized courtier, Niccolò Machiavelli (1469–1527) was laying the foundation for the realistic sixteenth-century ruler. No Renaissance work has been more important or more controversial than Machiavelli's The Prince (1513). With Machiavelli, for better or worse, begins the science of politics.

The Prince is a handbook for a ruler who would establish a lasting government. It attempts to set down principles culled from historical examples and contemporary events to aid the prince in attaining and maintaining power. By study of these precepts and by their swift and forceful application, Machiavelli believed, the prince might even control fortune itself. What made The Prince so remarkable in its day, and what continues to enliven debate over it, is that Machiavelli was able to separate all ethical considerations from his analysis. Whether this resulted from cynicism or from his own expressed desire for realism, Machiavelli uncompromisingly instructed the would-be ruler to be half human and half beast—to conquer neighbors, to murder enemies, and to deceive friends. Steeped in the humanist ideals of fame and virtù—a combination of virtue and virtuosity, of valor, character, and ability—he sought to reestablish Italian rule and place government on a stable scientific basis that would end the perpetual conflict among the Italian city-states.

The Politics of the Italian City-States

The absence of a unifying central authority in Italy, resulting from the collapse of the Holy Roman Empire and the papal schism, allowed ancient guilds and confraternities to transform themselves into self-governing societies. By the beginning of the fifteenth century, the Italian **city-states** were the center of power, wealth, and culture in the Christian world.

This dominion rested on several conditions. First, their geographical position favored the exchange of resources and goods between East and West. A great circular trade encompassed the Byzantine Empire, the North African coastal states, and the Mediterranean nations of western Europe. The Italian peninsula dominated the circumference of that circle. Its port cities, Genoa and Venice especially, became great maritime powers through their trade in spices and minerals. Moreover, just beyond the peninsula to the north lay the vast and populous territories of the Holy Roman Empire. Their continuous need for manufactured goods, especially cloth and metals, was filled by long caravans that traveled from Italy through the Alps. Finally, the city-states and their surrounding areas were agriculturally self-sufficient.

The Five Powers

Although there were dozens of Italian city-states, by the early fifteenth century five had emerged to dominate the politics of the peninsula. In the south was the kingdom of Naples, the only city-state governed by a hereditary monarchy. Its politics were mired in conflicts over its succession.

Bordering Naples were the Papal States, whose capital was Rome but whose territories stretched far to the north and lay on both sides of the spiny Apennine mountain chain that extends down the center of the peninsula. Throughout the fourteenth and early fifteenth centuries the territories under the nominal control of the Church were largely independent and included such thriving city-states as Bologna, Ferrara, and Urbino. Even in Rome the weakened papacy had to contend with noble families for control of the city.

The three remaining dominant city-states—Florence, Milan, and Venice—were bunched together in the north. Florence, center of Renaissance culture, was one of the wealthiest cities of Europe before the devastations of the plague and the sustained economic downturn of the late fourteenth century. Nominally, Florence was a republic, but during the fifteenth century it was ruled in effect by its principal banking family, the Medici.

To the north of Florence was the duchy of Milan, the major city in Lombardy. Milan's economic life was oriented northward to the Swiss and German towns beyond the Alps, and its major concern was preventing foreign invasions. The most warlike of the Italian cities, Milan was a despotism, ruled for nearly two centuries by the Visconti family.

The last of the five powers was the republic of Venice, which became the leading maritime power of the age. Until the fifteenth century, Venice was less interested in

ITALY, 1494

Notice how Italy was organized into city-states at the end of the fifteenth century. Which were the largest city-states? Which city-states seem most susceptible to foreign invasion? Which states had the best positioning for trade? When the wars of Italy began in 1494 (discussed later in this chapter), France sided with Milan against Naples, Florence, and the Papal States. Based on the positions of the combatants, what do you think would have been the likeliest route for the French invasion? Which city-states could the French avoid fighting?

securing a landed empire than in dominating a seaborne one. The republic was ruled by a hereditary elite, headed by an elected **doge**, who was the chief magistrate of Venice, and a variety of small elected councils.

The political history of the Italian peninsula during the late fourteenth and early fifteenth centuries is one of unrelieved turmoil. Wherever we look, the governments of the city-states were threatened by foreign invaders, internal conspiracies, or popular revolts. In the 1370s, the Genoese and Venetians fought their fourth war in little more than a century, this one so bitter that the Genoese risked much of their fleet in an unsuccessful effort to conquer Venice itself. Florence and Milan were constantly at war with each other. Nor were foreign threats the only dangers. In Milan, three Visconti brothers inherited power. Two murdered the third, and then the son of one murdered the other to reunite the inheritance. The Venetians executed one of their military leaders, who was plotting treachery. One or another Florentine family usually faced exile when governments there changed hands. Popular revolts channeled social and economic discontent against the ruling elites in Rome, Milan, and Florence. The revolt of the "Ciompi" (the wooden shoes) in Florence in 1378 was an attempt by poorly paid wool workers to reform the city's exclusive guild system and give guild protection to the wage laborers lower down the social scale.

By the middle of the fifteenth century, however, two trends were apparent amid this political chaos. The first was the consolidation of strong centralized governments within the large city-states. These took different forms but yielded a similar result: internal political stability. The return of the popes to Rome after the Great Schism restored the pope to the head of his temporal estates and began a long period of papal dominance over Rome and its satellite territories. In Milan, one of the great military leaders of the day, Francesco Sforza (1401–1466), seized the reins of power after the failure of the Visconti line. The succession of King Alfonso I in Naples ended a half century of civil war. In both Florence and Venice, the grip of the political elite over high offices was tightened by placing greater power in small advisory councils and, in Florence, by the ascent to power of the Medici family. In sum, this process is known as the rise of signorial rule.

The rise of the signories made possible the second development of this period: the establishment of a balance of power within the peninsula. Sforza's consolidation of power in Milan initially led to warfare, but ultimately it formed the basis of the Peace of Lodi (1454). This established two balanced alliances, one between Florence and Milan and the other between Venice and Naples. These states, along with the papacy, pledged mutual nonaggression, a policy that lasted for nearly 40 years.

The Peace of Lodi did not bring peace. It only halted the long period in which the major city-states struggled against one another. Under cover of the peace, the large states continued the process of swallowing up their smaller neighbors and creating quasi-empires. Civilian populations were overrun, local leaders were exiled or exterminated, tribute money was taken, and taxes were levied. Each of the five states either increased its mainland territories or strengthened its hold on them. Venice and Florence especially prospered.

Venice: A Seaborne Empire

Venice owed its prosperity to trade rather than conquest. Its position at the head of the Adriatic permitted access to the raw materials of both East and West. The rich Alpine timberland behind the city provided the hardwoods necessary for ship-building. The inhabitants of the hinterland were steady consumers of grain, cloth, and the new manufactured goods—glass, silk, jewelry, and cottons—that came pouring onto the market in the late Middle Ages.

But the heart of Venetian success lay in the way in which it organized its trade and its government. The key to Venetian trade was its privileged position with the Byzantine Empire. Venice had exchanged with the Byzantines military support for tax concessions that gave Venetian traders a competitive edge in the spice trade with the East. The spice trade was so lucrative that special ships were built to accommodate it. These galleys were constructed at public expense and doubled as the Venetian navy in times of war. By controlling these ships, the government strictly regulated the spice trade. Rather than allow the wealthiest merchants to dominate it, as they did in other cities, Venice specified the number of annual voyages and sold shares in them at auction based on a fixed price. This practice allowed big and small merchants to gain from the trade and encouraged all merchants to find other trading outlets.

Like its trade, Venetian government was also designed to disperse power. Although it was known as the Most Serene Republic, Venice was not a republic in the sense that we use the word; it was rather an oligarchy—a government by a restricted group. Political power was vested in a Great Council whose membership had been fixed at the end of the thirteenth century. From the body of the Great Council, which numbered about 2,500 at the end of the fifteenth century, was chosen the Senate, a council about one-tenth the size, whose members served a one-year term. It was from the Senate that the true officers of government were selected: the doge, who was chosen for life, and members of a number of small councils, who administered affairs and advised the doge. Members of these councils were chosen by secret ballot in an elaborate process by which nominators were selected at random. Terms of office on the councils were extremely short in order to limit factionalism and to prevent any individual from gaining too much power.

With its mercantile families firmly in control of government and trade, Venice created a vast overseas empire in the East during the thirteenth and fourteenth centuries. Naval supremacy allowed the Venetians to offer protection to strategic outposts in return for either privileges or tribute. But in the fifteenth century, Venice turned westward. In a dramatic reversal of its centuries-old policy, it began a process of conquest in Italy itself. There were several reasons for this new policy. First, the Venetian navy was no longer the unsurpassed power that it once had been. Wars with Genoa had drained resources, and the revival of the Ottoman Turks in the East posed a growing threat that ultimately resulted in the fall of Constantinople (1453) and the end of Venetian trading privileges. Outposts in Dalmatia and the Aegean came under assault from both the Turks and the king of Hungary, cutting heavily into the complicated system by which goods were circulated by Venetian merchants. It was not long before Portuguese competition affected the most lucrative of all the commodities traded by the Venetians: pepper. Perhaps more important, mainland expansion offered new opportunities for Venice. Not all Venetians were traders, and the new industries that were being developed in the city could readily benefit from control of mainland markets. Most decisive of all, opportunity was knocking. In Milan, Visconti rule was weakening, and the Milanese territories were ripe for picking.

Venice reaped a rich harvest. From the beginning of the fifteenth century to the Peace of Lodi, the Most Serene Republic engaged in unremitting warfare. Its successes were remarkable. It pushed out to the north to occupy all the lands between the city and the Habsburg territories; it pushed to the east until it straddled the entire head of the Adriatic; and it pushed to the west almost as far as Milan itself. The western conquests, in particular, brought large populations under Venetian control, which, along with their potential as a market, provided a ready source of taxation. By the end of the fifteenth century, the mainland dominions of Venice were contributing nearly 40 percent of the city's revenue at a cost far smaller than that of the naval empire a century earlier.

Florence: Spinning Cloth into Gold

Florentine prosperity was built on banking and wool. Beginning in the thirteenth century, Florentine bankers were among the wealthiest and most powerful in the world. Florentine financiers established banks in all the capitals of Europe and the East. In the Middle Ages, bankers served more functions than simply handling and exchanging money. Most were also tied to mercantile adventures and underwrote industrial activity. So it was in Florence that international bankers purchased high-quality wool to be manufactured into the world's finest woven cloth.

The activities of both commerce and cloth manufacture depended on external conditions, and so the wealth of Florence was potentially unstable. In the mid-fourteenth century, instability came with the plague that devastated the city. Nearly 40 percent of the entire population was lost in the single year 1348, and recurring outbreaks continued to ravage the survivors. Loss of workers and markets seriously disrupted manufacturing. By 1380, cloth production had fallen to less than a quarter of pre-plague levels. On the heels of plague came wars. The costs of warfare created a massive public debt. Every Florentine of means owned shares in this debt, and the republic was continually devising new methods for borrowing and staving off crises of repayment.

As befitted a city whose prosperity was based on manufacturing, Florence had a strong guild tradition. The most important guilds were associated with banking and cloth manufacture, but they included the crafts and food processing trades as well. Only guild members could participate in government, electing the nine *Signoria* who administered laws, set tax rates, and directed foreign and domestic policy. Like that of Venice, Florentine government was a republican oligarchy, and like Venice, it depended on rotated short periods in office and selections by lot to avoid factionalism. But Florence had a history of factionalism that was longer than its history of republican government. Its formal structures were occasionally altered so that powerful families could gain control of the real centers of political power, the small councils and emergency assemblies through which the Signoria governed. Conservative leadership drawn from the upper ranks of Florentine society guided the city through the wars of the early fourteenth century. But soon afterward, the leaders of its greatest families—the Albizzi, the Pazzi, and the Medici—again divided Florentine politics into factions.

The ability of the Medici to secure a century-long dynasty in a government that did not have a head of state is just one of the mysteries surrounding the history of this remarkable family. Cosimo de Medici (1389–1464) was one of the richest men in Christendom when he returned to the city in 1434 after a brief exile. His leading position in government rested on supporters who were able to gain a controlling influence on the Signoria. Cosimo built his party carefully, banishing his Albizzi enemies, recruiting followers among the craftsmen he employed, and even paying delinquent taxes to maintain his voters' eligibility. Most important, emergency powers were invoked to reduce the number of citizens qualified to vote for the Signoria until the majority were Medici backers.

Cosimo's grandson, Lorenzo (1449–1492), held strong humanist values instilled in him by his mother, Lucrezia Tornabuoni, who organized his education. He brought Michelangelo and other leading artists to his garden; he brought Pico della Mirandola and other leading humanists to his table. Lorenzo's power was based on his personality and reputation. His diplomatic abilities were the key to his survival. Almost immediately after Lorenzo came to power, Naples and the papacy began a war with Florence, a war that was costly to the Florentines in both taxation and lost territory. In 1479, Lorenzo traveled to Naples and personally convinced the

A view of Florence in 1490.

Neapolitan king to sign a separate treaty. This restored the Italian balance of power and ensured continued Medici rule in Florence.

There is some doubt whether Lorenzo should be remembered by the title "the Magnificent" that was bestowed on him. His absorption in politics came at the expense of the family's commercial enterprises, which were nearly ruined during his lifetime. Moreover, the emergency powers that Lorenzo invoked to restrict participation in government changed forever the character of Florentine republicanism, irredeemably corrupting it. There is no reason to accept his enemies' judgment that Lorenzo was a tyrant, but the negative consequences of his rule cannot be ignored. In 1494, two years after Lorenzo's death, the peninsula was plunged into the wars that turned it from the center of European civilization into a satellite region.

The End of Italian Hegemony, 1450–1527

In the course of the Renaissance, western Europe was Italianized. For a century, the city-states dominated the trade routes that connected East and West. Italian manufactures, such as Milanese artillery, Florentine silk, and Venetian glass, were prized above all others. The ducat and the florin, two Italian coins, were universally accepted in an age when every petty prince minted his own. The peninsula exported culture in the same way that it exported goods. Humanism quickly spread across the Alps, aided by the recent invention of printing (which the Venetians soon dominated), and Renaissance standards of artistic achievement were known worldwide and everywhere imitated. The city-states shared their technology as well. The compass and the navigational chart, projection maps, double-entry bookkeeping, eyeglasses, the telescope—all profoundly influenced what could be undertaken.

Political and Military Unrest. But it was not in Italy that the rewards of such achievement were enjoyed. There, the seeds of political turmoil and military imperialism, combined with the rise of the Ottoman Turks, were to reap a not unexpected harvest. Under the cover of the Peace of Lodi, the major city-states had scrambled to enlarge their mainland empires. By the end of the fifteenth century, they eyed one another warily. Each expected the others to begin a peninsulawide war for hegemony and took the steps that ultimately ensured the contest. Each shared the dream of recapturing the glory that was Rome. Long years of siege and occupation had militarized the Italian city-states.

The Italian Decline. The disunited Italians were not able to meet the challenge of the most remarkable military leader of the age, the Ottoman prince Mehmed II (1451–1481), who conquered Constantinople and Athens and threatened Rome itself.

Venice was most directly affected by the Ottoman advance. Not only was its favored position in eastern trade threatened, but during a prolonged war at the end of the fifteenth century the Venetians lost many of their most important commercial outposts. Ottoman power closed off the markets of eastern Europe, and by 1480, Venetian naval supremacy was a thing of the past.

Successive popes pleaded in vain for holy wars to halt the advance of the Ottoman Turks. The fall of Constantinople in 1453 was an event of epochal proportions for Europeans; many believed that it foreshadowed the end of the world. Yet it was Italians rather than Ottomans who plunged the peninsula into the wars from which it never recovered.

The Wars of Italy (1494–1529) began when Naples, Florence, and the Papal States united against Milan. At first this alliance seemed little more than another shift in the balance of power. But rather than call on Venice to redress the situation, the Milanese leader, Ludovico Sforza, sought help from the French. An army of French cavalry and Swiss mercenaries, led by Charles VIII of France (1483–1498), invaded the peninsula in 1494. With Milanese support, the French swept all before them. Florence was forced to surrender Pisa, a humiliation that led to the overthrow of the Medici and the establishment of French sovereignty. The Papal States were next to be occupied, and within a year Charles had conquered Naples without engaging the Italians in a single significant battle. Unfortunately, the Milanese were not the only ones who could play at the game of foreign alliances. The Venetians and the pope united and called on the services of King Ferdinand of Aragon and the Holy Roman Emperor. Italy was now a battleground in what became a total European war for dynastic supremacy. The city-states used their foreign allies to settle old scores and to extend their own mainland empires. At the turn of the century, Naples was dismembered. In 1509, the pope conspired to organize the most powerful combination of forces yet known against Venice. All of the mainland possessions of the Most Serene Republic were lost, but by a combination of good fortune and skilled diplomacy, Venice itself survived. Florence was less fortunate, becoming a pawn first of the French and then of the Spanish. The final blow to Italian hegemony was the sack of Rome in 1527 by German mercenaries.

Chronology

ITALIAN POLITICS

1378	Ciompi revolt in Florence
1389–1464	Cosimo de Medici; leads rise of Medici to domination of Florence
1400–1450	Ottomans establish domination of the Balkans
1443	Naples and Sicily reunited under Alfonso I of Aragon
1449–1492	Lorenzo de Medici; plays important role as patron of the arts
1453	Fall of Constantinople
1454	Peace of Lodi
1494–1529	Wars of Italy
1494	Charles VII of France invades Italy
1509	Pope organizes successful coalition aimed at Venice
1527	German mercenaries sack Rome

SUMMARY

Renaissance Society   Italy was far more urban than other parts of Europe. Urban populations were organized by occupation, which largely corresponded to social position and wealth. City governments reflected the centrality of commerce and trade to city life. Economic conditions promoted the production and consumption of luxury items. Renaissance children who survived infancy found their lives governed by parentage and by gender. Most city dwellers lived at subsistence. For many people, life improved in the aftermath of the plague. Towns and cities introduced a new sense of social and political cohesiveness. The Church remained the spatial, spiritual, and social center of people's lives.

Renaissance Art   The social, economic, and political context of Renaissance Italy shaped the era's remarkable artistic achievements. In painting, sculpture, and architecture, Renaissance artists challenged old models, developed new techniques, and created a new style. By reviving classical themes, geometric principles, and a spirit of human vitality, artists broke decisively from the dominant medieval traditions. The artistic achievements of the Renaissance culminated in the creative outpourings of Michelangelo Buonarroti.

Renaissance Ideals   It was the humanists' goal to discover as much as had survived from the ancient world and to provide texts of classical authors that were as full and accurate as possible. The humanist emphasis on the humanistic disciplines fostered new educational ideals. Humanists furthered the secularization of Renaissance society through their emphasis on the study of the classical world. Although humanists were scholars, they made no distinction between an active and a contemplative life. Castiglione tried to define the perfect Renaissance courtier. Renaissance scientific inquiry focused on analysis of classical works and experiment-based knowledge. Machiavelli's *The Prince* set down rules for attaining and maintaining power.

The Politics of the Italian City-States   At the beginning of the fifteenth century the Italian city-states were the center of power, wealth, and culture in the Christian world. Five city-states dominated Italy: Naples, Venice, Florence, Milan, and the Papal States. Venice's wealth and power were initially based on seaborne trade with the East. Venetian government was designed to disperse power. In the fifteenth century, Venice turned West and engaged in wars of conquest. Florentine prosperity was built on banking and cloth manufacture. The Medici came to dominate Florence. The Peace of Lodi did not end competition between the Italian city-states. Invasion by France and Spain marked the beginning of Italian decline.

QUESTIONS FOR REVIEW

1. What social and cultural conditions were peculiar to the Italian peninsula, and how might those conditions have contributed to the Renaissance?
2. What were the principal characteristics of the Renaissance style in the visual arts?
3. What is humanism, and why was the study of languages so important to the humanists?
4. In what ways did the ideas of Niccolò Machiavelli reflect the reality of politics in the city-states of Renaissance Italy?

The European Empires

European Encounters

The sixteenth century was an age of exploration. Knowledge bequeathed from the past created curiosity about the present. Technological change made long sea voyages possible, and the demands of commerce provided incentives. Ottoman expansion on the southern and eastern frontiers of the Continent threatened access to the goods of the East on which Europeans had come to rely.

To pay for eastern goods, especially spices, Western gold and silver flowed steadily eastward. As supplies of precious metals dwindled, economic growth in Europe slowed. Throughout the fifteenth century, ever-larger amounts of Western specie were necessary to purchase ever-smaller amounts of Eastern commodities. Europe faced a severe shortage of gold and silver, a shortage that threatened its standard of living and its prospects for economic growth. The search was on for new sources of gold.

Africa and a Passage to India

It was the Portuguese who made the first dramatic breakthroughs in exploration and colonization. The Portuguese had long sailed the Atlantic, where they had established bases in the Azores and Madeira islands. Their small ships, known as **caravels**, were ideal for ocean travel, and their navigators were among the most skillful in the world. Yet they were unable to participate in the lucrative Mediterranean trade in bullion and spices until the expanding power of the Ottomans threatened the traditional eastern sea routes.

Prince Henry the Navigator. In the early fifteenth century, the Portuguese gained a foothold in northern Africa and used it to stage voyages along the continent's unexplored western coast. Like most explorers, the Portuguese were motivated by a mixture of faith and greed. Establishing southern bases would enable them to surround their Muslim enemies while also giving them access to the African bullion trade. Under the energetic leadership of Prince Henry the Navigator (1394–1460), the Portuguese pushed steadily southward.

Prince Henry's systematic program paid off in the next generation. By the 1480s, Portuguese outposts had reached almost to the equator, and in 1487, Bartolomeu Dias (ca. 1450–1500) rounded the tip of Africa and opened the eastern African shores to Portuguese traders. The aim of these enterprises was access to Asia rather than Africa. A decade later, Vasco da Gama (ca. 1460–1524) rounded the Cape of Good Hope and crossed into the Indian Ocean. When he returned to Lisbon in 1499, laden with the most valuable spices of the East, Portuguese ambitions were achieved. Larger expeditions followed, one of which, blown off course, touched the South American coast of Brazil, which was soon subsumed within the Portuguese dominions.

The Beginnings of the Slave Trade. The exploration of the African coast also brought the Portuguese into contact with Muslim traders who had developed connections between North Africa and the middle of the continent. They bartered for gold, ivory, and exotic spices, and slaves. Slavery was a common feature of the cultures that interacted in Africa. Europeans had used slaves in ancient times and had developed a theory that justified slavery by capture. Muslims were dependent upon them for their armies and bought many slaves from European sources. Africans enslaved those who were captured in tribal wars and sold them out of Africa, first to Muslim traders and then to the Portuguese. By the 1470s it was estimated that over a thousand African slaves a year were being imported into Portugal and that a significant percentage of those were sold to Spanish masters who also saw their value in farming.

In these early decades, slaves were viewed as just another trading commodity and valued only in regard to their profit. Ships were still small, voyages still risky, and capital still scarce. The agricultural use of African slaves was limited by the small amount of commercial agriculture undertaken by Europeans. The Portuguese held a monopoly on transporting slaves from Africa, but the trade soon centered in

Seville where Italians dominated it. This was a significant, if unplanned development. Seville would soon become the center of the Spanish overseas empire, and the Spanish colonies in America would soon become the destination for most of the African slaves bought by Europeans.

MAP DISCOVERY

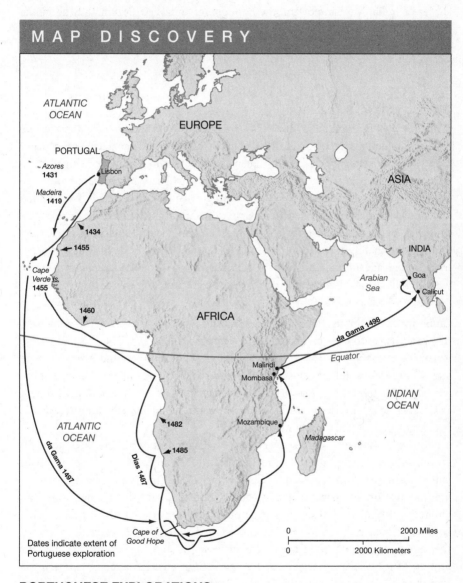

Dates indicate extent of Portuguese exploration

PORTUGUESE EXPLORATIONS

Examine the routes of the Portuguese explorers. What was their strategy of exploration? How long did it take for explorers to round the tip of Africa? What was the ultimate goal of Portuguese seafarers?

The Asian Trade. Building on their experience in West Africa, the Portuguese came to the East as traders rather than as conquerors. They developed a policy of establishing military outposts to protect their investments and subduing native populations only when necessary. By the beginning of the sixteenth century, the Portuguese Empire spanned both the eastern and western coasts of Africa and the western shores of India. Most important, the Portuguese controlled Ceylon and Indonesia, the precious Spice Islands from which came cloves, cinnamon, and pepper. Almost overnight, Lisbon became one of the trading capitals of the world, tripling in population between 1500 and 1550.

Mundus Novus

While the bulk of Portuguese resources were devoted to the Asian trade, those of the Spanish kingdom came to be concentrated in the New World. Though larger and richer than its western neighbor, Spain had been segmented into a number of small kingdoms and principalities and divided between Christians and Muslims. Not until the end of the fifteenth century, when the crowns of Aragon and Castile were united and the Muslims were expelled from Granada, could the Spanish concentrate their resources. By then they were far behind in establishing commercial enterprises. With Portugal dominating the African route to India, Queen Isabella of Castile was persuaded by a Genoese adventurer, Christopher Columbus (ca. 1446–1506), to take an interest in a western route. That interest resulted in one of the greatest accidents of history.

Christopher Columbus. Like all well-informed people of his day, Columbus believed the world was round. He calculated that a westward course would be shorter and less expensive than the path that the Portuguese were breaking around Africa—but he was wrong. He misjudged the size of the globe by a quarter and the distance of the journey by 400 percent. Columbus sailed westward into the unknown in 1492, and on 12 October he landed in the Bahamas, on an island that he named San Salvador. He had discovered a *Mundus Novus*, a New World.

Initially, Columbus's discovery was a disappointment. He had gone in search of a western passage to the Indies and he had failed to return to Spain laden with Eastern spices. Despite his own belief that the islands he had discovered lay just off the coast of Japan, it was soon apparent that he had found an altogether unknown landmass. Columbus's own explorations and those of his successors continued to focus on discovering a route to the Indies. This was all the more imperative once the Portuguese succeeded in finding the passage around Africa. Rivalry between the two nations intensified after 1500, when the Portuguese began exploring the coast of Brazil. In 1494, the **Treaty of Tordesillas** had confined Portugal's right to the eastern route to the Indies as well as to any undiscovered lands east of an imaginary line fixed west of the Cape Verde Islands. This entitled Portugal to Brazil. The Spanish received whatever lay west of the line.

This sixteenth-century map of Java and the Moluccas shows European traders bartering for spices. At the upper left, a ship laden with the rich cargo sails for markets in Europe.

Spanish-backed explorations soon proved the value of the newly discovered lands. In 1513, Vasco Núñez de Balboa (1475–1517) crossed the Isthmus of Panama and became the first European to view the Pacific Ocean. The discovery of this ocean refueled Spanish ambitions to find a western passage to the Indies.

Ferdinand Magellan. In 1519, Ferdinand Magellan (ca. 1480–1521), a Portuguese mariner in the service of Spain, set sail in pursuit of Columbus's goal of reaching the Spice Islands by sailing westward. His voyage, which he did not live to complete, remains the most astounding of the age. It was left to his navigator, Sebastian Elcano (ca. 1476–1526), to complete the first circumnavigation of the globe. In 1522, three years and one month after setting out, Elcano returned to Spain with a single ship and 18 survivors of the crew of 280. But in his hold were spices of greater value than the cost of the expedition. His return provided practical proof that the world was round, but it also demonstrated that the vastness of the Pacific Ocean made a western passage to the Indies uneconomical. The circumnavigation of Magellan and Elcano brought to an end the first stage of the Spanish exploration of the New World.

The Spanish Conquests

The exploits of Hernando Cortés (1485–1547) opened the next stage of Spanish discovery. The Spanish colonized the New World along the model of their reconquest of Spain. Individuals were given control over land and the people on it in return for military service. The interests of the crown were threefold: to convert the natives to

Christianity, to extend sovereignty over new dominions, and to gain profit from the venture. The colonial entrepreneurs had a singular interest: to grow rich. Most of the colonizers came from the lower orders of Spanish society.

Many of the protective measures taken by the crown to ensure orderly colonization and fair treatment of the natives were ineffective in practice. During the first decades of the sixteenth century, Spanish captains and their followers subdued the Indian populations of the Caribbean Islands and put them to work on the agricultural haciendas they had carved out for themselves.

Life on the hacienda, however, did not always satisfy the ambitions of the Spanish colonizers. Hernando Cortés was one such conquistador. Having participated in the conquest of Cuba, Cortés sought an independent command to lead an expedition into the hinterland of Central America, where a fabulous empire was rumored to exist. Having gathered a force of 600 men, Cortés sailed across the Gulf of Mexico in 1519 and established a fort at Vera Cruz, where he garrisoned 200 men. With 400 soldiers, he marched 250 miles through steamy jungles and over rugged mountains before glimpsing the first signs of the great Aztec civilization. The Aztec Empire was a loose confederation of native tribes that the Aztec had conquered during the previous century. It was ruled by the emperor Montezuma II (1502–1520) from his capital at Tenochtitlán. Invited to an audience with the Aztec emperor, Cortés and his men saw vast stores of gold and silver.

The conquest of the Aztecs took nearly a year and remains an overwhelming feat of arms. Nearly 100,000 natives from the tribes that the Aztecs had conquered supported the Spanish assault.

By 1522, Cortés was master of an area larger than all of Spain. But the cost in native lives was staggering. In 30 years, a population of approximately 25 million had been reduced to fewer than 2 million. Most of the loss was due to exposure to European diseases such as smallpox, typhoid, and measles, against which the indigenous peoples had no immunity. Their labor-intensive system of agriculture could not survive the rapid decrease in population, and famine followed pestilence.

This tragic sequence was repeated everywhere the Europeans appeared. In 1531, Francisco Pizarro (ca. 1475–1541) conquered the Peruvian Empire of the Incas, vastly extending the territory under Spanish control. A huge silver mine was discovered in 1545 at Potosí in what is now southern Bolivia, and the gold and silver that poured into Spain in the next quarter century helped to support Spanish dynastic ambitions in Europe. During the course of the sixteenth century, over 200,000 Spaniards migrated across the ocean. Perhaps one in ten were women, who married and set up families. Succeeding generations created huge haciendas built with the forced labor of black African slaves.

The Legacy of the Encounters

By the seventeenth century, long-distance trade had begun to integrate the regions of the world into a single marketplace. Slaves bought in Africa mined silver in South America. The bullion was shipped to Spain, where it was distributed across Europe.

Most went to Amsterdam to settle Spanish debts, Dutch bankers having replaced the Italians as the paymasters of Europe. From Holland, some of the silver traveled east to the Baltic Sea, the Dutch lifeline, where vital stores of grain and timber were purchased for home consumption. Even more of this silver was carried to Asia to buy spices in the Spice Islands, cottons in India, or silk in China. Millions of ounces flowed from America to Asia via the European trading routes. On the return voyage, Indian cottons were traded in Africa to purchase slaves for the South American silver mines.

Gold, God, and Glory. Gold, God, and glory neatly summarized the motives of the European explorers. Yet many technological problems had to be overcome before these goals could be achieved. Advances in navigational skills, especially in dead reckoning and later in calculating latitude from the position of the sun, were essential preconditions for covering the distances that were to be traveled. Ship designs became more sophisticated. The magnetic compass and the astrolabe were indispensable tools. Better maps and charts fueled both ambitions and abilities.

Nor was it happenstance that European forces conquered the peoples they encountered in both the east and west. Generations of warfare against Muslims had honed the skills of Christian warriors. European ships were sturdily built and armed with cannons that could be used on land or at sea. Soldiers were well-equipped and battle-tested. Military leaders were trained and experienced in the arts of siege and the tactics of divide and conquer.

The Columbian Exchange. The encounters between Europeans and native Americans were a cultural and intellectual event of the first magnitude. But it was also an ecological and biological event with enormous consequences—a transfer of microbes, animals, and plants known as the **Columbian Exchange**.

The mixing of populations that had historically remained separate had effects that no one could have foreseen. First and foremost were issues of public health. When the Spanish explorers arrived in the Caribbean islands, they carried agents of common diseases such as measles, smallpox, and influenza that raged in European population centers and killed many thousands each year but to which survivors carried a lifetime immunity. The native populations of the Americas endured their first exposure to these diseases all at once and millions succumbed in the first half-century of contact.

Disease was not the only unanticipated exchange that resulted from the encounters. On their ships the Spanish explorers brought horses, pigs, cows, and other domesticated animals unknown in the Americas. Not only did these new animals change patterns of work among the native populations, but they also changed dietary customs. Pork and beef gradually entered the diet of those who traded with the colonists and ultimately that of the general population.

Nor was the exchange one-sided. Beginning in the 1550s, European naturalists catalogued thousands of unknown species, a small number of which were suited to the different climates and soils of Europe. Among the most important of these

MAP DISCOVERY

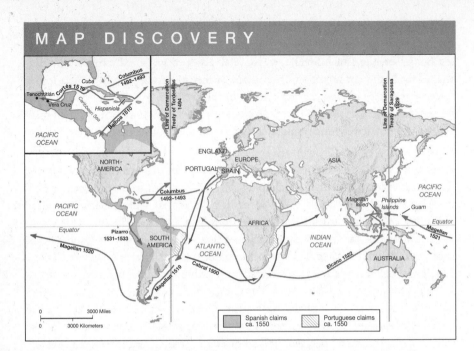

CLAIMS OF SPAIN AND PORTUGUAL TO OVERSEAS EMPIRES

Examine the voyages of discovery and the claims to overseas empires. How did Portuguese and Spanish exploration differ? What was the effect of the Treaty of Tordesillas on their travel and claims? Why was it believed at the time that Portugal was the more powerful empire?

species were a number of foodstuffs that ultimately had a transforming effect on the European diet. They included tomatoes, potatoes, chili peppers, and chocolate.

European Reflections. Riches and converts, power and glory, all came in the wake of exploration. But in the process of discovering new lands and new cultures, Europe also learned something of its own aspirations. Early Portuguese voyagers went in quest of the mythical Prester John, a saintly figure who was said to rule a heaven on earth in the middle of Africa. The first children born on Madeira were named Adam and Eve, though this slave plantation of sugar and wine was an unlikely Garden of Eden. The optimism of those who searched for the fountain of youth in the Florida swamps was not only that they would find it there, but that a long life was worth living. Contact with the cultures of the New World also forced a different kind of thinking about life in the old one. The supposed customs of strange lands provided the setting for one of the great works of English social criticism, Sir Thomas More's *Utopia* (1516).

Europe also discovered and revealed a darker side of itself in the age of exploration. Accompanying the boundless optimism and assertive self-confidence that made so much possible was a tragic arrogance and callous disregard toward native

Contact with cultures of the New World forced Europeans into a different way of thinking about the old world. In this detail from *The Cognoscenti*, a seventeenth-century Flemish painting, English scholars and navigators examine European encounters with new lands and new cultures.

peoples. Though they encountered heritages that were in some ways richer than their own, few westerners harbored any appreciation of them. European expansion revealed the rapaciousness, greed, and cruelty of many European conquerors. These were the impulses of the Crusades rather than of the Renaissance.

Chronology

EUROPEAN ENCOUNTERS

1394–1460	Henry the Navigator; leads Portuguese effort to increase sea power
1487	Bartolomeu Dias rounds tip of Africa
1492	Columbus arrives in New World
1497–1499	Vasco da Gama leads expedition to India
1498	Castilian women begin arriving in the New World
1500–1550	Population of Lisbon triples
1516	Publication of Thomas More's *Utopia*
1519–1522	Ferdinand Magellan leads expedition that circumnavigates globe
1522	Hernando Cortés completes conquest of Aztecs
1531	Francisco Pizarro conquers Incas

The Formation of States

In the middle of the fifteenth century there were many factors working against the formation of large states in Europe. The most obvious involved simple things such as transportation and communication. The distance that could be covered quickly was very small. In wet and cold seasons, travel was nearly impossible. Large areas were difficult to control and to defend. Communication was not only subject to the hazards of travel. Distinct languages or dialects, a principal feature of small states, contributed to separate cultures. Customary practices, common ancestry, and shared experiences helped to define a sense of community through which small states defined themselves.

To these natural forces that acted to maintain the existence of small units of government were added invented ones. To succeed, a prince had to establish supremacy over a number of rivals. For the most part, states were inherited. Short lives meant prolonged disputes about inheritance. Rulers had to defend their thrones from rivals with strong claims to legitimacy.

Rulers also had to defend themselves from the ambitions of their mightiest subjects. The constant warfare of the European nobility was one of the central features of the later Middle Ages. To avoid resort to arms, princes and peers entered into all manner of alliances, using their children as pawns and the marriage bed as the chessboard. Rulers also faced independent institutions within their states, powerful organizations that had to be won over or crushed. By the end of the fifteenth century, the long process of taming the Church was about to enter a new stage. Fortified towns presented a different problem. They possessed both the labor and the wealth necessary to raise and maintain armies. They also jealously guarded their privileges. Rulers who could not tax their towns could not rule their state. Finally, most kingdoms had assemblies representing the propertied classes, especially in matters of taxation. Some, like the English Parliament and the Spanish Cortes, were strong; others, like the Imperial Diet and the French Estates-General, were weak. But everywhere, they posed an obstacle to the extension of the power of princes.

In combination, these factors slowed and shaped the process of state formation. But neither separately nor together were they powerful enough to overcome it. The fragmentation of Europe into so many small units of government made some consolidation inevitable; and as the first large states took shape, the position of smaller neighbors grew ever more precarious.

This was especially true by the end of the fifteenth century because of the increase in the destructive power of warfare. Technological advances in cannonry and in the skills of gunners and engineers made medieval fortifications untenable. Gunpowder decisively changed battlefield tactics. It made heavy armor obsolete and allowed for the development of a different type of warfare. Infantry armed with long pikes or small muskets became the crucial components of armies that were growing ever larger. Systems of supply were better, sources of small arms were more available, and the rewards of conquest were more tangible. What could not be inherited or married could be conquered.

Eastern Configurations

The interplay of factors that encouraged and inhibited the formation of states is most easily observed in the eastern parts of Europe. There the different paths taken by Muscovy and Poland-Lithuania stand in contrast. At the beginning of the sixteenth century, the principality of Muscovy was the largest European political unit. Muscovy's growth was phenomenal. Under Ivan III, "the Great" (1462–1505), Muscovy expanded to the north and west. During a long series of wars it annexed Novgorod and large parts of Livonia and Lithuania. Between 1460 and 1530, Muscovy increased its territory by 1.5 million square miles.

A number of factors led to the rise of Muscovy. First, external threats had diminished. The deterioration of the Mongol Empire, which had dominated south-central Russia, allowed Ivan to escape the yoke of Mongol rule that the Russian princes had worn for centuries. Second, the fall of Constantinople made Muscovy the heir to eastern Christendom, successor to the Roman and Byzantine empires. Third, Ivan the Great was fortunate in having no competitors for his throne. He was able to use other social groups to help administer the new Muscovite territories without fear of setting up a rival to power.

Ivan extended the privileges of his nobility and organized a military class, the members of which received land as a reward for their fidelity. He also developed a new theory of sovereignty that rested on divine rather than temporal power. Traditionally, Russian princes ruled their lands by patrimony. They owned both estates and occupants. Ivan the Great extended this principle to cover all lands to which there was an ancient Russian claim and combined it with the religious authority of the Orthodox Church. Both he and his successors ruled with the aid of able Church leaders, who were normally part of the prince's council.

Ivan the Terrible. What made the expansion of Muscovy so impressive is that land once gained was never lost. The military and political achievements of Ivan the Great were furthered by his son Vasili and his more famous grandson Ivan IV, "the Terrible" (1533–1584). Ivan IV defeated the Mongols on his southeastern border and incorporated the entire Volga basin into Muscovy. But his greatest ambition was to gain a port on the Baltic Sea and establish a northern outlet for commerce. His objective was to conquer Livonia, but in nearly three decades of warfare between Muscovy and Poland-Lithuania, with whom Livonia had allied itself, Muscovy's territorial victories fell short of the real prize. Furthermore, Ivan's northern campaigns seriously weakened the defense of the south. In 1571, the Crimean Tatars advanced from their territories on Muscovy's southwestern border and inflicted a powerful psychological blow when they burned the city of Moscow. Although the Tatars were eventually driven off Muscovite soil, expansion in both north and south was at an end for the next 75 years.

By the reign of Ivan IV, Muscovite society was divided roughly into three groups: the hereditary nobility, known as the boyars; the military service class; and the peasantry, who were bound to the land. There was no large mercantile presence in Muscovy, and its urban component remained small. The boyars, who were powerful landlords of great estates, owed little to the tsar. They inherited their lands and did not necessarily benefit from expansion and conquest. Members of the military service class, on the other hand, were bound to the success of the crown. Their military service was a requirement for the possession of their estates, which were granted out of lands gained through territorial expansion. Gradually, the new military service class grew in power and prestige, largely at the expense of the older boyars. Ivan IV used members of the military service class as legislative advisers and elevated them in his parliamentary council (the Zemsky Sobor), which also contained representatives of the nobility, clergy, and towns.

Unlike his grandfather, Ivan IV had an abiding mistrust of the boyars and it was his treatment of them that earned him the nickname "the Terrible." During his brutal suppression of supposed conspiracies, several thousand families were massacred by Ivan's own orders and thousands more by the violent excesses of his agents. He also forcibly relocated boyar families. This practice made the boyars' situation similar to that of the military service class, whose members owed their fortunes to the tsar. For the first time the boyars were required to perform military service to the tsar.

All of these measures contributed to the breakdown of local networks of influence and power and to a disruption of local governance. But they also made possible a system of central administration, one of Ivan IV's most important achievements. Ivan IV promoted the interests of the military service class over those of the boyars, but he did not destroy the nobility. New boyars were created, especially in conquered territories, and these new families owed their positions and loyalty to the prince. Both boyars and the military benefited from Ivan's policy of binding the great mass of people to the land. Serfdom made possible the prolonged absence of military leaders from their estates and contributed to the creation of the military service class. In the long term, however, serfdom retarded economic development by removing the incentive for large landholders to make investments in commerce or to improve agricultural production.

Poland-Lithuania. The growth of an enlarged and centralized Muscovy stands in contrast to the experiences of Poland-Lithuania during the same period. At the end of the fifteenth century, Casimir IV (1447–1492) ruled the kingdom of Poland and the grand duchy of Lithuania. His son Wladislaw II ruled Bohemia (1471–1516) and Hungary (1490–1516).

While the Polish-Lithuanian monarchs enjoyed longevity similar to that of the Muscovites, those who ruled Hungary and Bohemia were not so fortunate. By the sixteenth century, a number of claimants to both crowns existed, and the competition was handled by diplomacy rather than war. The formal union of the Polish and

Lithuanian crowns in 1569 also involved the decentralization of power and the strengthening of the rights of the nobility in both countries. In the end, the states split apart. The Russians took much of Lithuania; the Ottomans took much of Hungary. Bohemia, which in the fifteenth century had been ruled more by its nobles than by its king, was absorbed into the Habsburg territories after 1526.

There were many reasons why a unified state failed to develop in east-central Europe. First, wars with the Ottomans and the Russians absorbed resources. Second, the princes faced rivals to their crowns. These contests for power necessitated concessions to leading citizens, which decreased the princes' ability to centralize their kingdoms or to effect real unification among them. The nobility of Hungary, Bohemia, and Poland-Lithuania all developed strong local interests that increased over time. War, rivalries for power, and a strong nobility prevented any one prince from dominating this area as the princes of Muscovy dominated theirs.

The Western Powers

As in the east, there was no single pattern to the consolidation of the large western European states. They, too, were internally fragmented and externally imperiled. While England had to overcome the ruin of decades of civil war, France and Spain faced the challenges of invasion and occupation. Each nation formed its state differently: England by administrative centralization, France by good fortune, and Spain by dynastic marriage.

The Taming of England. Alone among European states, England suffered no threat of foreign invasion during the fifteenth century. This island fortress might easily have become the first consolidated European state were it not for the ambitions of the nobility and the weakness of the crown. For 30 years, the English aristocracy fought over the spoils of a helpless monarch. The Wars of the Roses (1455–1485) were as much a free-for-all among the English peerage as they were a contest for the throne between the houses of Lancaster and York.

Three decades of intermittent warfare had predictable results. The houses of Lancaster and York were both destroyed. Edward IV (1461–1483) succeeded in gaining the crown for the house of York, but he was never able to wear it securely. When he died, his children, including his heir, Edward V (1483), were placed in the protection of their uncle Richard III (1483–1485). Richard's usurpation led to civil war, and he was killed by the forces of Henry Tudor at the battle of Bosworth Field in 1485. By the end of the Wars of the Roses, the monarchy had lost both revenue and prestige.

It was left to Henry Tudor to deal with the power of the nobility and the poverty of the monarchy. No English monarch had held secure title to the throne for over a century. Henry Tudor, as Henry VII (1485–1509), put an end to this dynastic instability at once. He married Elizabeth of York, in whose heirs would rest the legitimate claim to the throne. He also began the long process of taming his overmighty subjects.

Traitors were hanged and turncoats were rewarded. He and his son Henry VIII (1509–1547) adroitly created a new peerage, which soon was as numerous as the old feudal aristocracy. These new nobles owed their titles and loyalty to the Tudors.

The financial problems of the English monarchy were not so easily overcome. The English landed classes had established the principle that only on extraordinary occasions were they to be required to contribute to the maintenance of government. This principle was defended through their representative institution, the Parliament. When the kings of England wanted to tax their subjects, they had first to gain the assent of Parliament. Though Parliaments did grant requests for extraordinary revenue, especially for national defense, they did so grudgingly. The English landed elites were not exempt from taxation, but they were able to control the amount of taxes they paid.

Since the king was, therefore, dependent on the efficient management of his own estates, English state building required the growth of centralized institutions that could oversee royal lands and collect royal customs. Gradually, medieval institutions such as the Exchequer were supplanted by newer organs that were better able to adjust to modern methods of accounting, record keeping, and enforcement.

Not until the middle of the next reign was the English monarchy again solvent. As a result of his dispute with the papacy, Henry VIII confiscated the enormous wealth of the Catholic church and, with one stroke, solved the Crown's monetary problems (see Chapter 13). But the real contribution that Henry and his chief minister, Thomas Cromwell (ca. 1485–1540), made to forming an English state was the way in which this windfall was administered. Cromwell accelerated the process of centralizing government that had begun under Edward IV. He divided administration according to its functions by creating separate departments of state, modeled on courts. These new departments were responsible for record keeping, revenue collection, and law enforcement. Each had a distinct jurisdiction and a permanent trained staff. Cromwell coordinated the work of these distinct departments by expanding the power of the Privy Council, which included the heads of these administrative bodies. Through a long evolution, the Privy Council came to serve as the king's executive body. Cromwell also saw the importance of Parliament as a legislative body. Through Parliament, royal policy could be turned into statutes that had the assent of the political nation. If Parliament was well managed, issues that were potentially controversial could be defused. Laws passed by Parliament were more easily enforced locally than were proclamations issued by the king.

The Unification of France. The forces working against the consolidation of a French state were formidable. France was surrounded by aggressive and powerful neighbors with whom it was frequently at war. Its greatest nobles were semi-independent princes who were constant rivals for the throne. French people were primarily loyal to their province and viewed the pretensions of the monarchy with deep suspicion. France was also splintered by profound regional differences. The north and south were divided by culture and by language (the *langue d'oc* in the south and the *langue d'oil* in the north).

The first obstacles to unification that were overcome were the external threats to French security. For over a century the throne of France had been contested by the kings of England. The so-called Hundred Years' War, which was fought intermittently between 1337 and 1453, originated in a dispute over the inheritance of the French crown and English possessions in Gascony in southern France (see Chapter 10).

The struggle between the kings of England and the kings of France allowed French princes and dukes, who were nominally vassals of the king, to enhance their autonomy by making their own alliances with the highest bidder. When the English were finally driven out of France in the middle of the fifteenth century, the kings of France came into a weakened and divided inheritance.

Nor was England the only threat to the security of the French monarchy. On France's eastern border, in a long arching semicircle, were the estates of the dukes of Burgundy. While England and France were locked in deadly embrace, Burgundy systematically grew, absorbing territory from both the Holy Roman Empire and France. The conquest of Lorraine finally connected the ducal estates in one long, unbroken string. The power of Burgundy threatened its neighbors in all directions. Both France and the empire were too weak to resist its expansion, but the confederation of Swiss towns to the southwest of Burgundy was not. In a series of stunning military victories, Swiss forces repelled the Burgundians from their lands and demolished their armies. Charles the Bold, the last Valois duke of Burgundy, fell at the Battle of Nancy in 1477. His estates were quickly dismembered. France recovered its ancestral territories, including Burgundy itself, and through no effort of its own was now secure on its eastern border.

The king who was most associated with the consolidation of France was Louis XI (1461–1483). He inherited an estate that had been exhausted by warfare and civil strife. More by chance than by plan, he vastly extended the territories under the dominion of the French crown and, more important, subdued the nobility. But during the course of his reign, Louis XI gradually won back what he had been forced to give away. Years of fighting both the English and each other left the ranks of the French aristocracy depleted. As blood spilled on the battlefields, the stocks of fathers and sons ran low. Estates to which no male heirs existed fell forfeit to the king. In this manner, the crown absorbed Anjou and Maine in the northwest and Provence in the south. More important, Louis XI ultimately obtained control of the two greatest independent fiefs, Brittany and Orléans, by marrying his son Charles to the heiress of Brittany and his daughter Jeanne to the heir of Orléans. When, in 1527, the lands of the duke of Bourbon fell to the crown, the French monarch ruled a unified state.

Long years of war established the principle of royal taxation, which was essential to the process of state building in France. This enabled the monarchy to raise money for defense and for consolidation. Because of the strength of the nobles, most taxation fell only on the commoners, the so-called third estate. Although there was much complaint about taxes, the French monarchy established a broad base for taxation and a high degree of compliance long before any other European nation.

Along with money went soldiers, needed to repel the English and to defend the crown against rebels and traitors. Again the French monarchy was the first to establish the principle of a national army, raised and directed from the center but quartered and equipped regionally. From the nobility were recruited the cavalry, from the towns and countryside the massive infantry. Fortified towns received privileges in return for military service to the king. Towns supplied small arms, pikes, and swords and later pistols and muskets. By the beginning of the sixteenth century, the French monarch could raise and equip an army of his own.

The Marriages of Spain. Before the sixteenth century there was little prospect of a single nation emerging on the Iberian peninsula. North African Muslims, called Moors, occupied the province of Granada in the south; the stable kingdom of Portugal dominated the western coast. The Spanish peoples were divided among a number of separate states. The two most important were Castile, the largest and wealthiest kingdom, and Aragon, which was composed of a number of quasi-independent regions, each of which maintained its own laws and institutions. Three religions and four languages (not including dialects) widened these political divisions. And the different states had different outlooks. Castile was, above all, determined to rid itself of the Moors in Granada and to convert to Christianity its large Jewish population. Aragon played in the high-stakes game for power in the Mediterranean. It claimed sovereignty over Sicily and Naples and exercised it whenever it could.

When Ferdinand of Aragon and Isabella of Castile secretly exchanged wedding vows in 1469, both their homelands were rent by civil war. In Castile, Isabella's brother Henry IV (1454–1474) struggled unsuccessfully against the powerful Castilian nobility. In Aragon, Ferdinand's father, John II (1458–1479), faced a revolt by the rich province of Catalonia on one side and the territorial ambitions of Louis XI of France on the other. Joining the heirs together increased the resources of both kingdoms.

Ferdinand and Isabella (1479–1516) took the first steps toward forging a Spanish state. Their most notable achievement was the final recovery of the lands that had been conquered by the Moors. For centuries the Spanish kingdoms had fought against the North African Muslims who had conquered large areas of the southern peninsula. The *reconquista* was characterized by short bursts of warfare followed by long periods of wary coexistence. By the middle of the fifteenth century, the Moorish territory had been reduced to the province of Granada. The final stage of the reconquista began in 1482 and lasted for a decade. It was waged as a holy war and was financed in part by grants from the pope and the Christian princes of Europe. In 1492, Granada finally fell, and the province was absorbed into Castile.

The reconquista played an important part in creating a national identity for the Christian peoples of Spain. To raise men and money for the war effort, Ferdinand and Isabella mobilized their nobility and town governments and created a central organization to oversee the invasion. The conquered territories were used to reward the men who had aided the effort, though the crown maintained control and jurisdiction over most of the province. But the idea of the holy war also had a darker side and an unanticipated consequence. The Jewish population that had lived peacefully in Castile and Aragon became another object of hostility. Many Jews had risen to prominence in government and in skilled professions. Others, who had accepted conversion to Christianity and were known as *conversos*, had become powerful figures in church and state.

Both groups were now attacked. The conversos fell prey to a special church tribunal created to examine their sincere devotion to Catholicism. This was the **Spanish Inquisition**, which, though it used traditional judicial practices—torture to gain confessions, public humiliation to show contrition, and burnings at the stake to maintain purity—used them on a scale never before seen. Thousands of conversos were killed, and many more families had their wealth confiscated to be used for the reconquista. In 1492, the Jews were expelled from Spain. Though the reconquista and the expulsion of the Jews inflicted great suffering on victims and incalculable loss to the Castilian economy, both events enhanced the prestige of the Catholic monarchs.

The joint presence of Ferdinand and Isabella in the provinces of Spain was symbolic of the unity they strove to achieve. Ferdinand made Castilian the official language of government in Aragon and even appointed Castilians to Aragonese posts. He and Isabella actively encouraged the intermarriage of the two aristocracies and the expansion of the number of wealthy nobles who held land in both kingdoms. Nevertheless, these measures did not unify Spain or erase the centuries-long tradition of hostility among the diverse Iberian peoples.

It was left to the heirs of Ferdinand and Isabella to forge together the Spanish kingdoms, and the process was a painful one. The hostility to a foreign monarch that both the Castilian nobility and the Aragonese towns had shown to Ferdinand and Isabella increased dramatically at the accession of their grandson Charles V (1516–1556), who had been born and raised in the Low Countries, where he ruled over Burgundy and the Netherlands. Through a series of dynastic accidents, Charles was heir to the Spanish crown with its possessions in the New World and to the vast Habsburg estates that included Austria. Charles established his rule in Spain gradually. For a time he was forced to share power in Castile and to suppress a disorganized aristocratic rebellion.

Because of his foreign obligations, Charles was frequently absent from Spain. During those periods he governed through regents and royal councils that did much to centralize administration. Though Castile and Aragon had separate councils, they were organized similarly and had greater contact than before. Charles V realized the importance of Spain, especially of Castile, in his empire. He established a permanent bureaucratic court, modeled on that of Burgundy, and placed able Spaniards at the head of its departments.

Flemish tapestry showing Isabella and Ferdinand attended by courtiers and ladies-in-waiting.

The most important factor in uniting the Spanish kingdoms, however, was the fact that Charles V brought Spain to the forefront of European affairs in the sixteenth century. Spanish prowess, whether in arms or in culture, became a source of national pride that helped to erode regional identity. Gold and silver from the New World helped to finance Charles's great empire, and he achieved nearly all of the ancient territorial ambitions of the Spanish kingdoms. In Italy, he prosecuted Aragonese claims to Sicily and Naples. In the north, he held on firmly to the kingdom of Navarre, which had been annexed by Ferdinand, and secured Spain's border with France. In the south, he blocked off Ottoman and Muslim expansion. The reign of Charles V ushered in the dawn of Spain's golden age.

The Dynastic Struggles

The formation of large states throughout Europe led inevitably to conflicts among them. Long chains of marriages among the families of the European princes meant that sooner or later the larger powers would lay claim to the same inheritances and test the matter by force. Thus the sixteenth century was a period of almost unrelieved general warfare in Europe.

Power and Glory

Wars were fought to further the interests of princes rather than the interests of national sovereignty or international Christianity. They were certainly not fought in the interests of their subjects. States were an extension of a prince's heritage. The wars of the sixteenth century were dynastic wars.

The New Monarchs waged war and defended their territories in new ways. Internal security depended on locally raised forces or hired mercenaries. Both required money, which was becoming available in unprecedented quantities as a result of the increasing prosperity of the early sixteenth century and the windfall of gold and silver from the New World. Developments in transport and supply enabled campaigns to take place far from the center of a state. Finally, communications were improving. The need for knowledge about potential rivals or allies had the effect of expanding the European system of diplomacy. Resident agents were established in all the European capitals, and they had a decisive impact on war and peace. Their dispatches formed the most reliable source of information about the strengths of armies or the weaknesses of governments, about the births of heirs or the deaths of princes.

The Italian Wars

The struggle for supremacy in Europe in the sixteenth century pitted the French house of Valois against the far-flung estates of the Habsburg Empire. Yet the wars took place in Italy. The rivalries among the larger Italian city-states proved to be fertile ground for the newly consolidated European monarchies. Both French and Spanish monarchs had remote but legitimate claims to the kingdom of Naples in southern Italy. In 1494, the French king, Charles VIII, took up an invitation from the ruler of Milan to intervene in Italian affairs. His campaign was an unqualified, if fleeting, success. He marched the length of the peninsula, overthrew the Medici in Florence, forced the pope to open the gates of Rome, and finally seized the crown of Naples. But the French appetite for Italian territory was not sated. Soon a deal was struck with Ferdinand of Aragon to divide the kingdom of Naples in two. All went according to plan until these thieves fell out among themselves. In the end, Spain wound up with all of Naples and France was left with nothing but debts and grievances.

Therefore, when Francis I came to the French throne and Charles V came to the Spanish, Naples was just one of several potential sources of friction. Not only had Ferdinand betrayed the French in Naples, he had also broken a long-standing peace on the Franco-Spanish border by conquering the independent but French-speaking kingdom of Navarre. Francis could be expected to avenge both slights. Charles, on the other hand, was the direct heir of the dukes of Burgundy. From his childhood he longed for the restoration of his ancestral lands, including Burgundy itself, which had been gobbled up by Louis XI after the death of Charles the Bold. Competition between Francis and Charles became all the more ferocious when Charles's grandfather, the Holy Roman Emperor Maximilian I (1486–1519), died in 1519. Both monarchs launched a vigorous campaign for the honor of succeeding him.

Charles V, who now inherited the Habsburg lands in Austria and Germany, succeeded to this eminent but empty dignity. His election as Holy Roman Emperor not only aggravated the personal animosity among the monarchs, but added another source of conflict in Italy. When Louis XII (1498–1515) had succeeded to the throne of France, he had laid claim to the duchy of Milan through an interest of his wife's, though he was unable to enforce it. Francis I proved more capable. In 1515, he stunned all of Europe by crushing the vaunted Swiss mercenaries at the battle of Marignano. But the duchy of Milan was a territory under the protection of the Holy Roman Emperor, and it soon appealed for imperial troops to help repel the French invaders. Milan was strategically important to Charles V because it was the vital link between his Austrian and Burgundian possessions. Almost as soon as he took up the imperial mantle, Charles V was determined to challenge Francis I in Italy.

The key to such a challenge was the construction of alliances among the various Italian city-states and most especially with England, whose aid both Charles and Francis sought to enlist in the early 1520s. Henry VII had found foreign alliances a ready source of cash, and he was always eager to enter into them as long as they did not involve raising armies and fighting wars. Henry VIII was made of sterner stuff. He longed to reconquer France and to cut a figure on the European scene. Charles V made two separate trips to London, and Henry crossed the Channel in 1520 to meet Francis I.

The result of these diplomatic intrigues was an alliance between England and the Holy Roman Empire. English and Burgundian forces would stage an invasion of northern France, while Spanish and German troops would again attempt to dislodge the French from Italy. The strategy worked better than anyone could have imagined. In 1523, Charles's forces gained a foothold in Milan by taking the heavily fortified town of Pavia. Two years later, Francis was ready to strike back. At the head of his own royal guards, he massed Swiss mercenaries and French infantry outside Pavia and made ready for a swift assault. Instead, a large imperial army arrived to relieve the town, and in the subsequent battle, the French suffered a shattering defeat. Francis I was captured.

The victory at Pavia, which occurred on Charles V's twenty-fifth birthday, seemingly made him master of all of Europe. His ally Henry VIII urged an immediate invasion and dismemberment of France and began raising an army to spearhead the attack. But Charles's position was much less secure than it appeared. The Ottomans threatened his Hungarian territories, and the Protestants threatened his German lands. He could not afford a war of conquest in France. His hope now was to reach an agreement with Francis I for a lasting European peace, and for this purpose the French king was brought in captivity to Madrid. Charles's terms, however, led not to peace but to 30 years of warfare.

Jean Clouet, *Portrait of Francis I* (sixteenth century). Rivalry between Francis and Charles V plunged Europe into decades of war.

Charles demanded that Burgundy be returned to him. Though Francis was hardly in a position to bargain, he held out on this issue for as long as possible and secretly prepared a disavowal of the final agreement before it was made. By the Treaty of Madrid in 1526, Francis I yielded Burgundy and recognized the Spanish conquest of Navarre and Spanish rule in Naples. The agreement was sealed by the marriage of Francis to Charles's sister, Eleanor of Portugal. But marriage was not sufficient security for such a complete capitulation. To secure his release from Spain, Francis was required to leave behind as hostages his seven- and eight-year-old sons until the treaty was fulfilled. For three years the children languished in Spanish captivity.

No sooner had he set foot on French soil than Francis I renounced the Treaty of Madrid. Despite the threat that this posed to his children, Francis argued that the terms had been extracted against his will, and he even gained the sanction of the pope for violating his oath. Setting France on a war footing, he began seeking new allies. Henry VIII, disappointed with the meager spoils of his last venture, switched sides. So, too, did a number of Italian city-states, including Rome. Most important, Francis I entered into an alliance with the Ottoman sultan, Suleiman the Magnificent (1520–1566), whose armies were pressing against the southeastern borders of the Holy Roman Empire. In the year following Pavia, the Ottomans secured an equally decisive triumph at Mohacs, which cut Hungary in two and threatened Vienna, the eastern capital of the Habsburg lands. Almost overnight, Charles V had been turned from hunter into hunted. The Ottoman threat demanded immediate attention in Germany, the French and English were preparing to strike in the Low Countries, and the Italian wars continued. In 1527, Charles's unpaid German mercenaries stormed through Rome, sacked the papal capital, and captured the pope. Christian Europe was mortified.

The struggle for European mastery ground on for decades. The Treaty of Cateau-Cambrésis in 1559 brought to a close 60 years of conflict. In the end, the French were no more capable of dislodging the Habsburgs from Italy than were the Habsburgs of forcing the Ottomans out of Hungary. The great stores of silver that poured into Castile from the New World were consumed in the fires of continental warfare. In 1557, both France and Spain declared bankruptcy to avoid foreclosures by their creditors. For the French, the Italian wars were disastrous. They seriously undermined the state's financial base, eroded confidence in the monarchy, and thinned the ranks of the ruling nobility. The adventure begun by Charles VIII in search of glory brought France nearly to ruin. It ended with fitting irony. After the death of Francis I, his son Henry II (1547–1559) continued the struggle. Henry never forgave his father for abandoning him in Spain, and he sought revenge on Charles V, who had been his jailer. He regarded the Treaty of Cateau-Cambrésis as a victory and celebrated it with great pomp and pageantry. Among the feasts and festivities were athletic competitions for the king's courtiers and attendants. Henry II entered the jousting tournament and there was killed.

SUMMARY

European Encounters The need to establish secure trade routes with the East fueled early European expansion. Portugal, under the leadership of Prince Henry the Navigator, explored the coast of Africa. Portuguese exploration resulted in a commercial empire in the East and the acceleration of the slave trade. The voyages of Columbus initiated the process of Spanish conquest in the Americas. Profit, the spread of Christianity, and glory drove European expansion.

The Formation of States Although the obstacles to large state formation were formidable in the fifteenth century, they were not powerful enough to stop the process from moving forward. The rulers of Muscovy took advantage of favorable circumstances to create a vast state. In the aftermath of the Wars of the Roses, Henry VII helped transform England's poor and weak monarchy into a stable and efficient institution. Luck played an important role in the consolidation of royal authority in France under Louis XI. The marriage of Ferdinand of Aragon and Isabella of Castile started the process of national unification in Spain.

The Dynastic Struggles The sixteenth century was a period of almost constant dynastic warfare. The New Monarchs waged war and defended their territories in new ways. The struggle for supremacy in Europe in the sixteenth century pitted the

French house of Valois against the far-flung estates of the Habsburg Empire. Most of the actual fighting took place in Italy. Emperor Charles V secured the support of Henry VIII of England in his battle with France for supremacy in Italy. French defeat and the capture of Francis I allowed Charles V to force the French king to accept the harsh terms of the Treaty of Madrid. The situation soon reversed itself with a number of Charles's allies, including Henry VIII, switching sides and supporting the French. The struggle for European mastery ground on for decades, with the Treaty of Cateau-Cambrésis in 1559 finally bringing the conflict to a close.

QUESTIONS FOR REVIEW

1. What impulses in European society were revealed by the global exploration and conquests of the Portuguese and the Spanish?
2. What qualities characterized the New Monarchies and what are some of the best examples of such princely states?
3. How and why did the experience of political and territorial unification differ in England, France, and Spain?
4. How did war between the great European monarchies contribute to unity within each?

The Reform of Religion

The Intellectual Reformation

In the early sixteenth century, reformers throughout western Europe preached new ideas about religious doctrine and religious practice. At first these ideas took the form of a sustained critique of the Roman Catholic Church, but they soon developed a momentum of their own. Some reformers remained within traditional Catholicism; others moved outside and founded new Protestant churches. Wherever this movement for religious reform, whether Catholic or Protestant, appeared, it was fed by new ideas. And the rapid communication of new ideas was made possible by the development of printing, which appeared in Germany in the late fifteenth century and spread across Europe in the succeeding decades. Yet printing was as much a result as a cause of the spread of ideas. The humanist call for a return to the study of the classics and for the creation of accurate texts, first heard in Italy, aroused scholars and leaders in all of the European states. Their appetite for manuscripts exhausted the abilities of the scribes and booksellers who reproduced texts. Printing responded to that demand.

The Print Revolution

Printing, one of the true technological revolutions in western history, was not invented. It developed as a result of progress made in allied industries, especially papermaking and goldsmithing. A number of German craftsmen experimented with using movable metal type to make exact reproductions of manuscripts on paper. In the 1450s in Mainz, Johannes Gutenberg (ca. 1400–1468) and his partners succeeded and published their famous Bibles.

Once it was begun, printing spread like wildfire. Most of the early printed works were either religious or classical. Bibles, church service books, and the commentaries of the Church Fathers were most common. Cicero topped the list of classical authors.

An early German print shop. The man at the left operates the screw press while an apprentice (right) stacks the printed sheets. The man in the back is setting type for the next impression.

Printing rapidly came to be a basic part of life. In the first 40 years after the presses were first set up, perhaps as many as 20 million books were produced and distributed. Printing changed the habits of teachers and students, the way in which the state conducted its business, and the methods of legal training and legal proceedings. Compilations of laws could now be widely distributed and more uniformly enforced. Printing had a similar effect on the development of scientific study. The printing press popularized the discoveries of the New World and contributed to the reproduction of more accurate charts and maps, which in turn facilitated further discovery. Printing also helped to standardize language by frequent repetition of preferred usage and spelling. Perhaps most important, printing created an international intellectual community whose ideas could be dispersed the length and breadth of the Continent. The printing press enhanced the value of ideas and of thinking. Nothing could be more central to the reform of religion.

Christian Humanism

Many of the ideas that spread across Europe as the result of the printing revolution originated in Italian humanism (see Chapter 11). The revival of classical literature, with its concern for purity in language and eloquence in style, was one of the most admired achievements of the Renaissance. By the beginning of the sixteenth century, the force of humanism was felt strongly in northern and western Europe, where it was grafted onto the traditional theological teaching. The combination was a new and powerful intellectual movement known as **Christian humanism.**

The humanism of the north differed from that of the Italian city-states. Although the Italian humanists were certainly Christian, they were interested in secular subjects, especially in mastering classical languages and translating classical texts. Italian humanists had established techniques for the recovery of accurate texts and had developed principles for compiling the scholarly editions that now poured forth from the printing presses. Christian humanists applied these techniques to the study of the authorities and texts of the Church. Most of the new humanists had been trained in Italy, where they devoted themselves to the mastery of Greek and Latin. They had imbibed the idea that scholars, using their own critical faculties, could establish the authority of texts and the meaning of words. Building on the patient work of their predecessors and the advantages offered by printing, this new generation of humanists brought learning to educated men and women throughout Europe.

Christian humanism was a program of reform rather than a philosophy. It aimed to make better Christians through better education. Humanists were especially interested in the education of women. Thomas More (1478–1535) raised his daughters to be among the educated elite of England. Renowned women scholars held places at Italian universities. Humanist educational principles posed an implicit challenge to Roman Catholicism. Schools had once been the monopoly of the

Church, which used them to train clergymen. Literacy itself had been preserved over the centuries so that the gospel could be propagated.

By the sixteenth century these purposes had been transformed. Schools now trained many people who were not destined for careers in the Church, and literacy served the needs of the state, the aristocracy, and the merchant classes. More important, as the humanists perfected their techniques of scholarship, the Church continued to rely on traditional methods of training and traditional texts. Rote memorization of the opinions of others was more highly valued than critical thinking. The Vulgate Bible was used throughout western Christendom. It was now a thousand years old.

The Humanist Movement

Many humanist criticisms of Church teaching focused on its failure to inspire individuals to live a Christian life. Humanist writers were especially scathing about popular practices that bordered on superstition, such as pilgrimages to holy places or the worship of relics from the early history of the Church. Christian humanists wanted to inspire Christians.

Christian humanism was an international movement. The humanists formed the elite of the intellectual world of the sixteenth century, and their services were sought by princes and peers as well as by the most distinguished universities. In fact, the New Monarchs supported the humanists and protected them from their critics.

The centerpiece of humanist reforms was the translation of Christian texts. Skilled in Greek and Latin, informed by scholars of Hebrew and Aramaic, humanist writers prepared new editions of the books of the Bible and of the writings of the early Church Fathers.

The Wit of Erasmus

Orphaned at an early age, Desiderius Erasmus of Rotterdam (ca. 1466–1536) was educated by the Brothers of the Common Life, a lay brotherhood that specialized in schooling children and preparing them for a monastic life. Marked out early by his extraordinary intellectual gifts, Erasmus entered a monastery and was then allowed to travel to pursue his studies, first in France and then in England.

Erasmus devoted his life to restoring the direct connection between the individual Christian and the textual basis of Christian doctrine. Although he is called the father of biblical criticism, Erasmus was not a theologian. He was more interested in the practical impact of ideas than in the ideas themselves. His scathing attacks on the Scholastics, popular superstition, and the pretensions of the traditionalists in the Church and the universities all had the same goal: to restore the experiences of Christ to the center of Christianity.

Though his patrons were the rich and his language was Latin, Erasmus also hoped to reach men and women lower down the social order, those whom he believed the Church had failed to educate. "The doctrine of Christ casts aside no age, no sex, no fortune or position in life. It keeps no one at a distance."

The Lutheran Reformation

On the surface, the Roman Catholic Church appeared to be as strong as ever at the beginning of the sixteenth century. Yet everywhere in Europe, the cry was for reform. Wherever one turned, one saw abuses. Parish livings were sold to the highest bidder to raise money. This was simony. Rich appointments were given to the kinsmen of powerful Church leaders rather than to those who were most qualified. This was nepotism. Individual clergymen accumulated numerous positions whose responsibilities they could not fulfill. This was pluralism. Some priests who took the vow of chastity lived openly with their concubines. Some mendicants who took the vow of poverty dressed in silk and ate from golden plates.

The Spark of Reform

Europe was becoming more religious. The signs of religious fervor were everywhere. Cities hired preachers to expound the gospel. Pilgrims to the shrines of saints clogged the roadways every spring and summer. Endowments of masses for the dead increased. Henry VII of England provided money for 10,000 masses to be said for his soul. Even city merchants might bequeath funds for several hundred masses. In the chantries, where such services were performed, there were neither enough priests nor enough altars to supply the demand.

People wanted more from the Church than the Church could possibly give them. Humanists condemned visits to the shrines as superstitious; pilgrims demanded that the relics be made more accessible. Reformers complained of pluralism; the clergy complained that they could not live on the salary of a single office. Civic authorities demanded that the established Church take greater responsibility for good works; the pope demanded that civic authorities help to pay for them.

Contradiction and paradox dominated the movements for reform. Though the most vocal critics of the Church complained that its discipline was too lax, for many ordinary people its demands were too rigorous. The obligations of penance and confession weighed heavily on them. Church doctrine held that sins had to be washed away before the souls of the dead could enter heaven. Until then, they suffered in purgatory. Sins were cleansed through penance, the performance of acts of contrition assigned after confession. But the ordeal of confession kept many people away. It is hardly surprising that the sale of **indulgences** became a popular substitute for penance and confession.

The Sale of Indulgences

An indulgence was a portion of the treasury of good works performed by righteous Christians throughout the ages. Indulgences could be granted to people who wanted to atone for their sins. Strictly speaking, an indulgence supplemented penance rather than substituted for it. It was effective only for the contrite—for sinners who repented of their sins. But as the practice of granting indulgences spread, this subtle distinction largely disappeared. The living bought indulgences to cleanse the sins of the dead, and some even bought indulgences in anticipation of sins they had not yet committed.

By the sixteenth century, to limit abuses by local church authorities, only the pope, through his agents, could grant indulgences. Popes used special occasions to offer an indulgence for pilgrimages to Rome or for contributions to special papal projects. Other indulgences were licensed locally, usually at the shrines of saints or at churches that contained relics.

The indulgence controversy was a symptom rather than a cause of the explosion of feelings that erupted in the small German town of Wittenberg in 1517. In that year the pope was offering an indulgence to help finance the rebuilding of Saint Peter's Basilica in Rome. The pope chose Prince Albert of Brandenburg (1490–1545) to distribute the indulgence in Germany, and Albert hired the Dominican friar Johann Tetzel (ca. 1465–1519) to preach its benefits.

Martin Luther Challenges the Church

Enthusiasm for the indulgence spread to the neighboring state of Saxony, where the ruler, Frederick III, the Wise (1463–1525), banned its sale. Frederick's great collection of relics carried their own indulgences, and Tetzel offered unwelcome competition. But

An anonymous caricature of Johann Tetzel, whose sale of an indulgence inspired Martin Luther's Ninety-five Theses. Tetzel answered with 122 theses of his own but was rebuked and disowned by the Catholics.

Saxons flocked into Brandenburg to make their purchases, and by the end of October, Tetzel was not very far from Wittenberg Castle, where Frederick's relics were housed. On All Saints' Day the relics would be opened to view. On the night before, Martin Luther (1483–1546), a professor of theology at Wittenberg University, posted on the door of the castle church ninety-five theses attacking indulgences and their sale.

In so doing, Luther was following the Scholastic tradition of disputation, in which scholars presented propositions, or theses, for open debate with all comers. Luther's theses were controversial, but they were meant to be. Only circumstance moved Luther's theses from the academic to the public sphere. Already there was growing concern among clergy and theologians about Tetzel's blatant sale of indulgences.

Luther's theses focused this concern and finally communicated it beyond the walls of the Church and the university. The theses were quickly translated into German and spread throughout the Holy Roman Empire.

Martin Luther's Faith

In his youth Martin Luther had studied for a career in law, but against his father's wishes he entered an Augustinian monastery and was ordained a priest in 1507. He received his doctorate at the university in Wittenberg and was appointed to the theology faculty in 1512.

In all outward appearances, Luther was successful and contented, but beneath this tranquil exterior lay a soul in torment. Despite his devotion, he could not erase his sense of sin; he could not convince himself that he could achieve the righteousness God demanded of him.

Knowledge of his salvation came to Luther through study. His internal agonies led him to ponder over and over again the biblical passages that described the righteousness of God. In the intellectual tradition in which he had been trained, that righteousness was equated with law. The righteous person either followed God's law or was punished by God's wrath. It was this understanding that tormented him.

Even before he wrote his Ninety-five Theses, Luther had made the first breakthrough by a unique reading of the writings of Saint Paul. "I pondered night and day until I understood the connection between the righteousness of God and the sentence 'The just shall live by faith.' Then I grasped that the justice of God is the righteousness by which through grace and pure mercy, God justifies us through faith. Immediately I felt that I had been reborn and that I had passed through wide open doors into paradise!" Finally he came to believe that the righteousness of God was a gift freely given to the faithful and that to receive God's righteousness, one had only to believe in God's infinite mercy. It was this belief that fortified Luther during his years of struggle with both civil and Church powers.

Over the next several years, Luther refined his spiritual philosophy and drew out the implications of his newfound beliefs. His religion was shaped by three interconnected tenets. First came justification by faith alone—**sola fide**. An individual's everlasting salvation came from faith in God's goodness rather than from the performance of good works. Sin could not be washed away by penance, and it could not be forgiven by indulgence. Second, faith came only through the knowledge and contemplation of the Word of God—*sola scriptura*. All that was needed to understand the justice and mercy of God was contained in the Bible. Reading the Word, hearing the Word, expounding on and studying the Word—this was the path to faith and through faith to salvation. Third, all who believed in God's righteousness and had achieved their faith through the study of the Bible were equal in God's eyes. The priesthood included all believers. Each followed his or her own calling and found his or her own faith through Scripture. Ministers and preachers could help others to learn God's Word, but they could not confer faith.

From Luther to Lutheranism

The first to feel the seriousness of Luther's challenge to the established order was the reformer himself. The head of Luther's order, a papal legate, and finally the Emperor Charles V all called for Luther to recant his views on indulgences. Luther was excommunicated by Pope Leo X in 1521 and ordered by Charles V to appear before the diet, or assembly, in Worms, Germany, in April of that year. There he gave the same infuriating reply: If he could be shown the places in the Bible that contradicted his views, he would gladly change them. Charles V declared Luther an enemy of the empire. In both Church and state he was now an outlaw.

In fact, during the three years between the posting of his theses and his appearance before the emperor, Luther came to conclusions that were much more radical than his initial attack on indulgences. He came to believe that the papacy was a human rather than a divine invention. Therefore, he denounced both the papacy and the general councils of the Church. In his *Address to the Christian Nobility of the German Nation* (1520) he called on the princes to take the reform of religion into their own hands.

But Luther had attracted powerful supporters as well as powerful enemies. Prince Frederick III of Saxony consistently intervened on his behalf, and the delicate international situation forced Luther's chief antagonists to move more slowly than they might have wished. The pope hoped first to keep Charles V off the imperial throne and then to maintain a united front with the German princes against him. Charles V, already locked in his lifelong struggle with the French, needed German military support and peace in his German territories. These factors consistently played into Luther's hands.

While the pope and the emperor were otherwise occupied, Luther refined his ideas and won important converts. As time passed, Luther's reputation grew, not only in Germany, but all over Europe. Between 1517 and 1520, he published 30 works, all of which achieved massive sales. Luther's individual accomplishments were remarkable, but what turned his theology into a movement, which after 1529 came to be known as Protestantism, was the support he received among German princes and within German cities.

Princes and Cities. Individual princes turned to Luther's theology for several reasons. First and foremost was sincere religious conviction. Second were political and economic factors. As German princes worked to centralize their administrations, protect themselves from predatory neighbors, and increase their revenues, they felt the burden of papal exactions. Taxes and gifts flowed south to a papacy dominated by Italians. Luther's call for civil rulers to lead their own churches meant that civil rulers could keep their own revenues.

The Reformation spread particularly well in the German cities, especially those to which the emperor had granted the status of freedom from the rule of any prince. The cities had long struggled with the tension of the separate jurisdictions of state and Church. Much urban property was owned by the Church and so was exempt from taxation and law enforcement, and the clergy constituted a significant proportion of urban populations. Reformed religion stressed the equality of clergy and laity and thus the indisputable power of civil authorities. Paradoxically, it was because the cities contained large numbers of priests that Luther's ideas reached the cities quickly. Many of his earliest students served urban congregations and began to develop doctrines and practices that, though based on Luther's ideas, were adapted to the circumstances of city life. Moreover, the imperial free cities were also centers of the printing trade and home to many of the most noted humanists who were initially important in spreading Luther's ideas.

Luther's message held great appeal for the middle orders in the towns. These groups resented the privileges given to priests and members of religious orders who paid no taxes and were exempt from the obligations of citizenship. The level of anticlericalism, always high in Germany, was especially acute in cities that were suffering economic difficulties. Pressure from ordinary people and petty traders forced town leaders into action. The evangelism of reforming ministers created converts and an atmosphere of reform. Support from members of the ruling oligarchy both mobilized these pressures and capitalized on them. Town governments secured their own autonomy over the Church, tightening their grip on the institutions of social control and enhancing the social and economic authority of their members.

The Appeal for Women. Religious reform appealed to women as well as men, but it affected them differently. Noblewomen were among the most important defenders of Protestant reformers, especially in states in which the prince opposed it. Marguerite of Navarre (1492–1549), sister of Francis I, frequently intervened with her brother on behalf of individual Lutherans who fell afoul of Church authorities. Mary of Hungary (1505–1558) played a similar role in the Holy Roman Empire. Bona, wife of Sigismund I of Poland, was especially important in eastern reform. An Italian by birth, Bona (1493–1558) was a central figure in spreading both Renaissance art and humanist learning into Poland.

Luther's reforms also appealed to women who were not so highly placed in society. The doctrine of the equality of all believers put men and women on an equal spiritual footing even if it did nothing to break the male monopoly of the ministry. In the private sphere, family life became the center of faith when salvation was removed from the control of the Church.

By following humanist teaching on the importance of educating women of the upper orders and by encouraging literacy, the reformers did much that was uplifting. Girls' schools were founded in a number of German cities, and townswomen could use their newly acquired skills in their roles as shopkeepers, family accountants, and teachers of their children. But there were losses as well as gains. The attack on the worship of saints and especially of the Virgin Mary removed female images from religion. Protestantism was male-dominated in a way that Catholicism was not. Moreover, the emphasis on reading the Bible tended to reinforce the image of women as weak and inherently sinful. The dissolution of the convents took away the one institution that valued women's gender and allowed them to pursue a spiritual life outside marriage.

The Spread of Lutheranism

By the end of the 1520s, the empire was divided between cities and states that accepted reformed religion and those that adhered to Roman Catholicism. Large German communities across northern Europe, mostly founded as trading outposts, became focal points for the penetration of reformist ideas.

Merchants and students carried Luther's ideas into Scandinavia, but there the importance of political leaders was crucial. Christian III (1534–1559) of Denmark had been present at the Diet of Worms when Luther made his famous reply to Charles V. Christian was deeply impressed by the reformer, and after a ruinous civil war he confiscated Catholic Church property in Denmark and created a reformed religion under Luther's direct supervision.

Paradoxically, Lutheranism came to Sweden as part of an effort to throw off the yoke of Danish dominance. When Gustav I Vasa (1523–1560) led a successful uprising against the Danes and became king of Sweden, he encouraged the spread of Protestant ideas.

As important as Protestant ideas were in northern and central Europe, they proved most fertile in the Swiss towns of the empire. Here was planted the second generation of reformers, theologians who drew radical new conclusions from Luther's insights. In the east, Huldrych Zwingli (1484–1531) brought reformed religion to the town of Zurich. Educated at the University of Basel and deeply influenced by humanist thought early in his career, Zwingli was a preacher among the Swiss mercenary troops that fought for the empire. In 1516, he met Erasmus in Basel and, under his influence, began a study of the Greek writings of the Church Fathers and of the New Testament. Zwingli was also influenced by reports of Luther's defiance of the pope, for his own antipapal views were already developing.

MAP DISCOVERY

THE SPREAD OF LUTHERANISM

Observe the extent of Lutheranism across Europe in the sixteenth century. Where was Lutheranism concentrated? Notice how Lutheranism swept through entire states. How was Europe divided between Protestants and Catholics?

Perhaps most decisively for his early development, Zwingli was stricken by plague in 1519. In his life-and-death struggle he came to a profoundly personal realization of the power of God's mercy.

These experiences became the basis for the reform theology that Zwingli preached in Zurich. He believed that the Church had to recover its earlier purity and to reject the innovations in practices that successive popes and general councils had brought in. He stressed the equality of believers, justification by faith alone, and the sufficiency of the gospel as authority for church practice. He attacked indulgences, penance, clerical celibacy, prayers to the Virgin, statues and images in churches, and a long list of other practices. He regarded the Mass as a commemorative event rather than one that involved the real presence of Christ. His arguments were so effective that the town council adopted them as the basis for a reform of religion.

The principles that Zwingli preached quickly spread to neighboring Swiss states. Practical as well as theological, Zwingli's reforms were carried out by the civil government with which he allied himself. This was not the same as the protection that princes had given to Lutherans. Rather, in the places that came under Zwingli's influence, there was an important integration of church and state. He stressed the divine origins of civil government and the importance of the magistrate as an agent of Christian reform.

This theocratic idea—that the leaders of the state and the leaders of the church were linked—became the basis for further social and political reform.

The Protestant Reformation

By the middle of the 1530s, Protestant reform had entered a new stage. Luther did not intend to form a new religion; his struggle had been with Rome. His religion was one of protest. The second generation of reformers faced a different task. The new reformers were the church builders who had to systematize doctrine for a generation that had already accepted religious reform. Their challenge was to draw out the logic of reformed ideas and to create enduring structures for reformed churches.

Geneva and Calvin

The Reformation came late to Geneva. In the sixteenth century, Geneva was under the dual government of the duchy of Savoy and the Catholic bishop of the town, who was frequently a Savoy client. The Genevans also had their own town council, which traditionally struggled for power against the bishop. By the 1530s the council had gained the upper hand. The council confiscated Church lands and institutions, secularized the Church's legal powers, and forced the bishop and most of his administrators to flee the city. War with Savoy inevitably followed, and Geneva would certainly have been crushed into submission except for its alliance with neighboring Bern, a potent military power among the Swiss towns.

Geneva was saved and was free to follow its own course in religious matters. In 1536, the adult male citizens of the city voted to become Protestant. But there was as yet no reformer in Geneva to establish a Protestant program and no clear definition of what that program might be.

John Calvin (1509–1564) was born in France, the son of a bishop's secretary. His education was based on humanist principles, and he learned Greek and Hebrew, studied theology, and received a legal degree from the University of Orléans.

This painting depicts a Calvinist service in Lyon, France, in 1564. The men and women are segregated, and the worshippers are seated according to rank. An hourglass times the preacher's sermon.

Around the age of 20 he converted to Lutheranism. Francis I was determined to root Protestants out of France, and Calvin fled Paris. Persecution of Protestants continued in France, and one of Calvin's close friends was burned for heresy. Ultimately, Calvin decided to settle in Strasbourg, where he could retire from public affairs and live out his days as a scholar.

War between France and the empire clogged the major highways to Strasbourg. Therefore Calvin and his companions detoured through Geneva, where Guillaume Farel (1489–1565), one of Geneva's leading Protestant reformers, persuaded Calvin to remain in Geneva and lead its reformation.

Calvin's greatest contributions to religious reform came in church structure and discipline. Like Luther and Zwingli, he believed that salvation came from God's grace. But more strongly than his predecessors, he believed that the gift of faith was granted only to some and that each individual's salvation or damnation was predestined before birth. The doctrine of **predestination** was a traditional one, but Calvin emphasized it differently and brought it to the center of the problem of faith. Those who were predestined to salvation were obliged to govern; those who were predestined to damnation were obliged to be governed.

Calvin structured the institution of the Genevan church in four parts: the pastors, who preached the Word to their congregations; the doctors, who studied and wrote; the deacons, who oversaw the institutions of social welfare, such as hospitals and schools, run by the church; and finally the elders of the church, who governed the church in all moral matters. They were the most controversial part of Calvin's establishment and the most fundamental. They had the power to discipline. Chosen from among the elite of the city, the 12 elders enforced the strict Calvinist moral code that extended into all aspects of private life.

The structure that Calvin gave to the Genevan church soon became the basis for reforms throughout the Continent. The Calvinist church was self-governing, independent of the state, and therefore capable of surviving and even flourishing in a hostile environment. Expanded over the course of several editions, Calvin's *The Institutes of the Christian Religion* became the most influential work of Protestant theology. Perhaps its greatest impact was in Britain, where the reformation took place not once but twice.

The English Reformation

The king of England wanted a divorce. Henry VIII had been married to Catherine of Aragon (1485–1536) as long as he had been king, and she had borne him no male heir to carry on his line. She had given birth to six children and endured several miscarriages, yet only one daughter, Mary, survived. Henry came to believe that this was God's punishment for his marriage. Catherine had been married first to Henry's older brother, who had died as a teenager, and there was at least one scriptural prohibition against marrying a brother's wife. A papal dispensation had been provided for the marriage; now Henry wanted a papal dispensation for an annulment. For three years his case ground its way through the papal courts. Catherine of Aragon was the aunt of the Emperor Charles V, and the emperor had taken her side in the controversy. With imperial power in Italy at its height, the pope was content to hear all of the complex legal and biblical precedents argued at leisure.

By 1533, Henry could wait no longer. He had already impregnated Anne Boleyn (ca. 1507–1536), one of the ladies-in-waiting at his court, and for the child—which Henry was certain would be a boy—to be legitimate, a marriage would have to take place at once. Legislation was prepared in Parliament to prevent papal interference in the decisions of England's courts, and Thomas Cranmer (1489–1556), archbishop of Canterbury, England's highest ecclesiastical officer, agreed to annul Henry's first marriage and celebrate his second. This was the first step in a complete break with Rome. Under the guidance of Thomas Cromwell (ca. 1485–1540), the English Parliament passed statute after statute that made Henry supreme head of the Church in England and owner of its vast wealth. Monasteries were dissolved, and a Lutheran service was introduced. On 7 September 1533, Anne Boleyn gave birth not to the expected son, but to a daughter, the future Queen Elizabeth I.

The Church of England. Henry's reformation was an act of state, but the English Reformation was not. There was an English tradition of dissent from the Roman Church that stretched back to the fourteenth century. Anticlericalism was especially virulent in the towns, where citizens refused to pay fees to priests for performing services such as burial. And humanist ideas flourished in England, where Thomas More, John Colet, and a host of others supported both the new learning and its efforts to reform spiritual life. Luther's attack on ritual and the Mass and his emphasis on Scripture and faith echoed the lost Lollard program and found many recruits in London and the northern port towns.

Protestantism grew slowly in England because it was vigorously repressed. Like Francis I and Charles V, Henry VIII viewed actual attacks on the established church as potential attacks on the established state. Henry had earned the title Defender of the Faith from the pope in 1521 for authoring an attack on Luther.

Henry's divorce unleashed a groundswell of support for religious change. The king's own religious beliefs remained a secret, but Anne Boleyn and Thomas Cromwell sponsored Lutheran reforms, and Thomas Cranmer put them into practice. Religion was legislated through Parliament, and the valuable estates of the Church were sold to the gentry. These practices found favor with both the legal profession and the landed elites and made Protestantism more palatable among these conservative groups. It was in the reign of Edward VI (1547–1553), Henry's son by his third wife, that the central doctrinal and devotional changes were made. Church service was now conducted in English, and the first two English prayer books were created. The Mass was reinterpreted along Zwinglian lines and became the Lord's Supper, the altar became the communion table, and the priest became the minister. Preaching became the center of the church service, and concern about the education of learned ministers resulted in commissions to examine and reform the clergy.

Beginning in the 1530s, state repression turned against Catholics. Those who would not swear the new oaths of allegiance or recognize the legality of Henry VIII's marriage suffered for their beliefs as the early Protestants had suffered for theirs. Thomas More and over 40 others paid with their lives for their opposition. An uprising in the north in 1536, known as the Pilgrimage of Grace, was suppressed, but Catholicism continued to flourish in England, surviving underground during the reigns of Henry and Edward and reemerging under Mary I (1553–1558).

The Successors of Henry VIII. Mary Tudor, the first woman to rule England, held to the Catholic beliefs in which her mother, Catherine of Aragon, had raised her, and she vowed to bring the nation back to her mother's church. She reestablished papal sovereignty, abolished Protestant worship, and introduced a crash program of education in the universities to train a new generation of priests. Catholic retribution for the blood of their martyrs was not long in coming. Cranmer and three other bishops were burned for heresy.

Nearly 800 Protestants fled the country rather than suffer a similar fate. These Marian exiles, as they came to be called, settled in a number of reformed communities, Zurich, Frankfurt, and Geneva among them. There they imbibed the second generation of Protestant ideas, especially Calvinism, and from there they began a propaganda campaign to keep reformed religion alive in England. It was the Marian exiles who were chiefly responsible for the second English reformation, which began in 1558 when Mary died and her half-sister, Elizabeth I (1558–1603), came to the throne.

Under Elizabeth, England returned to Protestantism, but not the Protestantism that had come before. Even the most advanced reforms during Edward's reign now seemed too moderate for the returning exiles. Against Elizabeth's wishes, the English church adopted the Calvinist doctrine of predestination and the simplification (but not wholesale reorganization) of the structure of the church. But it did not become a model of thoroughgoing reformation. The Thirty-nine Articles (1563) continued the English tradition of compromising points of disrupted doctrine and of maintaining traditional practices wherever possible.

The Reformation of the Radicals

Schism breeds schism. That was the stick with which Catholic Church and civil authorities beat Luther from the beginning. By attacking the authority of the established church and flouting the authority of the established state, he was fomenting social upheaval. But he insisted that his own ideas buttressed rather than subverted authority, especially civil authority under whose protection he had placed the Church. As early as 1525, peasants in Swabia appealed to Luther for support in their social rebellion. They based some of their most controversial demands, such as the abolition of tithes and labor service, on biblical authority. Luther instructed the rebels to lay down their arms and await their just rewards in heaven. But Luther's ideas had a life of their own. He clashed with Erasmus over free will and with Zwingli over the Mass. Toward the end of his life he felt that he was holding back the floodgates against the second generation of Protestant thinkers. Time and again, serious reformers wanted to take one or another of his doctrines further than he was willing to go himself.

The most dangerous threat to the establishment of an orthodox Protestantism came from groups who were described, not very precisely, as **Anabaptists**. Though this label—which means, literally, "baptism again"—identified people who practiced adult baptism, it was mainly used to tar religious opponents with the brush of extremism. Anabaptists appeared in a number of German and Swiss towns in the 1520s. Taking seriously the doctrine of justification by faith, Anabaptists argued that only believers could be members of the true church of God. Because baptism was the sacrament through which entry into the church took place, Anabaptists reasoned that it was a sacrament for adults rather than infants. But infant baptism was a core doctrine for both Catholics and Protestants. It symbolized the acceptance of Christ, and without it, eternal salvation was impossible. It was a practical doctrine. Unbaptized infants who died could not be accepted in heaven, and infant mortality was appallingly common.

Thus the doctrine of Anabaptism posed a psychological as well as a doctrinal threat to the reformers. But the practice of adult baptism paled in significance compared to many of the other conclusions that religious radicals derived from the principle of sola scriptura—by the Word alone. Some groups argued the case that since true Christians were only those who had faith, all others must be cast out of the church. These true Christians formed small separate sects. Many believed that their lives were guided by the Holy Spirit, who directed them from within. Some went further and denied the power of civil authority over true believers. Some argued for community of goods among believers and rejected private property. Others literally followed passages in the Old Testament that suggested polygamy and promiscuity.

Wherever they settled, these small bands of believers were persecuted to the brutal extent of the laws of heresy. Catholics burned them, Protestants drowned them, and they were stoned and clubbed out of their communities. There was enough substance in their ideas and enough sincerity in their patient sufferings that they continued to recruit followers as they were driven from town to town, from Germany into the Swiss cities, and from Switzerland into Bohemia and Hungary. There, on the eastern edges of the empire, the largest groups of Anabaptists finally settled.

The Catholic Reformation

Catholics felt the same impulses toward a more fulfilling religious life as Protestants and complained of the same abuses of clerical, state, and papal powers. But the Catholic response was to reform the church from within. A new personal piety was stressed, which led to the founding of additional spiritual orders. The ecclesiastical hierarchy became more concerned with pastoral care and initiated reforms of the clergy at the parish level. The challenge of converting other peoples, Asians and Amerindians especially, led to the formation of missionary orders and to a new emphasis on preaching and education. Protestantism itself revitalized Catholicism.

The Spiritual Revival

The quest for individual spiritual fulfillment dominated later medieval Roman Catholicism. Erasmus, Luther, and Zwingli were all influenced by a Catholic spiritual movement known as the **New Piety**. It was propagated in Germany by the Brethren of the Common Life, a lay organization that stressed the importance of personal meditation on the life of Christ. The Brethren taught that a Christian life should be lived according to Christ's dictates as expressed in the Sermon on the Mount. They instructed their pupils to lead a simple ascetic life with personal devotion at its core. These were the lessons that the young Erasmus found so liberating and the young Luther so stifling.

The New Piety, with its emphasis on a simple personal form of religious practice, was a central influence on Christian humanism. It is important to realize that humanism developed within the context of Catholic education and that many churchmen embraced the new learning and supported educational reform or patronized works of humanist scholarship. The leading Christian humanists remained within the Catholic Church even after many of their criticisms had formed the basis of Protestant reforms.

This combination of piety and humanism imbued the ecclesiastical reforms initiated by Church leaders. Cardinal Jiménez de Cisneros, who also served as inquisitor-general of the Spanish Inquisition, undertook a wide-ranging reorganization of Spanish religious life in the late fifteenth century. Though not every project was successful, Jiménez de Cisneros's program took much of the sting out of Protestant attacks on clerical abuse, and there was never a serious Protestant movement in Spain.

The most influential reforming bishop was Gian Matteo Giberti (1495–1543) of Verona. Using his own frugal life as an example, Giberti rigorously enforced vows, residency, and the pastoral duties of the clergy. He founded almshouses to aid the poor and orphanages to house the homeless. In Verona, Giberti established a printing press, which turned out editions of the central works of Roman Catholicism, especially the writings of Augustine.

The most important indication of the reforming spirit within the Roman Church was the foundation of new religious orders in the early sixteenth century. Devotion to a spiritual life of sacrifice was the chief characteristic of the lay and clerical orders that had flourished throughout the Middle Ages. In one French diocese, the number of clergy quadrupled in the last half of the fifteenth century. Although the number of entrants to the traditional orders of Franciscans and Dominicans did not rise as quickly, the growth of lay communities such as the Brethren of the Common Life attested to the continuing appeal of Catholic devotionalism. Devotionalism was particularly strong in Italy, where a number of new orders received papal charters.

In Spain, Saint Teresa of Ávila (1515–1582) led the reform of the Carmelites. She believed that women had to withdraw totally from the world around them to achieve true devotion. Against the wishes of the male superiors of her order, she founded a convent to put her beliefs into practice and began writing devotional tracts such as *The Way of Perfection* (1583). In 1535, Angela Merici (ca. 1474–1540) established the Ursulines, one of the most original of the new foundations, composed of young unmarried girls who remained with their families but lived chaste lives devoted to the instruction of other women.

Loyola's Pilgrimage

The thirteenth child of a Spanish noble family, Saint Ignatius Loyola (1491–1556) trained for a military life in the service of Castile. In 1521, he was one of the garrison defenders when the French besieged Pamplona. A cannonball shattered his leg, and he was carried home for a long enforced convalescence. There, he slowly and carefully read the only books in the castle: a life of Christ and a history of the saints. His reading inspired him. Before, he had sought glory and renown in battle. But when he compared the truly heroic deeds of the saints to his own vainglorious exploits, he decided to give his life over to spirituality.

Loyola was not a man to do things by halves. He resolved to model his life on the sufferings of the saints about whom he had read. He renounced his worldly goods and endured a year-long regimen of physical abstinence and spiritual nourishment in the town of Manresa. During this period, he began to have visions, which later culminated in a mystical experience in which Loyola believed Christ called him directly to His service.

Like Luther, Loyola was tormented by his perceived inability to achieve grace through penance, but unlike Luther he redoubled his efforts. He recorded the techniques he used during this vigil in *The Spiritual Exercises*, which became a handbook for Catholic devotion. In 1523, crippled and barefoot, he made a pilgrimage to Jerusalem. He returned to Spain intent on becoming a priest.

Rubens's (1577–1640) *The Miracles of Saint Ignatius Loyola*. Founder of the Society of Jesus, Loyola prepared his Jesuit recruits for an active, rather than a contemplative, life.

By this time, Loyola had adopted a distinctive garb that attracted both followers and suspicion. Twice, the Spanish ecclesiastical authorities summoned him to be examined for heresy. In 1528, he decided to complete his studies in France, where he and a small group of friends eventually decided to form a brotherhood after they became priests. They devoted themselves to the cure of souls and took personal vows of poverty, chastity, and obedience to the pope. On a pilgrimage to Rome, Loyola and his followers again attracted the attention of ecclesiastical authorities. Loyola explained his mission to them and in 1540 won the approval of Pope Paul III to establish a new holy order, the Society of Jesus.

Loyola's Society was founded at a time when the spiritual needs of the Church were being extended beyond the confines of Europe. Loyola volunteered his followers, who came to be known as Jesuits, to serve in the remotest parts of the world. One disciple, Francis Xavier (1506–1552), made converts to Catholicism in the Portuguese port cities in the East and then in India and Japan. Other Jesuits became missionaries to the New World, where they offered Christian consolation to the Amerindian communities. By 1556, the Society of Jesus had grown from 10 to 1,000, and Loyola had become a full-time administrator in Rome.

Loyola's most fundamental innovation in these years was the founding of schools to train recruits for his order. Jesuit training was rigorous. Since they were being prepared for an active rather than a contemplative life, Jesuits were not cloistered during their training. Jesuit schools were opened to the laity, and lay education became one of the Jesuits' most important functions.

Chronology

THE REFORMATION AND THE COUNTER-REFORMATION

Year	Event
1517	Luther writes his Ninety-five Theses
1521	Luther is excommunicated and declared an enemy of the empire; Henry VIII receives title Defender of the Faith
1523	Zwingli expounds his faith in formal disputation
1533	Henry VIII divorces Catherine of Aragon, marries Anne Boleyn, and breaks with the Church of Rome
1536	Calvin publishes *Institutes of the Christian Religion*
1540	Loyola receives papal approval for Society of Jesus
1545–1563	Council of Trent
1553	Mary I restores Catholicism in England
1563	Elizabeth I enacts the Thirty-nine Articles, which restores Protestantism to England

The Counter-Reformation

The Jesuits were both the culmination of one wave of Catholic reform and the advance guard of another. They combined the piety and devotion that stretched from medieval mysticism through humanism, diocesan reforms, and the foundations of new spiritual orders. But they also represented an aggressive Catholic response that was determined to meet Protestantism head on and repel it—the **Counter-Reformation**. This was the Church militant. Old instruments such as the Inquisition were revived, and new weapons such as the Index of Prohibited Books were forged. But the problems of fighting Protestantism were not only those of combating Protestant ideas. Like oil and water, politics and religion failed to combine. Emperor Charles V and the hierarchy of the German church demanded thoroughgoing reform of the Catholic Church; the pope and the hierarchy of the Italian church resisted the call. Brothers in Christ, pope and emperor were mortal enemies in everything else.

At the emperor's instigation, the first serious preparations for a general council of the Church were made in the 1530s. The papacy warded it off. The complexities of international diplomacy were one factor—the French king was even less anxious to bring peace to the empire than the pope was—and the complexities of papal politics were another. The powers of a general council in relation to the powers of the papacy had never been clarified. After the advent and spread of Protestantism, successive popes had little reason to believe that in this gravest crisis of all, a council would be mindful of papal prerogatives. In fact, Catholic reformers were as bitter in their denunciations of papal abuses as Protestants were. The second attempt to arrange a general council of the Church occurred in the early 1540s. Again the papacy warded it off.

These factors ensured that when a general council of the Church finally did meet, its task would not be an easy one. The northern churches, French and German alike, wanted reforms of the papacy; the papacy wanted a restatement of orthodox doctrine. Many princes whose states were divided among Catholics and Protestants wanted compromises that might accommodate both. Ferdinand I, king of Bohemia, saw the council as an opportunity to bring the Hussites back into the fold. Charles V and the German bishops wanted the leading Protestant church authorities to offer their own compromises on doctrine that might form a basis for reuniting the empire. The papacy wanted traditional church doctrine reasserted.

The general council of the Church that finally met in Trent from 1545 to 1563 thus had nearly unlimited potential for disaster, but it ended in total victory for the views of the papacy. For all of the papacy's seeming weaknesses, an Italian pope always held the upper hand at the council. Fewer than one-third of the delegates came from outside Italy. The French looked on the council suspiciously and played only a minor role, and the emperor forbade his bishops to attend after the council moved to Bologna.

Yet for all of these difficulties, the councillors at Trent made some real progress. They corrected a number of abuses, of which the sale of indulgences was the most substantive. They formulated rules for the better regulation of parish priests and stressed the obligation of priests and bishops to preach to their congregations. They ordered seminaries to be founded in all dioceses where there was not already a university so that priests could receive sufficient education to perform their duties. They prepared a new modern and uniform Catholic service and centralized and updated the Index of Prohibited Books to include Protestant writings from all over the Continent.

The Council of Trent made no concessions to Protestants, moderate or radical. The redefinition of traditional Roman Catholicism drew the doctrinal lines clearly and ended decades of confusion. But it also meant that the differences between Catholics and Protestants could now be settled only by the sword.

MAP DISCOVERY

THE RELIGIOUS DIVISIONS OF EUROPE, CA. 1555

Which was the largest religious denomination by the middle of the sixteenth century? Which states were most at risk of internal religious warfare? Notice the difference in the ways in which Lutheranism and Calvinism spread. Where did Catholicism remain untouched by the new religions?

The Empire Reacts

Warfare dominated the reform of religion almost from its beginning. The burnings, drownings, and executions by which both Catholics and Protestants attempted to maintain religious purity were but raindrops compared to the sea of blood that was shed in sieges and on battlefields beginning in the 1530s. The Catholic divisions were clear. The empire continued to be engaged in the west with its archenemy, France, and in the south with the ever-expanding Ottoman Empire. Charles V needed not only peace within his own German realms, but positive support for his offensive and defensive campaigns. He could never devote his full resources to suppressing Protestant dissent.

Yet there was never a united Protestant front to suppress. The north German towns and principalities that accepted Lutheranism in the 1520s had had a long history of warfare among themselves. Added to this was the division between Luther and Zwingli over doctrinal issues that effectively separated the German and Swiss components of the Reformation from each other.

Although both the Protestant and the Catholic sides were internally weak, it was the greater responsibilities of Charles V that allowed for the uneasy periods of peace. Each pause gave the Protestant reformers new life. Lutheranism continued to spread in the northern part of the empire, Zwinglian reform in the south. Charles V asked the papacy to convoke a general council and the Protestants to stop evangelizing in new territories. But Protestant leaders were no more capable of halting the spread of the Reformation than were Catholics. Thus each violation of each uneasy truce seemed to prove treachery. In 1546, just after Luther's death, both sides raised armies in preparation for renewed fighting. In the first stage of war, Charles V scored a decisive victory, capturing the two leading Protestant princes and conquering Saxony and Thuringia, the homeland of Lutheran reform.

Charles V's greatest victories were always preludes to his gravest defeats. The remaining Protestant princes were driven into the arms of the French, who placed dynastic interests above religious concerns. Again Europe was plunged into general conflict, with the French invading the German states from the west, the Turks from the south, and the Protestant princes from the north. Charles V, now an old and broken man, was forced to flee through the Alps in the dead of winter and was brought to the bargaining table soon after. By the Peace of Augsburg in 1555 the emperor agreed to allow the princes of Germany to establish the religion of their people. Protestant princes would govern Protestant states, and Catholic princes would govern Catholic states. The Peace of Augsburg ended 40 years of religious struggle in Germany.

SUMMARY

The Intellectual Reformation Printing played a key role in the promotion and development of religious reform. Christian humanists applied the tools of Italian humanists to the Bible and the works of the Church fathers. Christian humanists emphasized education, especially of women. The life and work of Erasmus epitomized Christian humanism.

The Lutheran Reformation Europe was becoming more religious in the late fifteenth and early sixteenth centuries. People wanted more from the Church than it could give, stimulating criticism as well as devotion. Martin Luther was tormented by the question of how salvation was attained. His eventual solution focused on three principles: a foundation built on the Word, justification by faith alone, and the priesthood of all believers. The political conflict between the pope and the emperor created both allies and enemies for Luther. By the end of the 1520s, the Holy Roman Empire was split between Catholics and adherents to the reformed religion. Lutheranism spread beyond Germany, its reception varying with local conditions.

The Protestant Reformation In the 1530s Protestantism entered a new phase, with a second generation of reformers establishing new churches at the same time as they expanded on reformed ideas. John Calvin's theology emphasized predestination. Under his leadership, Geneva became a theocracy. Politics was the driving force behind Henry VIII's decision to break with the Catholic Church. Under his successors, England went back and forth between Protestantism and Catholicism, ending with a Protestant compromise under Elizabeth I. Throughout Europe, some Protestants pushed the reformed theology to radical conclusions.

The Catholic Reformation A desire for spiritual fulfillment dominated later medieval Roman Catholicism. New religious orders were established to meet the needs of changing times. Saint Ignatius of Loyola founded the Jesuits, an order that played a key role in combating Protestantism and promoting Catholic education throughout the world. The Counter-Reformation saw the advent of new tools for imposing orthodoxy. Tensions between the pope and the emperor delayed the convening of a general council to forge the Catholic response to the Protestant challenge. The Council of Trent promulgated many reforms, but made no compromises with Protestantism. Warfare in the Holy Roman Empire culminated with the Peace of Augsburg (1555). Henceforth, the emperor would allow the princes of Germany to establish the religion of their people.

QUESTIONS FOR REVIEW

1. How did humanism prepare the way for the Reformation?
2. What motivated Martin Luther?
3. What were the differences between the reforming ideas of Luther, Zwingli, and Calvin?
4. How did the Catholic Church respond to the challenges posed by the Protestant Reformation?

Europe at War, 1555–1648

The Crises of the Western States

"Un roi, une foi, une loi"—"One king, one faith, one law." This was a prescription that members of all European states accepted without question in the sixteenth century. Society was an integrated whole, equally dependent on monarchical, ecclesiastical, and civil authority for its effective survival. A European state could no more tolerate the presence of two churches than it could the presence of two kings. But the Reformation had created two churches. The coexistence of Catholics and Protestants in a single realm posed a stark challenge to accepted theory and traditional practice.

The problem proved intractable because it admitted only one solution: total victory. There could be no compromise for several reasons. Religious beliefs were profoundly held. Religious controversy was more than a life-and-death struggle: It was a struggle between everlasting life and eternal damnation. Doomed, too, was the practical solution of toleration. To the modern mind, toleration seems so logical that it is difficult to understand why it took over a century of bloodshed before it came to be grudgingly accepted by the most bitterly divided countries. But toleration was not a practical solution in a society that admitted no principle of organization other than one king, one faith.

The French Wars of Religion

No wars are more terrible than civil wars. The loss of lives and property is staggering, but the loss of communal identity is greater still. Generations pass before societies recover from their civil wars. Such was the case with the **French wars of religion**.

The Spread of Calvinism and Religious Division. Protestantism came late to France. Not until after Calvin reformed the Church in Geneva and began to export his brand of Protestantism did French society begin to divide along religious lines. By 1560, there were over 2,000 Protestant congregations in France, and their membership totaled nearly 10 percent of the French population. Calvin and his successors achieved their greatest following among the middle ranks of urban society: merchants, traders, and artisans. They also found a receptive audience among aristocratic women, who eventually converted their husbands and children.

However, the wars of religion were brought on by more than the rapid spread of Calvinism. Equally important was the vacuum of power that had been created when Henry II (1547–1559) died in a jousting tournament. Surviving Henry were his extraordinary widow, Catherine de Médicis, three daughters, and four sons, the oldest of whom, Francis II (1559–1560), was only 15 years old. Under the influence of his beautiful young wife, Mary, Queen of Scots, Francis allowed Mary's relatives, the Guise family, to dominate the great offices of state and to exclude their rivals from power. The Guises controlled the two most powerful institutions of the state: the army and the Church.

The Guises were staunchly Catholic, and among their enemies were the Bourbons, princes of the blood with a direct claim to the French throne but also a family with powerful Protestant members. The revelation of a Protestant plot to remove the king

Catherine de Médicis (1519–1598), the wife of Henry II of France, was the real power behind the throne during the reigns of her sons Charles IX (1560–1574) and Henry III (1574–1589). Her overriding concern was to ensure her sons' succession and to preserve the power of the monarchy.

from Paris provided the Guises with an opportunity to eliminate their most potent rivals. The Bourbon duc de Condé, the leading Protestant peer of the realm, was sentenced to death. But five days before Condé's execution, Francis II died, and Guise power evaporated. The new king, Charles IX (1560–1574), was only 10 years old and firmly under the grip of his mother, Catherine de Médicis, who now declared herself regent of France.

Civil War. Condé's death sentence convinced him that the Guises would stop at nothing to gain their ambitions. Force would have to be met with force. Protestants and Catholics alike raised armies and, in 1562, civil war ensued. Once the wars began, the leading Protestant peers fled the court, but the position of the Guises was not altogether secure. Henry Bourbon, king of Navarre, was the next in line to the throne should Charles IX and his two brothers die without male heirs. Henry had been raised in the Protestant faith by his mother, Jeanne d'Albret, whose own mother, Marguerite of Navarre, was among the earliest protectors of the **Huguenots**, as the French Calvinists came to be called.

The inconclusive nature of the early battles might have allowed for the pragmatic solution by Catherine de Médicis had it not been for the assassination of the duc de Guise in 1563 by a Protestant fanatic. This act added a personal vendetta to the religious passions of the Catholic leaders. They encouraged the slaughter of Huguenot congregations and openly planned the murder of Huguenot leaders. Protestants gave as good as they got. In open defiance of Valois dynastic interests, the Guises courted support from Spain, while the Huguenots imported Swiss and German mercenaries to fight in France. Noble factions and irreconcilable religious differences were pulling the government apart.

The Saint Bartholomew's Day Massacre. By 1570, Catherine was ready to attempt another reconciliation. She announced her plans for a marriage between her daughter Margaret and Henry of Navarre, a marriage that would symbolize the spirit of conciliation between the crown and the Huguenots. The marriage was to take place in Paris during August 1572. The arrival of Huguenot leaders from all over France to attend the marriage ceremony presented an opportunity of a different kind to the Guises and their supporters. If leading Huguenots could be assassinated in Paris, the Protestant cause might collapse, and the truce that the wedding signified might be turned instead into a Catholic triumph.

Saint Bartholomew was the apostle whom Jesus described as a man without guile. Ironically, it was on his feast day that the Huguenots who had innocently come to celebrate Henry's marriage were led like lambs to the slaughter. On 24 August 1572 the streets of Paris ran red with Huguenot blood. Although frenzied, the slaughter was inefficient. Henry of Navarre and a number of other important Huguenots escaped the carnage and returned to their urban strongholds. In the following weeks, the violence spread from Paris to the countryside, and thousands of Protestants paid for their beliefs with their lives.

One King, Two Faiths

The Saint Bartholomew's Day Massacre was a transforming event in many ways. In the first place, it prolonged the wars. A whole new generation of Huguenots now had an attachment to the continuation of warfare: Their fathers and brothers had been mercilessly slaughtered. By itself, the event was shocking enough; in the atmosphere of anticipated reconciliation created by the wedding, it screamed out for revenge. And the target for retaliation was no longer limited to the Guises and their followers. By accepting the results of the massacre, the monarchy sanctioned it and spilled Huguenot blood on itself. For more than a decade, Catherine de Médicis had maintained a distance between the crown and the leaders of the Catholic movement. That distance no longer existed.

The Theory of Resistance. After Saint Bartholomew's Day, Huguenot theorists began to develop the idea that resistance to a monarch whose actions violated divine commandments or civil right was lawful. For the first time, Huguenot writers provided a justification for rebellion. Perhaps most importantly, a genuine revulsion against the massacres swept the nation. A number of Catholic peers now joined with the Huguenots to protest the excesses of the crown and the Guises. These Catholics came to be called the **politiques**, from their desire for a practical settlement of the wars. They were led by the duke of Anjou, who was next in line to the throne when Charles IX died in 1574 and Henry III (1574–1589) became king.

Painting of the Saint Bartholomew's Day Massacre. The massacre began in Paris on 24 August 1572, and the violence soon spread throughout France.

Against them, in Paris and a number of other towns, the Catholic League was formed, a society that pledged its first allegiance to religion. The League took up where the Saint Bartholomew's Day Massacre left off, and the slaughter of ordinary people who professed the wrong religion continued. Matters grew worse in 1584 when the duke of Anjou died. With each passing year it was becoming apparent that Henry III would produce no male heir. After the duke's death, the Huguenot Henry of Navarre was the next in line for the throne. Catholic Leaguers talked openly of altering the royal succession and began to develop theories of lawful resistance to monarchical power. By 1585, when the final civil war began—the war of the three Henrys, named for Henry III, Henry Guise, and Henry of Navarre—the crown was in the weakest possible position. Paris and the Catholic towns were controlled by the League, and the Protestant strongholds were controlled by Henry of Navarre. King Henry III could not abandon his capital or his religion, but neither could he gain control of the Catholic party. The extremism of the Leaguers kept the politiques away from court; without the politiques there could be no settlement.

In December 1588, Henry III summoned Henry Guise and Guise's brother to a meeting in the royal bedchamber. There, they were murdered by the king's order. The politiques were blamed for the murders—revenge was taken on a number of them—and Henry III was forced to flee his capital. He made a pact with Henry of Navarre, and together royalist and Huguenot forces besieged Paris. All supplies were cut off from the city, and only the arrival of a Spanish army prevented its fall. In 1589, Catherine de Médicis died, her ambition to reestablish the authority of the monarchy in shambles, and in the same year a fanatic priest gained revenge for the murder of the Guises by assassinating Henry III.

Henry IV. Now Henry of Navarre came into his inheritance. But after nearly 30 years of continuous civil war, it was certain that a Huguenot could never rule France. If Henry was to become king of all France, he would have to become a Catholic king. It is not clear when Henry made the decision to accept the Catholic faith—"Paris is worth a Mass," he reportedly declared—but he did not announce his decision at once. Rather, he strengthened his forces, tightened his bonds with the politiques, and urged his countrymen to expel the Spanish invaders. He finally made his conversion public and in 1594 was crowned Henry IV (1589–1610). A war-weary nation was willing to accept him.

In 1598, Henry proclaimed the **Edict of Nantes**, which granted limited toleration to the Huguenots. It was the culmination of decades of attempts to find a solution to the existence of two religions in one state. It was a compromise that satisfied no one, but it was a compromise that everyone could accept. "One king, two faiths" was as apt a description of Henry IV as it was of the settlement. Yet neither Henry's conversion nor the Edict of Nantes stilled the passions that had spawned and sustained the French wars of religion. Sporadic fighting between Catholics and Huguenots continued, and fanatics on both sides fanned the flames of religious hatred. Henry IV survived 18 attempts on his life before he was finally felled by an assassin's knife in 1610, but by then he had established the monarchy and brought a semblance of peace to France.

Chronology

THE FRENCH WARS OF RELIGION

1559	Death of Henry II
1560	Protestant duc de Condé sentenced to death
1562	First battle of wars of religion
1563	Catholic duc de Guise assassinated; Edict of Amboise grants limited Protestant worship
1572	Saint Bartholomew's Day Massacre
1574	Accession of Henry III
1576	Formation of Catholic League
1584	Death of duc d'Anjou makes Henry of Navarre heir to throne
1585	War of the three Henrys
1588	Duc de Guise murdered by order of Henry III
1589	Catherine de Médicis dies; Henry III assassinated
1594	Henry IV crowned
1598	Edict of Nantes

The World of Philip II

While France was caught up in religious strife, Spain, by the middle of the sixteenth century, had achieved the status of the greatest power in Europe. The dominions of Philip II (1556–1598) of Spain stretched from the Atlantic to the Pacific; his continental territories included the Netherlands in the north and Milan and Naples in Italy. In 1580, Philip became king of Portugal, uniting all the states of the Iberian peninsula. With the addition of Portugal's Atlantic ports and its sizable fleet, Spanish maritime power was now unsurpassed. Philip saw himself as a Catholic monarch fending off the spread of heresy. He came to the throne at just the moment that Calvinism began its rapid growth in northern Europe and provided the impetus for the greatest crisis of his reign: the revolt of the Netherlands.

Though Philip's father, Charles V, amassed a great empire, he had begun only as the duke of Burgundy. Charles's Burgundian inheritance encompassed a diverse territory in the northwestern corner of Europe. The 17 separate provinces of this territory were called the Netherlands, or the Low Countries, because of the flooding that kept large portions of them under water. The Netherlands, one of the richest and most populous regions of Europe, was an international leader in manufacturing, banking, and commerce. In the southern provinces, French was the background and language of the inhabitants; in the northern ones, Germans had settled, and Dutch was spoken.

The Low Countries had accepted the Peace of Augsburg in a spirit of conciliation in which it was never intended. Here, Catholics, Lutherans, Anabaptists, and Calvinists peaceably coexisted. As in France, this situation changed dramatically with the spread of Calvinism. The heavy concentration of urban populations in the Low Countries provided the natural habitat for Calvinist preachers, who made converts across the entire social spectrum. As Holy Roman Emperor, Charles V may have made his peace with Protestants, but as king of Spain he had not. Charles V had maintained the purity of the Spanish Catholic Church through a careful combination of reform and repression.

Philip II intended to pursue a similar policy in the Low Countries. With papal approval, he initiated a scheme to reform the hierarchy of the Church by expanding the numbers of bishops, and he invited the Jesuits to establish schools for orthodox learning. Simultaneously, he strengthened the power of the Inquisition and ordered the enforcement of the decrees of the Council of Trent. The Protestants sought the protection of their local nobles, who, Catholic or Protestant, had their own reasons for opposing the strict enforcement of heresy laws. Provincial nobles and magistrates resented both the policies that were being pursued and the fact that they disregarded local autonomy. Town governors and noblemen refused to cooperate in implementing the new laws.

MAP DISCOVERY

HABSBURG LANDS AT THE ABDICATION OF CHARLES V

Notice how dispersed were the states controlled by Charles V when he abdicated the throne in 1556. Why did he divide his empire between son Philip II and brother Ferdinand I? What made it possible for the Netherlands to revolt from Spanish control?

The Revolt of the Netherlands

The passive resistance of nobles and magistrates was soon matched by the active re-sistance of the Calvinists. Unable to enforce Philip's policy, Margaret of Parma, his half-sister, whom Philip had made regent, agreed to a limited toleration. But in the summer of 1566, before this toleration could be put into effect, bands of Calvinists unleashed a storm of iconoclasm in the provinces, breaking stained glass windows and statues of the Virgin and the saints, which they claimed were idolatrous. Helpless in the face of determined Calvinists and apathetic Catholics, local authori-ties could not protect Church property. Iconoclasm gave way to open revolt. Fearing social rebellion, even the leading Protestant noblemen took part in suppressing these riots.

Rebellion and War. In Spain, the events in the Netherlands were treated for what they were: open rebellion. Despite the fact that Margaret had already restored order, Philip II was determined to punish the rebels and enforce the heresy laws. A large military force under the command of the duke of Alba (1507–1582) was sent from Spain as an army of occupation. Alba lured leading Protestant noblemen to Brussels, where he publicly executed them in 1568. He also established a military court to punish participants in the rebellion, a court that came to be called the Council of Blood. The Council handed down over 9,000 convictions, 1,000 of which carried the death penalty. As many as 60,000 Protestants fled beyond Alba's jurisdiction. Alba next made an example of several small towns that had been implicated in the iconoclasm. He allowed his soldiers to pillage the towns at will before slaughtering their entire populations and razing them to the ground. By the end of 1568, royal policy had gained a sullen acceptance in the Netherlands, but for the next 80 years, with only occasional truces, Spain and the Netherlands were at war.

Chronology

REVOLT OF THE NETHERLANDS

1559	Margaret of Parma named regent of the Netherlands
1566	Calvinist iconoclasm begins revolt
1567	Duke of Alba arrives in Netherlands and establishes Council of Blood
1568	Protestant Count Egmont executed
1572	Protestants capture Holland and Zeeland
1573	Alba relieved of his command
1576	Sack of Antwerp; Pacification of Ghent
1581	Catholic and Protestant provinces split
1585	Spanish forces take Brussels and Antwerp
1609	Twelve Years' Truce

The Protestants Rebel. Alba's policies had driven Protestants into rebellion, and this forced the Spanish government to maintain its army by raising taxes from the provinces that had remained loyal. Soon the loyal provinces were also in revolt, not over religion but over taxation and local autonomy. Tax resistance and fear of an invasion from France left Alba unprepared for the series of successful assaults Protestants launched in the northern provinces during 1572. The Protestant generals established a permanent base in the northwestern provinces of Holland and Zeeland. By 1575, they had gained a stronghold that they would never relinquish. Prince William of Orange (1533–1584) assumed the leadership of the two provinces, which were now united against the tyranny of Philip's rule.

Spanish government was collapsing all over the Netherlands. William ruled in the north, and the States-General, a parliamentary body composed of representatives from the separate provinces, ruled in the south. Margaret of Parma had resigned in disgust at Alba's tactics, and Alba had been relieved of his command when his tactics failed. No one was in control of the Spanish army. The soldiers, who had gone years with only partial pay, now roamed the southern provinces looking for plunder. Brussels and Ghent had both been targets, and in 1576 the worst atrocities of all occurred when mutinous Spanish troops sacked Antwerp. Over 7,000 people were slaughtered, and nearly one-third of the city burned to the ground.

The "Spanish fury" in Antwerp effectively ended Philip's rule over his Burgundian inheritance. The Protestants had established a permanent home in the north. The States-General had established its ability to rule in the south, and Spanish policy had been totally discredited. To achieve a settlement, the Pacification of Ghent of 1576, the Spanish government conceded local autonomy in taxation, the central role of the States-General in legislation, and the immediate withdrawal of all Spanish troops from the Low Countries. This rift among the provinces was soon followed by a permanent split. In 1581, one group of provinces voted to depose Philip II while a second group decided to remain loyal to him. Philip II refused to accept the dismemberment of his inheritance or to recognize the independent Dutch state that now existed in Holland.

Meanwhile, Protestant England under Elizabeth I (1558–1603) had sided with the Dutch Protestants opposing Philip II. During Elizabeth's reign, England and Spain entered a long period of hostility. English pirates raided Spanish treasure ships returning to Europe, and Elizabeth covertly aided both French and Dutch Protestants. Finally, in 1588, Philip decided to invade England. A great fleet set sail from the Portuguese coast to the Netherlands, where a large Spanish army was waiting to be conveyed to England.

The **Spanish Armada** comprised over 130 ships, many of them the pride of the Spanish and Portuguese navies. They were bigger and stronger than anything possessed by the English, whose forces were largely merchant vessels hastily converted for battle. But the English ships were faster and more easily maneuverable in the unpredictable winds of the English Channel. They also carried guns that could easily be reloaded for multiple firings, whereas the Spanish guns were designed to discharge only one broadside before hand-to-hand combat ensued. With these advantages, the

The defeat of the immense armada that Philip II sent to invade England in 1588 dealt a serious blow to Spain's standing in Europe.

English were able to prevent the Armada from reaching port in the Netherlands and to destroy many individual ships as they were blown off course.

Throughout the 1580s and 1590s, Spanish military expeditions attempted to reunite the southern provinces and to conquer the northern ones. But Spanish successes in the south were outweighed by the long-term failure of their objectives in the north. In 1609, Spain and the Netherlands concluded the Twelve Years' Truce, which tacitly recognized the existence of the state of Holland. By the beginning of the seventeenth century, Holland was not only an independent state; it was one of the greatest rivals of Spain and Portugal.

The Struggles in Eastern Europe

In eastern Europe, dynastic struggles outweighed the problems created by religious reform. Muscovy remained the bulwark of Eastern Orthodox Christianity, immune from the struggles over the Roman faith. Protestantism did spread into Poland-Lithuania, but its presence was tolerated by the Polish state. The spread of dissent was checked not by repression, but by a vigorous Catholic reformation led by the Jesuits. The domestic crises in the East were crises of state rather than of the Church. In Muscovy, the disputed succession that followed the death of Ivan the Terrible plunged the state into anarchy and civil war. Centuries of conflict between Poland-Lithuania and Muscovy came to a head with the Poles' desperate gamble to seize control of their massive eastern neighbor. War between Poland-Lithuania and Muscovy inevitably dominated the politics of the entire region. The Baltic states, most notably Sweden, soon joined the fray.

Kings and Diets in Poland

Until the end of the sixteenth century, Poland-Lithuania was the dominant power in the eastern part of Europe. It was economically healthy and militarily strong. Through its Baltic ports, especially Gdansk, Poland played a central role in international commerce and a dominant role in the northern grain trade. The vast size of the Polish state made defense difficult, and during the course of the sixteenth century it had lost lands to Muscovy in the east and to the Crimean Tatars in the south. But the permanent union with Lithuania in 1569 and the gradual absorption of the Baltic region of Livonia more than compensated for these losses. Matters of war and peace, of taxation, and of reform were placed under the strict supervision of the Polish Diet, a parliamentary body that represented the Polish landed elite. The diet also carefully controlled religious policy. Roman Catholicism was the principal religion in Poland, but the state tolerated numerous Protestant and Eastern creeds. In the Warsaw Confederation of 1573, the Polish gentry vowed "that we who differ in matters of religion will keep the peace among ourselves."

The biological failure of the Jagiellon monarchy in Poland ended that nation's most successful line of kings. Without a natural heir, the Polish nobility and gentry, who officially elected the monarch, had to peddle their throne among the princes of Europe. When Sigismund III (1587–1632) was elected to the Polish throne in 1587, he was also heir to the crown of Sweden. Sigismund accepted the prohibitions against religious repression outlined in the Warsaw Confederation, but he actively encouraged the establishment of Jesuit schools, the expansion of monastic orders, and the strengthening of the Roman Catholic Church.

All of these policies enjoyed the approval of the Polish ruling classes. But the diet would not support Sigismund's efforts to gain control of the Swedish crown, which he inherited in 1592 but from which he was deposed three years later. If Sigismund triumphed in Sweden, all Poland would get was a part-time monarch. The Polish Diet consistently refused to give the king the funds necessary to invade Sweden successfully. Nevertheless, Sigismund mounted several unsuccessful campaigns against the Swedes that sapped Polish money and manpower.

Muscovy's Time of Troubles

The wars of Ivan the Great and Ivan the Terrible in the fifteenth and sixteenth centuries were waged to secure agricultural territory in the west and a Baltic port in the north. Both objectives came at the expense of Poland-Lithuania. But after the death of Ivan the Terrible in 1584, the Muscovite state began to disintegrate. For years it had been held together only by conquest and fear. Ivan's conflicts with the boyars, the hereditary nobility, created an aristocracy that was unwilling and unable to come to the aid of Ivan's successors. By 1601, the crown was plunged into a crisis of legitimacy known as the **Time of Troubles**. Ivan had murdered his heir in a fit of anger and left his half-witted son to inherit the throne. This led to a vacuum of power at the center as well as a struggle for the spoils of government. Private armies ruled great swaths of the state, and pretenders to the crown—all claiming

EASTERN EUROPE, CA. 1550 after the consolidation of Russia and the growth of Poland. The eastern part of Europe was still sparsely populated and economically underdeveloped.

to be Dimitri, the lost brother of the last legitimate tsar—appeared everywhere. Ambitious groups of boyars backed their own claimants to the throne. So, too, did ambitious foreigners who eagerly sought to carve up Muscovite possessions.

Muscovy's Time of Troubles was Poland's moment of opportunity. While Muscovy floundered in anarchy and civil war, Poland looked to regain the territory that it had lost to Muscovy over the previous century. Sigismund abandoned war with Sweden to intervene in the struggle for the Russian crown. Polish forces crossed into Muscovy, and Sigismund's generals backed one of the strongest of the false Dimitris, but their plan to put him on the throne failed when he was assassinated. Sigismund used the death of the last false Dimitri as a pretext to assert his own claim to the Muscovite crown. More Polish forces poured across the frontier. In 1610, they took Moscow, and Sigismund proclaimed himself tsar, intending to unite the two massive states.

The Russian boyars, so long divided, now rose against the Polish enemy. The Polish garrison in Moscow was starved into submission, and a native Russian, Michael Romanov (1613–1645), was chosen tsar by an assembly of landholders, the Zemsky Sobor. He made a humiliating peace with the Swedes—who had also taken advantage of the Time of Troubles to invade Muscovy's Baltic provinces—in return for Swedish assistance against the Poles. Intermittent fighting continued for another 20 years. In the end, Poland agreed to peace and a separate Muscovite state but only in exchange for large territorial concessions.

The Rise of Sweden

Sweden's rise to power during the seventeenth century was as startling as it was swift. Until the Reformation, Sweden had been part of the Scandinavian confederation ruled by the Danes. Although the Swedes had a measure of autonomy, they were very much a junior partner in Baltic affairs. Denmark controlled the narrow sound that linked the Baltic Sea with the North Sea, and its prosperity derived from the tolls it collected on imports and exports. When, in 1523, Gustav I Vasa led the uprising of the Swedish aristocracy that ended Danish domination, he won the right to rule over a poor, sparsely populated state with few towns or developed seaports. The Vasas ruled Sweden in conjunction with the aristocracy. Although the throne was hereditary, the part played by the nobility in elevating Gustav I Vasa (1523–1560) gave the nobles a powerful voice in Swedish affairs. Through the council of state, known as the Rad, the Swedish nobility exerted a strong check on the monarch.

Sweden's aggressive foreign policy began accidentally. When in the 1550s the Teutonic Knights found themselves no longer capable of ruling in Livonia, the Baltic seaports that had been under their dominion scrambled for new alliances. Muscovy and Poland-Lithuania were the logical choices, but the town of Reval, an important outlet for Russian trade near the mouth of the Gulf of Finland, asked Sweden for protection. After some hesitation, since the occupation of territory on the southern shores of the Baltic would involve great expense, Sweden fortified Reval in 1560. A decade later, Swedish forces captured Narva, farther to the east, and consolidated Sweden's hold on the Livonian coast. By occupying the most important ports on the Gulf of Finland, Sweden could control a sizable portion of the Muscovite trade. As the Swedes secured the northern Livonian ports, more of the Muscovy trade moved to the south and passed through Riga, which would have to be captured or blockaded if the Swedes were to control commerce in the eastern Baltic.

Sigismund's aggressive alliance with the Polish Jesuits had persuaded the Swedish nobility that he would undermine their Lutheran church, and Sigismund was deposed in favor of his uncle Charles IX (1604—1611). War between Sweden and Poland resulted from Sigismund's efforts to regain the Swedish crown, and the Swedes used the opportunity to blockade Riga and to occupy more Livonian territory. The Swedish navy was far superior to any force that the Poles could assemble, but on land, Polish forces were masters. The Swedish invasion force suffered a crushing defeat and had to retreat to its coastal enclaves. The Poles now had an opportunity to retake all of Livonia, but, as always, the Polish Diet was reluctant to finance Sigismund's wars. Furthermore, Sigismund had his eyes on a bigger prize. Rather than follow up its Swedish victory, Poland invaded Muscovy.

Meanwhile, the blockade of Riga and the assembly of a large Swedish fleet in the Baltic threatened Denmark. The Danes continued to claim sovereignty over Sweden and took the opportunity of the Polish-Swedish conflict to reassert it. In 1611, under the energetic leadership of the Danish king Christian IV (1588–1648), Denmark invaded Sweden from both the east and the west. The Danes captured the towns of Kalmar and Alvsborg and threatened to take Stockholm. To end the Danish war, Sweden accepted humiliating terms in 1613, renouncing all claims to the northern coasts and recognizing Danish control of the Arctic trading route.

Paradoxically, these setbacks became the springboard for Swedish success. Fear of the Danes led both the English and the Dutch into alliances with Sweden. These countries all shared Protestant interests, and the English were heavily committed to the Muscovy trade, which was still an important part of Swedish commerce. Fear of the Poles had a similar effect on Muscovy. In 1609, the Swedes agreed to send 5,000 troops to Muscovy to help repel the Polish invasion. In return, Muscovy agreed to cede to Sweden its Baltic possessions. This was accomplished in 1617 and gave Sweden complete control of the Gulf of Finland.

In 1611, during the middle of the Danish war, Charles IX died and was succeeded by his son Gustavus Adolphus (1611–1632), one of the leading Protestant princes of his day. Gustavus's greatest skills were military, and he inherited an ample navy and an effective army. Unlike nearly every other European state, Sweden raised its forces from its own citizens. Gustavus introduced new weapons such as

THE RISE OF SWEDEN. For the only time in its history, Sweden acquired territories on the European mainland.

the light mobile gun and reshaped his army into standard-size squadrons and regiments, which were easier to administer and deploy.

The calamitous wars that Gustavus inherited from his father occupied him during the early years of his reign. He was forced to conclude the humiliating peace with the Danes in 1613 and to go to war with the Russians in 1614 to secure the Baltic coastal estates that had been promised in 1609. Gustavus's first military initiative was to resume war with Poland to force Sigismund to renounce his claim to the Swedish throne. In 1621, Gustavus landed in Livonia and in two weeks captured Riga, the capstone of Sweden's Baltic ambitions. Occupation of Riga increased Swedish control of the Muscovy trade and deprived Denmark of a significant portion of its customs duties. Gustavus now claimed Riga as a Swedish port and successfully demanded that ships sailing from there pay tolls to Sweden rather than Denmark. By the mid-seventeenth century, Sweden ranked among the leading Protestant powers.

The Thirty Years' War, 1618–1648

In time, the isolated conflicts that dotted the corners of Europe were joined together. In 1609, Spain and the Dutch Republic had signed a truce that was to last until 1621. In over 40 years of nearly continuous fighting, the Dutch had carved out a state in the northern Netherlands. They used the truce to consolidate their position and increase their prosperity. Spain had reluctantly accepted Dutch independence, but Philip III (1598–1621), like his father before him, never abandoned the objective of recovering his Burgundian inheritance. By the beginning of the seventeenth century, Philip had good reasons for hope. Beginning in the 1580s, Spanish forces had reconquered the southern provinces of the Netherlands. The prosperous towns of Brussels, Antwerp, and Ghent were again under Spanish control, and they provided a springboard for another invasion.

The Twelve Years' Truce gave Spain time to prepare for the final assault. During this time, Philip III attempted to resolve all of Spain's other European conflicts so that he could then give full attention to a resumption of the Dutch war. Circumstance smiled on his efforts. In 1603, the pacific James I (1603–1625) came to the English throne. Secure in his island state, James I desired peace among all Christian princes. He quickly concluded the war with Spain that had begun with the attempted invasion of the Spanish Armada, and he entered into negotiations to marry his heir to a Spanish princess. In 1610, the bellicose Henry IV of France was felled by an assassin's knife. French plans to renew war with Spain were abandoned with the accession of the eight-year-old Louis XIII (1610–1643). The **Thirty Years' War** was about to begin.

Bohemia Revolts

The Peace of Augsburg had served the German states well. The principle that the religion of the ruler was the religion of the state complicated the political life of the Holy Roman Empire, but it also pacified it. Though rulers had the right to enforce uniformity on their subjects, in practice many of the larger states tolerated more than one religion. By the beginning of the seventeenth century, Catholicism and Protestantism had achieved a rough equality within the German states, symbolized by the fact that of the seven electors who chose the Holy Roman Emperor, three were Catholic, three were Protestant, and the seventh was the emperor himself, acting as king of Bohemia. This situation was not unwelcome to the leaders of the Austrian Habsburg family who succeeded Emperor Charles V. By necessity, the eastern Habsburgs were more tolerant than their Spanish kinfolk. The head of their house was elected king of Bohemia and king of Hungary, both states with large Protestant populations.

A Fatal Election. In 1617, Mathias, the childless Holy Roman Emperor, began making plans for his cousin, Ferdinand Habsburg, to succeed him. Ferdinand was a very devout and very committed Catholic. To ensure a Catholic majority among the electors, the emperor relinquished his Bohemian title and pressed for Ferdinand's election as the new king of Bohemia. The Protestant nobles of Bohemia forced the new king to accept the strictest limitations on his political and religious powers, but once elected, Ferdinand had not the slightest intention of honoring the provisions that had been thrust on him. His opponents were equally strong willed. When Ferdinand violated Protestant religious liberties, a group of noblemen marched to the royal palace in Prague in May 1618, found two of the king's chief advisers, and hurled them out of an upper-story window.

The Defenestration of Prague, as this incident came to be known, initiated a Protestant counteroffensive throughout the Habsburg lands. Fear of Ferdinand's policies led to Protestant uprisings in Hungary as well as Bohemia. The men who seized control of the government declared Ferdinand deposed and the throne vacant. But they had no candidate to accept their crown. Whatever their religion, princes were always uneasy about the overthrow of a lawful ruler. Whoever came to be called king of Bohemia in place of Ferdinand would have to face the combined might of the Habsburgs. When Emperor Mathias died in 1619, Ferdinand succeeded to the imperial title as Ferdinand II (1619–1637), and Frederick V, one of the Protestant electors, accepted the Bohemian crown.

Frederick V, the "Winter King." Frederick was a sincere but weak Calvinist whose credentials were much stronger than his abilities. His mother was a daughter of Prince William of Orange and his wife, Elizabeth, was a daughter of James I of England. It was widely believed that Elizabeth's resolution that she would "rather eat sauerkraut with a king than roast meat with an elector" decided the issue. No decision could have been more disastrous for the fate of Europe. Frederick ruled a geographically divided German state known as the Palatinate. One hundred miles separated the two segments of his lands, but both were strategically important. The Lower Palatinate bordered on the Catholic Spanish Netherlands and the Upper Palatinate on Catholic Bavaria.

Once Frederick accepted the Bohemian crown, he was faced with a war on three fronts. Ferdinand II had no difficulty enlisting allies to recover the Bohemian crown, since he could pay them with the spoils of Frederick's lands. Spanish troops from the Netherlands occupied the Lower Palatinate, and Bavarian troops occupied the Upper Palatinate. Frederick, by contrast, met rejection wherever he turned. Neither the Dutch nor the English would send more than token aid; both had advised him against breaking the imperial peace. The Lutheran princes of Germany would not enter into a war between Calvinists and Catholics, especially after Ferdinand II promised to protect the Bohemian Lutherans.

At the Battle of the White Mountain in 1620, Ferdinand's Catholic forces annihilated Frederick's army. Frederick and Elizabeth fled to Denmark, and Bohemia was left to face the wrath of Ferdinand, the victorious king and emperor. The retribution was horrible. Mercenaries who had fought for Ferdinand II were allowed to sack Prague for a week. Elective monarchy was abolished, and Bohemia became part of the hereditary Habsburg lands. Free peasants were enserfed and subjected to imperial law. Nobles who had supported Frederick lost their lands and their privileges. Calvinism was repressed and thoroughly rooted out, consolidating forever the Catholic character of Bohemia. Frederick's estates were carved up, and his rights as elector were transferred to the Catholic duke of Bavaria. The Battle of the White Mountain was a turning point in the history of central Europe, for it forced all Protestant nations to arm for war.

The War Widens

For the Habsburgs, religious and dynastic interests were inseparable. Ferdinand II and Philip III of Spain fought for their beliefs and for their patrimony. Their victory gave them more than they could have expected. Ferdinand swallowed up Bohemia and strengthened his position in the empire. Philip gained possession of a vital link in his supply route between Italy and the Netherlands. Spanish expansion threatened France. The occupation of the Lower Palatinate placed a ring of Spanish armies around France from the Pyrenees to the Low Countries. The French too searched for allies. But French opinion remained divided over which was the greater evil: Spain or Protestantism.

Chronology

THE THIRTY YEARS' WAR

1618	Defenestration of Prague
1619	Ferdinand Habsburg elected Holy Roman Emperor; Frederick of the Palatinate accepts the crown of Bohemia
1620	Catholic victory at Battle of the White Mountain
1621	End of Twelve Years' Truce; war between Spain and Netherlands
1626	Danes form Protestant alliance under Christian IV
1627	Spain declares bankruptcy
1630	Gustavus Adolphus leads Swedish forces into Germany
1631	Sack of Magdeburg; Protestant victory at Breitenfeld
1632	Protestant victory at Lützen; death of Gustavus Adolphus
1635	France declares war on Spain
1640	Portugal secedes from Spain
1643	Battle of Rocroi; French forces repel Spaniards
1648	Peace of Westphalia

The Danes Respond. Frederick, now in Holland, refused to accept the judgment of battle. He lobbied for a grand alliance to repel the Spaniards from the Lower Palatinate and to restore the religious balance in the empire. Though his personal cause met with little sympathy, his political logic was impeccable, especially after Spain again declared war on the Dutch. A grand Protestant alliance—secretly supported by the French—brought together England, Holland, a number of German states, and Denmark. It was the Danes who led this potentially powerful coalition. In 1626, a large Danish army under the command of King Christian IV engaged imperial forces on German soil. But Danish forces could not match the superior numbers and the superior leadership of the Catholic mercenary forces under the command of the ruthless and brilliant Count Albrecht von Wallenstein (1583–1634). In 1629, the Danes withdrew from the empire and sued for peace.

If the Catholic victory at the White Mountain in 1620 threatened the well-being of German Protestantism, the Catholic triumph over the Danes threatened its survival. More powerful than ever, Ferdinand II was determined to turn the religious clock back to the state of affairs that had existed when the Peace of Augsburg was concluded in 1555. He demanded that all lands that had then been Catholic but had since become Protestant must now be returned to the Catholic fold. He also proclaimed that because the Peace of Augsburg made no provision for the toleration of Calvinists, they would no longer be tolerated in the empire. These policies together constituted a virtual revolution in the religious affairs of the German states, and they proved impossible to impose. Ferdinand succeeded in only one thing: He united Lutherans and Calvinists against him. Moreover, the costs of the war were heavy even for the victors. Wallenstein, who had over 130,000 men in arms, would no longer take orders from anyone, and Ferdinand II was forced to dismiss him from service.

Protestant Gains. In 1630, King Gustavus Adolphus of Sweden decided to enter the German conflict to protect Swedish interests. While Gustavus Adolphus struggled to construct his alliance, imperial forces continued their triumphant progress. In 1631, they besieged, captured, and put to the torch the town of Magdeburg. Perhaps three-fourths of the 40,000 inhabitants of the town were brutally slaughtered. The sack of Magdeburg marked a turning point in Protestant fortunes. It gave the international Protestant community a unifying symbol that enhanced Gustavus's military efforts. Brandenburg and Saxony joined Gustavus Adolphus, allowing him to open a second front in Bohemia. In the autumn of 1631, this combination overwhelmed the imperial armies. Gustavus won a decisive triumph at Breitenfeld, while the Saxons occupied Prague.

Gustavus Adolphus lost no time in pressing his advantage. While Ferdinand II pleaded with Wallenstein to again lead the imperial forces, the Swedes marched west to the Rhine, easily conquering the richest of the Catholic cities and retaking the Lower Palatinate. In early 1632, Protestant forces plundered Bavaria, but Wallenstein resumed his command and chose to chase the Saxons from Bohemia rather than the Swedes from Bavaria. Not until the winter of 1632 did the armies of Gustavus and Wallenstein finally meet. At the Battle of Lützen, the Swedes won the field but lost their beloved king. Wounded in the leg, the back, and the head, Gustavus Adolphus died. In less than two years he had decisively transformed the course of the war and the course of Europe's future. Protestant forces now occupied most of central and northern Germany.

The Long Quest for Peace

The final stages of the war involved the resumption of the century-old struggle between France and Spain. When the Twelve Years' Truce expired in 1621, Spain again declared war on the Dutch. Dutch naval power was considerable, and the Dutch took the war to the far reaches of the globe, attacking Portuguese settlements in Brazil and in the East and harassing Spanish shipping on the high seas. In 1628, the Dutch captured the entire Spanish treasure fleet as it sailed from the New World. Spain had declared bankruptcy in 1627, and the loss of the whole of the next year's treasure from America exacerbated an already catastrophic situation.

These reversals, combined with the continued successes of Habsburg forces in central Europe, convinced Louis XIII and his chief minister, Cardinal Richelieu, that the time for active involvement in European affairs was now at hand. Throughout the early stages of the war, France had secretly aided anti-Habsburg forces. Gustavus Adolphus's unexpected success dramatically altered French calculations. Now it was evident that the Habsburgs could no longer combine their might, and Spanish energies would be drained off in the Netherlands and central Europe. The time had come to take an open stand. In 1635, France declared war on Spain.

Gustavus Adolphus of Sweden, shown at the battle of Breitenfeld in 1631. The battle was the first important Protestant victory of the Thirty Years' War. Gustavus died on the battlefield at Lützen in the following year.

France took the offensive first, invading the Spanish Netherlands. In 1636, a Spanish army struck back, pushing to within 25 miles of Paris before it was repelled. Both sides soon began to search for a settlement, but pride prevented them from laying down their arms. Spain toppled first. Its economy in shambles and its citizens in revolt over high prices and higher taxes, it could no longer maintain its many-fronted war. The Swedes again defeated imperial forces in Germany. The Dutch destroyed much of Spain's Atlantic fleet in 1639, and the Portuguese rose up against the union of crowns that had brought them nothing but expense and the loss of crucial portions of their empire. In 1640, the Portuguese regained their independence. In 1643, Spain gambled once more on a knockout blow against the French. But at the Battle of Rocroi, exhausted French troops held out, and the Spanish invasion failed.

By now, the desire for peace was universal. Most of the main combatants had long since perished: Philip III, ever optimistic, in 1621; Frederick V, an exile to the end, in 1632; Gustavus Adolphus, killed at Lützen in the same year; Wallenstein, murdered by order of Ferdinand II in 1634; Ferdinand himself in 1637; and Louis XIII in 1643, five days before the French triumph at Rocroi. Those who succeeded them did not have the same passions, and after so many decades the longing for peace was the strongest emotion on the Continent.

In 1648, a series of agreements, collectively known as the Peace of Westphalia, established the outlines of the political geography of Europe for the next century. Its focus was on the Holy Roman Empire, and it reflected Protestant successes in the final two decades of war. Sweden gained further territories on the Baltic, making it master of the north German ports. France, too, gained in territory and prestige. It kept the vital towns in the Lower Palatinate through which Spanish men and matériel had moved, and though it did not agree to come to terms with Spain immediately, France's fear of encirclement was at an end. The Dutch gained statehood through official recognition by Spain and through the power they had displayed in building and maintaining an overseas empire.

Territorial boundaries were reestablished as they had existed in 1624, giving the Habsburgs control of both Bohemia and Hungary. The independence of the Swiss cantons was now officially recognized as were the rights of Calvinists to the protection of the Peace of Augsburg, which again was to govern the religious affairs of the empire. Two of the larger German states were strengthened as a counterweight to the emperor's power. Bavaria was allowed to retain the Upper Palatinate, and Brandenburg, which ceded some of its coastal territory to Sweden, gained extensive territories in the east. The emperor's political control over the German states was also weakened. German rulers were given independent authority over their states and the imperial diet, rather than the emperor, was empowered to settle disputes. Thus weakened, future emperors ruled in the Habsburg territorial lands with little ability to control, or influence, or even arbitrate German affairs. The judgment that the Holy Roman Empire was neither holy, nor Roman, nor an empire was now irrevocably true.

The Peace of Westphalia, 1648, recognized the new boundaries of European states that included an independent Portugal and the United Netherlands. It also recognized the growth of the Ottoman Empire into the Balkans.

SUMMARY

The Crises of the Western States   The Reformation created two churches, setting off a series of political conflicts that could only be resolved by war. Calvinism found a receptive audience in France among the middle ranks of urban society and aristocratic women. The French Wars of Religion were brought about by the spread of Calvinism and the political vacuum created when Henry II died unexpectedly. Civil war broke out in France in 1562. The assassination of the duc de Guise in 1563 pushed the violence to new levels. The Saint Bartholomew's Day Massacre in 1572 prolonged the war and prompted Protestants to develop theories of resistance to unjust monarchs. Henry IV brought the wars to an end and proclaimed the Edict of Nantes. Philip II of Spain took the lead in fighting for Catholic dominance in Europe. His efforts to restore Catholicism to England failed. His religious policies in the Low Countries led to rebellion and war.

The Struggles in Eastern Europe   Dynastic issues, rather than religious conflict, led to political upheaval in eastern Europe. Conflict between Sigismund III and the Polish Diet over war with Sweden weakened the state. Following the death of Ivan the Terrible, Muscovy descended into a Time of Troubles. Poland and Sweden took advantage of Muscovy's problems. Michael Romanov became tsar. Fighting continued for 20 years, ending with territorial concessions to Poland. Sweden made a rapid rise to power in the seventeenth century. War broke out between Sweden and Poland when the Swedes deposed Sigismund III. Sweden was saved from crushing defeat by the recalcitrance of the Polish Diet and Sigismund's decision to invade Muscovy. Under Gustavus, Sweden rose to become one of Europe's leading Protestant powers.

The Thirty Years' War, 1618–1648   The isolated conflicts of the late sixteenth and early seventeenth centuries joined together in the Thirty Years' War. The Peace of Augsburg helped Protestants and Catholics to achieve rough equality within the German states. Once elected king of Bohemia, Ferdinand Habsburg attempted to impose Catholicism on his Protestant subjects. Protestant uprisings in Hungary and Bohemia led to Ferdinand's deposition. In 1619, Ferdinand became Emperor Ferdinand II and the Protestant elector Frederick V became king of Bohemia. War followed quickly. Frederick's defeat at the Battle of the White Mountain in 1620 forced all Protestants in central Europe to prepare for war. Ferdinand's efforts to reverse the Peace of Augsburg united Lutherans and Calvinists against him. King Gustavus Adolphus of Sweden led the Protestant counterattack. After his death in 1632, the war entered a new phase focused on the struggle between France and Spain. Peace was finally achieved in 1648 with the Treaty of Westphalia.

QUESTIONS FOR REVIEW

1. How was Henry IV able to bring peace to France after decades of civil war?
2. What were the political and religious connections between the armada launched against England by Philip II and the revolt of the Netherlands?
3. How did Sweden rise to become one of Europe's great powers in the first half of the seventeenth century?
4. How did religion help spark and spread the Thirty Years' War?
5. What were the effects of the Peace of Westphalia on political arrangements in the heart of Europe?

CHAPTER 15

The Experiences of Life in Early Modern Europe, 1500–1650

Economic Life

There was no typical sixteenth-century European. Language, custom, geography, and material conditions separated people in one place from those in another. Contrasts between social groups were more striking still.

Nonetheless, one distinctive sixteenth-century experience that all groups shared, though they could only dimly perceive it, was change. In general, one generation improved on the situation of the last. Agriculture increased; more land was cleared, more crops were grown, and better tools were crafted. On the negative side, irreplaceable resources were lost as more trees were felled, more soil was eroded, and more fresh water was polluted. These changes and dynamic transformations in economic and social conditions affected everyday life in the sixteenth century.

Rural Life

In the sixteenth century, as much as 90 percent of the European population lived on farms or in small towns in which farming was the principal occupation. Villages were small and relatively isolated. These villages, large or small, prosperous or poor, were the bedrock of the sixteenth-century state. The manor, the parish, and the rural administrative district were the institutional infrastructures of Europe. Each organized the peasantry for its own purposes. Manorial rents supported the lifestyle of the nobility; parish tithes supported the works of the Church; local taxes supported the power of the state. Rents, tithes, and taxes easily absorbed more than half of the wealth produced by the land.

To survive on what remained, the village community had to be self-sufficient. In good times, there was enough to eat and some to save for the future. Hard times meant hunger and starvation. One in every three harvests was bad; one in every five was disastrous.

The Sixteenth-Century Household. Hunger and cold were the constant companions of the average European. Everywhere in Europe, homes were inadequate shelter against the cold and damp. Most were built of wood and roofed in thatch. The typical house was one long room with a stone hearth at the end.

People had relatively few household possessions. The essential piece of furniture was the wooden chest, which was used for storage. A typical family could keep all of its belongings in the chest, which could then be buried or carried away in time of danger. The chest had other uses as well. Its flat top served as a table or bench or a raised surface on which food could be placed. Tables and stools were becoming more common during the sixteenth century, though chairs were still a great luxury.

The scale of life was small, and its pace was controlled by nature: up at dawn, asleep at dusk, long working hours in summer, short ones in winter. For most people, the world was bounded by the distance that could be traveled on foot. Those who stayed all their lives in their rural villages may never have seen more than a hundred other people at once. Their wisdom, handed down through generations, was of the practical experience that was necessary to survive the struggle with nature.

Reliance on Agriculture. Peasant life centered on agriculture. Technology and technique varied little across the Continent, but there were significant differences depending on climate and soil. Across the great plain, the breadbasket that stretched from the Low Countries to Poland-Lithuania, the most common form of crop growing was still the three-field rotation system. In this method, winter crops such as wheat or rye were planted in one field; spring crops such as barley, peas, or beans were planted in another; and the third field was left fallow. More than 80 percent of what was grown on the farm was consumed on the farm. Rye and barley were the staples for peasants. Most was baked into the coarse black bread that was the mainstay of the peasant diet. In one form or another, grain provided over 75 percent of the calories in a typical diet.

GRAIN SUPPLY AND TRADE IN SIXTEENTH-CENTURY EUROPE

Where were the breadbaskets of Europe located? What was the relationship between urban areas and grain supply? How did grain move from suppliers to consumers?

The warm climate and dry weather of Mediterranean Europe favored a two-crop rotation system. With less water and stronger sunlight, half the land had to be left fallow each year to restore its nutrients. Here, fruit, especially grapes and olives, was an essential supplement to the diet. With smaller cereal crops, wine replaced beer as a beverage.

Animal husbandry was the main occupation in the third agricultural area of Europe, the mountainous and hilly regions. Sheep, the most common animal, provided the raw material for almost all clothing. In western Europe, their wool was the main export of both England and Spain. Pigs were prevalent in woodland settlements. They foraged for food and were kept, like poultry, for slaughter. Oxen were essential as draft animals. In the dairying areas of Europe, cattle produced milk, cheese, and butter; in Hungary and Bohemia, the great breeding center of the Continent, they were raised for export; almost everywhere else, they were used as beasts of burden.

Most agricultural land was owned not by those who worked it, but by lords who let it out in various ways. The land was still divided into manors, and the manor lord, or **seigneur**, was still responsible for maintaining order, administering justice, and arbitrating disputes. Lords were not necessarily individual members of the nobility; in fact, the lords were more commonly the Church or the state. In western Europe, peasants generally owned between one-third and one-half of the land they worked; eastern European peasants owned little if any land. But by the sixteenth century, almost all peasants enjoyed security of tenure on the land they worked. In return for various forms of rents, they used the land as they saw fit and could hand it down to their children. Labor service was being replaced by monetary payments in northern and western Europe, but it continued in the east. German and Hungarian peasants normally owed two or three days' labor on the lord's estate each week, while Polish peasants might owe as much as four days. Labor service tied the peasants to the land they worked. Eastern European peasants were less mobile than peasants in the west, and as a result, towns were fewer and smaller in the east.

Though the land in each village was set out in large fields so that crops could be rotated, families owned their own pieces within the field, usually in scattered strips. There were also large common fields used as pasture, as well as common woodlands where animals foraged, fuel was gathered, and game was hunted.

Farm work was ceaseless toil. Six or seven times a year, farmers tilled the fields to spread animal manure below the surface of the soil. Calamities lurked everywhere, from rain and drought to locusts and crows. Most farms could support only one family at subsistence level, and excess sons and daughters had to fend for themselves, either through marriage in the village or by migration to a town.

Town Life

In the country, people worked to the natural rhythm of the day and season. In the town, the bell tolled every hour. In the summer, the laborers gathered at the town gates at four in the morning, in the winter at seven. The bell signaled the time for morning and afternoon meals as well as the hour to lay down tools and return home. Wages were paid for hours worked—seven in winter, as many as sixteen in midsummer.

The Heart of Commerce. In all towns, an official guild structure organized and regulated labor. Rules laid down the requirements for training, the standards for quality, and the conditions for exchange. Only those who were officially sanctioned could work in trades, and each trade could perform only specified tasks.

While the life of the peasant community turned on self-sufficiency, that of the town turned on interdependence. The town was one large marketplace in which the circulation of goods dictated the residents' survival. Men and women in towns worked as hard as people on farms, but town dwellers generally received a more varied and more comfortable life in return. This is not to suggest that hunger and hardship were unknown in towns. Urban poverty was endemic and grew worse as the century wore on. In most towns, as much as one-quarter of the entire population might be destitute, living on casual day labor, charity, or crime. But the institutional network of support for the poor and homeless was stronger. The urban poor fell victim more often to disease than to starvation.

Towns were distinguished by the variety of occupations that existed within them. The preparation and exchange of food dominated small market towns. In these small towns, men divided their time between traditional agricultural pursuits—there were always garden plots and even substantial fields attached to towns—and manufacturing.

Almost every town made and distributed to the surrounding area some special product that drew to the town the wealth of the countryside.

The Workforce. In larger towns, the specialization of labor was more intense, and wage earning was more essential. Large traders dominated the major occupations such as baking, brewing, and cloth manufacture, leaving distribution in the hands of the family economy, where there might still be a significant element of bartering. Piecework handicrafts became the staple for less prosperous town families, who prepared raw materials for the large manufacturers or finished products before their sale.

In large towns there were also specialized trades that women performed. There were 55 midwives in Nuremberg in the middle of the sixteenth century, and a board of women chosen from among the leading families of the town supervised their work. Nursing the sick also seems to have been an exclusively female occupation. So, too, was prostitution, which was officially sanctioned in most large towns in the early sixteenth century.

Most town dwellers, however, lived by unskilled labor. The most lucrative occupations were strictly controlled, so people who flocked to towns in search of employment usually hired themselves out as day laborers, hauling and lifting goods onto carts or boats or delivering water and food. After the first decades of the century, the supply of laborers exceeded the demand, and town authorities were constantly attempting to expel the throngs of casual workers. The most fortunate of such workers might succeed in becoming servants.

Domestic service was a critical source of household labor. Even families who were on the margins of subsistence employed servants to undertake innumerable household tasks, which allowed parents to pursue their primary occupations.

Just as towns grew by the influx of surplus rural population, they sustained themselves by the import of surplus agricultural production. Most towns owned vast tracts of land, which they leased to peasants or farmed by hired labor. All towns had municipal storehouses of grain to preserve their inhabitants from famine during harvest failures.

Economic Change

Over the course of the sixteenth century, the European population increased by about one-third, much of the growth taking place in the first 50 years. Rough estimates suggest the rise to have been from about 80 million to 105 million. Europe had finally recovered from the devastation of the Black Death, and by 1600 its population was greater than it had ever been. Demographic growth was even more dramatic in the cities. In 1500, only four cities had populations greater than 100,000; in 1600, there were eight. Fifteen large cities more than doubled their populations.

The rise in population dramatically affected the lives of ordinary Europeans. In the early part of the century, the first phase of growth brought prosperity. Because there was uncultivated land that could be plowed and enough commons and woodlands to be shared, population increase was a welcome development. Even when rural communities began to reach their natural limits, opportunity still existed in the burgeoning towns and cities. At first the cycle was beneficial. Surplus on the farms led to economic growth in the towns. Growth in the towns meant more opportunities for people on the farms. The first waves of migrants to the towns found opportunity everywhere. Apprenticeships were easy to find, and the shortage of casual labor kept wages at a decent rate.

This window of opportunity could not remain open forever. With more mouths to feed, more crops had to be planted, and new fields were carved from less fertile areas. In England and the Low Countries, large drainage projects were undertaken to reclaim land for crops. In the east, so-called forest colonies sprang up, clearing space in the midst of woodlands for new farms.

By midcentury, the window of opportunity shut more firmly on people who were attempting to enter the urban economy. New restrictions were put in place that meant that newly arrived immigrants could enter only the less profitable small crafts.

As workers continued to flood into the towns, real wages began to fall, not only among the unskilled but throughout the workforce. The fall in real wages took place against a backdrop of inflation that has come to be called the **Price Revolution**. Over the course of the century, cereal prices increased between fivefold and sixfold, and prices of manufactured goods increased between twofold and threefold. Most of the rapid increase came in the second half of the century, a result of both population growth and the import of precious metals from the New World. The Price Revolution was felt throughout the Continent and played havoc with government finances, international trade, and the lives of ordinary people.

Ever-increasing prices created profound social dislocation and threw into turmoil all groups and sections of the European economy. Some people became destitute; others became rich beyond their dreams. The towns were particularly hard hit, for they exchanged manufactured goods for food and so suffered when grain prices rose faster than those of other commodities. Landholders who derived their income from rents were squeezed; those who received payment in kind reaped a windfall of more valuable agricultural goods. As long as ordinary peasants consumed what they raised, the nominal value of commodities did not matter. But if some part of their subsistence was obtained by labor, they were in grave peril.

There was now an enormous incentive to produce a surplus for market and to begin to specialize in particular grains that were in high demand. Every small scrap of land that individual peasant families could bring under cultivation would now yield foodstuffs that could be exchanged for manufactured goods that had been unimaginable luxuries a generation earlier. The tendency for all peasants to hold roughly equivalent amounts of land abruptly ceased. The fortunate could now become prosperous by selling their surplus. The unfortunate found ready purchasers for their strips and common rights.

The beneficial cycle now turned vicious. Those who had sold out and left the land looking for prosperity in the towns were forced to return to the land as agrarian laborers. In western Europe, they became the landless poor, seasonal migrants without the safety net of rooted communal life. In eastern Europe, labor service enriched

POPULATION DENSITY IN EUROPE, CA. 1600

Which parts of Europe were most populated in the early seventeenth century? Which were least populated? What was the relationship between population and water route access?

the landed nobility, who were able to sell vast stores of grain in the export market. Poland-Lithuania became a major supplier of cereals to northern Europe. But agricultural surplus from the east could not make up for the great shortfall in the west. By the end of the sixteenth century, the western European states faced a crisis of subsistence.

SOCIAL LIFE

The basic assumption of sixteenth-century European society was inequality. The group, rather than the individual, was the predominant unit in society. The first level of the social order was the family and the household, then came the village or town community, and finally the gradations of ranks and orders of society at large. Each group had its own place in the social order, and each performed its own essential function. Society was the sum of its parts. This traditional social organization was severely tested over the course of the sixteenth century.

Social Constructs

Hierarchy was the dominant principle of social organization in the sixteenth century. The hierarchy of masters, journeymen, and apprentices dominated trades; trades themselves existed in a hierarchy. Civic government was a hierarchy of officials led by the elite of councillors and mayors. Among the peasants was the hierarchy of freeholder, laborer, and leaseholder, as well as the more flexible social hierarchy among the ancient and prosperous families and the newer and struggling ones. The family itself was hierarchically organized, with the wife subordinate to her husband, the children to their parents, and the apprentices and servants to their master and mistress. Hierarchy was a principle of orderliness that helped to govern social relations.

Status rather than wealth determined the social hierarchy of the sixteenth century. It conferred privileges and exacted responsibilities according to rank. Status was everywhere apparent. It was confirmed in social conventions such as bowing and hat doffing. In towns and cities, the clothing people were allowed to wear, even the foods they were allowed to eat, reflected status. Status was signified by titles, not just in the ranks of the nobility, but even in ordinary communities of masters and mistresses, goodmen and goodwives. The acceptance of status was an everyday, unreflective act. Inequality was an unquestioned fact of life.

Images that people used to describe both the natural world and their social world reinforced the functional nature of hierarchy. The most elaborate image was that of the **Great Chain of Being**, a description of the universe in which everything had a place, from God at the top to inanimate objects such as rocks and stones at the bottom. For ordinary people, the Great Chain of Being expressed the belief that all life was interconnected, that every link was a part of a divinely ordered universe and was as necessary as every other.

The second metaphor that was used to describe society stressed this notion of interdependency even more strongly. This was the image of the Body Politic, in which the head ruled, the arms protected, the stomach nourished, and the feet labored. In the state, the king was the head, the church was the soul, the nobles were the arms, the artisans were the hands, and the peasants were the feet. Like the Chain of Being, the Body Politic was a profoundly conservative concept of social organization that precluded the idea of social mobility.

Social Structure

The Great Chain of Being and the Body Politic were static concepts of social organization. But in the sixteenth century, European society was in a state of dynamic change. Fundamentally, all European societies were divided between nobles and commoners, though relationships between the two orders differed from place to place.

The Nobles. Nobility was a legal status that conferred certain privileges on its holders and passed by inheritance from one generation to the next. Though various systems of title were in use across the Continent, the hierarchy of prince, duke, earl, count, and baron was roughly standard.

Because rulers conferred these titles on individuals, elevating some to higher ranks and others from commoner to noble, the nobility was a political order as well as a social one. Political privileges were among the nobility's most important attributes. In many countries, the highest offices of the state and the military were reserved for members of the nobility. Noblemen were also granted rights of political participation in the deliberative bodies of the state.

Finally, members of the nobility held economic privileges, a result both of their rank and of their role as lords on the lands they owned. In almost every state, the nobility was exempt from most kinds of taxation. The interests of the nobles conflicted directly with those of the ruler, and the larger the number of tax exemptions for the nobility, the stronger was its power in relation to the monarch.

Privileges implied obligations. Initially, the nobility was the warrior caste of the state, and its primary obligations were to raise, equip, and lead troops into battle. By the sixteenth century, the military needs of the state had far surpassed the military power of its nobility. Warfare had become a national enterprise that required central coordination. Nobles became administrators as much as warriors, though it is fair to say that many did both. The French nobility came to be divided into the nobility of the sword and the nobility of the robe—that is, warriors and officeholders.

Nobles also had the obligation of governing at both the national and the local level. At the discretion of the ruler, they could be called to engage in any necessary occupation, no matter how disruptive to their economic or family affairs. They administered their estates and settled the disputes of their tenants. In times of want, they were expected to provide for the needy. The obligation of good lordship was implicitly understood, if not always explicitly carried out, between lord and peasant.

Town Elite and Gentry. The principal distinction in sixteenth-century society was between lord and commoners, but it was not the only one. A new social group was emerging in the towns—a group that had neither the legal nor the social privileges of nobility but performed many of the same functions. The towns remained a separate unit of social organization in most states, enjoying many of the same political and economic privileges as the nobility. Representatives of the towns met with the nobles and the king and were the most important part of the national deliberative assemblies, like the English Parliament or the French estates. Towns were granted legal rights to govern their own citizens, to engage in trade, and to defend themselves by raising and storing arms. Though they paid a large share of most taxes, towns also received large tax concessions.

Georges de La Tour, *The Fortune Teller*. In the painting, which serves as a warning to the naive about the wicked ways of the world, a fashionably dressed young innocent is drawn into the snare of the wily fortune teller.

As individuals, members of the town elite held no special status in society at large. Some were among the richest people in the state, but they had to devise their own systems of honor and prestige. In Venice, the *Book of Gold* distinguished the local elite from the ranks of ordinary citizens. In France and Spain, some of the highest officers of leading towns were granted noble status. In England, wealthy guild members could become knights, a rank just below noble status.

In rural society, the transformation of agricultural holdings in many places also created a group that fit uncomfortably between lords and commoners. The accumulation of larger and larger estates, by purchase from the nobility, the state, or the church, made lords—in the sense of landowners with tenants—of many who were not lords in rank. They received rents and dues from their tenants, administered their estates, and preserved the so-called moral economy that sustained the peasants during hard times. In England, this group came to be known as the gentry, and there were parallel groups in Spain, France, and the Holy Roman Empire. The gentry aspired to the privileges of the nobility.

Social stratification also marked rural communities. In many German villages, a principal distinction was made between those who held land in the ancient part of the settlement—the Esch—and those who held land in those areas into which the village had expanded. The Esch was normally the best land. But interestingly, the holders of the Esch were tied to the lord of the estate, while holders of the less desirable lands were free peasants. Here, freedom to move from place to place was less valued than was the right to live in the heart of the village.

Just the opposite set of values prevailed in English villages, where freeholders were in the most enviable position. They led the movements to break up the common fields for planting and were able to initiate legal actions against their lord. Whenever village land was converted to freehold, unfree tenants would go into debt to buy it.

In towns, the order of rank below the elite pertained as much to the kind of work that one performed as it did to the level at which the work was undertaken. The critical division in town life was between those who had the freedom of the city—citizens—and those who did not. Citizenship was restricted to membership in certain occupations and was closely regulated. It could be purchased, but most citizenship was earned by becoming a master in one of the guilds. Only males could be citizens.

Social Change

In the sixteenth century, social commentators believed that change was transforming the world in which they lived.

The New Rich. Many factors promoted social change during the course of the sixteenth century. First, population increase necessitated an expansion of the ruling orders. With more people to govern, there had to be more governors who could perform the military, political, and social functions of the state. Second, opportunities to accumulate wealth expanded dramatically with the Price Revolution. Traditionally, wealth was calculated in land and tenants rather than in

Feeding the Hungry, by Cornelius Buys, 1504. A maidservant is doling out small loaves to the poor and the lame at the door of a wealthy person's home. The poor who flocked to the towns were often forced to rely on charity to survive.

the possession of liquid assets such as gold and silver. But with the increase in commodity prices, surplus producers could rapidly improve their economic position. Moreover, state service became a source of unlimited riches. The profits to be made from tax collecting, officeholding, or the law could easily surpass those to be made from landholding. And the newly rich clamored for privileges.

The New Poor. Social change was equally apparent at the bottom of the social scale, but here it could not be so easily absorbed. The continuous growth of population created a group of landless poor who squatted in villages and clogged the streets of towns and cities. Rough estimates suggest that as many as one-quarter of all Europeans were destitute.

Traditionally, local communities cared for their poor. Widows, orphans, and the handicapped, who would normally constitute over half of the poor in a village or town, were viewed as the "deserving poor," worthy of the care of the community through the Church or private almsgiving. Catholic communities such as Venice created a system of private charity that paralleled the institutions of the Church. Though Protestant communities took charity out of the control of the Church, they were no less concerned about the plight of the deserving poor. In England, a special tax, the poor rate, supported the poor.

Charity was an obligation of the community, but as the sixteenth century wore on, the number of destitute people grew beyond the ability of the local community to care for them. Many of those who now begged for alms fell outside the traditional categories of the deserving poor. They were men and women who were capable of working but incapable of finding more than occasional labor. They left their native communities in search of employment and thus forfeited their claims on local charity. Most wound up in the towns and cities, where as strangers they had no claim on local charity.

The problem of crime complicated the problems of poverty and vagrancy. Increasing population and increasing wealth equaled increasing crime; the addition of the poor to the equation aggravated the situation. The poor, outsiders to the community without visible means of support, were the easiest targets of official retribution. Throughout the century, numerous European states passed vagrancy laws. Sexual offenses were criminalized, especially bastardy, since the birth of illegitimate children placed an immediate burden on the community. Prostitutes, who had long been tolerated and regulated in towns, were now persecuted. Rape increased. Capital punishment was reserved for the worst crimes—murder, incest, and grand larceny being most common—but, not surprisingly, executions were carried out mostly on outsiders to the community.

Peasant Revolts

The economic and social changes of the sixteenth century had serious consequences. Most telling was the upswing of violent confrontations between peasants and their lords. Across Europe and with alarming regularity, peasants took up arms to defend themselves from what they saw as violations of traditional rights and obligations. Most revolts chose leaders, drew up petitions of grievances, and organized the rank and file into a semblance of military order. Leaders were literate—drawn more commonly from among the lower clergy or minor gentry than from the peasantry—political demands were moderate, and tactics were sophisticated. But peasant revolts so profoundly threatened the social order that they were met with the severest repression.

Agrarian Changes. It is essential to realize that while peasants revolted against their lords, at bottom their anger and frustration were caused by agrarian changes that could be neither controlled nor understood. As population increased and market production expanded, many of the traditional rights and obligations of lords and peasants became oppressive.

For example, conflict arose over enclosing crop fields. An **enclosure** was a device—normally a fence or hedge that surrounded an area—to keep a parcel of land separate from the planted strips of land owned by the villagers. It could be used for grazing animals or raising a specialty crop for the market. But an enclosure destroyed the traditional form of village agriculture whereby decisions on which crops to plant were made communally. It became one of the chief grievances of the English peasants. But while enclosures broke up the old field system in many villages, they were a logical response to the transformation of land ownership that had already taken place. As more and more land was accumulated by fewer and fewer families, it made less and less sense for them to work widely scattered strips all over the village. If a family could consolidate its holdings by swaps and sales, it could gain an estate that was large enough to be used for both crops and grazing. An enclosed estate allowed wealthy farmers to grow more luxury crops for market or to raise only sheep on a field that had once been used for grain.

Enclosure was a process that both lord and rich peasant undertook, but it drove the smallholders from the land and was thus a source of bitter resentment for the poorer peasants. It was easy to protest the greed of the lords who, owning the most land, were the most successful enclosers. But enclosures resulted more from the process whereby villages came to be characterized by a very small elite of large landholders and a very large mass of smallholders and landless poor. It was an effect rather than a cause.

Uprising in Germany. The complexity of these problems is perhaps best revealed in the series of uprisings that are known collectively as the German Peasants' War. It involved tens of thousands of peasants, and it combined a whole series of agrarian grievances with an awareness of the new religious spirit preached by Martin Luther. Luther condemned both lords and peasants—the lords for their rapaciousness, the peasants for their rebelliousness. Though he had a large following among the peasants, his advice that earthly oppressions be passively accepted was not followed. The Peasants' War was directed against secular and ecclesiastical lords, and the rebels attacked both economic and religious abuses. The combination of demands, such as the community's right to select its own minister and the community's right to cut wood freely, attracted a wide following in the villages and small towns of southern and central Germany. The printed demands of the peasantry, the most famous of which was the Twelve Articles of the Peasants of Swabia (1525), helped to spread the movement far beyond its original bounds. The peasants organized themselves into large armies led by experienced soldiers, but ultimately, movements that refused compromise were ruthlessly crushed.

At base, the demands of the peasantry addressed the agrarian changes that were transforming German villages. Population growth was creating more poor villagers who could only hire out as laborers but who demanded a share of common grazing and woodlands. Because the presence of these poor people increased the taxable wealth of the village, they were advantageous to the lord. But the strain they placed on resources was felt by both the subsistence and surplus farmers. Tensions within the village were all the greater in that the landless members were the kin of the landed. If they were to be settled properly on the land, then the lord would have to let the village expand. If they were to be kept on the margins of subsistence, then the more prosperous villagers would have to be able to control their numbers and their conduct. In either case, the peasants needed more direct responsibility for governing the village than existed in their traditional relationship with their lord. Therefore, the peasants of Swabia demanded release of the village peasantry from the status of serfs. They wanted to be allowed to move off the land, to marry out of the village without penalty, and to be free of the death taxes that further impoverished their children. They also wanted stable rents fixed at fair rates, a limit placed on labor service, and a return to the ancient customs that governed relations between lords and peasants. All of these proposals were backed by an appeal to Christian principles of love and charity. They were profoundly conservative.

The demands of the German peasants reflected a traditional order that no longer existed. In many places, the rents and tithes that the peasants wanted to control no longer belonged to the lords of the estates. They had been sold to town corporations or wealthy individuals who purchased them as an investment and expected to realize a fair return. Most tenants did enjoy stable and fixed rents, but only on their traditional lands. As they increased their holdings, perhaps to keep another son in the village or to expand production for the market, they were faced with the fact that rents were higher and land was more expensive than it had been before. Marriage fines, death duties, and labor service were oppressive, but they balanced the fact that traditional rents were very low. In many east German villages, peasants willingly increased their labor service for a reduction in their money rents. It was hardly likely that they could have both. If the peasants were being squeezed, and there can be little doubt that they were, it was not only the lords who were doing the squeezing. The Church took its tenth, the state increased its exactions, and the competition for survival and prosperity among the peasants themselves was ferocious. Peasants were caught between the jaws of an expanding state and a changing economy. When they rebelled, the jaws snapped shut.

Chronology

SOCIAL AND ECONOMIC CHANGE

1450–1550	Population of France doubles
1500–1600	Population of Europe increases by about one-third
1500–1600	Population of England doubles; population of London quadruples
1500–1600	Price revolution leads to declines in real wages
1514	Revolt of Hungarian peasants
1524–1525	German Peasants' War
1600	Europe reaches new population high of about 105 million

Private and Community Life

The great events of the sixteenth century—discovery of the New World, consolidation of states, increasing incidence and ferocity of war, and reform of religion—all had a profound impact on the lives of ordinary people. However slowly and intermittently these developments penetrated to isolated village communities, they were inextricably bound up with the experiences and world view of all Europeans.

The Family

Sixteenth-century life centered on the family, the primary kinship group. European families were predominantly nuclear, composed of a married couple and their children. Yet, however families were composed, kinship had a wider orbit than just parents and children. In-laws, step relations, and cousins were considered part of the kin group and could be called on for support in a variety of contexts from charity to employment and business partnerships. In towns, such family connections created large and powerful clans.

In a different sense, family was lineage, the connections between preceding and succeeding generations. This was an important concept among the upper ranks of society, in which ancient lineage, genuine or fabricated, was a valued component of nobility. Even in peasant communities, however, lineage existed in the form of the strips in the field that were passed from generation to generation and named for the family that owned them.

The family was also an economic unit. It was the basic unit for the production, accumulation, and transmission of wealth. Occupation determined the organization of the economic family. Every member of the household had his or her own functions that were essential to the survival of the unit. Tasks were divided by gender and by age, but there was far more intermixture than is traditionally assumed.

Finally, the family was the primary unit of social organization. It was in the family that children were educated and the social values of hierarchy and discipline were taught. Authority in the family was strictly organized in a set of three overlapping categories. At the top was the husband, head of the household, who ruled over his wife, children, and servants. All members of the family owed obedience to the head. Children owed obedience to their parents, male or female. Similarly, servants owed obedience to both master and mistress. Male apprentices were under the authority of the wife, mother, and mistress of the household. The importance of the family as a social unit was underscored by the fact that people who were not attached to families attracted suspicion in sixteenth-century society. Single men were often viewed as potential criminals, single women as potential prostitutes.

Though the population of Europe was increasing in the sixteenth century, families were not large. Throughout northern and western Europe, the size of the typical family was two adults and three or four children. Women married around age 25, men slightly later. Most women could expect about 15 fertile years and seven or eight pregnancies if neither they nor their husbands died in the interim. Only three or four children were likely to survive beyond the age of 10. In her fertile years, a woman was constantly occupied with infants. Constant pregnancy and child care may help explain some of the gender roles that men and women assumed in the sixteenth century. Biblical injunctions and traditional stereotypes help explain others. Whether a woman was pregnant or not, her labor was a vital part of the domestic economy, especially until the first surviving children were strong enough to assume their share. The woman's sphere was the household. On the farm, she was in charge of the preparation of food, the care of domestic animals, the care and education of children, and the manufacture and cleaning of the family's clothing. In towns, women supervised the shop that was part of the household. They sold goods, kept accounts, and directed the work of domestics or apprentices.

Jan Vermeer's, *The Milkmaid* (1658–1660) shows a domestic servant absorbed in her household tasks. Homes were sparsely furnished, though this family was rich enough to possess a table, an earthenware bowl and jug, and a footstove that held hot coals (seen on the floor behind the maid).

The man's sphere was the public one: the fields in rural areas, the streets in towns. Men plowed, planted, and did the heavy reaping work of farming. They made and maintained essential farm equipment and had charge of the large farm animals. They marketed surplus produce and made the few purchases of equipment or luxury goods. Men performed the labor service that was normally due the lord of the estate, attended the local courts in various capacities, and organized the affairs of the village. In towns, men engaged in heavy labor, procured materials for craft work, and marketed their product if it was not sold in the household shop. Only men could be citizens of the towns or full members of most craft guilds, and only men were involved in civic government.

While male roles were constant throughout the life cycle, as men trained for and performed the same occupations from childhood to death, female roles varied greatly depending on the situation. While under the care of fathers, masters, or husbands, women worked in the domestic sphere; once widowed, they assumed the public functions of head of household. Many women inherited shops or farmland; most became responsible for the placement and training of their children. But because of the division of labor on which the family depended and because of the inherent social and economic prejudices that segregated public and domestic roles, widows were particularly disadvantaged.

Communities

The family was part of a wider community. On the farm, this community was the rural village; in the town, it was the ward, quarter, or parish in which the family lived.

Community life must not be romanticized. Interpersonal violence, lawsuits, and feuds were common in both rural and urban communities. Like every other aspect of society, the community was socially and economically stratified, gender roles were segregated, and resources were inequitably divided. But the community was also the place where people found their social identity. It provided marriage partners for its families, charity for its poor, and a local culture for all of its inhabitants.

Identities and Customs. The two basic forces that tied the rural community together were the lord and the priest. The lord set conditions for work and property ownership that necessitated common decision making on the part of the village farmers. Use of the common lands, the rotation of labor service, and the form in which rents in kind were paid were all decisions that had to be made collectively. Communal agreement was also expressed in communal resistance to violations of custom or threats to the moral economy. All these forms of negotiation fused individual families into a community. So, too, in a different way did the presence of the parish priest or minister, who attended all the pivotal events of life—birth, marriage, and death. The church was the only common building of the community; it was the only space that was not owned outright by the lord or an individual family. The scene of village meetings and ceremonies, it was the center of both spiritual and social life. The parish priest served as a conduit for all the news of the community and the focal point for the village's festive life.

Weddings and Festivals. The most common ceremony was the wedding, a public event that combined a religious rite and a community procession with feasting and festivity. It took different forms in different parts of Europe and in different social groups. Many couples were engaged long before they were married, and in many places it was the engagement that was most important to the individuals and the wedding that was most important to the community. Traditional weddings involved the formal transfer of property, an important event in rural communities where the ownership of strips of land or common rights concerned everyone. The public procession, "the marriage in the streets," as it was sometimes called in towns, proclaimed the union throughout the community.

Other ceremonies were equally important in creating a shared sense of identity within the community. In both town and countryside, the year was divided by a number of festivals that defined the rhythm of toil and rest. They coincided with both the seasonal divisions of agricultural life and the central events of the Christian calendar. Christmas and Easter were probably the most widely observed Christian holidays, but **Carnival**, which preceded Lent, was a frenzied round of feasts and parties that resulted in a disproportionate number of births nine months later.

In addition to feasting, dancing, and play, festivals often included sports, such as soccer or wrestling, which served to channel aggressions. At such times, village elders would also arbitrate disputes, and marriage alliances or property transactions would be arranged.

Festivals further cemented the political cohesion of the community. Seating arrangements signaled the hierarchy of the community, and public punishment of offenders reinforced deference and social and sexual mores. Youth groups or the village women might band together to shame a promiscuous woman or to place horns on the head of a cuckolded husband. These forms of community ritual worked not only to punish offenders but also to reinforce the social and sexual values of the village as a whole.

Popular Beliefs and the Persecution of Witches

Ceremony and festival are reminders that sixteenth-century Europe was still a pre-literate society. Despite the introduction of printing and the millions of books that were produced during the period, the vast majority of Europeans conducted their affairs without the benefit of literacy. Outside a small circle of intellectuals, there was little effective knowledge about either human or celestial bodies. But this does not mean that ordinary people lived in a constant state of terror and anxiety. They used the knowledge they did have to form a view of the universe that conformed to their experiences and responded to their hopes.

Magical Practices. These beliefs blended Christian teaching and folk wisdom with a strong strain of magic. Popular belief in magic could be found everywhere in Europe, and it operated in much the same way as science does today. Only skilled practitioners could perform magic. It was a technical subject that combined expertise in the properties of plants and animals with theories about the composition of human and heavenly bodies. It had its own language, a mixture of ancient words and sounds with significant numbers and catch phrases. Magicians specialized. Alchemists worked with rocks and minerals, astrologers with the movement of the stars. Witches were thought to understand the properties of animals especially well.

Magical practices appealed to people at all levels of society. The wealthy favored astrology and paid handsomely to discover which days and months were the most auspicious for marriages and investments. The poorest villagers sought the aid of herbalists to help control the constant aches and pains of daily life. Sorcerers and wizards were called on in more extreme circumstances, such as a threatened harvest or matters of life and death. These magicians competed with the remedies offered by the Church. Special prayers and visits to the shrines of particular saints were believed to have similar curative value. Magical and Christian beliefs were often practiced simultaneously. It was not until the end of the century, when Protestant and Catholic leaders condemned magical practices and began a campaign to root them out, that magic and religion came into conflict.

Magical practices served a variety of purposes. Healing was the most common, and many "magical" brews were effective remedies for the minor ailments for which they were prescribed. Most village magicians were women because it was believed that women had unique knowledge and understanding of the body.

Magic was also used for predictive purposes. Certain charms and rituals were believed to have the power to affect the weather, the crops, and even human events. As always, affairs of the heart were as important as those of the stomach. Magicians advised the lovesick on potions and spells that would gain them the object of their desires. Finally, it was believed that magic had the power to alter the course of nature and could be used for both good and evil purposes.

The Witch Craze. Magic for evil was black magic, or witchcraft. Witches were believed to possess special powers that put them into contact with the devil and the forces of evil, which they could then use for their own purposes. Belief in the prevalence of good and evil spirits was Christian as well as magical. But the Church had gradually consigned the operation of the devil to the afterlife and removed his direct agency from earthly affairs. Beginning in the late fifteenth century, Church authorities began to prosecute large numbers of suspected witches. By the end of the sixteenth century, there was a continentwide witch craze. Confessions were obtained under torture, as were further accusations.

Witches were usually women, most often unmarried or widowed. In a sample of more than 7,000 cases of witchcraft prosecuted in early modern Europe, over 80 percent of the defendants were women. There is no clear explanation for why women fulfilled this important and powerful role. Belief in women's special powers over the body through their singular ability to give birth is certainly one part of the explanation, for many stories about the origins of witches suggest that they were children fathered by the devil and left to be raised by women. This sexual element of union with the devil and the common belief that older women were sexually aggressive combined to threaten male sexual dominance. Witches were also believed to have peculiar physical characteristics. Accused witches were strip-searched to find the devil's mark, which might be any bodily blemish. Another strand of explanation lies in the fact that single women existed on the fringes of society, isolated and exploited by the community at large. Their occult abilities thus became a protective mechanism that gave them a function within the community while they remained outside it.

It is difficult to know how important black magical beliefs were in ordinary communities. Most of the daily magic that was practiced was a mixture of charms, potions, and prayers that mingled magical, medical, and Christian beliefs. Misfortunes that befell particular families or social groups were blamed on the activities of witches. The campaign of the established churches to root out magic was directed largely against witches. The churches transposed witches' supposed abilities to communicate with the devil into the charge that they worshiped the devil. Because there was such widespread belief in the presence of diabolical spirits and in the capabilities of witches to control them, Protestant and Catholic church courts could easily find witnesses to testify in support of the charges against individual witches. Over 100,000—perhaps several times that many—condemned witches in Europe were burned, strangled, drowned, or beheaded. Yet wherever sufficient evidence exists to understand the circumstances of witchcraft prosecutions, it is clear that the community itself was under some form of social or economic stress rather than that there was any increase in the presence or use of witches.

SUMMARY

Economic Life Roughly 90 percent of Europe's population lived on farms or in small farming towns. Most Europeans faced the constant threat of famine, cold, and disease. Peasant life centered on agriculture. In towns, life revolved around commerce. Most town dwellers were unskilled laborers. Europe's population grew rapidly in the sixteenth century. Population growth led to inflation. The Price Revolution had dramatic consequences for all Europeans.

Social Life A belief in hierarchy and a static society underlay European social thought. The belief in hierarchy was expressed through the metaphors of the Great Chain of Being and the Body Politic. Europeans were divided between nobles and commoners. Nobility conferred privileges and responsibilities. Town elites and gentry occupied a social space between lord and commoners. Social change transformed European society at both the top and bottom. Economic and social change created tensions that were expressed in peasant revolts such as the German Peasants' War.

Private and Community Life Sixteenth-century life centered on the family. European families were predominantly nuclear. Within the family, tasks were organized by gender and by age. The family mirrored the hierarchy of the larger society. The woman's sphere was the home. The man's sphere was the public world. Families were part of wider communities. The lord and the priest helped tie communities together. Ceremonies and festivals served to reinforce community identity. There was widespread belief in magic and witchcraft. The sixteenth century saw a dramatic increase in the number of prosecutions of suspected witches.

QUESTIONS FOR REVIEW

1. What physical forces and social customs shaped the everyday life of Europe's rural population?
2. What was the nature of demographic change in the sixteenth century, and what was its impact on the European economy?
3. How are the terms "stratification," "hierarchy," and "status" useful for understanding social relations in early modern Europe?
4. How were the different roles of men and women within the family reflected in the different lives of men and women in the wider community?

The Royal State in the Seventeenth Century

The Rise of the Royal State

The wars that dominated the early part of the seventeenth century had a profound impact on the western European states. Not only did they cause terrible suffering and deprivation, but they also demanded efficient and better-centralized states to conduct them. War was both a product of the European state system and a cause of its continued development. As armies grew in size, their matériel needs grew in volume. As the battlefield spread from state to state, defense became government's most important function. More and more power was absorbed by the monarch and his chief advisers; more and more of the traditional privileges of aristocracy and of towns were eroded. At the center of these rising states, particularly in western Europe, were the king and his court. In the provinces were tax collectors and military recruiters.

Divine Kings

In the early sixteenth century, monarchs treated their states and subjects as personal property. Correspondingly, rulers were praised in personal terms, for their virtue, wisdom, or strength. By the early seventeenth century, the monarchy had been transformed into an office of state. Now rulers embodied their nation, and, no matter what their personal characteristics, they were held in awe because they were monarchs.

Thus, as rulers lost direct personal control over their territory, they gained indirect symbolic control over their nation. This symbolic power was manifested everywhere. By the beginning of the seventeenth century, monarchs had permanent seats of government attended by vast courts of officials, place seekers, and servants. The idea of the capital city emerged, with Madrid, London, and Paris as models. Here, the grandiose style of the ruler stood proxy for the wealth and glory of the nation.

Portraits of rulers conveyed the central message. Elizabeth I was depicted astride a map of England or clutching a rainbow and wearing a gown woven of eyes and ears to signify her power to see and hear her subjects. Peter Paul Rubens (1577–1640) represented 21 separate episodes in the life of Marie de Médicis, queen regent of France.

Monarchy was also glorified in literature. National history, particularly of recent events, enjoyed wide popularity. Its avowed purpose was to draw the connection between the past and the present glories of the state.

Shakespeare and Kingship. Many of the plays of William Shakespeare (1564–1616) dealt with monarchy. He set many of his plays at the courts of princes, and even comedies such as *Measure for Measure* (1604) and *The Tempest* (1611) centered on the power of the ruler to dispense justice and to bring peace to his subjects. Shakespeare's history plays focused entirely on the character of kings. In Shakespeare's tragedies, a

Queen Elizabeth I of England. This portrait was commissioned by Sir Henry Lee to commemorate the queen's visit to his estate at Ditchley. Here the queen is the very image of Gloriana—ageless and indomitable.

flaw in the ruler's personality brought harm to the world around him. Shakespeare's concentration on the affairs of rulers helped to reinforce their dominating importance in the lives of all of their subjects.

Monarchy and Law. The political theory of the **divine right of kings** further enhanced the importance of monarchs. This theory held that the institution of monarchy had been created by God and the monarch functioned as God's representative on earth.

The idea of divine origin of monarchy was uncontroversial, and it was espoused not only by kings. In 1614, the French Estates-General agreed that "the king is sovereign in France and holds his crown from God only." This sentiment echoed the commonplace view of French political theorists. The greatest writer on the subject, Jean Bodin (1530–1596), called the king "God's image on earth."

Kings were nevertheless bound by the law of nature and the law of nations. They could not deprive their subjects of their lives, their liberties, or their property without due cause established by law.

The Court and the Courtiers

In reality, the day-to-day affairs of government had grown beyond the capacity of any monarch to handle them. The expansion in the powers of the western states absorbed more officials than ever. At the beginning of the sixteenth century, the French court of Francis I employed 622 officers; at the beginning of the seventeenth century, the court of Henry IV employed over 1,500. Yet the difference was not only in size. Members of the seventeenth-century court were becoming servants of the state as well as of the monarch.

Expanding the court was one of the ways in which monarchs co-opted potential rivals within the aristocracy. In return, those who were favored received royal grants of titles, lands, and income. As the court expanded, so did the political power of courtiers. Royal councils—a small group of leading officeholders who advised the monarch on state business—grew in significance. The council assumed management of the government and soon began to advocate policies for the monarch to adopt.

Yet the court still revolved around the monarch. The monarch appointed, promoted, and dismissed officeholders at will. As befitted this type of personal government, most monarchs chose a single individual to act as a funnel for private and public business. This was the "favorite," whose role combined varying proportions of best friend, right-hand man, and hired gun. Favorites lasted only as long as they retained their influence with the monarch.

The Drive to Centralize Government

Europe's divine monarchs shared a common goal: to extend the authority of the monarch over his state and to centralize his control over the machinery of governance. One of the chief means by which kings and councilors attempted to expand the authority of the state was through the legal system.

Administering justice was one of the sacred duties of the monarchy. The complexities of ecclesiastical, civil, and customary law gave trained lawyers an essential role in government. As the need for legal services increased, royal law courts multiplied and expanded. In France, the Parlement of Paris, the main law court of the state, became a powerful institution that contested with courtiers for the right to advise the monarch.

In Spain, the *letrados*—university-trained lawyers who were normally members of the nobility—were the backbone of royal government. Formal legal training was a requirement for many of the administrative posts in the state. In Castile, members of all social classes frequently used the royal courts to settle personal disputes. The expansion of a centralized system of justice thus joined the interests of subjects and the monarchy.

In England, central courts situated in the royal palace of Westminster grew, and the lawyers and judges who practiced in them became a powerful profession. They were especially active in the House of Commons of the English Parliament, which, along with the House of Lords, had extensive advisory and legislative powers. More important than the rise of the central courts, however, was the rise of the local ones. The English crown extended royal justice to the counties by granting legal authority to members of the local social elite. These justices of the peace, whose position can be traced to medieval times, became agents of the crown in their own localities. Justices were given power to hear and settle minor cases and to imprison people who had committed serious offenses until the assizes, the semiannual sessions of the county court.

Assizes combined the ceremony of rule with its process. Royal authority was displayed in a great procession to the courthouse that was led by the judge and the county justices, followed by the grand and petty juries of local citizens who would hear the cases, and finally by the carts carrying the prisoners to trial. Along with the legal business that was performed, assizes were occasions for edifying sermons, typically on the theme of obedience.

Efforts to integrate center and locality extended to more than the exercise of justice. The monarch also needed officials who could enforce royal policy in localities where the special privileges of groups and individuals remained strong. By the beginning of the seventeenth century, the French monarchy had begun to rely on new central officials known as **intendants** to perform many of the tasks of the provincial governors. During the reign of Louis XIII, Cardinal Richelieu (1585–1642) expanded the use of the intendants, and by the middle of the century they had become a vital part of royal government.

The Lords Lieutenant were a parallel institution created in England. Unlike every other European state, England had no national army. Every English county was required to raise, equip, and train its own militia. Lords Lieutenant were in charge of these trained bands. The lieutenants were chosen from the greatest nobles of the realm, but they delegated their work to members of the local gentry, large landholders who took on their tasks as a matter of prestige rather than profit.

Efforts to centralize the Spanish monarchy could not proceed so easily. The separate regions over which the king ruled maintained their own laws and privileges.

Attempts to apply Castilian rules or implant Castilian officials always drew opposition from other regions. In 1625, Count-Duke Olivares (1587–1645), favorite of King Philip IV (1621–1665), proposed a plan to help unify Spain and solve the dual problems of military manpower and military finance. After 1621, Spain was fighting in the Netherlands and Germany. Olivares called for a Union of Arms to which all the separate regions of the empire, including Mexico, Peru, Italy, and the dominions in Iberia, would contribute. Olivares was able to establish at least the principle of unified cooperation, but not all of the Iberian provinces were persuaded to contribute. Catalonia stood on its ancient privileges and refused to grant either troops or funds.

The Taxing Demands of War

More than anything else, the consolidation of the state was propelled by war, which required increased governmental powers of taxation. Perhaps half of all revenue of the western states went to finance war. To maintain its military forces, the state had to squeeze every penny from its subjects. Old taxes had to be collected more efficiently, and new taxes had to be introduced and enforced. Such unprecedented demands for money on the part of the state were always resisted. The privileged challenged the legality of levying taxes; the unprivileged tried to avoid paying them.

The economic hardships caused by the ceaseless military activity touched everyone. Those in the direct path of battle had little left to feed themselves, let alone to provide to the state. The disruption of the delicate cycle of planting and harvesting devastated local communities. Armies plundered ripened grain and trampled seedlings as they moved through fields. The conscription of village men and boys removed vital skills and labor from the community. Peasants were squeezed by the armies for crops, by the lords for rents, and by the state for taxes.

In fact, the inability of the lower orders of European society to finance a century of warfare was clear from the beginning. In Spain and France, much wealth was beyond the reach of traditional royal taxation. The nobility and many of the most important towns had long enjoyed exemption from basic taxes on consumption and wealth. European taxation was regressive, falling most heavily on those who were least able to pay. Rulers and subjects alike recognized the inequities of the system, and regime after regime considered overhauling the national tax system but ultimately settled for new emergency levies. Nevertheless, the fiscal crisis that the European wars provoked did result in an expansion of state taxation.

Still, no matter how much new revenue was provided for war finance, more was needed. New taxes and increased rates of traditional taxation created suffering and a sense of grievance throughout the western European states. Opposition to taxation was not based on greed. The state's right to tax was not yet an established principle. Monarchs received certain forms of revenue in return for grants of immunities and privileges to powerful groups in their state. The state's efforts to go beyond these restricted grants was viewed as theft of private property.

Throughout the seventeenth century, monarchy was consolidating its position as a form of government. The king's authority came from God, but his power came from his people. By administering justice, assembling armies, and extracting resources through taxation, the monarch ruled as well as governed. The richer and more powerful the king, the more potent was his state. His subjects began to identify themselves as citizens of a nation and to see themselves in distinction to other nations.

The Crises of the Royal State

The expansion of the functions, duties, and powers of the state in the early seventeenth century was not universally welcomed in European societies. The growth of central government came at the expense of local rights and privileges held by organized bodies such as the Church and the towns or by individuals such as provincial officials and aristocrats. The state proved to be a powerful competitor for the meager surplus produced on the land. As rents and prices stabilized in the early seventeenth century, after a long period of inflation, taxation increased, especially with the gathering momentum of the Thirty Years' War.

It was not only taxation that aroused opposition. Social and economic regulation meant more laws, more lawyers, and more agents of enforcement. State regulation was disruptive and expensive at a time when the fragile European economy was in decline. The early seventeenth century was a time of hunger in most of western Europe. Subtle changes in climate reduced the length of growing seasons and the size of crops. Bad harvests in the 1620s and 1640s left disease and starvation in their wake. And the wars ground on.

By the middle of the seventeenth century, a Europe-wide crisis was taking shape. Bread riots and tax revolts had become increasingly common in the early seventeenth century. As the focus of discontent moved from local institutions to the state, the forms of revolt and the participants also changed. Members of the political elite began to formulate their own grievances against the expansion of state power. A theory of resistance, first developed in the French wars of religion, came to be applied to political tyranny and posed a direct challenge to the idea of the divine right of kings. By the 1640s, all of these forces converged, and rebellion exploded across the Continent.

The Need to Resist

Europeans lived more precariously in the seventeenth century than in any period since the Black Death. One benchmark of crisis was population decline. In the Mediterranean, the Spanish population fell from 8.5 million to 7 million, and the Italian population from 13 million to 11 million. The ravages of the Thirty Years' War were most clearly felt in central Europe. Germany lost nearly one-third of its people; Bohemia lost nearly half. England, the Netherlands, and France were hardest hit in the first half of the century and only gradually recovered by 1700. Population decline had many causes, and direct casualties from warfare were only a very small component.

The indirect effects of war—the disruption of agriculture and the spread of disease—were far more devastating.

All sectors of the European economy from agriculture to trade stagnated or declined in the early seventeenth century, but peasants were hardest hit. The surplus from good harvests did not remain in rural communities to act as a buffer for bad ones. Tens of thousands died during the two great subsistence crises in the late 1620s and the late 1640s.

Acute economic crisis led to rural revolt. As the French peasants reeled from visitations of plague, frost, and floods, the French state was raising the taille, the tax on basic commodities that fell most heavily on the lower orders. A series of French rural revolts in the late 1630s protested tax increases. The *Nu-Pieds* ("barefooted") rose against changes in the salt tax; other peasants rose against new levies on wine. These revolts typically began with the murder of a local tax official, the organization of a peasant militia, and the recruitment of local clergy and notables. The rebels forced temporary concessions from local authorities but never achieved lasting reforms. Each revolt ended with the reimposition of order by the state.

The most spectacular popular uprisings occurred in Spanish-occupied Italy. In the spring of 1647, in the Sicilian city of Palermo, violence broke out in the wake of a disastrous harvest, rising food prices, and relentless taxation. As grain prices rose, the city government subsidized the price of bread, running up huge debts in the process. When the town governors could no longer afford the subsidies, they decided to reduce the size of the loaf rather than increase its price. The women of the city rioted when the first undersized loaves were placed on sale, and soon the entire city was in revolt. Commoners who were not part of the urban power structure led the revolt, and for a time they achieved the abolition of Spanish taxes on basic foodstuffs. Their success provided the model for a similar uprising in Naples, the largest city in Europe. The revolt began in 1647 after the Spanish placed a tax on fruit. A crowd gathered in protest, burned the customs house, and murdered several local officials. The rebels again achieved the temporary suspension of Spanish taxation. But neither of the Italian urban revolts could attract support from the local governors or the nobility. Both uprisings were eventually crushed.

EUROPEAN POPULATION DATA (IN MILLIONS)							
Year	1550	1575	1600	1625	1650	1675	1700
England	3.0	—	4.0	4.5	—	5.8	5.8
France	—	20.0	—	—	—	—	19.3
Italy	11.0	13.0	13.0	13.0	12.0	11.5	12.5
Russia	9.0	—	11.0	8.0	9.5	13.0	16.0
Spain	6.3	—	7.6	—	5.2	—	7.0
All Europe	85.0	95.0	100.0	100.0	80.0	90.0	100.0

The Right to Resist

Rural and urban revolts by members of the lower orders of European society were doomed to failure. Not only did the state control vast military resources, but it could count on the loyalty of the governing classes to suppress local disorder. Only when disgruntled local elites joined the angry peasants did the state face a genuine crisis. Traditionally, aristocratic rebellion was sparked by rival claimants to the throne. By the early seventeenth century, however, hereditary monarchy was too firmly entrenched to be threatened by aristocratic rebellions. The principles of hereditary monarchy and the divine right of kings laid an unshakable foundation for royal legitimacy. But if the monarch's right to rule could no longer be challenged, was the method of rule equally unassailable? Were subjects bound to their sovereign in all cases whatsoever?

Resistance Theory. Luther and Calvin had preached a doctrine of passive obedience. Magistrates ruled by divine will and must be obeyed in all things, they argued. Both left a tiny crack in the door of absolute submission, however, by recognizing the right of lesser magistrates to resist their superiors if divine law was violated. During the French civil wars, a broader theory of resistance began to develop. In attempting to defend themselves from accusations that they were rebels, a number of Huguenot writers responded with an argument that accepted the divine right of kings but maintained that kings were placed on earth by God to uphold piety and justice. When they failed to do so, lesser magistrates were obliged to resist them. Because God would not institute tyranny, oppressive monarchs could not be acting by divine right. Therefore, the king who violated divine law could be punished. In the most influential of these writings, *A Defense of Liberty Against Tyrants* (1579), Philippe Duplessis-Mornay (1549–1623) took the critical next step and argued that the king who violated the law of the land could also be resisted.

In the writings of both the French Huguenots and the Dutch Protestants there remained strict limits to this right to resist. These authors accepted divine right theory and restricted resistance to other divinely ordained magistrates.

Logic soon drove the argument further. If it was the duty of lesser magistrates to resist monarchical tyranny, why was it not the duty of all citizens to do so? This question was posed by the Jesuit professor Juan de Mariana (1536–1624) in *The King and the Education of the King* (1598). Since magistrates were first established by the people and then legitimated by God, magistrates were nothing other than the people's representatives. If it was the duty of magistrates to resist the tyranny of monarchs, Mariana reasoned, then it must also be the duty of every individual citizen.

In defense of the English Revolution, the great English poet John Milton (1608–1674) built on traditional resistance theory. In *The Tenure of Kings and Magistrates* (1649), Milton expanded on the conventional idea that society was formed by a covenant, or contract, between ruler and ruled. The king, in his coronation oath, promised to uphold the laws of the land and to rule for the benefit of his subjects. The subjects promised to obey. Either side's failure to meet obligations broke the contract.

Resistance and Rebellion. By the middle of the seventeenth century, resistance theory provided the intellectual justification for a number of attacks on monarchical authority. In 1640, simultaneous rebellions in the ancient kingdoms of Portugal and Catalonia threatened the Spanish monarchy. The Portuguese successfully dissolved the rather artificial bonds that had been created by Philip II and resumed their separate national identity. Catalonia, the easternmost province of Spain, which Ferdinand of Aragon had brought to the union of crowns in the fifteenth century, presented a more serious challenge. Throughout the 1620s, Catalonia, with its rich Mediterranean city of Barcelona, had consistently rebuffed Olivares's attempts to consolidate the Spanish provinces. The Catalan Cortes—the representative institution of the towns—refused to make even small contributions to the Union of Arms or to successive appeals for emergency tax increases. Catalonian leaders feared that these demands were only an entering wedge. They did not want their province to go the way of Castile, where taxation was as much an epidemic as was plague.

Catalonia resisted demands for contributions to the Spanish military effort, but soon the province was embroiled in the French war, and Olivares was forced to bring troops into Catalonia. The presence of the soldiers and their conduct inflamed the local population. In the spring of 1640, an unconnected series of peasant uprisings took place. Soldiers and royal officials were slain, and the Spanish viceroy of the province was murdered. But the violence was not directed only against outsiders. Attacks on wealthy citizens raised the specter of social revolt.

It was at this point that a peasant uprising broadened into a provincial rebellion. The political leaders of Barcelona sanctioned the rebellion and decided to lead it. They declared that Philip IV had violated the fundamental laws of Catalonia and that in consequence their allegiance to the crown of Spain was dissolved. They turned to Louis XIII of France, offering him sovereignty if he would preserve their liberties. In fact, the Catalonians simply exchanged a devil they knew for one they did not. The French happily sent troops into Barcelona to repel a Spanish attempt to crush the rebellion. Now two armies occupied Catalonia. The Catalan rebellion lasted for 12 years. When the Spanish finally took Barcelona in 1652, both rebels and ruler were exhausted from the struggle.

The revolt of the Catalans posed a greater external threat to the Spanish monarchy than it did an internal one. In contrast, the French **Fronde**, an aristocratic rebellion that began in 1648, was more directly a challenge to the underlying authority of the state. It too began in response to fiscal crises brought on by war. Throughout the 1640s, the French state, tottering on the edge of bankruptcy, had used every means of creative financing that its ministers could devise. Still, it was necessary to raise traditional taxes and to institute new ones. The first tactic revived peasant revolts, especially in the early years of the decade; the second led to the Fronde.

The Fronde was a rebellion against the regency government of Louis XIV (1643–1715), who was only four years old when he inherited the French throne. His mother, Anne of Austria (1601–1666), ruled as regent with the help of her Italian adviser, Cardinal Mazarin (1602–1661). In the circumstances of war, agricultural crisis, and financial stringency, no regency government was going to be popular, but Anne and Mazarin made the worst of a bad situation. They initiated new taxes on office-holders, Parisian landowners, and the nobility. Soon all three groups united against them, led by the Parlement of Paris, the highest court in the land, in which new decrees of taxation had to be registered. When the Parlement refused to register a number of the new taxes proposed by the government and soon insisted on the right to control the crown's financial policy, Anne and Mazarin struck back by having a number of Parlement members arrested. But in 1648, barricades went up in Paris, and the court, along with the nine-year-old king, fled the capital. Quickly, the Fronde—which took its name from the slingshots that children used to hurl stones at carriages—became an aristocratic revolt aimed not at the king but at his advisers. Demands for Mazarin's resignation, the removal of the new taxes, and greater participation in government by nobles and Parlement were coupled with profuse statements of loyalty to the king.

The duc de Condé, leader of the Parisian insurgents, courted Spanish aid against Mazarin's forces, and the cardinal was forced to make concessions to prevent a Spanish invasion of France. The leaders of the Fronde agreed that the crown must overhaul its finances and recognize the rights of the administrative nobility to participate in formulating royal policy. But they had no concrete proposals to accomplish either aim. Nor could they control the deteriorating political situation in Paris and a number of provincial capitals, where urban and rural riots followed the upper-class attack on the state. The catastrophic winter of 1652, with its combination of harvest failure, intense cold, and epidemic disease, brought the crisis to a head. Louis XIV was declared old enough to rule, and his forces recaptured Paris, where he was welcomed as a savior. The Fronde accomplished little other than to demonstrate that the French aristocracy remained an independent force in politics. Like the Catalonian revolt, it revealed the fragility of the absolute state on the one hand, yet its underlying stability on the other.

The English Civil War

The most profound challenge to monarchical authority in the seventeenth century took place in England. In 1603, James I succeeded his cousin Elizabeth I without challenge. He was not a lovable monarch, but he was capable, astute, and generous. Though he relied on Elizabeth's most trusted ministers to guide state business, James was soon plunged into financial and political difficulties. He never escaped either.

Charles I. James's financial problems resulted directly from the fact that the tax base of the English monarchy was undervalued. For decades the monarchy had staved off a crisis by selling lands that had been confiscated from the Church in the mid-sixteenth century. But this solution reduced the Crown's long-term revenues and made it dependent on extraordinary grants of taxation from Parliament. Royal demands for money were met by parliamentary demands for political reform. The most significant, in 1628, during the reign of Charles I, led to the formulation of the Petition of Right, which restated the traditional English freedoms from arbitrary arrest and imprisonment (habeas corpus), from nonparliamentary taxation, and from the confiscation of property by martial law.

Religious problems mounted on top of economic and political difficulties. **Puritans** were demanding thoroughgoing church reforms. One of the most contentious issues raised by some Puritans was the survival in the Anglican Church of the Catholic hierarchy of archbishops and bishops. These Puritans demanded the abolition of this episcopal form of government and its replacement with a presbyterial system similar to that in Scotland, in which congregations nominated their own representatives to a national assembly. Neither James I nor his son, Charles I, opposed religious reform, but to achieve their reforms, they strengthened episcopal power. In the 1620s, Archbishop William Laud (1573–1645) rose to power in the English church by espousing a Calvinism so moderate that many denied it was Calvinism at all. One of Laud's first projects after he was appointed archbishop of Canterbury was to establish a consistent divine service in England and Scotland by creating new prayer books.

It fell to the unfortunate dean of St. Giles Cathedral in Edinburgh to introduce the new Scottish prayer book in 1637. The reaction was immediate: Someone threw a stool at his head, and dozens of women screamed that "popery" was being brought to Scotland. Citizens rioted, and the clergy and the nobility resisted the use of the new prayer book. To Charles I the opposition was rebellion, and he began to raise forces to suppress it. But the Scots fought back, and by the end of 1640 an army of Charles's Scottish subjects had successfully invaded England.

Now the fiscal and political problems of the Stuart monarchs came into play. For 11 years, Charles I had managed to live from his own revenues. He had accomplished this by a combination of economy and the revival of ancient feudal rights that struck hard at the governing classes. He levied fines for unheard-of offenses, expanded traditional taxes, and added a brutal efficiency to the collection of

Charles I by Daniel Myrtens. The antagonism between Charles and Parliament sparked a civil war in England.

revenue. While these expedients sufficed during peacetime, they could not support an army and war. Charles I was again dependent on grants from Parliament, which he reluctantly summoned in 1640.

The Long Parliament. The **Long Parliament**, which met in November 1640 and sat for 13 years, saw little urgency in levying taxes to repel the Scots. Parliament proposed a number of constitutional reforms that Charles I reluctantly accepted. The Long Parliament would not be dismissed without its own consent. In the future, Parliaments

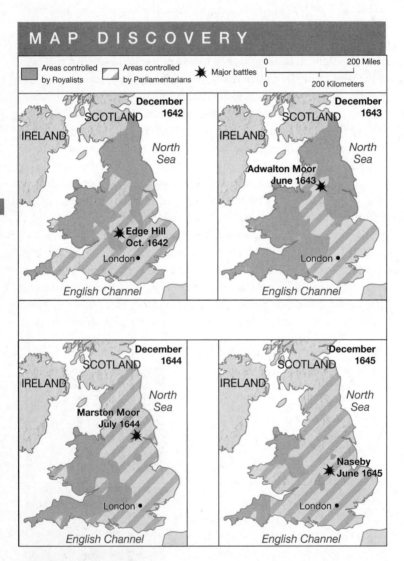

MAP DISCOVERY

Areas controlled by Royalists

Areas controlled by Parliamentarians

Major battles

0   200 Miles
0   200 Kilometers

December 1642
SCOTLAND
IRELAND
North Sea
Edge Hill Oct. 1642
London

December 1643
SCOTLAND
IRELAND
North Sea
Adwalton Moor June 1643
London

December 1644
SCOTLAND
IRELAND
North Sea
Marston Moor July 1644
London

December 1645
SCOTLAND
IRELAND
North Sea
Naseby June 1645
London

ENGLISH CIVIL WAR

How would you describe the geographical divisions at the beginning of the war in 1642? Who appears to have been winning the war by December 1643? How did the war progress between 1644 and 1645?

would be summoned once in every three years. Due process in common law would be observed, and the ancient taxes that the Crown had revived would be abolished.

At first, Charles I could do nothing but bide his time and accept these assaults on his power and authority. Once he had crushed the Scots, he would be able to bargain from a position of strength. But as the months passed, it became clear that Parliament had no intention of providing him with money or forces. By the end of 1641, Charles's patience had worn thin. In the summer of 1642, he left the capital and headed north where he raised the royal standard and declared the leaders of Parliament rebels and traitors. England was plunged into civil war.

After nearly three years of inconclusive fighting, Parliament won a decisive victory at Naseby in June 1645 and brought the war to an end the following summer. The king was in captivity, bishops had been abolished, a Presbyterian church had been established, and limitations were placed on royal power. All that was necessary to end three years of civil war was the king's agreement to abide by the judgment of battle.

But Charles I had no intention of surrendering either his religion or his authority. Despite the rebels' successes, they could not rule without him, and he would concede nothing as long as opportunities to maneuver remained. In 1647 there were opportunities galore. The war had proved ruinously expensive to Parliament. It owed enormous sums to the Scots, to its own soldiers, and to the governors of London. Each of these elements had its own objectives in a final settlement of the war, and they were not altogether compatible. London feared the parliamentary army, unpaid and camped dangerously close to the capital. The Scots and the English Presbyterians in Parliament feared that the religious settlement that had already been made would be sacrificed by those known as Independents, who desired a more decentralized church. The Independents feared that they would be persecuted just as harshly by the Presbyterians as they had been by the king. In fact, the war had settled nothing.

The English Revolutions

Charles I happily played both ends against the middle until the army decisively ended the game. In June 1647, parliamentary soldiers kidnapped the king and demanded that Parliament pay their arrears, protect them from legal retribution, and recognize their service to the nation. Those in Parliament who opposed the army's intervention were impeached, and when London Presbyterians rose up against the army's show of force, troops moved in to occupy the city. The civil war, which had come so close to resolution in 1647, had now become a military revolution. Religious and political radicals flocked to the army and encouraged the soldiers to support their programs and to resist disbandment. New fighting broke out in 1648, as Charles encouraged his supporters to resume the war. But forces under the command of Sir Thomas Fairfax (1612–1671) and Oliver Cromwell (1599–1658) easily crushed the royalist uprisings in England and Scotland. The army now demanded that Charles I be brought to justice for his treacherous conduct both before and during the war. When the majority in Parliament refused, still hoping to reach an accommodation with the king, the soldiers again acted decisively. In December 1648, army regiments were sent to London to purge the two houses of Parliament of those who opposed the army's demands. The remaining members, contemptuously called the Rump Parliament, voted to bring the king to trial for his crimes against the liberties of his subjects. On 30 January 1649, Charles I was executed, and England was declared to be a commonwealth. The monarchy and the House of Lords were abolished, and the nation was to be governed by what was left of the membership of the House of Commons.

Oliver Cromwell. For four years, the members of the Rump Parliament struggled with proposals for a new constitution, achieving little. In 1653, Oliver Cromwell, with the support of the army's senior officers, forcibly dissolved the Rump and became the leader of the revolutionary government. When Cromwell's Parliament proved no more capable of governing than had the Rump, a written constitution, The Instrument of Government (1653), established a new polity. Cromwell was given the title Lord Protector, and he was to rule along with a freely elected Parliament and an administrative body known as the council of state.

Cromwell was able to smooth over conflicts and hold the revolutionary cause together through the force of his own personality. Though many urged him to accept the crown of England and begin a new monarchy, Cromwell steadfastly held out for a government in which fundamental authority resided in Parliament. Until his death he defended the achievements of the revolution.

But a sense that only a single person could effectively rule a state remained strong. When Cromwell died in 1658, his oldest son Richard was proposed as the new lord protector, but Richard had very little experience in either military or civil affairs. Without an individual to hold the movement together, the revolution fell apart. In 1659, the army again intervened in civil affairs, dismissing the recently elected Parliament and calling for the restoration of the monarchy. After a period of negotiation in which the king agreed to a general amnesty with only a few exceptions, the Stuarts were restored when Charles II (1649–1685) took the throne in 1660.

Twenty years of civil war and revolution had their effect. Absolute monarchy had become constitutional monarchy with the threat of revolution behind the power of Parliament and the threat of anarchy behind the power of the Crown.

The Glorious Revolution. The threats of revolution and of anarchy proved potent in 1685 when James II (1685–1688) came to the throne. A declared Catholic, James attempted to use his power of appointment to foil the constraints that Parliament imposed on him. He elevated Catholics to leading posts in the military and in the central government and began a campaign to pack a new Parliament with his supporters. This proved to be too much for the governing classes, which entered into negotiations with William, prince of Orange, who was the husband of Mary Stuart, James's eldest daughter. In 1688, William landed in England with a small force. Without support, James II fled to France, the English throne was declared vacant, and William and Mary were proclaimed king and queen of England. There was little bloodshed and little threat of social disorder, and the event soon came to be called the **Glorious Revolution.** Its achievements were set down in the Declaration of Rights (1689), which was presented to William and Mary before they took the

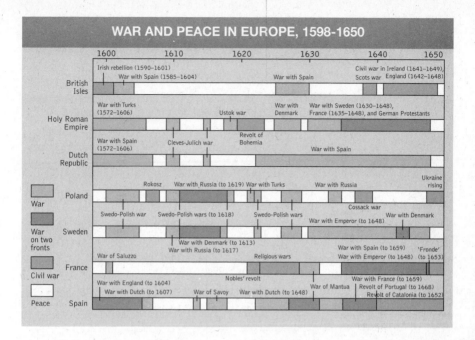

WAR AND PEACE IN EUROPE, 1598-1650

throne. The declaration reasserted the fundamental principles of constitutional monarchy as they had developed over the previous half-century. Security of property and the regularity of Parliaments were guaranteed. The Toleration Act (1689) granted religious freedom to nearly all groups of Protestants. The liberties of the subject and the rights of the sovereign were to be in balance.

The events of 1688 in England reversed a trend toward increasing power on the part of the Stuarts. This second episode of resistance resulted in the development of a unique form of government, which, a century later, spawned dozens of imitators. John Locke (1632–1704) was the theorist of the Revolution of 1688. He was heir to the century-old debate on resistance, and he carried the doctrine to a new plateau. In *Two Treatises on Government* (1689), Locke developed the contract theory of government. Political society was a compact that individuals entered into freely for their own well-being. It was designed to maintain each person's natural rights: life, liberty, and property. Natural rights were inherent in individuals; they could not be given away. The contract between rulers and subjects was an agreement for the protection of natural rights. When rulers acted arbitrarily, they were to be deposed by their subjects, preferably in the relatively peaceful manner in which James II had been replaced by William III.

The Zenith of the Royal State

The midcentury crises tested the mettle of the royal states. Over the long term, the seventeenth-century crises had two different consequences. First, they provided a check to the exercise of royal power. Fear of recurring rebellions had a chilling effect on policy, especially taxation. Reforms of financial administration, long overdue, were one

CIVIL WAR AND REVOLUTION IN ENGLAND

Chronology

1603–1625	Reign of James I
1620s	Rise to power of Archbishop Laud in the Anglican Church
1625–1649	Reign of Charles I
1637	Scottish rebellion in response to introduction of Anglican prayer book
1640	Scottish army invades England; Charles I summons Parliament
1640–1653	Long Parliament
1642–1649	Civil War
1648–1653	Rump Parliament
1649	Charles I tried and executed; monarchy and the House of Lords abolished
1653–1658	Oliver Cromwell establishes commonwealth and holds title of Lord Protector of England
1659	Army dissolves Parliament and calls for restoration of monarchy
1660	Charles II takes the throne and monarchy is restored
1685–1688	Reign of James II
1688	Glorious Revolution brings William and Mary to the throne
1689	Declaration of Rights and Toleration Act
1689	Publication of John Locke's *Two Treatises on Government*

of the themes of the later seventeenth century. Even as royal government strengthened itself, it remained concerned about the impact of its policies. The memory of rebellion also served to control the ambitions of factious noblemen and town oligarchies.

If nothing else, these episodes of opposition to the rising royal states made clear the universal desire for stable government, which was seen as the responsibility of both subjects and rulers. The natural advantages of monarchy had to be merged with the interests of the citizens of the state and their desires for wealth, safety, and honor. After so much chaos and instability the monarchy had to be elevated above the fray of day-to-day politics to become a symbol of the nation's power and glory.

In England, Holland, and Sweden a form of constitutional monarchy developed in which rulers shared power, in varying degrees, with other institutions of state. In England it was Parliament; in Holland, the town oligarchies; in Sweden, the nobility. But in most other states in Europe there developed a pure form of royal government known as **absolutism**. Absolute monarchy revived the divine right theories of kingship and added to them a cult of the personality of the ruler.

The Nature of Absolute Monarchy

Locke's theory of contract provided one solution to the central problem of seventeenth-century government: how to balance the monarch's right to command and the subjects' duty to obey.

The English solution was most suited to a state that was largely immune from invasion and land war. Constitutional government required a higher level of political participation of citizens than did absolute monarchy. Greater participation meant greater freedom of expression, greater toleration of religious minorities, and greater openness in the institutions of government. All were dangerous. The price that England paid was a half-century of governmental instability.

The alternative to constitutional monarchy was absolute monarchy. It, too, found its leading theorist in England. Thomas Hobbes (1588–1679), in his greatest work, *Leviathan* (1651), argued that people came together to form a government for the most basic of all purposes: self-preservation. Without government they were condemned to a life that was "solitary, poor, nasty, brutish, and short." To escape, individuals pooled their power and granted it to a ruler. The terms of the Hobbesian contract were simple: Rulers agreed to rule; subjects agreed to obey.

The main features of absolute monarchy were all designed to extend royal control. As in the early seventeenth century, the person of the monarch was revered. Courts grew larger and more lavish in an effort to enhance the glory of the monarchy and thereby of the state. "*L'état, c'est moi*" ("I am the state"), Louis XIV was supposed to have said. As the king grew in stature, his competitors for power all shrank. Large numbers of nobles were herded together at court under the watchful eye of monarchs who now ruled rather than reigned. The king shed the cloak of his favorites and rolled up his own sleeves to manage state affairs. Representative institutions were weakened or cast aside. Monarchs needed standing armies trained in the increasingly sophisticated arts of war, so the military was expanded and made an integral part of the machinery of government.

Yet the absolute state was never as powerful in practice as it was in theory. Nor did it ever exist in its ideal shape. Absolutism was always in the making, never quite made. Its success depended on a strong monarch who knew his own will and could enforce it. It depended on unity within the state, on the absence or ruthless suppression of religious or political minorities. The absolute ruler needed to control information and ideas to limit criticism of state policy. Ultimately, the absolute state rested on the will of its citizens to support it.

Absolutism in the East

Frederick William, the Great Elector of Brandenburg-Prussia (1640–1688), made highly effective use of the techniques of absolutism. In 1640, he inherited a scattered and ungovernable collection of territories. The nobility, known as *die Junker*, enjoyed immunity from almost all forms of direct taxation, and the towns had no obligation to furnish men or supplies for military operations beyond their walls.

When Frederick William attempted to introduce an excise—the commodity tax on consumption that had so successfully financed the Dutch Revolt and the English Revolution—he was initially rebuffed. But military emergency overcame legal precedents. By the 1650s, Frederick William had established the excise in the towns, though not in the countryside.

With the excise as a steady source of revenue, the Great Elector set about forming one of the most capable and best disciplined standing armies of the age. He organized one of the first departments of war to oversee all of the details of the creation of his army, from housing and supplies to the training of young officer candidates. This department was also responsible for the collection of taxes. By integrating military and civilian government, Frederick William established an efficient state bureaucracy that was particularly responsive in times of crisis. The creation of the Prussian army was the force that led to the creation of the Prussian state.

The same materials that forged the Prussian state led to the transformation of Russia. Soon after the young Tsar Peter I, known later as "the Great" (1682–1725), came to the throne, he realized that he could compete with the western states only by learning to play their game.

Like Frederick William, Peter concentrated on military reform. He understood that if Russia was to flourish in a world dominated by war and commerce, it would have to reestablish its hold on the Baltic ports. This meant dislodging the Swedes from the Russian mainland and creating a fleet to protect Russian trade. Neither goal seemed likely. The Swedes were one of the great powers of the age, constant innovators in battlefield tactics and military organization. Peter studied their every campaign. His first wars against the Swedes ended in humiliating defeats, but with each failure came a sharper sense of what was needed to succeed.

First Peter introduced a system of conscription and created a standing army. He unified the military command at the top and stratified it in the field. He established promotion based on merit and established military schools to train cadets for the next generation of officers.

Finally, in 1709, Peter realized his ambitions. At the battle of Poltava, the Russian army routed the Swedes, wounding King Charles XII, annihilating his infantry, and capturing dozens of his leading officers. After the battle of Poltava, Russia gradually replaced Sweden as the dominant power in the Baltic.

As an absolute ruler, Peter the Great's power was unlimited, but it was not uncontested. He secularized the Russian Orthodox church, subjecting it to state control and confiscating much of its wealth. He broke the old military service class, which attempted a coup d'état when he was abroad in the 1690s. By the end of his reign, the Russian monarchy was among the strongest in Europe.

The Origins of French Absolutism

Nowhere was absolutism as successfully implanted as in France. Louis XIII (1610–1643) was only eight years old when he came to the throne, and he grew slowly into his role under the tutelage of Cardinal Richelieu. It was Richelieu's vision that stabilized French government. As chief minister, Richelieu saw clearly that France's survival and prosperity depended on strengthening royal power. He preached a doctrine of *raison d'état* ("reason of state"), in which he placed the needs of the nation above the privileges of its most important groups. Richelieu saw three threats to stable royal government: the Huguenots, the nobles, and the most powerful provincial governors.

Legend:
- Russia in 1689
- Territory added by Peter
- Peter's trip to Western Europe, 1697–1698
- ✳ Major battles

EXPANSION OF RUSSIA UNDER PETER THE GREAT

Notice the extent of the Russian Empire in 1689 and territory added by Peter the Great. What was important about the new territory? What was the role of the battle of Poltava in expanding the empire? The route of Peter's trip to western Europe is marked here. Why did he travel where he did? Based on the chapter discussion, what impact did his trip have on the way he ruled his empire?

Richelieu took measures to control all three. The power of the nobles was the most difficult to attack. The nobles' long tradition of independence from the crown had been enhanced by the wars of religion. The ancient aristocracy, the nobility of the sword, felt themselves to be in a particularly vulnerable position. Their world was changing, and their traditional roles were becoming obsolete. Professional soldiers replaced them at war, professional administrators at government. Mercantile wealth threatened their economic superiority, and the growth of the nobility of the robe—lawyers and state officials—threatened their social standing. They were hardly likely to take orders from a royal minister such as Richelieu.

To limit the power of local officials, Richelieu used intendants to examine their conduct and reform their administration. He made careful appointments of local governors and brought more regions under direct royal control. Against the Calvinists, who were called Huguenots in France, Richelieu's policy was more subtle. He was less interested in challenging their religion than their autonomy. In 1627, when the English sent a force to aid the Huguenots against the government, Richelieu and Louis XIII abolished the Huguenots' privileges. They were allowed to maintain their religion but not their special status. Finally, in 1685, Louis XIV revoked the Edict of

Nantes, which had guaranteed civil and religious rights to the Huguenots. All forms of Protestant worship were outlawed, and the ministers who were not hunted down and killed were forced into exile. Despite a ban on Protestant emigration, over 200,000 Huguenots fled the country, many of them carrying irreplaceable skills with them to Holland and England in the west and to Brandenburg in the east.

Richelieu's program was a vital prelude to the development of absolute monarchy in France. The cardinal did not act without the full support of Louis XIII, but there can be no doubt that Richelieu was the power behind the throne.

Louis le Grand

Not quite five years old when Louis XIII died, Louis XIV was tutored by Cardinal Jules Mazarin (1602–1661), Richelieu's successor as chief minister. Mazarin was more ruthless and less popular than his predecessor, but like Richelieu, he was an excellent administrator.

The King and His Ministers. In order to pacify the rebellious nobility of the Fronde, who opposed Mazarin's power, Louis XIV was declared to have reached his majority at the age of 13. But it was not until Mazarin died 10 years later, in 1661, that the king began to rule.

Louis was blessed with able and energetic ministers. The two central props of his state—money and might—were in the hands of dynamic men, Jean-Baptiste Colbert (1619–1683) and the Marquis de Louvois (1639–1691). Colbert was Louis's chief minister for finance. Colbert's fiscal reforms were so successful that in less than six years a debt of 22 million French pounds had become a surplus of 29 million. Colbert achieved this astonishing feat not by raising taxes but by increasing the efficiency of their collection. Until Louis embarked on his wars, the French state was solvent.

To Louvois, Louis's minister of war, fell the task of reforming the French army. During the Fronde, royal troops were barely capable of defeating the makeshift forces of the nobility. By the end of the reign, the army had grown to 400,000, and its organization had been thoroughly reformed.

Louis XIV furthered the practice of relying on professional administrators to supervise the main departments of state and to offer advice on matters of policy. He built on the institution of the intendant that Richelieu had developed with so much success. Intendants were now a permanent part of government, and their duties expanded from their early responsibilities as coordinators and mediators into areas of policing and tax collection. It was through the intendants that the wishes of central government were made known in the provinces.

The Court of Versailles. Though Louis XIV was well served, it was the king himself who set the tone for French absolutism. The acting of majesty was central to Louis's rule. His residence at Versailles was the most glittering court of Europe. When the court and king moved there permanently in 1682, Versailles became the envy of the Continent. But behind the imposing facade of Versailles stood a well-thought-out plan for domestic and international rule.

This Hyacinthe Rigaud portrait of Louis XIV in his coronation robes shows the splendor of *Le Roi Soleil* (the Sun King), who believed himself to be the center of France as the sun is the center of the solar system.

Louis XIV attempted to tame the French nobles by requiring their attendance at his court. Louis established a system of court etiquette so complex that constant study was necessary to prevent humiliation. While the nobility studied decorum, they could not plot rebellion.

During Louis's reign, France replaced Spain as the greatest nation in Europe. Massive royal patronage of art, science, and thought brought French culture to new heights. The French language replaced Latin as the universal European tongue. France was the richest and most populous European state, and Louis's absolute rule finally harnessed these resources to a single purpose. France became a commercial power rivaling the Netherlands, a naval power rivaling England, and a military power without peer. It was not only for effect that Louis took the image of the sun as his own. In court, in the nation, and throughout Europe, everything revolved around him.

Louis XIV made his share of mistakes. His aggressive foreign policy ultimately bankrupted the crown. But without doubt, his greatest error was to persecute the Huguenots. As an absolute ruler, Louis regarded the Huguenots, with their separate communities and distinct forms of worship, as an affront to his authority. Supporters of the monarchy celebrated the revocation of the Edict of Nantes in 1685 as an act of piety. But the persecution of the Huguenots was a social and political disaster for France. The Huguenots who fled to other Protestant states spread stories of atrocities that stiffened European resolve against Louis. Those who remained became an embittered minority who pulled at the fabric of the state at every chance. Nor did the official abolition of Protestantism have much effect on its existence. Against these policies the Huguenots held firmly to their beliefs. There were well over one million French Protestants, undoubtedly the largest religious minority in any state. Huguenots simply went underground, practicing their religion secretly and gradually replacing their numbers. No absolutism, however powerful, could succeed in eradicating religious beliefs.

SUMMARY

The Rise of the Royal State Monarchs became the symbolic center of the state. Their power was based on the theory of the divine right of kings. As the scope of affairs of government grew, so too did the number and importance of royal officials. Europe's monarchs sought to extend their authority and centralize their states. The consolidation of the state was driven by the demands of war. War required ever-increasing state revenues.

The Crises of the Royal State The expansion of royal power met stiff resistance. The ravages of war, famine, and disease pushed Europeans toward rebellion. Europeans developed new political theories to justify resistance to tyrannical monarchs. Major rebellions shook Spain and France. In England, the policies of the Stuart kings led to civil war and the execution of Charles I. Oliver Cromwell ruled England as Lord Protector until his death in 1658. The Stuarts were restored in 1660 when Charles II took the throne. The policies of James II led to the Glorious Revolution in 1688. He was replaced by William and Mary, who accepted the provisions of the Declaration of Rights.

The Zenith of the Royal State England became a constitutional monarchy. Most other European states moved in the direction of absolutism. Absolute monarchs revived the theory of the divine right of kings and added a cult of personality of the ruler. The main features of absolute monarchy were designed to extend royal control. Absolute monarchies were never as powerful in practice as in theory. Frederick William of Prussia and Peter the Great of Russia used reform of the military to strengthen their states and consolidate central control. Cardinal Richelieu laid the foundations of French absolutism. Louis XIV benefited from active and able ministers. He used compulsory attendance at his court at Versailles to limit the independence of the nobility. His aggressive foreign policy ultimately bankrupted the crown. His greatest mistake was his persecution of the Huguenots.

QUESTIONS FOR REVIEW

1. How did war in the seventeenth century contribute to the creation of more powerful monarchical states?
2. What religious and political ideas were developed to justify resistance to monarchical authority?
3. What political and religious problems combined to bring England to civil war, and what results did the conflict produce in English government?
4. How did rulers such as Frederick William of Brandenburg, Peter the Great, or Louis XIV, and theorists such as Hobbes, justify absolute monarchical power?

Science and Commerce in Early Modern Europe

The New Science

The **scientific revolution** was the opening of a new era in European history. After two centuries of classical revival, European thinkers had finally come up against the limits of ancient knowledge. The explanations of the universe and the natural world that had been advanced by Aristotle and codified by his followers no longer seemed adequate.

The two essential characteristics of the new science were that it was materialistic and mathematical. Its materialism was contained in the realization that the universe was composed of matter in motion. This meant that the stars and planets were made not of some perfect ethereal substance but of the same matter that was found on the earth. They were therefore subject to the same rules of motion as were earthly objects. The mathematics of the new science was contained in the realization that calculation had to replace common sense as the basis for understanding the universe. Mathematics itself was transformed with the invention of logarithms, analytic geometry, and calculus. Scientific experimentation took the form of measuring repeatable phenomena.

The new science was a Europe-wide movement. The spirit of scientific inquiry flourished everywhere among the educated. By and large, these scientists operated outside the traditional seats of learning at the universities. Though most were university-trained and not a few taught the traditional Aristotelian subjects, theirs was not an academic movement. Rather, it was a public one that was made possible by the printing press. Once published, findings became building blocks for scientists throughout the Continent and from one generation to the next. Many discoveries were made in the search for practical solutions to ordinary problems, and what was learned fueled advances in technology and the natural sciences. The new science gave seventeenth-century Europeans a sense that they might finally master the forces of nature.

Heavenly Revolutions

Aristotle had presented a view of the physical world that coincided with a view of the spiritual and moral one. The heavens were unchangeable, and therefore they were better than the earth. The sun, moon, and planets were all faultless spheres, unblemished and immune from decay. Their motion was circular because the circle was the perfect form of motion. The earth was at the center of the universe because it was the heaviest planet and because it was at the center of the Great Chain of Being, between the underworld of spirits and the upperworld of gods.

In the 1490s, Nicolaus Copernicus (1473–1543) came to the Polish University of Krakow, where the latest astronomical theories were vigorously debated. He became fascinated by astronomy and puzzled by the debate over planetary motion. Copernicus believed, like Aristotle, that the simplest explanations were the best. If the sun was at the center of the universe and the earth was simply another planet in orbit, then many of the most elaborate explanations of planetary motion were unnecessary. Because Copernicus accepted most of the rest of the traditional Aristotelian explanation, especially the belief that the planets moved in perfect circles, his sun-centered universe was only slightly better at predicting the position of the planets than the traditional earth-centered one, but Copernicus's idea stimulated other astronomers to make new calculations.

Brahe and Kepler. Under the patronage of the king of Denmark, Tycho Brahe (1546–1601) built a large observatory to study planetary motion. Brahe and his students compiled the largest and most accurate mathematical tables of planetary motion yet known. From this research, Brahe's pupil, Johannes Kepler (1571–1630), one of the great mathematicians of the age, formulated laws of planetary motion.

Kepler discovered that planets orbited the sun in an elliptical rather than a circular path. This accounted for their movements nearer to and farther from the earth. He further demonstrated that there was a precise mathematical relationship between the speed with which a planet revolved and its distance from the sun. Kepler's findings supported the view that the solar system was heliocentric and that the heavens, like the earth, were made of matter that was subject to physical laws.

Galileo. What Kepler demonstrated mathematically, the Italian astronomer Galileo Galilei (1564–1642) confirmed by observation. With a telescope that he had created by using magnifying lenses and a long tube, Galileo saw parts of the heavens that had never been dreamt of before. In 1610, he discovered four moons of Jupiter, proving conclusively that not all heavenly bodies revolved around the earth. He observed the landscape of the earth's moon and described it as being full of mountains, valleys, and rivers. It was of the same imperfect form as the earth itself. He even found spots on the sun, which suggested that it, too, was composed of ordinary matter. Many of Galileo's scientific discoveries had to do with motion—he was the first to posit a law of inertia—but his greatest contribution to the new science was his popularization of the Copernican theory.

As news of his experiments and discoveries spread, Galileo became famous throughout the Continent, and his support for heliocentrism became a celebrated cause. In 1616, the Roman Catholic Church cautioned him against promoting his views. In 1633, a year after publishing *A Dialogue Between the Two Great Systems of the World*, the Inquisition tried Galileo and forced him to recant the idea that the earth moves. He spent the rest of his life under house arrest.

The Natural World

The new science originated from a number of traditions that were anything but scientific. Inquiry into nature and the environment grew out of the discipline of natural philosophy and was nurtured by spiritual and mystical traditions. Much of the most useful medical knowledge had come from the studies of herbalists; the most reliable calculations of planetary motion had come from astrologers. Though the first laboratories and observatories were developed in aid of the new science, practice in them was as much magical as experimental. The modern emphasis on experimentation and empirical observation developed only gradually. What was new about the new science was the determination to develop systems of thought that could help humans to understand and control their environment. There was a greater openness and spirit of cooperation about discoveries than in the past, when experiments were conducted secretly and results were kept hidden away.

Neoplatonism and the New Scientists. Aristotelianism was not the only philosophical system to explain the nature and composition of the universe. During the Renaissance, the writings of Plato attracted a number of Italian humanists, most

Andreas Cellarius created this artistic depiction of the solar system in the late seventeenth century. The chart portrays the heliocentric universe described by Copernicus and Galileo and the elliptical orbits of the planets posited by Kepler. An outsized earth is shown in four different positions as it orbits the sun.

notably Marsilio Ficino (1433–1499) and Pico della Mirandola (1463–1494). These Neoplatonic humanists believed that the architect of the universe possessed the spirit of a geometrician and that the perfect disciplines were music and mathematics. These elements of Neoplatonism created an impetus for the mathematically based studies of the new scientists. They were especially important among the astronomers, who used both calculation and geometry in exploring the heavens. But they also served to bolster the sciences of alchemy and astrology. **Alchemy** was the use of fire in the study of metals, an effort to find the essence of things through their purification. Astrology was the study of the influence of the stars on human behavior, calculated by planetary motion and the harmony of the heavenly spheres. Astrologers made careful calculations based on the movement of the planets and were deeply involved in the new astronomy.

Paracelsus. The Swiss alchemist Paracelsus (1493–1541) studied alchemy before becoming a physician. Paracelsus taught that all matter was composed of combinations of three principles: salt, sulfur, and mercury. This view replaced the traditional belief in the four elements of earth, water, fire, and air.

The Paracelsian system transformed ideas about chemistry and medicine. Paracelsus rejected the theory that disease was caused by an imbalance in the humors of the body—the standard view of Galen, the great Greek physician of the second century C.E. Instead, Paracelsus argued that each disease had its own cause, which could be diagnosed and remedied through the ingestion of particular chemicals.

Boyle and Chemistry. Although established physicians and medical faculties rejected Paracelsian cures and methods, his influence spread among ordinary practitioners. It ultimately had a profound impact on the studies of Robert Boyle (1627–1691), an Englishman who helped to establish the basis of the science of chemistry. Boyle devoted his energies to raising the study of medical chemistry above that of merely providing recipes for the cure of disease. He worked carefully and recorded each step in his experiments. Boyle's first important work, *The Sceptical Chymist* (1661), attacked both the Aristotelian and Paracelsian views of the basic components of the natural world. Boyle rejected both the four elements and the three principles. Instead, he favored an atomic explanation in which matter "consisted of little particles of all sizes and shapes." Changes in these particles, which would later be identified as the chemical elements, resulted in changes in matter. Boyle's most important experiments were with gases—a word that Paracelsus invented. Boyle formulated the relationship between the volume and pressure of a gas (Boyle's Law), and he invented the air pump.

Medical Science. The new spirit of scientific inquiry also affected medical studies. The study of anatomy through dissection had helped the new scientists to reject many of the descriptive errors in Galen's texts. The Belgian doctor Andreas Vesalius (1514–1564) published the first modern set of anatomical drawings in 1543. But accurate knowledge of the composition of the body did not mean better understanding of its operation. One of the greatest mysteries was how blood moved through the vital organs. William Harvey (1578–1657), an Englishman who had received his medical education in Italy, was interested in the anatomy of the heart. He examined hearts in more than 40 species before concluding that the heart worked like a pump and that the valves of the heart chambers allowed the blood to flow in only one direction. He concluded that the blood was pumped by the heart and circulated throughout the entire body.

Sir Isaac Newton. The greatest of all English scientists was the mathematician and physicist Sir Isaac Newton (1642–1727). Newton was the first to understand the composition of light, the first to develop a calculus, the first to build a reflecting telescope. He made stunning contributions to the sciences of optics, physics, astronomy, and mathematics. His magnum opus, *Mathematical Principles of Natural Philosophy* (1687), is one of the most important scientific works ever composed. Newton offered a solution to the following problem: If the world was composed of matter in motion, what was motion?

Though Galileo had first developed a theory of inertia—the idea that a body at rest stays at rest—most materialists believed that motion was inherent in objects. In contrast, Newton believed that motion was the result of the interaction of objects and that it could be calculated mathematically. From his experiments he formulated the concept of force and his famous laws of motion: (1) that objects that are at rest or in uniform linear motion remain in such a state unless acted on by an external force; (2) that changes in motion are proportional to force; and (3) that for every action there is an equal and opposite reaction. From these laws of motion, Newton advanced one step further: If the world was no more than matter in motion and if all motion was subject to the same laws, then the movement of the planets could be explained in the same way as the movement of an apple falling from a tree. There was a mathematical relationship between attraction and repulsion—a universal gravitation, as Newton called it—that governed the movement of all objects. Newton's theory of gravity joined Kepler's astronomy and Galileo's physics. The mathematical, materialistic world of the new science was now complete.

Science Enthroned

By the middle of the seventeenth century, the new science was firmly established throughout Europe. Royal and noble patrons supported the enterprise by paying some of the costs of equipment and experimentation. Royal observatories were created for the astronomers, colleges of physicians for the doctors, laboratories for the chemists. Both England and France established royal societies of learned scientists.

Support for the new science was not, however, universal. Embattled by the Reformation and the wars of religion, the Church regarded the new science as another heresy. Not only did it confound ancient wisdom and contradict Church teachings, but it was also a lay movement that was neither directed nor controlled from Rome. Galileo's trial slowed the momentum of scientific investigation in Catholic countries and starkly posed the conflict between authority and knowledge. Nevertheless, the Church's stand was based on more than narrow self-interest. Ever since Copernicus had published his views, a new skepticism had emerged among European intellectuals. The skeptics concluded that nothing was known and nothing was knowable. Their position led inevitably to the most shocking of all possible views: atheism.

But the new science was not necessarily an attack on established religion. Few of the leading scientists saw a contradiction between their studies and their faith. Still, by the middle of the century, attacks on the Church were increasing, and some people blamed the new science for them. Therefore, it was altogether fitting that one of the leading mathematicians of the day should provide the method for harmonizing faith and reason.

In the *Discourse on Method* (1637), René Descartes (1596–1650) demonstrated how skepticism could be used to produce certainty. He began by declaring that he would reject everything that could not be clearly proven beyond doubt. Thus he rejected the material world, the testimony of his senses, and all known or imagined opinions. He was left only with doubt. But what was doubt if not thought, and what was thought if not the workings of his mind? The only thing of which he could be certain, then, was that he had a mind. Thus his famous formulation: "I think, therefore I am." From this first certainty came another, the knowledge of perfectibility. He knew that he was imperfect and that a perfect being had to have placed that knowledge within him. Therefore a perfect being—God—existed.

Descartes's philosophy, known as **Cartesianism**, rested on the dual existence of matter and mind. Matter was the material world, which was subject to the incontrovertible laws of mathematics. Mind was the spirit of the creator. Descartes was one of the leading mechanistic philosophers, believing that all objects operated in accord with natural laws. He invented analytic geometry and made important contributions to the sciences of optics and physics on which Newton would later build. But his proof that the new science could be harmonized with the old religion was his greatest contribution.

Though many of the pathbreaking discoveries of the new scientists would not find practical use for centuries, the spirit of discovery had a great impact in an age of commerce and capital. The quest for mathematical certainty and prime movers led directly to improvements in agriculture, mining, navigation, and industrial activity. The new sense of control over the material world provided a new optimism for generations of Europeans and bolstered the desire to expand commerce at home and abroad.

MAP DISCOVERY

DUTCH TRADE ROUTES, CA. 1650

The Dutch were the greatest commercial nation of the seventeenth century. According to the trade routes shown here, how would you describe the extent of Dutch trade? Why are there so many trading centers in the East? Based on information provided in the chapter, what were some of the major goods exchanged in the various trade regions? Why did the Dutch not secure major colonial possessions in the East?

Chronology

THE NEW SCIENCE

1433–1499	Marsilio Ficino, Renaissance Neoplatonist
1463–1494	Pico della Mirandola, Renaissance Neoplatonist
1473–1543	Nicolaus Copernicus; proposed heliocentric model of the solar system
1493–1541	Paracelsus; rejected Galenic theory of disease
1543	Publication of Copernicus's *On the Revolutions of the Heavenly Spheres*
1543	Publication of Andreas Vesalius's anatomical drawings
1546–1601	Tycho Brahe; along with his students, compiled crucial astronomical data
1564–1642	Galileo Galilei; popularized Copernican theory
1571–1630	Johannes Kepler; discovered elliptical orbits of planets
1578–1657	William Harvey; argued for circulation of blood
1632	Publication of Galileo's *A Dialogue Between the Two Great Systems of the World*
1633	Inquisition forces Galileo to recant position that the earth is in motion
1642–1727	Sir Isaac Newton, greatest mathematician and physicist of his age
1661	Publication of Robert Boyle's *The Sceptical Chymist*
1687	Publication of Newton's *Mathematical Principles of Natural Philosophy*

Empires of Goods

Under the watchful eye of the European states, a worldwide marketplace for the exchange of commodities had been created. First the Dutch and then the English had established monopoly companies to engage in exotic trades in the East. The Spanish and Portuguese, then the English and French had established colonial dependencies in the Atlantic, which they carefully nurtured in hope of economic gain. Protected trade had flourished beyond the wildest dreams of its promoters. Luxury commodities became staples; new commodities became luxuries. Trade enhanced the material life of all European peoples, though it came at great cost to the Asians, Africans, and Latin Americans whose labor and raw materials were converted into the new crazes of consumption. Though long-distance trade was never as important to the European economy as was inland and intracontinental trade, its development in the seventeenth and eighteenth centuries had a profound impact on lifestyles, economic policy, and ultimately warfare.

The Marketplace of the World

By the sixteenth century, all the major trading routes had already been opened. The Spanish moved back and forth across the Atlantic; the Dutch and Portuguese sailed around the tip of Africa to the Indian Ocean. The Baltic trade connected the eastern and western parts of Europe as Danes, Swedes, and Dutch exchanged Polish and Russian raw materials for English and French manufactured goods. The Mediterranean was still a vital artery of intercontinental trade, but its preeminent role was diminishing. Commercial power was shifting to the northern European states just as dramatically as military and political power.

The Evolution of Long-Distance Travel. The technology that was associated with commerce achieved no major breakthroughs to compare with the great transformations of the fifteenth century, when new techniques of navigation made transatlantic travel possible. There continued to be improvements, however. The new astronomical findings were a direct aid to navigation, as were the recorded experiences of so many practiced sea travelers. The single most important innovation in shipbuilding was the Dutch flyboat, which helped traders gain maximum profit from their journeys to the Baltic. Flyboats sacrificed speed and maneuverability for economy and capacity.

Innovation, organization, and efficient management were the principal elements of what historians have called the commercial revolution. Concerted efforts to maximize opportunities and advantages accounted for the phenomenal growth in the volume and value of commercial exchange. One of the least spectacular and most effective changes was the replacement of bilateral trade with **triangular trade**. In bilateral trade, the surplus commodities of one community were exchanged for those of another. Triangular trade created a larger pool of desirable goods. British manufactured goods could be traded to Africa for slaves, the slaves could be traded in the West Indies for sugar, and the sugar could be consumed in Britain. Moreover, the merchants who were involved in shifting these goods from place to place could achieve profits on each exchange. Indeed, their motive in trading could now change from dumping surplus commodities to matching supply and demand.

The New Forms of Banking. Equally important were the changes made in the way trade was financed. Because states, cities, and even individuals could stamp their own precious metal, there were hundreds of different European coins with different nominal and metallic values. The influx of American silver further destabilized an already unstable system of exchange. The Bank of Amsterdam was created in 1609 to establish a uniform rate of exchange for the various currencies that were traded in that city. From this useful function developed transfer banking, or giro banking, a system that had been invented in Italy. In giro banking, various merchant firms held money on account and issued bills of transfer from one to another. This transfer system meant that merchants in different cities did not have to transport their precious metals or endure long delays in having their accounts settled.

Giro banking also aided the development of bills of exchange, an early form of checking. Merchants could conclude trades by depositing money in a given bank or merchant house and then having a bill drawn for the sum they owed. Bills of exchange were especially important in international trade, as they made large-scale shipments of precious metals to settle trade deficits unnecessary. By the end of the seventeenth century, bills of exchange had become negotiable; that is, they could pass from one merchant to another without being redeemed.

The effects of these and many other small-scale changes in business practice helped to fuel prolonged growth in European commerce. It was the European merchant who made this growth possible, accepting the risks of each individual transaction and building up small pools of capital from which successive transactions could take place.

Consumption Choices

As long-distance trade became more sophisticated, merchants became more sensitive to consumer tastes. Low-volume, high-quality goods such as spices and silks, which were the preserve of the largest trading companies, had reached saturation levels by the early seventeenth century. The price of pepper, the most used of all spices, fell nearly continuously after 1650. Triangular trade allowed merchants to provide a better match of supplies and demands. The result was the rise to prominence of a vast array of new commodities, which not only continued the expansion of trade but also reshaped diet, lifestyles, and patterns of consumption. New products came from both the East and the West. Dutch and English incursions into the Asian trade provoked competition with the Portuguese and enlarged the range of commodities that were shipped back to Europe. An aggressive Asian triangle was created in which European bullion bought Indonesian spices that were exchanged for Persian silk and Chinese and Japanese finished goods. In the Atlantic, the English were quick to develop both home and export markets for a variety of new or newly available products.

The New Commodities. The European trade with Asia had always been designed to satisfy consumer demand rather than to exchange surplus goods. Europeans manufactured little that was desired in Asia, so the chief commodity imported to the East was bullion: tons of South American silver, perhaps one-third of all that was produced. In return came spices, silk, coffee, jewels, jade, porcelain, dyes, and a wide variety of other exotic goods. By the middle of the seventeenth century, the Dutch dominated the spice trade. Both the Dutch and the English competed for preeminence in the silk trade.

The most important manufactured articles imported from the East to Europe were the lightweight, brightly colored Indian cottons known as calicoes. Until the middle of the seventeenth century, cotton and cotton blended with silk were used in Europe only for wall hangings and table coverings. The material, which was soft and smooth to the touch, soon replaced linen for use as underwear and close-fitting garments among the well-to-do. The fashion quickly caught on, and the Dutch, who were first to realize the potential of the cotton market, began to export calicoes throughout the Continent. The English and French followed suit, establishing their own trading houses in India and bringing European patterns and designs with them for the Asians to copy.

Along with the new apparel from the East came new beverages. Coffee, which was first used in northern Europe in the early seventeenth century, had become a fashionable drink by the end of the century. Coffee houses sprang up in the major urban areas of northern Europe. As a basic beverage and import commodity, coffee was surpassed in importance only by tea. While coffee drinking remained the preserve of the wealthy, tea consumption spread throughout European society. It was probably most important in England, where the combination of Chinese tea and West Indian sugar created a phenomenal growth in consumption. The English imported most of their tea directly from China, where an open port had been established at Canton. Tea soon became the dominant cargo of the large English merchant ships coming from Asia.

Colonial Trade: The Demand for Sugar. The success of tea was linked to the explosive growth in the development of sugar in Europe's Atlantic colonies. The Portuguese found Brazil's hot, humid climate to be well suited for cultivation of the cane plants. The island of Barbados became the first English sugar colony. The planters modeled their development on Brazil, where African slaves were used to plant, tend, and cut the giant canes from which the sugar was extracted. By 1700, the English were sending home over 50 million pounds of sugar besides what they were shipping directly to the North American colonies.

The African Slave Trade. The triangular trade of manufactures—largely reexported calicoes—to Africa for slaves, who were exchanged in the West Indies for sugar, became the dominant form of English overseas trade. Colonial production depended on the enforced labor of hundreds of thousands of Africans. Africans were enslaved by other Africans and then sold to Europeans to be used in the colonies. More than six million black slaves were imported into the Americas during the course of the eighteenth century. Although rum and calicoes were the main commodities exchanged for slaves, the Africans who dominated the slave trade organized a highly competitive market. Every colonial power participated in this lucrative trade.

Dutch Masters

For the nearly 80 years between 1565 and 1648 that the Dutch were at war, they grew ever more prosperous. While the economies of most other European nations were sapped by warfare, the Dutch seemed to draw strength from their interminable conflict with the Spanish Empire. The Dutch became expert at attacking the Spanish silver fleets, singling out the slower and smaller vessels for capture. The Dutch also benefited from the massive immigration into their provinces of Protestants who had lived and worked in the southern provinces. The immigrants brought vital skills in manufacturing and large reserves of capital for investment in Dutch commerce.

Though the Dutch Republic comprised seven separate political entities, with a total population of about two million, the province of Holland was preeminent among them. Holland contained more than one-quarter of this population, and its trading port of Amsterdam was one of the great cities of Europe. The city had grown from a mid-sized urban community of 65,000 in 1600 to a metropolis of 170,000 50 years later. The port was one of the busiest in the world, for it was built to be an **entrepôt**. Vast warehouses and docks lined its canals. Visitors were impressed by Amsterdam's bustle, cleanliness, and businesslike appearance. The central buildings were the Bank and the Exchange, testimony to the dominant activities of the residents.

The Dutch dominated all types of European trade. Dutch ships outnumbered all others in every important port of Europe. Goods were brought to Amsterdam to be redistributed throughout the world. Dutch prosperity rested first on the Baltic trade. Even after it ceased to expand in the middle of the seventeenth century, the Baltic trade made up over one-quarter of all of Holland's commercial enterprise. The Dutch also were the leaders in the East Indian trade throughout the seventeenth century. They held a virtual monopoly on the sale of exotic spices and the largest share of the pepper trade. Their imports of cottons and especially of porcelain began new consumer fads that soon resulted in the development of European industries. Dutch potteries began to produce china, as lower-quality ceramic goods came to be known. Dutch trade in the Atlantic was of less importance, but the Dutch did have a colonial presence in the New World, controlling a number of small islands and the rapidly growing mainland settlement of New Netherland. Yet the Dutch still dominated the secondary market in tobacco and sugar, becoming the largest processor and refiner of these important commodities.

There were many explanations for the unparalleled growth of this small maritime state into one of the greatest of European trading empires. Geography and climate provided one impetus; the lack of sufficient foodstuffs provided another. Yet there were cultural characteristics as well. One was the openness of Dutch society. Even before the struggle with Spain, the northern provinces had shown a greater inclination toward religious toleration than had most parts of Europe. Amsterdam became a unique center for religious and intellectual exchange. European Jews flocked there, as did Catholic dissidents such as Descartes. They brought with them a wide range of skills and knowledge along with capital that could be invested in trade. By the middle of the seventeenth century, the Dutch Republic enjoyed a reputation for cultural creativity that was the envy of the Continent. A truly extraordinary school of Dutch artists led by Rembrandt celebrated this new state born of commerce with vivid portrayals of its people and its prosperity.

Scale of Feet

PLAN OF A SLAVE VESSEL.

THE SLAVE TRADE.

THE motion in the House of Lords made by Lord Denman, on Tuesday night, has naturally revived the interest of the measures for the extinction of this vile traffic of "man-selling and man-stealing." The close of the session is marked by these humane exertions, as was its commencement, in the comprehensive speech of Lord George Bentinck, in the House of Commons, on February 3. His Lordship then held in his hand a communication from Captain Pilkington, of the Royal Navy, on the subject of the slave-trade, accompanied with a plan of one of the slave vessels (which we now Engrave). They were sit-

Water Line

entertainment enlivened by some most exquisite performances on the national instrument, the harp, much to the delight of all assembled. From the dinner-table the company retired at an early hour to the School-rooms, where the *conversazioni* were held.

WEDNESDAY.

On Wednesday, as the Geological and Natural History Sections were unable to fin'sh the business before them, they each held meetings; but as a great number of members had left Swansea that morning by the *Lord Beresford* steamer, and others were examining the works in the neighbourhood, the Sections were very slightly attended, and the papers communicated were of small general interest.

A dinner, given by Lewis W. Dillwyn, Esq., who is himself one of the oldest members of the Royal Society, may be regarded as the close of the proceedings.

The last General Meeting was held in the afternoon, when it appeared, that, notwithstanding the inferiority of Swansea as respects population, this meeting has added considerably to the funds of the Association.

In concluding our notice of an Association which numbers among its members all the most eminent men in every department of physical and natural science, we cannot but express our satisfaction at the business-like character of this meeting. It is true that it has not startled the wor d by the announcement of any great discovery; but it will be found, upon examination, to present a fair average rate of progress. The vulnerable points have been less apparent than hitherto; and by the exclusion from the sections of all subjects which were not purely scientific, and by particularly avoiding those communications which have frequently been introduced as mere trading advertisements, of which we witnessed but one, that on gutta percha, which in our opinion should not have

This diagram shows how slaves were packed into cargo holds for the notorious Middle Passage to the Americas. The plan was a model of efficiency, for slave traders sought to maximize profits.

397

Mercantile Organization

Elsewhere in Europe, trade was the king's business. The wealth of the nation was part of the prestige of the monarch, and its rise or fall was part of the crown's power. In all European states except the Dutch Republic, the activities of merchants were scorned by both the landed elite and the salaried bureaucrats. Yet the activities of the mercantile classes took on increasing importance for the state for two reasons. First, imported goods, especially luxuries, were a noncontroversial target for taxation. Customs duties and excise taxes grew all over Europe. Second, the competition for trade was seen as a competition for power and glory between states rather than between individual merchants.

Mercantilism. The competition for power and glory derived from the theory of **mercantilism**, a set of assumptions about economic activity that were commonly held throughout Europe and that guided the policies of almost every government. Mercantilists believed that the wealth of a nation resided in its stock of precious metal and that economic activity was a zero-sum game. What one country gained, another lost. If England bought wine from France and paid £100,000 in precious metal for it, then England was £100,000 poorer and France was £100,000 richer. If one was to trade profitably, it was absolutely necessary to wind up with a surplus of precious metal.

These ideas about economic activity led to a variety of forms of economic regulation. The most common was the **monopoly**, a grant of special privileges in return for both financial considerations and an agreement to abide by the rules set out by the state. Some monopolies were granted by the crown as a reward for past favors or to purchase future support. Monopolists usually paid considerable fees for their rights, but they could make capital investments with the expectation of long-term gains. This advantage was especially important in attracting investors for risky and expensive ventures such as long-distance trade. Monopolists also benefited the economy as a whole by increasing productive investment at a time when most capital was being used to purchase land, luxury goods, or offices.

The East India Companies. Two monopoly companies, the English and the Dutch East India Companies, dominated the Asian trade. The English East India Company, founded in 1600 with a capital of £30,000, was given the exclusive right to the Asian trade and immediately established itself throughout the Indian Ocean. The Dutch East India Company was formed two years later with ten times the capital of its English counterpart. By the end of the century, the Dutch company employed over 12,000 people. Both companies were **joint-stock companies**, a new form of business organization. Subscribers owned a percentage of the total value of the company, based on the number of shares they bought, and were entitled to a distribution of profits on the same basis. Shares could be exchanged without the breakup of the company as a whole. Both Amsterdam and London soon developed stock markets to trade the shares of monopoly companies.

Protective Trade Regulations. Monopolies were not the only form of regulation in which seventeenth-century governments engaged. For states with Atlantic colonies, regulation took the form of restricting markets rather than traders. In the 1660s, the English government, alarmed at the growth of Dutch mercantile activity in the New World, passed a series of **Navigation Acts** designed to protect English shipping. Colonial goods—primarily tobacco and sugar—could be shipped to and from England only in English boats. If the French wanted to purchase West Indian sugar, they could not simply send a ship to the English colony of Barbados loaded with French goods and exchange them for sugar. Rather, they had to make their purchases from an English import-export merchant, and the goods had to be unloaded in an English port before they could be reloaded to be shipped to France. As a result of these protective measures, the English reexport trade skyrocketed. With such a dramatic increase in trading, all moved in English ships, shipbuilding boomed, and English ports and coastal towns enjoyed heightened prosperity. For a time, colonial protection proved effective.

The French entered the intercontinental trade later than their North Atlantic rivals, and they were less dependent on trade for their subsistence. French protectionism was as much internal as colonial. Of all the states of Europe, only France could satisfy its needs from its own resources. Achieving such self-sufficiency, however, required coordination and leadership. In the 1670s, Louis XIV's finance minister, Jean-Baptiste Colbert (1619–1683), developed a plan to bolster the French economy by protecting it against European imports. First Colbert followed the English example of restricting the reexport trade by requiring that imports come to France either in French ships or in the ships of the country from which the goods originated. In addition, he used tariffs to make imported goods unattractive in France. He sponsored a drive to increase French manufacturing, especially of textiles, tapestries, linens, glass, and furniture. To protect the investments in French manufacturing, enormous duties were placed on the import of similar goods manufactured elsewhere. At the same time, the English had already begun to imitate this form of protection. In the early eighteenth century, England attempted to limit the importation of cotton goods from India to prevent the collapse of the domestic clothing industry.

The Navigation Acts and Colbert's program of protective tariffs were directed specifically against Dutch reexporters. The Dutch were the acknowledged leaders in all branches of commerce in the seventeenth century. Restrictive navigation practices were one way to combat an advantage that the Dutch had built through heavy capital investment and by breaking away from the prevailing theories about the relationship between wealth and precious metals. English and French economic protectionism cut heavily into the Dutch trade, and ultimately, both the English and French overtook the Dutch. But protectionism had its price. Just as the dynastic wars were succeeded by the wars of religion, the wars of religion were succeeded by the wars of commerce.

The Wars of Commerce

Competition for trade was part of the struggle by which the state grew powerful. It was not inevitable that economic competition would lead to warfare, but restrictive competition was another matter.

Thus the scramble for colonies in the seventeenth century led to commercial warfare in the eighteenth. As the English gradually replaced the Dutch as the leading commercial nation, so the French replaced the English as the leading competitor. Their struggles for the dominance of world markets brought European warfare to every corner of the globe.

The Mercantile Wars

Commercial warfare in Europe began between the English and the Dutch in the middle of the seventeenth century. Both had established aggressive overseas trading companies in the Atlantic and in Asia. Conflict was inevitable, and the result was three naval wars fought between 1652 and 1674.

The Dutch had little choice but to strike out against English policy, but they also had little chance of overall success. The wars were costly to both states, nearly bankrupting the English crown in 1672. Anglo-Dutch rivalry was finally laid to rest after 1688, when William of Orange, stadtholder of Holland, became William III (1689–1702), king of England.

The Anglo-Dutch commercial wars were just one part of a larger European conflict. Dutch commerce was as threatening to France as it was to England, though in a different way. Under Colbert, France pursued a policy of economic independence. The state supported internal industrial activity through the financing of large workshops and the encouragement of new manufacturing techniques. To protect French products, Colbert levied punitive tariffs on Dutch imports; these tariffs severely depressed both trade and manufacture in Holland. Though the Dutch retaliated with restrictive tariffs of their own—in 1672 they banned the import of all French goods for an entire year—the Dutch economy depended on free trade. The Dutch had much more to lose than did France in a battle of protective tariffs.

The battle that Louis XIV had in mind, though, was more deadly than one of tariffs. Greedily, he eyed the Spanish Netherlands—to which he had a weak claim through his Habsburg wife—and believed that the Dutch stood in the way of his plans. In 1672, Louis's army, over 100,000 strong, invaded the Low Countries and swept all before them. Only the opening of the dikes by the Dutch prevented the French from entering the province of Holland itself.

The French invasion coincided with the third Anglo-Dutch war, and the United Provinces found themselves besieged on land and sea. Their international trade was disrupted, their manufacturing industries were in ruins, and their military budget skyrocketed. Only able diplomacy and skillful military leadership prevented their total demise. A separate peace was made with England; Spain, whose sovereign territory had been invaded, entered the war on the side of the Dutch, as did a number of German states. Louis's hope for a lightning victory faded, and the war settled into a series of interminable sieges and reliefs of fortified towns. The Dutch finally persuaded France to come to terms in the Treaty of Nijmegen (1678–1679). While Louis XIV retained a number of the territories he had taken from Spain, his armies withdrew from the United Provinces, and he agreed to lift most of the commercial sanctions against Dutch goods. The first phase of mercantile warfare was over.

The Wars of Louis XIV

It was Louis XIV's ambition to restore the ancient Burgundian territories to the French crown and to provide secure northern and eastern borders for his state. Pursuit of these aims involved him in conflicts with nearly every other European state.

The Balance of Power. In the late seventeenth century, ambassadors and ministers of state began to develop the theory of a **balance of power** in Europe. This was a belief that no state or combination of states should be allowed to become so powerful that its existence threatened the peace of the others. Behind this purely political idea of the balance of power lay a theory of collective security that knit together the European state system. French expansion in either direction not only threatened the other states that were directly involved but also posed a threat to European security in general.

Louis showed his hand clearly enough in the Franco-Dutch war that had ended in 1679. Though he withdrew his forces from the United Provinces and evacuated most of the territories he had conquered, by the Treaty of Nijmegen France absorbed Franche-Comté as well as portions of the Spanish Netherlands. Louis began plotting his next adventure almost as soon as the treaty was signed. War finally came in 1688, when French troops poured across the Rhine to seize Cologne. A united German Empire led by Leopold I, archduke of Austria, combined with the maritime powers of England and Holland, led by William III, to form the Grand Alliance, the first of the great balance of power coalitions. In fact, the two sides proved to be so evenly matched that the Nine Years' War (1688–1697) settled very little, but it did demonstrate that a successful European coalition could be formed against France. It also signified the permanent shift in alliances that resulted from the Revolution of 1688 in England. Although the English had allied with France against the Dutch in 1672, after William became king he persuaded the English Parliament that the real enemy was France. Louis's greatest objective, to secure the borders of his state, had withstood its greatest test. He might have rested satisfied but for the vagaries of births, marriages, and deaths.

Like his father, Louis XIV had married a daughter of the king of Spain. Philip IV had married his eldest daughter to Louis XIV and a younger one to Leopold I of Austria, who subsequently became the Holy Roman Emperor (1658–1705). Before he died, Philip finally fathered a son, Charles II (1665–1700), who attained the Spanish crown at the age of four but was mentally and physically incapable of ruling his vast empire. For decades, it was apparent that there would be no direct Habsburg successor to the Spanish Empire. Louis XIV and Leopold I both had legitimate claims to an inheritance that would have irreversibly tipped the European balance of power.

The War of the Spanish Succession. As Charles II grew increasingly feeble, efforts to find a suitable compromise to the problem of the Spanish succession were led by William III, who, as stadtholder of Holland, was vitally interested in the fate of the Spanish Netherlands and, as king of England, was equally interested in the fate of the Spanish American colonies. In the 1690s, two treaties of partition were drawn up, neither of which was implemented.

All of these plans had been made without consulting the Spanish, who wanted to maintain their empire intact. To this end, they devised a brilliant plan. Charles II bequeathed his entire empire to Philip of Anjou, the younger grandson of Louis XIV, with two stipulations: that Philip renounce his claim to the French throne and that he accept the empire intact, without partition. If he—or, more to the point, his grandfather, Louis XIV—did not accept these conditions, the empire would pass to Archduke Charles, the younger son of Leopold I. Such provisions virtually ensured war between France and the empire unless compromise between the two powers could be reached. Before terms could even be suggested, however, Charles II died, and Philip V (1700–1746) was proclaimed king of Spain and its empire.

Thus the eighteenth century opened with the War of the Spanish Succession (1702–1714). Emperor Leopold rejected the provisions of Charles's will and sent his troops to occupy Italy. Louis XIV confirmed the worst fears of William III when he provided his grandson with French troops to "defend" the Spanish Netherlands. William III revived the Grand Alliance and initiated a massive land war against the combined might of France and Spain. The allied objectives were twofold: to prevent the unification of the French and Spanish thrones and to partition the Spanish Empire so that both Italy and the Netherlands were ceded to Austria. Louis XIV's objective was simply to preserve as much as possible of the Spanish inheritance for the house of Bourbon.

William III died in 1702 and was succeeded by Anne (1702–1714). John Churchill (1650–1722), Duke of Marlborough and commander-in-chief of the army, continued William's policy. England and Holland again provided most of the finance and sea power, but the English also provided a land army that was nearly 70,000 strong. Prussia joined the Grand Alliance, and disciplined Prussian troops helped to offset the addition of the Spanish army to Louis's forces. Churchill defeated French forces in 1704 at Blenheim in Germany and in 1706 at Ramillies in the Spanish Netherlands. France's military ascendancy was over.

Between 1713 and 1714, a series of treaties at Utrecht settled the War of the Spanish Succession. Spanish possessions in Italy and the Netherlands were ceded

GENEALOGY
THE SPANISH SUCCESSION

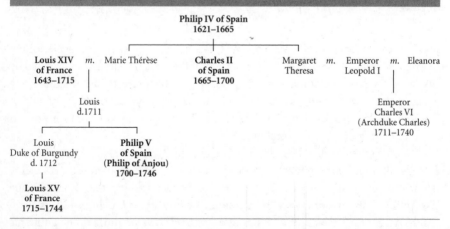

to Austria; France abandoned all its territorial gains east of the Rhine and ceded its North American territories of Nova Scotia and Newfoundland to England. England also acquired from Spain Gibraltar, on the southern coast of Spain, and the island of Minorca in the Mediterranean. Both were strategically important to English commercial interests. English intervention in the Nine Years' War and the War of the Spanish Succession did not result in large territorial gains, but it did result in an enormous increase in English power and prestige. Over the next 30 years, England would assert its own imperial claims.

War of the Spanish Succession. The great British victories in this war were in the Spanish Netherlands and the Holy Roman Empire. They established Britain as a great power.

The Colonial Wars

The Treaty of Utrecht (1713–1714) ushered in almost a quarter century of peace in western Europe. Peace allowed Europe to rebuild its shattered economy and resume the international trade that had been so severely disrupted over the past 40 years. The Treaty of Utrecht had resolved a number of important trading issues, all in favor of Great Britain, as England was known after its union with Scotland in 1707. In addition to receiving Gibraltar and Minorca from Spain, Britain was granted the monopoly to provide slaves to the Spanish American colonies and the right to send one trading ship a year to them. In the East and in the West, Britain was becoming the dominant commercial power in the world.

Part of the reason for Britain's preeminence was the remarkable growth of its Atlantic colonies. Like every other colonial power, the British held a monopoly on their colonial trade. They were far less successful than were the Spanish and French in enforcing the notion that colonies existed only for the benefit of the parent country, but the English Parliament continued to pass legislation aimed at restricting colonial trade with other nations and other nations' colonies. Like most other mercantile restrictions, these efforts were stronger in theory than in practice. Tariffs on imports and customs duties on British goods provided a double incentive for smuggling.

France emerged as Britain's true colonial rival. In the Caribbean, the French had the largest and most profitable of the West Indian sugar islands, Saint Domingue (modern-day Haiti). In North America, France not only held Canada but also laid claim to the entire continent west of the Ohio River. The French did not so much settle their colonial territory as occupy it. They surveyed the land, established trading relations with the Native Americans, and built forts at strategic locations. The English, in contrast, had developed fixed communities, which grew larger and more prosperous by the decade. France decided to defend its colonies by establishing an overseas military presence. Regular French troops were shipped to Canada and installed in Louisbourg, Montreal, and Quebec. The British responded with troops of their own and sent an expeditionary force to clear the French from the Ohio River Valley. This action was the immediate cause of the Seven Years' War (1756–1763).

Although the Seven Years' War had a bitter Continental phase, it was essentially a war for empire between the English and the French. There were three main theaters: the North American mainland, the West Indian sugar plantations, and the eastern coast of India. All over the globe, the British won smashing victories. The French were chased from their major trading zone, and English dominance was secured.

By the end of the Seven Years' War, Britain had become a global imperial power. In the Peace of Paris (1763), France ceded all of Canada in exchange for the return of its West Indian islands. British dominion in the East Indian trade was recognized and led ultimately to British dominion in India itself. In less than a century, France's ascendancy was broken, and Europe's first modern imperial power had been created.

Territory awarded to
House of Bourbon

Territory added to Austria

Territory added to Savoy

THE TREATY OF UTRECHT

What critical gains did Britain make as a result of the 1714 Treaty of Utrecht? Notice the extent of Austria after the treaty. What problems was the Austrian government most likely to face? What did Savoy gain?

SUMMARY

The New Science   The scientific revolution challenged prevailing assumptions about the natural world. The new science was materialistic, mathematical, and a Europe-wide movement. Nicolaus Copernicus developed a heliocentric model of the universe. Johannes Kepler formulated laws of planetary motion. Galileo developed laws of motion and popularized Copernican theory. Spiritual and mystical traditions played an important role in the scientific revolution. Paracelsus transformed ideas about chemistry and medicine. Robert Boyle helped establish the science of chemistry. William Harvey demonstrated the circulation of blood. Sir Isaac Newton discovered fundamental laws of motion. The state provided support for scientific inquiry. René Descartes argued for the harmony of faith and reason. Cartesianism rested on a division between mind and matter.

Empires of Goods   The development of long-distance trade had a profound impact on lifestyles, economic policy, and warfare. In the seventeenth century, commercial power shifted from the Mediterranean countries to the northern European states. Innovation, organization, and efficient management all played a role in producing the commercial revolution. Consumer tastes came to exert a strong influence on trade and commercial patterns. The demand for sugar was linked to the success of tea. Sugar cultivation stimulated the African slave trade. The Dutch were the preeminent commercial power in the first part of the seventeenth century. Outside of the Dutch Republic, monarchs played a central role in trade. According to the theory of mercantilism, trade was a zero-sum game in which the object was to amass as much precious metal as possible. States granted monopolies and regulated trade to further mercantilist goals.

The Wars of Commerce   Economic competition developed into military conflict. After the Anglo-Dutch commercial wars, England was the dominant commercial power in Europe. The French pursued a policy of economic independence that included the use of punitive tariffs against the Dutch. Louis XIV invaded the Netherlands but was prevented from attaining an easy victory by a Dutch, Spanish, German, and English coalition. Louis XIV aimed to restore the Burgundian territories to France and to secure northern and eastern borders for his state. The claims of Louis XIV and Leopold I to the Spanish throne threatened to destroy the balance of power in Europe. The War of the Spanish Succession ended with France's defeat by the Grand Alliance. The Seven Years' War was essentially a war for empire between England and France. England's triumph made it a global imperial power.

QUESTIONS FOR REVIEW

1. What was new about the methods and ideas of Copernicus, Brahe, Kepler, and Galileo, and why were they threatening to Catholic doctrine?
2. In what ways did the new science build upon traditional ideas associated with alchemy and astrology? In what ways was it a departure?
3. What new technologies, trading practices, and financial devices assisted the expansion of long-distance trading?
4. Why were the Dutch especially well-suited to participate in the worldwide expansion of European commerce?
5. How did the governments of the various European nations promote their own commercial interests?

The Balance of Power in Eighteenth-Century Europe

The Rise of Russia

At the beginning of the eighteenth century, Russia was scarcely of concern to the rest of Europe. Peter the Great changed that. The Treaty of Nystad had confirmed the magnitude of his victory over the Swedes in the Great Northern War. The change created consternation in the courts of Europe. Little was known about the Russian ruler or his state.

Peter the Great sought greater contact with western Europe. Twice he visited Europe to discover the secrets of western prosperity and might. He arranged marriages between the closest heirs to his throne, including his son Alexis, and the sons and daughters of German princes and dukes. By 1721, he had established 21 separate foreign embassies. The sons of the Russian gentry and nobility were sent to the west— sometimes forcibly—to further their education and to learn to adapt to western outlooks. Peter recruited foreign engineers and gunners to serve in his army, foreign architects to build his new capital at Saint Petersburg, foreign scholars to head the new state schools, and foreign administrators to oversee the new departments of state.

By 1721, Russia was recognized all over Europe as an emerging power. The Russian navy, built mostly by foreigners, was now capable of protecting Russian interests and defending important ports such as Riga and Saint Petersburg. Even the Dutch, who had long plotted the decline of Swedish might, now became nervous. It was therefore unsettling that the Russian ruler now wanted to be recognized as an emperor.

The Reforms of Peter the Great

Peter the Great was not the first Russian tsar to attempt to borrow from the West. The process had been under way for decades. But Russia was a vast state, and Europe was only one of its neighbors. Russia's religion had come from Byzantium

This portrait of Peter the Great by his court painter Louis Caravaque pays homage to Peter's intense interest in naval matters. Ships flying English, Dutch, Danish, and Russian flags prepare for maneuvers under his command.

rather than Rome, thus giving Russian Christianity an eastern flavor. Its Asian territories mixed the influence of Mongols and Ottomans; its southern borders met Tatars and Cossacks. While most European states were racially and ethnically homogeneous, Russia was a loose confederation of diverse peoples. Yet the western states posed the greatest threat to Russia in the seventeenth century, and it was to the West that Peter, like his father before him, turned his attention.

Nearly all of Peter's reforms—economic, educational, administrative, social, military—were aimed at enhancing military efficiency rather than civil progress. In his 30 years of active rule, there was only one year—1724—during which he was not at war. Vital reforms such as the poll tax (1724), which changed the basis of taxation from the household to the individual adult male, had enormous social consequences. The new policy of taxing individuals officially erased whole social classes. A strict census, taken (and retaken) to inhibit tax evasion, became the basis for further governmental encroachments on the tsar's subjects. Yet the poll tax was designed not for any of these purposes but to increase tax revenue for war.

Although Peter's reforms were developed from little other than military necessity, they constituted a fundamental transformation in the life of all Russian people. The creation of a gigantic standing army and an entirely new navy meant conscription of the Russian peasantry on a grand scale. Military service was not confined to the peasantry. Most of the gentry lived on estates that had been granted to them along with the resident peasants as a reward for their military contributions. Peter the Great intensified the obligations of the gentry. Not only were they to serve the state for life, but they were to accompany their regiments to the field and lead them in battle. When too old for active military service, they were to perform administrative service in the new departments of state.

The expansion of military forces necessitated an expansion of military administration as well. Peter's first innovation was the creation of the Senate, a group of nine senior administrators who were to oversee all aspects of military and civil government. The Senate became a permanent institution of government led by an entirely new official, the Procurator-General, who presided over its sessions and could propose legislation as well as oversee administration. From the Senate emanated 500 officials known as the fiscals, who traveled throughout the state looking for irregularities in tax assessment and collection. They quickly developed into a hated and feared internal police force.

Peter's efforts to reorganize his government went a step further in 1722, when he issued the **Table of Ranks**. This was an official hierarchy of the state that established the social position or rank of individuals. It was divided into three categories: military service, civil service, and owners of landed estates. Each category contained 14 ranks, and it was decreed that every person who entered the hierarchy did so at the bottom and worked his way up. The creation of the Table of Ranks demonstrated Peter's continued commitment to merit as a criterion for advancement. Equally important was Peter's decision to make the military service the highest of the three categories. This reversed the centuries-old positions of the landed aristocracy and the military service class. Though the old nobility also served in the military and continued to dominate state service, the Table of Ranks opened the way for the infusion of new elements into the Russian elite.

Many of the men who were able to advance in the Table of Ranks did so through attendance at the new institutions of higher learning that Peter founded. His initial educational establishments were created to further the military might of the state. Peter was also interested in liberal education, and he had scores of Western books translated into Russian. He had a press established in Moscow to print original works, including the first Russian newspaper. He decreed that a new, more Westernized alphabet replace the one used by the Russian Orthodox church and that books be written in the vernacular rather than in the formal literary language of religious writers. He also introduced Arabic numerals into official accounting records.

In all of these ways and more, Peter the Great transformed Russia, but the changes did not come without cost. The traditions of centuries were not easily broken. In the end, the great costs of westernization were paid by the masses of people, who benefited little from the changes.

Life in Rural Russia

At the beginning of the eighteenth century, nearly 97 percent of the Russian people lived on the land and practiced agriculture. Their lifestyles and farming methods had changed little for centuries. A harsh climate and low yields characterized Russian agriculture. One-third of the annual harvests during the eighteenth century were poor or disastrous, yet throughout the century, state taxation was making ever larger demands on the peasantry. During Peter's reign alone, direct taxation increased by 500 percent.

The theory of the Russian state was one of service, and the role of Russian peasants was to serve their master. The law code of 1649 formalized a process that had been under way for over a century whereby peasants lost status and became the property of their landlords. During the next century, laws curtailed the ability of peasants to move freely from one place to another, eliminated their right to hold private property, and abolished their freedom to petition the tsar against their masters. At the same time that landlords increased their hold over peasants, the state increased its hold over landlords. They were made responsible for the payment of taxes owed by their peasants and for the military service due from the peasants. By the middle of the eighteenth century, over half of all peasants—6.7 million adult males by 1782—had become serfs, the property of their masters, without any significant rights or legal protection.

If serfs made up the bottom half of the Russian peasantry, there were few advantages to being in the top half among the state peasants. State peasants lived on lands owned by the monarchy itself. Like the serfs, state peasants were subject to the needs of the state for soldiers and workers. Forced labor was used in all of

Peter's grandiose projects. Saint Petersburg was built by the backbreaking labor of peasant conscripts.

The Enlightened Empress Catherine

Of all the legacies of Peter the Great, perhaps the one of most immediate consequence was that government could go on without him. During the next 37 years, six tsars ruled Russia, "three women, a boy of twelve, an infant, and a mental weakling," as one commentator acidly observed. Although each succession was contested, the government continued to function smoothly, and Peter's territorial conquests were largely maintained. Russia also experienced a remarkable increase in population during this period. Between 1725 and 1762, the population grew from 13 to 19 million, a jump of nearly one-half in a single generation. This explosion of people dramatically increased the wealth of the landholding class, whose members reckoned their status by the number of serfs they owned.

The expansion of the economic resources of the nobility was matched by a rise in their legal status and political power. This period was sarcastically dubbed "the emancipation of the nobility," a phrase that captures not only the irony of the growing gap between rich and poor but also the contrast between the social structures of Russia and those of western Europe. In return for their privileges and status, Peter the Great extended the duties that the landowning classes owed to the state. By granting unique rights, such as the ownership of serfs, to the descendants of the old military service class, Peter had forged a Russian nobility. However, lifetime service was the price of nobility.

To gain and hold the throne, each succeeding tsar had to make concessions to the nobles to win their loyalty. The requirement of service to the state was gradually weakened until finally, in 1762, the obligation was abolished entirely.

Catherine's Accession. The abolition of compulsory service was not the same as the abolition of service itself. In fact, the end of compulsory service enabled Catherine II, the Great (1762–1796), to enact some of the most important reforms of her reign. Her first two acts as empress—having her husband, Peter III, murdered and lowering the salt tax—strengthened her position.

The most important event in the early years of Catherine's reign was the establishment of a legislative commission to review the laws of Russia. Catherine herself wrote the Instruction (1767) by which the elected commissioners were to operate. She borrowed her theory of law from the French jurist Baron de Montesquieu (1689–1755) and her theory of punishment from the Italian reformer Cesare Beccaria (1738–1794). Among other things, Catherine advocated the abolition of capital punishment, torture, serf auctions, and the breakup of serf families by sale. Few of these radical reforms were ever put into practice.

In 1775, Catherine restructured local government. Russia was divided into 50 provincial districts, each with a population of between 300,000 and 400,000 inhabitants. Each district was to be governed by both a central official and elected local noblemen. This reform was modeled on the English system of justices of the peace. In 1785, Catherine issued the Charter of the Nobility, a formal statement of the rights and privileges of the noble class. The charter incorporated all the gains the nobility had made since the death of Peter the Great, but it also instituted the requirements for local service that had been the basis of Catherine's reforms. District councils with the right to petition the tsar directly became the centerpiece of Russian provincial government.

Catherine's reforms did little to enhance the lives of the vast majority of her people. She took no effective action to end serfdom or to soften its rigors. In fact, by grants of state land, Catherine gave away 800,000 state peasants, who became serfs. So, too, did millions of Poles who became her subjects after the partition of Poland in 1793 and 1795.

Pugachev's Revolt. Popular discontent fueled the most significant uprising of the century, Pugachev's Revolt (1773–1775), which took place during Catherine's reign. Emelyan Pugachev (1726–1775) was a Cossack who had been a military adventurer in his youth. Disappointed in his career, he made his way to the Ural Mountains, where he recruited Asian tribesmen and laborers who were forced to work in the mines. By promising freedom and land ownership, he drew peasants to his cause. In 1773, Pugachev declared himself to be Tsar Peter III, the murdered husband of Catherine II. He began with small raiding parties against local landlords and military outposts and soon gained the allegiance of tens of thousands of peasants. In 1774, with an army of nearly 20,000, Pugachev took the city of Kazan and threatened to advance on Moscow. It was another year before state forces could effectively control the rebellion. Finally, Pugachev was betrayed by his own followers and sent to Moscow, where he was executed.

During the reigns of Peter and Catherine the Great, Russia was transformed into an international power. Saint Petersburg, a window to the West, attracted many of Europe's leading luminaries. At court, French was spoken, the latest fashions were worn, and the newest ideas for economic and educational reform were aired. The Russian nobility mingled comfortably with its European counterparts, while the military service class developed into bureaucrats and administrators. Although court society glittered, for millions of peasants the quality of life was no better at the end of the campaign of westernization than it had been at the beginning.

The Two Germanies

The Thirty Years' War, which ended in 1648, initiated a profound transformation of the Holy Roman Empire. Warfare had devastated imperial territory and left a legacy of political consequences. There were now two empires—a German and an

Austrian—though both were ruled by the same person. In the German territories, whether Catholic or Protestant, the Holy Roman Emperor was more a constitutional monarch than the absolute ruler he was in Austria. The larger states such as Saxony, Bavaria, and Hanover made their own political alliances despite the jurisdictional control that the emperor claimed to exercise. Most decisively, so did Brandenburg-Prussia. By the beginning of the eighteenth century, the electors of Brandenburg had become the kings of Prussia, and Prussian military power and efficient administrative structure became the envy of its German neighbors.

The Austrian Empire was composed of Austria and Bohemia, the Habsburg hereditary lands, and as much of Hungary as could be controlled. Austria remained the center of the still-flourishing Counter-Reformation and a stronghold of Jesuit influence. The War of the Spanish Succession, which gave the Habsburgs control of the southern Netherlands and parts of Italy, brought Austria an enhanced role in European affairs. Austria remained one of the great powers of Europe and the leading power in the Holy Roman Empire, despite the rise of Prussia. Indeed, from the middle of the eighteenth century the conflict between Prussia and Austria was the defining characteristic of central European politics.

The Rise of Prussia

The transformation of Brandenburg-Prussia from a petty German principality to a great European power was one of the most significant developments of the eighteenth century. Frederick William, the Great Elector (1640–1688), had begun the process of forging Brandenburg-Prussia into a power in its own right by building a large and efficient military machine. At the beginning of the eighteenth century, Prussia was on the winning side in both the War of the Spanish Succession and the Great Northern War. When the battlefield dust had settled, Prussia possessed Pomerania and the Baltic port of Stettin. It was now a recognized power in eastern Europe.

Frederick William I. Frederick William I (1713–1740) and his son Frederick II, the Great (1740–1786), turned this promising beginning into an astounding success. A devout Calvinist, Frederick William I deplored waste and display. The reforms he initiated were intended to subordinate both aristocracy and peasantry to the needs of the state and to subordinate the needs of the state to the demands of the military.

Because of its exposed geographical position, Prussia's major problem was to maintain an efficient and well-trained army during peacetime. Security required a constant state of military preparedness, yet the relaxation of military discipline and the desertion of troops to their homes inevitably followed the cessation of hostilities. Frederick William I solved this problem by integrating the economic and military structures of his state. First, he appointed only German officers to command his troops, eliminating mercenaries. Then he placed these noblemen at the head of locally recruited regiments. Each adult male in every district was required to register for military service in the regiment of the local landlord. These reforms dramatically increased the effectiveness of the army by shifting the burden of recruitment and training to the localities.

Yet despite all the attention that Frederick William I lavished on the military—by the end of his reign, nearly 70 percent of state expenditures went to the army—his foreign policy was largely pacific. In fact, his greatest achievements were in civil affairs, reforming the bureaucracy, establishing a sound economy, and raising state revenues. Through generous settlement schemes and by welcoming Protestant and Jewish refugees, Frederick William was able to expand the economic potential of these eastern territories. Frederick William I pursued an aggressive policy of land purchase to expand the royal domain, and the addition of so many new inhabitants in Prussia further increased his wealth.

Frederick the Great. Financial security was vital to Frederick the Great's success. With his throne, Frederick II inherited the fourth largest army in Europe and the richest treasury. He wasted no time in putting both to use. His two objectives were to acquire the Polish corridor of West Prussia that separated his German and Prussian territories and the agriculturally and industrially rich Austrian province of Silesia to the southeast of Berlin. Just months after his coronation, Frederick conquered Silesia, which soon came to dominate the Prussian economy.

It was Frederick's military prowess that earned him the title "the Great." However, his achievements went beyond the military arena. More than his father, Frederick II forged an alliance with the Prussian nobility, integrating the nobles into a unified state. A tightly organized central administration, which depended on the cooperation of the local nobility, directed both military and bureaucratic affairs. At the center, Frederick worked tirelessly to oversee his government. He codified the laws of Prussia, abolished torture and capital punishment, and instituted agricultural techniques imported from the states of western Europe. By the end of Frederick's reign, Prussia had become a model for bureaucratic organization, military reform, and enlightened rule.

Austria Survives

Austria was the great territorial victor in the War of the Spanish Succession, acquiring both the Netherlands and parts of Italy. Austrian forces recaptured a large part of Hungary from the Turks, thereby expanding Austria's territory to the south and the east. Charles VI (1711–1740), hereditary ruler of Austria and Bohemia, king of Hungary, and Holy Roman Emperor of the German nation, was recognized as one of Europe's most potent rulers—but appearances were deceptive. The apex of Austrian power and prestige had already passed, and Austria's rivals in eastern Europe, Russia, and Prussia were on the rise.

Decentralized Rule. The difficulties facing Austria ran deep. The Thirty Years' War had made the emperor more an Austrian monarch than an imperial German ruler.

On the Austrian hereditary estates, the Catholic Counter-Reformation continued unabated, bringing with it the benefits of Jesuit education, cultural revival, and the religious unity that was necessary to motivate warfare against the Ottomans. But these benefits came at a price. Perhaps as many as 200,000 Protestants fled Austria and Bohemia, taking their skills and capital with them. For centuries the vision of empire had dominated Habsburg rule. This meant that the Austrian monarchy was a multiethnic confederation of relatively autonomous lands loosely tied together by loyalty to a single head. Hungary even elected the Habsburg emperor its king in a separate ceremony. Therefore it was hard for Austria to centralize in the same way as had Prussia.

Austria was predominantly rural and agricultural. Less than 5 percent of the population lived in towns of 10,000 or more; less than 15 percent lived in towns at all. The landed aristocracy exploited serfs to the maximum. When serfs married, when they transferred property, even when they died, they paid taxes to their lord. As a result, they had little left to give the state. In consequence, the Austrian army was among the smallest and poorest of the major powers, despite the fact that it had the most active enemies along its borders.

Lack of finance, lack of human resources, and lack of governmental control were not the only problems facing Charles VI. With no sons to succeed him, Charles feared that his hereditary and elective states would go their separate ways after his death and that the great Habsburg monarchy would end. For 20 years, his abiding ambition was to gain recognition for the principle that his empire would pass intact to his daughter, Maria Theresa. He expressed the principle in a document known as the **Pragmatic Sanction**, which stated that all Habsburg lands would pass intact to the eldest heir, male or female. Charles VI made concession after concession to gain acceptance of the Pragmatic Sanction. But the leaders of Europe licked their lips at the prospect of a dismembered Austrian Empire.

Maria Theresa. In 1740, soon after Maria Theresa (1740–1780) inherited the imperial throne, Frederick of Prussia invaded the rich Austrian province of Silesia and attracted allies for an assault on Vienna. Faced with Bavarian, Saxon, and Prussian armies, Maria Theresa appeared before the Hungarian estates, accepted their crown, and persuaded them to provide her with an army capable of halting the allied advance. Though she was unable to reconquer Silesia, Hungarian aid helped her to hold the line against her enemies.

The loss of Silesia, the most prosperous part of the Austrian domains, signaled the need for fundamental reform. The new eighteenth-century idea of building a state replaced the traditional Habsburg concern with maintaining an empire. Maria Theresa and her son Joseph II (1780–1790) began the process of transformation. For Austria, state building meant first the reorganization of the military and civil bureaucracy to clear the way for fiscal reform. As in Prussia, a central directory was created to oversee the collection of taxes and the disbursement of funds. Maria

Theresa personally persuaded her provincial estates both to increase taxation and to extend it to the nobles and the clergy. Although her success was limited, she finally established royal control over the raising and collection of taxes.

Maria Theresa also improved the condition of the Austrian peasantry. She limited labor service to two days per week and abolished the most burdensome feudal dues. Joseph II ended serfdom altogether. The new Austrian law codes guaranteed peasants' legal rights and established their ability to seek redress through the law. Joseph II hoped to extend reform even further. In the last years of his life, he abolished obligatory labor service and ensured that all peasants kept one-half of their income before paying local and state taxes. Such a radical reform met a storm of opposition and was abandoned at the end of Joseph's reign.

The reorganization of the bureaucracy, the increase in taxation, and the social reforms that created a more productive peasantry revitalized the Austrian state. The efforts of Maria Theresa and Joseph II to overcome provincial autonomy worked better in Austria and Bohemia than in Hungary. The Hungarians declined to contribute at all to state revenues, and Joseph II took the unusual step of refusing to be crowned king of Hungary so that he would not have to make any concessions to Hungarian autonomy. He even imposed a tariff on Hungarian goods sold in Austria. More seriously, parts of the empire had already been lost before the process of reform could begin. Prussia's seizure of Silesia was the hardest blow of all. Yet in 1740, when Frederick the Great and his allies had swept down from the north, few would have predicted that Austria would survive.

The Politics of Power

Frederick the Great's invasion of Silesia in 1740 was callous and cynical. Since the Pragmatic Sanction bound him to recognize Maria Theresa's succession, Frederick calculatingly offered her a defensive alliance in return for which she would simply hand over Silesia. It was an offer she should not have refused. Though Frederick's action initiated the War of the Austrian Succession, he was not alone in his desire to shake loose parts of Austria's territory. Soon nearly the entire Continent became embroiled in the conflict.

The War of the Austrian Succession. The War of the Austrian Succession (1740–1748) resembled a pack of wolves stalking its injured prey. It quickly became a major international conflict involving Prussia, France, and Spain on one side and Austria, Britain, and Holland on the other. Spain joined the fighting to recover its Italian possessions, Saxony claimed Moravia, France entered Bohemia, and the Bavarians moved into Austria from the south. With France and Prussia allied, it was vital that Britain join with Austria to maintain the balance of power. Initially, the British did little more than subsidize Maria Theresa's forces, but once France renewed its efforts to conquer the Netherlands, both Britain and the Dutch Republic joined in the fray.

Maria Theresa and her family. Eleven of Maria Theresa's 16 children are posed with the empress and her husband, Francis of Lorraine. Standing next to his mother is the future emperor Joseph II.

That the British cared little about the fate of the Habsburg Empire was clear from the terms of the treaty that they dictated at Aix-la-Chapelle (Aachen) in 1748. Austria recognized Frederick's conquest of Silesia as well as the loss of parts of its Italian territories to Spain. France, which the British had always regarded as the real enemy, withdrew from the Netherlands in return for the restoration of a number of colonial possessions. The War of the Austrian Succession made Austria and Prussia permanent enemies and gave Maria Theresa a crash course in international diplomacy. She learned firsthand that self-interest rather than loyalty underlay power politics.

The Seven Years' War. This lesson was reinforced in 1756, when Britain and Prussia entered into a military accord at the beginning of the Seven Years' War (1756–1763). Frederick's actions drove France into the arms of both the Austrians and the Russians, and an alliance that included the German state of Saxony was formed in defense. Thus was initiated a diplomatic revolution in which France and Austria became allies after 300 years as enemies.

Once again, Frederick the Great took the offensive, and once again, he won his risk against the odds. His attack on Saxony and Austria in 1756 brought a vigorous response from the Russians, who interceded on Austria's behalf with a massive army. Three years later, at the battle of Kunersdorf, Frederick suffered the worst military defeat of his career when the Russians shattered his armies. In 1760, his forces were barely one-third of the size of those massed by his opponents, and it was only a matter of time before he was fighting defensively from within Prussia.

In 1762, Russian Empress Elizabeth died. She was succeeded by her nephew, the childlike Peter III, a German by birth who worshipped Frederick the Great. When

Peter came to the throne, he immediately negotiated peace with Frederick, abandoning not only his allies but also the substantial territorial gains that the Russian forces had made within Prussia. It was small wonder that the Russian military leadership joined in the coup d'état that brought Peter's wife, Catherine, to the throne in 1762. With Russia out of the war, Frederick was able to fend off further Austrian offensives and to emerge with his state, including Silesia, intact.

The Seven Years' War did little to change the boundaries of the German states, but it had two important political results. The first was to establish beyond doubt the status of Prussia as a major power and a counterbalance to Austria in central Europe. The second result of the Seven Years' War was to initiate a long period of peace in eastern Europe. Both Prussia and Austria were financially exhausted from two decades of fighting. Both states needed a breathing spell to initiate administrative and economic improvements, and the period following the Seven Years' War witnessed the sustained programs of internal reforms for which Frederick the Great, Maria Theresa, and Joseph II were famous in the decades following 1763.

The Partitions of Poland. In Poland the autonomous power of the nobility remained as strong as ever. No monarchical dynasty was ever established, and each elected ruler not only confirmed the privileges of the nobility but usually was forced to extend them. In the Diet, the Polish representative assembly, small special-interest groups could bring legislative business to a halt by exercising their veto power. Given the size of Poland's borders, its army was pathetically inadequate, and the Polish monarchy was helpless to defend its subjects from the destruction on all sides.

In 1764, Catherine the Great and Frederick the Great combined to place one of Catherine's former lovers on the Polish throne and to turn Poland into a weak dependent. Russia and Prussia had different interests in Poland's fate. For Russia, Poland represented a vast buffer state that kept the German powers at a distance from Russia's borders. It was more in Russia's interest to dominate Polish foreign policy than to conquer its territory. For Prussia, Poland looked like another helpless flower, "to be picked off leaf by leaf," as Frederick observed. Poland seemed especially appealing because Polish territory, including the Baltic port of Gdansk, separated the Prussian and Brandenburg portions of Frederick's state.

By the 1770s, the idea of carving up Poland was being actively discussed in Berlin, Saint Petersburg, and Vienna. In 1772, the three great eastern powers struck a deal. Russia would take a large swath of the grain fields of northeast Poland, which included over one million people; Frederick would unite his lands by seizing West Prussia; and Austria would gain both the largest territories, including Galicia, and the greatest number of people, nearly two million Polish subjects.

In half a century, the balance of power in central Europe had shifted decisively. Prussia's absorption of Silesia and parts of Poland made it a single geographical entity as well as a great economic and military power. Austria fought off an attempt to dismember its empire and went on to participate in the partition of Poland. From one empire there were now two states, and the relationship between Prussia and Austria would dominate central Europe for the next century.

This engraving by Le Mire is called "The Cake of the Kings: First Partition of Poland, 1773." The monarchs of Russia, Austria, and Prussia join in carving up Poland. The Polish king is clutching his tottering crown.

The Greatness of Great Britain

By the middle of the eighteenth century, Great Britain had become the leading power of Europe. Britain was unsurpassed as a naval power, able to protect its far-flung trading empire and to make a show of force in almost any part of the world. Perhaps more impressively, for a nation that did not support a large standing army, British soldiers had won decisive victories in the European land wars. In addition, Britain enjoyed economic preeminence. British colonial possessions in the Atlantic and Indian oceans poured consumer products into Britain for export to the European marketplaces. The manufacturing industries that other European states attempted to create with huge government subsidies flourished in Britain through private enterprise.

British military and economic power was supported by a unique system of government. In Britain, the nobility served the state through government. The British constitutional system, devised in the seventeenth century and refined in the eighteenth, shared power between the monarchy and the ruling elite through the institution of Parliament. Central government integrated monarch and ministers with chosen representatives from the localities. Such integration not only provided the Crown with the vital information it needed to formulate national policy, but also eased acceptance and enforcement of government decisions. Government was seen as the rule of law, which, however imperfect, was believed to operate for the benefit of all. The relative openness of the British system hindered diplomatic and colonial affairs, in which secrecy and rapid changes of direction were often the monarch's most potent weapons. These weaknesses came to light most dramatically during the struggle for independence waged by Britain's North American colonists.

The British Constitution

The British Constitution was a patchwork of laws and customs that was gradually sewn together. Many of its greatest innovations came about through circumstance rather than design, and circumstance continued to play an essential role in its development in the eighteenth century. At the apex of the government stood the king, not an absolute monarch like his European counterparts, but not necessarily less powerful for having less arbitrary power. The British people revered monarchy and the monarch. The theory of mixed government depended on the balance of interests represented by the monarchy, the aristocracy in the House of Lords, and the people in the House of Commons.

The partnership between the Crown and the representative body was best expressed in the idea that the British government was composed of King-in-Parliament. Parliament consisted of three separate organs: monarch, lords, and commons. Though each existed separately as a check on the potential excesses of the others, parliamentary government could operate only when the three functioned together. The king was charged with selecting ministers, initiating policy, and supervising administration. The two houses of Parliament were charged with raising revenue, making laws, and presenting subjects' grievances to the Crown.

The British gentry dominated the Commons, occupying over 80 percent of the 558 seats in any session. Most of these members also served as unpaid local officials in the counties, as justices of the peace, captains of the local militias, or collectors of local taxes. They came to Parliament not only as representatives of the interests of their class, but as experienced local governors who understood the needs of both Crown and subject.

Nevertheless, the Crown had to develop methods to coordinate the work of the two houses of Parliament and facilitate the passage of governmental programs. The king and his ministers began to use the deep royal pockets of offices and favors to bolster their friends in Parliament. Not only were those employed by the Crown encouraged to find a place in the House of Commons, but those who had a place in Parliament were encouraged to take employment from the Crown. Despite its potential for abuse, this was a political process that integrated center and locality, and at first it worked rather well. Men with local standing were brought into central offices, where they could influence central policymaking while protecting their local constituents. These officeholders, who came to be called *placemen*, never constituted a majority of the members of Parliament. They formed the core around which eighteenth-century governments operated, but it was a core that needed direction and cohesion. Such leadership and organization were the essential contribution of eighteenth-century politics to the British Constitution.

Parties and Ministers

Although parliamentary management was vital to the Crown, it was not the Crown that developed the basic tools of management. Rather, these techniques originated within the political community itself, and their usefulness was only slowly grasped by the monarchy. The first and, in the long term, most important tool was the party system. Political **parties** initially developed in the late seventeenth century around the issue of the Protestant succession. Those who opposed James II because he was a Catholic attempted to exclude him from inheriting the Crown. They came to be called by their opponents **Whigs**, which meant "Scottish horse thieves." Those who supported James's hereditary rights but who also supported the Anglican Church came to be called by their opponents **Tories**, which meant "Irish cattle rustlers."

The Whigs supported a Protestant monarchy and a broad-based Protestantism. They attracted the allegiance of large numbers of dissenters, heirs to the Puritans of the seventeenth century who practiced forms of Protestantism different from that of the Anglican Church. The struggle between Whigs and Tories was less a struggle for power than one for loyalty to their opposing viewpoints. As the Tories tended to oppose the succession of Prince George of Hanover and the Whigs to support it, it was no mystery which party would find favor with George I (1714–1727). Moreover, as long as there was a pretender to the British throne—another rebellion took place in Scotland in 1745 led by the grandson of James II—the Tories continued to be tarred with the brush of disloyalty.

The division of political sympathies between Whigs and Tories helped to create a set of groupings to which parliamentary leadership could be applied. A national rather than a local or regional outlook could be used to organize support for royal policy as long as royal policy conformed to that national outlook. The ascendancy of the Whigs enabled George I and his son George II (1727–1760) to govern effectively through Parliament, but at the price of dependence on the Whig leaders. Though the monarch had the constitutional freedom to choose his ministers, realistically he could choose only Whigs and practically none but the Whig leaders of the House of Commons. Fortunately for the first two Georges, they found a man who was able to manage Parliament but desired only to serve the Crown.

Sir Robert Walpole (1676–1745), who came from a gentry family in Norfolk, was an early supporter of the Hanoverian succession. Once George I was securely on the throne, Walpole became an indispensable leader of the House of Commons. Walpole became First Lord of the Treasury, a post that he transformed into first minister of state. From his treasury post, Walpole assiduously built a Whig parliamentary party. He carefully dispensed jobs and offices, using them as bait to lure parliamentary supporters. Walpole's organization paid off both in the passage of legislation desired by the Crown and at the polls, where Whigs were returned to Parliament time and again.

From 1721 to 1742, Walpole was the most powerful man in the British government. His long tenure in office was as much a result of his policies as of his methods of governing. He brought a measure of fiscal responsibility to government by establishing a fund to pay off the national debt. In foreign policy, he pursued peace with the same fervor with which both his predecessors and his successors pursued war. The long years of peace brought prosperity to both the landed and merchant classes, but they also brought criticism of Walpole's methods. His use of government patronage to build his parliamentary party was attacked as corruption. So too were the ways in which the pockets of Whig officeholders were lined.

Walpole's 20-year rule established the pattern of parliamentary government. The Crown needed a "prime" minister who was able to steer legislation through the House of Commons. It also needed a patronage broker who could take control of the treasury and dispense its largess in return for parliamentary backing. Walpole's personality and talents had combined these two roles. Thereafter, they were divided. Those who had grown up under Walpole had learned their lessons well. The Whig monopoly of power continued unchallenged for nearly another 20 years. The patronage network that Walpole had created was vastly extended by his Whig successors. Even minor posts in the customs or the excise offices were exchanged for political favor, and only those approved by the Whig leadership could claim them. The cries of corruption grew louder, and in London a popular radicalism developed in opposition to the Whig oligarchy. The outcry was taken up as well in the North American colonies, where two million British subjects champed at the bit of imperial rule.

Chronology

THE NEW EUROPEAN POWERS

1707	England and Scotland unite to form Great Britain
(1713–1714)	Peace of Utrecht ends War of the Spanish Succession (1702–1714)
1714	British Crown passes to house of Hanover
1721	Treaty of Nystad ends Great Northern War (1700–1721)
1721–1742	Sir Robert Walpole leads British House of Commons
1722	Peter the Great of Russia creates Table of Ranks
1740	Frederick the Great of Prussia invades Austrian province of Silesia
1748	Treaty of Aix-la-Chapelle ends War of the Austrian Succession (1740–1748)
(1756–1763)	Seven Years' War pits Prussia and Britain against Austria, France, and Russia
1773–1775	Pugachev's Revolt in Russia
1774	Boston Tea Party
1775	American Revolution begins
1785	Catherine the Great of Russia issues Charter of the Nobility

America Revolts

Britain's triumph in the Seven Years' War (1756–1763) had come at great financial cost to the nation. Then, as now, the cost of world domination was staggering. George III (1760–1820) came to the throne with a taste for reform and a desire to break the Whig stranglehold on government. He was to have limited success on both counts. In 1763, the king and his ministers agreed that reform of colonial administration was long overdue. Such reform would have the twin benefit of shifting part of the burden of taxation from Britain to North America and of making the commercial side of colonization pay.

This was sound thinking all around, and in due course, Parliament passed a series of duties on goods imported into the colonies, including glass, wine, coffee, tea, and most notably sugar. The so-called Sugar Act (1764) was followed by the Stamp Act (1765), a tax on printed papers such as newspapers, deeds, and court documents. Both acts imposed taxes in the colonies similar to those that already existed in Britain. Accompanying the acts were administrative orders designed to cut into the lucrative black market trade. The government instituted new rules for searching ships and transferred authority over smuggling from the local colonial courts to Britain's Admiralty courts. Though British officials could only guess at the value of the new duties imposed, it was believed that with effective enforcement, £150,000 would be raised. All this would go toward paying the vast costs of colonial administration and security.

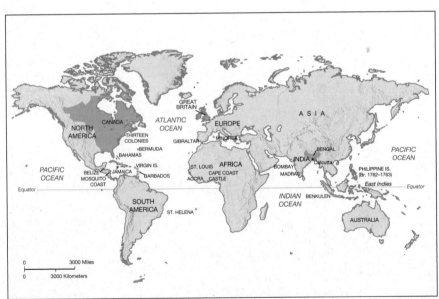

THE FIRST BRITISH EMPIRE, CA. 1763. The empire was the result of commercial enterprise and Britain's military successes.

British officials were perplexed when these mild measures met with a ferocious response. Assemblies of nearly every colony officially protested the Sugar Act and petitioned for its repeal. Riots followed passage of the Stamp Act. Tax collectors were hounded out of office, their resignations precipitated by threats and acts of physical violence. In Massachusetts, mobs that included political leaders in the colony razed the homes of the collector and the lieutenant-governor. However much the colonists might have regretted the violence that was done, they believed that an essential political principle was at stake. It was a principle of the freedom of an Englishman.

At their core, the American colonists' protests underscored the vitality of the British political system. The Americans argued that they could not be taxed without their consent and that their consent could come only through representation in Parliament. Since there were no colonists in Parliament, Parliament had no jurisdiction over the property of the colonists. Taxation without representation was tyranny. There were a number of subtleties to this argument that were quickly lost as political rhetoric and political action heated up. First, the colonists did tax themselves through their own legislatures, and much of that money paid the costs of administration and defense. Second, as a number of pamphleteers pointed out, no one in the colonies had asked the British government to send regiments of the army into North America. When defense was necessary, the colonists had proven themselves both able and cooperative in providing it. A permanent tax meant a permanent army, and a standing army was as loathed in the colonies as it was in Britain.

The passion generated in the colonies over the issue of taxation without parliamentary representation was probably no greater than that generated in Britain. For the British, the principle at issue was parliamentary sovereignty. Once the terms of debate had been so defined, it was difficult for either side to find a middle ground.

Parliamentary moderates managed repeal of the Stamp Act and most of the clauses of the Sugar Act, but they also joined in passing the **Declaratory Act** (1766), which stated unequivocally that Parliament held sovereign jurisdiction over the colonies "in all cases whatsoever." This claim became more and more difficult to sustain as colonial leaders began to cite the elements of resistance theory that had justified the Revolution of 1688. Then the protest had been against the tyranny of the king; now it was against the tyranny of Parliament. American propagandists claimed that a conspiracy existed to deprive the colonists of their property and rights, to enslave them for the benefit of special interests and corrupt politicians.

The techniques of London radicals who opposed parliamentary policy were adopted by colonists. Newspapers were used to whip up public support; boycotts brought ordinary people into the political arena; public demonstrations such as the Boston Tea Party (1774) were carefully designed to intimidate; and mobs were occasionally given free rein. Violence was met by violence, and in 1775, full-scale fighting was under way. Eight years later, Britain withdrew from a war it could not win, and the American colonies were left to govern themselves.

SUMMARY

The Rise of Russia Peter the Great guided Russia's development into a major European power. Peter borrowed from the West in an effort to increase Russia's power. His reforms were aimed at enhancing military efficiency. Nonetheless, they transformed many aspects of Russian life. Peter's policies made a bad situation worse for Russia's serfs and peasants. Population growth increased the wealth of the landowning class. Catherine the Great drew on Enlightenment ideas to enhance the effectiveness of her government. Her reforms did little to improve the lives of the vast majority of her people.

The Two Germanies Conflict between Prussia and Austria was at the heart of central European politics from the mid-eighteenth century on. Frederick William, the Great Elector, began the process of turning Brandenburg-Prussia into a military power. Frederick II built on the successes of his father, using the army and state resources he inherited to expand Prussia's territory. By the end of Frederick II's reign, Prussia had become a model for bureaucratic organization, military reform, and enlightened rule. Austria faced a number of challenges including: powerful rivals, decentralized government, and insufficient revenue. Charles V designated his daughter Maria Theresa as his heir in the Pragmatic Sanction. Prussia invaded shortly after she assumed the throne. Despite Hungarian help, Austria lost Silesia. Maria Theresa and her son Joseph II carried out a series of important reforms. The War of the Austrian Succession made Austria and Prussia permanent enemies. The Seven Years' War established Prussia as a major power and initiated a long period of peace in eastern Europe. Prussia, Russia, and Austria partitioned Poland, each taking a piece.

The Greatness of Great Britain By the middle of the eighteenth century, Great Britain had become the leading power of Europe. British military and economic power was supported by its constitutional government. The constitution established a limited, but nonetheless important, role for the monarch. The Crown worked to coordinate the work of the two houses of Parliament and facilitate the passage of governmental programs. The advent of political parties was critical to parliamentary management. Britain's triumph in the Seven Years' War came at a great financial cost. Efforts to impose some of those costs on its North American colonies created tensions that culminated in the American Revolution.

QUESTIONS FOR REVIEW

1. What were the great powers of Europe in the eighteenth century and in what ways was there a balance of power among them?
2. What did Peter I and Catherine II of Russia accomplish during their reigns that justifies the title "the Great"?
3. How was the tiny state of Brandenburg-Prussia able to make itself into one of Europe's major powers, and what did that mean for the Austrian Empire?
4. How did Britain's theory of mixed government and its parliamentary party system assist its rise to become Europe's great imperial power?
5. How and why did the balance of power shift during the eighteenth century?

Culture and Society in Eighteenth-Century Europe

Eighteenth-Century Culture

The eighteenth century spawned a rich and costly culture. Decorative architecture, especially interior design, reflected the increasing sociability of the aristocracy. Entertainment, especially music, became a central part of aristocratic culture.

Musical entertainments in European country houses were matched by the literary and philosophical entertainments of the urban salons. The salons, especially in Paris, blended the aristocracy and bourgeoisie with the leading intellectuals of the age. At formal meetings, papers on scientific or philosophical topics were read and discussed. At informal gatherings, new ideas were examined and exchanged. The most influential thinkers of the day presented the ideas of the **Enlightenment,** a new European outlook on religion, society, and politics.

The Enlightenment

The Enlightenment was less a set of ideas than it was a set of attitudes. At its core was a critical questioning of traditional institutions, customs, and morals.

In France, Enlightenment intellectuals were called **philosophes** and claimed all the arts and sciences as their purview. *The Encyclopedia* (35 volumes, 1751–1780), edited by Denis Diderot (1713–1784), was one of the greatest achievements of the age. Entitled the *Systematic Dictionary of the Sciences, Arts, and Crafts*, it attempted to summarize all acquired knowledge and to dispel all imposed superstitions.

The Enlightenment was by no means a strictly French phenomenon. Its greatest figures included the Scottish economist Adam Smith (1723–1790), the Italian legal reformer Cesare Beccaria (1738–1794), and the German philosopher Immanuel Kant (1724–1804). In France, it began among anti-establishment critics; in Scotland and the German states it flourished in the universities; and in Prussia, Austria, and Russia it was propagated by the monarchy.

No brief summary can do justice to the diversity of enlightened thought in eighteenth-century Europe. Because it was an attitude of mind rather than a set of shared beliefs, there are many contradictory strains to follow. In his famous essay *What Is Enlightenment?* (1784), Immanuel Kant described it simply as freedom to use one's own intelligence.

During the Enlightenment, salons showcased the most influential thinkers of the day. Here, a lecture is being given at the house of Madame Geoffrin.

The Spirit of the Enlightenment

In 1734, a small book entitled *Philosophical Letters Concerning the English Nation* appeared in France. Its author, Voltaire (1694–1778), who had spent two years in Britain, demonstrated again and again the superiority of the British. They practiced religious toleration and were not held under the sway of a venal clergy. They valued people for their merits rather than their birth. Their political constitution placed limits on the power of kings. They made national heroes of their scientists, poets, and philosophers. In all of this, Voltaire contrasted British virtue with French vice. He attacked the French clergy and nobility directly and the French monarchy implicitly.

Voltaire. In France, Voltaire's book *Philosophical Letters* was officially banned and publicly burned, and a warrant was issued for his arrest. Nonetheless, it ignited a movement that would soon spread to nearly every corner of Europe.

Born in Paris in 1694 into a bourgeois family with a court office, François-Marie Arouet began his public career as a poet and playwright. It was not long before he was imprisoned in the Bastille for penning verses that maligned the honor of the regent of France. When released from prison, he insulted a nobleman, who retaliated by having his servants publicly beat Voltaire. Voltaire issued a challenge for a duel, a greater insult than the first, given his low birth. He was again sent to the Bastille and was released only on the promise that he would leave the country immediately.

Thus Voltaire found himself in Britain. When he returned to Paris in 1728, it was with the intention of popularizing Britain to Frenchmen. He wrote and produced a number of plays and began writing the *Philosophical Letters*, a work that not only secured his reputation but also forced him into exile at the village of Cirey, where he moved in with the Marquise du Châtelet (1706–1749).

The Marquise du Châtelet, though only 27 at the time of her liaison with Voltaire, was one of the leading advocates of Newtonian science in France. She built a laboratory in her home and introduced Voltaire to experimental science. While she undertook the immense challenge of translating Newton into French, Voltaire worked on innumerable intellectual projects. It was one of the most productive periods of his life, and when the Marquise du Châtelet died in 1749, Voltaire was crushed.

Then older than 50, Voltaire began his travels. He was invited to Berlin by Frederick the Great, but the relationship between these two great egotists was predictably stormy and resulted in Voltaire's arrest in Frankfurt. Finally allowed to leave Prussia, Voltaire eventually settled in Geneva, where he quickly became embroiled in local politics and was asked to leave.

Voltaire was tired of wandering and tired of being chased. He was also deeply affected by the tragic earthquake in Lisbon in 1755, when thousands of people attending church services were killed. Optimism in the face of such a senseless tragedy was no longer possible. His black mood was revealed in *Candide* (1759), which was to become his enduring legacy.

Voltaire's greatest contribution to Enlightenment attitudes was probably his capacity to challenge all authority. He held nothing sacred. At the height of the French Revolution, Voltaire's body was removed from its resting place in Champagne and taken with great pomp to Paris and interred in the Pantheon, where the heroes of the nation were put to rest. When the monarchy was restored after 1815, his bones were unceremoniously dumped in a lime pit.

Hume. Some enlightened thinkers based their critical outlook on skepticism, the belief that nothing could be known for certain. When the Scottish philosopher David Hume (1711–1776) was accused of being an atheist, he countered the charge by saying that he was too skeptical to be certain that God did not exist.

Hume made two seminal contributions to Enlightenment thought. He exploded the synthesis of Descartes by arguing that neither matter nor mind could be proved to exist with any certainty. Only perceptions existed, either as impressions of material objects or as ideas. If human understanding was based on sensory perception rather than on reason, then there could be no certainty in the universe. Hume's second point launched a frontal attack on established religion. If there could be no certainty, then the revealed truths of Christian religion could have no basis. In his historical analysis of the origins of religion, Hume argued that "religion grows out of hope or fear." He attacked the core of Christian explanations that were based on either Providence or miracles by arguing that for anyone who understood the basis of human perception, it would take a miracle to believe in miracles.

Montesquieu. In 1749, Hume received in the mail a work from an admiring Frenchman, entitled *The Spirit of the Laws* (1748). The sender was Charles-Louis de Secondat, Baron Montesquieu (1689–1755). Born in Bordeaux, he ultimately inherited both a large landed estate and the office of president of the Parlement of Bordeaux. His novel *Persian Letters* (1721) was a brilliant satire of Parisian morals, French society, and European religion all bound together by the story of a Persian despot who leaves his harem to learn about the ways of the world. The use of the Persian outsider allowed Montesquieu to comment on the absurdity of European customs in general and French practices in particular. The device of the harem allowed him to titillate his audience with exotic sexuality.

In both *Persian Letters* and *The Spirit of the Laws*, Montesquieu explored how liberty could be achieved and despotism avoided. He divided all forms of government into republics, monarchies, and despotisms. Each form had its own peculiar spirit: virtue and moderation in republics, honor in monarchies, and fear in despotisms. Like each form, each spirit was prone to abuse and had to be restrained if republics were not to give way to vice and excess, monarchies to corruption, and despotisms to repression.

For Montesquieu, a successful government was one in which powers were separated and checks and balances existed within the institutions of the state. As befitted a provincial magistrate, he insisted on the absolute separation of the judiciary from all other branches of government. The law needed to be independent, impartial, and just. Montesquieu advocated that law codes be reformed and reduced mainly to regulate crimes against persons and property. Punishment should fit the crime but should be humane. Montesquieu was one of the first to advocate the abolition of torture. Like most Europeans of his age, he saw monarchy as the only realistic form of government, but he argued that for a monarchy to be successful, it needed a strong and independent aristocracy to restrain its tendency toward corruption and despotism.

Enlightened Education and Social Reform. Enlightened thinkers attacked established institutions, above all the Church. Most were **deists** who believed in the existence of God on rational grounds only. Following the materialistic ideas of the new science, deists believed that nature conformed to its own material laws and operated without divine intervention. God, in a popular Enlightenment image, was like a clockmaker who constructed the elaborate mechanism, wound it, and gave the pendulum its first swing. After that, the clock worked by itself. Deists were accused of being anti-Christian, and they certainly opposed the ritual forms of both Catholic and Protestant worship as well as the role of the Church in education, for education was the key to an enlightened view of the future.

Jean-Jacques Rousseau (1712–1778) attacked the educational system. His tract on education, disguised as the romantic novel *Émile* (1762), argued that children should be taught by appealing to their interests rather than with strict discipline. Education was crucial because the Enlightenment was dominated by the idea of the British philosopher John Locke (1632–1704) that the mind was blank at birth, a *tabula rasa*—"white paper void of all characters"—and that it was filled up by experience. Contrary to the arguments of Descartes, Locke wrote, in *An Essay Concerning Human Understanding* (1690), that there were no innate ideas and no good or evil that was not conditioned by experience. For Locke, as for a host of thinkers after him, good and evil were defined as pleasure and pain. We do good because it is pleasurable, and we avoid evil because it is painful. Morality was a sense experience rather than a theological one. It was also relative rather than absolute. This was an observation that derived from increased interest in non-European cultures.

By the middle of the eighteenth century, the pleasure/pain principle enunciated by Locke had come to be applied to the foundations of social organization. If personal good was pleasure, then social good was happiness. The object of government, in the words of the Scottish moral philosopher Francis Hutcheson (1694–1746), was "the greatest happiness of the greatest number." This principle was at the core of *Crimes and Punishments* (1764), Cesare Beccaria's pioneering work of legal reform. Laws were instituted to promote happiness within society. They had to be formulated equitably for both criminal and victim. Punishment was to act as a deterrent to crime rather than as retribution. Therefore Beccaria advocated the abolition of torture to gain confessions, the end of capital punishment, and the rehabilitation of criminals through the improvement of penal institutions.

It was in refashioning the world through education and social reform that the Enlightenment revealed its orientation toward the future. "Optimism" was a word invented in the eighteenth century to express this feeling of liberation from the weight of centuries of traditions.

Chronology

MAJOR WORKS OF THE ENLIGHTENMENT

1690	An Essay Concerning Human Understanding (Locke)
1721	Persian Letters (Baron Montesquieu)
1734	Philosophical Letters Concerning the English Nation (Voltaire)
1739	A Treatise of Human Nature (Hume)
1740	Pamela (Richardson)
1748	An Enquiry Concerning Human Understanding (Hume); The Spirit of the Laws (Baron Montesquieu)
1751–1780	Encyclopedia (Diderot)
1759	Candide (Voltaire)
1762	Émile; The Social Contract (Rousseau)
1764	Crimes and Punishments (Beccaria)
1784	What Is Enlightenment? (Kant)
1795	The Progress of the Human Mind (Marquis de Condorcet)
1798	An Essay on the Principles of Population (Malthus)

The Impact of the Enlightenment

Paradoxically, enlightened political reform took firmer root in eastern Europe, where the ideas were imported, than in western Europe, where they originated. It was absolute rulers who were most successful in borrowing Enlightenment reforms.

Enlightened ideas informed the eastern European reform movement that began around mid-century, especially in the areas of law, education, and the extension of religious toleration. The Prussian jurist Samuel von Cocceji (1679–1755) initiated the reform of Prussian law and legal administration. Cocceji's project was to make the enforcement of law uniform throughout the realm, to prevent judicial corruption, and to produce a single code of Prussian law. The code, finally completed in the 1790s, reflected the principles of criminal justice articulated by Beccaria. In Russia, the Law Commission summoned by Catherine the Great in 1767 never did complete its work. Nevertheless, profoundly influenced by Montesquieu, Catherine attempted to abolish torture and to introduce the Beccarian principle that the accused was innocent until proven guilty. In Austria, Joseph II presided over a wholesale reorganization of the legal system. Courts were centralized, laws were codified, and torture and capital punishment were abolished.

Enlightenment ideas also underlay the efforts to improve education in eastern Europe. Efforts at compulsory education were first undertaken in Russia under Peter the Great, but these were aimed at the compulsory education of the nobility. Catherine extended the effort to the provinces, attempting to educate a generation of Russian teachers. She was especially eager for women to receive primary schooling, although the prejudice against educating women was too strong to overcome. Austrian and Prussian reforms were more successful in extending the reach of primary education, even if its content remained weak.

Religious toleration was the area in which the Enlightenment had its greatest impact in Europe, though again this was most visible in the eastern countries. Freedom of worship for Catholics was barely whispered about in Britain, and neither France nor Spain was moved to tolerate Protestants. Nevertheless, within these parameters there were some important changes in the religious makeup of the western European states. In Britain, Protestant dissenters were no longer persecuted for their beliefs. By the end of the eighteenth century, the number of Protestants outside the Church of England was growing, and by the early nineteenth century, discrimination against such Protestants was all but eliminated. In France and Spain, relations between the national church and the papacy were undergoing a reorientation. Both states were asserting more independence—both theologically and financially—from Rome.

In eastern Europe, enlightened ideas about religious toleration did take effect. Catherine the Great abandoned persecution of a Russian Orthodox sect known as the Old Believers. Prussia had always tolerated various Protestant groups, and with the conquest of Silesia it acquired a large Catholic population. Catholics were guaranteed freedom of worship; Frederick the Great even built a Catholic church in Berlin to symbolize this policy. Austria extended enlightened ideas about toleration furthest. Maria Theresa was a devout Catholic and actually increased religious persecution in her realm, but Joseph II rejected his mother's dogmatic position. In 1781, he issued the **Patent of Toleration,** which granted freedom of worship to Protestants and members of the Eastern Orthodox church. The following year he extended this toleration to Jews. Joseph's attitude toward toleration was as practical as it was enlightened. He believed that the revocation of the Edict of Nantes— which had granted limited toleration to Protestants—at the end of the seventeenth century had been an economic disaster for France, and he encouraged religious toleration as a means to economic progress.

Joseph's belief that religious toleration could promote economic progress was in keeping with the ferment of new ideas on economics in Europe. A science of economics was first articulated during the Enlightenment. A group of French thinkers known as the **physiocrats** subscribed to the view that land was wealth and thus argued that agricultural activity, especially improved means of farming and livestock breeding, should take first priority in state reforms. Because wealth came from land, taxation should be based only on land ownership, a principle that was coming into increased prominence, despite the opposition of the landowning class. Physiocratic ideas combined a belief in the sanctity of private property with the need for the state to increase agricultural output. Ultimately, the physiocrats, like the great Scottish economic theorist Adam Smith, came to believe that government should cease to interfere with private economic activity. They articulated the doctrine *laissez faire, laissez passer*—"let it be, let it go." The ideas of Adam Smith and the physiocrats, particularly the **laissez-faire** doctrine, ultimately formed the basis for nineteenth-century economic reform.

If the Enlightenment did not initiate a new era, it did offer a new vision. Enlightened thinkers challenged existing ideas and existing institutions. A new emphasis on self and on pleasure led to a new emphasis on happiness. All three fed into the distinctively Enlightenment idea of self-interest. Happiness and self-interest were values that would inevitably corrode the old social order, which was based on principles of self-sacrifice and corporate identity. It was only a matter of time.

Eighteenth-Century Society

Eighteenth-century society was a hybrid of old and new. It remained highly stratified socially, politically, and economically. Birth and occupation determined wealth, privilege, and quality of life as much as they had in the past. But in the eighteenth century, the gulf between top and bottom was being filled by a thriving middle class, a **bourgeoisie,** as they were called in France. There were now more paths toward the middle and upper classes and more wealth to be distributed among people living above the level of subsistence, but at the top of society the nobility remained the privileged order in every European state.

The Nobility

Nobles were defined by their legal rights. They had the right to bear arms, the right to special judicial treatment, and the right to tax exemptions.

Though all who enjoyed these special rights were noble, not all nobles were equal. In England, the elite class was divided between the peers and the gentry. The peers held titles, were members of the House of Lords, and had a limited range of judicial and fiscal privileges. In the mid-eighteenth century there were only 190 British peers. The gentry, which numbered over 20,000, dominated the House of Commons and local legal offices but were not strictly members of the nobility. The French nobility was informally divided into the small group of peers known as the *Grandes*, whose ancient lineage, wealth, and power set them apart from all others; a rather larger service nobility whose privileges derived in one way or another from municipal or judicial service; and what might be called the country nobility, whose small estates and local outlook made their exemption from taxes vital to their survival.

These distinctions among the nobilities of the European states masked a more important one: wealth. In the eighteenth century, despite the phenomenal increase in mercantile activity, wealth was still calculated in profits from the ownership of land, and it was the wealthy landed nobility who set the tone of elite life in Europe.

Most nobles maintained multiple residences. The new style of aristocratic entertainment required more public space on the first floor, while the increasing demand for personal and familial privacy necessitated more space in the upper stories. The result was larger and more opulent homes.

The building of country houses was only one part of the conspicuous consumption of the privileged orders. Improvements in travel, in both transport and roads, permitted increased contact between members of the national elites. The grand tour of historical sites continued to be used as a substitute for formal education. The grand tour was also a means of introducing the European aristocracies to each other. Whether it was a Russian noble in Germany or a Briton in Prussia, all spoke French and shared a common cultural outlook.

Much of that outlook was cultivated in the **salons,** a social institution begun in the seventeenth century by French women that gradually spread throughout the continent. In the salons, especially those in Paris, the aristocracy and the bourgeoisie mingled with the leading intellectuals of the age, examining and exchanging new ideas. It was in the salons that the impact of the Enlightenment, the great European intellectual movement of the eighteenth century, first made itself felt.

The Bourgeoisie

The bourgeoisie provided the safety valve between the nobility and those who were acquiring wealth and power but who lacked the advantages of birth and position. They served vital functions in all European societies, dominating trade, both nationally and internationally. They made their homes in cities and did much to improve the quality of urban life. They developed their own culture and class identity and permitted successful individuals to enjoy a sense of pride and achievement.

In the eighteenth century, the bourgeoisie was growing in numbers and importance. Some of its members were able to pass into the nobility through the purchase of land or office. But for most, their own social group began to define its own values, which centered on the family and the home. Their homes became a social center for kin and neighbors, and their outlook on family life reflected new personal relationships.

Marriages were made for companionship as much as for economic advantage. Romantic love between husbands and wives was newly valued. So were children, whose futures came to dominate familial concern. Childhood was recognized as a separate stage of life and the education of children as one of the most important of parental concerns.

William Hogarth was famous for his satirical series paintings. *Marriage à la Mode*, ca. 1743, depicts the complicated negotiations between a wealthy merchant and an aristocrat for a marriage between their families and shows the progress of the arranged match to its end. In this scene of domestic disarray, second in the series, the marriage quickly proves to be a disaster.

Urban Elites. The bourgeoisie was strongest where towns were strongest: in western rather than in eastern Europe and in northern rather than southern Europe, with the notable exception of Italy. Holland was the exemplar of a bourgeois republic. More than half of the Dutch population lived in towns, and there was no significant aristocratic class to compete for power. At the end of the eighteenth century, the British middle classes probably constituted around 15 percent of the population, the French bourgeoisie less than 10 percent. By contrast, the Russian and Hungarian urban elites were less than 2 percent of the population of those states.

Like the nobility, the bourgeoisie constituted a diverse group. At the top were great commercial families engaged in the expanding international marketplace and reaping the profits of trade. In wealth and power they were barely distinguishable from the nobility. At the bottom were the so-called petite bourgeoisie: shopkeepers, craftsmen, and industrial employers. The solid core of the bourgeoisie was employed in trade, exchange, and service. Most were engaged in local or national commerce. Trade was the lifeblood of the city, for by itself the city could neither feed nor clothe its inhabitants. Most bourgeois fortunes were first acquired in trade. Finance was the natural outgrowth of commerce, and another segment of the bourgeoisie accumulated or preserved capital through the sophisticated financial instruments of the eighteenth century. Finally, the bourgeoisie were members of the burgeoning professions that provided services for the rich. Medicine, law, education, and the bureaucracy were all bourgeois professions, for the cost of acquiring the necessary skills could be borne only by those who were already wealthy.

The bourgeoisie grew as European urbanization continued steadily throughout the eighteenth century. In 1600, only 20 European cities contained as many as 50,000 people; in 1700, that number had risen to 32, and by 1800 it had increased to 48. In such cities, the demand for lawyers, doctors, merchants, and shopkeepers was almost insatiable.

Besides wealth, the urban bourgeoisie shared another characteristic: mobility. The aspiration of the bourgeoisie was to become noble, either through office or by acquiring rural estates. Many trading families left their wharves and counting-houses to acquire rural estates and live off rents. For the greater bourgeoisie the transition was easy; for the lesser it was usually just beyond their grasp. The bourgeoisie did not only imagine their discomfort; they were made to feel it at every turn. Despised from above, envied from below, they were the subject of jokes, of theater, and of popular songs. They were the first victims in the shady financial dealings of the crown and court, the first casualties in urban riots. Their one consolation was that as a group they got richer and richer. And as a group they began to develop a distinctive culture that reflected their qualities and aspirations.

Bourgeois Values. Although many members of the bourgeoisie aspired to noble status, others had no desire to wear the silks and furs that were reserved for the nobility or to attend the opening night at the opera decked in jewels and finery. In fact, such ostentation was alien to them. A real tension existed between the values of noble and bourgeois. The ideal noble was idle, wasteful, and ostentatious; the ideal bourgeois was industrious, frugal, and sober.

Even if the bourgeoisie did not constitute a class, they did share certain attitudes that constituted a culture. The wealthy among them participated in the new world of consumption, whether they did so lavishly or frugally. For those who aspired to more than their birth allowed, there was a loosening of the strict codes of dress that reserved certain fabrics, decorative materials, and styles to the nobility. They might acquire coaches and carriages to take them on the Sunday rides through the town gardens or to their weekend retreats in the suburbs.

Increasingly, the bourgeoisie was also beginning to travel. In Britain, whole towns were established to cater to leisure travelers. The southwestern town of Bath, famous since Roman times for the soothing qualities of its waters, was the most popular of all European resort towns. Brighton, a seaside resort on the south coast, quadrupled in size in the second half of the eighteenth century.

Leisure and Entertainment. Leisure activities of the bourgeoisie quickly became commercialized. Theaters and music halls proliferated. Voltaire's plays were performed before packed houses in Paris. In Venice, it was estimated that over 1,200 operas were produced in the eighteenth century.

Theater and concertgoing were part of the new attitude toward socializing that was one of the greatest contributions of the Enlightenment. Enlightened thinkers spread their views in the salons, and the salons soon spawned the academies, local scientific societies that, though led and patronized by provincial nobles, included large numbers of bourgeois members. The academies sponsored essay competitions, built up libraries, and became the local center for intellectual interchange. A less-structured form of sociability took place in the coffeehouses and tearooms that came to be a feature of even small provincial towns. In the early eighteenth century, there were over 2,000 London coffee shops where men—for the coffeehouse was largely a male preserve—could talk about politics, read the latest newspapers and magazines, and indulge their taste for this still-exotic beverage.

Above all, bourgeois culture was literate culture. Wealth and leisure led to mental pursuits—if not always to intellectual ones. The proliferation of relatively cheap printed material had an enormous impact on the lives of those who were able to afford it. This was the first great period of the newspaper and the magazine. The first daily newspaper appeared in London in 1702; 80 years later, 37 provincial towns had their own newspapers, and the London papers were read all over Britain.

For entertainment and serious political commentary the British reading public turned to magazines, of which there were over 150 separate titles by the 1780s. The most famous were *The Spectator*, which ran in the early part of the century and did much to set the tone for a cultured middle-class life, and the *Gentleman's Magazine*, which ran in the mid-century and was said to have had a circulation of nearly 15,000. The longest-lived of all British magazines was *The Ladies' Diary*, which continued in existence from 1704 to 1871 and doled out self-improvement, practical advice, and fictional romances in equal proportion.

The Ladies' Diary was not the only publication aimed at lettered bourgeois women. A growing body of both domestic literature and light entertainment was available to them. This included a vast number of teach-yourself books aimed at instructing women how best to organize domestic life or how to navigate the perils of polite society. Moral instruction, particularly on the themes of obedience and sexual fidelity, was also popular. But the greatest output directed toward women was in the form of fanciful romances, from which a new genre emerged. The novel first appeared in its modern form in the 1740s.

Family Life. In the eighteenth century, a remarkable transformation in home life was under way, one that the bourgeoisie shared with the nobility: the celebration of domesticity. The image—and sometimes the reality—of the happy home, where love was the bond between husband and wife and between parents and children, came to dominate both the literary and visual arts. Only those who were wealthy enough to afford to dispense with women's work could partake of the new domesticity, and only those who had been touched by Enlightenment ideas could attempt to make the change. But where it occurred, the transformation in the nature of family life was one of the most profound alterations in eighteenth-century culture.

The first step toward the transformation of family relationships was in centering the conjugal family in the home. In the past, the family was a less important structure for most people than the social groups to which they belonged or the neighborhood in which they lived. Marriage was an economic partnership at one end and a means to carry on lineage at the other. Individual fulfillment was not an object of marriage, and this attitude could be seen among the elites in the high level of arranged marriages, the speed with which surviving spouses remarried, and the formal and often brutal personal relationships between husbands and wives.

Patriarchy was the dominant value within the family. Husbands ruled over wives and children, making all of the crucial decisions that affected both the quality of their lives and their futures. It was believed that children were stained with the sin of Adam at birth and that only the severest upbringing could clean some of it away. Children were sent out first for wet-nursing, then at around the age of seven for boarding, either at school or in a trade, and finally into their own marriages.

This profile of family life began to change, especially in western Europe, during the second half of the eighteenth century. Though the economic elements of marriage remained strong, romantic and sexual attraction became a factor. Even in earlier centuries, parents did not simply assign a spouse to their children, but by the eighteenth century, adolescents themselves searched for their own marriage partners and exercised a strong negative voice in identifying unsuitable ones.

Companionate Marriage. The quest for compatibility, no less than the quest for romantic love, led to a change in personal relationships between spouses. Husbands and wives began spending more time with each other, developing common interests and pastimes. For the first time, houses were built to afford the couple privacy from their children, their servants, and their guests.

Couples had more time for each other because they were beginning to limit the size of their families. There were a number of reasons for this development, which again pertained only to the upper classes. For one thing, child mortality rates were declining among wealthy social groups. Virulent epidemic diseases like the plague, which knew no class lines, were gradually disappearing, and sanitation was improving. Bearing fewer children had an enormous impact on women's lives, reducing the danger of death and disablement in childbirth and giving women time to pursue domestic tasks. Many couples appear to have made a conscious decision to space births, though success was limited by the fact that the most common technique of birth control was coitus interruptus, or withdrawal.

New Attitudes Toward Children. The transformation in the quality of relationships between spouses was mirrored by an even greater transformation in attitudes toward children. Childhood now took on a new importance for many reasons. With the decline in mortality rates, parents could feel that their emotional investment in their children had a greater chance of fulfillment. Equally important were the new ideas about education, especially Locke's belief that the child enters into the world a blank slate whose personality is created through early education. This view placed a new responsibility on parents and gave them the concept of childhood as a stage through which individuals passed. This idea could be seen in the commercial sphere as well as in any other. In 1700, there was not a single shop in London that sold children's toys exclusively; by the 1780s, toy shops were everywhere. There were also shops that sold clothes specifically designed for children. Most important of all was the development of materials for the education of children.

The Snatched Kiss, or *The Stolen Kiss* (1750s), by Jean-Honoré Fragonard, was one of the "series paintings" popular in the late eighteenth century. A later canvas entitled *The Marriage Contract* shows the next step in the lives of the lovers.

The commercialization of childhood was, of course, directed at adults. More and more mothers were devoting their time to their children. Among the upper classes, the practice of wet-nursing began to decline. Children became companions to be taken on outings to the increasing number of museums or shows of curiosities.

The emergence of the bourgeoisie was one of the central social developments of the eighteenth century. The bourgeois culture, which emphasized a fulfilling home life, leisure pursuits, and literacy, soon came to dominate the values of educated society in general. But the population at large could not share this transformation of family life. Working women could afford neither the cost of instructional materials for their children nor the time to use them. Working women enjoyed no privacy in the hovels in which they lived with large families in single rooms. Wives and children were still beaten by husbands and fathers. By the end of the eighteenth century, two distinct family cultures coexisted in Europe, one based on companionate marriage and the affective bonds of parents and children and the other based on patriarchal dominance and the family as an economic unit.

The Masses

Although more Europeans were surviving than ever before, with more food, more housing, better sanitation, and even better charities, there was also more misery. Those who would have succumbed to disease or starvation a century before now survived from day to day, beneficiaries—or victims—of increased farm production and improved agricultural marketing. The market economy organized a more effective use of land as large farming enterprises gobbled up smaller units, but it created a widespread social problem. The landless agrarian laborer of the eighteenth century was the counterpart of the sixteenth century wandering beggar. In the cities, the plight of the poor was as desperate as ever.

Even the most openhearted charitable institutions were unable to cope with the massive increase in the poor.

Despite widespread poverty, many members of the lower orders were able to gain some benefit from existing conditions. The richness of popular culture, signified by a spread of literacy into the lower reaches of European society, was one indication of this change. So, too, were the reforms urged by enlightened thinkers to improve basic education and to improve the quality of life in the cities. For that segment of the lower orders that could keep its head above water, the eighteenth century offered new opportunities and new challenges.

Breaking the Cycle. Of all the legacies of the eighteenth century, none was more fundamental than the steady increase in European population that began around 1740. This was not the first time that Europe had experienced sustained population growth, but it was the first time that such growth was not checked by a demographic crisis. In 1700, the European population is estimated to have been 120 million. By 1800, it had grown 50 percent to over 180 million.

Ironically, the traditional pattern of European population found its theorist at the very moment that it was about to disappear. In 1798, Thomas Malthus (1766–1834) published *An Essay on the Principles of Population*. Reflecting on the history of European population, Malthus observed the cyclical pattern by which growth over one or two generations was checked by a crisis that significantly reduced population. From these lower levels, new growth began until it was checked and the cycle repeated itself. Because the number of people increased more quickly than did food supplies, the land could sustain only a certain level of population. When that level was near, the population became prone to a demographic check.

Patterns of Population. In the sixteenth and seventeenth centuries, the dominant pattern of the life cycle was high infant and child mortality, late marriages, and early death. All controlled population growth. Infant and child mortality rates were staggering; only half of those born reached the age of 10. On average, the child-bearing period for most women was 10 to 12 years, long enough to endure six pregnancies, which would result in three surviving children.

Three surviving children for every two adults would, of course, have resulted in a 50 percent rise in population in every generation. Celibacy was one limiting factor; urban death rates were another. Perhaps as much as 15 percent of the population in western Europe remained celibate either by entering religious orders that imposed celibacy or by lacking the personal or financial attributes necessary to marry. In the cities, rural migrants accounted for the appallingly high death rates. In addition, plagues carried away hundreds of thousands of people, wars halved populations of places in their path, and famine overwhelmed the weak and the poor.

The late seventeenth and early eighteenth centuries were a period of population stagnation if not actual decline. Not until the third or fourth decade of the eighteenth century did another growth cycle begin. It rapidly gained momentum throughout the Continent and showed no signs of abating after two full generations. Fertility was increasing as some women were marrying younger, thereby increasing their childbearing years. Illegitimacy rates were also rising.

But increasing fertility was only part of the picture. More significant was decreasing mortality. European warfare not only diminished in scale after the middle of the eighteenth century, it changed location as well. Rivalry for colonial empires removed the theater of conflict from European communities. So did the increase in naval warfare. As warfare abated, so did epidemic disease. The plague had all but disappeared from western Europe by the middle of the eighteenth century.

Public health improvements also played a role in population increases. Urban sanitation was becoming more effective. Clean water supplies, organized waste and sewage disposal, and strict quarantines were increasingly part of urban regulations. The use of doctors and trained midwives helped to lower the incidence of stillbirth and decreased the number of women who died in childbirth. Almost everywhere, levels of infant and child mortality were decreasing. More people were being born, and more were surviving to adulthood. The result was renewed population growth.

Agricultural Improvements. In the past, if warfare or epidemic diseases failed to check population growth, famine would have done the job. How the European economy conquered famine in the eighteenth century is a complicated story. There was no single breakthrough that accounts for the ability to feed the tens of millions of additional people who now inhabited the Continent. Holland and Britain used dynamic new agricultural techniques, but most European agriculture was still mired in the time-honored practices that had endured for centuries. Not everyone could be fed or fed adequately. Widespread famine might have disappeared, but slow starvation and chronic undernourishment had not. Hunger was more common at the end of the eighteenth century than at the beginning, and the nutritional content of a typical diet may have reached its lowest point in European history.

Nevertheless, Europe's capacity to sustain rising levels of population can be explained only in terms of agricultural improvement. Quite simply, European farmers were now producing more food and marketing it better. In the most advanced societies, this was a result of conscious efforts to make agriculture more efficient. In traditional open-field agriculture, communities quickly ran up against insurmountable obstacles to growth. The three-field crop rotation system left a significant proportion of land fallow each year, while the concentration on subsistence cereal crops progressively eroded the land that was in production. Common farming was only as strong as the weakest member of the community. There was little incentive for successful individuals to plow profits back into the land, through either the purchase of equipment or the increase of livestock.

Livestock was a crucial variable in agricultural improvement. As long as there was barely enough food for humans to eat, only essential livestock could be kept alive over the winter. Oxen, which were still the ordinary beasts of burden, and pigs and poultry, which required only minimal feed, were the most common. But few animals meant little manure, and without manure the soil could not easily be regenerated.

Around the middle of the seventeenth century, solutions to these problems began to appear. The first change was consolidation of landholdings so that traditional crop rotations could be abandoned. A second innovation was the introduction of **fodder crops,** some of which—such as clover—added nutrients to the soil, while others—such as turnips—were used to feed livestock. Better grazing and better winter feed increased the size of herds, and new techniques of animal husbandry, particularly crossbreeding, produced hardier strains. It was quite clear that the key to increased production lay in better fertilization, and by the eighteenth century, some European farmers had broken through the "manure barrier." Larger herds, the introduction of clover crops, the use of human waste from towns, and even the first experiments with lime as an artificial fertilizer were all part of the new agricultural methods.

The New Staples. Along with the new crops that helped to nourish both soil and animals came new crops that helped to nourish people. Indian corn, or maize, was a staple crop for Native Americans and gradually came to be grown in most parts of western Europe. Maize not only had higher nutritional value than most other cereals, it also yielded more food per acre than did traditional grains. So, too, did the potato, which also entered the European diet from the New World. The potato grew in poor soil, required less labor, and yielded an abundant and nutritious harvest. It rapidly took hold in Ireland and parts of Prussia, from which it spread into eastern Europe.

It must be stressed, however, that these new developments involved only a very narrow range of producers. The new techniques were expensive, and knowledge of the new crops spread slowly. The most important improvements in agricultural production were more traditional ones. Basically, there was an increase in the amount of land that was used for growing. In Russia, Prussia, and Hungary, hundreds of thousands of new acres came under the plow; in the west, drainage schemes and forest clearance expanded productive capacity.

There was also an upswing in the efficiency with which agricultural products were marketed. From the seventeenth century onward, market agriculture was gradually replacing subsistence agriculture in most parts of Europe. Market agriculture had the advantage of allowing specialization on farms. Single-crop farming enabled farmers to benefit from the peculiarities of their own soil and climate. They could then exchange their surplus for the range of crops they needed to subsist. Market exchange was facilitated by improved transportation and communication and above all by the increase in the population of towns, which provided demand. The new national and international trade in large quantities of grain evened out regional variations in harvests and went a long way toward reducing local grain shortages. The upkeep of roads, the building of canals, and the clearing of waterways created a national lifeline for the movement of grain.

Finally, it is believed that the increase in agricultural productivity owed something to a change in climate that took place in the late eighteenth century. The European climate is thought to have been unusually cold and wet during the seventeenth century, and it seems to have gradually warmed during the eighteenth century.

The Plight of the Poor. Incremental improvements in agriculture, transportation, and climate contributed to the most serious social problem of the eighteenth century: the dramatic population increase of poor people throughout Europe.

It is impossible to gauge the number of European poor or to separate them into categories of greater and greatest misery. The truly indigent—the starving poor—probably made up 10 to 15 percent of most societies, perhaps as many as 20 million people throughout the Continent. They were most prevalent in towns but were an increasing burden on the countryside, where they wandered in search of agricultural employment. Yet the problem of poverty was not to be seen only among the destitute. In fact, the uniqueness of the poor in the eighteenth century is that they were drawn from social groups that even in the hungry times of the early seventeenth century had been successful subsistence producers.

It was easy to see why poverty was increasing. The relentless advance of population drove up the price of food and drove down the price of wages. Only in Britain did wages nearly keep pace with prices. Rising prices made land more valuable. At the beginning of the eighteenth century, as the first wave of population expansion hit western Europe, smallholdings began to decrease in size. The custom of partible inheritance, by which each son received a share of land, shrank the average size of a peasant holding below that necessary to sustain an average-size family, let alone a family that was growing larger.

As holdings contracted, the portion of the family income that was derived from wage labor expanded. In such circumstances, males were more valuable than females, either as farmers or laborers, and there is incontrovertible evidence that European rural communities practiced female infanticide. In the end, however, it became increasingly difficult for the peasant family to remain on the land. Small freeholders were forced to borrow against future crops until a bad harvest led to foreclosure. Many were allowed to lease back their own lands, on short terms and at high rents, but most swelled the ranks of agricultural laborers, migrating during the planting and harvest seasons, suffering cruelly during winter and summer.

Emigration was the first logical consequence of poverty. In places where rural misery was greatest, such as Ireland, whole communities pulled up stakes and moved to America. Frederick the Great attracted hundreds of thousands of emigrants to Prussia by offering them land. But most rural migrants did not move to new rural environments. Rather, they followed the well-trodden paths to the cities. Many traditional domestic crafts were evolving into industrial

The poverty of eighteenth-century London slums was a favorite subject of the English artist William Hogarth. *Gin Lane* depicts the London poor in alcoholic delirium, their only escape from the misery of their daily lives.

activities. In the past, peasants supplemented their family income by processing raw materials in the home. Spinning, weaving, and sewing were common cottage industries in which the workers took in the work, supplied their own equipment, and were paid by the piece. Now, especially in the cloth trades, a new form of industrial activity was being organized. Factories, usually located in towns or larger villages, assembled workers together, set them at larger and more efficient machines, and paid them for their time rather than for their output. Families who were unable to support themselves from the land had no choice but to follow the movement of jobs.

Caring for the Poor. Neither state nor private charities could cope with the flood of poor immigrants. Hospitals, workhouses, and, more ominously, prisons were established or expanded to deal with them. Hospitals were residential asylums rather than places for health care. They took in the old, the incapacitated, and, increasingly, the orphaned young. Workhouses existed for those who were capable of work but incapable of finding it. In most places, workhouses, which were supposed to improve the values of the idle poor by keeping them busy, served only to improve the profits of the industrialists, who rented out workhouse inmates at below-market wages. Prisons grew with crime. There were spectacular increases in crimes against property in all eighteenth-century cities, and despite severe penalties that could include hanging for petty theft, more criminals were incarcerated than executed.

Popular Culture. While many people endured unrelieved misery, others lived comfortably by the standards of the age, and almost everyone believed that things were better than they had ever been before. Popular culture was a rich mixture of family and community activities that provided outlets from the pressures of work and the vagaries of fortune. It was no less sustaining to the population at large than was the purely literate culture of the elite and no less vital as a means of explanation for everyday events than the theories of the philosophers or the programs of the philosophes.

In fact, the line between elite and popular culture in the eighteenth century was a thin one. For one thing, there was still much mixing of social classes in both rural and urban environments. Occasions of display, such as festivals, village fairs, or religious holidays, brought entire communities together and reinforced their collective identities. Moreover, there were many shared elements between the two cultures. All over Europe, literacy was increasing. Men were more likely to have learned to read than women, as were inhabitants of urban areas. As the rates of female literacy rose, so did overall rates, for women took the lead in teaching children.

Popular literacy spawned popular literature in remarkable variety. Religious tracts were found throughout Europe. Romances, the staple of lending libraries, were usually published and sold in inexpensive installments. The best-selling popular fiction, at least in western Europe, was melodramatic tales of knights and ladies from the age of chivalry.

Popular social activities continued to reflect the violent and even brutal nature of day-to-day existence. Village festivals were still the safety valve of youth gangs who enforced sexual morals by shaming husbands whose wives were unfaithful or women whose reputations were sullied. Many holidays were celebrated by sporting events that pitted inhabitants of one village against those of another. These almost always turned into free-for-alls in which broken bones were common and deaths were not unknown.

Even more popular were the so-called blood sports involving animals. Dogfighting and cockfighting are among those that still survive today. Less attractive to the modern mind were bearbaiting or bull running, in which the object was the slaughter of a large beast over a prolonged period of time. Blood sports were not confined to the masses—foxhunting and bullfighting were pastimes for the very rich—but they formed a significant part of local social activity.

SUMMARY

Eighteenth-Century Culture   At the heart of the Enlightenment was a questioning of traditional institutions, customs, and morals. Voltaire embodied the spirit of the Enlightenment and played a key role in the popularization of Enlightenment thought. David Hume's skepticism was the basis for his attack on established religion. Baron Montesquieu took an enlightened approach to the problem of creating and maintaining a good government. Enlightened thinkers attacked established institutions, above all the Church. Jean-Jacques Rousseau contributed to the vigorous eighteenth-century debate about education. Absolute rulers in eastern Europe were influenced by Enlightenment ideas. Religious toleration was the area in which the Enlightenment had its greatest impact. A science of economics was first articulated during the Enlightenment.

Eighteenth-Century Society   In the eighteenth century a new and vital middle class, the bourgeoisie, emerged to fill the gap between the top and bottom of society. Nobles were defined by their legal rights. There was considerable diversity within the nobility. The nobility set the cultural tone. The bourgeoisie served vital functions in all European societies, dominating trade, both nationally and internationally. In the eighteenth century, the bourgeoisie was growing in numbers and importance, particularly in areas where urban centers were strongest. The bourgeoisie developed their own distinctive attitudes towards family, marriage, and childhood. Like the nobility, the bourgeoisie were a diverse group. Rapid population growth brought with it a massive increase in the poor. Despite widespread poverty, many members of the lower orders were able to gain some benefit from existing conditions. The eighteenth century saw a fundamental departure from traditional population cycles. Increased fertility, decreased mortality, and agricultural improvements all contributed to population growth. Hospitals, workhouses, and prisons were established or expanded to deal with the social and economic problems associated with the growth of the European poor.

QUESTIONS FOR REVIEW

1. What were the main elements of Enlightenment thought?
2. What social, moral, and religious traditions were challenged by the ideas of thinkers such as Voltaire, Hume, Montesquieu, and Rousseau?
3. How did the European nobility maintain its social eminence in the face of a new bourgeois culture created by an expanding middle class?
4. Why did Europe's population begin to grow so dramatically in the eighteenth century, and how did society respond to the challenges that it posed?

CHAPTER 20

The French Revolution and the Napoleonic Era, 1789–1815

The French Revolution and the Fall of the Monarchy

At the end of the eighteenth century France was a state in trouble, but it was not alone. Revolutionary incidents flared up throughout Europe in the second half of the eighteenth century in the Netherlands, Belgium, and Ireland. Absolute authority was challenged and sometimes modified. Across the Atlantic, American colonists concerned with the principle of self-rule had thrown off the yoke of the British in the War of Independence. But none of the events, including the American Revolution, was so violent in breaking with the old order, so extensive in involving millions of men and women in political action, and so consequential for the political futures of other European states as was the French Revolution. The triumphs and contradictions of the revolutionary experiment in democracy marked the end of the old order and the beginning of modern history. Politics would never be the same again.

The Political and Fiscal Crisis of Eighteenth-Century France

The French monarchy was in a state of perpetual financial crisis across the eighteenth century. Louis XV, like his great-grandfather Louis XIV, ruled as an absolute monarch, but he lacked sufficient funds to run the state. He sought loans to meet his needs as well as to pay the interest on existing debts, but the cycle of borrowing only made the situation worse. The monarchy tried to reduce expenditures, but such attempts were limited by the necessity of maintaining an effective and costly army and navy because of wars on both the Continent and in the colonies.

The nadir of Louis XV's reign came in 1763, with the French defeat in the Seven Years' War. The defeat not only left France barren of funds, it also promoted further expenditures for strengthening the French navy against the superior British fleet. The king saw taxation as the only way out of the financial trap in which he now found himself.

But raising taxes was far from an easy undertaking, and it was one that required the support of the aristocracy. The heightened tensions between the monarch and the aristocracy found expression in various institutions, especially the parlements, which were the 13 sovereign courts in the French judicial system, with their seats in Paris and a dozen provincial centers. Following the costly Seven Years' War, the parlements chose to exercise the power of refusal by blocking a proportional tax to be imposed on nobles and commoners alike.

By challenging the king, the parlements became a battleground between the elite, who claimed that they represented the nation, and the king, who said the nation was himself. As the king's needs increased in the second half of the eighteenth century, the situation was becoming intolerable for those exercising power and those aspiring to rule in the name and for the good of the nation. This tension between a growing debt that was undermining the monarchy and the increased ascendancy of an elite of nobles and bourgeois came to characterize the **Old Regime** in France.

When Louis XVI assumed the French throne in 1774, he was only 20 years old. He inherited a monarchy in a state of perpetual financial crisis. Not only did he inherit a trouble-ridden fiscal structure, but Louis XVI also made his own contributions to it, increasing the debt greatly by his involvement in the War of American Independence (1775–1783). Following the advice of a series of ministers, Louis sought structural solutions to the debt through a reformed fiscal policy, taxation, and other new sources of revenue, but each set of reforms offended different established interests. In the end, he resorted to an unusual but available step—the convening of the **Estates-General**—as a means of achieving reforms and providing financial stability for the state.

Historically, the Estates-General was the representative body of the three "estates," or social groups, of France—the clergy (the First Estate), the nobility (the Second Estate), and the commoners (the Third Estate). The **Third Estate** was composed of all those members of the realm who enjoyed no special privilege—28 million French people. The Estates-General had not been convened since 1614. Through this body and its duly chosen representatives, Louis XVI sought the consent of the nation to levy taxes. In the political organizing that took place in the winter of 1788–1789 the seeds of revolution were sown.

Convening the Estates-General

When Louis XVI announced in August 1788 that the Estates-General would meet at Versailles in May 1789, people from all walks of life hoped for some redress of their miseries. The king hoped that the clergy, nobility, and commoners would solve his fiscal problems. Every social group, from the nobles to the poorest laborers, had its own agenda and its own ideas about justice, social status, and economic well-being.

It was a time of great hope, especially for workers and peasants who had been buffeted by the rise in prices, decline in real wages, and the hunger that followed crop failures and poor harvests. There was new promise of a respite and a solution. Taxes could be discussed and changed, the state bureaucracy could be reformed—or better, abolished. Intellectuals discussed political alternatives in the salons of the wealthy. Nobles and bourgeois met in philosophical societies dedicated to enlightened thought. Commoners gathered in cafes to drink and debate. Although the poor often fell outside of the network of communication, they were not immune to the ideas that emerged. In the end, people of all classes had opinions and were more certain than ever of their right to express their ideas. Absolutism was in trouble, though Louis XVI did not know it, as people began to forge a collectively shared idea of politics. People now had a forum—the Estates-General—and a focus—the politics of taxation.

"If Only the King Knew." In conjunction with the political activity and in scheduled meetings, members of all three estates drew up lists of their problems. The people of France drew up grievance lists—known as **cahiers de doléances**—that were then carried to Versailles by the deputies elected to the Estates-General. The grievance lists contained the collective outpouring of problems of each estate and are important for two major reasons. First, they made clear the similarity of grievances shared throughout France. Second, they indicated the extent to which a common political culture, based on a concern with political reform, had permeated different levels of

This cartoon depicts the plight of the French peasants. An old farmer is bowed down under the weight of the privileged aristocracy and clergy while birds and rabbits, protected by unfair game laws, eat his crops.

French society. Both the privileged and the nonprivileged identified a common enemy in the system of state bureaucracy to which the monarch was so strongly tied. Although the king was still addressed with respect, new concerns with liberty, equality, property, and the rule of law were voiced.

"If only the king knew!" In that phrase, French men and women had for generations expressed their belief in the inevitability of their fate and the benevolence of their king. In 1789, peasants and workers were questioning why their lives could not be better, but they continued to express their trust in the king. Combined with their old faith was a new hope that a better time was coming.

The elected deputies arrived at Versailles at the beginning of May 1789 carrying in their valises and trunks the grievances of their estates.

The Crisis in Voting by Estate. Traditionally, each of the three orders was equally weighted. The arrangement favored the nobility, who controlled the first two estates, since the clergy themselves were often noble.

The Third Estate was adamant in its demand for vote by head. The privileged orders were equally firm in insisting on vote by order. Paralysis set in, as days dragged into weeks and the estates were unable to act. The body that was to save France from fiscal collapse was hopelessly deadlocked.

Abbé Emmanuel Joseph Sieyès (1748–1836), a member of the clergy, emerged as the critical leader of the Third Estate. He understood that although eighteenth-century French society continued to be divided by law and custom into a pyramid of three tiers, these orders or estates were obsolete in representing social realities. The base of the pyramid was formed by the largest of the three estates, those who worked—the bourgeoisie, the peasantry, and urban and rural workers—and produced the nation's wealth. He argued that as long as the First and Second Estates did not share their privileges and rights, the Third Estate were not a part of the French nation.

Under the influence of Sieyès and the reformist consensus that characterized their ranks, the delegates of the Third Estate decided to proceed with their own meetings. On 17 June 1789, joined by some sympathetic clergy, the Third Estate changed its name to the National Assembly as an assertion of its true repre-sentation of the French nation. Three days later, members of the new National Assembly found themselves locked out of their regular meeting room by the king's guard. Outraged by the insult, they moved to a nearby indoor tennis court, where they vowed to stay together for the purpose of writing a constitution. The event, known as the Oath of the Tennis Court, marked the end of the absolutist monarchy and the beginning of a new concept of the state that power resided in the people. The revolution had begun.

The Importance of Public Opinion. Throughout May and June 1789, Parisians trekked to Versailles to watch the deliberations and then they brought the news back to the capital. Deputies wrote home to their constituents to keep them abreast of events. Newspapers that reported daily on the wranglings and pamphleteers who analyzed them spread the news throughout the nation. Information, often conflicting, stirred up anxiety; news of conflict encouraged action.

The frustration and stalemate of the Estates-General threatened to put the spark to the kindling of urban unrest. The people of Paris had suffered through a harsh winter and spring under the burdens of high prices (especially of bread), lim-ited supplies, and relentless tax demands. The rioting of the spring had for the moment ceased as people waited for their problems to be solved by the deputies of the Estates-General. The suffering of the urban poor was not new, but their ability to connect economic hardships with the politics at Versailles and to blame the govern-ment was. As hopes began to dim with the news of political stalemate, news broke of the creation of the National Assembly. It was greeted with new anticipation.

The Outbreak of Revolutionary Action in 1789

The king, who had temporarily withdrawn from sight following the death of his son at the beginning of June, reemerged to meet with the representatives of each of the three estates and propose reforms, including a constitutional monarchy. But Louis XVI refused to accept the now popularly supported National Assembly as a legitimate body, insisting instead that he must rely on the three estates for advice.

MAP DISCOVERY

GREAT
BRITAIN

HOLY
ROMAN
EMPIRE

English Channel

AUSTRIAN
NETHERLANDS

Rhine R.

★ Lille
★ Arras
★ Le Havre ★ Amiens
Rouen
Brest ★
★ Reims ★ Metz
Caen
Dol
Rennes ★ Versailles ★ Paris ★ Nancy
Quiberon ● Seine R. ★ Troyes Strasbourg
Nantes ★ ★ Angers ★ Orléans Colmar
● Cholet Sancerre ★ Dijon ● ★ Besançon
Bourges
★ Poitiers Loire R. SWISS
CONFED.

Bay of
Biscay

FRANCE

Lyon ●
★ Bordeaux Grenoble
★ Valence
Garonne R. Rhone R.

Montauban ● Nîmes Avignon
Montpellier ★
SPAIN ★ Marseille ★ Toulon

Mediterranean Sea

Boundaries, 1789

★ Revolutionary centers

Areas of the Great Fear,
July – Aug. 1789

French boundaries, 1793

Counterrevolutionary activity

● Centers of counter-
revolutionary activity

Areas of insurrection

0   200 Miles
0   200 Kilometers

REVOLUTIONARY FRANCE

The French Revolution was not merely a Parisian phenomenon, as this map shows. Locate the revolutionary centers on the map. What feature is common to all of these centers? How do you explain their distribution throughout France? Pockets of insurrection and counter-revolution were scattered for the most part in the southeast and west. What did they have in common? What territories did France gain between 1789 and 1793 and why did it expand?

He simply did not understand that the choice was no longer his to make. He summoned troops to Versailles and began concentrating soldiers in Paris. Civilians continually clashed with members of the military, whom they jostled and jeered. The urban crowds recognized the threat of repression that the troops represented. People decided to meet force with force. To do so, they needed arms themselves—and they knew where to get them.

The Storming of the Bastille. On 14 July 1789, the irate citizens of Paris stormed the Bastille, a royal armory that also served as a prison for a handful of debtors. The storming of the Bastille became the great symbol in the revolutionary legend of the overthrow of the tyranny and oppression of the Old Regime. But it is significant for another reason. It was an expression of the power of the people to take politics into their own hands. Parisians were following the lead of their deputies in Versailles. They had formed a citizen militia known as the National Guard, and they were prepared to defend their concept of justice and law.

The people who stormed the Bastille were not the poor, the unemployed, the criminals, or the urban rabble, as their detractors portrayed them. They were petty tradesmen, shopkeepers, and wage-earners, who considered it their right to seize arms in order to protect their interests. The Marquis de Lafayette (1757–1834), a noble beloved of the people because of his participation in the American Revolution, helped organize the National Guard.

The king could no longer dictate the terms of the constitution. By their actions, the people in arms had ratified the National Assembly. Louis XVI was forced to yield. The events in Paris set off similar uprisings in cities and towns throughout France. But the revolution was not just an urban phenomenon: The peasantry had their own grievances and their own way of making a revolution.

Peasant Fear of an Aristocratic Plot. The precariousness of rural life and the increase in population in the countryside contributed to the permanent displacement and destitution of a growing sector of rural society. Without savings and destroyed by poor harvests, impoverished rural inhabitants wandered the countryside looking for odd jobs and eventually begging to survive. All peasants endured common obligations placed on them by the crown and the privileged classes. In spite of various strategies for survival, the lives of more and more peasant families were disrupted by the end of the eighteenth century as they were displaced from the land.

News of the events of Versailles and then of the revolutionary action in Paris did not reassure rural inhabitants. By the end of June the hope of deliverance from crippling taxes and dues was rapidly fading. The news of the Oath of the Tennis Court and the storming of the Bastille terrified country folk, who saw the actions as evidence of an aristocratic plot that threatened sorely needed reforms. As information moved along postal routes in letters from delegates to their supporters, and as news was repeated in the Sunday market gatherings, distortions and exaggerations crept in. It seemed to rural inhabitants that their world was falling apart.

That state of affairs was aggravated as increasing numbers of peasants were pushed off the land to seek employment as transient farm laborers, moving from one area to another with the cycles of sowing and harvesting. Often traveling in groups, hordes of vagabonds struck fear into the hearts of farm workers, trampling crops and sleeping in open fields. Peasants were sure that the unfortunate souls were brigands paid by the local aristocracy to persecute a peasantry already stretched to the breaking point.

The Peasant Revolt. Hope gave way to fear. Beginning on 20 July 1789, peasants in different areas of France reacted collectively throughout France, spreading false rumors of a great conspiracy. Fear gripped whole villages and in some areas spawned revolt. Just as urban workers had connected their economic hardships to politics, so too did desperate peasants see their plight in political terms. They banded together and marched to the residences of the local nobility, breaking into chateaux with a single mission in mind: to destroy all legal documents by which nobles claimed payments, dues, and services from local peasants. They drove out the lords and in some cases burned their chateaux, putting an end to the tyranny of the privileged over the countryside.

The overthrow of privileges rooted in a feudal past was not as easy as that. Members of the National Assembly were aghast at the eruption of rural violence. They knew that to stay in power they had to maintain peace. They also knew that to be credible they had to protect property. Peasant destruction of seigneurial claims posed a real dilemma for the bourgeois deputies directing the revolution. If they gave in to peasant demands, they risked losing aristocratic support and undermining their own ability to control events. If they gave in to the aristocracy, they risked a social revolution in the countryside, which they could not police or repress. Liberal members of the aristocracy cooperated with the bourgeois leaders in finding a solution.

In a dramatic meeting that lasted through the night of 4 August 1789, the National Assembly agreed to abolish the principle of privilege. The peasants had won—or thought they had. In the weeks and months ahead, rural people learned that they had lost their own prerogatives—the rights to common grazing and gathering—and were expected to buy their way out of their feudal services. In the meantime, parliamentary action had saved the day. The deputies stabilized the situation through legislating compromise.

Women on the March. Women participated with men in both urban and rural revolutionary actions. Acting on their own, women were responsible for one of the most dramatic events of the early years of the revolution: In October 1789, they forced the king and the royal family to leave Versailles for Paris to deal in person with the problems of bread supply, high prices, and starvation.

On the morning of 5 October 1789, 6,000 Parisian women marched out of the city and toward Versailles. They were taking their problem to the king with

A contemporary print of the women of Paris advancing on Versailles. The determined marchers are shown waving pikes and dragging an artillery piece. The women were hailed as heroines of the revolution.

Depart des Heroines de Paris pour Versailles le 5 Octobre 1789.

the demand that he solve it. Later in the day, Lafayette led the Parisian National Guard to Versailles to mediate events. The battle came early the next morning, when the women, now accompanied by revolutionary men, tired and cold from waiting all night at the gates of the palace, invaded the royal apartments and chased Marie Antoinette from her bedroom. A shocked Louis XVI agreed to return with the crowd to Paris. Louis XVI was now captive to the revolution, whose efforts to form a constitutional monarchy he purported to support.

Declaring Political Rights

"Liberty consists in the ability to do whatever does not harm another." So wrote the revolutionary deputies of 1789. Sounding a refrain similar to that of the American Declaration of Independence, the Declaration of the Rights of Man and Citizen appeared on 26 August 1789. The document amalgamated a variety of Enlightenment ideas drawn from the works of political philosophy, including those of Locke and Montesquieu. "Men are born and remain free and equal in rights. Social distinctions may be based only on common utility." Perhaps most significant of all was the attention given to property, which was declared a "sacred and inviolable," "natural," and "imprescriptible" right of man.

In the year of tranquility that followed the violent summer of 1789, the new politicians set themselves the task of creating institutions based on the principle of liberty and others embodied in the Declaration of the Rights of Man and Citizen. The result was the Constitution of 1791, a statement of faith in a progressive constitutional monarchy. A king accountable to an elected parliamentary body would lead France into a prosperous and just age. The constitution acknowledged the people's sovereignty as the source of political power. It also enshrined the principle of property by making voting rights dependent on property ownership. All men might be equal before the law, but by the Constitution of 1791 only wealthy men had the right to vote for representatives and hold office.

Civil Liberties. All titles of nobility were abolished. In the early period of the revolution, civil liberties were extended to Protestants and Jews, who had been persecuted under the Old Regime. Previously excluded groups were granted freedom of thought, worship, and full civil liberties. More reluctantly, deputies outlawed slavery in the colonies in 1794. Slave unrest in Saint Domingue (modern-day Haiti) had coincided with the political conflicts of the revolution and exploded in rebellion in 1791, driving the revolutionaries in Paris to support black independence although it was at odds with French colonial interests. Led by Toussaint L'Ouverture (1743–1803), black rebels worked to found an independent Haitian state, which was declared in 1804. But the concept of equality with regard to race remained incompletely integrated with revolutionary principles, and slavery was reestablished in the French colonies in 1802.

Women's Rights. Men were the subject of the newly defined rights. No references to women or their rights appear in the constitutions or the official Declaration of Rights. Women's organizations agitated for an equitable divorce law, and divorce was legalized in September 1792. Women were critical actors in the revolution from its very inception, and their presence shaped and directed the outcome of events, as the women's march to Versailles in 1789 made clear. The Marquis de Condorcet (1743–1794), elected to the Legislative Assembly in 1791, was one of the first to chastise the revolutionaries for overlooking the political rights of women who, he pointedly observed, were half of the human race.

The revolutionaries had declared that liberty was a natural and inalienable right, a universal right that was extended to all with the overthrow of a despotic monarch and a privileged elite. The principle triumphed in religious toleration. Yet the revolutionary concept of liberty foundered on the divergent claims of excluded groups—workers, women, and slaves—who demanded full participation in the world of politics. In 1792, revolutionaries confronted the contradictions inherent in their political beliefs of liberty and equality that were being challenged in the midst of social upheaval and foreign war. In response, the revolution turned to more radical measures to survive.

The Trials of Constitutional Monarchy

The disciplined deliberations of committees intent on fashioning a constitutional monarchy replaced the passion and fervor of revolutionary oratory. The National, or Constituent, Assembly divided France into new administrative units—*départements*—for the purpose of establishing better control over municipal governments. Along with new administrative trappings, the government promoted its own rituals. On 14 July 1790, militias from each of the newly created 83 départements of France came together in Paris to celebrate the first anniversary of the storming of the Bastille. A new national holiday was born and with it a sense of devotion and patriotism for the new France liberated by the revolution.

In spite of the unifying elements, however, the newly achieved revolutionary consensus began to show signs of breaking down.

The Counterrevolution. In February 1790, legislation dissolved all monasteries and convents, except for those that provided aid to the poor or that served as educational institutions. As the French church was stripped of its lands, Pope Pius VI (1775–1799) denounced the principles of the revolution. In July 1790, the government approved the Civil Constitution of the Clergy: Priests now became the equivalent of paid agents of the state. By requiring an oath of loyalty to the state from all practicing priests, the National Assembly created a new arena for dissent. Catholics were forced to choose to embrace or reject the revolution. The wedge driven between the Catholic Church and revolutionary France allowed a mass-based counterrevolution to emerge. Aristocratic émigrés who had fled the country because of their opposition to the revolution were languishing for lack of a popular base. From his headquarters in Turin, the king's younger brother, the Comte d'Artois, was attempting to incite a civil war in France. When the revolutionaries decided to attack the Church not just as a landed and privileged institution but also as a religious one, the counterrevolution rapidly expanded.

Late one night in June 1791, Louis XVI, Marie Antoinette, and their children disguised themselves as commoners, crept out of the royal apartments in the Tuileries Palace, and fled Paris. Louis intended to leave France to join royalist forces opposing the revolution at Metz. He got as far as Varennes, where he was captured by soldiers of the National Guard and brought back to a shocked Paris. The king had abandoned the revolution. Although he was not put to death for another year and a half, he was more than ever a prisoner of the revolution.

The Fiscal Crisis. The defection of the king was certainly serious, but it was not the only problem facing the revolutionaries. Other problems plagued the revolutionary government, notably foreign war and the fiscal crisis, coupled with inflation. In order to establish its seriousness and legitimacy, the National Assembly had been willing in 1789 to absorb the debts of the Old Regime. The new government could not sell titles and offices, as the king had done to deal with financial problems, but it did confiscate Church property. In addition, it issued treasury bonds in the form of assignats in order to raise money. The assignats soon assumed the status of bank notes, and by the spring of 1790 they had become compulsory legal tender. Initially they were to be backed by land confiscated from the Church and sold by the state. But the need for money soon outran the value of the land available, and the government continued to print assignats according to its needs. Depreciation of French currency in international markets and inflation at home resulted. The revolutionary government found itself in a situation which in certain respects was worse than that experienced by Louis XVI before the calling of the Estates-General. Assignat-induced inflation produced a sharp decline in the fortunes of bourgeois investors living on fixed incomes. Rising prices meant increased misery for workers and peasants.

New counterrevolutionary groups were becoming frustrated with revolutionary policies. Throughout the winter and spring of 1791–1792, people rioted and demanded that prices be fixed, while the assignat dropped to less than half its face value. Peasants refused to sell crops for the worthless paper. Hoarding further drove up prices. Angry crowds turned to pillaging, rioting, and murder, which became more frequent as the value of the currency declined and prices rose.

Foreign war beginning in the fall of 1791 also challenged stability. Some moderate political leaders welcomed war as a blessing in disguise, since it could divert the attention of the masses away from problems at home and promote loyalty to the revolution. Others envisioned war as a great crusade to bring revolutionary principles to oppressed peoples throughout Europe. The king and queen, trapped by the revolution, saw war as their only hope of liberation. Louis XVI could be rightfully restored as the leader of a France defeated by the sovereigns of Europe. Some who opposed the war believed it would destabilize the revolution. France must solve its problems at home, they argued, before fighting a foreign enemy. Louis, however, encouraged those ministers and advisers eager for battle. In April 1792, France declared war against Austria.

Experimenting with Democracy, 1792–1799

The revolution was a school for the French nation. A political universe populated by individual citizens replaced the eighteenth-century world of subjects loyal to their king. The new construction of politics, in which all individuals were equal, ran counter to prevailing ideas about collective identities defined in guilds and orders. People on all levels of society learned politics by doing it.

After 1789, all men were declared free and equal, in opportunity if not in rights. Men of ability and talent, who had served as middlemen for the privileged elite under the Old Regime, now claimed power as their due. But the school of the revolution did not remain the domain of a special class. Women demanded their places but continued to be excluded from the political arena, though the importance of their participation in the revolution was indisputable. Workers talked of seizing their rights, but because of the inherent contradictions of representation and participation, experimenting with democracy led to outcomes that did not look very democratic at all.

The Revolution of the People

The first stage of the French Revolution, lasting from 1789 through the beginning of 1792, was based on liberty—the liberty to compete, to own, and to succeed. The second stage of the French Revolution, which began in 1792, took equality as its rallying cry. It was the revolution of the working people of French cities. The popular movement that spearheaded political action in 1792 was committed to equality of rights in a way not characteristic of the leaders of the revolution of 1789. Urban workers were not benefiting from the revolution, but they had come to believe in their own power as political beings. Organized on the local level into sections, artisans in cities identified themselves as **sans-culottes**—literally, those trousered citizens who did not wear knee breeches (*culottes*)—to distinguish themselves from the privileged elite.

On 10 August 1792, the people of Paris stormed the Tuileries, chanting their demands for "Equality!" and "Nation!" The people tramped across the silk sheets of the king's bed and broke his fine furniture, reveling in the private chambers of the royal family. Love and respect for the king had vanished. What the people of Paris demanded was the right to vote and participate in a popular democracy. Working people were acting independently of other factions, and the bourgeois political leadership became quickly aware of the need to scramble to maintain order. The people were now a force to be reckoned with and feared.

"Terror Is the Order of the Day"

The Convention was the legislative body elected in September 1792 that succeeded the Legislative Assembly and had as its charge determining the best form of government after the collapse of the monarchy. On 21 September 1792, the monarchy was abolished in France; on the following day the Republic, France's first, came into being. Members of the Convention conducted the trial of Louis XVI for treason and pronounced his sentence: execution by the guillotine in January 1793.

The various political factions of the Convention were described in terms borrowed from geography. The Mountain, sitting on the upper benches on the left, was made up of members of the Jacobin Club (named for its meeting place in an abandoned monastery). The **Jacobins** were the most radical element in the National Convention, supporting democratic solutions and speaking in favor of the cause of people in the streets.

Jacobin Ascendancy. Both **Girondins**, the more moderate revolutionary faction, and Jacobins were from the middle ranks of the bourgeoisie, and both groups were dedicated to the principles of the revolution. Although they controlled the ministries, the Girondins began to lose their hold on the revolution and the war. The renewed European war fragmented the democratic movement, and the Girondins, unable to control violence at home, saw political control slipping away. They became prisoners of the revolution when 80,000 armed Parisians surrounded the National Convention in June 1793.

Girondin power had been eroding in the critical months between August 1792 and June 1793. A new leader was working quietly and effectively behind the scenes to weld a partnership between the popular movement of sans-culottes and the

Jacobins. He was Maximilien Robespierre (1758–1794), leader of the Mountain and the Jacobin Club. Although neither an original thinker nor a compelling orator, Robespierre discovered with the revolution that he was an adroit political tactician. He gained a following and learned how to manipulate it. It was he who engineered the Jacobins' replacement of the Girondins as leaders of the government.

Robespierre and the Reign of Terror. Robespierre's chance for real power came when he assumed leadership of the Committee of Public Safety in July 1793. Faced with the threat of internal anarchy and external war, the elected body, the National Convention, yielded political control to the 12-man Committee of Public Safety that ruled dictatorially under Robespierre's direction. The Great Committee, as it was known at the time, orchestrated the **Reign of Terror** (1793–1794), a period of systematic state repression that meted out justice in the people's name. Summary trials by specially created revolutionary tribunals were followed by the swift execution of the guilty under the blade of the guillotine.

Influenced by *The Social Contract* (1762) and other writings of Jean-Jacques Rousseau, Robespierre believed that sovereignty resided with the people. For him, individual wills and even individual rights did not matter when weighed against the will of the nation. Robespierre saw himself in the all-important role of interpreting and shaping the people's will. As head of the Great Committee, Robespierre oversaw a revolutionary machinery dedicated to economic regulation, massive military mobilization, and a punitive system of revolutionary justice characterized by the slogan, "Terror is the Order of the Day." Militant revolutionary committees and revolutionary tribunals were established throughout France to identify traitors and to mete out the harsh justice that struck hardest against those members of the bourgeoisie perceived as opponents of the government. The bureaucratized Reign of Terror was responsible for about 40,000 executions in a nine-month period, resulting in the image of the republicans as "drinkers of blood."

The Cult of the Supreme Being, a civic religion without priests or churches and influenced by Rousseau's ideas about nature, followed de-Christianization. The cathedral of Notre Dame de Paris was turned into the Temple of Reason, and the new religion established its own festivals to undermine the persistence of Catholicism. The cult was one indication of the Reign of Terror's attempt to create a new moral universe of revolutionary values.

Women Excluded. Women remained conspicuously absent from the summit of political power. After 1793, Jacobin revolutionaries, who had been willing to empower the popular movement of workers, turned against women's participation and denounced it. Women's associations were outlawed and the Society of Revolutionary Republican Women was disbanded. Olympe de Gouges, revolutionary author of the Declaration of the Rights of Woman and Citizen, was guillotined. Women were declared unfit for political participation, according to the Jacobins, because of their biological functions of reproduction and childrearing. Rousseau's ideas about family policy were probably more influential than his political doctrines. Following Rousseau's lead, Robespierre and the Jacobins insisted that the role of women as mothers was incompatible with women's participation in the political realm.

The Thermidorian Reaction. By attacking his critics on both the Left and the Right, Robespierre undermined the support he needed to stay in power. He abandoned the alliance with the popular movement that had been so important in bringing him to power. Robespierre's enemies—and he had many—were able to break the identification between political power and the will of the people that Robespierre had established. As a result, he was branded a traitor by the same process that he had used against many of his own enemies. He saved France from foreign occupation and internal collapse, but he could not save democracy through terror. In the summer of 1794, Robespierre was guillotined. The Reign of Terror ceased with his death in the revolutionary month of Thermidor 1794.

The End of the Revolution

The revolution did not end with the **Thermidorian Reaction**, as the fall of Robespierre came to be known, but his execution initiated a new phase. In the four years after Robespierre's fall, a new government by committee, called the Directory, appeared to offer mediocrity, caution, and opportunism in place of the idealism and action of the early years of the revolution. Most people, numbed after years of change, barely noticed that the revolution was over. Ordinary men in parliamentary institutions effectively did the day-to-day job of running the government. They tried to steer a middle path between royalist resurgence and popular insurrection. This nearly forgotten period in the history of the French Revolution was the fulfillment of the liberal hopes of 1789 for a stable constitutional rule.

The Directory, however, continued to be dogged by European war. A mass army of conscripts and volunteers had successfully extended France's power and frontiers. France expelled foreign invaders and annexed territories, including Belgium, while increasing its control in Holland, Switzerland, and Italy. But the expansion of revolutionary France was expensive and increasingly unpopular. Military defeats and the corruption of the Directory undermined government control. The Directory might have succeeded in the slow accretion of a parliamentary tradition, but reinstatement of **conscription** in 1798 met with widespread protest and resistance. No matter what their political leanings, people were weary. They turned to those who promised stability and peace.

The Thermidorian Reaction and the elimination of Robespierre as the legitimate interpreter of the people's will ushered in a period of conciliation, opportunism, and a search for stability. Ironically, the savior that France found to answer its needs for peace and a just government was a man of war and a dictator.

Chronology

THE FRENCH REVOLUTION

August 1788	Louis XVI announces meeting of Estates-General to be held May 1789
5 May 1789	Estates-General convenes
17 June 1789	Third Estate declares itself the National Assembly
20 June 1789	Oath of the Tennis Court
14 July 1789	Storming of the Bastille
20 July 1789	Revolution of peasantry begins
26 August 1789	Declaration of the Rights of Man and Citizen
5 October 1789	Parisian women march to Versailles; force Louis XVI to return to Paris
February 1790	Monasteries, convents dissolved
July 1790	Civil Constitution of the Clergy
June 1791	Louis XVI and family attempt to flee Paris; are captured and returned
September 1791	France's First Constitution
April 1792	France declares war on Austria
10 August 1792	Storming of the Tuileries
22 September 1792	Revolutionary calendar implemented
January 1793	Louis XVI executed
July 1793	Robespierre assumes leadership of Committee of Public Safety
1793–1794	Reign of Terror
1794	Robespierre guillotined
1799	Napoleon overthrows the Directory and seizes power

The Reign of Napoleon, 1799–1815

The great debate that rages to this day about Napoleon revolves around the question of whether he fulfilled the aims of the French Revolution or perverted them. In his return to a monarchical model, Napoleon resembled the enlightened despots of eighteenth-century Europe. In a modern sense, he was also a dictator, manipulating the French people through a highly centralized administrative apparatus. He locked French society into a program of military expansion that depleted its human and material resources. Yet in spite of destruction and war, he dedicated his reign to building a French state according to the principles of the revolution.

Bonaparte Seizes Power

Napoleon's Training and Experience. Napoleon Bonaparte (1769–1821) was born into an Italian noble family in Corsica. He secured a scholarship to the French military school at Brienne, graduating in 1784. He then spent a year at the Military Academy in Paris and received a commission as a second lieutenant of artillery in January 1786.

The revolutionary wars had begun in 1792 as wars to liberate humanity in the name of liberty, equality, and fraternity. Yet concerns for power, territory, and riches replaced earlier French concerns with defense of the nation and of the revolution.

This aggrandizement was nowhere more evident than in the Egyptian campaign of 1798, in which Napoleon Bonaparte headed an expedition whose goal was to enrich France by hastening the collapse of the Turkish Empire, crippling British trade routes, and handicapping Russian interests in the region. With Napoleon's highly publicized campaigns in Egypt and Syria, the war left the European theater and moved to the east, leaving behind the original revolutionary ideals.

The Egyptian campaign, which was in reality a disaster, made Napoleon a hero at home. His victories in the Italian campaign in 1796–1797 had launched his political career. As he extended French rule into central Italy, he became the embodiment of revolutionary values and energy.

Napoleon as First Consul. In 1799, Napoleon Bonaparte readily joined a conspiracy that pulled down the Directory and became the first consul of a triumvirate of consuls. Napoleon set out to secure his position of power by eliminating his enemies on the Left and weakening those on the Right. He guaranteed the security of property acquired in the revolution, a move that undercut royalists who wanted to return property to its original owners. Through policing forces and special criminal courts, law and order prevailed and civil war subsided. The first consul promised a balanced budget and appeared to deliver it. Realizing the importance of religion in maintaining domestic peace, Napoleon reestablished relations with the pope in 1801 by the Concordat, which recognized Catholicism as the religion of the French and restored the Roman Catholic hierarchy.

Napoleon came to power in 1799 by appealing for the support of the army. In 1802, Napoleon decided to extend his power by calling for a plebiscite in which he asked the electorate to vote him first consul for life. Public support was overwhelming. An electoral landslide gave Napoleon greater political power than any of his Bourbon predecessors had known.

Napoleon at War with the European Powers

By 1802, Napoleon had signed favorable treaties with both Austria and Great Britain. He appeared to deliver a lasting peace and to establish France as the dominant power in Europe. But the peace was short-lived. In 1803, France embarked on an 11-year period of continuous war. Under Napoleon's command, the French army delivered defeat after defeat to the European powers. Austria fell in 1805, Prussia fell in 1806, and the Russian armies of Alexander I were defeated at Friedland in 1807. In 1808, Napoleon invaded Spain to drive out British expeditionary forces intent on invading France. Spain became a satellite kingdom of France, although the conflict continued.

MAP DISCOVERY

Major battles

France in 1799

Napoleon's additions to France by 1812

States under Napoleon's control, 1812

Napoleon's allies 1812

NAPOLEON'S EMPIRE

Note the expansion of France under Napoleon's rule. How much of western and central Europe did Napoleon control by 1812? Why did Great Britain remain outside of Napoleon's influence? Why were Prussia, Austria, Denmark, and Norway allies of France in 1812?

Britain was the one exception to the string of Napoleonic victories. Napoleon initially considered sending a French fleet to invade the island nation. Lacking the strength necessary to achieve this, he turned to economic warfare and blockaded European ports against British trade. Beginning in 1806, the **Continental System**, as the blockade was known, erected a structure of protection for French manufactures in all continental European markets. The British responded to the tariff walls and boycotts with a naval blockade that cut French commerce off from its Atlantic markets. The Continental System did not break the British economy, however, and the French economy did not flourish when faced with restricted resources and the persistence of a black market in smuggled goods.

Still, by 1810, Napoleon was master of the Continent. French armies had extended revolutionary reforms and legal codes outside France and brought with them civil equality and religious toleration. They had also drained defeated countries of their resources and had inflicted the horrors of war with armies of occupation, forced billeting, and pillage.

Chronology

THE REIGN OF NAPOLEON

1799	Napoleon establishes consulate, becomes first consul
1801	Napoleon reestablishes relations with pope, restores Roman Catholic hierarchy
1802	Plebiscite declares Napoleon first consul for life
1804	Napoleon proclaims himself emperor of the French
1806	Continental System implemented
1808–1814	France engaged in Peninsular War with Spain
June 1812	Napoleon invades Russia
September 1812	French army reaches Moscow, is trapped by Russian winter
1813	Napoleon defeated at Battle of Nations at Leipzig
March 1814	Napoleon abdicates and goes into exile on island of Elba
March 1815	Napoleon escapes Elba and attempts to reclaim power
15 June 1815	Napoleon is defeated at Waterloo and exiled to island of Saint Helena

The First Empire and Domestic Reforms

Through the 1802 plebiscite that voted him first consul for life, Napoleon maintained the charade of constitutional rule while ruling as virtual dictator. In 1804, he abandoned all pretense and had himself proclaimed emperor of the French. He staged his own coronation and that of his wife Josephine at the cathedral of Notre Dame de Paris.

The Importance of Science and Economic Reforms. Secure in his regime, Napoleon set about implementing sweeping reforms in every area of government. He recognized the importance of science for both industry and war. Napoleon became a patron of science, supporting important work in the areas of physics and chemistry. Building for the future, Napoleon made science a pillar in the new structure of higher education.

Napoleon's contribution to the French economy was the much needed reform of the tax system. He authorized the creation of a central banking system. French industries flourished under state protection. The blockade forced the development of new domestic crops such as beet-sugar and indigo, which became substitutes for colonial products. Napoleon extended the infrastructure of roads, so necessary for the expansion of national and European markets.

The New Legal System. Perhaps his greatest achievement was the codification of law, a task begun under the revolution. Combined with economic reforms, the new **Napoleonic Code** facilitated trade and the development of commerce by regularizing contractual relations and protecting property rights and equality before the law. The civil laws of the new code carved out a family policy characterized by hierarchy and subordination. Married women were neither independent nor equal to men in ownership of property, custody of children, and access to divorce. Women also lacked political rights. In the Napoleonic Code, women, like children, were subjected to paternal authority.

Decline and Fall

Militarily, Napoleon went too far. The first cracks in the French facade began to show in the Peninsular War (1808–1814) with Spain, as Spanish guerrilla tactics proved costly for French troops. But Napoleon's biggest mistake occurred when he decided to invade Russia in June 1812.

The Invasion of Russia and the Battle of Nations. Having decisively defeated Russian forces in 1807, Napoleon entered into a peace treaty with Tsar Alexander I that guaranteed Russian allegiance to French policies. But Alexander repudiated the Continental System in 1810 and appeared to be preparing for his own war against France. Napoleon seized the initiative, sure that he could defeat Russian forces once again. With an army of 500,000 men, Napoleon moved deep into Russia in the summer of 1812. The tsar's troops fell back in retreat, and when Napoleon and his men entered Moscow in September, they found a city in flames. The people of Moscow had destroyed their own city to deprive the French troops of winter quarters. Napoleon's men found themselves facing a severe Russian winter without overcoats, without supplies, and without food. The starving and frostbitten French army was forced into retreat. Fewer than 100,000 men made it back to France.

The empire began to crumble. Britain, unbowed by the Continental System, remained Napoleon's sworn enemy. Prussia joined Great Britain, Sweden, Russia, and Austria in opposing France anew. In the Battle of Nations at Leipzig in October 1813, France was forced to retreat. Napoleon refused a negotiated peace and fought on until the following March, when the victorious allies marched down the streets of Paris and occupied the French capital. Deserted by his allies, Napoleon abdicated

This 1835 painting by De Boisdenier depicts the suffering of Napoleon's Grand Army on the retreat from Moscow. The Germans were to meet a similar fate more than 100 years later when they invaded Russia without adequate supplies for the harsh winter.

in April 1814 in favor of his young son, the titular king of Rome (1811–1832). When the allies refused to accept the young "Napoleon II," the French called on the Bourbon Louis XVIII and crowned him king. Napoleon was then exiled to the Mediterranean island of Elba.

Napoleon's Final Defeat: Waterloo. Still, it was not quite the end for Napoleon. While the European heads of state sat in Vienna trying to determine the future of Europe and France's place in it, Napoleon returned from his exile on Elba. On 15 June 1815, Napoleon once again confronted the European powers in one of the most famous battles in history: Waterloo. With 125,000 loyal French forces, Napoleon seemed within hours of reestablishing the French Empire in Europe, but the defeat of his forces was decisive. Napoleon's return proved brief, lasting only 100 days. He was exiled to the island of Saint Helena in the South Atlantic. For the next six years, Napoleon wrote his memoirs under the watchful eyes of his British jailors. He died a painful death on 5 May 1821 from what today is believed to have been cancer.

SUMMARY

The French Revolution and the Fall of the Monarchy The financial problems of the French monarchy forced Louis XVI to call the Estates-General. People from all walks of life hoped the Estates-General would provide relief for their problems. A crisis over voting procedures prompted the Third Estate to leave the Estates-General and form the National Assembly. The storming of the Bastille demonstrated that a new political reality was emerging in which the king was no longer in control of events. Rioting in the countryside sparked by fear of aristocratic conspiracy forced the National Assembly to abolish the system of privileges. Six thousand Parisian women forced Louis XVI and his family to return to Paris. The Declaration of the Rights of Man and Citizen and the Constitution of 1791 encapsulated the goals of the first phase of the revolution. War, fiscal crisis, and counterrevolutionary activity pushed the revolution into a new and more radical phase.

Experimenting with Democracy, 1792–1799   Starting in 1792, the watchword of the revolution changed from liberty to equality. The working people of Paris pushed for popular democracy. The Convention abolished the monarchy and carried out the trial and execution of Louis XVI. Under the leadership of Robespierre, the Jacobins dominated the revolutionary government and orchestrated the Reign of Terror. The fall of Robespierre in the Thermidorian Reaction led to the creation of the Directory. Military defeats and corruption undermined the Directory and created the conditions for Napoleon's rise to power.

The Reign of Napoleon, 1799–1815   Napoleon's victories in Italy and his Egyptian campaign made him a hero in France. In 1799 he was part of a successful coup that toppled the Directory. As first consul, he consolidated his power by maintaining domestic peace and by reestablishing relations between France and the Catholic Church. A series of military victories made Napoleon the master of Europe. Napoleon attempted to use an economic blockade to defeat Britain. In 1804 Napoleon had himself crowned emperor. He carried out a series of reforms, most notably of the legal system. His decision to invade Russia in 1812 was the beginning of the end. Defeat in Russia led to abdication and exile on Elba for Napoleon in 1814. After escaping Elba, Napoleon tried one last time to reclaim control of Europe in 1815. He was defeated at Waterloo and exiled again, this time to Saint Helena in the South Atlantic.

QUESTIONS FOR REVIEW

1. To what extent was the French nobility responsible for the crisis that destroyed the Old Regime?
2. How did commoners, men and women, transform a crisis of government into a revolution?
3. Why did the leaders of the revolution resort to a "reign of terror" and what effect did that have on the revolution?
4. What problems in France and beyond contributed to the rise of Napoleon?
5. What did Napoleon accomplish in France, and what brought about his fall?

Industrial Europe

The Traditional Economy

By the eighteenth century, a process of industrialization that would ultimately transform the traditional economy was already under way. It began with the **agricultural revolution** (discussed below), one of the great turning points in human history. After the agricultural revolution, an inadequate food supply was a political rather than an economic fact of life. Fewer and fewer farmers were required to feed more and more people. By the middle of the nineteenth century, the most advanced economies were capable of producing vast surpluses of basic commodities. The agricultural revolution was not an event, and it did not happen suddenly. It would not deserve the label "revolution" at all were it not for its momentous consequences: Europe's escape from the shackles of the traditional economy.

Rural Manufacture

By the end of the eighteenth century, the European population was reaching the point at which another check on its growth might be expected. Between 1700 and

1800, total European population had increased by nearly 50 percent, and the rate of growth was continuing to accelerate. This vast expansion of rural population placed a grave strain on agricultural production.

The crisis of overpopulation meant that not only were there more mouths to feed, there were more bodies to clothe. This increased the need for cloth and thus for spinners and weavers. Traditionally, commercial cloth production was the work of urban artisans, but the expansion of the marketplace and the introduction of new fabrics, especially cotton and silk, had eroded the monopoly of most of the clothing guilds. Merchants could sell as much finished product as they could find, and the teeming rural population provided a tempting pool of inexpensive labor for anyone who was willing to risk the capital to purchase raw materials. Initially, farming families took manufacturing work into their homes to supplement their income. Spinning and weaving were the most common occupations, and they were treated as occasional work, reserved for the slow times in the agricultural cycle. This was known as cottage industry.

But by the middle of the eighteenth century, cottage industry was developing in a new direction. As landholdings grew smaller, even good harvests did not promise subsistence to many families. This oversupply of labor was soon organized into the **putting-out system**, which mobilized the resources of the rural labor force for commercial production of large quantities of manufactured goods. The characteristics of the putting-out system were similar throughout Europe. The entrepreneur purchased raw materials, which were "put out" to the homes of workers, where the manufacture took place, most commonly spinning or weaving. The finished goods were returned to the entrepreneur, who sold them at a profit, with which he bought raw materials to begin the process anew.

Putting-out required only a low level of skill and inexpensive common tools. Rural families did their own spinning, and rural villages did their own weaving. Thus putting-out demanded little investment, in plant, equipment, or education. Nor did it inevitably disrupt traditional gender-based tasks in the family economy. Spinning was women's work, weaving was men's, and children helped at whichever task was under way.

As long as rural manufacture supplemented agricultural income, it was seen as a benefit for everyone involved—the entrepreneur, the individual worker, and the village community. But gradually, the putting-out system came to dominate the lives of many rural families. Long hours in dank cottages performing endlessly repetitive tasks became the lot of millions of rural inhabitants. And their numbers increased annually. Whereas the sons of farmers waited to inherit land before they formed their families, the sons of cottage weavers needed only a loom to begin theirs. They could afford to marry younger and to have more children, for children could contribute to manufacturing from an early age. Consequently, the expansion of the putting-out system contributed to overpopulation.

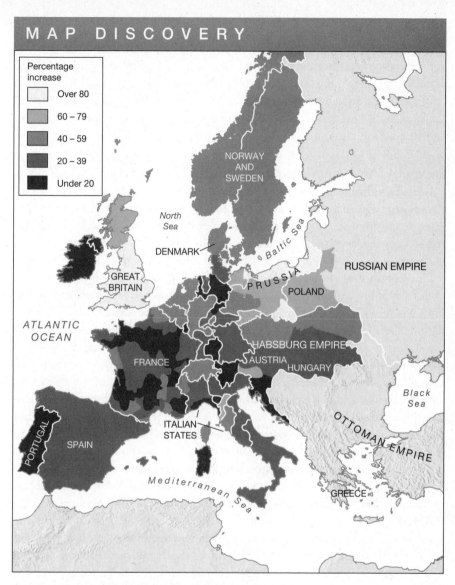

POPULATION GROWTH IN EUROPE, 1800–1850

Notice which parts of Europe experienced the largest growth in population in the first half of the nineteenth century. Compare the rate of population growth in Spain and Norway and Sweden. Which grew faster? In which parts of Europe did the population increase the most during this period? What impact would you expect such growth to have on the agricultural economy? On the rate of industrialization?

The Agricultural Revolution

The continued growth of Europe's population necessitated an expansion of agricultural output. In most places, this was achieved by intensifying traditional practices, bringing more land into production, and using more labor to work the land. But in the most advanced European economies, first in Holland and then in England, traditional agriculture underwent a long but dynamic transformation, an agricultural revolution.

Enclosures. As long as farming was practiced in open fields, there was little incentive for individual landowners to invest in improvements to their scattered strips. Commercial agriculture was more suited to large estates than small ones and was more successful when the land could be utilized in response to market conditions rather than the necessities of subsistence. The consolidation of estates and the enclosure of fields were thus the initial steps in a long-term process of change.

In England, where enclosure was to become most advanced, it was already under way in the sixteenth century. Prosperous families had long been consolidating their strips in the open fields, and at some point, the lord of the manor and the members of the community agreed to carve up the common fields and make the necessary exchanges to consolidate everyone's lands. Perhaps as much as three-quarters of the arable land in England was enclosed by agreement before 1760. Enclosure by agreement did not mean that the breakup of the open-field community was always a harmonious process. Riots before or after agreed enclosures were not uncommon. Poor farmers who had once enjoyed the right to use certain strips of land for cultivation and pasture often found themselves reduced to working as hired hands for larger landowners.

Opposition to enclosure by agreement led, in the eighteenth century, to enclosure by act of Parliament. Parliamentary enclosure was legislated by government, a government that was composed for the most part of large landowners. Between 1760 and 1815, more than 1.5 million acres of farmland were enclosed by act of Parliament.

The enclosure of millions of acres of land was one of the largest expenses of the new commercial agriculture. As hedging or fencing off the land and plowing up the commons proceeded, more and more agricultural activity become market-oriented. Single crops were sown in large enclosed fields and exchanged at market for the mixture of goods that had previously been grown in the village. Market production turned farmers' attention from producing a balance of commodities to increasing the yield of a single commodity.

Agricultural Innovations. The first innovation was the widespread cultivation of fodder crops such as clover and turnips. Crops like clover restore nutrients to the soil as they grow, shortening the period in which land has to lie fallow. Moreover, farm animals grazing on clover or feeding on turnips return more manure to the land, further increasing its productivity.

The ability of farmers to increase their livestock was as important as their ability to grow more grain. Not only were horses and oxen more productive than humans—a horse could perform seven times the labor of a man while consuming only five times the food—but the animals also refertilized the land as they worked. But animals competed with humans for food, especially during the winter months, when little grazing was possible. To conserve grain for human consumption, some livestock had to be slaughtered in the autumn. Therefore the development of the technique of meadow floating was a remarkable breakthrough. By flooding low-lying land near streams in the winter, English and Dutch farmers could prevent the ground from freezing during their generally mild winters. When the water was drained, the land beneath it would produce an early grass crop on which the beasts could graze. This meant that more animals could be kept alive during the winter.

The relationship between animal husbandry and grain growing became another feature of commercial agriculture. In many areas, farmers could choose between growing grain and pasturing animals. When prices for wool or meat were relatively higher than those for grain, fields could be left in grass for grazing. When grain prices rose, the same fields could be plowed. Consolidated enclosed estates made this convertible husbandry possible. The decision to hire field workers or shepherds could be taken only by large agricultural employers.

Convertible husbandry was but the first step in the development of a true system of regional specialization in agriculture. Different soils and climates favored different uses of the land. The introduction of fodder crops and increased fertilization rejuvenated thin soils, and southeastern England became the nation's breadbasket. Large enclosed estates provided a surplus of grain throughout the eighteenth century. Similarly, the midlands became the location of great sheep runs and cattle herds. Experiments in herd management, crossbreeding, and fattening all resulted in increased production of wool, milk, meat, leather, soap, and tallow for candles.

There can be no doubt about the benefits of the transformation of agricultural practices that began in Holland and England in the seventeenth century and spread slowly to all corners of the Continent over the next 200 years. Millions more mouths were fed at lower cost than ever before. Cheaper food allowed more discretionary spending, which fueled the demand for consumer goods, which in turn employed more rural manufacturers. But there are no benefits without costs. The transformation of agriculture was also a transformation in a way of life. The plight of the rural poor was tragic enough in villages of kin and neighbors, where face-to-face charity might be returned from one generation to the next. As landless laborers, however, the rural poor became fodder for the factories, the "dark satanic mills" that came to disfigure the land. For the destitute, charity was now bestowed on them in anonymous parish workhouses or by the good works of the comfortable middle class. In all of these ways the agricultural revolution changed the face of Europe.

Yield Ratios for Grain Crops, 1400–1800

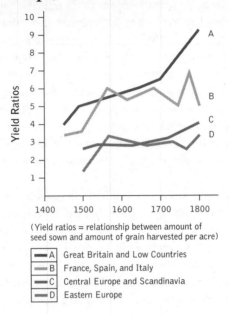

(Yield ratios = relationship between amount of seed sown and amount of grain harvested per acre)

- A Great Britain and Low Countries
- B France, Spain, and Italy
- C Central Europe and Scandinavia
- D Eastern Europe

The Industrial Revolution in Britain

The **Industrial Revolution** was a sustained period of economic growth and change brought about by the application of mineral energy and technological innovations to the process of manufacturing. It took place largely during the century between 1750 and 1850, though different industries moved at different paces and sustained economic growth continued in Britain until the First World War. It is difficult to define precisely the timing of the Industrial Revolution because, unlike a political event, an economic transformation does not happen all at once. Before 1750, innovations made their way slowly into general use, and after 1850 the pace of growth slowed appreciably. By then, Britain had a manufacturing economy, less than one-quarter of its labor force engaged in agriculture, and nearly 60 percent was involved in industry, trade, and transport.

Britain First

The Industrial Revolution occurred first in Britain, but even in Britain, industrialization was a regional phenomenon rather than a national one. This was the result of both national conditions and historical developments. When industrialization spread to the Continent, it took hold, as it had in Britain, in regions where mineral resources were abundant or where domestic manufacturing was a traditional activity. There was no single model for European industrialization, however often contemporaries looked toward Britain for the key to unlock the power of economic growth.

Water and Coal. Among Britain's blessings, water was foremost. Britain was favored by an internal water system that tied inland communities together. In the eighteenth century, no place in Britain was more than 70 miles from the sea or more than 30 miles from a navigable river. Water transport was far cheaper than hauling goods overland. Small wonder that river transport was one of the principal interests of merchants and traders. Beginning in the 1760s, private concerns began to invest in the construction of canals, first to move coal from inland locations to major arteries and then to connect the great rivers themselves. Over the next 50 years, several hundred miles of canals were built by authority of Navigation Acts, which allowed for the sale of shares to raise capital.

Coal was the second of Britain's natural blessings. Coal had been in use as a fuel for several centuries, it was abundant, and it was easily transported on water. The location of large coalfields along waterways was a vital condition of its early use. As canals and roadways improved, more inland coal was brought into production for domestic use. Yet it was in industry rather than in the home that coal was put to its greatest use. Here again, Britain was favored, for large seams of coal were also located near large seams of iron.

Economic Infrastructure. The factors that contributed to Britain's early industrialization were not only those of natural advantage. Over the course of years, Britain had developed an infrastructure for economic advancement. The transformation of domestic handicrafts to industrial production depended as much on the abilities of merchants as on those of manufacturers. The markets for domestic manufacturing had largely been overseas, where British merchants built up relationships over generations. Export markets were vital to the success of industrialization as production grew dynamically, and most ventures needed a quick turnaround of sales to reinvest their profits in continued growth. Equally important, increased production meant increased demand for raw materials. The expansion of shipping mirrored the expansion of the economy, tripling during the eighteenth century to over one million tons of cargo capacity.

The expansion of shipping, agriculture, and investment in machines, plant, and raw material all required capital. Not only did capital have to exist, but it had to be made productive. At the end of the seventeenth century, the creation of the Bank of England had begun the process of constructing a reliable banking system. Bank of England notes could be exchanged between merchants, and this increased the liquidity of the English economy, especially in London. It also became the model for provincial banking by the middle of the eighteenth century.

Though the banking system was vital to large enterprises, in fact the capital for most industry was raised locally, from kin and neighbors, and it grew by plowing profits back into the business. At least at the beginning, manufacturers were willing to take risks and to work for small returns to ensure the survival and growth of their business.

Minerals and Metals

The Industrial Revolution could not have occurred without coal. It was the black gold of the eighteenth century, the fuel that fed the furnaces and turned the engines of industrial expansion. The coal produced by one miner generated as much energy as 20 horses. Coal mining was the first capital-intensive industry in Britain and was already well developed by the seventeenth century.

Early Coal Mining. The technical problems of coal mining grew with demand. As surface seams were exhausted it became necessary to dig deeper shafts, to lower miners farther underground, and to raise the coal greater heights to the surface. As pits were sunk deeper, they reached pools of groundwater, which enlarged as the coal was stripped away from the earth. The pit acted like a riverbed and was quickly filled. Water drainage presented the greatest obstacle to deep-shaft mining. In 1709, Thomas Newcomen (1663–1729) introduced a steam-driven pump, which enabled water to be sucked through a pipe directly from the pit bottom to the surface.

Innovations like Newcomen's engine helped to increase coal output at just the time that it became needed as an industrial fuel. Eventually, the largest demand for coal came from the iron industry. In 1793, just two ironworks consumed as much coal as the entire population of Edinburgh. Like coal mining, iron making was both capital- and labor-intensive. Iron making depended on an abundance of wood, for it took the charcoal derived from ten acres of trees to refine one ton of iron ore.

The great innovations in the production of iron came with the development of techniques that allowed for the use of coal rather than wood charcoal in smelting and forging. As early as 1709, Abraham Darby (ca. 1678–1717), a Quaker nail maker, experimented with smelting iron ore with coke, coal from which most of the gas has been burned off. Iron coking greatly reduced the cost of fuel in the first stages of production, but because most ironworks were located in woodlands rather than near coal pits, the method was not widely adopted. Moreover, although coke made from coal was cheaper than charcoal made from wood, coke added its own impurities to

Women and children often labored in horrible conditions that were cramped, lacked fresh air, and offered little sunlight.

the iron ore. Nor could it provide the intense heat needed for smelting without a large bellows. The cost of the bellows offset the savings from the coke until James Watt (1736–1819) invented a new form of steam engine in 1775.

The Steam Engine. Like most innovations of the Industrial Revolution, James Watt's steam engine was an adaptation of existing technology. An instrument maker in Glasgow, Watt was asked to repair a model of a Newcomen engine and immediately realized that it would work more efficiently if there were a separate chamber for the condensation of the steam. Though his idea was sound, Watt spent years attempting to implement it. He did not succeed until he became partners with the Birmingham iron maker and manufacturer Matthew Boulton (1728–1809). At Boulton's works, Watt found craft workers who could make precision engine valves, and at the foundries of John Wilkinson (1728–1808) he found workers who could bore the cylinders of his engine to exact specifications.

Watt's engine received its first practical application in the iron industry. Wilkinson became one of the largest customers for steam engines, using them for pumping, moving wheels, and ultimately increasing the power of the blast of air in the forge. Increasing the heat provided by coke in the smelting and forging of iron led to the transformation of the industry. In the 1780s, Henry Cort (1740–1800), a naval contractor, experimented with a technique for using coke as fuel in removing the impurities from pig iron. The iron was melted into puddles and stirred with rods. As a result of his innovations, iron could now be made entirely with coke, so ironworks moved to the coalfields. Forges, furnaces, and rolling machines were brought together and powered by steam engines. By 1808, output of pig iron had grown from 68,000 to 250,000 tons and that of bar iron from 32,000 to 100,000 tons.

Cotton Is King

Traditionally, British commerce was dominated by the woolen cloth trade, in which techniques of production had not changed for hundreds of years. During the course of the seventeenth century, new fabrics appeared on the domestic market, particularly linen, silk, and cotton. It was cotton that captured the imagination of the eighteenth-century consumer, especially brightly colored, finely spun Indian cotton.

Domestic Industries. Limited output and variable quality characterized British textile production throughout the early part of the eighteenth century. The breakthrough came with technological innovation. Beginning in the mid-eighteenth century, a series of new machines dramatically increased output and, for the first time, allowed English textiles to compete with Indian imports.

The first innovation was the flying shuttle, invented by John Kay (1704–1764) in the 1730s. The flying shuttle allowed weavers to work alone rather than in pairs, but it was adopted slowly, for it increased the demand for spun thread, which was already in short supply. The spinning bottleneck was opened by James Hargreaves

(d. 1778), who devised a machine known as the jenny. The first jennies allowed for the spinning of eight threads at once, and improvements brought the number to more than 100. Jennies replaced spinning wheels by the tens of thousands. The jenny was a crucial breakthrough in redressing the balance between spinning and weaving, though it did not solve all problems. Jenny-spun thread was not strong enough to be used as warp, which continued to be wheel spun.

The need to provide stronger warp threads was ultimately solved by the development of the water frame. It was created in 1769 by Richard Arkwright (1732–1792), whose name was also to be associated with the founding of the modern factory system. Arkwright's frame consisted of a series of water-power-driven rollers, which stretched the cotton before spinning. These stronger fibers could be spun into threads that were suitable for warp, and English manufacturers could finally produce an all-cotton fabric. It was not long before another innovator realized that the water frame and the jenny could be combined into a single machine, one that would produce an even finer cotton yarn than that made in India. The mule, so named because it was a cross between a frame and a jenny, was invented by Samuel Crompton (1753–1827). It was the decisive innovation in cotton cloth production.

The original mules were small machines that could be used for domestic manufactures. But increasingly, the mule followed the water frame into purposely built factories, where it became larger and more expensive. The need for large rooms to house the equipment and the need for a ready source of running water to power it provided an incentive for the creation of factories where manufacturers could maintain control over the quality of products through strict supervision of the workforce.

In the eighteenth century, a number of British inventors patented new machines that transformed the British textile industry and marked the beginning of the Industrial Revolution. Among the inventions was the spinning jenny, invented by James Hargreaves in 1764, and named for his daughter. The jenny, which permitted the spinning of a number of threads at the same time, made possible the automatic production of cotton thread.

Cotton Factories. Richard Arkwright constructed the first cotton factories in Britain, all of which were designed to house water frames. The organization of the cotton industry into factories was one of the pivotal transformations in economic life. Domestic spinning and weaving took place in agricultural villages; factory production took place in mill towns. The location of the factory determined population movements, and from the first quarter of the eighteenth century onward, a great shift toward the northeast of England took place. Moreover, the character of the work itself changed. The operation of heavy machinery reversed the traditional gender-based tasks. Mule spinning became men's work; hand-loom weaving was taken over by women. The mechanization of weaving took longer than that of spinning because of difficulties in perfecting a power loom and because of opposition to its introduction by workers known as Luddites, who organized machine-breaking riots in the 1810s. The Luddites attempted to maintain the traditional organization of their industry and the independence of their labor. For a time, hand-loom weavers managed to survive by accepting lower and lower piece rates. It was not long, however, before weaving as well as spinning became factory work.

The transformation of cotton manufacture had a profound effect on the overall growth of the British economy. By the mid-nineteenth century, nearly half a million people earned their living from cotton, which alone accounted for over 40 percent of the value of all British exports. Cotton was undeniably the king of manufactured goods.

The Iron Horse

The greatest complaint of industrialists was that they could not get enough raw materials or fuel, nor could they ship their finished products fast enough to keep up with demand. Transportation was becoming a serious stumbling block to continued economic growth.

It was the need to ship increasing amounts of coal to foundries and factories that provided the spur for the development of railways. Ever since the seventeenth century, coal had been moved from the seam to the pit on rails, constructed first of wood and later of iron. By 1800, there were perhaps 300 miles of iron rail in British mines. In the same year, Watt's patent on the steam engine expired, and inventors began to apply the engine to a variety of mechanical tasks.

The First Railways. In 1830, the first modern railway, the Manchester-to-Liverpool line, was opened. Like the canals, it was designed to move coal and bulk goods, but surprisingly, its most important function came to be moving people. In its first year, the Manchester-Liverpool line carried over 400,000 passengers, who generated double the revenue derived from freight. The London–Birmingham and London–Bristol lines were both designed with passenger traffic in mind. Railway building was one of the great boom activities of British industrialization. By 1835, Parliament had passed 54 separate acts establishing over 750 miles of railways. By 1852, over 7,500 miles of track were in use.

From Goods to Passengers. By the 1850s, coal was the dominant cargo shipped by rail, and the speedy, efficient service continued to drive prices down. The iron and steel industries were modernized on the back of demand for rails, engines, and cast-iron seats and fittings.

Most of all, the railroads changed the nature of people's lives. Whole new concepts of time, space, and speed emerged to govern daily activities. The cheap railway excursion was born to provide short holidays or even daily returns. Over six million people visited London by train to view the **Crystal Palace Exhibition** in 1851, a number equivalent to one-third of the population of England and Wales. By speeding all forms of communication, the railways brought people together and helped to develop a sense of national identity.

Entrepreneurs and Managers

The Industrial Revolution in Britain was not simply invented. Too much credit is given to a few breakthroughs, and too little is given to the ways in which they were improved and dispersed. Societies for the advancement of knowledge sprang up all over Britain. Journals and magazines promoted new ideas and techniques. Competitions were held for the best invention of the year, and prizes were awarded for agricultural achievements. Practical science rather than pure science was the hallmark of industrial development.

Yet technological innovation was not the same as industrialization. A vital change in economic activity took place in the organization of industry. Putters-out, with their circulating capital and hired laborers, could never make the economies necessary to increase output and quality while simultaneously lowering costs. This was the achievement of industrialists, producers who owned workplace, machinery, and raw materials and who invested fixed capital by plowing back their profits. Moreover, industrial enterprises were not sure-fire investments. There were over 30,000 bankruptcies in the eighteenth century, testimony both to the risks of business and the willingness of entrepreneurs to take them.

To survive against these odds, successful industrialists had to be both entrepreneurs and managers. As entrepreneurs they raised capital, almost always locally from relatives, friends, or members of their church. The industrial entrepreneur also had to understand the latest methods for building and powering machinery and the most up-to-date techniques for performing the work. Finally, entrepreneurs had to know how to market their goods. In these functions, industrial entrepreneurs developed logically from putters-out.

But industrialists also had to be managers. The most difficult task was organization of the workplace. Most gains in productivity were achieved through the specialization of function. The processes of production were divided and subdivided until workers performed a basic task over and over. The education of the workforce was the industrial manager's greatest challenge. Workers had to be

Honoré Daumier (1808–1879), *The Third-Class Carriage.* Daumier captured a human condition peculiar to the modern era: "the lonely crowd."

taught how to use and maintain their machines and disciplined to apply themselves continuously.

Who were the industrialists who transformed the traditional economy? Because British society was relatively open, they came from every conceivable background. Wealthy landowners were prominent in capital-intensive aspects of industries, for example owning ironworks and mines, but few established factories. Most industrialists came from the middle classes, which comprised only one-third of the British population but provided as many as two-thirds of the first generation of industrialists. These included lawyers, bankers, merchants, and people who were already engaged in manufacturing, as well as tradespeople, shopkeepers, and self-employed craft workers. The career of every industrialist was unique, as a look at two—Josiah Wedgwood and Robert Owen—will show.

Josiah Wedgwood. Josiah Wedgwood (1730–1795) was the thirteenth child of a long-established English potting family. His head teemed with ideas for improving ceramic manufacturing, but it was not until he was 30 that he could set up on his own and introduce his innovations. These encompassed both technique and organization, the entrepreneurial and managerial sides of his business.

Wedgwood developed new mixtures of clays that took brilliant colors in the kiln and new glazes for both "useful" and "ornamental" ware. When he began his first works, he divided the making of pottery into distinct tasks and separated his workers among them. He invested in schools to help train young artists, in canals to transport his products, and in London shops to sell them. Wedgwood was a marketing genius. He named his famed cream-colored pottery Queen's ware and made special coffee and tea services for leading aristocratic families. He would then sell replicas by the thousands. In less than 20 years, Wedgwood pottery was prized all over Europe, and Wedgwood's potting works were the standard of the industry.

Robert Owen. Robert Owen (1771–1858), the son of a small tradesman, was apprenticed to a clothier at the age of 10. As a teenager he worked as a shop assistant in Manchester, where he audaciously applied for a job as manager of a cotton mill. At 19, he was supervising 500 workers and learning the cotton trade. Owen was immediately successful, increasing his workers' output and introducing new materials to the mill. In 1816, he entered a partnership to purchase the New Lanark mill in Scotland.

Owen found conditions in Scotland much worse than those in Manchester. Over 500 workhouse children were employed at New Lanark, where drunkenness and theft were endemic. Owen believed that to improve the quality of work, one had to improve the quality of the workplace. He replaced old machinery with new, reduced working hours, and instituted a monitoring system to check theft. To enhance life outside the factory, he established a high-quality company-run store, which plowed its profits into a school for village children.

Owen was struck by the irony that in the mills, machines were better cared for than humans. He thought that with the same attention to detail that had so improved the quality of commodities, he could make even greater improvements in the quality of life. He prohibited children under the age of 10 from mill work and instituted a 10-hour day for child labor. His local school took infants from one year old, freeing women to work and ensuring each child an education. Owen instituted old-age and disability pensions, funded by mandatory contributions from workers' wages. Taverns were closed, and workers were fined for drunkenness and sexual offenses. In the factory and the village, Owen established a principle of communal regulation to improve both the work and the character of his employees. New Lanark became the model of the world of the future, and each year, thousands of people made an industrial pilgrimage to visit it.

The Wages of Progress

Robert Owen ended his life as a social reformer. His efforts to improve the lot of his workers at New Lanark led to experiments to create ideal industrial communities throughout the world. Owen's agitation for social reform was part of a movement that produced results of lasting consequence. The **Factory Act (1833)** prohibited factory work by children under the age of nine, provided two hours of daily education, and effectively created a 12-hour day in the mills until the Ten Hours Act (1847). The Mines Act (1842) prohibited women and children from working underground.

Nor was Owen alone in dedicating time and money to the improvement of workers' lives. The rapid growth of unplanned cities exacerbated the plight of people who were too poor and overworked to help themselves. Conditions of housing and sanitation were appalling even by nineteenth-century standards. The Public Health Act (1848) established boards of health and the office of medical examiner. The Vaccination Act (1853) and the Contagious Diseases Act (1864) attempted to control epidemics.

The movement for social reform began almost as soon as industrialization. The Industrial Revolution initiated profound changes in the organization of British society. Cities sprang up from grain fields almost overnight. The lure of steady work and high wages prompted an exodus from rural Britain and spurred an unremitting boom in population. In 1750, about 15 percent of the population lived in urban areas; by 1850, about 60 percent did. Industrial workers married younger and produced more children than their agricultural counterparts. This was in part because factory hands did not have to wait until they inherited land or money and in part because they did not have to serve an apprenticeship. Early marriage and large families also signified a belief that things were better now and would be even better soon.

Expansion of Wealth. The Industrial Revolution brought a vast expansion of wealth and a vast expansion of people to share it. Despite the fact that population doubled between 1801 and 1851, per capita income rose by 75 percent, which means that had the population remained stable, per capita income would have increased by a staggering 350 percent. At the same time, untold millions of pounds had been sunk into canals, roads, railways, factories, mines, and mills.

But the expansion of wealth is not the same as the improvement in the quality of life, for wealth is not equally distributed. An increase in the level of wealth may mean only that the rich are getting richer more quickly than the poor are getting poorer. Similarly, economic growth over a century involved the lives of several generations, which experienced different standards of living. Finally, quality of life cannot be measured simply in economic terms. People with more money to spend may still be worse off than their ancestors, who may have preferred leisure to wealth or independence to the discipline of the clock.

There are no easy answers to the quality-of-life question. It seems clear that in the first stages of industrialization, only the wealthy benefited economically, though much of their increased wealth was reinvested in expansion. Under the impact of population growth, the Napoleonic wars, and regional harvest failure, real wages seem to have fallen from the levels reached in the 1730s. But beginning around 1820, there is convincing evidence that the real wages of industrial workers were rising, despite the fact that more and more work was semiskilled and unskilled machine-minding and more of it was being done by women, who were generally paid only two-thirds as much as men. Thus, in the second half of the Industrial Revolution, both employers and workers saw a bettering of their economic situation. This was one reason why rural workers flocked to the cities to take the lowest-paid and least desirable jobs in the factories.

Social Costs. But economic gain had social costs. The first was the decline of the family as a labor unit. In both agricultural and early industrial activity, families labored together. The early factories preferred family labor to workhouse conscripts, and it was traditional for children to work beside their parents, cleaning, fetching, or assisting in minding the machines. Paradoxically, it was the agitation for improvement in the conditions of child labor that spelled the end of the family work unit. At first, young children were barred from the factories, and older ones were allowed to work only a partial adult shift. Though reformers intended that schooling and leisure be substituted for work, the separation of children from parents in the workplace ultimately made possible the substitution of teenagers for adults, especially as machines replaced skilled human labor. The individual worker now became the unit of labor, and during economic downturns it was adult males with their higher salaries who were laid off first.

The decline of the family as a labor unit was matched by other changes in living conditions when rural dwellers migrated to cities. Many rural habits were unsuited to both factory work and urban living. The tradition of "Saint Monday," for example, was one that was deeply rooted in the pattern of agricultural life. Little effort was expended at the beginning of the work week, and progressively more was expended toward the end. The factory demanded constant application, six days a week. Strict rules were enforced to keep workers at their stations and their minds on their jobs. Similarly, industrial workers entered the world of the cash economy. Most agricultural workers were used to being paid in kind and to barter exchange. Money was an unusual luxury that was associated with binges of food, drink, and frivolities. This made adjustment to the wage packet as difficult as adjustment to the clock. Cash had to be set aside for provisions, rent, and clothing.

Such adjustments were not easy, and during the course of the nineteenth century a way of life passed from England forever. A vertically integrated society in which lord of the manor, village worthies, independent farmers, workers, and servants lived together interdependently was replaced by a society of segregated social classes. By the middle decades of the nineteenth century, a class of capitalists and a class of workers had begun to form and had begun to clash. The middle classes abandoned the city centers and built exclusive suburban communities in which to raise their children and insulate their families. Conditions in the cities deteriorated under the pressure of overcrowding, lack of sanitation, and the absence of private investment. The loss of interaction between these different segments of society had profound effects on the struggle to improve the quality of life for everyone. Leaders of labor saw themselves as fighting against profits, greed, and apathy; leaders of capital saw themselves as battling drunkenness, sloth, and ignorance. Between these two stereotypes there was little middle ground.

Chronology

THE INDUSTRIAL REVOLUTION IN BRITAIN

1709	Thomas Newcomen introduces steam-driven water pump
1709	Abraham Darby begins experiments with smelting iron ore with coke
1730s	John Kay invents flying shuttle
1760s	Private companies begin to invest in canals
1769	Richard Arkwright invents water frame
1775	James Watt invents improved steam engine
1780s	Henry Cort develops new method for removing impurities from pig iron
1794	Eli Whitney patents cotton gin
1801–1851	Population of England grows by 100 percent
1801–1851	Populations of Liverpool and Manchester grow by 1,000 percent
1810s	First Luddite riots
1830	Manchester-to-Liverpool railway line opened
1835	750 miles of railways in use in Britain
1852	7,500 miles of railways in use in Britain

The Industrialization of the Continent

Though Britain took the first steps along the road to an industrial economy, it was not long before other European nations followed. There was no single model for the industrialization of the continental states. Contemporaries continually made comparisons with Britain, but in truth the process of British industrialization was not well suited to any part of the Continent but the coal-rich regions in Belgium and the Rhineland. Nevertheless, all of Europe benefited from the British experience. No one else had to invent the jenny, the mule, or the steam engine. Therefore, although industrialization began later on the Continent, it could progress more quickly.

Britain shaped European industrialization in another way. Its head start made it very difficult for follower nations to compete against British commodities in the world market. This meant that European industrialization would be directed first and foremost to home markets, where tariffs and import quotas could protect fledgling industries. Britain's competitive advantage demanded that European governments become involved in the industrialization of their countries, financing capital-intensive industries, backing the railroads, and favoring the establishment of factories.

INDUSTRIAL REVOLUTION ON THE CONTINENT

What were the least industrial parts of Europe outside of Great Britain? In which directions did the major railroads run? How did the progress of industrialization in continental Europe compare with that in Britain? What impact did industrialization have on Spain and Italy?

France: Industrialization Without Revolution

The experience of France in the nineteenth century demonstrates that there was no single path in industrialization. Each state blended its natural resources, historical experiences, and forms of economic organization in unique combinations. While some mixtures resulted in explosive growth, as in Britain, others made for steady development, as in France.

French industrialization was keyed to domestic rather than export markets and to the application of new technology to a vast array of traditional crafts. France possessed a pool of highly skilled and highly productive labor, a manufacturing tradition that was oriented toward the creation of high-quality goods, and consumers who valued taste and fashion over cost and function. While the British dominated the new mass market for inexpensive cottons and cast-iron goods, a market with high sales but low profit margins, the French were producing luxury items whose scarcity kept both prices and profits high.

Two decisive factors determined the nature of French industrialization: population growth and the French Revolution.

Slow Growth. From the early eighteenth to the mid-nineteenth century, France grew slowly. In 1700, the French population stood at just under 20 million; in 1850, it was under 36 million, a growth rate of 80 percent. In contrast, Germany grew 135 percent, from 15 to 34 million, and England grew 300 percent, from 5 to 20 million, during the same period. Because of its moderate population growth, France was not pressured by the force of numbers to abandon its traditional agricultural methods, nor did it face a shortage of traditional supplies of energy.

The Impact of the French Revolution. The consequences of the French Revolution are less clear. Throughout the eighteenth century, the French economy performed at least as well as had the British and better in many areas. The revolution disrupted every aspect of economic life. Some of its outcomes were unforeseen and unwelcome. For example, Napoleon's Continental System, which attempted to close European markets to Britain, resulted in a shipping war, which the British won decisively and which eliminated France as a competitor for overseas trade in the mid-nineteenth century. But other outcomes were the result of direct policies, even if their impact could not have been entirely predicted. Urban guilds and corporations were abolished, opening trades to newcomers but destroying the close-knit groups that trained skilled artisans and introduced innovative products. Similarly, the breakup of both feudal and common lands to satisfy the hunger of the peasantry had the effect of maintaining a large rural population for decades.

Despite the efforts of the central government, there had been little change in the techniques used by French farmers over the course of the eighteenth century. French peasants clung tenaciously to traditional rights that gave even the smallest landholder a vital say in community agriculture. Landlords were predominantly absentee, less interested in the organization of their estates than in the dues and taxes that could be extracted from them. Therefore the policies of successive revolutionary governments strengthened the hold of small peasants on the land. With the abolition of many feudal dues and with careful family planning, smallholders could survive and pass a meager inheritance on to their children. French agriculture was able to supply the nation's need for food, but it could not release large numbers of workers for purely industrial activity.

Stages of Industrial Progress. French industrial growth was constrained on the one hand by the relatively small numbers of workers who could engage in manufacturing and on the other by the fact that a large portion of the population remained subsistence producers, cash-poor and linked only to small rural markets. Throughout the eighteenth century, the French economy continued to be regionally segregated rather than nationally integrated. The size of the state inhibited a highly organized internal trade, and there was little improvement of the infrastructure of transportation. Manufacturing concerns were still predominantly family businesses whose primary markets were regional rather than international. There was no national capital market until the mid-nineteenth century, and there were precious few regional ones.

It was not until midcentury that sustained industrial growth became evident in France. This was largely the result of the construction of railroads on a national plan, financed in large part by the central government. Whereas in Britain the railways took advantage of a national market, in France they created one. They also gave the essential stimulation to the modernization of the iron industry, of machine making, and of the capital markets.

The disadvantages of being on the trailing edge of economic change were mitigated for a time by conventional practices of protectionism. Except in specialty goods, agricultural produce, and luxury products, French manufacturers could not compete with either British or German commodities. Had France maintained its position as a world trader, this comparative disadvantage would have been devastating. But defeat in the wars of commerce had led to a drawing inward of French economic effort. Marseille and Bordeaux, once bustling centers of European trade, became provincial backwaters in the nineteenth century. But the internal market was still strong enough to support industrial growth, and domestic commodities could be protected by prohibitive tariffs, especially against British textiles, iron, and, ironically, coal.

While France achieved industrialization without an industrial revolution, it also achieved economic growth within the context of its traditional values. Agriculture may not have modernized, but the ancient village communities escaped the devastation that modernization would have brought. The orderly progression of generations of farming families characterized rural France until the shattering experiences of the Franco-Prussian War (1870) and the First World War (1914–1918). Nor did France experience the mushroom growth of new cities, with all of their problems of poverty, squalor, and homelessness. Slow population growth ameliorated the worst of the social diseases of industrialization, while traditional rural manufacturing softened the transformation of a way of life.

Germany: Industrialization and Union

The process of industrialization in Germany was dominated by the historic divisions of the empire of the German peoples. Before 1815, there were over 300 separate jurisdictional units within the empire, and after 1815 there were still more than 30. Each state clung tenaciously to its local laws and customs, which favored its citizens over outsiders. Merchants who lived near the intersection of separate jurisdictions could find themselves liable for several sets of tolls to move their goods and several sets of customs duties for importing and exporting them. These would have to be paid in different currencies at different rates of exchange according to the different regulations of each state. Small wonder that German merchants exhibited an intense localism, preferring to trade with members of their own state and supporting trade barriers against others. Such obstacles had a depressing effect on the economies of all German states but pushed with greatest weight against the manufacturing regions of Saxony, Silesia, and the Rhineland.

Agriculture. Most of imperial Germany was agricultural land that was suited to a diversity of uses. While English farmers were turning farms into commercial estates, German peasants were learning how to make do with less land.

Agricultural estates were organized differently in different parts of Germany. In the east, serfdom still prevailed. In central Germany, the long process of commuting labor service into rents was nearly complete by the end of the eighteenth century. The peasantry was not yet free, as a series of manorial relationships still tied them to the land, but they were no longer mere serfs. Finally, Western Germany was dominated by free farmers who either owned or leased their lands and who had a purely economic relationship with their landlords. The restriction of peasant mobility in much of Germany posed difficulties for the creation of an industrial workforce.

Though Germany was well endowed with natural resources and skilled labor in a number of trades, it had not taken part in the expansion of world trade during the seventeenth century, and the once bustling Hanseatic ports had been far outdistanced by the rise of the Atlantic economies. The principal exported manufacture was linen, which was expertly spun and woven in Saxony and the Prussian province of Silesia. The linen industry relied on the putting-out system and some factory spinning, especially after the introduction of British mechanical innovations. But even the most advanced factories were still being powered by water, and so they were located in mountainous regions where rapidly running streams could turn the wheels. Neither linens nor traditional German metal crafts could compete on the international markets, but they could find a wider market within Germany if only the problems of political division could be resolved.

The Zollverein. The problems of political division were especially acute for Prussia after the reorganization of European boundaries in 1815. Prussian territory now included the coal- and iron-rich Rhineland provinces, but a number of smaller states separated these areas from Prussia's eastern domain. Between 1815 and 1865, the population of Germany grew by 60 percent, to over 36 million. This was an enormous internal market, nearly as large as France, and the Prussians resolved to make it a unified trading zone by creating a series of alliances with smaller states, known as the **Zollverein** (1834). The Zollverein was not a free trade zone, like the British Empire, but rather a customs union in which member states adopted the liberal Prussian customs regulations.

The creation of the Zollverein was vital to German industrialization. It permitted the exploitation of natural advantages, such as plentiful supplies of coal and iron, and it provided a basis for the building of railroads. Germany was a follower nation in the process of industrialization. Seeking to learn from England, it brought British equipment and engineers to Germany, and German manufacturers sent their children to England to learn the latest techniques in industrial management. Steam engines were installed in German coal mines, if not in factories, and the process of puddling revolutionized iron making, though most iron was still smelted with charcoal rather than coke. Coal was plentiful in Prussia, but it was found at the eastern and western extremities of Germany. Therefore the railroads were the key to tapping German industrial potential. Here, they were a cause rather than a result of industrialization. The agreements that were hammered out in the creation of the Zollverein made possible the planning necessary to build single rail lines across the boundaries of numerous states.

As early as 1850, there were over 3,500 miles of rail in Germany, with important roads linking the manufacturing districts of Saxony and the coal and iron deposits of the Ruhr. Twenty years later, Germany was second only to Britain in the amount of track that had been laid and opened. By then, Germany was no longer simply a follower. German engineers and machinists, trained in Europe's best schools of technology, were turning out engines and rolling stock second to none. And the railroads transported a host of high-quality manufactures, especially durable metal goods that came to carry the most prestigious trademark of the late nineteenth century: "Made in Germany."

The Lands That Time Forgot

Nothing better demonstrates the point that industrialization was a regional rather than a national process than a survey of the states that did not develop industrial economies by the middle of the nineteenth century. These states ranged from the Netherlands, which was still one of the richest areas in Europe, to Spain and Russia, which were the poorest. Also included were Austria-Hungary, the states of the Italian peninsula, and Poland. In all of these nations there was some industrial progress. Nevertheless, the economies of all these states remained nonindustrial and, except that of the Netherlands, dominated by subsistence agriculture.

There were many reasons why these states were unable to develop their industrial potential. Some, such as Naples and Poland, were simply underendowed with resources; others, such as Austria-Hungary and Spain, faced difficulties of transport and communications that could not easily be overcome. Spain's modest resources were located on its northern and eastern edges, while a vast arid plain dominated the center. To move raw materials and finished products from one end of the country to the other was a daunting task, made more difficult by a lack of waterways and the rudimentary condition of Spanish roads. Two-thirds of Austria-Hungary was either mountains or hills, a geographic feature that presented obstacles that not even the railroads could easily solve. But there was far more than natural disadvantage behind the failure of these parts of Europe to move in step with the industrializing states. Their social structure, agricultural organization, and commercial policies all hindered the adoption of new methods, machines, and modes of production.

The leaders of traditional economies maintained tariff systems that insulated their own producers from competition. But protection was sensible only when it protected rather than isolated. Inefficiently produced goods of inferior quality were the chief results of the protectionist policies of the follower nations. Failure to adopt steam-powered machines made traditionally produced linens and silks so expensive that smuggling occurred on an international scale. Though these goods might find buyers in domestic markets, they could not compete in international trade, and one by one the industries of the follower nations atrophied. The economies that remained traditionally organized came to be exploited for their resources by those that had industrialized. Traditional agriculture could not produce the necessary surplus of either labor or capital to support industry, and industry could not economize sufficiently to make manufactured goods cheap enough for a poor peasantry.

There was more than irony in the fact that one of the first railroads built on the Continent was built in Austria but designed to be powered by horses rather than engines. The first railways in Italy linked royal palaces to capital cities; those in Spain radiated from Madrid and bypassed most centers of natural resources. In these states, the railroads were built to move the military rather than passengers or goods. They were state-financed, were occasionally state-owned, and almost always lost money. They were symbols of the industrial age, but in these states they were symbols without substance.

SUMMARY

The Traditional Economy   By the end of the eighteenth century, European population growth was placing a strain on agricultural production. Many rural workers turned to cottage industry and to participation in the putting-out system. In Britain and the Netherlands, the need to increase agricultural production was met with more efficient land management and a series of agricultural innovations. Collectively, these changes are known as the agricultural revolution. The transformation of agriculture came with significant social and cultural costs.

The Industrial Revolution in Britain   The Industrial Revolution occurred first in Britain. British advantages included: a strong water-based transportation system, abundant coal, and a well-developed economic infrastructure. The challenges of coal mining led to the development of the steam engine. More efficient engines were developed to solve problems in the iron industry. The textile industry led the way in the factory-based mechanized production. Railroads were both a response to the demands of industrialization and a cause of its acceleration. Industrial entrepreneurs had to learn the skills of management to succeed. Britain responded to the social costs of industrialization with a number of reform acts. Industrialization required painful adjustments from participants and produced profound changes in British society.

The Industrialization of the Continent While European industrialization was shaped by Britain, industrialization on the Continent was different in each country. In France, industrialization was a slow process that took advantage of traditional skills and occupations and gradually modernized the marketplace. In Germany, industrialization had to overcome political divisions within the empire. The creation of a customs union dominated by Prussia was vital to industrial development. For a variety of reasons, a number of states did not develop industrial economies in the nineteenth century, or saw only limited industrialization in particular regions.

QUESTIONS FOR REVIEW

1. Why did early manufacturing develop in the countryside, and what effect did that have on manufacturing practices and social relations?
2. In what ways were the ideas about organization of manufacturers such as Josiah Wedgwood and Robert Owen as significant as new technology in the development of industry in Britain?
3. How did British society address some of the changes in people's lives that were brought about by industrialization?
4. How did industrialization on the Continent differ from industrialization in England?
5. Why did some nations develop little industry at all?

CHAPTER 22

Political Upheavals and Social Transformations, 1815–1850

The New Ideologies

After 1815, the world was changing in many ways. As national boundaries were being redefined, the way in which Europeans regarded their world was also being transformed. Steam-driven mechanical power in production and transportation steadily replaced human and animal power. The new technology challenged old values; new definitions of worth emerged from the changing world of work. The fixed, castelike distinctions of the old aristocratic world were under attack or in disarray. Western intellectuals struggled to make sense of the new age and their place in it.

The political and economic upheavals of the first half of the nineteenth century encouraged a new breed of thinkers to search for ways to explain the transformations of the period. Before midcentury, Europeans witnessed one of the most intellectually fertile periods in the history of the West. This era gave birth to new ideologies—liberalism, nationalism, romanticism, conservatism, and socialism—that came to shape the ideas and institutions of the present day.

The New Politics of Preserving Order

European states had been dealing with war for over two decades. Now they faced the challenge of peace. The revolution and Napoleon had not only meant military engagements; they had also brought the force of revolutionary ideas to the political arena, and these ideas did not retire from the field after Waterloo. Nor did treaties restore an old order, despite their claims. Governments throughout Europe had to find new ways to deal with the tension between state authority and individual liberty. Conservative and liberal thinkers took very different paths in the pursuit of political stability.

Conservatism. **Conservatism** represented a dynamic adaptation to a social system in transition. In place of individualism, conservatives stressed the established institutions of European society; in place of reason and progress, conservatives advocated gradual, evolutionary growth and social stability. They opposed an abrupt break with tradition. Liberty, argued British statesman Edmund Burke (1729–1797) in *Reflections on the Revolution in France* (1790), must emerge out of the gradual development of the old order, not its destruction.

Conservatism took a reactionary turn in the hands of the Austrian statesman Prince Klemens von Metternich. The Carlsbad decrees of 1819 are a good example of the "Metternich system" of espionage, censorship, and university repression in central Europe, which sought to eliminate any constitutional or nationalist sentiments that had arisen during the Napoleonic period. The German Confederation approved the decrees against free speech and civil liberties and set up mechanisms to root out "subversive" university students. Students who had taken up arms in the Wars of Liberation (1813–1815) against France had done so in hopes of instituting liberal and national reforms. Metternich's system aimed at uprooting these goals. Student fraternities were closed, and police became a regular fixture in the university. Political expression was driven underground for at least a decade. Metternich set out to crush liberalism, constitutionalism, and parliamentarianism in central Europe.

Liberalism. Two main tenets of **liberalism** asserted the freedom of the individual and the corruptibility of authority. As a political doctrine, liberalism built on Enlightenment rationalism and embraced the right to vote, civil liberties, legal equality, constitutional government, parliamentary sovereignty, and a free market economy. Liberals firmly believed that less government was better government and that noninterference would produce a harmonious and well-ordered world. They also believed that human beings were basically good and reasonable and needed freedom in which to flourish, and that the sole end of government should be to promote that freedom.

Liberal thinkers grappled with the political conflicts of the revolutionary period and the economic disruptions brought on by industrialization. The Great Revolution at the end of the eighteenth century spawned a vast array of liberal thought in France. Republicans, Bonapartists, and constitutional monarchists cooperated as self-styled "liberals," who shared a desire to preserve the gains of the revolution while ensuring orderly rule. Liberal ideas also influenced a variety of political movements in the United States, including those demanding the liberation of slaves and the extension of legal and political rights to women.

By the mid-nineteenth century, liberal thinking constituted a dominant strain in British politics. Jeremy Bentham (1748–1832) founded **utilitarianism**, a fundamentally liberal doctrine that argued for "the greatest happiness of the greatest number." Bentham believed that government could achieve positive ends through limited and "scientific" intervention. John Stuart Mill (1806–1873) espoused social reform for the poor and championed the equality of women and the necessity of birth control. David Ricardo (1772–1823), in *Principles of Political Economy and Taxation* (1817), outlined his opposition to government intervention in foreign trade and elaborated his "iron law of wages," which contended that wages would stabilize at the subsistence level. Increased wages would cause the working classes to increase, and the resulting competition in the labor market would drive wages down to the subsistence level.

Romanticism and Change

Unlike liberalism and conservatism, which were fundamentally political ideologies, **romanticism** designated a variety of literary and artistic movements throughout Europe that spanned the period from the late eighteenth century to the mid-nineteenth century. One could be a liberal and a romantic just as easily as one could be a conservative and a romantic.

The Romantic World View. Above all, in spite of variations, romantics shared similar beliefs and a common view of the world. Romantics in general rebelled against the confinement of classical forms and refused to accept the supremacy of reason over emotions.

Intellectuals, Artists, and Freedom. By rooting artistic vision in spontaneity, romantics endorsed a concept of creativity based on the supremacy of human freedom. The artist was valued in a new way as a genius through whose insight and intuition great art was created. Intuition, as opposed to scientific learning, was endorsed as a valid means of knowing. Building on the work of the eighteenth-century philosopher Immanuel Kant

Liberty Leading the People (1831) by Eugène Delacroix captures the spirit of the French romantics, who looked upon revolutionary action as a way to achieve union with the spirit of history.

(1724–1804), romanticism embraced subjective knowledge. Inspiration and intuition took the place of reason and science in the romantic pantheon of values.

Germaine de Staël (1766–1817), whose writings influenced French political theory after 1815, is often hailed as the founder of French romanticism. Like many other romantics, she was greatly influenced by the writings of Jean-Jacques Rousseau, and through him she discovered that "the soul's elevation is born of self-consciousness." The recognition of the subjective meant for de Staël that women's vision was as essential as men's for the flowering of European culture.

The supremacy of emotions over reason found its way into the works of the great romantic composers of the age: Louis Hector Berlioz (1803–1869), the French composer who set Faust's damnation to music; Polish virtuoso Frédéric Chopin (1810–1849); and Hungarian concert pianist Franz Liszt (1811–1886). Artists such as J. M. W. Turner (1775–1851), the English landscape painter, and Eugène Delacroix (1798–1863), the leader of the French romantic school in painting, shared a rebellious experimentation with color and a rejection of classical conventions and forms.

In the postrevolutionary age of the years between 1815 and 1850, romanticism claimed to be no more than an aesthetic stance in art, letters, and music, a posture that had no particular political intent. Yet its validation of the individual as opposed to the caste or the estate was a revolutionary doctrine that helped to define a new political consciousness.

Reshaping State and Society

As another legacy of the French Revolution, the concept of the nation as a source of collective identity and political allegiance became a political force after 1815. Just as nationalism put the needs of the people at the heart of its political doctrine, so did socialism focus on the needs of society and especially of the poor.

Nationalism. In its most basic sense, nationalism before 1850 was the political doctrine that glorified the people united against the absolutism of kings and the tyranny of foreign oppressors. The success of the French Revolution and the spread of Napoleonic reforms boosted nationalist doctrines, which were most fully articulated on the Continent. The philosophers Johann Fichte (1762–1814) and Georg Wilhelm Friedrich Hegel (1770–1831) emphasized the importance of the state. There was a new concern with history, as nationalists sought to revive a common cultural past.

In the period between 1830 and 1850, many nationalists were liberals and many liberals were nationalists. The nationalist yearning for liberation meshed with the liberal political program of overthrowing tyrannical rule. Giuseppe Mazzini (1805–1872) represented the new breed of liberal nationalist. A less-than-liberal nationalist was political economist Georg Friedrich List (1789–1846), who formulated a statement of economic nationalism to counter the liberal doctrines of David Ricardo. Arguing that free trade worked only for the wealthy and powerful, List advocated a program of protective tariffs for developing German industries. British free trade, he perceived, was merely economic imperialism in disguise. List was one of the few nationalists who did not wholeheartedly embrace liberal economic doctrines. Beyond ideology and political practices, nationalism began to capture the imagination of groups who resented foreign domination. Expanding state bureaucracies did little to tame the centrifugal forces of nationalist feeling and probably exacerbated a desire for independence in eastern and central Europe, especially in the Habsburg-ruled lands.

Nationalists valued the authenticity of the vernacular and folklore over the language and customs imposed by a foreign ruler. Johann Gottfried von Herder (1744–1803) and the brothers Jacob Ludwig Grimm (1785–1863) and Wilhelm Carl Grimm (1786–1859) were German examples of the romantic appreciation of the roots of German culture. While French romantics emphasized the glories of their revolutionary heritage, German romantics stressed the importance of history as the source of one's identity. By searching for the self in a historic past, and especially in the Middle Ages, they glorified their collective cultural identity and national origins.

Socialism. Socialists rejected the world as it was. Socialism, like other ideologies of the first half of the nineteenth century, grew out of the changes in the structure of daily life and the structure of power. There were as many stripes of socialists as there were of liberals, nationalists, and conservatives.

Socialist thinkers in France theorized about alternative societies in which wealth would be more equitably distributed. To Henri de Saint-Simon (1760–1825) the accomplishments and potential of industrial development represented the highest stage in history. In a perfect and just society, productive work would be the basis of all prestige and power.

Like Saint-Simon, the French social theorist Pierre Joseph Proudhon (1809–1865) recognized the social value of work. But unlike Saint-Simon, Proudhon refused to accept the dominance of industrial society. In his famous pamphlet *What Is Property?* (1840), Proudhon answered, "Property is theft." However, this statement was not an argument for the abolition of private ownership. Proudhon reasoned that industrialization had destroyed workers' rights, which included the right to the profits of their own labor. In attacking "property," in its meaning of profits amassed from the labor of others, Proudhon was arguing for a socialist concept of limited possession—people had the right to own only what they had earned from their own labor—and for a potentially anarchist concept of limited government—people had the right to rule themselves.

At least one socialist believed in luxury. Charles Fourier (1772–1837) devoted himself to the study and improvement of society and formulated one of the most trenchant criticisms of industrial capitalism. In numerous writings between 1808 and his death, he put forward a vision of a utopian world organized into units called phalanxes that took into account their members' social, sexual, and economic needs. With a proper mix of duties, everyone in the phalanx would work only a few hours a day. In Fourier's phalanxes, every aspect of life would be organized communally, although neither poverty nor property would be eliminated. Education would help to dispel discord, and rich and poor would learn to live together in perfect harmony.

The emancipation of women was an issue acknowledged by socialists as well as liberals. Some social reformers, including Fourier, put the issue of women's freedom at the center of their plans to redesign society. Other social reformers joined with conservative thinkers in arguing that women must be kept in their place, which was in the home.

Socialists, along with other ideologues in the decades before the middle of the nineteenth century, were aware of how rapidly their world was changing. Many believed that a revolution that would eliminate poverty and the sufferings of the working class was at hand. Followers of Saint-Simon, Proudhon, and Fourier all hoped that their proposals and ideas would change the world and prevent violent upheaval. Not all social critics were so sanguine.

In *The Communist Manifesto*, Karl Marx (1818–1883) and Friedrich Engels (1820–1895) described the dire situation of the working classes throughout the 1840s. The growing poverty and alienation of the **proletariat**, the propertyless masses, the authors promised, would bring to industrialized Europe a class war against the capitalists. Exploited workers were to prepare themselves for the moment of revolution by joining with each other across national boundaries.

Intellectuals and reformers hoped with the force of their ideas to reshape the world in which they lived. The technology of industrial production informed people's values and required a new way of looking at the world. Liberals, nationalists, romantics, conservatives, and socialists addressed the challenges of a changing economy in a political universe buffeted by democratic ideas. Rather than providing neat answers, ideologies fueled actions, and often violent protest and revolution erupted in the streets.

Protest and Revolution

For European societies that had remained stable, if not stagnant, for centuries, the changes in the first half of the nineteenth century were undoubtedly startling and disruptive. New factories created the arena for exploitation and misery. More people than ever before lived in cities, and national populations faced the prospect of becoming urban. Urban congestion brought crime and disease; patterns of consumption demonstrated beyond dispute that people were not created equal. A new European society that challenged existing political ideas and demanded new political formulations was in the process of emerging.

Causes of Social Instability

The fabric of stability began unraveling throughout Europe beginning in the 1820s. The forces of order reacted to protest with repression everywhere in Europe. Yet armed force proved inadequate to contain the demands for political participation and the increased political awareness of whole segments of the population. Workers, the middle class, and women's political organizations now demanded, through the vote, the right to govern themselves.

Urban Miseries. In 1800, two of every one hundred Europeans lived in a city. By 1850, the number of urban dwellers per hundred had jumped to five and was rising rapidly. Massive internal migration caused most urban growth. People from the same rural areas often lived together in the same urban neighborhoods and even in the same boardinghouses. Until midcentury, many migrants returned to their rural homes for the winter when work, especially in the building trades, was scarce in the city. Young migrant women who came to the city to work as servants sent money home to support rural relatives or worked to save a nest egg—or dowry—in order to return to the village permanently.

Despite the neighborhood support networks that migrants constructed for themselves, the city was not always a hospitable place. Workers were poorly paid, and women workers were more poorly paid than men. When working women were cut free of the support of home and family, uncounted numbers were forced into part-time prostitution to supplement meager incomes.

Urban crime also grew astronomically, thefts accounting for the greatest number of crimes. Social reformers identified poverty and urban crowding as causes of the increase in criminal behavior. In 1829, both Paris and London began to create modern urban police forces to deal with the challenges to law and order. Crime assumed the character of disease in the minds of middle-class reformers. Statisticians and social scientists, themselves a new urban phenomenon, produced massive theses on social hygiene, lower-class immorality, and the unworthiness of the poor. The pathology of the city was widely discussed. Always at the center of the issue was the "social question": the growing problem of what to do with the poor.

The "Social Question." State-sponsored work relief expanded after 1830 for the deserving poor: the old, the sick, and children. Able-bodied workers who were idle were regarded as undeserving and dangerous, regardless of the causes of their unemployment. Performance of work became an indicator of moral worth, as urban and rural workers succumbed to downturns in the economic cycle. Those who were unable to work sought relief, as a last resort, from the state. What has been called "a revolution in government" took place in the 1830s and 1840s, as legislative bodies increased regulation of everything from factories and mines to prisons and schools.

Some argued, as in the case of the Irish famine, that the government must do nothing to intervene because the problem would correct itself, as Thomas Malthus had predicted 40 years earlier, through the "natural" means of famine and death that would keep population from outgrowing available resources and food supplies. Poverty was a social necessity; by interfering with it, this first group insisted, governments could only make matters worse.

Others contended that poverty was society's problem, not a law of nature. Therefore, it was the social responsibility of the state to take care of its members. The question of how to treat poverty, or "the social question" as it came to be known among contemporaries, underlay many of the protests and reforms of the two decades before 1850 and fueled the revolutionary movements of 1848. Parliamentary legislation attempted to improve the situation of the poor and especially the working class in the 1830s and 1840s.

In 1833, British reformers turned their attention to the question of child labor. Parliament passed the Factory Act of 1833, which prohibited the employment of children under nine years of age and restricted the work week of children under eighteen. The British Parliament commissioned investigations, compiled in the "Blue Books," that reported the abusive treatment of men, women, and children in factories.

This 1834 engraving from *The Oracle of Health* shows the brutal treatment of children working in an English textile factory. The meager wages of children were often necessary for the survival of their families.

The British legislation marked an initial step in state intervention in the workplace. Additional legislation over the next three decades further restricted children's and women's labor in factories and concerned itself with improvement of conditions in the workplace. At bottom the social question was: What was the state's responsibility in caring for its citizens?

The Revolutions of 1830

Few Europeans who were alive in 1830 remembered the age of revolution from 1789 to 1799. Yet the legends were kept alive from one generation to the next. Secret political organizations perpetuated Jacobin republicanism. Mutual-aid societies and artisan associations preserved the rituals of democratic culture. A revolutionary culture seemed to be budding in the student riots in Germany and in the revolutionary waves that swept across southern and central Europe in the early 1820s. Outside Manchester, England, in August 1819, a crowd of 80,000 people gathered in St. Peter's Field to hear speeches for parliamentary reform and universal male suffrage. The cavalry swept down on them in a bloody slaughter that came to be known as the **Peterloo massacre**, a bitter reference to the Waterloo victory four years before.

Poor harvests in 1829 followed by a harsh winter left people cold, hungry, and bitter. Misery fueled social protest, and the convergence of social unrest with long-standing political demands touched off apparently simultaneous revolutions all over Europe.

The French Revolution of 1830. In France, the late 1820s was a period of increasing political friction. Charles X (1824–1830), the former comte d'Artois, had never resigned himself to the constitutional monarchy accepted by his brother and predecessor, Louis XVIII. When Charles assumed the throne in 1824, he dedicated himself to a true restoration of kingship as it existed before the revolution. To this end, he realigned the monarchy with the Catholic Church and undertook several unpopular measures, including approval of the death penalty for people who were found guilty of sacrilege. The king's bourgeois critics, heavily influenced by liberal ideas about political economy and constitutional rights, sought increased political power through their activities in secret organizations and in public elections. The king responded to his critics by relying on his ultraroyalist supporters to run the government. In May 1830, the king dissolved the Chamber of Deputies and ordered new elections. The elections returned a liberal majority that was unfavorable to the king. Charles X retaliated with what proved to be his last political act, the Four Ordinances, in which he censored the press, changed the electoral law to favor his own candidates, dissolved the newly elected chamber, and ordered new elections.

Opposition to Charles X might have remained at the level of political wrangling and journalistic protest had it not been for the problems plaguing the people of Paris. A severe winter in France had driven food prices up by 75 percent. The king underestimated the extent of hardship and the political volatility of the population. Throughout the spring of 1830, prices continued to rise and Charles continued to blunder. In a spontaneous uprising in the last days of July 1830, workers took to the streets of Paris. The revolution that they initiated spread rapidly to towns and the countryside, as people throughout France protested the cost of living, hoarding by grain merchants, tax collection, and wage cuts. In "three glorious days" the restored Bourbon regime was pulled down, and Charles X fled to England.

The people fighting in the streets demanded a republic, but they lacked organization and political experience. Liberal bourgeois politicians quickly filled the power vacuum. They presented Charles's cousin, the duc d'Orléans, as the savior of France and the new constitutional monarch. This July Monarchy, born of a revolution, put an end to the Bourbon Restoration. Louis-Philippe, the former duc d'Orléans, became king of the French. The charter that he brought with him was, like its predecessor, based on restricted suffrage, with property ownership a requisite for voting.

Unrest in Europe. Popular disturbances did not always result in revolution. In Britain, rural and town riots erupted over grain prices and distribution, but no revolution followed. German workers broke their machines to protest low wages and loss of control of the workplace, but no prince was displaced.

In southern Europe, Turkish overlords ruled Greece as part of the Ottoman Empire. The longing for independence smoldered in Greece throughout the 1820s as public pressure to support the Greeks mounted in Europe. Greek insurrections were answered by Turkish retaliations throughout the Ottoman Empire. The sultan of Turkey had been able to call on his vassal, the pasha of Egypt, to subdue Greece. In response, Great Britain, France, and Russia signed the Treaty of London in 1827, pledging intervention on behalf of Greece. In a joint effort, the three powers defeated the Egyptian fleet. Russia declared war on Turkey the following year, seeking territorial concessions from the Ottoman Empire. Following the Russian victory, Great Britain and France joined Russia in declaring Greek independence.

Belgian Independence. The overthrow of the Bourbon monarch in France served as a model for revolution in other parts of Europe. In the midst of the Greek crisis the Belgian provinces revolted against the Netherlands. The Belgians' desire to have their own nation struck at the heart of the settlement reached at the Congress of Vienna in the aftermath of the Napoleonic Wars. Provoked by a food crisis similar to that in France, Belgian revolutionaries took to the streets in August 1830. Belgians protested the deterioration of their economic situation and made demands for their own Catholic religion, their own language, and constitutional rights. Bitter fighting on the barricades in Brussels ensued, and the movement for freedom and independence spread to the countryside.

The Great Powers disagreed about what to do. Russia, Austria, and Prussia were all eager to see the revolution crushed. France, having just established the new regime of the July Monarchy, and Great Britain, fearing the involvement of the central and eastern European powers in an area where Britain had traditionally had interests, were reluctant to intervene. A provisional government in Belgium set about the task of writing a constitution. All five Great Powers recognized Belgian independence, with the proviso that Belgium was to maintain the status of a neutral state.

The Forgotten Revolutions. Russia, Prussia, and Austria were convinced to accept Belgian independence because they were having their own problems in eastern and southern Europe. Revolution erupted in Warsaw when Polish army cadets and university students revolted in November 1830 to demand independence and a constitution. Landed aristocrats and gentry helped to establish a provisional government but soon split over how radical reforms should be. Polish peasants refused to support either landowning group. Within the year, Russia brought in 180,000 troops to crush the revolution and reassert its rule over Poland.

In February 1831, the Italian states of Modena and Parma rose up to throw off Austrian domination of northern Italy. The revolutionaries were ineffective against Austrian troops. Revolution in the Papal States resulted in French occupation that lasted until 1838 without serious reforms. Nationalist and republican yearnings were driven underground, kept alive there in the Young Italy movement under the leadership of Giuseppe Mazzini.

Although the revolutions of 1830 are called "the forgotten revolutions" of the nineteenth century, they are important for several reasons. First, they made clear to European states how closely tied together were their fates. True to the principles of the Vienna settlements of 1815, European leaders preserved the status quo and maintained the balance of power. Revolutions in Poland and Italy were contained by Russia and Austria without interference from the other powers. Where adaptation was necessary, as in Greece and Belgium, the Great Powers were able to compromise on settlements, even though the solutions ran counter to previous policies. Heads of state were willing to use the forces of repression to stamp out protest. The international significance of the revolutions reveals a second important aspect of the events of 1830: the vulnerability of international politics to domestic instability.

Finally, the 1830 revolutions exposed a growing awareness of politics at all levels of European society. If policies in 1830 revealed a shared consciousness of events and shared values among ruling elites, the revolutions disclosed a growing awareness among the lower classes of the importance of politics in their daily lives. In a dangerous combination, workers and the lower classes throughout Europe were politicized, yet they continued to be excluded from political power.

Reform in Great Britain

The right to vote had been an issue of contention in the revolutions of 1830 in western Europe. The July Revolution in France had doubled the electorate, but still only a tiny minority of the population (less than 1 percent) enjoyed the vote. Universal male suffrage had been mandated in 1793 during the Great Revolution but not implemented. Those in power believed that the wealthiest property owners were best qualified to govern, in part because they had the greatest stake in politics and society. One also needed to own property to hold office, since those who served in parliaments received no salary.

The Rule of the Land. Landowners also ruled Britain. Migration to cities had depleted the population of rural areas, but the electoral system did not adjust to these changes. Large towns had no parliamentary representation, while dwindling county electorates maintained their parliamentary strength. Areas that continued to enjoy representation greater than that justified by their population were dubbed "rotten boroughs" or "pocket boroughs" to indicate a corrupt and antiquated electoral system. In general, urban areas were grossly underrepresented, as the wealthy few controlled county seats.

After much parliamentary wrangling and popular agitation, the **Great Reform Bill of 1832** proposed a compromise. Although the vast majority of the population still did not have the vote, the new legislation strengthened the industrial and commercial elite in the towns, enfranchised most of the middle class, opened the way to social reforms, and encouraged the formation of political parties. In the 1830s, new radical reformers, disillusioned with the 1832 reform bill because it strengthened the power of a wealthy capitalist class, argued that democracy was the only answer to the problems plaguing British society.

The Chartist Movement. In 1838, a small group of labor leaders, including representatives of the London Working Men's Association, an organization of craft workers, drew up a document known as the People's Charter. The single most important demand of the charter was that all men must have the vote.

Chartism blossomed in working-class towns and appeared to involve all members of the family. Women organized Chartist schools and Sunday schools in radical defiance of local church organizations. Many middle-class observers were sure that

This English cartoon of 1832 is titled *The Clemency of the Russian Monster*. It shows Nicholas I in the guise of a bear with menacing teeth and claws addressing the Poles after crushing their rebellion against Russian rule.

the moment for class war and revolutionary upheaval had arrived. The government responded with force to the perceived threat of armed rebellion and imprisoned a number of Chartist leaders. The final moment for Chartism occurred in April 1848, when 25,000 Chartist workers, inspired by revolutionary events on the Continent, assembled in London to march on the House of Commons. They carried a newly signed petition demanding the enactment of the terms of their charter. In response, the government deputized nearly 200,000 "special" constables in the streets. These deputized private citizens were London property owners and skilled workers who were intent on holding back a revolutionary rabble. Tired, cold, and rain-soaked, the Chartist demonstrators disbanded. No social revolution took place in Great Britain, and the dilemma of democratic representation was deferred.

Workers Unite

The word *proletariat* entered European languages before the mid-nineteenth century to describe those workers afloat in the labor pool who owned nothing, not even the tools of their labor, and who were becoming appendages to the new machines that dominated production.

Luddism. Mechanization deprived skilled craftworkers of control of the workplace. In Great Britain, France, and Germany, groups of textile workers destroyed machines in protest. Machine-breakers tyrannized parts of Great Britain from 1811 to 1816 in an attempt to frighten masters. The movement was known as Luddism after its mythical leader, Ned Ludd. Workers damaged and destroyed property for more control over the work process, but such destruction met with severe repression. From the 1820s to the 1850s, sporadic but intense outbursts of machine-breaking occurred in continental Europe. Skilled workers, fearing that they would be pulled down into the new proletariat because of mechanization and the increased scale of production, organized in new ways after 1830.

Uprisings and strikes in France increased dramatically from 1831 to 1834 and favored the destruction of the monarchy and the creation of a democratic republic. Many French craft workers grew conscious of themselves as a class and embraced a socialism that was heavily influenced by their own traditions and contemporary socialist writings. Government repression drove worker organizations underground in the late 1830s, and secret societies proliferated.

Women in the Workforce. Women were an important part of the workforce in the industrializing societies. Working men were keenly aware of the competition with cheaper female labor in the factories. Women formed a salaried workforce in the home, too. To produce cheaply and in large quantities, some manufacturers turned to subcontractors for the simpler tasks in the work process. These new middlemen contracted out work such as cutting and sewing to needy women, who were often responsible for caring for family members in their homes.

Cheap female labor, paid by the piece, allowed employers to profit by keeping overhead costs low and by driving down the wages of skilled workers. Trade unions opposed women's work both in the home and in the factories. Unions argued that their members should earn a wage "sufficient to support a wife and children." Unions consistently excluded women workers from their ranks.

French labor leader Flora Tristan, speaking not only as a worker but also as a wife and mother, had a very different answer for those who wanted to remove women from the workplace. She recognized that working women needed to work in order to support themselves and their families. Tristan told audiences in Europe and Latin America that the emancipation of women from their "slave status" was essential if the working class as a whole was to enjoy a better future.

Working women's only hope, according to Tristan, lay in education and unionization. She urged working men and women to join together to lay claim to their natural and inalienable rights. In some cases, working women formed their own organizations, like that of the Parisian seamstresses who joined together to demand improved working conditions. On the whole, however, domestic workers in the home remained isolated from other working women, and many women in factories feared the loss of their jobs if they engaged in political activism. The wages of Europe's working women remained low, often below subsistence level.

Revolutions Across Europe, 1848–1850

Europeans had never experienced a year like 1848. Beginning soon after the ringing in of the New Year, revolutionary fervor swept through nearly every European country.

Hindsight reveals warning signs in the two years before the 1848 cataclysm. Beginning in 1846, a severe famine racked Europe. Lack of grain drove up prices. An increasing percentage of disposable income was spent on food for survival. Lack of spending power severely damaged markets and forced thousands of industrial workers out of their jobs. The famine hurt everyone—the poor, workers, employers, and investors—as recession paralyzed the economy.

The food crisis took place in a heavily charged political atmosphere. Throughout Europe during the 1840s, middle and lower classes had intensified their agitation for democracy. Chartists in Great Britain argued for a wider electorate. Bourgeois reformers in France campaigned for universal manhood suffrage. The movement was known as the "banquet" campaign because its leaders attempted to raise money by giving speeches at subscribed dinners. In making demands for political participation, those who were agitating for the vote necessarily criticized those who were in power. Freedom of speech and freedom of assembly were demanded as inalienable rights. The food crisis and political activism were the ingredients of an incendiary situation.

In addition to a burgeoning democratic culture, growing demands for national autonomy based on linguistic and cultural claims spread through central, southern, and eastern Europe. Although the revolts in Poland in 1846 failed, they encouraged similar movements for national liberation among Italians and Germans. Even in the relatively homogeneous nation of France, concerns with national mission and national glory grew among the regime's critics. National unity was primarily a middle-class ideal. Liberal lawyers, teachers, and businessmen from Dublin to Budapest to Prague agitated for separation from foreign rule. Austria, with an empire formed of numerous ethnic minorities, had the most to lose. Since 1815, Metternich had been ruthless in stamping out nationalist dissent. By the 1840s, nationalist claims were assuming a cultural legitimacy that was difficult to dismiss or ignore.

France Leads the Way. The events in France in the cold February of 1848 ignited the conflagration that swept Europe. On 22 February, bourgeois reformers had staged their largest banquet to date in Paris in support of extension of the vote. City officials became nervous at the prospect of thousands of workers assembling for political purposes and canceled the scheduled banquet. This was the spark that touched off the powder keg. In a spontaneous uprising, Parisians demonstrated against the government's repressive measures. Skilled workers took to the streets not only in favor of the banned banquet but also with the hope that the government would recognize the importance of labor to the social order. Shots were fired; a demonstrator was killed. The French Revolution of 1848 had begun.

Events moved quickly. The National Guard, a citizen militia of bourgeois Parisians, defected from Louis-Philippe. Many army troops that were garrisoned in Paris crossed the barricades to join revolutionary workers. The king attempted some reform, but it was too little and too late. Louis-Philippe fled. The Second Republic was proclaimed at the insistence of the revolutionary crowds on the barricades. The Provisional Government, led by the poet Alphonse de Lamartine (1790–1869), included members of both factions of political reformers of the July Monarchy: moderates who sought constitutional reforms and an extension of the suffrage and radicals who favored universal manhood suffrage and social programs to deal with poverty and work. Only the threat of popular violence held this uneasy alliance together.

The people fighting in the streets had little in common with the bourgeois reformers who assumed power on 24 February. Workers made a social revolution out of a commitment to their right to work, which would replace the right to property as the organizing principle of the new society. Only one member of the new Provisional Government was a worker, and he was included as a token symbol of the intentions of the new government. The government acknowledged the demand of the right to work and set up two mechanisms to guarantee workers' relief. First, a commission of workers and employers was created to act as a grievance and bargaining board and to settle questions of common concern in the workplace. Headed by the socialist Louis Blanc (1811–1882) and known as the Luxembourg Commission, the worker-employer parliament was an important innovation but accomplished little other than deflecting workers' attention away from the problems of the Provisional Government. The second measure was the creation of "national workshops" to deal with the problems of unemployment in Paris. Workers from all over France poured into Paris with the hope of finding jobs. However, the workshops had a residency requirement that even Parisians had difficulty meeting. As a result, unemployment skyrocketed. Furthermore, the government was going bankrupt trying to support the program. The need to raise taxes upset peasants in the provinces. National pressure mounted to repudiate the programs of the revolution.

French workers were too weak to dominate the revolution. The government recalled General Louis Cavaignac (1802–1857) from service in Algeria to maintain order. In a wave of armed insurrection, Parisian workers rebelled in June of 1848. Using troops from the provinces who had no identification with the urban population and employing guerrilla techniques he had mastered in Algeria, Cavaignac put down the uprising. The Second Republic was placed under the military dictatorship of Cavaignac until December, when presidential elections were scheduled.

Revolutions in Central and Eastern Europe. France was not alone in undergoing revolution in 1848. Long-suppressed desires for civil liberties and constitutional reforms erupted in widespread popular disturbances in Prussia and the German states. Fearing a war with France and unable to count on Austria or Russia for support, the princes who ruled Baden, Württemberg, Hesse-Darmstadt, Bavaria, Saxony, and Hanover followed the advice of moderate liberals and acceded quickly to revolutionary demands. In Prussia, King Frederick William IV (1840–1861) preferred to use military force to respond to popular demonstrations. Only in mid-March 1848 did the Prussian king yield to the force of the revolutionary crowds building barricades in Berlin by ordering his troops to leave the city and by promising to create a national Prussian assembly. The king was now a prisoner of the revolution.

Meanwhile, the collapse of absolute monarchy in Prussia gave further impetus to a constitutional movement among the liberal leaders of the German states. The governments of all the German states were invited to elect delegates to a national parliament in Frankfurt. The Frankfurt parliament, which was convened in May 1848, had as its dual charge the framing of a constitution and the unification of Germany. To most parliamentarians, who were trained in universities and shared a social and cultural identity, nationalism and constitutionalism were inextricably related.

As straightforward as the desire for a German nation appeared to be, it was complicated by two important facts. First, there were non-German minorities living in German states. What was to be done with the Poles, Czechs, Slovenes, Italians, and Dutch in a newly constituted and autonomous German nation?

MAP DISCOVERY

Revolutions of 1848

North Sea

IRELAND
Dublin

GREAT BRITAIN

PRUSSIA

POLAND
Berlin
March 1848

RUSSIA

BELGIUM

ATLANTIC OCEAN

Paris
February & June, 1848

FRANCE

Frankfurt
March 1848

Prague
April 1848

Vienna
April 1848

Budapest
April 1848

AUSTRIAN EMPIRE

Milan
Venice

PARMA
MODENA

PORTUGAL

SPAIN

PAPAL STATES
Rome **March 1848 – June 1849**

Naples

OTTOMAN EMPIRE

Mediterranean Sea

SICILY

GREECE

THE REVOLUTIONS OF 1848

In less than a generation, a second major wave of revolutions swept across Europe from west to east in 1848. What were the centers of revolutionary action in 1848 and what was their relationship to the seats of political power? How do you explain the timing of the eastern trajectory of successive revolutions? How did the map of Europe change as a result of these revolutions?

Second, there were Germans living outside the German states under Habsburg rule in Austria, in Danish Schleswig and Holstein, in Posen (Poznan), in Russian Poland, and in European Russia. How were they to be included within the linguistically and ethnically constituted German nation? After much wrangling over a "small" Germany that excluded Austrian Germans and a "large" Germany that included them, the Frankfurt parliament opted for the small-Germany solution in March 1849. The crown of the new nation was offered to the unpredictable Frederick William IV of Prussia (1840–1861), head of the largest and most powerful of the German states. Unhappy with his capitulation to the revolutionary crowd in March 1848, the Prussian king refused to accept a "crown from the gutter." He had his own plans to rule over a middle-European bloc, but not at the behest of liberal parliamentarians. The attempt to create a German nation crumbled with his unwillingness to lead.

Revolution in Austrian-dominated central Europe was concentrated in three places: Vienna, Budapest, and Prague. By April 1848, Metternich had fallen from power, and the Viennese revolutionaries had set up a constituent assembly. In Budapest, the initial steps of the patriot Lajos Kossuth (1802–1894) toward establishing a separate Hungarian state seemed equally solid, as the Magyars defeated Habsburg troops. Habsburg armies were more successful in Prague, where they crushed the revolution in June 1848.

In December 1848, Emperor Ferdinand I (1835–1848), whose authority had been weakened irreparably by the overthrow of Metternich, abdicated in favor of his 18-year-old nephew, Franz Josef I (1848–1916).

Italian Nationalism. The Habsburg Empire was also under siege in Italy, where the Kingdom of the Two Sicilies, Tuscany, and Piedmont declared new constitutions in March 1848. Championed by Charles Albert of Piedmont, Venice and Lombardy rose up against Austria. Nationalist sentiments had percolated underground in the Young Italy movement, founded in 1831 by Giuseppe Mazzini. Mazzini a tireless and idealistic patriot, favored a democratic revolution. In spite of a reputation for liberal politics, Pope Pius IX (1846–1878) lost control of Rome and was forced to flee the city. Mazzini became head of the Republic of Rome, created in February 1849.

The French government decided to intervene to protect the pope's interests and sent in troops to defeat the republicans. One of Mazzini's disciples, Giuseppe Garibaldi (1807–1882), returned from exile in South America to undertake the defense of Rome. Although his legion of poorly armed patriots and soldiers of fortune, known from their attire as the Red Shirts, waged a valiant effort to defend the city from April to June 1849, they were no match for the highly trained French army. French troops restored Pius IX as ruler of the Papal States.

Meanwhile, from August 1848 to the following spring, the Habsburg armies fought and finally defeated each of the revolutions throughout the Austrian Empire. Austrian success can be explained in part because the various Italian groups of Piedmontese, Tuscans, Venetians, Romans, and Neapolitans lacked coordination and central organization. Both Mazzini and Pius IX had failed to provide the focal point of leadership necessary for a successful national movement. By the fall of 1849, Austria had solved the problems in its own capital and with Italy and Hungary by military dominance. Austria understood that a Germany united under Frederick William IV of Prussia would undermine Austrian dominance in central Europe.

Chronology

PROTEST AND REVOLUTION

August 1819	Peterloo Massacre
1824	Charles X assumes French throne
1827	Treaty of London to support liberation of Greece
July 1830	Revolution in Paris; creation of July Monarchy under Louis-Philippe
August 1830	Revolution in Belgium
November 1830	Revolution in Poland
1831–1838	Revolutions in Italian states
1831–1834	Labor protests in France
1832	Britain's Great Reform Bill
1838	Drawing up of the first People's Charter in Britain
1846	Beginning of food crisis in Europe; revolts in Poland
1846–1848	Europe-wide movements for national liberation
February 1848	Revolution in France; overthrow of the July Monarchy; proclamation of the French Second Republic and creation of Provisional Government
March 1848	Uprisings in some German states; granting of a constitution in Prussia
March 1848–June 1849	Revolutions in Italy
April 1848	Revolutions in Vienna, Budapest, Prague
May 1848	Frankfurt Assembly
June 1848	Second revolution in Paris, severely repressed by army troops under General Cavaignac
December 1848	Presidential elections in France; Louis Napoleon wins

Europe in 1850. In 1850, Austrians threatened the Prussians with war if they did not give up their plans for a unified Germany. In November of that year, Prussian ministers signed an agreement with their Austrian counterparts in the Moravian city of Olmutz. The convention became known as "the humiliation of Olmutz" because Prussia was forced to accept Austrian dominance or go to war. In every case, military force and diplomatic measures prevailed to defeat the national and liberal movements within the German states and the Austrian Empire.

By 1850, a veneer of calm spread over central Europe. In Prussia, the peasantry was emancipated from feudal dues, and a constitution, albeit conservative and based on a three-class system, was established. Yet beneath the surface was the deeper reality of Austrian decline and Prussian challenge. In international relations, Austria's dominance in the German Confederation had diminished, as Prussia assumed greater political and economic power.

The 1848 revolutions spelled the end to the concert of Europe as it had been defined in the peace settlement of 1815, the harmonious cooperation of European nations to protect the status quo. The European powers were incapable of united action to defend established territorial interests.

The revolutions of 1848 failed in part because of the irreconcilable split between moderate liberals and radical democrats. The participation of the masses had frightened members of the middle classes who were committed to moderate reforms that did not threaten property. In the face of more extreme solutions, members of the middle class were willing to accept the increased authority of existing rule as a bulwark against anarchy. In December 1848, Prince Louis Napoleon, nephew of the former emperor, was elected president of the Second Republic by a wide margin. The first truly modern French politician, Louis Napoleon managed to appeal to everyone—workers, bourgeois, royalists, and peasants—by making promises that were vague or unkeepable. Severe repression forced radical protest into hiding. The new Bonaparte bided his time until the moment in 1851 when he seized absolute power.

Similar patterns emerged elsewhere in Europe. In Germany, the bourgeoisie accepted the dominance of the old feudal aristocracy as a guarantee of law and order. Repressive government, businessmen were sure, would restore a strong economy. The attempts in 1848 to create new nations based on ethnic identities were in shambles by 1850.

Nearly everywhere throughout Europe, constitutions had been systematically withdrawn with the recovery of the forces of reaction. The propertied classes remained in control of political institutions. Radicals willing to use violence to press electoral reforms were arrested, killed, or exiled. There seemed to be no effective opposition to the rise and consolidation of state power. The 1848 revolutions have been called a turning point at which modern history failed to turn. Contemporaries wondered how so much action could have produced so few lasting results.

SUMMARY

The New Ideologies The social, economic, and political challenges of the first half of the nineteenth century helped stimulate the development of new ideologies. Conservatives stressed tradition and established institutions. The two main tenets of liberalism were the freedom of the individual and the corruptibility of authority. Trusting in the goodness and rationality of free individuals, liberals believed that less government was better government. Romanticism encompassed a variety of literary and artistic movements. Romantics stressed the primacy of emotion and the importance of intuition and inspiration. Nationalism before 1850 glorified the people united against the absolutism of kings and the tyranny of foreigners. Between 1830 and 1850 there was a close connection between nationalism and liberalism. Socialist thinkers in France theorized about alternative societies in which wealth would be more equitably distributed. Karl Marx and Friedrich Engels argued that class conflict would bring about social revolution.

Protest and Revolution As European society became less stable in the 1820s, protest met repression across Europe. The problems associated with rapid, unplanned urban growth were a major cause of social instability. Governments grappled with the "social question," creating new laws and institutions to deal with poverty and crime. Protest led to revolution in 1830. In France, the reactionary policies of Charles X sparked widespread unrest, toppled his government, and led to the advent of the July Monarchy. With the help of Britain, Russia, and France, Greece gained independence from the Ottoman Empire. Belgium won recognition of its independence from all five Great Powers. Uprisings in eastern and southern Europe threatened Russia, Prussia, and Austria. The Great Reform Bill of 1832 moved Great Britain in the direction of significant political reform. The Chartists demanded universal male suffrage. Labor unrest grew more common across Europe. Famine and intensified demands for more democratic government fueled the revolutions of 1848. The overthrow of the July Monarchy in France set off protest movements elsewhere, most notably in Prussia and Austrian-dominated central Europe. Austria managed to suppress a nationalist uprising in Italy. The revolutions of 1848 ended with the forces of reaction in the ascendancy.

QUESTIONS FOR REVIEW

1. What problems did European peacemakers confront at the Congress of Vienna and how did they attempt to resolve the problems?
2. How did industrialization change European families?
3. In what ways were liberalism and nationalism compatible with each other; how were they in conflict?
4. What are the connections between various ideologies—for instance, liberalism, romanticism, or socialism—and the revolutions of 1830 and 1848?

State Building and Social Change in Europe, 1850–1871

Building Nations: The Politics of Unification

The revolutions of 1848 had occurred in a period of political experimentation. Radicals enlisting popular support had tried and failed to reshape European states for their own nationalist, liberal, and socialist ends. Governments in Paris, Vienna, Berlin, and a number of lesser states had been swept away as revolutions created a power vacuum but no durable solutions. To fill that vacuum, a new breed of politicians emerged in the 1850s and 1860s, men who understood the importance of the centralized nation-state and the need of reforms from above. They shared a new realism about means and ends, and about using foreign policy successes to further domestic programs.

The Crimean War

In 1849 and 1850, Russia had fulfilled its role as policeman of Europe by supporting Austria against Hungary and Prussia. Yet Russia was not merely content to keep the peace; it sought greater power to the south in the Balkans. The narrow straits connecting the Black Sea with the Aegean Sea were controlled by the Ottoman Empire. Russia hoped to benefit from Ottoman weakness caused by internal conflicts and gain control of the straits as an outlet for the Russian fleet to the Mediterranean.

At the center of the hope for Ottoman disintegration lay the **Eastern Question**, the term that was used in the nineteenth century to designate the problems surrounding the European territories controlled by the Ottoman Empire. Each of the Great Powers—Russia, Great Britain, Austria, Prussia, and France—hoped to benefit territorially from the collapse of Ottoman control. In 1853, Great Power rivalry over the Eastern Question created an international situation that led to war.

In 1853, the Russian government demanded that the Turkish government recognize Russia's right to protect Greek Orthodox believers in the Ottoman Empire. The Turkish government refused Russian demands, and the Russians ordered troops to enter the Danubian principalities of Moldavia and Wallachia, which were held by the Turks.

In October 1853, the Turkish government, counting on support from Great Britain and France, declared war on Russia. Russia easily prevailed over its weaker neighbor to the south. In a four-hour battle, a Russian squadron destroyed the Turkish fleet off the coast of Sinope. Tsar Nicholas I (1825–1855) drew up the terms of a settlement with the Ottoman Empire and submitted them to Great Britain and France for review.

The two western European powers, fearing Russian aggrandizement at Turkish expense, responded by declaring war on Russia on 28 March 1854, a date that marked a new phase in the Crimean War. The Italian kingdom of Sardinia also joined the war against Russia in January 1855, hoping to make its name militarily and win recognition for its aim to unite Italy into a single nation. Although Great Britain, France, and the Italian state of Sardinia did not have explicit economic interests, they were motivated by ambition, prestige, and rivalry in the Balkans.

British and French troops landed in the Crimea, the Russian peninsula extending into the Black Sea, in September 1854, with the intention of capturing Sevastopol, Russia's heavily fortified chief naval base on the Black Sea. The allies laid siege to the fortress at Sevastopol, which fell on 11 September 1855 after 322 days of battle. The defeated Russians abandoned Sevastopol, blew up their forts, and sank their own ships. Facing the threat of Austrian entry into the war, Russia agreed to preliminary peace terms.

In the Peace of Paris of 1856, Russia relinquished its claim as protector of Christians in Turkey. The British gained the neutralization of the Black Sea. The mouth of the Danube was returned to Turkish control, and an international commission was created to oversee safe navigation on the Danube. The Danubian principalities were placed under joint guarantee of the powers, and Russia gave up a small portion of Bessarabia. In 1861, the principalities were united in the independent nation of Romania.

The Crimean War had dramatic and enduring consequences. Russia ceased to play an active role in European affairs and turned toward expansion in central Asia. Its withdrawal opened up the possibility for a move by Prussia in central Europe.

Unifying Italy

The Kingdom of Sardinia, meanwhile, was leading the drive for Italian reunification. Italy had not been a single political entity since the end of the Roman Empire in the west in the fifth century. The movement to reunite Italy culturally and politically was known as the **Risorgimento** (literally, "resurgence").

Cavour's Political Realism. In 1848, both Giuseppe Mazzini's Young Italy movement and Giuseppe Garibaldi's Red Shirts had sought a united republican Italy achieved through direct popular action, but they had failed. It took a politician of aristocratic birth to recognize that Mazzini's and Garibaldi's model of revolutionary action was doomed against the powerful Austrian military machine. Mazzini was a moralist. Garibaldi was a fighter. But Camillo Benso di Cavour (1810–1861) was an opportunistic politician and a realist.

As premier of Sardinia from 1852 to 1859 and again in 1860–1861, Cavour was well placed to launch his campaign for Italian unity. The Kingdom of Sardinia, whose principal state was Piedmont, had made itself a focal point for unification efforts. Its king, Carlo-Alberto (1831–1849), had stood alone among Italian rulers in opposing Austrian domination of the Italian peninsula in 1848 and 1849. Severely defeated by the Austrians, he was forced to abdicate. He was succeeded by his son Victor Emmanuel II (1849–1861), who had the good sense to appoint Cavour as his first minister. From the start, Cavour undertook liberal administrative measures that included tax reform, stabilization of the currency, improvement of the railway system, the creation of a transatlantic steamship system, and the support of private enterprise. With these programs, Cavour created for Sardinia the dynamic image of progressive change. He involved Sardinia in the Crimean War, thereby securing its status among the European powers.

Most important, however, was Cavour's alliance with France against Austria in 1858. The alliance was quickly followed by an arranged provocation against the Habsburg monarchy. Austria declared war in 1859 and was easily defeated by French forces in the battles of Magenta and Solferino. The peace settlement joined Lombardy to the Piedmontese state.

Cavour's approach was not without its costs. His partnership with a stronger power meant sometimes following France's lead, and the need to cajole French support meant enriching France with territorial gain in the form of Nice and Savoy. However, Sardinia got more than it gave up. In the summer of 1859, revolutionary

Kingdom of Sardinia, to 1859

Acquisitions by Sardinia, 1859

Annexed by Sardinia, 1860; established Kingdom of Italy

To Kingdom of Italy, 1866

To Kingdom of Italy, 1870

THE UNIFICATION OF ITALY. **By 1860, the majority of the Italian "boot" was under the rule of Piedmont-Sardinia. By 1870, the unification was complete.**

assemblies in Tuscany, Modena, Parma, and the Romagna, wanting to eject their Austrian rulers, voted in favor of union with the Piedmontese. By April 1860, these four areas of central Italy were under Victor Emmanuel II's rule. Sardinia had doubled in size to become the dominant power on the Italian peninsula.

Southern Italians took their lead from events in central Italy and, in the spring of 1860, initiated disorders against the rule of King Francis II (1859–1861) of Naples. Uprisings in Sicily inspired Giuseppe Garibaldi to return from his self-imposed exile to organize his own army of Red Shirts, known as the Thousand, who liberated

Sicily and then crossed to the Italian mainland to expel Francis II from Naples. Garibaldi next turned his attention to the liberation of the Holy City, where a French garrison protected the pope.

As Garibaldi's popularity as a national hero grew, Cavour became alarmed at the competition in uniting Italy and took secret steps to block the advance of the Red Shirts and their leader. To seize the initiative, Cavour directed the Piedmontese army into the Papal States. After defeating the pope's troops, Cavour's men crossed into the Neapolitan state and scored important victories against forces loyal to the king of Naples. Cavour proceeded to annex southern Italy for Victor Emmanuel II, using plebiscites to seal the procedure.

A King for a United Italy. At this point, in 1860, Garibaldi yielded his own conquered territories to Sardinia, making possible the declaration of a united Italy under Victor Emmanuel II, who reigned as king of Italy from 1861 to 1878.

The new king of Italy was now poised to acquire Venetia, which was under Austrian rule, and Rome, which was ruled by Pope Pius IX, and Victor Emmanuel devoted much of his foreign policy in the 1860s to these ends. In 1866, when Austria lost a war with Prussia, Italy struck a deal with the victor and gained control of Venetia. When Prussia prevailed against France in 1870, Victor Emmanuel

In this British cartoon of 1860, Garibaldi surrenders his power to Victor Emmanuel II, king of Piedmont-Sardinia (soon to be king of a united Italy). The caption reads "Right Leg in the Boot at Last."

took over Rome. The boot of Italy, from top to toe, was now a single nation. The pope remained in the Vatican, opposed to an Italy united under King Victor Emmanuel II.

Unifying Germany

In this age of realistic politicians, Prussian statesman Otto von Bismarck (1815–1898) emerged as the supreme practitioner of **realpolitik**, the ruthless use of any means, including illegal and violent ones, to advance a country's interests. Bismarck was a Junker, an aristocratic estate-owner from east of the Elbe River, who entered politics in 1847. In the 1850s, he became aware of Prussia's future in the center of Europe; he saw that the old elites must be allied with the national movement to survive.

Prussia's Seven Weeks' War with Austria. In 1850, Prussia had been forced to accept Austrian dominance in central Europe or go to war. Throughout the following decade, however, Prussia systematically undermined Austrian power and excluded Austria from German economic affairs. In 1862, at the moment of a crisis provoked by the king over military reorganization, Bismarck became minister-president of the Prussian cabinet and foreign minister. He overrode the parliamentary body, the Diet, by reorganizing the army without a formally approved budget. In 1864, he constructed an alliance between Austria and Prussia for the purpose of invading Schleswig, a predominantly German-speaking territory controlled by the king of Denmark. Within five days of the invasion, Denmark yielded the duchies of Schleswig and Holstein, now to be ruled jointly by Austria and Prussia.

Counting on the neutrality of France and Great Britain, the support of Sardinia, and good relations with Russia, Bismarck promoted a crisis between Austria and Prussia over management of the formerly Danish territories and led his country into war with Austria in June 1866. In this Seven Weeks' War, Austrian forces proved to be no match for the better-equipped and better-trained Prussian army. Bismarck dictated the terms of the peace, excluding Austria from a united, Prussian-dominated Germany. In 1867, in response to pressures from the subject nationalities, the Habsburg Empire transformed itself into a dual monarchy of two independent and equal states under one ruler, who would be both the emperor of Austria and the king of Hungary. In spite of the reorganization, the problem of nationalities persisted, and ethnic groups began to agitate for total independence from imperial rule.

The Franco-Prussian War. Bismarck's biggest obstacle to German unification was laid to rest with Austria's defeat. The south German states continued to resist the idea of Prussian dominance, but growing numbers of people in Baden, Württemberg, Bavaria, and the southern parts of Hesse-Darmstadt recognized the value of uniting under Prussian leadership.

Legend:

- Prussia, 1815–1866
- Annexed by Prussia, 1866
- North German Confederation, 1866
- With Prussia, formed German Empire, 1871
- Ceded to German Empire by France, 1871
- German Confederation, 1815–1866

Map labels: EAST PRUSSIA, POLAND (RUSSIAN EMPIRE), HUNGARY, Baltic Sea, WEST PRUSSIA, POSEN, SILESIA, AUSTRO-HUNGARIAN EMPIRE, MORAVIA, POMERANIA, P R U S S I A, BOHEMIA, BRANDENBURG, Berlin, SAXONY, SCHLESWIG-HOLSTEIN, MECKLENBURG-SCHWERIN, Lübeck, ANHALT, THURINGIAN STATES, BAVARIA, TYROL, Hamburg, Bremen, HANOVER, HESSEN-NASSAU, WÜRTTEMBERG, ITALY, North Sea, WESTPHALIA, RHINELAND, BADEN

THE UNIFICATION OF GERMANY

In this map, regard the diversity in size and type of political entities that were combined to form the new state of Germany. What annexation did the War of 1866 make possible? How did the peace settlement with France affect the creation of the German state? Why was the North German Confederation so important in determining the formation of the new German Empire?

Many French observers were troubled by the Prussian victory over Austria and were apprehensive about what a united Germany might portend for the future of French dominance in Europe. Napoleon III attempted unsuccessfully to contain Prussian ambitions through diplomatic maneuverings. Instead, France found itself stranded without important European allies. In the spring of 1870, Bismarck seized the initiative and provoked a crisis with France. The issue of succession to the Spanish throne provided the pretext. On 13 July 1870, the Prussian king (later Emperor William I) sent a message to Napoleon III reporting a meeting with the French ambassador. Bismarck skillfully edited this "Ems Dispatch" to suggest that the French ambassador had insulted the Prussian king, then leaked news of the incident to the press in both countries.

As a direct result of this contrived misunderstanding, France declared war on Prussia in July 1870. As Bismarck hoped, the southern German princes immediately sided with the Prussian king. Unlike the Germans, who were well prepared for war, the French had not coordinated deployment with the new technology of the railroad. Although French troops had the latest equipment, they were sent into battle without instructions on how to use it. And they were outnumbered almost two to one. All these factors combined to spell disaster for the French. Within a matter of weeks it was obvious that France had lost the Franco-Prussian War. The path was now clear for the declaration of the German Empire in January 1871.

Prussian Dominance of United Germany. In unifying Germany, Bismarck built on the constitution of the North German Confederation formed in 1867, which guaranteed Prussian dominance. Bismarck used the bureaucracy as a mainstay of the emperor. The new **Reichstag**—the national legislative assembly—was to be elected by means of universal male suffrage, but it was not sovereign, and the chancellor was accountable only to the emperor.

The United States: Civil War and Reunification

In the 1860s, another crisis in state building was resolved across the Atlantic. The United States cemented political unity through the use of force in its Civil War (1861–1865). The president of the United States, Abraham Lincoln (1809–1865), mobilized the superior resources of the industrial Northern states against the heavily agrarian, slave-owning South. The United States worked to achieve national unity and territorial integrity in another sense through ongoing expansion westward by eliminating and subduing Native American peoples.

With the emancipation of the slaves, republican democracy appeared to triumph in the United States. Newly created European nation-states followed a different path: Plebiscites were manipulated by those in power in Italy, and a neo-absolutism emerged in Germany. Yet the Civil War in the United States and the successful bids for unification in Italy and Germany shared remarkable similarities. In all three countries, wars eventually resulted in a single national market and a single financial system without internal barriers. Unified national economies, particularly in Germany and the United States, paved the way for significant economic growth and the expansion of industrial power.

Nationalism and Force

The personification of nation-states was one of the great achievements of statesmen throughout Europe between 1850 and 1870. The language and symbols they put in place created the nation itself, a new political reality whose forms contained a modern political consciousness. The nation-state became an all-knowing being whose rights had to be protected, whose destiny had to be assured.

The nation was above all a creation that minimized or denied real differences in dialect and language, regional loyalties, local traditions, and village identities. No power was acknowledged to exist above the nation-state, and no power could sanction the nation's actions but itself. Force was an acceptable alternative to diplomacy. Violence and nationalism were inextricably linked in the unification of both Italy and Germany in the third quarter of the nineteenth century.

National unification had escaped the grasp of liberals and radicals between 1848 and 1850 with the failure of revolutionary and reform movements. In the 1850s and 1860s, those who were committed to radical transformations worked from within the existing system. The new realists subordinated liberal nationalism to conservative state-building. Under newly dynamic conservative leadership, military force would validate what intellectuals and idealistic revolutionaries had not been able to legitimate through ideological claims.

Reforming European Society

After the revolutions of 1848, government repression silenced radical movements throughout Europe. But repression could not maintain social harmony and promote growth and prosperity. In the third quarter of the nineteenth century, Europe's leaders recognized that reforms were needed to build dynamic and competitive states. Three different models for social and political reform developed in France, Great Britain, and Russia after 1850. All three sets of reforms took place in unified nation-states. The three societies had little in common with each other ideologically, but all reflected a commitment to progress and an awareness of the state's role and responsibility in achieving it.

The Second Empire in France, 1852–1870

One model for reform was that of France, where the French emperor worked through a highly centralized administrative structure and with a valued elite of specialists to achieve social and economic transformation.

Napoleon III. Under Napoleon III's direction the Second Empire achieved economic expansion and industrial development. A new private banking system enabled the pooling of investors' resources to finance industrial expansion. Napoleon III and his advisers believed that prosperity was the answer to all social problems. Between 1852 and 1860, the government supported a massive program of railroad construction. Jobs multiplied, and investment increased. Agriculture expanded as railroad lines opened new markets. The rich got richer, but the extreme poverty of the first half of the nineteenth century was diminishing. Brutal misery in the city and countryside did not disappear, but on the whole, the standard of living increased as wages rose faster than prices.

Rebuilding Paris. The best single example of the energy and commitment of the imperial regime was the rebuilding of the French capital. Before midcentury, Paris was one of the most unsanitary, crime-ridden, and politically volatile capitals in Europe. Within 15 years it had been transformed into a city of lights, wide boulevards and avenues, monumental vistas, parks, and gardens. Poor districts were cleared to make way for the elegant apartment buildings of the Parisian bourgeoisie. As workers from all over France migrated to the capital in search of jobs, the population nearly doubled, increasing by just under one million in the 1850s and 1860s. Wide, straight Parisian avenues served as an international model that was copied in Mexico City, Brussels, Madrid, Rome, Stockholm, and Barcelona between 1870 and 1900.

The Foreign Policy of the Second Empire. Just as a new Paris would make France a center of Western culture, Napoleon III intended his blueprint for foreign policy to restore France to its pre-1815 status as the greatest European power. By involving France in both the Crimean War and the war for Italian unification, Napoleon III returned France to adventurous foreign policies, acquired Nice and Savoy from Sardinia, and reversed the settlements of 1815.

French construction of the Suez Canal between the Red Sea and the Mediterranean created tensions with Great Britain, which was protective of its own dominance in the Mediterranean and the Near East. Nevertheless, the free trade agreement between the British and the French in 1860 was a landmark in overseas policy and a commitment to liberal economic policies.

The Second Empire's involvement in Mexico was a fiasco. The Mexican government had been chronically unable to pay its foreign debts, and France was Mexico's largest creditor. Napoleon III hoped that by intervening in Mexican affairs, he could strengthen ties with Great Britain and Spain, to whom the Mexicans also owed money. With the backing of Mexican conservatives who opposed Mexican president Benito Juárez (1806–1872), Napoleon III supported the Austrian archduke Maximilian (1832–1867) as emperor of Mexico. After he was crowned in 1863, the new Mexican emperor struggled to rule in an enlightened manner, but he was stymied from the beginning by his ineptitude and lack of popular support. Following the recall of the 34,000 French troops that, at considerable expense, were keeping Maximilian's troubled regime in place, Maximilian was captured and executed by a firing squad in the summer of 1867. The Mexican disaster damaged the prestige of Napoleon III's regime in the international arena, and in 1870 the humiliatingly rapid defeat of French imperial forces in the Franco-Prussian War ended the experiment in liberal empire.

The Victorian Compromise

Great Britain provided another model of reform, which was fostered through liberal parliamentary democracy. In government by "amateurs," with local rather than a highly centralized administration, British legislation alternated between a philosophy of freedom and one of protection. But reforms were always hammered out by parliamentary means with the support of a gradually expanding electorate.

Parliamentary Reforms. In contrast to France, Britain enjoyed apparent social harmony without revolution and without civil war. The relative calm of British society in the middle of the nineteenth century owed much to the fact that Great Britain had an enormously productive capitalist economy of sustained growth.

The stability and calm were undoubtedly exaggerated, however, for Great Britain at midcentury had its share of serious social problems. British slums rivaled any in Europe. Poverty, disease, and famine ravaged the kingdom. Social protests of the 1840s raised fears of upheavals similar to those in continental Europe. Yet Great Britain avoided a revolution. One explanation for the relative calm lay in Britain's parliamentary tradition, which emphasized liberty as the birthright of English citizens and was able slowly to adapt to the demands of an industrializing society. The great compromise of Victorian society was the reconciliation of industrialists' commitment to unimpeded growth with the workers' need for the state's protection.

As part of a pattern of slow democratization, the Reform Bill of 1832 gave increased political power to the industrial and manufacturing bourgeoisie, who joined a landed aristocracy and merchant class. But the property qualification meant that only 20 percent of the population could vote. In 1867, under conservative leadership, a second reform bill was introduced. Approval of this bill doubled the electorate, giving the vote to a new urban population of shopkeepers, clerks, and workers. In 1884, farm laborers were enfranchised. Women, however, remained barred from voting until after World War I.

Gladstone and Disraeli. The lives and careers of two men, William Ewart Gladstone (1809–1898) and Benjamin Disraeli (1804–1881), exemplify the particular path the British government followed in maintaining public peace. Rivals and political opponents, both men served as prime ministers and both left their mark on the age.

William Gladstone rides in an omnibus in this painting titled *One of the People*, by Alfred Morgan. This mode of transport was thought of as a social leveler because all classes of people could afford the fares.

William Gladstone was a classical liberal who believed in free enterprise and opposed state intervention. Good government, according to Gladstone, should remove obstacles to talent, competition, and individual initiative but should interfere as little as possible in economy and society. Gladstone's first term as prime minister (1868–1874) significantly advanced the British liberal state. Taking advantage of British prosperity, Gladstone abolished tariffs, cut defense expenditures, lowered taxes, and sponsored sound budgets. He furthered the liberal agenda by disestablishing the Anglican Church in Ireland in 1869. The Anglican Church had been the source of great resentment to the vast majority of Irish Catholics, who had been forced to pay taxes to support the Protestant state church.

Gladstone reformed the army and the civil service. His government introduced the secret ballot. Finally, the Liberal party stressed the importance of education for an informed electorate and passed an education act that aimed to make elementary schooling available to everyone. These reforms added up to a liberal philosophy of government. Liberal government was above all an attack on privilege. It sought to remove restraints on individual freedom and foster opportunity and talent.

During these years, another political philosophy—conservatism—also left its mark on British government. Under the flamboyant leadership of Benjamin Disraeli, the Conservative party, trusting the state to correct and protect, supported state intervention and regulation on behalf of the poor and disadvantaged. Disraeli sponsored the Factory Act of 1875, which set a maximum of 56 hours on the factory work week. The Public Health Act established a sanitary code. The Artisans Dwelling Act defined minimum housing standards. Probably the most important conservative legislation was the Trade Union Act, which permitted picketing and other peaceful labor tactics.

Disraeli championed protection against free trade. Unlike the Liberals, he insisted on the importance of traditional institutions such as the monarchy, the House of Lords, and the Church of England. His work in organizing a national party machinery facilitated the adaptation of the parliamentary system to mass politics. His methods of campaigning and building a mass base of support were used by successful politicians regardless of political persuasion.

As the intersecting careers of Gladstone and Disraeli demonstrate, the British model combined free enterprise with intervention and regulation. The clear issues and the clear choices of the two great parties—Liberal and Conservative—dominated parliamentary life after midcentury. In polarizing parliamentary politics, they also invigorated it.

The terms "liberal" and "conservative" hold none of the meaning today that they did for men and women in the nineteenth century. Classical liberalism has little in common with its twentieth-century counterpart, which favors an active, interventionist state. Disraeli is a far more likely candidate for the twentieth-century liberal label than is Gladstone, Britain's leading nineteenth-century liberal statesman.

Reforming Russia

Russia offered a third model for reform in the nineteenth century. Like Britain, Russia had avoided revolution at midcentury and hoped to preserve social peace. Yet the Russian model for reform stood in dramatic contrast to Britain's. Russia was an unreformed autocracy in which the tsar held absolute power. Without a parliament, without a constitution, and without civil liberties for his subjects, the Russian ruler governed through a bureaucracy and a police force. Economically, Russia was a semifeudal agrarian state with a class of privileged aristocrats supported by serf labor on their estates.

A Serf-Holding Nation. For decades—since the reign of Alexander I (1801–1825)—the tsars and their advisers realized that they were out of step with developments in western Europe. An awareness was growing that serfdom was uncivilized and morally wrong, as critics compared the Russian practice with the atrocities of American slavery. Among the European powers, only Russia remained a serf-holding nation. Russian serfs were tied to the land and owed dues and labor services in return for the lands they held. Peasant protests mounted, attracting public attention to the plight of the serfs. But in spite of growing moral concern, there were many reasons to resist the abolition of serfdom. How were serf-holders to be compensated for the loss of labor power? What was to be the freed serfs' relationship to the land?

Alexander II and the Emancipation of the Serfs. Hesitation about abolition evaporated with the Russian defeat in the Crimean War. The new tsar, Alexander II (1855–1881), viewed Russia's inability to repel an invasion force on its own soil as proof of its backwardness. Russia had no railroads and was forced to transport military supplies by carts to the Crimea. It took three months to provision troops; the enemy could do so in three weeks. Liberating the serfs would permit a well-trained reserve army to exist without fear of rebellion and would also create a system of free labor, so necessary for industrial development.

In March 1861, the tsar signed the emancipation edict that liberated 52 million serfs. Serfdom was eliminated in Poland three years later. Alexander II, who came to be known as the "Tsar-Liberator," compromised between landlord and serf by allotting land to freed peasants while requiring from the former serfs redemption payments that were spread out over a period of 49 years. To guarantee repayment, the land was granted not directly to individual peasants but to the village commune (*mir*), which was responsible for collecting redemption payments. The peasant paid the state in installments; the state reimbursed the landowner in the form of interest-bearing bonds and redemption certificates. Neither serf nor landholder benefited from these financial arrangements; the real winner in the abolition of serfdom was the state, which expanded its bureaucratic hierarchy and financial infrastructure.

The Great Reforms. The tsar introduced a vast array of "Great Reforms"—emancipating the serfs, creating local parliamentary bodies (**zemstvos**), reorganizing the judiciary, modernizing the army—yet Russia was not sufficiently liberalized or democratized to satisfy the critics of autocracy. Between 1860 and 1870, a young generation of intelligentsia, radical intellectuals who were influenced by the rhetoric of revolution in western Europe, protested against the existing order, traveling from village to village to educate the peasants and in some cases to attempt to radicalize them.

The Populist Movement. The radicals paid dearly for their commitment to populism when they were subjected to mass trials and repression in the late 1870s. Some of these critics fled into exile to reemerge as revolutionaries in western Europe, where they continued to oppose the tsarist regime and helped to shape the tradition of revolution and dissent in Western countries. Other educated men and women who remained in Russia chose violence as the only effective weapon against absolute rule. Terrorists who called themselves "Will of the People" decided to assassinate the tsar; in the "emperor hunt" that followed, numerous attempts were made on the tsar's life.

In response to attempts on his life and the assassination of public officials, which were intended to cripple the central regime, Alexander II put the brakes on reform in the second half of his reign. The Great Reforms could not be undone, however, and had set in motion sweeping economic and social changes. The state encouraged capitalist growth and witnessed the rise of a professional middle class and the formation of an embryonic factory proletariat. Yet reforms had increased expectations for an equally dramatic political transformation that failed to materialize. In the end, the Will of the People movement succeeded in its mission. In St. Petersburg in 1881, a terrorist bomb killed Alexander II, the Tsar-Liberator.

The Politics of Leadership

Political modernization was not achieved in Russia; and in western and central Europe, modern politics emerged only after 1850. Until that time, traditional political institutions had prevailed. When faced with revolutionary upheavals, regimes aimed for stability and preservation of their control. Only after 1850 did political leaders emerge who understood the world of politics and directed it to their own ends. Three statesmen typified the new approach to the public world of power: Camillo di Cavour, Otto von Bismarck, and Louis Napoleon.

The Demise of Royal Authority. In old-regime Europe, power flowed downward from the monarch, who was perched atop a hierarchically organized social system that is often depicted as a pyramid. In the first half of the nineteenth century, men and women learned that those in power could be questioned. The good of the people was the primary justification for government. Power now flowed upward from the citizens to their appointed and elected representatives. The new power brokers were those who could control and direct the flow, not merely be carried along or swept away by it. These were realists in the same tradition as Machiavelli and reflected the new political culture of the nineteenth century. They understood the importance of public opinion, which they used as a tool for the shaping of consensus, the molding of support. They also appreciated the power of the press.

The Supremacy of the Nation-State. The new political men also shared, to varying degrees, a disregard for traditional morality in decision making. The nation-state was the supreme justification for all actions. Realpolitik meant that statesmen had to think in terms of military capability, technological dominance, and the acceptable use of force. In the gamesmanship of statecraft, they were risk takers.

However, modern European statesmen did not share a common ideological outlook. Cavour leaned toward liberal ideas, while Bismarck was unquestionably conservative, and Louis Napoleon held a blend of liberal and conservative views. Yet these leaders enacted similar policies and sponsored similar legislation to strengthen and promote their states.

Changing Values and the Force of New Ideas

Just as the political world was undergoing transformation, the social, material, and intellectual world was also changing. As feminist thinkers struggled against entrenched prejudice against women, other thinkers brought new insights to the study of human society, some of which worked to impede women's progress toward equality. The third quarter of the nineteenth century opened an era that was especially rich in creativity in the natural and applied sciences.

The Politics of Homemaking

Industrialization had separated the workplace from the home, which was now glorified as a comfortable refuge from the harsh outside world. In 1870, an article in a popular Victorian magazine asserted, "Home is emphatically man's place of rest, where his wife is his friend who knows his mind, where he may be himself without fear of offending, and relax the strain that must be kept out of doors: where he may feel himself safe, understood, and at ease." Managing this domestic haven and her children was the middle-class woman's task, and "home economics" was invented during this period to help her organize her work.

This ideal of domestic order and tranquility was beyond the reach of the vast majority of the population. Working-class wives and mothers often had to earn wages if their families were to survive. In 1866, women constituted a significant percentage of the French labor force, including 45 percent of all textile workers. At the height of the rhetoric about the virtues of domesticity, as many as 40 percent of married Englishwomen worked in mills in industrial areas such as Lancashire. Others performed piecework in their homes so that they could care for their children.

Many middle-class women protested against the ideology that confined them to the domestic sphere. Earlier in the century, the great novelist Jane Austen had to keep a piece of muslin work on her writing table in the family drawing room to cover her papers lest visitors detect evidence of literary activity. In the next generation, Florence Nightingale refused to accept the embroidery and knitting to which she was assigned at home. Middle-class women's demands for equal treatment became more persistent after 1870. Patterns of behavior changed within the family, and they were not fixed immutably in social practice. Woman's place and woman's role proved to be much-disputed questions in the new politics of homemaking.

Realism in the Arts

Realism in the arts and literature was a rejection of romantic idealism and subjectivity. The realist response to the disillusionment with the political failures of the post-1848 era characterized a wide array of artistic and literary endeavors. Realists depicted the challenges of urban and industrial growth by confronting the alienation of modern life.

The Social World of the Artist. The term *realism* was first used to describe the paintings of Gustave Courbet (1819–1877). In *The Artist's Studio* (1855), Courbet portrayed himself surrounded by the intellectuals and political figures of his day. He may have been painting a landscape, but contemporary political life crowded in; a starving Irish peasant and her child crouch beneath the easel. Of his unrelenting canvases, none more fittingly portrays the harsh realism of bourgeois life than the funeral ceremony depicted in *Burial at Ornans* (1849–1850) or better depicts the brutality of workers' lives than *Stone Breakers* (1849).

Other artists shared Courbet's desire to reject the conventions prevailing in the art world in favor of portraying reality in its natural and social dimensions. Jean-François Millet's paintings of peasants and workers sought for a truth deeper than a surface beauty. Realist artists often strove to make a social commentary by

Gustave Courbet (1819–1877), *Burial at Ornans*. This painting portrays the harsh realism of a bourgeois funeral ceremony.

capturing scenes from the daily life of the poor that would not have been considered fit subjects for art a generation before.

Realist Novels. After midcentury, idealization in romantic literature yielded to novels depicting the objective and unforgiving social world. Through serialization in journals and newspapers, fiction reached out to mass audiences, who obtained their "facts" about modern life through stories that often cynically portrayed the monotony of daily existence. In *Hard Times* (1854), set in the imaginary city of Coketown, Charles Dickens (1812–1870) created an allegory that exposed the sterility and soullessness of industrial society.

In *Madame Bovary* (1856), Gustave Flaubert (1821–1880), the great French realist novelist, recounts the story of a young country doctor's wife whose desire to escape from the boredom of her provincial existence leads her into adultery and eventually results in her destruction. Flaubert was put on trial for obscenity and violating public morality with his tale of the unrepentant Emma Bovary. Mary Ann Evans (1819–1890), writing under the pseudonym George Eliot, was also concerned with moral choices and responsibilities in her novels, including *Middlemarch* (1871–1872), a tale of idealism disappointed by the petty realities of provincial English life.

The problem of morality in the realist novel is nowhere more apparent than in the works of the Russian writer, Fyodor Dostoyevsky (1821–1881), whose protagonists wrestle with a universe where God no longer exists and where they must shape their own morality. The impoverished student Raskolnikov in *Crime and Punishment* (1866) justifies his brutal murder of an old woman that occurs in the opening pages of the novel. Realist art and literature addressed an educated elite public but did not flinch before the unrelenting poverty and harshness of contemporary life. The morality of the realist vision lay in depicting the social evils for what they were: failures of a smug and progressive middle class.

Calotype of the Adamson family, ca. 1844, by pioneer photographers Robert Adamson (shown at far right) and David Octavius Hill of Scotland. The new technology of photography enabled middle-class families to have their portraits taken, a luxury once available only to those wealthy enough to commission artists.

The New World of Photography. Nineteenth-century photography was the result of wedding art and science. Although various techniques made it possible to capture images and landscapes on paper in the early decades of the nineteenth century, Louis Daguerre (1789–1851) can be credited as a pioneer in the photographic process with the invention of the daguerreotype in 1839. Daguerre was both a French scene painter and a physicist, and he brought both his sensibilities and scientific training to the process of capturing images on silver-coated copper plates treated with iodine vapor.

The fascination with photography in the nineteenth century can be observed in its use for portraits by growing numbers of ordinary people, just as in an earlier time the wealthy and powerful sat for oil portraits. In addition, the camera, still a cumbersome object, was used for country landscapes, urban landmarks, and recording the horrors and glory of battle. Within a generation, cameras altered the way people understood the world around them and how they recorded human life. An increasing emphasis on the real world, reflected in literature, art, and discoveries in science, was fueled by the altered worldview and the new consciousness that photography made possible.

Charles Darwin and the New Science

Science had a special appeal for a generation of Europeans disillusioned with the political failures of idealism in the revolutions of 1848. It was not an age of great scientific discovery, but rather one of synthesis of previous findings and their technological applications. Science was, above all, to be useful in promoting material progress.

The preeminent scientist of the age, Charles Darwin (1809–1882), was a great synthesizer. As a young man, he sailed around the world on the *Beagle* (1831–1836) as the ship's naturalist, collecting specimens and fossils. His greatest finds were in South America and especially on the Galapagos Islands. He spent the next 20 years of his life writing about his observations. The result, *On the Origin of Species by Means of Natural Selection* (1859), was a book that changed the world.

Darwin's argument was a simple one: Life forms originate in struggle and perpetuate themselves through struggle. The outcome of this struggle was determined by **natural selection**, or what came to be known as "survival of the fittest." Better-adapted individuals survived; others died out. Competition between species and within species produced a dynamic model of organic evolution and progress based on struggle. Darwin did not use the word "evolution" in the original edition, but a positivist belief in an evolutionary process permeated the text. Force explained the past and would guarantee the future, as the fittest survived. The general public found these ideas to be applicable to a whole range of human endeavors and to theories of social organization.

Karl Marx and the Science of Society

Another iconoclastic thinker of this creative period was Karl Marx (1818–1883). "Just as Darwin discovered the law of development of organic nature, Marx discovered the law of development of human history." So spoke Friedrich Engels (1820–1895), longtime friend of and collaborator with Karl Marx, over Marx's grave. The son of a Prussian lawyer, Marx had rejected the study of the law to become a philosopher. As a brilliant young scholar, Marx developed a materially grounded view of society. In 1844, he joined forces with Friedrich Engels, a wealthy German businessman whose father owned factories in Manchester, England. Engels had just written *The Condition of the Working Class in England in 1844*, an exposé of the social costs of industrialization. Marx and Engels found that they were kindred spirits, both moved by the struggles of the poor and the economic exploitation of workers.

The philosophy of Marx and Engels was built on a materialist view of society in which human beings were defined not by their souls but by their labor. Labor was a struggle to transform nature by producing commodities useful for survival. Building on this fundamental concept of labor, Marx and Engels saw society as being divided into two camps: those who owned property and those who did not. For Marx, every social system was divided into classes and carried within it the seeds of its own destruction. In a world of commerce and manufacturing, the capitalist bourgeoisie exploited labor for low wages; they were the new aristocracy against whom workers would eventually rebel.

Marx was more than an observer; he was a critic of capitalism who espoused revolutionary change. His labor theory of value was the wedge that he drove into the self-congratulatory rhetoric of the capitalist age. Labor was the source of all value, he argued, yet the bourgeois employers denied workers the profit of their work by refusing to pay them a decent wage. Instead, they pocketed the profits. He believed workers were separated, or alienated, from the product of their labor. But more profoundly, in his view of a capitalist system, all workers were alienated from the creation that made them human; they were alienated from their labor.

The force of Karl Marx's ideas mobilized thousands of contemporaries who were aware of the injustices of capitalism. Few thinkers have left a more lasting legacy than Karl Marx, which has survived distortion, opposition, and criticism from ideologues and scholars. Marx was a synthesizer who combined economics, philosophy, politics, and history in a wide-ranging critique of industrial society.

Marxism spread across Europe as workers responded to its message. Political parties coalesced around Marxist beliefs and programs, and Marxists were beginning to be heard in associations of workers. In London in 1864, they helped to found the International Working Men's Association, an organization of workers dedicated to "the end of all class rule." The promise of a common association of workers transcending national boundaries became a compelling idea to those who envisioned the end of capitalism. In 1871, Marx and his followers turned to Paris for proof that the revolution was at hand.

A New Revolution?

Soundly defeated on 2 September 1870, Napoleon III and his fighting force of 100,000 men became Prussia's prisoners of war. With the emperor's defeat, the Second Empire collapsed. But even with the capture of Napoleon III, the city of Paris refused to capitulate. The dedication of Parisians to the ongoing war with the Prussians was evident from the first. The regime's liberal critics in Paris seized the initiative to proclaim France a republic. If a corrupt and decadent empire could not save the nation, then France's Third Republic could.

The Siege of Paris. In mid-September 1870, two German armies surrounded Paris and began a siege that lasted for over four months. Bismarck's troops were intent on bringing the city to its knees not by fighting but by cutting off its vital supply lines. By November, food and fuel were dwindling, and Parisians were facing starvation. Undaunted, they began to eat dogs, cats, and rats. Soon horses disappeared from the streets, and the zoo was depleted of animals.

Despite food and fuel shortages, the proud Parisians fought on. The Germans began a steady bombardment of the city beginning in January 1871. Although Parisians continued to resist through three weeks of shelling, the rest of France wanted an end to the war. The Germans agreed to an armistice to allow French national elections. French citizens outside Paris repudiated the war and returned an overwhelmingly conservative majority to seek peace. Thus the siege came to an end, but it left deep wounds that continued to fester.

Chronology

STATE BUILDING AND SOCIAL CHANGE

1853–1856	Crimean War
1859	Austria declares war on Kingdom of Sardinia; France joins forces with Italy
1860	Piedmont-Sardinia annexes duchies in central Italy; France gains Nice and Savoy
3 March 1861	Emancipation of Russian serfs
14 March 1861	Kingdom of Italy proclaimed with Victor Emmanuel II as king
1861–1865	American Civil War
1863	Maximilian crowned emperor of Mexico
1863	Prussians and Austrians at war with Denmark
1866	Seven Weeks' War between Austria and Prussia; Italy acquires Venetia
1867	Emperor Maximilian executed
July 1870	Franco-Prussian War begins
2 September 1870	French Second Empire capitulates with Prussian victory at Sedan
20 September 1870	Italy annexes Rome
18 January 1871	German Empire proclaimed
March–May 1871	Paris Commune

The Paris Commune. Parisians felt betrayed by the rest of France. Through four months in a besieged city, they had sacrificed, suffered, and died. The war was over, but Paris was not at peace. The new national government, safely installed outside Paris at Versailles, attempted in March 1871 to disarm the Parisian citizenry by using army troops. Parisian men, women, and children poured into the streets to protect their cannons and to defend their right to bear arms. In the fighting that followed, the Versailles troops were driven from the city, and Paris was under siege again.

The spontaneity of the March uprising was soon succeeded by organization. Citizens rallied to the idea of the city's self-government and established the **Paris Commune**, as other French cities followed the capital's lead. Parisians were still at war, not against a foreign enemy but against the rest of France. The defense of the commune lasted for 72 days. Armed women formed their own fighting units, the city council regulated labor relations, and neighborhoods ruled themselves. The short-lived Paris Commune ended in May 1871, as government troops reentered the city and brutally crushed it. In one "Bloody Week," 25,000 Parisians were massacred, and 40,000 others were arrested and tried. Such reprisals inflamed radicals and workers all over Europe. The example of the commune became a rallying cry for revolutionary movements throughout the world and inspired the future leaders of the Russian revolutionary state.

The commune was important at the time, but not as a revolution. It offered two lessons: First, it demonstrated the power of patriotism. Competing images of the nation were at stake, one Parisian and the other French, but no one could deny the power of national identity to inspire a whole city to suffer and to sacrifice. Second, the commune made clear the power of the state. No revolutionary movement could succeed without controlling the massive forces of repression that were at the state's command. The commune had tried to recapture a local, federal view of the world but failed to take sufficient account of the power of the state that it opposed.

SUMMARY

Building Nations: The Politics of Unification   The desire of the Great Powers to benefit territorially from the collapse of the Ottoman Empire led to the Crimean War. Russia's invasion of the Ottoman Empire in 1853 triggered declarations of war against Russia by Great Britain, France, and Sardinia. Russian defeat ended its active role in European affairs and opened new possibilities for Prussia in central Europe. The Sardinian prime minister Camillo Benso di Cavour used political reform and an alliance with France to advance the cause of Italian unification. Giuseppe Garibaldi took the lead in southern Italy. Italy was united under Victor Emmanuel II. The Prussian statesman Otto von Bismarck believed that the use of any means was justified to advance his country's interests. He used wars with Denmark, Austria, and France to create a united Germany dominated by Prussia. Between 1850 and 1870, the nation-state became the highest form of authority.

Reforming European Society   After 1850, European leaders recognized that reforms were needed to build dynamic and competitive states. In France during the Second Empire, Napoleon III worked through a highly centralized administrative structure and with a valued elite of specialists to achieve social and economic transformation. Napoleon and his advisers believed that prosperity was the answer to all social problems. Napoleon hoped that an adventurous foreign policy would make France, once again, the greatest power in Europe. Defeat by Prussia in 1870 put an end to the experiment in liberal empire. Great Britain fostered reform through liberal parliamentary democracy. Britain's strong economy contributed to social stability. Political reform helped Britain meet the challenges of social and economic change. Russia was an autocratic, semifeudal agrarian state. Alexander II emancipated Russia's serfs, created local parliamentary bodies, reorganized the judiciary, and modernized the army. Between 1860 and 1870, radical intellectuals promoted revolutionary changes in Russia. Repression led to further radicalization and efforts to assassinate the tsar. This, in turn, put a halt to further reform from above.

Changing Values and the Force of New Ideas   Political change was matched by social, material, and intellectual change. Industrialization separated the workplace from the home. Women were expected to make the home a refuge from the outside world. The domestic ideal was beyond the reach of the vast majority of women and many middle-class women protested against the constraints of confinement to the domestic sphere. Realist artists and writers rejected romantic idealism and subjectivity. They attempted to create objective images of social reality. The general public applied Charles Darwin's theory of evolution to social, economic, and political issues. Karl Marx developed a materially grounded view of society, built around the notion of class conflict. Marxism spread across Europe, spawning new political parties and workers' associations. Even after the capture of Napoleon III, the people of Paris refused to capitulate to the Prussians. The national government of France made peace with Prussia and used force to overthrow the Paris Commune and regain control of Paris.

QUESTIONS FOR REVIEW

1. How did the process of creating nation-states in Germany and Italy differ?
2. What social and political circumstances explain the different reforms undertaken in France, Britain, and Russia?
3. How did industrialization change women's lives, and how did such changes depend on a woman's social class?
4. What were the connections between Darwin's ideas about nature and Marx's ideas about society?
5. What forces inspired the creation of the Paris Commune, and what did its fate suggest about the possibility of revolution in the late nineteenth century?

The Crisis of European Culture, 1871–1914

European Economy and the Politics of Mass Society

Between 1871 and 1914 the scale of European life was radically altered. Large-scale heavy industries fueled by new energy sources dominated the economic landscape. Great Britain, the leader of the first phase of the Industrial Revolution of the eighteenth century, slipped in prominence as an industrial power at the end of the nineteenth century, as Germany and the United States devised successful competitive strategies of investment, protection, and control.

Regulating Boom and Bust

The organization of factory production throughout Europe and the proximity of productive centers to distribution networks meant ever-greater concentration of populations in urban areas. Like factories, cities were getting bigger at a rapid rate and were proliferating in numbers. With every passing year, fewer people remained on the land, and those who stayed were increasingly linked to cities and tied into national cultures by new transportation and communications networks.

The Need for Regulation. Between 1873 and 1895, an epidemic of slumps battered the economics of European nations. These slumps, characterized by falling prices, downturns in productivity, and declining profits, did not strike European nations simultaneously, nor did they affect all countries with the same degree of severity. But the slumps of the late nineteenth century and the boom period of intense economic expansion from 1895 to 1914 did teach industrialists, financiers, and politicians one important lesson: Alternating booms and busts in the business cycle were dangerous and had to be regulated. Workers and their families suffered even more as the job market periodically shrank.

Too much of a good thing brought on the steady deflation of the last quarter of the nineteenth century. In the world economy there was an overproduction of agricultural products—a sharp contrast to the famines that had ravaged Europe only 50 years earlier. Overproduction resulted from two new factors in the world economy: technological advances in crop cultivation and the low cost of shipping and transport, which had opened European markets to cheap agricultural goods from the United States, Canada, and Argentina. The drop in food prices affected purchasing power in other sectors and resulted in long-term deflation and unemployment.

Financiers, politicians, and businessmen dedicated themselves to eliminating the boom-and-bust phenomenon, which they considered dangerous. The application of science and technology to industrial production required huge amounts of capital. The two new sources of power after 1880, petroleum and electricity, could be developed only with heavy capital investment. Large mechanized steel plants were too costly for small family firms of the scale that had industrialized textile production so successfully earlier in the century. Heavy machinery, smelting furnaces, buildings, and transport were all beyond the means of the small entrepreneur.

To raise the capital necessary for the new heavy industry at the end of the nineteenth century, firms had to look outside themselves to the stock market, banks, or the state to find adequate capital resources. But investors and especially banks refused to invest without guarantees on their capital. Because investment in heavy industry meant tying up capital for extended periods of time, banks insisted on safeguards against falling prices. The solution that they demanded was the elimination of uncertainty through the regulation of markets.

Cartels. Regulation was achieved through the establishment of **cartels**, combinations of firms in a given industry united to fix prices and to establish production quotas. Cartels were agreements among big firms intent on controlling markets and guaranteeing profits. Trusts were another form of collaboration that resulted in the elimination of unprofitable businesses. Firms joined together horizontally within the same industry; for example, all steel producers agreed to fix prices and set quotas. Or they combined vertically by controlling all levels of the production process from raw materials to the finished product and all other ancillary products necessary to or resulting from the production process.

Banks, which had been the initial impetus behind the transformation to a regulated economy, in turn formed consortia to meet the need for greater amounts of capital. A consortium, paralleling a cartel, was a partnership among banks, often international in character, in which interest rates and the movement of capital were regulated by mutual agreement.

The state, too, played an important role in directing the economy. Throughout Europe, nation-states protected domestic industries by erecting tariff barriers against foreign goods. Only Great Britain among the major powers stood by a policy of free trade. Europe was split into two tiers—the haves and have-nots: those countries with a solid industrial core and those that had remained unindustrialized. This division had a geographic character, the north and west of Europe being heavily developed and capitalized and the southern and eastern parts of Europe remaining heavily agricultural. For both the haves and have-nots, tariff policies were an attractive form of regulation by the state to protect established industries and to nurture industries that were struggling for existence.

Challenging Liberal England

Great Britain experienced the transformation in political organization and social structure before other European nations. But after 1870, changes in politics influenced by the scale of the new industrial society spread to every European country. The policies that the emerging mass society generated were making clearer the contradictions inherent in the ideal of democracy. Mass demands were pushing aside the liberal emphasis on individual rights valued by parliamentary governments everywhere.

Trade Unions. In the 1880s, issues of unemployment, public health, housing, and education challenged the attitudes of Britain's ruling elite and fostered the advent of independent working-class politics. Between 1867 and 1885, extension of suffrage increased the electorate fourfold. Protected by the markets of its empire, the British economy did not experience the roller-coaster effect of recurrent booms and busts after 1873. But after 1900, wages stagnated as prices continued to rise, and workers responded by supporting militant trade unions.

Trade unions, drawing on a long tradition of working-class associations, were all that stood between workers and the economic dislocation caused by unemployment,

A union leader addresses striking British coal miners in 1912. Labor unions became increasingly militant after the turn of the century as rising unemployment and declining real wages cut into the gains of the working class.

sickness, or old age. In addition, new unions of unskilled and semiskilled workers flourished, beginning in the 1880s and 1890s. A Scottish miner, James Keir Hardie (1856–1915), attracted national attention as the spokesman for a new political movement, the Labour party, whose goal was to represent workers in Parliament. In 1892, Hardie was the first independent working man to sit in the House of Commons. Hardie and his party convinced trade unions that it was in their best interests to support Labour candidates instead of Liberals in parliamentary elections after 1900. By 1906, the new Labour party had 29 seats in Parliament. Intellectuals now joined with trade unionists in demanding public housing, better public sanitation, municipal reforms, and improved pay and benefits for workers.

Parliamentary Reforms. The existence of the new Labour party pressured Conservatives and Liberals to develop more enlightened social programs. After 1906, under threat of losing votes to the Labour party, the Liberal party heeded the pressures for reform. The "new" Liberals supported legislation to strengthen the right of unions to picket peacefully. Led by David Lloyd George (1863–1945), who was chancellor of the exchequer, Liberals sponsored the National Insurance Act of 1911. The act provided compulsory payments to workers for sickness and unemployment benefits.

In order to gain approval to pay for this new legislation, Lloyd George recognized that Parliament itself had to be renovated. The Parliament Bill of 1911 reduced the House of Lords, dominated by Conservatives resistant to proposed welfare reforms, from its status as equal partner with the House of Commons. Commons could and now did raise taxes without the consent of the House of Lords to pay for new programs that benefited workers and the poor.

Extraparliamentary Protest. Social legislation did not silence unions and worker organizations. Between 1910 and 1914, waves of strikes broke over England. Coal miners, seamen, railroad workers, and dockers protested against stagnant wages and rising prices.

The high incidence of strikes was a consequence of growing distrust of Parliament and of a regulatory state bureaucracy responsible for the social welfare reforms. Labour's voice grew more strident. Only the outbreak of war in 1914 ended the possibility of a general strike by miners, railwaymen, and transport workers. The question of Irish home rule also plagued Parliament. In Ulster in northern Ireland, army officers of Protestant Irish background threatened to mutiny. In addition, women agitating for the vote shattered parliamentary complacence. The most advanced industrial nation, with its tradition of peaceful parliamentary rule, had entered the age of mass politics.

Political Struggles in Germany

During his reign as chancellor of the German Empire (1871–1890), Otto von Bismarck's objective remained always the successful unification of Germany, and he promoted cooperation with democratic institutions and parties only as long as that goal was enhanced.

Bismarck and the German Parliament. Throughout the 1870s, the German chancellor collaborated with the German liberal parties in constructing the legal codes, the monetary and banking system, the judicial apparatus, and the railroad network that pulled the new Germany together. Bismarck backed German liberals in their antipapal campaign, in which the Catholic Church was depicted as an authority in competition with the German nation-state. The anti-Church campaign, launched in 1872, was dubbed the *Kulturkampf* ("struggle for civilization") because its supporters contended that it was a battle waged in the interests of humanity.

The legislation of the *Kulturkampf* expelled Jesuits from Germany, removed priests from state service, attacked religious education, and instituted civil marriage. Many Germans grew concerned about the social costs of such widespread religious repression, and the Catholic Center party increased its parliamentary representation by rallying Catholics as a voting bloc in the face of state repression. With the succession of a new pontiff, Leo XIII (1878–1903), Bismarck negotiated a settlement with the Catholic Church, cutting his losses and bringing the *Kulturkampf* to a halt.

The Social Democrat Party. Bismarck's repressive policies also targeted the Social Democratic party. The Social Democrats were committed to a Marxist critique of capitalism and to international cooperation with other socialist parties. Seeing them as a threat to stability in Germany and in Europe as a whole, Bismarck set out to smash them. In 1878, using the opportunity for repression presented by two attempts on the emperor's life, Bismarck outlawed the fledgling Socialist party.

The Anti-Socialist Law forbade meetings among socialists, fund-raising, and distribution of printed matter. Nevertheless, individual Social Democratic candidates stood for election in this period and learned quickly how to work with middle-class parties to achieve electoral successes. By 1890, Social Democrats had captured 20 percent of the electorate and controlled 35 Reichstag seats in spite of Bismarck's anti-Socialist legislation.

Beginning in 1888, the chancellor found himself at odds with the new emperor Wilhelm II (1888–1918) over his foreign and domestic policies. The young emperor dismissed Bismarck in March 1890 and abandoned the chancellor's anti-Socialist legislation. The Social Democratic party became the largest Marxist party in the world and, by 1914, the largest single party in Germany.

In the end, the Reichstag failed to defy the absolute authority of Emperor Wilhelm II, who was served after 1890 by a string of ineffectual chancellors. Despite its constitutional forms, Germany was ruled by a state authoritarianism in which the bureaucracy, the military, and various interest groups exercised influence over the emperor. A high-risk foreign policy that had a mass appeal was one way to circumvent a parliamentary system incapable of decision making. Constitutional solutions had been short-circuited in favor of authoritarian rule.

Political Scandals and Mass Politics in France

The Third Republic in France had an aura of the accidental about its origins and of the precarious about its existence. Yet appearances were misleading. Founded in 1870 with the defeat of Napoleon III's empire by the Germans, the Third Republic claimed legitimacy by placing itself squarely within the revolutionary democratic tradition.

Creating Citizens. The Third Republic successfully worked toward the creation of a national community based on a common identity of citizens. Compulsory schooling, one of the great institutional transformations of French government in 1885, socialized French children in common values, patriotism, and identification with the nation-state. Old ways, local dialects, superstitious practices, and peasant insularity dropped away or were modified under the persistent pressure of a centralized curriculum of reading, writing, arithmetic, and civics. Compulsory service in the army for the generation of young men of draft age served the same end of communicating national values to a predominantly peasant population. Technology also accelerated the process of shaping a national citizenry, as railroad lines tied people together and new and better roads made distances shrink.

A truly national and mass culture emerged in the period between 1880 and 1914. French people were not necessarily more political, but they were political in a new way that enabled them to identify their own local interests with national issues.

The Boulanger Affair. A political crisis, known as the Boulanger Affair, temporarily threatened the stability of the republic and served as a good indication of the extent of the transformation in French political life at the end of the nineteenth century.

As minister of war, General Georges Boulanger (1837–1891) became a hero to French soldiers when he undertook needed reforms of army life. He won over businessmen by leading troops against strikers. Above all, he cultivated the image of a patriot ready to defend France's honor at any cost.

Boulanger's potential in the political arena attracted the attention of right-wing backers, including monarchists who hoped eventually to restore kingship to France. By 1889, Boulanger was able to amass enough national support to frighten the defenders of parliamentary institutions. The charismatic general ultimately failed in his bid for power and fled the country because of allegations of treason. But he left in his wake an embryonic mass movement on the Right that operated outside the channels of parliamentary institutions.

The Dreyfus Affair. A very different kind of crisis began to take shape in 1894 with the controversy surrounding the trial of Captain Alfred Dreyfus (1859–1935) that came to be known simply as "the Affair." Dreyfus was an Alsatian Jewish army officer who was accused of selling military secrets to the Germans. His trial for treason served as a lightning rod for xenophobia—the hatred of foreigners, in this case especially Germans—and anti-Semitism, the hatred of Jews. Dreyfus was stripped of his commission and honors and sentenced to solitary confinement for life on Devil's Island, a convict colony off French Guiana in South America.

Illegal activities and outright falsifications by Dreyfus's superiors to secure a conviction came to light in the mass press and divided the nation. Those who supported Dreyfus's innocence, the pro-Dreyfusards, were for the most part on the left of the political spectrum and spoke of the republic's duty to uphold justice and freedom. The anti-Dreyfusards were associated with the traditional institutions of the Catholic Church and the army and considered themselves to be defending the honor of France.

On the national level, the Affair represented an important transformation in the nature of French political life. Existing parliamentary institutions had been found wanting. They were unable to cope with the mass politics stirred up by Dreyfus's conviction. The newspaper press vied with parliament and the courts as a forum for investigation and decision making.

The crises provoked by Boulanger's attempt to gain power and the Dreyfus Affair demonstrated the major role of the press and the importance of public opinion in exerting pressure on the system of government. The press emerged as a myth-maker in shaping and channeling public opinion. Émile Zola (1840–1902), the great French novelist, spearheaded the pro-Dreyfusard movement with his damning article *"J'accuse!"* ("I Accuse!"), in which he pointed to the military and the judiciary as the "spirits of social evil" for persecuting an innocent man. The article appeared in a leading French newspaper and was influential in securing Dreyfus's eventual exoneration and the discovery of the real culprit, one of Dreyfus's colleagues on the general staff. The Third Republic was never in danger of collapsing, but it was transformed. The locus of power in parliament was challenged by pressure groups outside of it.

Defeating Liberalism in Austria

In the 1870s, the liberal values of the bourgeoisie dominated the Austro-Hungarian Empire. The Habsburg monarchy had adjusted to constitutional government, which was introduced throughout Austria in 1860. Faith in parliamentary government based on a restricted suffrage had established a tenuous foothold.

By 1900, however, the urban and capitalist middle class that ruled Austria by virtue of a limited suffrage based on property had lost ground to new groups that were essentially anticapitalist and antiliberal in their outlook. The new groups were peasants, workers, urban artisans and shopkeepers, and the colonized Slavic peoples of the empire. Bourgeois politics and laissez-faire economics had offered little or nothing to these varied groups, who were now claiming the right of participation. Mass parties were formed based on radical pan-Germanic feeling, anticapitalism that appealed to peasants and artisans, hatred of the Jews shared by students and artisans, and nationalist aspirations that attracted the lower middle classes.

Chronology

EUROPEAN POLITICS: 1871–1914

1867–1885	Fourfold increase in electorate in Britain
1871–1890	Otto von Bismarck chancellor of the German Empire
1872–1878	*Kulturkampf* in Germany
1878	Bismarck outlaws the Socialist party in Germany
1880s	Emergence of independent working-class politics in Britain
1885	Introduction of compulsory schooling in France
1889	General Georges Boulanger makes failed bid for power in France
1892	James Keir Hardie becomes first independent working man to win seat in British Parliament
1894	Captain Alfred Dreyfus convicted of treason in France
1906	Labor party wins 29 seats in British Parliament
1911	Britain: Passage of National Insurance Act and Parliament Bill
1910–1914	Widespread labor unrest in Britain
1914	German Social Democratic party largest single party in Germany

Outsiders in Mass Politics

By the end of the nineteenth century, a faceless, nameless electorate had become the basis of new political strategies and a new political rhetoric. A concept of class identification of workers was devalued in favor of interest-group politics in which lobbies formed around single issues to pressure European governments. But the apparently all-inclusive concept of mass society continued to exclude some groups: women, ethnic minorities, and Jews.

Feminists and Politics

Women's drive for emancipation had been a recurrent motif of European political culture throughout the nineteenth century. In the areas of civil liberties, legal equality with men, and economic autonomy, only the most limited reforms had been enacted. The glorification of domesticity was a kind of recognition of women's unique contribution to society, but it was also a means of keeping women "in their place."

Women's Rights. European women who worked outside of the family were paid one-third to one-half of what men earned for the same work. In Great Britain, women did not enjoy equal divorce rights until the twentieth century. In France, married women had no control over their own incomes; all their earnings were considered their husband's private property. From the Atlantic to the Urals, women were excluded from economic and educational opportunities.

Growing numbers of women, primarily from the middle classes, began calling themselves "feminist," a term that was coined in France in the 1830s. The new feminists throughout western Europe differed from earlier generations in their willingness to organize mass movements and to appropriate the techniques of interest-group politics. The first international congress of women's rights, held in Paris in 1878, initiated an era of international cooperation and exchange among women's organizations. Women's groups now positioned themselves for sustained political action.

Movements for the Vote. The lessons of the new electoral politics were not lost on feminists seeking women's emancipation through the vote. If women's organizations were to survive as competing interest groups, they needed to form political alliances, control their own newspapers and magazines, and keep their cause before the public eye.

There was a growing willingness on the part of a variety of women's organizations to use mass demonstrations, rallies, and violent tactics. No movement operated more effectively in this regard than the British suffrage movement. In 1903, a group of eminently respectable middle-class and aristocratic British women formed the Women's Social and Political Union (WSPU). At the center of the movement was Emmeline Pankhurst (1858–1928), a middle-aged woman of frail and attractive appearance who had a will of iron and a gift for oratory. Mrs. Pankhurst and her two daughters, Christabel (1880–1958), a lawyer by training, and Sylvia (1882–1960), an artist, succeeded in keeping women's suffrage before the British public and brought the plight of British women to international attention.

Women's demands for political power were the basis of an unheralded revolution in Western culture. In Great Britain, the decade before the Great War of 1914 was a period of profound political education for women seeking the vote. An unprecedented 250,000 women gathered in Hyde Park in 1908 to hear more about female suffrage.

TREATMENT OF POLITICAL PRISONERS UNDER A LIBERAL GOVERNMENT.

This British suffragette poster, published by the Women's Social and Political Union, graphically depicts the extreme methods used to force-feed women prisoners. A prison guard pulls back the prisoner's head, others hold down her arms and legs, and another ties her foot to the chair. A doctor holds a hose through which he forces gruel into the woman's nose.

European women did not gain the right to vote easily. In France and Germany, moderate and left-wing politicians opposed extension of the vote to women because they feared that women would strengthen conservative candidates. Many politicians thought that women were not "ready" for the vote and that they should receive it only as a reward—an unusual concept in democratic societies. Not until 1918 were British women granted limited suffrage, and not until 1928 did they gain voting rights that were equal to those of men. Only after war and revolution was the vote extended to other women in the West: Germany in 1918, the United States in 1920, and France at the end of World War II.

Women and Social Reform. Not all activist women saw the right to vote as the solution to women's oppression. Those who agitated for social reforms for poor and working-class women parted ways with the militant suffragists. Women socialists were concerned with working-class women's "double oppression" in the home and in the workplace. Working-class women, most notably in Germany, united feminism with socialism in search of a better life.

The Jewish Question and Zionism

Two million eastern European Jews migrated westward between 1868 and 1914 in search of peace and refuge. Seventy thousand settled in Germany. Others continued westward, stopping in the United States. Another kind of Jewish migration took place in the nineteenth century: the movement within nations of Jews from rural to urban areas. In eastern Europe, Jewish migrations coincided with downturns in the economic cycle, and Jews became scapegoats for the high rates of unemployment and high prices that seemed to follow in their wake. Most migrants were peddlers, artisans, or small shopkeepers who were seen as threatening to small businesses. Differing in language, culture, and dress, they were viewed as alien in every way.

Anti-Semitism. The term **anti-Semitism**, meaning hostility to Jews, was first used in 1879 to give a pseudoscientific legitimacy to bigotry and hatred. Persecution was a harsh reality for Jews in eastern Europe at the end of the nineteenth century. In Russia, Jews could not own property and were restricted to living in certain territories, areas referred to as "the Pale." Organized massacres, or **pogroms**, in Kiev, Odessa, and Warsaw followed the assassination of Tsar Alexander II in 1881 and occurred again after the failed Russian revolution of 1905. Russian authorities blamed the Jews, who were perennially perceived as outsiders, for the assassination and revolution and the social instability that followed them. Pogroms resulted in the death and displacement of tens of thousands of eastern European Jews.

In western Europe, Jews considered themselves to be assimilated into their national cultures, identifying with their nationality as much as with their religion. Austrian and German Jews were granted full civil rights in 1867 on the principle that citizens of all religions enjoyed full equality. In France, Jews had been legally emancipated since the end of the eighteenth century. But the western and central European politics of the 1890s had a strong dose of anti-Semitism. Demagogues such as Georg von Schönerer (1842–1921) of Austria were capable of whipping up a frenzy of riots and violence against Jews. Western and central European anti-Semitism assumed a new level of virulence at the end of the nineteenth century.

Fear of the Jews was connected with hatred of capitalism. In France and Germany, Jews controlled powerful banking and commercial firms that became the targets of blame in hard times. Upwardly mobile sons of Jewish immigrants entered the professions of banking, trading, and journalism. They were also growing in numbers as teachers and academics. Their professional success only heightened tensions and condemnations of Jews as an "alien race." Anti-Semitism served as a violent means of mobilizing mass support, especially among the groups that felt threatened by capitalist concentration and large-scale industrialization. For anti-Semitic Europeans, Jews embodied the democratic, liberal, and cosmopolitan tendencies of the new culture that they were consciously rejecting in their new political affiliations.

Zionism. A Jewish leadership emerged in central and western Europe that treated anti-Semitism as a problem that could be solved by political means. For the generation at the end of the nineteenth century, the assimilation of their fathers and mothers was not the answer. Jews needed their own nation, it was argued, since they were a people without a nation. Zionism was the solution to what Jewish intellectuals called "the Jewish problem." Zion, the ancient homeland of biblical times, would provide a national territory, and a choice, to persecuted Jews. Zionism became a Jewish nationalist movement dedicated to the establishment of a Jewish state.

Theodor Herzl (1860–1904), an Austrian Jew born in Budapest, was the founder of **Zionism** in its political form. In *The Jewish State* (1896), Herzl concluded that Jews must have a state of their own. Under his direction, Zionism developed a world organization with the aim of establishing a Jewish homeland in Palestine.

Legend:
- The Pale: area where Russian Jews allowed to live
- Other areas of large Jewish population
- Cities with large Jewish population
- General routes of Jewish exodus

0   400 Miles
0   400 Kilometers

JEWISH MIGRATION

Persecution and expulsions drove two million Jews out of Russia and eastern Europe between 1868 and 1914. Some settled in central Europe, while others traveled to Palestine and the Americas. According to this map, what features do the areas of large Jewish population have in common? What are the major general routes of Jewish exodus? Based on the chapter discussion, why did Jews migrate into and out of the Pale in western Russia? What were the major stopover points in the Jewish migrations to the south and west?

Maurycy Minkowski, *After the Pogrom* (ca. 1910). Minkowski's works depict Jewish life in Poland before the Russian Revolution. In this painting he expertly captured the weariness, hopelessness, and fear of the refugees who have interrupted their flight to rest. The sense of isolation and dislocation evoked in the painting may derive from the deaf and mute artist's personal perception of profound separation and detachment.

Jews began emigrating to Palestine. With the financial backing of Jewish donors such as the French banker Baron de Rothschild, nearly 90,000 Jews had established settlements there by 1914. Calculated to tap a common Jewish identification with an ancient heritage, the choice of Palestine as a homeland was controversial from the beginning, and the problems arising from the choice have persisted to the present day.

Some Jewish critics of Zionism thought that a separate Jewish state would prove that Jews were not good citizens of their respective nation-states and would exacerbate hostilities toward Jews as outsiders. Yet Zionism had much in common with the European liberal tradition, because it sought in the creation of a nation-state for Jews the solution to social injustice. Zion, the Jewish nation in the Middle East, was a liberal utopia for the Jewish people. Zionism learned from other mass movements of the period the importance of a broad base of support. By the time of the First Zionist Congress, held in Basel, Switzerland, in 1897, it had become a truly international movement. Zionism did not achieve its goals before World War I, and the Jewish state of Israel was not recognized by the world community until 1948.

Workers and Minorities on the Margins

Changes in the scale of political life paralleled the rise of heavy industry and the increasing urbanization of European populations. New industrial and financial leaders assumed positions among Europe's ruling elite. A new style of politics brought new political actors into the public arena at the beginning of the twentieth century. Extraparliamentary groups grew in influence and power and exerted pressure on the political process. The politics of mass society made clear the contradictions inherent in democracy. Propaganda, the ability to control information, became the avenue to success.

There was no single anarchist doctrine, but the varieties of **anarchism** all shared a hope in a future free from constraints. Mikhail Bakunin (1814–1876), a member of the Russian nobility, became Europe's leading anarchist spokesman. Bakunin was a man of revolutionary action who espoused the use of violence to achieve individual liberation. He believed that all existing institutions must be swept away before ownership of production could be collectivized.

In 1892, the trial in Paris of a bomb-throwing anarchist named Ravachol attracted great public attention. He and other French anarchists had captured the popular imagination with their threats to destroy bourgeois society by bombing private residences, public buildings, and restaurants. Ravachol opposed the state and the capitalist economy as the dual enemy that could be destroyed only through individual acts of random physical violence. For his crimes he was condemned to death and publicly executed.

The best-known anarchists of the late nineteenth century were those, like Ravachol, who engaged in terrorist assassinations and bombings. Although not all anarchists were terrorists intent on destruction, all shared a desire for a revolutionary restructuring of society. Most anarchists were loners. They dreamed of the collapse of the capitalist system with its exploitation and inequality and of the emergence of a society based on personal freedom, autonomy, and justice. Anarchists spurned the Marxist willingness to organize and participate in parliamentary politics. They disdained the tyranny of new organizations and bureaucracies that worked for gradual reforms at the expense of principles of justice.

Anarchism had special appeal to workers in trades that were staggering under the blows of industrial capitalism. Calling themselves anarcho-syndicalists, artisans—especially in France—were able to combine local trade union organization with anarchist principles. But, unlike union movements in the industrialized countries of Great Britain and Germany, French trade unions remained small, weak, and local. The contrast between the Labour party in Great Britain and the German Social Democrats on the one hand and the French anarcho-syndicalists on the other highlighted the split between advanced industrial countries and less-developed areas of Europe, where an artisan class was attempting to preserve autonomy and control.

The problems of disaffected groups in general intensified before 1914. The politics of mass society excluded diverse groups, including women, Jews, and ethnic minorities, from participation. Yet the techniques, values, and organization of the world of politics remained available to all these groups. It was the outbreak of war in 1914 that silenced, temporarily at least, the challenge of these outsiders.

Shaping the New Consciousness

Both science and art contributed to the new world view that emerged in western society in the late nineteenth century. Not only was the European imagination opened up to new influences from the culture and aesthetics of other lands, but Europeans developed a critique of traditional values and rationalist thought from within through new developments in philosophy and science.

The Authority of Science

New scientific disciplines claimed to study society with methods similar to those applied to the study of bacilli and the atom. A traditional world of order and hierarchy gave way to a new way of perceiving reality. The discoveries of science had ramifications that extended beyond the laboratory, the hospital, and the classroom.

Discoveries in the Physical Sciences. Scientific discoveries in the last quarter of the nineteenth century pushed outward the frontiers of knowledge. In physics, James Clerk Maxwell (1831–1879) discovered the relationship between electricity and magnetism. His theories led to the discovery of the electromagnetic spectrum, comprising radiation of different wavelengths, including X-rays, visible light, and radio waves. This discovery had important practical applications for the development of the electrical industry and led to the invention of radio and television. Within a generation, the names of Edison, Westinghouse, Marconi, Siemens, and Bell entered the public realm.

Discoveries in the physical sciences succeeded one another with great rapidity. The periodic table of chemical elements was formulated in 1869. Radioactivity was discovered in 1896. Two years later, Marie Curie (1867–1934) and her husband Pierre (1859–1906) discovered the elements radium and polonium. At the end of the century, Ernest Rutherford (1871–1937) identified alpha and beta rays in radioactive atoms. Building on the new discoveries, Max Planck (1858–1947), Albert Einstein (1879–1955), and Niels Bohr (1885–1962) dismantled the classical physics of absolute and determined principles and left in its place modern physics based on relativity and uncertainty. In 1900, Planck propounded a theory that renounced the emphasis in classical physics on energy as a wave phenomenon in favor of a new "quantum theory" of energy as emitted and absorbed in minute, discrete amounts.

In 1905, Albert Einstein formulated his special theory of relativity, in which he established the relationship of mass and energy in the famous equation $E = mc^2$. In 1916, he published his general theory of relativity, a mathematical formulation that created new concepts of space and time. Einstein disproved the Newtonian view of gravitation as a force and instead saw it as a curved field in the time-space continuum created by the presence of mass.

Achievements in Biology. Though the discoveries in the physical sciences were the most dramatic, the biological sciences, too, witnessed great breakthroughs. Research biologists dedicated themselves to the study of disease-causing microbes and to the chemical bases of physiology. French chemist Louis Pasteur (1822–1895) studied microorganisms to find methods of preventing the spread of diseases in humans, animals, and plants. He developed methods of inoculation to provide protection against anthrax in sheep, cholera in chickens, and rabies in animals and humans.

The pace of breakthroughs in biological knowledge and medical treatment was staggering. The malaria parasite was isolated in 1880. The control of diseases such as yellow fever contributed to improvement in the quality of life. Knowledge burst the bounds of disciplines, and new fields developed to accommodate new concerns. Research in human genetics, a field that was only starting to be understood, was begun in the first decade of the twentieth century. The studies of Austrian botanist Gregor Mendel (1822–1884) in the crossbreeding of peas in the 1860s led to the Mendelian laws of inheritance.

Applied Knowledge. Biological discoveries resulted in new state policies. Public health benefited from new methods of prevention and detection of diseases caused by germs. A professor at the University of Berlin, Rudolf Virchow (1821–1902), discovered the relationship between microbes, sewage, and disease that led to the development of modern sewer systems and pure water for urban populations. Biochemistry, bacteriology, and physiology promoted a belief in social progress through state programs. After 1900, health programs to educate the general public spread throughout Europe.

Discoveries that changed the face of the twentieth century proliferated in a variety of fields. This was a time of firsts in all directions: airplane flights and deep-sea expeditions, based on technological applications of new discoveries, pushed out boundaries of exploration above the land and below the sea. In 1909, the same year that work began in human genetics, U.S. explorer Robert E. Peary (1856–1920) reached the North Pole. In that year, too, plastic was first manufactured, under the trade name Bakelite. Irish-born British astronomer Agnes Mary Clerke (1842–1907) did pioneering work in the new field of astrophysics. Ernest Rutherford proposed a new spatial reality in his theory of the nuclear structure of the atom, which stated that the atom can be divided and consists of a nucleus with electrons revolving around it.

Establishing the Social Sciences

Innovations in the social sciences paralleled the drama of discovery in the biological and physical sciences. The "scientific" study of society purported to apply the methods of observation and experimentation to human interactions. After 1870, sociology, economics, history, psychology, anthropology, and archaeology took shape at the core of new social scientific endeavors. But just as scientific advances could be applied to destructive ends, so, too, did the social sciences promote inequities and prejudices in the Western world.

Economics. The social scientific study of economics came to the aid of businessmen. The neoclassical economic theory of Alfred Marshall (1842–1924) and others recognized the centrality of individual choice in the marketplace while dealing with the problem of how businesses can know they have produced enough to maximize profits. Economists who were concerned with how individuals responded to prices devised a theory of marginal utility, by which producers could calculate costs and project profits on the basis of a pattern of response of consumers to price changes.

Psychology and Human Behavior. "Scientific" psychology developed in a variety of directions. Wilhelm Wundt (1832–1920) established the first laboratory devoted to psychological research in Leipzig in 1879. From his experiments he concluded that thought is grounded in physical reality. The Russian physiologist Ivan Pavlov (1849–1936) won fame with a series of experiments demonstrating the conditioned reflex in dogs. Sigmund Freud (1859–1939) greatly influenced the direction of psychology with his theory of personality development and the creation of psychoanalysis, the science of the unconscious. Freudian probing of the unconscious was a model that was greatly at odds with the behavioral perspective of conditioned responses based on Pavlov's work.

Émile Durkheim (1858–1917), regarded as the founder of modern sociology, studied suicide as a social phenomenon. He pitted sociological theory against psychology and argued that deviance was the result not of psychic disturbances but of environmental factors and hereditary forces.

Heredity became a general explanation for behavior of all sorts. Everything from poverty, drunkenness, and crime to a declining birthrate could be attributed to biologically determined causes. For some theorists, this reasoning teetered on the edge of racism and ideas about "better blood." Science changed the way people thought and the way they lived. It improved the quality of life by defeating diseases, improving nutrition, and lengthening life span. But scientific knowledge was not without its costs. Scientific discoveries led to new forces of destruction. Scientific ideas challenged moral and religious beliefs. Science was invoked to justify racial and sexual discrimination. Traditional values and religious beliefs also did combat with the new god of science, with philosophers proclaiming that God was dead. Not least of all, science and the progress it promised came under attack by those like Friedrich Nietzsche (1844–1900), the German philosopher who questioned rational values as well as the emphasis on religion in Western thought.

The "New Woman" and the New Consciousness

As women continued to be excluded from national political participation, the right to vote was gradually being extended to all men in western Europe, regardless of property or social rank. New scientific ideas colluded with political prejudices to justify denying women equal rights. The natural sciences had a formative impact on prevailing views of gender relations and female sexuality and were used to attempt to prove women's inferiority.

Biology and Woman's Destiny. Most scientific opinion argued in favor of female frailty and inferiority. These "scientific" arguments justified excluding women from educational opportunities and from professions such as medicine and law. There was also a generalized fear in Western societies that women who tried to exceed their "natural" abilities would damage their reproductive functions and neglect their nurturing roles.

The New Woman. In this age of scientific justification of female inferiority, the "new woman" emerged. All over Europe the feminist movement had demanded social, economic, and political progress for women. But the "new woman" phenomenon exceeded the bounds of the feminist movement and can be described as a general cultural phenomenon. The "new woman" was characterized by intelligence, strength, and sexual desire—in every way man's equal.

The new woman's pursuit of independence included control over her own body. Margaret Sanger (1879–1966), an American, advocated birth control to help women take charge of their reproductive lives. She was arrested several times for her activities but helped to get laws passed that allowed doctors to disseminate information about birth control. Annie Besant (1847–1933) played a similar role in Great Britain. Aletta Jacobs (1849–1929), the first woman to practice medicine in Holland, opened a contraceptive clinic in 1882. By 1900, sexuality and reproduction were openly connected to discussions of women's rights.

Art and the New Age

In the last quarter of the nineteenth century, the world of art in western Europe and the United States was characterized by new discoveries, new subjects, and new modes of expression. At least a half dozen major and distinct art movements caught the imagination of artists and the general public. Beginning in the 1860s, impressionist painters led the way in rebelling against the conventions of the formal painting of the academic salons. Choosing unlikely subjects such as railway stations and haystacks in the works of Claude Monet (1840–1926), impressionists made a revolution in capturing on canvas the nature of light and atmosphere. Post-impressionists in the 1880s and 1890s built on the insights of their impressionist colleagues but went in new and less predictable directions, as exemplified in the work of Paul Cezanne (1839–1906), Vincent Van Gogh (1853–1890), and Henri Rousseau (1844–1910). Pointillism, well exemplified in the work of Georges Seurat (1859–1891), also followed the discoveries of the impressionists by using tiny dots to convey light and a spectrum of color.

All the art of this period also had certain features in common. The artists reflected the values and mores of a changing society in their work, both in their choice of subject matter and their choice of perspective. They were also influenced by breakthroughs in science and technology that allowed the understanding of how light worked through the new realism of the photographic medium and new discoveries in physics and the science of the material world. New knowledge about non-Western cultures and Europeans' widening view of the world also influenced artistic subjects and styles. The new art movements of the late nineteenth century also indicated a dramatic shift in the class base of art out of the salons of the elite and the aristocracy and into the venues of middle class life—the home, the public spheres of the café, the theater, and the railway station.

SUMMARY

European Economy and the Politics of Mass Society   Industrial development led to ever-greater concentrations of population in urban centers. Boom and bust cycles led to social and political unrest. Financiers, politicians, and businessmen developed strategies for reducing economic fluctuation and market uncertainty. In Britain, the Labor party emerged to represent the interests of British workers. The Liberal party responded to competition from Labour by heeding pressure for reform. Between 1910 and 1914, Britain experienced considerable labor unrest. In Germany, Otto von Bismarck used democratic institutions and parties when doing so enhanced the process of unification. The *Kulturkampf* pitted German liberals against the Catholic Church. Despite Bismarck's social legislation, the Social Democrat party grew in popularity. Under Wilhelm II, Germany remained an authoritarian state. In France, the Third Republic launched a successful effort to build a national community. The Boulanger and Dreyfus affairs revealed the weakness of the French parliament in the face of mass politics and mobilized public opinion. In Austria, new groups challenged the dominance of the urban and capitalist middle class in Austrian politics.

Outsiders in Mass Politics   Growing numbers of women, primarily from the middle class, worked to achieve greater equality. The women's emancipation movement used the tools of mass politics to get its message out. There was considerable opposition to female suffrage. Some activist women believed that social reforms were at least as important as the right to vote. In the second half of the nineteenth century, European Jews migrated from east to west and from rural to urban areas. Anti-Semitism in eastern Europe took the form of legal restrictions and organized violence. Jews in western Europe enjoyed full civil rights, but still were subject to discrimination and violence. For anti-Semitic Europeans, Jews embodied the general cultural and social trends they found most threatening. For some Jews, the best response to anti-Semitism was not assimilation, but Zionism. Anarchists hoped to create a future free from constraints on individual liberty. Some anarchists were willing to use violence to achieve their aims. Anarchism had particular appeal to workers in trades that had suffered under the pressure of industrial capitalism.

Shaping the New Consciousness   The late nineteenth century saw numerous breakthroughs in the physical and biological sciences. Scientific breakthroughs were applied to medicine, industry, technology, and public policy. The "scientific" study of society purported to apply the methods of observation and experimentation to human interactions. After 1870, sociology, economics, history, psychology, anthropology, and archaeology took shape at the core of new social scientific endeavors. New scientific knowledge came with considerable costs. Most scientific opinion argued in favor of female frailty and inferiority. The "new woman" was characterized by intelligence, strength, sexual desire, and by belief in her equality with men. The new woman's pursuit of independence included control over her own body. In the last quarter of the nineteenth century, the world of art in western Europe and the United States was characterized by new discoveries, new subjects, and new modes of expression.

QUESTIONS FOR REVIEW

1. Why did European economies run through cycles of boom and bust in the late nineteenth century, and how did European governments attempt to regulate the economy?
2. What challenges did liberal ideals and institutions confront in England, Germany, France, and Austria?
3. What social forces brought women and others into the new mass politics of the late nineteenth century?
4. What new ideas were being generated in psychology and the social sciences at the turn of the century, and what impact did they have on the way Europeans thought about gender relations?

Europe and the World, 1870–1914

The European Balance of Power, 1870–1914

Between 1870 and 1914, European states were locked in a competition within Europe for dominance and control. The European balance of power that Bismarck had so carefully crafted began to disintegrate with his departure from office in 1890. By 1914, a Europe divided into two camps was no longer the sure guarantee of peace that it had been a generation earlier.

Upsetting the European Balance of Power

The map of Europe had been redrawn in the two decades after 1850. By 1871, Europe consisted of the Big Five—Britain, France, Germany, Austria-Hungary, and Russia—and a handful of lesser states. The declaration of the German Empire in

1871 and the emergence of Italy with Rome as its capital in 1870 unified numerous disparate states. Although not always corresponding to linguistic and cultural differences among Europe's peoples, national boundaries appeared to be fixed, with no country aspiring to territorial expansion at the expense of its neighbors. But the creation of the two new national units of Germany and Italy had legitimized nationalist aspirations and the militarism necessary to enforce them.

The Three Emperors' League. Under the chancellorship of Otto von Bismarck, Germany led the way in forging a new alliance system based on the realistic assessment of power politics within Europe. In 1873, Bismarck joined together the three most conservative powers of the Big Five—Germany, Austria-Hungary, and Russia—into the Three Emperors' League. Consultation about mutual interests and friendly neutrality were the cornerstones of this alliance.

Each of the Great Powers had a vulnerability, a geographic Achilles' heel. Germany's vulnerability lay in its North Sea ports. German shipping along its only coast could easily be bottlenecked by a powerful naval force. Such an event, the Germans knew, could destroy their rapidly growing international trade. What was worse, powerful land forces could encircle Germany. As Germany surged forward to seize its share of world markets, it was acutely aware that it was hemmed in on the Continent. Germany could not extend its frontiers the way Russia had to the east. German gains in the Franco-Prussian war in Alsace and Lorraine could not be repeated without risking greater enmity. German leaders saw the threat of encirclement as a second geographic weakness. Bismarck's awareness of these geographic facts of life prompted his engineering of the Three Emperors' League in 1873, two years after the founding of the German Empire.

Austria-Hungary was Europe's second largest landed nation and the third largest in population. The same factors that had made it a great European power—its size and its diversity—now threatened to destroy it. The ramshackle empire of Europe was weakened by the centrifugal forces of linguistic and cultural diversity, by nationalities clamoring for independence and self-rule, and by an unresponsive political system. Austria-Hungary remained backward agriculturally and unable to respond to the industrial challenge of western Europe. It seemed most likely to collapse from social and political pressures.

Russia's vulnerability was reflected in its preoccupation with maintaining free access to the Mediterranean Sea. Russia, clearly Europe's greatest landed power, was vulnerable because it could be landlocked by frozen or blockaded ports in the north. Russia was equally obsessed with protecting its warm-water ports on the Black Sea. Whoever controlled the strait of the Bosporus controlled Russia's grain export trade, on which its economic prosperity depended.

The Ottoman Empire. Another great decaying conglomeration was the Ottoman Empire, bridging Europe and Asia. Politically feeble and on the verge of bankruptcy, the Ottoman Empire with Turkey at its core comprised a vast array of ethnically, linguistically, and culturally diverse peoples. In the hundred years before 1914,

A *Punch* cartoon shows European leaders trying to keep the lid on the simmering kettle of Balkan crises.

increasing social unrest and nationalist bids for independence had plagued the Ottoman Empire. As was the case with the Habsburgs in Austria-Hungary, the Ottomans maintained power with increasing difficulty over these myriad ethnic groups struggling to be free.

The Ottomans had already seen parts of their holdings lopped off in the nineteenth century. Britain had acquired Cyprus, Egypt, Aden, and Sudan from the Ottomans. Germany insinuated itself into Turkish internal affairs and financed the Baghdad Railway in an attempt to link the Mediterranean to the Persian Gulf. Russia acquired territories on the banks of the Caspian Sea and had plans to take Constantinople. But it was the volatile Balkan Peninsula that threatened to upset the European power balance. The Balkans appeared to be ripe for dismemberment. Internally, the Slavs sought independence from their Habsburg and Turkish oppressors. External pressures were equally great, with each of the major powers following its own political agenda.

The Instability of the Alliance System

The system of alliances formed between and among European states was guided by two realities of geopolitics: the tension between France and Germany and Russia's fear of becoming landlocked.

Franco-German Tensions. A major destabilizing factor in the European balance of power was the tension between France and Germany. France had lost its dominance on the Continent in 1870–1871, when it was easily defeated by Prussia at the head of a nascent German Empire. With its back to the Atlantic, France faced the smaller states of Belgium, Luxembourg, Switzerland, and Italy and the industrially and militarily powerful Germany. France had suffered the humiliation of losing territory to Germany—Alsace and Lorraine in 1871—and was well aware of its continued vulnerability. Geopolitically, France felt trapped and isolated and in need of powerful friends as a counterweight to German power.

Russian Aspirations and the Congress of Berlin. Ostensibly, Russia had the most to gain from the extension of its frontiers and the creation of pro-Russian satellites. It saw that by championing pan-Slavic nationalist groups in southeastern Europe, it could greatly strengthen its own position at the expense of the two great declining empires, Ottoman Turkey and Austria-Hungary. Russia hoped to draw the Slavs into its orbit by fostering the creation of independent states in the Balkans. A Serbian revolt began in two Ottoman provinces, Bosnia and Herzegovina, in 1874. International opinion pressured Turkey to initiate reforms. Serbia declared war on Turkey on 30 June 1876; Montenegro did the same the next day. Britain, supporting the Ottoman Empire because of its trading interests in the Mediterranean, found itself in a delicate position of perhaps condemning an ally when it received news of Turkish atrocities against Christians in Bulgaria. Prime Minister Disraeli insisted that Britain was bound to defend Constantinople because of British interests in the Suez Canal and India. While Britain stood on the sidelines, Russia, with Romania as an ally, declared war against the Ottoman Empire. The war was quickly over; Russia captured all of Armenia and forced the Ottoman sultan, Abdul Hamid II (1842–1918), to sue for peace on 31 January 1878.

As an island kingdom, Great Britain relied on imports for its survival. The first of the European nations to become an urban and industrial power, Britain was forced to do so at the expense of its agricultural sector. It could not feed its own people without importing foodstuffs. Britain's geographic vulnerability was its dependence on access to its empire and the maintenance of open sea lanes. Britain saw its greatest menace as coming from the rise of other sea powers—notably Germany.

Bismarck, a seemingly disinterested party acting as an "honest broker," hosted the peace conference that met at Berlin. The British succeeded in blocking Russia's intentions for a Bulgarian satellite and keeping the Russians from taking Constantinople. Russia abandoned its support of Serbian nationalism, and Austria-Hungary occupied Bosnia and Herzegovina. The peace that was concluded at the 1878 Congress of Berlin disregarded Serbian claims, thereby ensuring continuing conflict over the nationalities question.

The Berlin Congress also marked the emergence of a new estrangement among the Great Powers. Russia felt betrayed by Bismarck and abandoned in its alliance with Germany. Bismarck in turn cemented a Dual Alliance between Austria-Hungary and Germany in 1879 that survived until the collapse of the two imperial regimes in 1918. The Three Emperors' League was renewed in 1881 with stipulations regarding the division of the spoils in case of a war against Turkey.

In 1882, Italy was asked to join the Dual Alliance with Germany and Austria-Hungary, thus converting it into the **Triple Alliance**, which prevailed until the beginning of World War I in 1914. Germany, under Bismarck's tutelage, signed treaties with Italy, Russia, and Austria-Hungary and established friendly terms with Great Britain. However, a new Balkan crisis in 1885 shattered the illusion of stable relations.

Hostilities erupted between Bulgaria and Serbia. Russia threatened to occupy Bulgaria, but Austria stepped in to prevent Russian domination of the Balkans, thus threatening the alliance of the Three Emperors' League. Russia was further angered by German unwillingness to support its interests against Austrian actions in the Balkans. Germany maintained relations with Russia in a new Reinsurance Treaty drawn up in 1887, which stipulated that each power would maintain neutrality should the other find itself at war. Bismarck now walked a fine line, balancing alliances and selectively disclosing the terms of secret treaties to nonsignatory countries with the goal of preserving the peace.

Bismarck was dismissed from the chancellorship in 1890 by the Kaiser Wilhelm II, a long-time enemy of Bismarck who came to the throne in 1888. Under Wilhelm II, Germany allowed the arrangement with Russia to lapse. Russia, in turn, allied itself with France in 1894. Also allied with Great Britain, France had broken out of the isolation that Bismarck had intended for it two decades earlier. The **Triple Entente** came into existence following the Anglo-Russian understanding of 1907. Now it was the Triple Entente of Great Britain, France, and Russia against the Triple Alliance of Germany, Austria-Hungary, and Italy.

There was still every confidence that these two camps could balance each other and preserve the peace. But from 1908 to 1909 the unresolved Balkan problem threatened to topple Europe's precarious peace. Against Russia's objections, Austria-Hungary annexed Bosnia and Herzegovina, the provinces it had occupied since 1878. Russia supported Serbia's discontent over Austrian acquisition of these predominantly Slavic territories that Serbia believed should be united with its own lands. Germany had to contend with its great geopolitical fear: hostile neighbors, France and Russia, on its western and eastern frontiers.

A third Balkan crisis erupted in 1912 when Italy and Turkey fought over the possession of Tripoli in North Africa. The Balkan states took advantage of this opportunity to increase their holdings at Turkey's expense. This action quickly involved Great Power interests once again. A second war broke out in 1913 over Serbian interests in Bulgaria. Russia backed Serbia against Austro-Hungarian support of Bulgaria. The Russians and Austrians prepared for war, while the British and Germans urged peaceful resolution. Although hostilities ceased, Serbian resentment toward Austria-Hungary over its frustrated nationalism was greater than ever. Britain, in its backing of Russia, and Germany, in its support of Austria-Hungary, were enmeshed in alliances that could involve them in a military confrontation.

The New Imperialism

The concept of empire was certainly not invented by Europeans in the last third of the nineteenth century. What, then, was new about the "new imperialism" practiced by England, France, and Germany after 1870?

In part, the **new imperialism** was the acquisition of territories on an intense and unprecedented scale. Industrialization created the tools of transportation, communication, and domination that permitted the rapid pace of global empire building. Above all, the new imperialism meant domination by the industrial powers over the nonindustrial world. The forms of imperialism may have varied from nation to nation, but the basically unequal relationship between an industrial power and an undeveloped territory did not.

Industrial powers sought to take over nonindustrial regions, not in isolated areas but all over the globe. In the attempt, they necessarily competed with one another, successfully adapting the resources of industrialism to the needs of conquest.

The Technology of Empire

For Europeans at the end of the nineteenth century, the world had definitely become a smaller place. Technology based on steam, iron, and electricity—the great forces of western industrialization—was responsible for shrinking the globe.

Steam, which powered factories, proved equally efficient as an energy source in transportation. Great iron steamships fueled by coal replaced the smaller, slower, wind-powered, wooden sailing vessels that had plied the sea for centuries. Just as the imperial Romans had used their network of roads to link far-flung territories to the capital, Europeans used sea-lanes to join their colonies to the home country.

Until 1850, Europeans ventured no farther on the African continent than its coastal areas. Now the installation of coal-burning boilers on smaller boats permitted navigation of previously uncharted rivers. Steam power made exploration and migration possible and greatly contributed to knowledge of terrain, natural wealth, and resources. Smaller, steam-powered vessels also increased European inland trade with China, Burma, and India.

Engineering Empire. To accommodate the new iron- and then steel-hulled ships, harbors were deepened and canals were constructed. Completed in 1869, the Suez Canal joined the Mediterranean and Red seas and created a new, safer trade route to the east. No longer did trading vessels have to make the long voyage around Africa's Cape of Good Hope.

Similarly, the Panama Canal (completed in 1914) connected the Atlantic and Pacific oceans across the Isthmus of Panama by a waterway containing a series of locks. Both the Suez and Panama canals saved travel time, which meant higher profits.

Technology also increased the speed of communication. By the late nineteenth century, a vast telegraph network connected Europe to every major area of the world. Faster communications extended power and control throughout empires. Now Europeans could communicate immediately with their distant colonies, dispatching troops, orders, and supplies.

Medical Advances. Technological advances in other areas helped to foster European imperialism in the nineteenth century. Advances in medicine allowed European men and women to penetrate disease-laden swamps and jungles. The bitter-tasting derivative of cinchona-tree bark, **quinine** was discovered to be an effective treatment for malaria. This treatment got its first important test during the French invasion of Algeria in 1830, and it allowed the French to stay healthy enough to conquer that North African country between 1830 and 1847.

Europeans carried the technologies of destruction as well as survival with them into less-developed areas of the world. New types of firearms that were produced in the second half of the nineteenth century included breech-loading rifles, repeating rifles, and machine guns. The new weapons gave the advantages of both accurate aim and rapid fire.

The new technology did not cause the new imperialism. The Western powers used technological advances as a tool for establishing their control of the world. Viewed as a tool, however, the new technology does explain how vast areas of land and millions of people were conquered so rapidly.

Motives for Empire

If technology was not the cause but only a tool, what explains the new imperialism of the late nineteenth century? There are no easy or simple explanations. Individuals made their fortunes overseas, and heavy industries such as the Krupp firm in Germany prospered with the expansion of state-protected colonies. Yet many colonies were economically worthless. Each imperial power held one or more colonies whose costs outweighed the return. This does not mean, however, that some Europeans were simply irrational in their pursuit of empire and glory.

Economics. Imperialism was influenced by business interests, market considerations, and the pursuit of individual and national fortunes. Not by accident did the great industrial powers control the scramble and dictate the terms of expansion. Nor was it merely fortuitous that Great Britain, the nation that provided the model for European expansion, dedicated itself to the establishment of a profitable worldwide network of trade and investment. Above all, the search for investment opportunities, whether railroads in China or diamond mines in South Africa, lured Europeans into a world system that challenged capitalist ingenuity and imagination. Acquiring territory was only one means of protecting investments. But other benefits were associated with the acquisition of territory that cannot be reduced to economic terms, and those too must be considered.

Geopolitics. Statesmen influenced by geopolitical concerns recognized the strategic value of certain lands. France, for example, occupied thousands of square miles of the Sahara to protect its interests in Algeria.

Other territory was important because of its proximity to sea routes. Egypt had significance for Great Britain not because of its inherent economic potential but because it allowed the British to protect access to lucrative markets in India through the Suez Canal. Beginning in 1875, the British purchased shares in the canal. By 1879, Egypt was under the informal dual rule of France and Great Britain. The British used the deterioration of internal Egyptian politics to justify their occupation of the country in 1882. Protected access to India also accounted for Great Britain's maintenance of Mediterranean outposts, its acquisition of territory on the east coast of Africa, and its occupation of territory in southern Asia.

A third geopolitical motive for annexation was the necessity of having fueling bases throughout the world for coal-powered ships. Islands in the South Pacific and the Indian Ocean were acquired primarily to serve as coaling stations for the great steamers carrying manufactured goods to colonial ports and returning with foodstuffs and raw materials. Ports along the southern rim of Asia served the same purpose. The need to protect colonies, fueling ports, and sea-lanes led to the creation of naval bases like those on the Red Sea at Djibouti by the French, in southeast Asia at Singapore by the British, and in the Hawaiian Islands at Honolulu by the Americans.

Great Britain originally opposed construction of the Suez Canal but soon recognized its crucial role in the route to India. In this cartoon, *The Lion's Share,* British Prime Minister Disraeli purchases a controlling interest in the Suez Canal Company from the khedive of Egypt. The British lion in the foreground guards the key to India, the symbol of the canal.

THE LION'S SHARE.
"GARE À QUI LA TOUCHE!"

In turn, the acquisition of territories justified the increase in naval budgets and the size of fleets. Britain still had the world's largest navy, but by the beginning of the twentieth century, the United States and Germany had entered the competition for dominance of sea-lanes. Japan expanded its navy as a vehicle for its own claims to empire in the Pacific.

The politics of geography was land- as well as sea-based. As navies grew to protect sea-lanes, armies expanded to police new lands. Between 1890 and 1914, military expenditures of Western governments grew phenomenally; war machines doubled in size. A side effect of the growing importance of geopolitics was the increased influence of military and naval leaders in foreign and domestic policy making.

Nationalism. National prestige was not an absolute value but one that was weighed relatively. Possessing an empire may have meant "keeping up with the Joneses," as it did for smaller countries such as Italy. Imperial status was important to a country like Portugal, which was willing to go bankrupt to maintain its territories. But prestige without economic power was the form of imperialism without its substance. Nation-states could, through the acquisition of overseas territories, gain bargaining chips to be played at the international conference table. In this way, smaller nations hoped to be taken seriously in the system of alliances that preserved the balance of power in Europe.

Western newspapers deliberately fostered the desire for the advancement of national interests. Newspapers competed for readers, and their circulations often depended on the passions they aroused. The drama and vocabulary of sporting events, whose mass appeal as a leisure activity also dates from this era, were now applied to imperialist politics. Whether it was a rugby match or a territorial conquest, readers backed the "home" team, disdained the opposition, and competed for the thrill of victory. Newspapers forged a national consciousness whereby individuals identified with collective causes that they did not fully comprehend.

Information conveyed in newspapers shaped opinion, and opinion, in turn, could influence policy. Leaders had to reckon with this new creation of "public opinion."

Public opinion was certainly influential, but it could be manipulated. In Germany, the government often promoted colonial hysteria through the press to advance its own political ends. Chancellor Otto von Bismarck used his power over the press to support imperialism and to influence electoral outcomes in 1884. His successors were deft at promoting the "bread and circuses" atmosphere that surrounded colonial expansion to direct attention away from social problems at home and to maintain domestic stability.

The printed word was also manipulated in Britain during the Boer War (1899–1902), critics asserted, by business interests to keep public enthusiasm for the war effort high. J. A. Hobson (1858–1940), himself a journalist and theorist of imperialism, denounced the "abuse of the press" in his hard-hitting *Psychology of Jingoism* (1901), which appeared while the war was still being waged. Hobson recognized **jingoism** as the appropriate term for the "inverted patriotism whereby the love of one's own nation is transformed into hatred of another nation, and [into] the fierce craving to destroy the individual members of that other nation."

Jingoism was not a new phenomenon in 1900, nor was it confined to Britain. Throughout Europe, a mass public appeared increasingly willing to support conflict to defend national honor. Xenophobia, hatred of foreigners, melded with nationalism, both nurtured by the mass press, to put new pressures on the determination of foreign policy. Government elites, who formerly operated behind closed doors far removed from public scrutiny, were now accountable in new ways to faceless masses.

To varying degrees, all of these factors—economics, geopolitics, and nationalism—motivated the actions of the three great imperialist powers—Britain, France, and Germany—and their less-powerful European neighbors. The same reasons account for the global aspirations of non-European nations such as the United States and Japan. None of these powers acted independently; each was aware of what the others were doing and tailored its actions accordingly. Imperialism followed a variety of patterns but always with a built-in component of emulation and acceleration. It was both a cause and a proof of a world system of states in which the actions of one nation affected the others.

The nineteenth-century liberal belief in progress encouraged Europeans to impose their beliefs and institutions on captive millions. After all, industrial society had given Europe the technology, the wealth, and the power to tame nature and dominate the world. Imperialists moralized that they had not only the right but also the duty to develop the nonindustrialized world for their own purposes.

The Search for Territory and Markets

Most western Europeans who read about the distant regions that their armies and political leaders were bringing under control regarded these new territories as little more than entries on a great tally sheet or as distinctively colored areas on a map.

The daily press recorded the numbers of square miles acquired and the names of the peoples in the occupied territories, and that was that. Few Europeans looked on imperialism as a relationship of power between two parties and, like all relationships, one influenced by both partners. Fewer still understood or appreciated the distinctive qualities of the conquered peoples.

The Scramble for Africa: Diplomacy and Conflict

Between 1875 and 1912, Europeans participated in the so-called **scramble for Africa**, a mad rush to partition Africa into European colonies. By its end, Europeans controlled virtually all Africa.

One cannot detect one single reason for the scramble as it actually took place on the ground. Africa is a large and complex continent, and the reasons for which Europeans pursued specific pieces of African territory were similarly complex. The explanations for the acquisition of a given colony, therefore, depend largely on the historical context of that particular case. In certain areas, such as the West African Sudanic and Sahara desert zones, ambitious French military men sought to advance their careers by carving out grand colonies. The existence of valuable minerals motivated the scramble for the area now called Zimbabwe, the Zambian/Zairian copper belt, and other areas. Along the West African coast, chronic disputes between traders working in an economy soured by a deterioration in the terms of trade seemed to require European annexation. Some colonies, such as present-day Uganda and Malawi, were created to please missionaries already working there. Britain took Egypt, and France occupied Djibouti for strategic reasons. As often as not, as in Mozambique, Tanzania, Namibia, and Botswana, some Europeans seized areas to keep other Europeans from doing the same thing. Only Ethiopia escaped the European grasp.

The Drive for Markets and Profits. An important factor influencing imperialist expansion was the economic downturn in Europe that lasted from 1873 until 1896. This downturn, coupled with Germany's fast rise to economic power during the 1870s and 1880s, was deeply unsettling to many Europeans. Protectionist policies springing from new economic anxieties eroded earlier faith in free trade, and many Europeans became keen to acquire African territory just in case it should turn out to be useful in the long run. Even Britain, long the major champion of free trade, became ever-more protectionist and imperialistic as the century neared its end.

Historians generally agree that the person who provided the catalyst for the scramble was Leopold II, king of the Belgians (1865–1909). His motive was greed. Early in 1876, Leopold went to work to acquire the Congo Basin, one-third the size of the United States, for himself. Cloaking himself in the mantle of philanthropy and asserting that all he desired was to stamp out the remnants of the East African slave trade, he organized the International African Association in late 1876.

A contemporary cartoon characterized King Leopold of the Belgians as a monstrous snake crushing the life out of the black population of the Congo Free State. The territory was under the personal rule of the Belgian king from 1885 to 1908.

IN THE RUBBER COILS.

His association soon established stations on the region's rivers and robbed the people of much valuable ivory. Meanwhile, Leopold himself skillfully lobbied for formal recognition of his association's right to rule the Congo Basin. France and Portugal, also covetous of the area, objected, and after much diplomatic wrangling, an international conference was finally held in Berlin in late 1884 to decide the question. The Berlin Conference was important not only because it yielded the Congo Basin to Leopold as the Congo Free State, but also because it laid down the ground rules for the recognition of other colonial claims in Africa. No longer would merely planting a flag in an area be considered adequate to establish sovereignty; instead, the creation of a real presence calculated to produce "economic development" would be needed. If by panicking the European states, Leopold's actions began the scramble, the Berlin Conference organized and structured it.

European Agreements and African Massacres. In dividing Africa, the European states were remarkably cooperative. Deals that traded one piece of territory for another were common, and peace was maintained. Diplomats did not consider Africa worth a European war.

Yet despite the importance of diplomatic compromise among European states during the scramble, every instance of European expansion in Africa, no matter what its specific motive, was characterized by a readiness to shoot Africans. With Hiram Maxim's invention in 1884 of a machine gun that could fire eleven bullets per second, and with the banning by the Brussels Convention of 1890 of the sale of modern weapons to Africans, the military advantage passed overwhelmingly to the imperialists.

The conquest of Africa became more like hunting than warfare. In 1893, for example, in Zimbabwe, 50 Europeans, using only six machine guns, killed 3,000 Ndebele people in less than two hours. In 1897, in northern Nigeria, a force of 32 Europeans and 500 African mercenaries defeated the 31,000-man army of the emir of Sokoto. At the battle of Omdurman in the Sudan in 1898, after five hours of fighting, the numbers killed were 20 Britons, 20 Egyptian allies, and over 11,000 Sudanese.

Ethiopia as Exception. One exception to the general rule of easy conquest was Ethiopia. The history of the country illustrates the importance of guns in the dynamics of the scramble. In the middle of the nineteenth century, the emperor of Ethiopia possessed little more than a grand title. Yet while the empire had broken down into its ethnic and regional components, the dream of a united empire was still alive. In their successful efforts to rebuild the empire, Ethiopian emperors relied increasingly on modern weapons imported from Europe and stockpiled.

By the early 1870s, however, the emperor realized that his achievements in rebuilding the empire were endangered not merely by the resistance of those whom he was then trying to force into his empire, but, more ominously, by the outside world, especially by Egypt to the north and the Sudan to the west. Furthermore, the opening of the Suez Canal in 1869 had made the Red Sea and its surrounding areas attractive not only to Egypt but also to European countries eager to protect their trade routes to Asia.

The emperor, Menelik II (1889–1913), realized that he could exploit rival European interests in the area by playing off one European power against the others to obtain the weapons he needed for expanding his empire's boundaries. He therefore gave certain concessions to France in return for French weapons. Italy, upset at the growing French influence, offered weapons as well, and Menelik accepted them. Russia and Britain joined in. More and more modern weapons flowed into Ethiopia during the 1870s and 1880s and into the early 1890s, and Menelik steadily strengthened his ability both to suppress internal dissent and to block foreign encroachment.

Then, in the early 1890s, Menelik's strategy of balancing one European power against another began to unravel. In 1889, he had signed the Treaty of Wichale with Italy, granting it certain concessions in return for more arms shipments. Italy then claimed that Ethiopia had thus become an Italian protectorate and moved against Menelik when he objected. By 1896, Italy was ready for a major assault on the Ethiopian army, heady with the confident racism of the time that it could defeat the "primitive" Ethiopians with ease. Hopelessly outnumbered, the Italians lost over 8,000 men on 1 March 1896 at the decisive battle of Adowa. With its army destroyed and its artillery lost to the Ethiopians, Italy had no choice but to negotiate a peace.

France and Britain soon ratified Italy's acceptance of Ethiopia as a sovereign state with its greatly expanded imperial boundaries. As a consequence of its victory at Adowa—and attesting to the crucial importance of modern weaponry for survival in late nineteenth-century Africa—Ethiopia was the only African country aside from the U.S. quasi-colony of Liberia that Europeans did not occupy in the scramble for Africa. After 1896, Menelik, with his access to modern weapons assured by his country's international recognition, successfully continued his campaigns to extend his control over the Ethiopian Empire's subordinate peoples.

Gold, Empire Building, and the Boer War

Europeans were as willing to shoot white Africans as they were black Africans during the scramble as they seized land and resources. In South Africa, for example, the British engaged in a long war over possession of the world's largest supply of gold with a group of white Africans, the Afrikaners, or Boers, settlers of Dutch and French Huguenot background who had developed their own unique identity during the eighteenth and early nineteenth centuries.

Afrikaner Rule. After the Great Trek (1837–1844), in which a large number of Afrikaners had withdrawn from British control by leaving the Cape Colony, the British had grudgingly recognized the independence of the Orange Free State and the Transvaal, the Afrikaner republics in the interior, in a series of formal agreements. The British complacently believed that the Afrikaners, economically weak and geographically isolated, could never challenge British preeminence in the region. Two events of the mid-1880s shattered their complacence. First, in 1884, Germany, Britain's greatest international competitor, inserted itself into the region by annexing Namibia as part of the scramble. The British, aware that the Germans and the Afrikaners were sympathetic to each other, worried about the German threat to their regional hegemony and economic prospects.

Britain's War in South Africa. British fear of the Germans was redoubled in 1886 when, in the Transvaal Republic, in the Witwatersrand area, the world's largest deposits of gold were discovered. A group of British diamond mine owners moved in quickly to develop the Witwatersrand's gold. The best-known of these investors was Cecil Rhodes (1853–1902), a businessman and Cape Colony politician who was intent on expanding his wealth through an extension of British power to the north. Rhodes and his colleagues quickly identified Afrikaner governmental policies on agriculture, tariffs, and labor control as major impediments to profitable gold production. Therefore, in 1895 they organized, with the connivance of members of the British government, an attempt to overthrow the Afrikaner government of the Transvaal. It was faultily executed, however, and, to Rhodes's utter humiliation, it failed.

This failure prompted the British government to send a new agent, Alfred Milner (1854–1925), to the area in 1897. Milner was determined to push the Afrikaners into uniting with the British in South Africa, through either diplomacy

MAP DISCOVERY

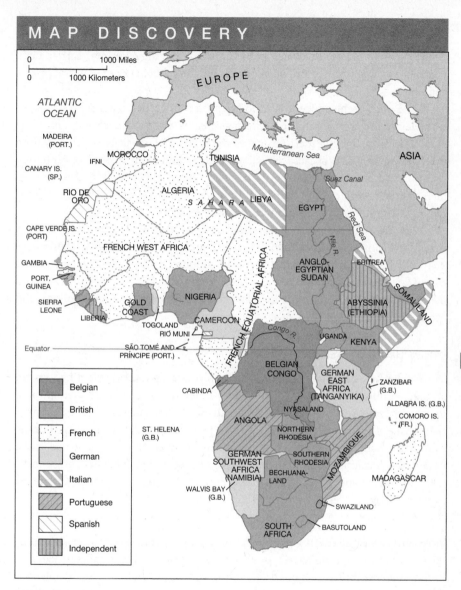

0   1000 Miles

0   1000 Kilometers

ATLANTIC OCEAN

EUROPE

ASIA

MADEIRA (PORT.)

CANARY IS. (SP.)

Mediterranean Sea

MOROCCO

IFNI

TUNISIA

Suez Canal

RIO DE ORO

ALGERIA

LIBYA

SAHARA

EGYPT

Red Sea

CAPE VERDE IS. (PORT)

FRENCH WEST AFRICA

Nile R.

GAMBIA

ANGLO-EGYPTIAN SUDAN

ERITREA

SOMALILAND

PORT. GUINEA

SIERRA LEONE

GOLD COAST

NIGERIA

FRENCH EQUATORIAL AFRICA

ABYSSINIA (ETHIOPIA)

LIBERIA

TOGOLAND

CAMEROON

RIO MUNI

Congo R.

UGANDA

KENYA

Equator

SÃO TOMÉ AND PRÍNCIPE (PORT.)

BELGIAN CONGO

GERMAN EAST AFRICA (TANGANYIKA)

ZANZIBAR (G.B.)

CABINDA

ALDABRA IS. (G.B.)

COMORO IS. (FR.)

ANGOLA

NYASALAND

NORTHERN RHODESIA

MOZAMBIQUE

ST. HELENA (G.B.)

GERMAN SOUTHWEST AFRICA (NAMIBIA)

SOUTHERN RHODESIA

BECHUANA-LAND

MADAGASCAR

WALVIS BAY (G.B.)

SWAZILAND

SOUTH AFRICA

BASUTOLAND

Legend:
- Belgian
- British
- French
- German
- Italian
- Portuguese
- Spanish
- Independent

AFRICA, 1914

By 1914, the map of Africa emerged as a patchwork indicating competing European interests. Do you perceive any patterns in the way the seven European nations laid claim to territory? What were the geopolitical imperatives that motivated the British to seek a swathe of territory from north to south? What are the only two states in 1914 not under the control or oversight of European powers? Based on the chapter discussion, how do you explain why they were exceptions?

or war. By 1899 it was clear that war was inevitable, and in October, British demands provoked a declaration of war from the Afrikaners. The British confidently expected to have the war over by Christmas, but the Afrikaners carried out a guerrilla war against inept British generals, and the so-called Boer War dragged on and on.

The British eventually sent 350,000 troops to South Africa, but these forces, even when reinforced by thousands of African auxiliaries, could not decisively defeat the 65,000 Afrikaner fighting men. Casualties were high on both sides, not merely from the fighting, but also because typhus epidemics broke out in the concentration camps in which the British interned Afrikaner women and children as they pursued their scorched-earth policies in the countryside. By the war's end, 25,000 Afrikaners, 22,000 British imperial troops, and 12,000 black Africans had died.

When World War I broke out in 1914, the scramble for Africa was over, and the map of the continent was colored in imperial inks. Only Ethiopia and Liberia were politically independent. Now that they had conquered Africa, the colonial powers had to face the issue of how their new colonies could be made to pay. And the conquered Africans had to face the issue of how they might regain their political and economic independence.

Imperialism in Asia

During the first half of the nineteenth century, strong Asian powers had grown stronger. China increased its control over inner Asian territories; Vietnam and Siam, predecessor to modern Thailand, enhanced their powers in southeast Asia. By the end of the nineteenth century, Asian political dynasties had suffered reversals. China had been permanently weakened in inner Asia; Vietnam had fallen under French colonial rule; Siam had lost half its territories. India had long constituted an important part of the British Empire. By contrast, Japan became an aggressive power, itself an imperial presence.

India. India was the starting point of all British expansion, and it stood at the center of British foreign policy. To protect its sea routes to India and to secure its Indian markets, Britain acquired territories and carved out concessions all over the world.

Formal British rule in India began in 1861 with the appointment of a viceroy, who was assisted by legislative and executive councils. Both of these bodies included some Indian representatives.

The special imperial relationship originated in the seventeenth century, when the British East India Company, a joint-stock venture free of government control, began limited trading in Indian markets. The need for regulation and protection firmly established British rule by the end of the eighteenth century. Conquest of the Punjab in 1849 brought the last independent areas under British control. Throughout this period, Britain invested considerable overseas capital in India, and in turn India absorbed one-fifth of total British exports. The market for Indian cotton, for centuries exported to Asia and Europe, collapsed under British tariffs, and India became a consumer of cheap Lancashire cotton. The British also exploited India's agriculture, salt, and opium production for profit.

China. At the end of the eighteenth century, the British traded English wool and Indian cotton for Chinese tea and textiles. But Britain's thirst for Chinese tea grew, while Chinese demand for English and Indian textiles slackened. Britain discovered that Indian opium could be used to balance the trade deficit created by tea. Opium exports to China mounted phenomenally—from 200 chests in 1729 to 40,000 chests in 1838. By the 1830s, opium was probably Britain's most important crop in world markets. Chinese buyers began paying for the drug with silver.

Concerned with the sharp rise in addiction, the accompanying social problems, and the massive outflow of silver, the Chinese government reacted. As Chinese officials saw it, they were exchanging their precious metal for British poison. In 1839, the Chinese government destroyed British opium in the port of Canton, touching off the Opium War (1839–1842).

Between 1842 and 1895, China fought five wars with foreigners and lost all of them. Defeat was expensive, as China had to pay costs to the winners. Before the end of the century, Britain, France, Germany, and Japan had managed to establish major territorial advantages in their **spheres of influence**, sometimes through negotiation and sometimes through force. By 1912, over 50 major Chinese ports had been handed over to foreign control as "treaty ports."

Spheres of influence grew in importance at the beginning of the twentieth century, when foreign investors poured capital into railway lines, which needed treaty protection from competing companies. Railways furthered foreign encroachment and opened up new territories to foreign claims. Foreigners established no formal empires in China, but the treaty ports certainly signaled both informal rule and indisputable foreign dominance.

Treaty ports were centers of foreign residence and trade, where rules of **extraterritoriality** applied. This meant that foreigners were exempt from Chinese law enforcement and that, although present on Chinese territory, they could be judged only by officials of their own countries. It also provoked resentment and growing antiforeign sentiments among the Chinese.

To preserve extraterritoriality and maintain informal empires, the European powers appointed civilian representatives known as consuls. Often merchants themselves, consuls acted as the chieftains of resident merchant communities, judges in all civil and criminal cases, and spokesmen for the commercial interests of the home country. Consuls were brokers for commerce and interpreted the international commercial law that was being forged. Consulates spread beyond China as Western nations used consuls to protect their own interests. In Africa, consuls represented the trading concerns of European governments and were instrumental in the transition to formal rule.

Chronology

THE NEW IMPERIALISM IN AFRICA AND ASIA

1837–1844	Great Trek
1839–1842	Opium War
1869	Suez Canal completed
1884	Berlin Conference held to regulate imperialism in Africa
1886	Gold discovered in the Transvaal Republic
1894–1895	Sino-Japanese War
1896	Battle of Adowa
1899–1902	Boer War
1900	Boxer Rebellion
1904–1905	Russo-Japanese War

Southeast Asia and Japan. European nations pursued imperialist endeavors elsewhere in Asia, acquired territories on China's frontiers, and took over states that had formerly paid tribute to the Chinese Empire. Thailand was the only country in southeast Asia to escape direct control by the Western powers. Yet it was forced to yield territory it once controlled and to accept the treaty port system with its tariffs and extraterritoriality.

The Sino-Japanese War of 1894–1895 revealed Japan's intentions to compete as an imperialist power in Asia. The modernized and westernized Japanese army easily defeated the ill-equipped and poorly led Chinese forces. As a result, Japan gained the island of Taiwan. Pressing its ambitions on the continent, Japan locked horns with Russia over claims to the Liaodong peninsula, Korea, and south Manchuria. Following its victory in the Russo-Japanese War of 1904–1905, Japan expanded into all of these areas, annexing Korea outright in 1910. The ease with which the small Asian nation had defeated the Russian giant and contributed to the heightening of anti-imperialist sentiments in China sent a strong message to the West.

The Imperialism of the United States

The United States provided another variation on imperial expansion. Its westward drive across the North American continent, beginning at the end of the eighteenth century, established the United States as an imperial power in the Western Hemisphere. By 1848, the relatively young American nation stretched over 3,000 miles from one ocean to the other. It had met the opposition and resistance of the Native Americans with armed force, decimated them, and "concentrated" the survivors in assigned territories, and later on reservations.

At the end of the nineteenth century, the United States, possessing both the people and the resources for rapid industrial development, turned to the Caribbean and the Pacific islands in pursuit of markets and investment opportunities. By acquiring stepping stones of islands across the Pacific Ocean in the Hawaiian Islands and Samoa, it secured fueling bases and access to lucrative east Asian ports. And by intervening repeatedly in Central America and building the Panama Canal, the United States had established its hegemony in the Caribbean by 1914. Growing in economic power and hegemonic influence, both Japan and the United States had joined the club of imperial powers and were making serious claims against European expansion.

Results of a European-Dominated World

Europeans fashioned the world in their own image, but in the process, Western values and Western institutions underwent profound and unintended transformations.

A World Economy

Imperialism produced an interdependent world economic system with Europe at its center. Industrial and commercial capitalism linked the world's continents in a communications and transportation network that would have been unimaginable in earlier ages.

Meeting Western Needs. Most trading in the age of imperialism still took place among European nations and North America. But entrepreneurs in search of new markets and new resources saw in Africa and Asia opportunities for protected exploitation. New markets were created in nonindustrialized areas of the world to meet the needs of Western producers and consumers. European landlords and managers trained Kenyan farmers to put aside their traditional agricultural methods and to grow more "useful" crops such as coffee, tea, and sugar. The availability of cheaper British textiles of inferior quality drove Indian weavers away from their handlooms. Chinese silk producers changed centuries-old techniques to produce silk thread and cloth that was suited to the machinery and mass-production requirements of the French. Trade permitted specialization but at the choice of the colonizer, not the colonized. World production and consumption were being shaped to suit the needs of the West.

Investment Abroad. Capital in search of profits flowed out of the wealthier areas of Europe into the nonindustrialized regions of Russia, the Balkans, and the Ottoman Empire, where capital-intensive expenditures (on railways, for instance) promised high returns. Capital investment in overseas territories also increased phenomenally as railroads were built to gain access to primary products. Great Britain led in overseas investment with loans abroad greater than those of its five major competitors— France, Germany, Holland, the United States, and Belgium—combined.

MAP DISCOVERY

MAJOR WORLD STATES AND COLONIAL POSSESSIONS, 1900

Belgium | German Empire | Italy | Portugal | United States
France | Great Britain | The Netherlands | Spain | Other Independent State

WORLD COLONIAL HOLDINGS

The European powers, great and small, competed with each other for world empires and world influence between 1870 and 1914. In terms of territory occupied, which nation held the largest global empire? What is the meaning of the expression, "The sun never sets on the British Empire"? Based on what you have read in the chapter, how do you explain the fact that the Netherlands held colonies in southeast Asia and Latin America, but had no holdings in Africa? How did the United States become an imperial power in this period? How do you explain the locations of U.S. colonial acquisitions?

The City of London had become the world's banker, and the adoption of gold as the standard for exchange for most European currencies by 1874 further facilitated the operation of a single, interdependent trading and investment system. Britain remained the world's biggest trading nation, with half of its exports going to Asia, Africa, and South America and the other half to Europe and the United States. But Germany was Britain's fastest-growing competitor, with twice as many exports to Europe and expanding overseas trade by 1914. The United States had recently joined the league of the world's great trading nations and was running a strong third in shares of total trade.

Foreign investments often took the form of loans to governments or to enterprises that were guaranteed by governments. Investors might be willing to take risks, but they also expected protection, as did merchants and industrialists trading in overseas territories. Together, trade and investment interests exerted considerable pressure on European states for control through acquisition and concessions.

The vast amounts of money involved help to explain the expectations of state involvement and the reasons why international competition, rivalry, and instability threatened to lead to conflict and to war.

Race and Culture

The West's ability to kill and conquer as well as to cure was, as one Victorian social observer argued, proof of its cultural superiority. Cultural superiority was only a short step from arguments for racial superiority. Race and culture were collapsed into each other. If Westerners were culturally superior, as they claimed, they must be racially superior as well. The "survival of the fittest" came to justify conquest and subjugation as "laws" of human interaction and, by extension, of relations among nations.

Women and Imperialism

Ideas about racial and cultural superiority were not confined to books by pseudo-scientists and to discussions among policy makers. Public discussions about marriage, reproduction, motherhood, and child-rearing reflected new concerns about furthering "the imperial race"—that is, white Westerners. Women throughout Western societies were advised by reformers, politicians, and doctors to have more children and instructed to take better care of them. Healthy young men were needed in the colonies, they were told, to defend Western values. State officials paid greater attention to infant mortality at the end of the nineteenth century, set up health programs for children, and provided young women with training in home management, nutrition, and child care.

All over Europe, newly formed associations and clubs stressed the need for careful mate selection. In Britain, Francis Galton (1822–1911) founded eugenics, the study of genetics for the purpose of improving inherited characteristics of the race. Imperialism, the propagandists proclaimed, depended on mothers, women who would nurture healthy workers, strong soldiers and sailors, and intelligent and capable leaders.

Some European women participated directly in the colonizing experience. As missionaries and nurses, they supported the civilizing mission. As wives of officials and managers, they were expected to embody the gentility and values of Western culture. Most men who traded and served overseas did so unaccompanied by women. But when women were present in any numbers, as they were in India before 1914, they were expected to preserve the exclusivity of Western communities.

Ecology and Imperialism

Ecology—the relationship and adjustment of human groups to their environment—was affected by imperial expansion, which dislocated the societies that it touched.

Early explorers had disrupted little as they arrived, observed, and then moved on. The missionaries, merchants, soldiers, and businessmen who came later required the inhabitants with whom they came into contact to change their thinking and behavior. In some cases, dislocation resulted in material improvements, better medical care, and the introduction of modern technology. For the most part, however, the initial ecological impact of the imperialist was negative. Western men and women carried diseases to people who did not share their immunity. Traditional village life was destroyed in rural India, and African societies disintegrated under the European onslaught.

Education of native populations had as its primary goal the improvement of administration and productivity in the colonies. When foreigners ruled indirectly through existing indigenous hierarchies, they often created corrupt and tyrannical bureaucracies that exploited natives. The indirect rule of the British in India was based on a pragmatic desire to keep British costs low.

When Asian and African laborers started producing for the Western market, they became dependent on its fluctuations. Victimized for centuries by the vagaries of weather, they now had to contend with the instability and cutthroat competition of cash crops in world markets. Men and women migrated from place to place in the countryside and from the countryside to newly formed cities.

Some European countries used their overseas territories as dumping grounds for criminals. Imitating the earlier example of the British in Australia, the French developed Guiana and New Caledonia as prison colonies in the hope of solving their social problems at home by exporting undesirables.

Critiquing Capitalism

One consequence of imperialism was the critique of capitalism it produced. Critics who condemned it as exploitative and racist saw imperialism as an expression of problems that were inherent in capitalism. In 1902, J. A. Hobson (1858–1940) published *Imperialism, A Study*, in which he argued that underconsumption and surplus capital at home drove Western industrial countries overseas in search of a cure for these economic ills. Rather than solving the problems by raising workers' wages and thereby increasing their consumption power and creating new opportunities for investment in home markets, manufacturers, entrepreneurs, and industrialists sought higher profits abroad. Hobson considered these business interests "economic parasites," making large fortunes at the expense of national interests.

In the midst of world war, the future leader of the Russian revolution, Vladimir Ilyich Ulyanov (1870–1924)—or, to use his revolutionary name, Lenin—added his own critique of capitalism. He did not share Hobson's belief that capitalism was merely malfunctioning in its imperialist endeavors. Instead, Lenin argued in *Imperialism, the Highest Stage of Capitalism* (1916) that capitalism was inherently and inevitably imperialistic.

SUMMARY

The European Balance of Power, 1870–1914   Between 1870 and 1914, European states were locked in a competition within Europe for dominance and control. Under the leadership of Otto von Bismarck, Germany led the way in forging a new alliance system. Each of the Great Powers had important geographical vulnerabilities. The weakness of the Ottoman Empire fueled conflict between the Great Powers. Russian fears of becoming landlocked and tensions between France and Germany were destabilizing factors. The Balkans became a focal point for European conflict. Following Bismarck's dismissal, a new alliance system emerged that pitted Great Britain, France, and Russia against Germany, Austria-Hungary, and Italy.

The New Imperialism   Imperialism, as it was practiced by European nations after 1870, involved acquisition of territories on an unprecedented scale. The new imperialism meant the domination by the industrial powers of the nonindustrial world. New technologies provided crucial tools for imperial domination. Economic interests, geopolitics, and nationalism all contributed to the drive for imperial expansion.

The Search for Territory and Markets   Between 1875 and 1912, Europeans participated in the so-called scramble for Africa. Reasons for colonial expansion in Africa varied from case to case. The drive for new markets spurred the acquisition of African colonies. There was little conflict between European states during the process of colonization. Ethiopia's acquisition of Western weapons allowed it to defeat Italian efforts at conquest. Fear of Germany and the discovery of gold led to the Boer War between Great Britain and the Afrikaners. In the second half of the nineteenth century, Asian powers, with the exception of Japan, suffered reversals. India was at the center of the British Empire. Formal rule of India by the British was established in 1861. Britain's insistence on importing opium to China led to war. China's defeat was only one of a series of losing wars with Europeans that severely weakened China's control over its territory and economy. Victory in wars with China and Russia established Japan as a major power in the Pacific. The United States provided another variation on imperial expansion, as it moved first across North America and then into the Caribbean and the Pacific.

Results of a European-Dominated World   Imperialism produced an interdependent world economic system with Europe at its center. While most trading took place between European nations and North America, entrepreneurs looked to Africa and Asia for opportunities for protected exploitation. World production and consumption were shaped to suit the needs of the West. Investment capital flowed into nonindustrialized regions. Government involvement in overseas investment created a close relationship among commerce, expansion, and politics. Imperialism stimulated belief in the racial superiority of Westerners. Women's reproductive and child-rearing functions were linked to national strength and imperial expansion. The impact of imperialism on colonized populations was mostly negative. Imperialism led to new critiques of capitalism.

QUESTIONS FOR REVIEW

1. What geopolitical factors made the European balance of power so unstable around the turn of the century?
2. What social, political, and economic forces encouraged the nations of Europe to create overseas empires in the late nineteenth century?
3. How and why did European imperialism differ in Africa and Asia?
4. How did imperial expansion around the globe transform the lives of Europeans at home?

War and Revolution, 1914–1920

The War Europe Expected

Many Europeans took stability and harmony for granted as preconditions for progress; yet they also recognized the usefulness of war. No one expected or wanted a general war, but liberal values served the goals of limited war, just as they had justified imperial conquest. Statesmen decided that there were rules to the game of war that could be employed in the interests of statecraft. Science and technology also served the interests of war. Statesmen and generals were sure that modern weapons would prevent a long war. Superiority in armed force became a priority for European states seeking to protect the peace.

EUROPEAN ALLIANCES ON THE EVE OF WORLD WAR I. Alliance systems divided Europe into two great blocs with few countries remaining neutral.

The beginning of the modern arms race resulted in "armed peace" as a defense against war. Leaders nevertheless expected and planned for a short and limited war. Previous confrontations among European states had been limited in duration and destruction, as in the case of Prussia and France in 1870, or confined to peripheries, as squabbles among the Great Powers in Africa indicated. The alliance system was expected to defend the peace by defining the conditions of war.

When war did come in 1914, it was a choice, not an accident. Yet it was a choice that Europeans did not understand, one whose limits they could not control. Their unquestioned pride in reason and progress that ironically had led them to this war did not survive the four years of barbaric slaughter that followed.

Separating Friends from Foes

After 1905, the intricate defensive alliances between and among the European states maintained the balance of power between two blocs of nations and helped to prevent one bloc from dominating the other. Yet by creating blocs, alliances identified foes as well as friends. On the eve of the war, France, Great Britain, and Russia stood together in the Triple Entente. Since 1882, Germany, Austria-Hungary, and Italy had joined forces in the Triple Alliance. Other states allied with one or the other of these blocs in pacts of mutual interest and protection. Throughout the world, whether in North Africa, the Balkans, or Asia, the power of some states was intended to balance the power of others.

The alliance system of blocs reflected the growing impact of public opinion on international relations. Statesmen had the ability to manipulate the newspaper images of allies as good and rivals as evil. But controlling public opinion served to lock policy makers into permanent partnerships and "blank checks" of support for their allies. Western leaders understood that swings in public opinion in periods of crisis could hobble their efforts to act in the nation's best interest. Permanent military alliances with clearly identified "friends" therefore took the place of more fluid arrangements.

Because of treaty commitments, no country expected to face war alone. Alliances that guaranteed military support permitted weak nations to act irresponsibly, with the certainty that they would be defended by their more powerful partners. At base, the alliance system stood as both a defense against war and an invitation to it.

Military Timetables

As Europe soon discovered, military timetables restricted a country's options at times of conflict. Military general staffs assumed increasing importance in state policy making. War planners became powerful as war was accepted as an alternative to negotiation. Germany's military preparations are a good example of how war strategy exacerbated crises and prevented peaceful solutions.

The Schlieffen Plan. Alfred von Schlieffen's (1833–1913) war plan was designed to make Germany the greatest power on the Continent. The **Schlieffen Plan**, which he set before his fellow officers in 1905, was bold and daring: In the likely event of war with Russia, Germany would launch a devastating offensive against France. Schlieffen reasoned that France, with its strong military forces, would come to the aid of its ally, Russia. Russia, lacking a modern transportation system, could not mobilize as rapidly as France.

Russia also had the inestimable advantage of the ability to retreat into its vast interior. If Germany were pulled into a war with Russia, its western frontier would be vulnerable to France, Russia's powerful ally. The Schlieffen Plan recognized that France would have to be defeated before Germany could turn its forces eastward against Russia. The Schlieffen Plan thus committed Germany to a war with France, regardless of particular circumstances.

Russia's Mobilization Plan and the French Plan XVII. Germany was not alone in being driven by military considerations. Russian military strategists planned full mobilization if war broke out with Austria-Hungary, which was menacing the interests of Russia's ally Serbia. Russia foresaw the likelihood that Germany would come to the aid of Austria-Hungary. Russia knew, too, that because of its primitive railway network, it would be unable to mobilize troops rapidly. To compensate for this weakness, Russian leaders planned to mobilize *before* war was declared. German military leaders had no choice in the event of full Russian mobilization but to mobilize their own troops immediately and to urge the declaration of war. Once a general mobilization was under way on both sides, conflict could hardly be avoided. Mobilization would mean war.

Like the Schlieffen Plan, the French Plan XVII called for the concentration of troops in a single area with the intention of decisively defeating the enemy. The French command, not well informed about German strengths and strategies, designated Alsace and Lorraine for the immediate offensive against Germany in the event of war.

Military leaders throughout Europe argued that if their plans were to succeed, speed was essential. Delays to consider peaceful solutions would cripple military responses. Diplomacy bowed to military strategy.

Assassination at Sarajevo

On 28 June 1914, in Sarajevo, the sleepy capital of the Austro-Hungarian province of Bosnia, Gavrilo Princip (1895–1918), a 19-year-old Bosnian Serb, repeatedly pulled the trigger of his Browning revolver, killing the designated heir of the Habsburg throne, Archduke Franz Ferdinand, and his wife, Sophie. Princip was part of a growing movement of South Slavs struggling for national liberation from Austria-Hungary.

Struggle over control of the Balkans had been a long-standing issue that had involved all the major European powers for decades. As Austria-Hungary's ally since 1879, Germany was willing to support Vienna's showdown in the Balkans as a way of stopping Russian advances in the area. The alliance with Germany gave Austria-Hungary a sense of security and confidence to pursue its Balkan aims. Germany had its own plans for domination of the Continent and feared that a weakened Austria-Hungary would undermine its own position in central Europe. Independent Balkan states to the south and east were also a threat to Germany's plans. German leaders hoped that an Austro-Serbian war would remain localized and would strengthen their ally, Austria-Hungary. While Austria-Hungary had Germany's support, Serbia was backed by a sympathetic Russia favoring nationalist movements in the Balkans. Russia had, in turn, been encouraged by France, its ally by military pact since 1894, to take a firm stand in its struggle with Austria-Hungary for dominance among Balkan nationalities.

On 23 July 1914, Austria-Hungary issued an ultimatum to Serbia and secretly decided to declare war regardless of the Serbs' response. In spite of a conciliatory, although not capitulatory, reply from Serbia to its ultimatum, Austria-Hungary declared war on the Balkan nation on 28 July 1914. Russia mobilized two days later. Germany mobilized in response to the Russian action and declared war on Russia on 1 August and on France on 3 August. France had begun mobilizing on 30 July, when its ally, Russia, entered the war.

Great Britain briefly attempted to mediate a settlement in the Austro-Serbian conflict, but once France declared war, the domino effect of the alliance system was triggered. On 4 August, after Germany had violated Belgian neutrality in its march to France, Great Britain honored its treaty obligations and declared war on Germany. Great Britain entered the war because it judged that a powerful Germany could use ports on the English Channel to invade the British Isles. Italy alone of the major powers remained for the moment outside the conflict.

A New Kind of Warfare

Early in the war, the best-laid plans of political and military leaders collapsed. First, Europe got a war that was not limited but spread quickly throughout Europe and became global. Switzerland, Spain, the Netherlands, and all of Scandinavia remained neutral, but every other European nation was pulled into the war. In August 1914, Japan cast its lot with the **Allies**, as the Triple Entente came to be known, and in November, the Ottoman Empire joined the **Central Powers** of Germany and Austria-Hungary. In the following year, Italy joined the war, not on the side of its long-term treaty partners, Germany and Austria-Hungary, but on the side of the Allies, with the expectation of benefiting in the Balkans from Austrian defeat. Bulgaria joined Germany and Austria-Hungary in 1915, seeking territory at Serbia's expense. By the time the United States joined the fray in 1917, the war had become a world war.

The second surprise for the European powers was that they did not get a preventive war of movement or one of short duration. Within weeks that pattern had given way to what promised to be a long and costly war of attrition. Technology was the key to understanding the change and to explaining the surprises.

Technology and the Trenches

Digging In. At the beginning of the twentieth century, soldiers were trained for a moving war, high maneuverability, and maximum territorial conquest. Yet after the first six weeks of battle, soldiers found themselves having to dig ditches and fight from fixed positions. Soldiers on both sides shoveled out trenches four feet deep, piled up sandbags, mounted their machine guns, and began to fight an unplanned, defensive war.

The front lines of Europe's armies in the west wallowed in the trenches that ran from the English Channel to the Swiss frontier. The British and French on one side and the Germans on the other fought each other with machine guns and mortars, backed up by heavy artillery to the rear. Strategists on both sides believed that they could break through enemy lines. As a result, the gruesome monotony of trench warfare was punctuated periodically by infantry offensives in which large concentrations of artillery caused immense bloodshed. Ten million men were killed in this bizarre and deadly combination of old and new warfare.

New Weapons. The shovel and the machine gun transformed war. The machine gun was not new in 1914, but its strategic value was not fully appreciated before then.

Military strategists continued to plan an offensive strategy when the weaponry developed for massive destruction had pushed them into fighting a defensive war from the trenches. Both sides resorted to concentration of artillery, increased use of poison gas, and unrestricted submarine warfare in desperate attempts to break the deadlock caused by meeting armed force with force.

The new emphasis on total victory drove the Central Powers and the Allies to grisly new inventions. Late in the war, the need to break the deadlock of trench warfare ushered in the airplane and the tank. Chlorine gas was first used in warfare by the Germans in 1915. Mustard gas, which was named for its distinctive smell and which caused severe blistering, was introduced two years later. The Germans were the first to use flamethrowers. Barbed wire, invented in the American Midwest to contain farm animals, became an essential aspect of trench warfare as it marked off the no-man's-land between combatants and prevented surprise attacks. The technology that had been viewed as a proof of progress was now channeled toward engineering new instruments of death.

The German Offensive

German forces seized the offensive in the west and invaded neutral Belgium at the beginning of August 1914. After the fall of Belgium, German military might swept into northern France with the intention of defeating the French in six weeks.

Germany on Two Fronts. In the years preceding the war, the German General Staff, unwilling to concentrate all of their troops in the west, had modified the Schlieffen Plan by committing divisions to Germany's eastern frontier. The absence of the full German fighting force in the west did not appreciably slow the

A typical World War I trench. Millions of soldiers lived amid mud, disease, and vermin, awaiting death from enemy shells. After the French army mutiny in 1916, the troops wrung the concession from their commanders that they would not have to charge German machine guns while armed only with rifles.

German advance through Belgium. Yet the Germans had underestimated both the cost of holding back the French in Alsace-Lorraine and the difficulty of maneuvering German forces and transporting supplies in an offensive war. Eventually, unexpected Russian advances in the east also siphoned off troops from the west. German forces in the west were so weakened by their offensive that they were unable to swing west of Paris, as planned, and instead chose to enter the French capital from the northeast by crossing the Marne River. This shift exposed the German First Army on its western flank and opened up a gap on its eastern flank.

The First Battle of the Marne. In a series of battles between 6 and 10 September 1914 that came to be known as the First Battle of the Marne, the Allies counterattacked and advanced into the gap. The German army was forced to drop back. In the following months, each army tried to outflank the other in what has been called "the race to the sea." By late fall, it was clear that the battles from the Marne north to the border town of Ypres in northwest Belgium near the English Channel had ended an open war of movement on the western front.

War on the Eastern Front

War on Germany's eastern front was a mobile war, fought over vast distances. The Russian army was the largest in the world. Yet it was crippled from the outbreak of the war by inadequate supplies and poor leadership. At the end of August 1914, the smaller German army, supported by divisions drawn from the west, delivered a devastating defeat to the Russians at Tannenberg, in the one great battle on the eastern front.

The German general Paul von Hindenburg (1847–1934) followed the stunning victory of Tannenberg two weeks later with another devastating blow to Russian forces at the Masurian Lakes.

The Russians were holding up their end of the bargain in the Allied war effort, but at great cost. They kept the Germans busy and forced them to divert troops to the eastern front, weakening the German effort to knock France out of the war. However, the Russian army, as one of its own officers described it, was being bled to death. Russian soldiers were poorly led into battle or not led at all because of the shortage of officers. Munitions shortages meant that soldiers often went into battle without rifles, armed only with the hope of scavenging arms from their fallen comrades.

War on the Western Front

Along hundreds of miles of trenches, the French and British tried repeatedly to expel the Germans from northern France and Belgium. Long periods of inactivity were punctuated by orgies of heavy bloodletting.

MAP DISCOVERY

WORLD WAR I

The Central Powers were in the unenviable position of fighting wars on two major fronts. The inset shows the stabilized western front of trench warfare in northern France and Belgium. Why did warfare focus in the west in this area, and why did it bog down for such a long period along this front? How did warfare along the eastern front differ, and why did the eastern front cover a much greater expanse? You will note the major battles in western and eastern Europe and the Ottoman Empire. Why was none of these battles decisive in ending the war? Were the British naval blockade and the German submarine war zone effective? Finally, note the reduced Russian territory as a result of the Treaty of Brest-Litovsk. Why was Russia willing to agree to such a loss of land to Germany before the war ended?

Verdun. Military leaders on both sides hoped for a decisive breakthrough that would win the war. In 1916, the Allies planned a joint strike at the Somme, a river in northern France that flowed west into the English Channel, but the Germans struck first at Verdun, a small fortress city in northeast France. By concentrating great numbers of troops, the Germans outnumbered the French five to two.

The German troops advanced easily through the first lines of defense. But the French held their position for ten long, horrifying months of continuous mass slaughter from February to December 1916. General Henri Philippe Pétain (1856–1951) bolstered morale by constantly rotating his troops such that most of the French army—259 of 330 infantry battalions—saw action at Verdun.

Yet no real winners emerged from the scorched earth of Verdun, where observers could see the nearest thing to desert created in Europe. Verdun was a disaster. The French suffered over half a million total casualties. German casualties were almost as high. A few square miles of territory had changed hands back and forth. In the end, no military advantage was gained, though almost 700,000 lives had been lost. Verdun demonstrated that an offensive war under these conditions was impossible.

The Somme. Still, new offensives were devised. The British went ahead with their planned offensive on the Somme in July 1916. For an advance of seven miles, 400,000 British and 200,000 French soldiers were killed or wounded. German losses brought the total casualties of this offensive to one million men. Despite his experience at Verdun, French general Robert Nivelle planned his own offensive in the Champagne region in spring 1917. Nivelle's offensive resulted in 40,000 deaths, and he was dismissed. The French army was falling apart; mutiny and insubordination were everywhere.

The British believed that they could succeed where the French had failed. Under General Douglas Haig (1861–1928), the commander-in-chief of British expeditionary forces on the Continent, the British launched an attack in Flanders through the summer and fall of 1917. Known as the Passchendaele offensive, this campaign resulted in almost 400,000 British soldiers slaughtered for insignificant territorial gain. The Allies and the Germans finally recognized that "going over the top" in offensives was not working and could not work. The war must be won by other means.

War on the Periphery

Recognizing the stalemate in the west, the Allies attempted to open up other fronts where the Central Powers might be vulnerable. In the spring of 1915, the Allies were successful in convincing Italy to enter the war on their side by promising that it would receive, at the time of the peace, the South Tyrol and the southern part of Dalmatia and key Dalmatian islands, which would assure Italy's dominance over the Adriatic Sea. By thus capitalizing on Italian antagonism toward Austria-Hungary over control of this territory, the Allies gained 875,000 Italian soldiers for their cause.

Germany, in turn, was well aware of the need to expand its alliances beyond Austria-Hungary if it was to compete successfully against superior Allied forces. Trapped as they were to the east and west, the Central Powers established control over a broad corridor stretching from the North Sea through central Europe and down through the Ottoman Empire to the Suez Canal, which was so vital to British interests.

In the Balkans, where the war had begun, the Serbs were consistently bested by the Austrians. By late 1915, the Serbs were knocked out of the war, having lost one-sixth of their population through war, famine, and disease. The promise of booty persuaded Bulgaria to join Germany and Austria-Hungary. Over the next year and a half, the Allies responded by convincing Romania and then Greece to join them.

War in the Ottoman Empire. The theater of war continued to expand. Although the Ottoman Empire had joined the war in late 1914 on the side of the Central Powers, its own internal difficulties attenuated its fighting ability. Hence the Ottoman Empire was the weakest link in the chain of German alliances. Yet it held a crucial position. The Turks could block shipping of vital supplies to Russia through the Mediterranean and Black seas. Coming to the aid of their Russian ally, a combined British and French fleet attacked Turkish forces at the strait of the Dardanelles in April 1915. In the face of political and military opposition, First Lord of the Admiralty Winston Churchill (1874–1965) supported the idea of opening a new front by sea. Poorly planned and mismanaged, the expedition was a disaster.

Britain sought to protect its interests in the Suez Canal. Turkish troops menaced the canal effectively enough to terrify the British into maintaining an elaborate system of defense in the area and concentrating large troop reinforcements in Egypt. War with the Ottoman Empire also extended battle into the oil fields of Mesopotamia and Persia. British forces took Baghdad in 1917, while Australian and New Zealand troops captured Jerusalem. The tentacles of war spread out, following the path of Western economic and imperial interests throughout the world.

War at Sea. Most surprising of all was the indecisive nature of the war at sea. The great battleships of the British and German navies avoided confrontation on the high seas. The only major naval battle of the Great War, the Battle of Jutland in the North Sea, took place in early 1916. Each side inflicted damage on the other but, through careful maneuvering, avoided a decisive outcome to the battle. Instead,

Crew on the deck of a German World War I submarine at sea.

the British used their seapower as a policing force to blockade German trade and strangle the German economy.

The German navy, much weaker than the British, relied on a new weapon, the submarine, which threatened to become decisive in the war at sea. *Unterseebooten,* or U-boats, as German submarines were called, torpedoed six million tons of Allied shipping in 1917. With cruising ranges as high as 3,600 miles, German submarines attacked Allied and neutral shipping as far away as off the shore of the United States and the Arctic supply line to Russia. Outraged neutral powers considered the Germans to be in violation of international law. The Germans also rejected the requirements of warning an enemy ship and boarding it for investigation as too dangerous for submarines, which were no match for battleships above water. The Allies invented depth charges and mines that were capable of blowing German submarines out of the water. These weapons, combined with the use of the convoy system in the Atlantic and the Mediterranean, produced a successful blockade and antisubmarine campaign that put an end to the German advantage.

Adjusting to the Unexpected: Total War

The period from 1914 to 1918 marked the first time in history that the productive activities of entire populations were directed toward a single goal: military victory. The Great War became a war of peoples, not just of armies. For this reason the Great War became known as history's first **total war**.

Mobilizing the Home Front

While soldiers were fighting on the eastern and western fronts, businessmen and politicians at home were creating bureaucratic administrations to control wages and prices, distribute supplies, establish production quotas, and, in general, mobilize human and material resources. The Allies and Central Powers organized civilians of all ages and both sexes to work for the war.

Women's Roles. Women played an essential role on the home front. They had never been isolated from the experiences and hardships of war, but they now found new ways to support the war effort. In cities, women went to work in munitions factories and war-related industries that had previously employed only men. Women filled service jobs, from firefighters to trolley-car conductors, jobs that were essential to the smooth running of industrial society and that men had left vacant. On farms, women literally took up the plow, as both men and horses were requisitioned for the war effort. Women also served in the auxiliary units of the armed services in the clerical and medical corps. In eastern European nations, women entered combat as soldiers.

Government Controls. In the first months of the war, the private sector had been left to its own devices, with nearly disastrous results. Shortages, especially of shells, and bottlenecks in production threatened military efforts. Governments were forced to establish controls and to set up state monopolies to guarantee the supplies necessary to wage war. Through government intervention, France improvised and relocated its war industries. The British government became involved in production, too, by establishing in 1915 the first Ministry of Munitions under the direction of David Lloyd George (1863–1945). Distinct from the Ministry of War, the Ministry of Munitions was to coordinate military needs with the armaments industry.

In a war that leaders soon realized would be a long one, food supplies assumed paramount importance. As the war pulled men off the farms, production declined. Germany, dependent on food imports and isolated from the world market by the Allied blockade, introduced rationing five months after the outbreak of the war. Other Continental nations followed suit. Government agents set quotas for agricultural producers. Armies were fed and supplied at the expense of domestic populations. Great Britain, which enjoyed a more reliable food supply by virtue of its sea power, did not impose food rationing until 1917.

Silencing Dissent

The strains of total war were becoming apparent. Two years of sacrificing and, in some areas, starving began to take their toll among soldiers and civilians on both sides. With the lack of decisive victories, war weariness was spreading. Work stoppages and strikes, which had virtually ceased with the outbreak of war in 1914, began to increase rapidly in 1916. Social peace between unions and governments was no longer held together by patriotic enthusiasm for war.

Politicians, too, began to rethink their suspension of opposition to government policies as the war dragged on. By 1916, the united front that political opponents had presented against the enemy was crumbling under growing demands for peace.

In a total war, unrest at home guaranteed defeat. Governments knew that all opposition to war policies had to be eliminated. In a dramatic extension of the police powers of the state, among both the Allies and the Central Powers, criticism of the government became treason. Censorship was enforced. Propaganda became more virulent. Anyone who spoke for peace was no better than the enemy. The governments of every warring nation resorted to harsh measures. Parliamentary bodies were stripped of power, civil liberties were suspended, and democratic procedures were ignored.

Every warring nation also sought to promote dissension among the populations of its enemies. Germany aided the Easter Rebellion in Ireland in 1916 in the hope that the Irish demand for independence would damage British fighting strength and morale. Germany also supported separatist movements among minority nationalities in the Russian Empire and was responsible for returning the avowed revolutionary V. I. Lenin under escort to Russia in April 1917. The British engaged in similar tactics. The British foreign secretary Arthur Balfour (1848–1930) worked with Zionist leaders in 1917 in drawing up the **Balfour Declaration**, which promised to "look with favor" on the creation of a Jewish homeland in Palestine. The British thereby encouraged Zionist hopes among central European Jews, with the intent of creating difficulties for German and Austrian rulers. Similarly, the British encouraged Arabs to rebel against Turks with the same promise of Palestine.

The Russian Revolution and Allied Victory

Two events proved decisive in 1917 in determining the course of the war: the collapse of the Russian army and the entry of the United States.

Revolution in Russia

In order to understand Russia's withdrawal from the war, it is important to understand that Russia's ruler, Tsar Nicholas II (1894–1917), presided over an empire in the process of modernization with widening social divisions in 1914. Nicholas believed that a short, successful war would strengthen his monarchy against the domestic forces of change. Little did Nicholas know, when he committed Russia to the path of war instead of revolution, that he had guaranteed a future of war *and* revolution.

The Last Tsar. In 1914, Russia was considered backward by the standards of Western industrial society. The serfs had been freed in the 1860s, but the nature of the emancipation exacerbated tensions in the countryside and peasant hunger for land. Russia's limited, rapid industrialization in the 1880s and 1890s was an attempt to catch up with Great Britain, France, and Germany as a world industrial power. But the speed of such change brought with it severe dislocations, especially in the industrial city of Moscow and the capital, St. Petersburg.

In 1905, the workers of St. Petersburg protested hardships due to cyclical downturns in the economy. On a Sunday in January 1905, the tsar's troops fired on a peaceful mass demonstration in front of the Winter Palace, killing and wounding scores of workers, women, and children who were appealing to the tsar for relief. The event, which came to be known as Bloody Sunday, set off a revolution that spread to Moscow and the countryside. In October 1905, the regime responded to the disruptions with a series of reforms that legalized political parties and established the Duma, or national parliament. Peasants, oppressed by their own burdens of taxation and endemic poverty, launched mass attacks on big landowners throughout 1905 and 1906. The government met workers' and peasants' demands with a return to repression in 1907.

What workers had learned in 1905 was the power and the means of independent organization. Factory committees, trade unions, and **soviets**, or elected workers' councils, proliferated. Unrest among factory workers revived on the eve of the Great War, a period of rapid economic growth and renewed trade-union activity. Between January and July 1914, Russia experienced 3,500 strikes.

Russia was less prepared for war than any of the other belligerents. Undoubtedly, it had more soldiers than other countries, but it lacked arms and equipment. Problems of provisioning such a huge fighting force placed great strains on the domestic economy and on the workforce. Under government coercion to meet the needs of war, industrial output doubled between 1914 and 1917, while agricultural production plummeted. The tsar, who unwisely insisted on commanding his own troops, left the government in the hands of his wife, the Tsarina Alexandra, a German princess by birth, and her eccentric peasant-priest adviser, Rasputin. Scandal, sexual innuendo, and charges of treason surrounded the royal court. The incompetence of a series of unpopular ministers further eroded confidence in the regime.

In the end, the war sharpened long-standing divisions within Russian society. Led by exhausted and starving working women, poorly paid and underfed workers toppled the regime in the bitter winter of March 1917. This event was the beginning of a violent process of revolution and civil war. The tsar abdicated, and all public symbols of the tsardom were destroyed. The banner bearing the Romanov two-headed eagle was torn down; in its place, the Red Flag, the international symbol of revolution, flew over the Winter Palace.

Dual Power. With the tsar's abdication, two centers of authority replaced autocracy. One was the Provisional Government, appointed by the Duma and made up of progressive liberals led by Prince Georgi Lvov (1861–1925), prime minister of the new government, who also served as minister of the interior. Aleksandr Kerenski (1881–1970), the only Socialist in the Provisional Government, served as minister of justice. The members of the new government hoped to establish constitutional and democratic rule.

The other center of authority was the soviets—committees or councils elected by workers and soldiers and supported by radical lawyers, journalists, and intellectuals in favor of socialist self-rule. Party organization and ideological consensus were generally lacking among the soviets, which were quite heterogeneous. The Petrograd Soviet was the most prominent among the councils. (In 1914, the name of St. Petersburg had been changed to the Russian "Petrograd.") This duality of power was matched by duality in policies and objectives and guaranteed a short-lived and unstable regime.

The problems facing the new regime soon became apparent as revolution spread to the provinces and to the battlefront. Peasants, who made up 80 percent of the Russian population, accepted the revolution and demanded land and peace. Without waiting for government directives, peasants began seizing the land. Peasants tried to alleviate some of their suffering by hoarding what little they had. The food crisis of winter persisted throughout the spring and summer, as bread lines lengthened and prices rose.

In addition to the problems of land and bread, the war itself presented the new government with other insurmountable difficulties. Hundreds of thousands of Russian soldiers at the front deserted the war, having heard news from home of peasant land grabs and rumors of a new offensive planned for July. By spring 1917, six to eight million Russian soldiers had been killed, wounded, or captured. The Russian army was incapable of fighting.

The Provisional Government was caught in an impossible situation. It could not withdraw from the war, but neither could it fight. Continued involvement in the lost cause of the war blocked any consideration of social reforms.

While the Provisional Government was trying to deal with the calamities, many members of the intelligentsia, Russia's educated class, whom the tsar had exiled for their political beliefs, now rushed back from western Europe to take part in the great revolutionary experiment. During the months between February and July 1917, theorists of all stripes put their cases before the people, but it was the Marxists, or Social Democrats, who had the greatest impact on the direction of the revolution.

Like Marxists in the West, the Russian Social Democrats split over how best to achieve a socialist state. The more moderate majority, the Mensheviks (meaning "minority"), wanted to work through parliamentary institutions and were willing to cooperate with the Provisional Government. A smaller faction—despite its name—calling themselves **Bolsheviks** (meaning "majority") dedicated themselves to preparation for a revolutionary upheaval. After April 1917, the Bolsheviks refused to work with the Provisional Government and organized themselves to take control of the Petrograd Soviet.

Lenin and the Opposition to War. The leader of the Bolsheviks was Vladimir Ilyich Ulyanov (1870–1924), best known by his revolutionary name, Lenin. More a pragmatist than a theoretician, he argued for a disciplined party of professional revolutionaries, a vanguard who would lead the peasants and workers in a socialist revolution against capitalism. In contrast to the Mensheviks, he argued that the time was ripe for a successful revolution and that it could be achieved through the soviets.

Immediately on arrival in Petrograd, Lenin threw down the gauntlet to the Provisional Government. In his **April Theses** he promised the Russian people peace, land, and bread. The war must be ended immediately, he argued, because it represented an imperialist struggle that was benefiting capitalists. Russia's duty was to withdraw and wait for a world revolution.

Dissatisfaction with the Provisional Government increased as the war dragged hopelessly on and bread lines lengthened. In the midst of these calamities a massive popular demonstration erupted in July 1917 against the Provisional Government and in favor of the soviets, which excluded the upper classes from voting. The Provisional Government responded with repressive force reminiscent of the tsardom. The July Days were proof of the growing influence of the Bolsheviks among the Russian people. Although the Bolshevik leadership had withdrawn support for the demonstrations at the last moment, Bolshevik rank-and-file party members strongly endorsed the protest. Indisputably, Bolshevik influence was growing in the soviets despite repression and persecution of its leaders. Lenin was forced to flee to Finland.

As a result of the July Days, Kerenski, who had been heading the Ministry of Justice, was named prime minister and continued the Provisional Government's moderate policies. To protect the government from a coup on the right, Kerenski permitted the arming of the Red Guards, the workers' militia units of the Petrograd Soviet. The traditional chasm between the upper and lower classes was widening as the policies of the Provisional Government conflicted with the demands of the soviets.

The October Revolution. The second revolution came in November (October in the Russian calendar). This time it was not a spontaneous street demonstration but the seizure of the Russian capital by the Red Guards of the Petrograd Soviet. The revolution was carefully planned and orchestrated by Lenin, who had returned surreptitiously from Finland, and his vanguard of Bolsheviks, who now possessed majorities in the soviets in Moscow, Petrograd, and other industrial centers. The military action was directed by Lev Bronstein, better known by his revolutionary name, Leon Trotsky (1879–1940). The Bolshevik chairman of the Petrograd Soviet, Trotsky used the Red Guard to seize political control and arrest the members of the Provisional Government. Kerenski escaped and fled the city.

The takeover was achieved with almost no bloodshed and was immediately endorsed by an All-Russian Congress of Soviets, which consisted of representatives

REVOLUTION AND CIVIL WAR IN RUSSIA, 1914–1920. Revolutionary and civil unrest was greatest in those areas of Russia with the greatest concentrations of peasants. Kulaks, the more prosperous peasants, were severely repressed for resisting the requisitioning of food after 1918.

of local soviets from throughout the nation who were in session amid the takeover of the capital. A Bolshevik regime under Lenin now ruled Russia. Tsar Nicholas II and the royal family were executed by Bolshevik revolutionaries in July 1918.

Chronology

THE RUSSIAN REVOLUTION

January–July 1914	Protests and strikes
30 July 1914	Russia enters World War I
March 1917	First Russian Revolution: Abdication of Tsar Nicholas II
March 1917	Creation of Provisional Government
April 1917	Bolsheviks take control of Petrograd
July 1917	Massive demonstration against Provisional Government; Lenin is forced to flee Russia
November 1917	Bolsheviks and Red Guards seize political control in what comes to be known as the October Revolution
March 1918	Russia withdraws from World War I and signs Treaty of Brest-Litovsk
July 1918	Tsar Nicholas II and family are executed

The Treaty of Brest-Litovsk. Lenin immediately set to work to end the Great War for Russia. After months of negotiation, Russia signed a separate peace with the Germans in March 1918 in the **Treaty of Brest-Litovsk**. By every measure, the treaty was a bitter humiliation for the new Soviet regime. Lenin believed that he had no choice: He needed to buy time in order to consolidate the revolution at home, and he hoped for a socialist revolution in Germany that would soften the results of the treaty.

The Treaty of Brest-Litovsk was judged a betrayal, not only outside Russia among the Allied powers, but also inside Russia among some army officers who had sacrificed much for the tsar's war. To those military men, the Bolsheviks were no more than German agents who held the country in their sway.

To deal with the anarchy caused by the fratricidal struggle, Lenin had to strengthen the government's dictatorial elements at the expense of its democratic ones. The new Soviet state used state police to suppress all opposition. The dictatorship of the proletariat yielded to the dictatorship of the repressive forces.

In the course of the civil war, Lenin was no more successful than Kerenski and the Provisional Government had been in solving the problems of food supplies. Human costs of the civil war were high, with more than 800,000 soldiers dead on both sides and two million civilian deaths from dysentery and diseases caused by poor nutrition. Industrial production ceased, and people fled towns to return to the countryside.

The United States Enters the Great War

The Allies longed for the entry of the United States into the war. Although the United States was a neutral country, it had become an important supplier to the Allies from early in the war. American bankers also made loans and extended credit to the Allies to the amount of $2.2 billion. The United States had made a sizable investment in the Allied war effort, and its economy was prospering.

Beginning with the sinking of the *Lusitania* in 1915, German policy on the high seas had incensed the American public. Increased U-boat activity in 1916 led President Woodrow Wilson (1856–1924) to issue a severe warning to the Germans to cease submarine warfare. However, the Germans were desperate, and the great advantage of submarines was in sneak attacks, a procedure that was against the international rules that required a warning. Germany initiated a new phase of unrestricted submarine warfare on 1 February 1917, when the German ambassador informed the U.S. government that U-boats would sink on sight all ships, including passenger ships, even those that were neutral and unarmed.

The United States Declares War. German machinations in Mexico were also revealed on 25 February 1917, with the interception of a telegram from Arthur Zimmermann (1864–1940), the German foreign minister. The telegram communicated Germany's willingness to support Mexico's recovery of "lost territory" in New Mexico, Arizona, and Texas in return for Mexican support of Germany in the event of U.S. entry into the war. American citizens were outraged. On 2 April 1917, Wilson, who had won the presidential election of 1916 on the promise of peace, asked the U.S. Congress for a declaration of war against Germany.

The entry of the United States was the turning point in the war, tipping the scales dramatically in favor of the Allies. The United States contributed its naval power to the large Allied convoys that formed to protect shipping against German attacks. By July 1918, the Americans were sending a phenomenal 300,000 soldiers a month to Europe. By the end of the war, two million Americans had traveled to Europe to fight in the war.

U.S. troops, although numerous, were not well trained, and they relied on France and Great Britain for their arms and equipment. But the Germans were aware that they could not hold out indefinitely against this superior Allied force. Realizing that its only chance of victory lay in swift action, the German high command decided on a bold measure: one great, final offensive that would knock the combined forces of Great Britain, France, and the United States out of the war once and for all by striking at a weak point and smashing through enemy lines. It almost worked.

FIGHTING THE GREAT WAR

1905	Development of the Schlieffen Plan
28 June 1914	Assassination of Archduke Franz Ferdinand and his wife, Sophie
28 July 1914	Austria-Hungary declares war on Serbia
30 July–4 August 1914	Russia, France, Britain, and Germany declare war in accordance with system of alliances
August 1914	Germany invades Belgium
6–10 September 1914	First Battle of the Marne
1915	Germany introduces chlorine gas
April 1915–January 1916	Gallipoli Campaign
May 1915	Sinking of the *Lusitania*
February–December 1916	Battle at Verdun
1917	First use of mustard gas
2 April 1917	United States enters war
March 1918	Russia withdraws
11 November 1918	Armistice

German Defeat. Known as the Ludendorff offensive, after the general who devised it, the final German push began in March 1918. Secretly amassing tired troops from the eastern front who had been pulled back after the Russian withdrawal, the Germans counted on the element of surprise to enable them to break through a weak sector in the west. On the first day of spring, Ludendorff struck. The larger German force gained initial success against weakened British and French forces. Yet in spite of breaches in defense, the Allied line held.

The final drive came in mid-July. More than one million German soldiers had already been killed, wounded, or captured in the months between March and July. German prisoners of war gave the French details of Ludendorff's plan. The Germans, now exposed and vulnerable, were placed on the defensive. The German army was rapidly disintegrating. On the other side, tanks, plentiful munitions, and U.S. reinforcements fueled an Allied offensive that began in late September. The end finally came after four years of war. On 11 November 1918, an armistice signed by representatives of the German and Allied forces took effect.

Settling the Peace

From January to June 1919, an assembly of nations convened in Paris to draw up the new European peace. Although the primary task of settling the peace fell to the Council of Four—Premier Georges Clemenceau of France, Prime Minister David

Lloyd George of Great Britain, Prime Minister Vittorio Emanuele Orlando of Italy, and President Woodrow Wilson of the United States—small states, newly formed states, and non-European states, Japan in particular, joined in the task of forging the peace. The states of Germany, Austria-Hungary, and Soviet Russia were excluded from the negotiating tables where the future of Europe was to be determined.

Wilson's Fourteen Points

President Wilson, who captured international attention with his liberal views on the peace, was the central figure of the conference. He was firmly committed to the task of shaping a better world. Before the end of the war, he had proclaimed the **Fourteen Points** as a guideline to the future peace and as an appeal to the people of Europe to support his policies. Believing that secret diplomacy and the alliance system were responsible for the events leading up to the declaration of war in 1914, he put forward as a basic principle "open covenants of peace, openly arrived at." Other points included the reduction of armaments, freedom of commerce and trade, self-determination of peoples, and a general association of nations to guarantee the peace. Point 14, which stipulated "mutual guarantees of independence and territorial integrity" through the establishment of the League of Nations, was endorsed by the peace conference. The League of Nations, which the United States refused to join in spite of Wilson's advocacy, was intended to arbitrate all future disputes among states and to keep the peace.

Georges Clemenceau of France was motivated primarily by a concern for his nation's security. France had suffered the greatest losses of the war in both human lives and property destroyed. To prevent a resurgent Germany, Clemenceau supported a variety of measures to cripple Germany as a military force on the Continent. Germany was disarmed. The territory west of the Rhine River was demilitarized, with occupation by Allied troops to last for a period of 15 years.

The representatives of the victorious Allies at Versailles: (left to right) David Lloyd George of Great Britain, Vittorio Orlando of Italy, Georges Clemenceau of France, and Woodrow Wilson of the United States.

Much time and energy were devoted to redrawing the map of Europe. New states were created out of the lands of three failed empires. On the basis of self-determination, Finland, Latvia, Estonia, Lithuania, Poland, Czechoslovakia, Austria, Hungary, and Yugoslavia were all granted nation-state status. However, the rights of ethnic and cultural minorities were violated in some cases because of the impossibility of redrawing the map of Europe strictly according to the principle of self-determination. In spite of good intentions, every new nation had its own national minority, a situation that held the promise of future troubles.

EUROPE AFTER WORLD WAR I. The need for security on the Continent led France to support a buffer zone of new nations between Russia and Germany, carved out of the former Austrian Empire. German territory along the French border was demilitarized out of the same concern for protection.

Treaties and Territories

The peace conference produced separate treaties with each of the defeated nations: Austria, Hungary, Turkey, Bulgaria, and Germany. The Austria settlement acknowledged the fundamental disintegration of the Austrian Empire, recognizing an independent Czechoslovakian republic and preparing the way for a fusing of Croatia, Dalmatia, Bosnia and Herzegovina with the Kingdom of Serbia, into the nation of Yugoslavia. Hungary and Poland also emerged as independent nations thanks to territorial losses by Germany and Austria-Hungary. Bulgaria lost territory on the Aegean Sea to Greece, and Yugoslavia assumed control of Bulgarian holdings in Macedonia. Romania gained Hungarian and Bulgarian territory.

In the Middle East, a separate treaty acknowledged Great Britain's mandate in Palestine, Mesopotamia, and Transjordan; and France's mandate in Syria.

In November 1917, Britain affirmed its support of the creation in Palestine of a national home for the Jewish people. This affirmation, known as the Balfour Declaration, was made by Lord Balfour on behalf of "His Majesty's Government" and was considered as a violation of promises made to the Arabs during the war that they would be given control of Palestine in return for supporting the Allied war effort. Although Arab rulers were given control of British mandates, and Prince Faisal assumed the title of king of Iraq, Arab resentment festered as increased numbers of European Jews moved into Palestine and Arab hopes for the creation of an Arab kingdom were dashed.

Amidst these other treaty negotiations, the treaty signed with Germany on 28 June 1919, known as the **Treaty of Versailles**, dealt exclusively with defeated Germany. In that treaty, the Allies imposed blame for the war on Germany and its expansionist aims in the famous War Guilt Clause. According to that clause, the war was Germany's fault, and Germany must be made to pay. Reparations, once the price of defeat, were now exacted as compensation for damages inflicted by a guilty aggressor.

The principle of punitive reparations was included in the German settlement. Germany learned it had to make a down payment of $5 billion against a future bill of $32 billion; had to hand over a significant proportion of its merchant ships, including all vessels of more than 1,600 tons; had to lose all German colonies; and had to deliver coal to neighboring countries. In addition, Germany lost the territory gained from Russia in 1918; returned Alsace and Lorraine to France; ceded territory to Belgium and eventually to Lithuania; and gave up parts of Prussia with large Polish populations. Furthermore, Germany lost control of the Saar, a coal-producing region, to France for fifteen years; and the German Baltic port of Danzig was declared an international "free city." By stripping Germany of key resources, territory and population, its ability to pay reparations was also weakened. These harsh clauses dictated by the determination of German war guilt, more than any other aspect of the peace settlement, came to haunt the Allies in the succeeding decades.

In the end, no nation obtained what it wanted from the peace settlement. The defeated nations believed that they had been badly abused. The victorious nations were aware of the compromises they had reluctantly accepted. Cooperation among nations was essential if the treaty was to work successfully. A new and stable balance of power depended on the participation of Russia, the United States, and the British Empire. But Russia was excluded from and hostile to the peace settlement, the United States was uncommitted to it, and the British Empire declined to guarantee it. All three Great Powers backed off from their European responsibilities at the end of the war. By 1920, all aspects of the treaty, but especially the reparations clause, had been questioned and criticized by the very governments that had written and accepted them. The search for a lasting peace had just begun.

SUMMARY

The War Europe Expected By 1914, Europe had divided into two blocs. The alliance system reduced diplomatic flexibility and increased the chances of general war. Military planning further limited political and diplomatic flexibility. The assassination of Archduke Franz Ferdinand and his wife Sophie sparked a new conflict in the Balkans which, in turn, led to the outbreak of World War I.

A New Kind of Warfare New technology transformed the nature of warfare. On the western front, machine guns and artillery created conditions in which defensive advantages made successful attacks almost impossible. Germany's initial attack on France stalled at the Battle of the Marne. On the eastern front, Germany overmatched its Russian opponent. The enormous casualties suffered at the Battle of Verdun and the Battle of the Somme demonstrated the futility of the war on the western front. The war expanded on Europe's periphery and in the Middle East. The war at sea was indecisive.

Adjusting to the Unexpected: Total War World War I was a total war, pitting the entire populations of nations against one another. Governments reorganized their economies to meet the demands of war. Women played a crucial role in the wartime labor force. As the war dragged on, governments took ever more repressive measures to stifle dissent, at the same time as they sought to stimulate dissension among the populations of their enemies.

The Russian Revolution and Allied Victory Rapid industrialization and modernization in the late nineteenth century caused considerable social upheaval in Russia. The 1905 Bloody Sunday demonstration set off a revolution. The government responded with a series of reforms, but repression had returned by 1907. Russia was unprepared for war in 1914. The strains of war intensified Russia's social and economic problems. The tsar's regime was toppled in March 1917, an event that marked the beginning of a process of revolution and civil war. Power was initially shared between the Provisional Government and committees, called soviets, that were elected by workers and soldiers. A food crisis and a war it could not end hamstrung the new government. Led by Lenin, the Bolsheviks overthrew the Provisional Government and took power in November 1917. The Bolsheviks made peace with Germany in the Treaty of Brest-Litovsk. Russia's withdrawal from World War I was followed by civil war in Russia. Unrestricted submarine warfare and the Zimmermann telegram helped pull the United States into the war. American forces and resources tipped the balance in the Allies' favor. An armistice was signed on November 11, 1918.

Settling the Peace The United States, France, Great Britain, and Italy took the lead creating the peace settlement that followed the war. Germany, Austria-Hungary, and Soviet Russia were excluded from the negotiations. President Woodrow Wilson of the United States pressed for the treaty to conform to his Fourteen Points, including the creation of a new international body, the League of Nations. The French were most interested in preventing Germany from reemerging as a military power. New states were created in central, eastern, and southern Europe. Separate peace treaties were concluded with Austria, Hungary, Turkey, Bulgaria, and Germany. The Treaty of Versailles imposed war guilt and war reparations on Germany, at the same time as it stripped Germany of provinces and colonies. In the end, both the victorious and defeated nations were unhappy with the peace settlement.

QUESTIONS FOR REVIEW

1. Why did so many in Europe look forward to war by the summer of 1914, and what had they done to bring it about?
2. How and why did the Great War differ so much from the expectations of both the generals and the majority of Europeans?
3. What is total war, and what made World War I the first such war in history?
4. In what ways did the Great War contribute to revolution in Russia?
5. How was peace at last achieved, and what were the terms of that peace?

The European Search for Stability, 1920–1939

Crisis and Collapse in a World Economy

In 1918, the belligerent nations—winners and losers alike—had big bills on their hands. Although nations at war had borrowed abroad and from their own populations through the sale of war bonds, private citizens could not provide all the money needed to finance four years of war.

International Loans and Trade Barriers

France borrowed from Great Britain. Both Great Britain and France took loans from the United States. When these sources proved insufficient, they printed more money. Because more money had claims on the same amount of national wealth, the money in circulation was worth less. When the people who had purchased war bonds were then paid off with depreciated currency, they lost real wealth. Inflation had the same effect as taxation. The people had less wealth, and the government had less debt.

The United States, for the first time in history the leading creditor nation in the world, had no intention of wiping the slate clean by forgiving war debts. Nor did it intend to accept repayment in less-valuable postwar currencies. Britain, France, and Belgium counted on reparations from Germany to pay their war debts and to rebuild their economies.

For the German people and for German leaders, reparations were an unacceptable, punitive levy that mortgaged the prosperity of future generations. Transferring wealth would have cut into any increase in the German standard of living in the 1920s, and it would have diminished the investment needed to make the German economy grow. Instead, the German government printed huge amounts of currency. The mark collapsed and world currencies were endangered.

With financial disaster looming, the British and Americans decided to intervene. A plan had to be devised that would permit Germany to prosper while funneling payments to France, which depended on reparations for its own recovery and for its war debt payments to the United States. The 1924 Dawes Plan aimed to end inflation and restore economic prosperity in Germany by giving Germany a more modest and realistic schedule of payments and by extending a loan from U.S. banks to get payments started.

As important as reparations and war debts are in any understanding of the Western world in the 1920s, they cannot be considered in isolation. Debtor nations, whether Allies paying back loans to the United States or defeated nations paying reparations to the victors, needed to be able to sell their goods in world markets.

If trade was to be the stepladder out of the financial hole of indebtedness, open markets and stable currencies were its rungs. Yet the Republican political leaders in the United States insisted on high tariffs to protect domestic goods against imports, and high tariffs prevented Europeans from selling in the United States and earning the dollars they needed to repay war debts.

While blocking imports, the United States planned to expand its own exports to world markets, especially to Europe. The problem for U.S. exporters, however, was the instability of European currencies in the first half of the 1920s. All over Europe, governments allowed inflation to rise with the expectation that depreciating currencies would make their goods cheaper in world markets and hence more salable.

Depreciating European currencies on the one hand meant an appreciating dollar on the other. More and more German marks, British pounds, and French francs had to be spent to purchase U.S. goods. The result was that fewer U.S. exports were sold in European markets. Because two-thirds of Germany's long-term credits came from the United States, Germany's fate was directly linked to the fortunes of U.S. financial centers. Conversely, the soundness of U.S. banks depended on a solvent Germany, which now absorbed 18 percent of U.S. capital exports.

Despite the scaled-down schedule of the Dawes Plan, reparations remained a bitter pill for German leaders and the German public to swallow. In 1929, U.S. bankers devised another plan, known as the Young Plan. Although the plan initially transferred $100 million to Germany, Germans saw the twentieth century stretching before them as year after year of nothing but humiliating reparations payments. To make matters worse, after 1928, U.S. private loans shriveled in Germany as U.S. investors sought the higher yields of a booming stock market at home.

Europe as a whole made rapid progress in manufacturing production during the second half of the decade and by 1929 had surpassed its prewar (1913) per capita income. Yet structural weaknesses were present. The false security of a new gold standard masked the instability and interdependence of currencies. Low prices prevailed in the agricultural sector, keeping the incomes of a significant segment of the population depressed. But the low rate of long-term capital investment was obscured in the flurry of short-term loans, whose disappearance in 1928 spelled the beginning of the end for European recovery. The protectionist trade policy of the United States conflicted with its insistence on repayment of war debts. Germany's resentment over reparations was in no way alleviated by the Dawes and Young repayment plans. The irresponsibility of U.S. speculation in the stock market pricked the bubble of prosperity. None of these factors operated in isolation to cause the collapse that began in 1929. Taken together, however, they caused a depression of previously unimagined severity in the international economic system.

The Great Depression

In October 1929 the stock market in the United States collapsed. This crash set off the **Great Depression** in an international economic system that was already plagued with structural problems. It also marked the beginning of a long period of worldwide economic stagnation and depression.

Dependence on the American Economy. A confluence of factors made Europe and the rest of the world vulnerable to reversals in the U.S. economy. Heavy borrowing and reliance on U.S. investment throughout the 1920s contributed to the inherent instability of European economies. Excessive lending and leniency were fatal mistakes of creditor nations, especially the United States. When, in the summer of 1929, U.S. investors turned off the tap of the flow of capital to search for higher profits at home, a precarious situation began to get worse.

The Great Depression was more serious in extent and duration than any depression before or since. In 1932, one in four American workers was without a

This poster for the October 1931 British general election reflects the National Government's concern over mass unemployment and industrial stagnation. The coalition National Government swamped the opposition Labour Party, taking 556 Parliament seats to Labour's 51.

job. One in three banks had closed its doors. People lost their homes, unable to pay their mortgages; farmers lost their land, unable to earn enough to survive. The great prosperity of the 1920s had vanished overnight.

The plight of the United States rippled through world markets. Americans stopped buying foreign goods. The Smoot-Hawley Tariff Act, passed by the U.S. Congress in 1930, created an impenetrable tariff fortress against agricultural and manufactured imports. The major trading nations of the world, including Great Britain, enacted similar protectionist measures. U.S. investment abroad dried up.

European nations tried to stanch the outward flow of capital and gold by restricting the transfer of capital abroad. Nevertheless, large amounts of foreign-owned gold ($6.6 billion from 1931 to 1938) were deposited in U.S. banks. In 1931, President Herbert Hoover supported a moratorium on the payment of reparations and war debts. The moratorium, combined with the pooling of gold in the United States, led to a run on the British pound sterling in 1931 and the collapse of Great Britain as one of the world's great financial centers.

Political Repercussions. The gold standard disappeared from the international economy, never to return. So did reparations payments and war debts when the major nations of Europe met without the United States at a special conference held in Lausanne, Switzerland, in 1932. Something else died at the end of the 1920s: confidence in a self-adjusting economy, an "invisible hand" by which the business cycle would be righted. In 1932–1933 the Depression reached its nadir and became a global phenomenon.

Chronology

INTERNATIONAL POLITICS

1919	Creation of the League of Nations
1922	Germany and Russia sign Treaty of Rapallo
1924	Dawes Plan
1929	Young Plan
October 1929	Collapse of the U.S. stock market; beginning of the Great Depression
1936	Germany stations troops in the Rhineland in violation of the Treaty of Versailles

The Soviet Union's Separate Path

In the 1920s, the Soviet state was also faced with solving its economic problems. Lenin's successor, Joseph Stalin (1879–1953), obliged the Soviet people to achieve in a single generation what it had taken western Europe a century and a half to accomplish.

The Soviet Regime at the End of the Civil War

Soviet Russia's small industrial sector was in total disarray by 1921. Famine and epidemics in 1921–1922 killed and weakened more people than the Great War and the civil war combined. The countryside had been plundered to feed the Red and White armies. The combination of empty promises and a declining standard of living left workers and peasants frustrated and discontented. The Bolshevik Party now faced the task of restoring a country exhausted by war and revolution.

At the head of the Soviet state was Lenin, the first among equals in the seven-man Politburo. Among the Politburo seven, three men in particular attempted to leave their mark on the direction of Soviet policy: Leon Trotsky (1879–1940), Nikolai Bukharin (1888–1938), and Joseph Stalin (1879–1953).

As members of the Politburo, Leon Trotsky (left), Nikolai Bukharin (center), and Joseph Stalin (right) each tried to direct Soviet economic policy. Only the politically shrewd Stalin would emerge victorious.

In the debate over the direction economic development should take, proposals ranged from a planned economy totally directed from above to an economy controlled from below. Lenin's primary goal was to stabilize Bolshevik rule in its progress toward socialism. He recognized that nothing could be achieved without the peasants. As a result, Lenin found himself embracing a new economic policy that he termed a "temporary retreat" from Communist goals.

The New Economic Policy, 1921–1928

In 1921, Lenin ended the forced requisitioning of peasant produce, which had been in effect during the civil war. In its place, peasants were to pay a tax in kind, that is, a fixed portion of their yield, to the state. Peasants in turn were permitted to reinstate private trade on their own terms. Party leaders accepted this shift in policy because it held the promise of prosperity, so necessary for political stability. Lenin's actions to return the benefits of productivity to the economy, combined with those of the peasants to reestablish markets, created the **New Economic Policy (NEP)** that emerged in the spring and summer of 1921.

Bukharin's Role. It remained for Nikolai Bukharin to tackle Russia's single greatest problem: How could Russia, crippled by poverty, find enough capital to industrialize? Insisting on the need for long-term economic planning, Bukharin counted on a prosperous and contented peasantry as the mainstay of his policy. He also hoped to attract foreign investment in Soviet endeavors as a way of ensuring future productivity.

Bukharin appreciated the importance of landholding to Russian peasants and defended a system of individual farms and private accumulation. Agriculture would operate through a market system, and the peasants would have the right to control their own surpluses. Rural prosperity would generate profits that could be used for gradual industrial development. Bukharin's policy stood in stark contrast to Stalin's later plan to feed industry by starving the agricultural sector.

Beginning in 1922, Lenin suffered a series of strokes that virtually removed him from power by March 1923. When he died on 21 January 1924, the Communist leadership split over the ambiguities of the NEP. The backward nature of agriculture did not permit the kind of productivity that the NEP policy makers anticipated. Cities demanded more food as their populations swelled with the influx of unskilled workers from rural areas. In 1927, peasants held back their grain. The Soviet Union was then experiencing a series of foreign policy setbacks in the West and in China, and Bolshevik leaders spoke of an active anti-Soviet conspiracy by the capitalist powers, led by Great Britain. The Soviet state lowered the price of grain, thereby squeezing the peasantry. The war scare, combined with the drop in food prices, soon led to an economic crisis.

Stalin Takes Charge. By 1928, the NEP was in trouble. Stalin, general secretary of the Communist Party of the Soviet Union, saw his chance. Under his supervision, the state intervened to prevent peasants from disposing of their own grain surpluses. The peasants responded to requisitioning by hoarding their produce and violent rioting. Bukharin and the NEP were in danger. Stalin exploited the internal crisis and external dangers to eliminate his political rivals. Stalin's rival Trotsky had been expelled from the Communist Party in November 1927 on charges that he had engaged in antiparty activities. Banished from Russia in 1929, Trotsky eventually found refuge in Mexico, where he was assassinated in 1940 at Stalin's command.

Bukharin's popularity in the party also threatened Stalin's aspirations. Bukharin was dropped from the Politburo in 1929. He was arrested in 1937 and was tried and executed for alleged treasonous activities the following year. The fate that befell Trotsky and Bukharin was typical of that which afflicted anyone who stood in the way of Stalin's pursuit of dictatorial control. Beneath his apparently colorless personality, Stalin was a dangerous man of great political acumen, a ruthless, behind-the-scenes politician who controlled the machinery of the party to his own ends and was not averse to using violence to achieve them.

Stalin's Rise to Power

Joseph Stalin was born Iosif Vissarionovich Dzhugashvili in 1879. His self-chosen revolutionary name, Stalin, means "steel" in Russian and is as good an indication as any of his opinion of his own personality and will.

Stalin was an early follower of Lenin and his close association with Lenin kept Stalin close to the center of power after the October Revolution of 1917. First as people's commissar for nationalities (1920–1923) and then as general secretary of the Central Committee of the Communist Party (1922–1953), Stalin showed natural talent as a political strategist.

After Lenin's death in 1924, Stalin shrewdly bolstered his own reputation by orchestrating a cult of worship for Lenin. In 1929, Stalin used the occasion of his fiftieth birthday to fashion for himself a reputation as the living hero of the Soviet state. Icons, statues, busts, and images of all sorts of both Lenin and Stalin appeared everywhere in public buildings, schoolrooms, and homes. Stalin systematically began eliminating his rivals so that he alone stood unchallenged as Lenin's true successor.

The First Five-Year Plan

The cult of Stalin coincided with the First Five-Year Plan (1929–1932), which launched Stalin's program of rapid industrialization. Between 1929 and 1937, the period covered by the first two five-year plans (truncated because of their proclaimed success), Stalin laid the foundation for an urban industrial society in the Soviet Union. By brutally squeezing profits out of the agricultural sector, Stalin managed to increase heavy industrial production between 300 and 600 percent.

Stalin committed the Soviet Union to rapid industrialization as the only way to preserve socialism. An industrial labor force was created virtually overnight as peasant men and women were placed at workbenches and before the vast furnaces of modern metallurgical plants. The number of women in the industrial workforce tripled in the decade after 1929. Heavy industrial production soared between 1929 and 1932.

When he first began to deal with the grain crisis of 1928, Stalin did not intend collective agriculture as a solution. But by the end of 1929, the increasingly repressive measures instituted by the state against the peasants had led both to **collectivization** and to the deportation of *kulaks*, the derisive term for wealthy peasants that literally means "tight-fisted ones." Stalin achieved forced collectivization by confiscating land and establishing collective farms run by the state. Within a few months, half of all peasant farms were collectivized. By 1938, private land was virtually eliminated. The state set prices, controlled distribution, and selected crops with the intention of ensuring a steady food supply and freeing a rural labor force for heavy industry.

Collectivization meant misery for the 25 million peasant families who suffered under it. At least five million peasants died between 1929 and 1932. Collectivization ripped apart the fabric of village life, destroyed families, and sent homeless peasants into exile. Some peasants retaliated by destroying their own crops and livestock. Ultimately, the peasants were to bear the chief burdens of industrialization.

The Comintern, Economic Development, and the Purges

After the Bolshevik revolution in 1917, Lenin had fully expected that other socialist revolutions would follow throughout the world. But as the prospects for world proletarian revolution evaporated, Soviet leaders sought to protect their revolutionary country from the hostile capitalist world through diplomacy. The end of the Allied intervention in Russia allowed the Bolshevik state to initiate diplomatic relations with the West, beginning with the Treaty of Rapallo signed with Germany in 1921. By 1924, all the major countries of the world—except the United States—had established diplomatic relations with the Soviet Union. In 1928, the Soviet Union cooperated in the preparation of a world disarmament conference to be held in Geneva and joined western European powers in a commitment to peace. The United States and the Soviet Union exchanged ambassadors for the first time in 1933.

THE SOVIET UNION'S SEPARATE PATH

November 1917	Bolsheviks and Red Guard seize power
1919	Creation of the Communist International (Comintern)
1920	Legalization of abortion and divorce
1921	End of the civil war
1921	Introduction of the New Economic Policy
3 April 1922	Stalin becomes secretary general of the Communist Party
21 January 1924	Lenin dies
1924–1929	Comintern policy of "Unity of the Working Classes"
1927	Dissatisfied peasants hoard grain
November 1927	Trotsky expelled from Communist Party
1928	Stalin introduces grain requisitioning
November 1929	Bukharin expelled from Politburo
1929	Introduction of First Five-Year Plan and the collectivization of agriculture
1929–1933	Comintern policy of noncooperation with Social Democratic parties
1933–1937	Second Five-Year Plan
1934–1938	Great Purge
1936	Abortion declared illegal
1938	Third Five-Year Plan

The Comintern. In addition to diplomatic relations, the Soviet state in 1919 encouraged various national Communist parties to form an association for the purpose of promoting and coordinating the coming world revolution. This Communist International, or Comintern, was based in Moscow and included representatives from 37 countries by 1920.

From 1924 to 1929, Bukharin and Stalin shared the view that the Comintern should promote the unity of working classes everywhere and should cooperate with existing worker organizations. In 1929, however, Stalin argued that advanced capitalist societies were teetering on the brink of new wars and revolutions. As a result, the Comintern must seek to sever the ties between Communist parties and social democratic parties in other countries to prepare for the revolutionary struggle. Stalin purged the Comintern of dissenters, and he decreed a policy of noncooperation in Europe from 1929 to 1933. As a result, socialism in Europe was badly split between Communists and democratic socialists, greatly facilitating the triumph of fascist movements, especially Nazism in Germany.

The Great Purge. Amid rapid industrialization, Stalin inaugurated the **Great Purge**, actually a series of purges lasting from 1934 through 1938. People whom Stalin believed to be his opponents—real and imagined, past, present, and future— were labeled "class enemies." The most prominent of them were given show trials. They were intimidated and tortured into false confessions of crimes against the regime and condemned to death or imprisonment. Stalin wiped out the Bolshevik old guard and all potential opposition within the Communist Party to his personal rule. Probably 300,000 people were put to death, among whom were engineers, managers, technologists, and officers of the army and navy. In addition, seven million people were placed in labor camps. The purges dealt a severe blow to the command of the army and resulted in a shortage of qualified industrial personnel, slowing industrial growth. But Stalin now had unquestioned control of the Party and the country.

Coerced and planned industrial growth brought with it a top-heavy and often inefficient bureaucracy, and that bureaucracy ensured that the Soviet Union was the most highly centralized of the European states. The growing threat of war posed by Nazi Germany meant an even greater diversion of resources from consumer goods to war industries, beginning with the Third Five-Year Plan in 1938.

Women and the Family in the New Soviet State

The building of the new Soviet state exacted particularly high costs from women. Soviet women had been active in the revolution from the beginning. Lenin and the Bolshevik leaders were committed to the liberation of women, who, like workers, were considered to be oppressed under capitalism.

After the October Revolution of 1917, the Bolsheviks passed a new law establishing equality for women within marriage. In 1920, abortion was legalized. New legislation established the right to divorce and removed the stigma from illegitimacy. Communes, calling themselves "laboratories of revolution," experimented with sexual equality. Russian women were enfranchised in 1917, the first women in a major country to win this right in national elections.

By the early 1930s, however, reforms affecting women were in trouble, largely because of a plummeting birthrate, which alarmed Soviet planners. In 1936, women's right to choose to end a first pregnancy was revoked. In the following decade, all abortions were made illegal. Homosexuality was declared a criminal offense. The family was glorified as the mainstay of the socialist order, and the independence of women was challenged as a threat to Soviet productivity. While motherhood was idealized, the Stalinist drive to industrialize could not dispense with full-time women workers.

Women's double burden in the home and workplace became heavier during Stalin's reign. Most Russian women held full-time jobs in the factories or on the farms. They also worked what they called a "second shift" in running a household and taking care of children. In the industrialized nations of western Europe, the growth of a consumer economy lightened women's labor in the home to some extent. In the Soviet Union, procuring the simplest necessities was women's work that required waiting in long lines for hours. Lack of indoor plumbing meant that women spent hours hauling water for their families at the end of a working day. In such ways, rapid industrialization exacted its special price from Soviet women.

The Rise of Fascist Dictatorship in Italy

Throughout western Europe, parliamentary institutions, representative government, and electoral politics offered no ready solutions to the problems of economic collapse and the political upheaval on the left and the right. **Fascism** promised what liberal democratic societies failed to deliver: a way out of the economic and political morass. Ruling by means of dictatorship by a charismatic leader, fascism promised an escape from parliamentary chaos, party wranglings, and the threat of communism. It also promised order and security.

Fascism was rooted in the mass political movements of the late nineteenth century, which emphasized nationalism, antiliberal values, and a politics of the irrational. The electoral successes of the German variant—National Socialism or **Nazism**—were just beginning in the late 1920s. In the same period, fascist movements appeared in England, Hungary, Spain, and France. But none was more successful than the fascist experiment in Italy.

Mussolini's Italy

Although Italy was one of the victorious Allies in World War I, Italians felt that their country had been betrayed by the peace settlement of 1919 by being denied the territory and status it deserved. A recently created electoral system based on universal manhood suffrage had produced parliamentary chaos and ministerial instability. People were beginning to doubt the parliamentary regime's hold on the future. It was under these circumstances that the Fascist Party, led by Benito Mussolini (1883–1945), entered politics in 1920 by attacking the large Socialist and Popular (Catholic) parties.

The Rise of Mussolini. Mussolini had begun his political career as a Socialist. An ardent nationalist, he volunteered for combat in World War I and was promoted to the rank of corporal. Injured in early 1917 by an exploding shell detonated during firing practice, he returned to Milan to continue his work as editor of *Il Populo d'Italia* ("The People of Italy"), the newspaper he founded in 1914 to promote Italian participation in the war.

Emphasizing nationalist goals and vague measures of socioeconomic transformation, Mussolini identified a new enemy for Italy: Bolshevism. He organized his followers into a highly disciplined Fascist Party, which quickly developed its own national network.

Many Fascists were former socialists and war veterans like Mussolini who were disillusioned with postwar government. They dreamed of Italy as a great world power, as it had been in the days of ancient Rome. Their enemies were not only the Communists with their international outlook but also the big businesses and unions. Panicky members of the lower middle classes sought security against the economic uncertainties of inflation and were willing to endorse violence to achieve it. Near civil war erupted as Italian Communists and Fascists clashed violently in street battles in the early 1920s. The Fascists entered the national political arena and succeeded on the local level in overthrowing city governments.

The March on Rome. On 28 October 1922, the Fascists, still a minority party, undertook their famous March on Rome, which followed similar Fascist takeovers in Milan and Bologna. Mussolini's followers occupied the capital. King Victor Emmanuel III invited Mussolini to form a government. Nationalist conservatives fully expected to be able to use the Fascists for their own ends. The accession of the new premier, however, marked the beginning of the end of parliamentary government and the emergence of Fascist dictatorship and institutionalized violence. Rising unemployment and severe inflation contributed to the politically deteriorating situation that helped to bring Mussolini to power.

Destruction and violence became fascism's most successful tools for securing political power. *Squadristi*, armed bands of Fascist thugs, attacked their political enemies, both Catholic and Socialist, destroyed private property, dismantled the printing presses of adversary groups, and generally terrorized both rural and urban populations.

The Fascists also used intimidation to secure votes. One outspoken Socialist critic of Fascist violence, Giacomo Matteotti, was murdered by Mussolini's subordinates in 1924. The deed threatened the survival of Mussolini's government as 150 Socialist, Liberal, and Popular party deputies resigned in protest. Mussolini chose that moment to consolidate his position by arresting and silencing his enemies. Within two years, Fascists were firmly in control, monopolizing politics, suppressing a free press, creating a secret police force, and transforming social and economic policies. Mussolini made Italy into a one-party dictatorship.

Dealing with Big Business and the Church. In 1925, the Fascist Party entered into an agreement with Italian industrialists that gave industry a position of privilege protected by the state in return for its support. Mussolini presented this partnership as the end to class conflict, but in fact it ensured the dominance of capital and the control of labor and professional groups. A corrupt bureaucracy run on bribes orchestrated the new relationship between big business and the state.

Mussolini, himself an atheist, recognized the importance of the Catholic Church in securing his regime. In 1870, when Italy was unified, the pope was deprived of his territories in Rome. This event, which became known as the "Roman Question," proved to be the source of ongoing problems for Italian governments.

In February 1929, in the Lateran Treaty and the accompanying Concordat, Mussolini granted the pope sovereignty over the territory around St. Peter's Basilica and the Vatican. The treaty also protected the role of the Catholic Church in education and guaranteed that Italian marriage laws would conform to Catholic dogma.

By 1929, as the Great Depression loomed, *Il Duce* ("the leader"), as Mussolini preferred to be called, was at the height of his popularity and power. Apparent political harmony had been achieved by ruthlessly crushing fascism's opponents. The agreement with the pope, which restored harmony with the Church, was matched by a new sense of order and accomplishment in Italian society and the economy.

Mussolini's Plans for Empire

As fascism failed to initiate effective social programs, Mussolini's popularity plummeted. In the hope of boosting his sagging image, Il Duce committed Italy to a foreign policy of imperial conquest.

Italy had conquered Ottoman-controlled Libya in North Africa in 1911. Now, in October 1935, Mussolini's troops invaded Ethiopia. Using poison gas and aerial bombing, the Italian army defeated the forces of Ethiopian emperor Haile Selassie (1930–1974).

The invasion of Ethiopia exposed the inability of the League of Nations to stop such flagrant violations. Great Britain and France protested Italy's conquest, and a rift opened up between these two western European nations and Italy. Mussolini had distanced himself from Nazi Germany. Now, however, in light of the disapproval of Britain and France, Mussolini turned to Germany for support. In October 1936, Italy and Germany concluded a friendship alliance. In May 1939, in an agreement known as the Pact of Steel, Germany and Italy drew closer, each agreeing to offer support to the other in any offensive or defensive war.

Hitler and the Third Reich

Repeated economic, political, and diplomatic crises of the 1920s buffeted Germany's internal stability. The German government did not actually promote inflation to avoid paying reparations, but it did do so to avoid a postwar recession, revive industrial production, and maintain high employment. But in 1923, the moderate inflation that stimulated the economy spun out of control into destructive hyperinflation.

The fiscal problems of the **Weimar Republic**, the new German government formed in 1919, obscure the fact that in the postwar period, Germany experienced real economic growth. Weimar committed itself to large expenditures for social welfare programs, including unemployment insurance. By 1930, social welfare was responsible for 40 percent of all public expenditures, compared to 19 percent before the war. All these changes, apparently fostering the well-being of the German people, aggravated the fears of German big businessmen, who resented the trade unions and the perceived trend toward socialism. The lower middle classes also felt cheated and economically threatened by inflation.

Growing numbers of Germans expressed disgust with parliamentary democracy. The Great Depression dealt a staggering blow to the Weimar Republic in 1929 as U.S. loans were withdrawn and German unemployment skyrocketed. By 1930, the antagonisms among the parties were so great that the parliament was no longer effective in ruling Germany. As chancellor from 1930 to 1932, Centrist leader Heinrich Brüning (1885–1970) tried to break this impasse by overriding the Weimar constitution. This move opened the door to enemies of the republic, and Brüning was forced to resign.

Hitler's Rise to Power

Aimlessness and failure marked Adolf Hitler's (1889–1945) early life. Denied admission to architecture school, he took odd jobs to survive. When war broke out in 1914, he volunteered immediately for service in the German army. Wounded and gassed at the front, he was twice awarded the Iron Cross for bravery in action.

The army provided Hitler with a sense of security and direction. The peace that followed determined his commitment to a career in politics. Hitler believed that Germany had not lost the war; it had been defeated from within, stabbed in the back by communists, socialists, liberals, and Jews. The Weimar Republic signed the humiliating Treaty of Versailles and continued to betray the German people by taxing wages to pay reparations. His highly distorted and false view of the origins of the Republic and its policies was the basis for his demand that the "Weimar System" be abolished and replaced by a Nazi regime.

The Beer Hall Putsch of 1923. In 1923, Hitler, now leading a small National Socialist German Workers party, the Nazis, attempted to seize control of the Munich municipal government. This effort, known as the Beer Hall Putsch, failed, and Hitler served nine months of a five-year sentence in prison. There he began writing the first volume of his autobiography, *Mein Kampf* ("My Struggle"). In this turgid work, he condemned the decadence of Western society and singled out for special contempt Jews, Bolsheviks, and middle-class liberals. From the Munich episode, Hitler learned that he could succeed against the German republic only from within, by coming to power legally. By 1928, he had a small party of about 100,000 Nazis. Modifying his anticapitalist message, Hitler appealed to the discontented small farmers and tailored his nationalist sentiments to a frightened middle class.

Hitler as Chancellor. Adolf Hitler became chancellor of Germany in January 1933 by legal, constitutional, and democratic means. The Nazi party received its heaviest support from farmers, small businessmen, civil servants, and young people. In the elections of 1930 and 1932, the voters made the Nazi party the largest party in the country—although not the majority one. President Paul von Hindenburg invited Hitler to form a government. Hitler claimed that Germany was on the verge of a Communist revolution, and he persuaded Hindenburg and the Reichstag to consent to a series of emergency laws, which the Nazis used to establish themselves firmly in power. Legislation outlawed freedom of the press and public meetings and approved the use of violence against Hitler's political enemies, particularly the Socialists and the Communists. Within two months after Hitler came to office, Germany was a police state, and Hitler was a legal dictator who could issue his own laws without having to gain the consent of either the Reichstag or the president. After carrying out this "legal revolution," the Nazis abolished all other political parties, established single-party rule, dissolved trade unions, and put their own people into state governments and the bureaucracy.

Hitler's political alliance with traditional conservative and nationalist politicians, industrialists, and military men helped to give the state created by Adolf Hitler, which he called the **Third Reich**, a claim to legitimacy based on continuity with the past. (The First Reich was the medieval German Empire; the Second Reich was the German Empire created by Bismarck in 1871.)

Nazi Goals

Hitler identified three organizing goals for the Nazi state: **Lebensraum** ("living space"), rearmament, and economic recovery. The goals were the basis of the new foreign policy Hitler forged for Germany, and they served to fuse that foreign policy with the domestic politics of the Third Reich. All three were based on Hitler's version of social Darwinism—that the German race was the fittest and would survive and prosper at the expense of others.

Living Space. Hitler first stated his ideals about *Lebensraum* in *Mein Kampf,* in which he argued that superior nations had the right to expand into the territories of inferior states. Living space meant for him German domination of central and eastern Europe at the expense of Slavic peoples. Germany had to annex territories, and Hitler's primary target was what he called "Russia and her vassal border states."

Rearmament. Hitler greatly escalated the secret rearmament of Germany begun by his Weimar predecessors in violation of the Treaty of Versailles. He withdrew Germany from the League of Nations and from the World Disarmament Conference, signaling a new direction for German foreign policy. In 1935, he publicly renounced the Treaty of Versailles and declared that Germany was rearming. The following year, he openly defied the French and moved German troops into the demilitarized Rhineland. In 1933, the German state was illicitly spending one billion Reichsmarks on arms, a figure that climbed to 30 billion by 1939.

Hitler knew that preparation for war would require full economic recovery. One of Germany's great weaknesses in World War I had been its dependence on imports of raw materials and foodstuffs. To avoid a repetition of this problem, Hitler instituted a program of autarky, or economic self-sufficiency, by which Germany aimed to produce everything that it consumed. He encouraged the efforts of German industry to develop synthetics for petroleum, rubber, metals, and fats.

Economic Recovery. The state pumped money into the private economy, creating new jobs and achieving full employment after 1936, an accomplishment that was unmatched by any other European nation. Recovery was built on armaments as well as consumer products. The Nazi state's concentration of economic power in the hands of a few strengthened big businesses. The victims of corporate consolidation were the small firms that could no longer compete with government-sponsored corporations such as the chemical giant I. G. Farben.

In 1936, Hitler introduced his Four-Year Plan, which was dedicated to the goals of full-scale rearmament and economic self-sufficiency. Before the third year of the Four-Year Plan, however, Hitler was aware of the failure to develop sufficient synthetic products to meet Germany's needs. But if Germany could not create substitutes, it could take over territories that provided the products Germany lacked.

Propaganda, Racism, and Culture

To reinforce his personal power and to sell his program for the total state, Hitler created a Ministry of Propaganda under Joseph Goebbels (1897–1945), a former journalist and Nazi Party district leader in Berlin. Goebbels was a master of manipulating emotions in mass demonstrations. With his magnetic appeal, Hitler inspired and manipulated the devotion of hundreds of thousands of those who heard him speak. Leni Riefenstahl, a young filmmaker working for Hitler, made a documentary of a National Socialist Party rally at Nuremberg. In scenes of swooning women and cheering men, her film, called *Triumph of the Will,* recorded the dramatic force of Hitler's rhetoric and his ability to move the German people. Hitler's public charisma masked a profoundly troubled and warped individual. Yet millions, including admirers in western Europe and the United States, succumbed to his appeal.

NATIONAL INCOME OF THE POWERS IN 1937 AND PERCENTAGE SPENT ON DEFENSE		
	National Income (billions of dollars)	Percentage Spent on Defense
United States	68	1.5
British Empire	22	5.7
France	10	9.1
Germany	17	23.5
Italy	6	14.5
USSR	19	26.4
Japan	4	28.2

Adolf Hitler salutes a huge crowd of Hitler Youth at a rally. The mass meetings were used by the Nazi mythmakers to enhance Hitler's image as the savior of Germany.

Targeting the Young and Women. The Nazi total state also sought to regulate family life. Special youth organizations were created for boys and girls between the ages of 10 and 18. After passage of the Hitler Youth Law in 1936, boys were required to join the Hitler Youth, which indoctrinated them with nationalistic and military values. Girls had to join the League of German Girls, which was intended to mold them into worthy wives and mothers. A woman's natural function, Hitler argued, was to serve in the home. Education for women beyond the care of home and family was a waste. In an effort to promote large families, the state paid allowances to couples for getting married, subsidized families according to their size, and gave tax breaks to large families. Abortion and birth control were outlawed.

Enemies of the State. Nazi propaganda condemned everything foreign, including Mickey Mouse, which was declared an enemy of the state in the 1930s. Purging foreign influences meant purging political opponents, especially members of the Communist Party, who were rounded up and sent to concentration camps in Germany. Communism was identified as an international Jewish conspiracy to destroy the German *Volk* (people of Aryan descent). Nazi literature also identified "asocials," those who were considered deviant in any way, including homosexuals, who were likewise to be expelled. Euthanasia was used on the mentally ill and the developmentally disabled in the 1930s. Concentration camps were expanded to contain enemies of the state. Later, when concentration camps became sites of extermination and forced labor, gypsies, homosexuals, criminals, and religious offenders had to wear insignia of different colors to indicate their basis for persecution. The people who received the greatest attention for elimination from Nazi Germany, and then from Europe, were Jews.

Scapegoating Jews. The first measures against the German Jews—their exclusion from public employment and higher education—began in 1933. In 1935, the Nuremberg Laws were enacted to identify Jews, to deprive them of their citizenship, and to forbid marriage and extramarital sexual relations between Jews and non-Jews. On the night of 9 November 1938, synagogues were set afire, and books and valuables owned by Jews were confiscated throughout Germany. Jews were beaten, about 91 were killed, and 20,000 to 30,000 were imprisoned in concentration camps. The night came to be called **Kristallnacht** ("night of broken glass"), which referred to the Jewish shop windows smashed by storm troopers under orders from Goebbels. The government claimed that *Kristallnacht* was an outpouring of the German people's will. An atmosphere of state-sanctioned hatred prevailed.

In addition to anti-Semitism, Hitler also placed other racist theories at the core of his fascist ideology. "Experts" decided that sterilization was the surest way to protect "German blood." In 1933, one of the early laws of Hitler's new Reich decreed compulsory sterilization of "undesirables" to "eliminate inferior genes." The Nazi state decided who these "undesirables" were and forced the sterilization of 400,000 men and women.

The Third Reich delivered on its promises to end unemployment, to improve productivity, to break through the logjam of parliamentary obstacles, and to return Germany to the international arena as a contender for power. Yet Hitler's Nazi government ruled by violence, coercion, and intimidation. With a propaganda machine that glorified the leader and vilified groups singled out as scapegoats for Germany's problems, Hitler destroyed democratic institutions and civil liberties in his pursuit of German power.

Democracies in Crisis

In contrast to the fascist mobilization of society and the Soviet restructuring of the economy, European democracies responded to the challenges of the Great Depression with small, tentative steps.

The Failure of the Left in France

France's Third Republic, like most European parliamentary democracies in the 1930s, was characterized by a multiparty system. Genuine political differences often separated one party from another. The tendency to parliamentary stalemate was aggravated by the depression and by the increasingly extremist politics on both the Left and the Right in response to developments in the Soviet Union and Germany.

In 1936, an electoral mandate for change swept the Left into power. The new premier, Léon Blum (1872–1950), was a Socialist. Lacking the votes to rule with an exclusively Socialist government, Blum formed a coalition of Left and Center parties that were intent on economic reforms, known as the **Popular Front**. Before Blum's government could take power, a wave of strikes swept France, and the

Popular Front was pushed to intervene. It promised wage increases, paid vacations, and collective bargaining to French workers. The reduced work week of 40 hours caused a drop in productivity, as did the short-lived one-month vacation policy. The government did nothing to prevent the outflow of investment capital from France. Higher wages failed to generate increased consumer demand because employers raised prices to cover their higher operating costs.

German rearmament, now publicly known, forced France into rearmament, which France could ill afford. Blum's government failed in 1937, with France still bogged down in a sluggish and depressed economy.

The radical Right drew strength from the Left's failures. Right-wing leagues and organizations multiplied, appealing to a frightened middle class. The failure of the Socialists, in turn, drove many sympathizers further to the Left to join the Communist Party. A divided France could not stand up to the foreign policy challenges of the 1930s posed by Hitler's provocations.

Muddling Through in Great Britain

Great Britain was hard hit by the Great Depression in the 1930s; only Germany and the United States experienced comparable economic devastation. The socialist Labour government of the years 1929 to 1931 under Prime Minister Ramsay MacDonald (1866–1937) was unprepared to deal with the 1929 collapse. It took a coalition of moderate groups from the three parties—Liberal, Conservative, and Labour—to address the issues of high unemployment, a growing government deficit, a banking crisis, and the flight of capital. The National Government (1931–1935) was a nonparty, centrist coalition whose members included Ramsay MacDonald, retained as prime minister, and Stanley Baldwin (1867–1947), a Conservative with a background in iron and steel manufacturing.

Slow Recovery. In response to the endemic crisis, the National Government took Britain off the international gold standard and devalued the pound. To protect domestic production, tariffs were established. The British economy showed signs of slow recovery, and the government survived the crisis. Moderates and classical liberals in Great Britain persisted in defending the nonintervention of the government in the economy, despite new economic theories, such as that of John Maynard Keynes (1883–1946), who urged government spending to stimulate consumer demand as the best way to shorten the duration of the depression.

The British Union of Fascists. Sir Oswald Mosley (1896–1980) promoted a fascist response to Britain's problems. In 1932, he founded the British Union of Fascists (BUF), consisting of goon squads and bodyguards. The BUF was opposed to free trade liberalism and communism alike. Like other European fascist organizations, BUF squads beat up their political opponents and began attacking Jews, especially eastern European émigrés living in London. Popular support for the group was already beginning to erode when the BUF was outlawed in 1936. By this time, anti-Hitler feeling was spreading in Great Britain. In Great Britain, the traditional party system prevailed not because of its brilliant solutions to difficult economic problems but because of the willingness of moderate parliamentarians to cooperate and to adapt, however slowly, to the new need for economic transformation.

Chronology

THE RISE OF FASCISM AND DEMOCRACY IN CRISIS

28 October 1922	Italian Fascists march on Rome
November 1923	Beer Hall Putsch in Munich
1924	Fascists achieve parliamentary majority in Italy
1929	Lateran Treaty between Mussolini and Pope Pius XI
1932	Nazi party is single largest party in German parliament
January 1933	Hitler becomes chancellor of Germany
March 1935	Hitler publicly rejects Treaty of Versailles and announces German rearmament
15 September 1935	Enactment of Nuremberg Laws against Jews and other minorities
3 October 1935	Italy invades Ethiopia
1936	Popular Front government elected in Spain
July 1936	Beginning of Spanish Civil War
October 1936	Rome-Berlin Axis Pact, an Italo-German accord
1936–1937	Popular Front government in France
27 April 1937	Bombing of the Spanish town of Guernica
9 November 1938	*Kristallnacht* initiates massive violence against Jews
March 1939	Fascists defeat the Spanish Republic
April 1939	Italy annexes Albania
May 1939	Pact of Steel between Germany and Italy

The Spanish Republic as Battleground

In 1931, Spain became a democratic republic after centuries of Bourbon monarchy and almost a decade of military dictatorship. In 1936, the voters of Spain elected a Popular Front government. The Popular Front in Spain was more radical than its French counterpart. The property of aristocratic landlords was seized; revolutionary workers went on strike; the Catholic Church and its clergy were attacked. This social revolution initiated three years of civil war. On one side were the Republicans, the Popular Front defenders of the Spanish Republic and of social revolution in Spain. On the other side were the Nationalists, those who sought to overthrow the Republic: aristocratic landowners, supporters of the monarchy and the Catholic Church, and much of the Spanish army.

The Spanish Civil War began in July 1936 with a revolt against the Republic from within the Spanish army. It was led by General Francisco Franco (1892–1975), a tough, shrewd, and stubborn conservative nationalist allied with the Falange, the fascist party in Spain.

Almost from the beginning, the Spanish Civil War was an international event. Mussolini sent "volunteer" ground troops to fight alongside Franco's forces. Hitler dispatched technical specialists, tanks, and the Condor Legion, an aviation unit, to support the Nationalists. The Germans regarded Spain as a testing ground for new equipment and new methods of warfare, including aerial bombardment. The Soviet Union intervened on the side of the Republic, sending armaments, supplies, and technical and political advisers. Because the people of Britain and France were deeply divided in their attitudes toward the war in Spain, the British government stayed neutral, and the government of France was unable to aid its fellow Popular Front government in Spain. Although individual Americans volunteered to fight with the Republicans, the U.S. government did not prevent the Texas Oil Company from selling oil to Franco's insurgents, nor did it block the Ford Motor Company, General Motors, and Studebaker from supplying them with trucks.

In response to the Spanish government's pleas for help, 2,800 American volunteers, among them college students, professors, intellectuals, and trade unionists, joined the loyalist army and European volunteers in defense of the Spanish Republic. Britons and antifascist émigrés from Italy and Germany also joined international brigades. The Russians withdrew from the war in 1938, disillusioned by the failure of the French, British, and Americans to come to the aid of the Republicans. Madrid fell to the Nationalists in March 1939. The government that Franco established sent one million of its enemies to prison or concentration camps.

SUMMARY

Crisis and Collapse in a World Economy   When World War I ended all of the belligerent nations carried enormous war debts. The issue of debt was compounded by the problem of Germany's reparation obligations and German hyperinflation. Trade barriers and depreciating currencies further complicated matters. The 1929 stock market crash in the United States triggered the Great Depression which, as a result of the pivotal role of the U.S. economy in the world, quickly became a global phenomenon.

The Soviet Union's Separate Path   The devastation of revolution and civil war forced Lenin to move away from Communist goals and adopt the New Economic Policy (NEP). After Lenin's death, Stalin rose to power and quickly moved to end the NEP and begin a series of five-year plans designed to produce rapid industrialization. The peasantry bore much of the burden of Soviet industrialization.

Collectivization of agriculture produced misery, famine, and death for millions. The Soviet Union established diplomatic relations with western nations in the 1920s. The Comintern involved itself in the affairs of Communist parties outside of the Soviet Union. Stalin's purges established him as the sole source of power and authority in the Soviet Union. Early reforms designed to liberate women were reversed in response to the challenges of the 1930s.

The Rise of Fascist Dictatorship in Italy   Political and economic instability in post-war Italy paved the way for the rise of Benito Mussolini and Italian fascism. Mussolini and his followers used violence and intimidation to rise to power. They promised a return to national glory and profound socioeconomic change. Accommodation with big business and the Catholic Church cemented Mussolini's hold on power. When his popularity began to fall, Mussolini launched a foreign policy of imperial conquest in an effort to revive his image. Italian conquest of Egypt brought condemnation from Britain and France, but little else. From the mid-1930s on, Italy and Germany grew closer together.

Hitler and the Third Reich   The Great Depression undermined the Weimar Republic and opened the door for Adolf Hitler and the Nazis. Hitler's political views were informed by his belief that Germany had not lost World War I, but had been betrayed by internal enemies. The failure of the 1923 Beer Hall Putsch demonstrated to Hitler that he could only come to power by working within the political system. Once appointed chancellor of Germany in 1933, Hitler and his party quickly moved to consolidate power in their own hands. Hitler had three organizing goals for the Nazi state: *Lebensraum* ("living space"), rearmament, and economic recovery. All three were based on his vision of German racial superiority. Propaganda played an important role in the Nazi state. The Nazis paid considerable attention to the regulation of family life. Jews were singled out as the particular enemies of the people and were subject to repression, discriminatory legislation, and violence.

Democracies in Crisis   European democracies responded to the challenges of the Great Depression with small, tentative steps. In 1936, the Popular Front, a coalition of Left and Center parties intent on economic reforms, came to power in France. Labor unrest and the costs of rearmament undermined the Popular Front. In Britain, a coalition of moderate groups from the three parties formed the National Government. The National Government's cautious policies produced slow recovery. As elsewhere, fascist groups arose in Britain to challenge the existing government. Civil war in Spain between Republicans and Nationalists became an international event. Italy and Germany supported the Nationalists and the Soviet Union supported the Republicans. General Francisco Franco and the Nationalists emerged victorious in 1939.

QUESTIONS FOR REVIEW

1. What problems for European stability were created or left unresolved by the armistice ending World War I?
2. What did Stalin's victory over Trotsky mean for economic development in the Soviet Union?
3. What is fascism, and why was it so alluring to Italians, Germans, and other Europeans?
4. How were rearmament, anti-Semitism, and economic self-sufficiency all part of Hitler's vision of *Lebensraum*?
5. Why did Europe's remaining democracies prove to be so frail during the 1930s?

Global Conflagration: World War II, 1939–1945

Aggression and Conquest

The years between 1933 and 1939 marked a bleak period in international affairs when the British, the French, and the Americans were unwilling or unable to recognize the dire threat to world peace of Hitler and his Nazi state. The war that began in Europe in 1939 eventually became a great global conflict that pitted Germany, Italy, and Japan—the **Axis Powers**—against the British Empire, the Soviet Union, and the United States—the Grand Alliance.

Even before war broke out in Europe, there was armed conflict in Asia. The rapidly expanding Japanese economy depended on Manchuria for raw materials and on China for markets. Chinese boycotts against Japanese goods and threats to

Japanese economic interests in Manchuria led to a Japanese military occupation of Manchuria and the establishment of the Japanese puppet state of Manchukuo there in 1931–1932. When the powers of the League of Nations, led by Great Britain, refused to recognize this state, Japan withdrew from the League. Fearing that the Chinese government was becoming strong enough to exclude Japanese trade from China, Japanese troops and naval units began an undeclared war in China in 1937. Thus the stage was set for a major military conflict in Asia and in Europe.

Hitler's Foreign Policy and Appeasement

For Hitler, a war against the Soviet Union for living space was inevitable. However, he wanted to avoid fighting anew the war that had led to Germany's defeat in 1914–1918. In World War I, Germany fought on two fronts, and German soldiers, civilians, and resources were exhausted. In the next war, Hitler wanted to avoid fighting Great Britain while battling Russia. He convinced himself that the British would remain neutral if Germany agreed not to attack the British Empire.

The Campaign Against Czechoslovakia. Encouraged by his success in annexing Austria in 1938, Hitler provoked a crisis in Czechoslovakia in the summer of the same year. He demanded "freedom" for the German-speaking people of the Sudetenland area of Czechoslovakia. His main objective, however, was to smash the Czech state, the major obstacle in central Europe to the launching of an attack on living space farther east.

Britain, seeking to avoid war, sent Prime Minister Neville Chamberlain (1869–1940) to reason with Hitler. Believing that transferring the Sudetenland, the German-speaking area of Czechoslovakia, to Germany was the only solution—and one that would redress some of the wrongs done to Germany after World War I— Chamberlain convinced France and Czechoslovakia to yield to Hitler's demands.

Appeasement at Munich. Chamberlain's actions were the result of British self-interest. British leaders agreed that their country could not afford another war like the Great War of 1914–1918. Defense expenditures had been dramatically reduced to devote national resources to improving domestic social services, protecting world trade, and fortifying Britain's global interests. Britain understood well its weakened position in its dominions. In the British hierarchy of priorities, defense of the British Empire ranked first, above defense of Europe, and Britain's commitment to western Europe ranked above the defense of eastern and central Europe.

Hitler's response to being granted everything he requested was to renege and issue new demands. One final meeting was held at Munich to avert war. On 29 September 1938, one day before German troops were scheduled to invade Czechoslovakia, Mussolini and the French prime minister, Edouard Daladier (1884–1970), joined Hitler and Chamberlain at Munich to discuss a peaceful resolution to the crisis.

At Munich, Chamberlain and Daladier again yielded to Hitler's demands. The Sudetenland was ceded to Germany, and German troops quickly moved to occupy the area. The policy of the British and French was dubbed "**appeasement**" to indicate the willingness to concede to demands to preserve peace. Yet Chamberlain was neither weak nor cowardly. His great mistake in negotiating with Hitler was assuming that Hitler was a reasonable man who, like all reasonable people, wanted to avoid another war.

Chamberlain thought that his mediation at Munich had won for Europe a lasting peace—"peace for our time," he reported. In fact, the policy of appeasement further destabilized Europe and accelerated Hitler's plans for European domination. Within months, Hitler cast aside the Munich agreement by annihilating Czechoslovakia. At the same time, Lithuania was pressured into surrendering Memel to Germany, and Hitler demanded control of Gdansk and the Polish Corridor. No longer could Hitler's goals be misunderstood.

Hitler's War, 1939–1941

In the tense months that followed the Munich meeting and the occupation of Prague, Hitler readied himself for war in western Europe. In May 1939, he formed a military alliance, the Pact of Steel, with Mussolini's Italy. Then Hitler and Stalin, previously self-declared enemies, shocked the West by joining their two nations in a pact of mutual neutrality, the Non-Aggression Pact of 1939. Opportunism lay behind Hitler's willingness to ally with the Communist state that he had denounced throughout the 1930s. A German alliance with the Soviet Union would, Hitler believed, force the British and the French to back down and to remain neutral while Germany conquered Poland—the last obstacle to a drive for expansion eastward—in a short, limited war. Stalin recognized the failure of the western European powers to stand up to Hitler. There was little possibility, he thought, of an alliance against Germany with the virulently anti-Communist Neville Chamberlain. The best Stalin could hope for was that the Germans and the Western powers would fight it out while the Soviet Union waited to enter the war at the most opportune moment. As an added bonus, Germany promised not to interfere if the Soviet Union annexed eastern Poland, Bessarabia, and the Baltic republics of Latvia and Estonia.

Finally recognizing Hitler's intent, the British and the French also signed a pact in the spring of 1939, promising assistance to Poland in the event of aggression. On 1 September 1939, Germany attacked Poland, and by the end of the month the vastly outnumbered Poles surrendered. Although the German army needed no assistance, the Soviet Union invaded Poland ten days before its collapse, and Germany and the Soviet Union divided the spoils.

War in Europe. Hitler's war, the war for German domination of Europe, had begun. But it had not begun the way he intended. Great Britain and France, true to their alliance with Poland and contrary to Hitler's expectations, declared war on Germany on 3 September 1939, even though they were unable to give any help to Poland. In the six months after the fall of Poland, no military action took place between Germany and the Allies, because Hitler postponed offensives in northern and western Europe due to poor weather conditions. This strange interlude, which became known as "the phony war," was a period of suspended reality in which France and Great Britain waited for Hitler to make his next move.

With the arrival of spring, Germany attacked Denmark and Norway in April 1940. Then on 10 May 1940, Hitler's armies invaded the Netherlands, Belgium, and Luxembourg. By the third week of May, German mechanized forces were racing through northern France toward the English Channel, cutting off the British and Belgian troops and 120,000 French forces from the rest of the French army.

In France, the German army fought a new kind of war called **blitzkrieg** ("lightning war"), so named because of its speed. The British and the French had expected the German army to behave much as it had in World War I, concentrating its striking forces in a swing through coastal Belgium and Holland to capture Paris. French strategists believed that France was safe because of the hilly and forested terrain that they thought was impassable. They also counted on the protection of the fortress wall known as the Maginot Line that France had built in the interwar period. The Maginot Line stretched for hundreds of miles but was useless against mobile tank divisions that outflanked it. With stunning speed, Germany drove its tanks—panzers—through the French defenses at Sedan in eastern France.

A German motorized detachment rides through a bomb-shattered town during the Nazi invasion of Poland in 1939. The invasion saw the first use of the *blitzkrieg*—lightning war—in which air power and rapid tank movement combined for swift victory.

MAP DISCOVERY

Axis powers
August 1939

Extent of Axis
control, May 1941

Allies

Neutral nations

Axis offenses

Allied offenses

Major battles

WORLD WAR II IN EUROPE

Note the movement of Axis armies in four different directions: north, south, east, and west. How were the Axis forces able to sustain a multifront war? The Axis Powers controlled most of Europe and north Africa by 1941. How do you explain the success of major Allied offensives?

The Fall of France. The French could have pinched off the advance of the overextended panzers, but the French army, suffering from severe morale problems, collapsed and was in retreat. On 17 June 1940, only weeks after German soldiers had stepped on French soil, Marshal Henri-Philippe Pétain, the great hero of the battle of Verdun in World War I, petitioned the Germans for an armistice. Threefifths of France, including the entire Atlantic seaboard, was occupied by the German army and placed under direct German rule. In the territory that remained unoccupied, Pétain created a collaborationist government that resided at Vichy, a spa city in central France, and worked in partnership with the Germans for the rest of the war. Charles de Gaulle (1890–1970), a brigadier general who was opposed to the armistice, fled to London, where he set up a Free French government in exile.

The Battle of Britain. French capitulation in June 1940 followed Italian entry into the war on the side of Germany in the same month. The British were now alone in a war against the two Axis powers as Germany made plans for an invasion of the British Isles from across the English Channel. To prepare the way, the German air

The London Underground was pressed into service as a bomb shelter during the Battle of Britain.

force under Reichsmarshal Hermann Göring (1893–1946) launched a series of air attacks against England, which became known as the Battle of Britain.

Under the leadership of Winston Churchill the British resisted these attacks. Churchill had succeeded Chamberlain as prime minister in 1940. He was a master public speaker who, in a series of radio broadcasts, inspired the people of Britain with the historic greatness of the task confronting them: holding out against Nazism until the forces of the overseas British Empire and the United States could be marshaled to liberate Europe. The British Royal Air Force inflicted serious losses on German aircraft, while British industry was able to maintain steady production of planes, bombs, and armaments. Recognizing his lack of success in establishing air superiority over the Channel or in breaking the will of the British people, Hitler abandoned the Battle of Britain and canceled the invasion.

It was not in Great Britain but in the Balkans that Hitler was able to engage the British enemy and inflict serious losses. The British had a presence in the Greek peninsula, where their air units were deployed to support the valiant resistance of the Greeks against Italian aggression. In his original plans for a limited war, Hitler hoped to establish control over the Balkans by peaceful, diplomatic means. But Mussolini's disastrous attempt to achieve military glory by conquering Greece impelled Hitler to make his own plans to attack Greece. Yugoslavia and Greece fell in April 1941.

The Balkans were important to Hitler for a number of reasons. Half of Germany's wheat and livestock came from the countries of southeastern Europe.

Romanian and Hungarian oil fields supplied Germany's only non-Russian oil. Greece and Yugoslavia were important suppliers of metal ores—including aluminum, tin, lead, and copper—so necessary for industry and the war effort.

The necessity of protecting resources, especially the Romanian oil fields, also gave the area geopolitical importance for Germany. Hitler was well aware of the strategic significance of controlling the Dardanelles in launching an attack against the Soviet Union. Potentially, the British lifeline to its empire could also be cut by control of the eastern Mediterranean.

Collaboration and Resistance

No one nation has ever controlled the Balkans, and Hitler understood that he must rule not by occupation but by collaboration. Some Balkan collaborators joined puppet governments out of an ideological commitment to fascism. Some governments collaborated with the Germans out of national self-interest. The government of Hungary, for example, allied with Germany in the hope of winning back territory lost at the end of World War I. Other collaborators were pragmatists who believed that by taking political office, they could negotiate with the German conquerors and soften the effects of the Nazi conquest on their people.

Resistance against German occupation and collaborationist regimes took many forms. Resisters wrote subversive tracts, distributed them, gathered intelligence information for the Allies, sheltered Jews or other enemies of the Nazis, committed acts of sabotage, assassination or other violent acts, and carried on guerrilla warfare against the German army. Resistance movements developed most strongly after the German attack on the Soviet Union in 1941, when the Communist parties of occupied Europe formed the core of the violent resistance against the Nazi regime. Resistance grew stronger when the Germans began to draft young European men for work on German farms and in German factories.

One of the great resistance fighters of the Second World War was Josip Broz (1892–1980), alias Tito. He was a Croatian communist and a Yugoslav nationalist. His partisans fought against Italian and German troops and kept 10 or more German divisions tied up in Yugoslavia. Tito gained the admiration and the support of Churchill, Roosevelt, and Stalin. After liberation, Tito's organization won 90 percent of the vote in the Yugoslav elections, and he became the leader of the country in the postwar era.

Racism and Destruction

In both the European and Asian theaters of battle, claims of racial superiority were invoked to justify inhuman atrocities. The Germans and Japanese used spurious arguments of racial superiority to fuel their war efforts. But the Germans and the Japanese were not alone in using racist propaganda. The United States employed racial stereotypes to depict the inferiority of the enemy. They seized the property of Japanese-Americans living on the West Coast and interned them in "relocation" camps. Nowhere, however, was the use of racism by the state more virulent than in Germany.

Enforcing Nazi Racial Policies

Social policies that were erected on horrifying biomedical theories discriminated against a variety of social groups in the Third Reich. Beginning in 1933, police harassment of those identified as gypsies began in earnest. Gypsies were subject to all racialist legislation and could be sterilized for their "inferiority" without any formal hearing process. Over 200,000 German, Russian, Polish, and Balkan gypsies were killed in the course of the war by internment in camps and by systematic extermination.

People who suffered from hereditary illnesses were also labeled a biological threat to the racial purity of the German people. Medical officials examined children, and those who were judged to be deformed were separated from their families and transferred to special pediatric clinics, where they were either starved to death or injected with lethal drugs. In the summer of 1939, the government organized euthanasia programs for adults and identified 65,000 to 70,000 Germans for death. The government required asylums to rank patients according to their race, state of health, and ability to work. These rankings were used to determine candidates for death. In Poland, mental patients were simply shot; in other places they were starved to death. The uncooperative, the sick, and the disabled were purged as racially undesirable.

The category covering the "asocial" was even broader than that covering hereditary illness. Under this designation, criminals, beggars, vagrants, and the homeless could be compulsorily sterilized. Alcoholics, prostitutes, and people with sexually transmitted diseases could be labeled asocial and treated accordingly. These forms of behavior were considered to be hereditary and determined by blood.

Nazi social policies likewise treated homosexuals as "community aliens." The persecution of homosexual men intensified after 1934, when any form of "same-sex immorality" became subject to legal prosecution. But because homosexuality was judged to be a sickness rather than an immutable biological trait, gays did not become the primary object of Nazi extermination policies that began to be enforced against the "biologically inferior." Treatment of homosexuality might involve psychoanalysis, castration, or indefinite incarceration in a concentration camp. Although it is not clear how many homosexuals were actually killed by the Nazis, estimates run as high as 200,000.

The Destruction of Europe's Jews

In 1933, when Hitler and the Nazis came to power, they did not have a blueprint for the destruction of Europe's Jews. The anti-Semitic policies of the Third Reich evolved incrementally in the 1930s and 1940s. After 1938, German civil servants expropriated Jewish property as rightfully belonging to the state. When the war began, Jews were rounded up and herded into urban ghettos in Germany and in the large cities of Poland. Until 1941, Nazi policies against the Jews were often uncoordinated and unfocused.

The Final Solution. Confinement in urban ghettos was the beginning of a policy of concentration that ended in annihilation. After identifying Jews, seizing their property, and confining them to ghettos, German authorities began to implement a step-by-step plan for extermination. There appears to have been no single order from Hitler that decreed what became known to German officials as the **Final Solution**—the total extermination of European Jews. But Hitler's recorded remarks make it clear that he knew and approved of what was being done to the Jews. A spirit of shared purpose permeated the entire administrative system from the civil service through the judiciary.

Mass racial extermination began with the German conquest of Poland, where both Jews and non-Jews were systematically killed. It continued when Hitler's army invaded the Soviet Union in 1941. This campaign, known as Operation Barbarossa, set off the mass execution of eastern Europeans who were declared to be enemies of the Reich. The tactics of the campaign pointed the way to the Final Solution. To the Nazi leadership, Slavs were subhuman, and by extension, Russian Jews were the lowest of the low, even more despised than German Jews.

The executions were the work of the SS, the elite military arm of the Nazi Party. Special mobile murder squads of the SD under Reinhard Heydrich (1904–1942) were organized behind the German lines in Poland and Russia. Members of the army were aware of what the SS squads were doing and participated in some of the extermination measures.

Firing squads shot Russian victims en masse, then piled their bodies on top of one another in open graves. Reviewing these procedures for mass killings, SS chief Heinrich Himmler—ever competitive with other Nazi agencies—suggested a more efficient means of extermination that would require less labor power and would enhance the prestige of the SS. As a result, extermination by gas was introduced; the exhaust fumes of vans were piped into the enclosed cargo areas that served as portable gas chambers. In Poland, Himmler replaced the vans with permanent buildings housing gas chambers, which used Zyklon B, a gas developed for the purpose by the chemical firm I. G. Farben. The chambers could annihilate thousands of people at a time.

The Third Reich began erecting its vast network of death in 1941. The first extermination camp was created in Chelmno, Poland, where 150,000 people were killed between 1941 and 1944. The camps practiced systematic extermination of the groups that were deemed racially inferior, sexually deviant, and politically dangerous. The term **Holocaust** has been used to describe the mass slaughter of European Jews, most of which took place in five major killing centers in what is now Polish territory: Chelmno, Belzec, Sobibor, Treblinka, and Auschwitz.

Seizing Jews in Warsaw. Nazi soldiers rounded up men, women, and children for "resettlement" in the east.

Many victims, transported for days in sealed railroad cars without food, water, or sanitation facilities, died before ever reaching the camps. Others died within months as forced laborers for the Reich. People of all ages were starved, beaten, and systematically humiliated. Guards taunted their victims verbally, degraded them physically, and tortured them with false hope. Having been promised clean clothes and nourishment, camp internees were herded into "showers" that dispensed gas rather than water. Descriptions of life in the camps reveal a systematized brutality and inhumanity on the part of the German, Ukrainian, and Polish guards toward their victims. In all, 11 million people died by the extermination process—6 million Jews and almost as many non-Jews, including children, the aged, homosexuals, Slavic slave laborers, Soviet prisoners of war, Communists, members of the Polish and Soviet leadership, various resisters, gypsies, and Jehovah's Witnesses.

On entering the camps, the sick and the aged were automatically designated for extermination because of their uselessness as a labor force. Many children were put to work, but some were designated for extermination. Many mothers chose to accompany their children to their deaths to comfort them in their final moments. Pregnant women, too, were considered useless in the forced labor camps and were sent immediately to the "showers." The number of German Jewish women who died in the camps was 50 percent higher than the number of German Jewish men. Starvation diets meant that women stopped menstruating. Because the Nazis worried that women of childbearing age would continue to reproduce, women who showed signs of menstruation were killed immediately. Women who were discovered to have given birth in the camp were killed, as were their infants. Family relations were completely destroyed, as inmates were segregated by sex. It soon became clear that even those who were allowed to live were intended only to serve the Nazis' short-term needs.

Resisting Destruction. The impossibility of any effective resistance was based on two essential characteristics of the process of extermination. First, the entire German state and its bureaucratic apparatus were involved in the policies, laws, and decrees of

THE HOLOCAUST. The greatest loss of Jewish life in the Holocaust took place in Poland and the Soviet Union.

the 1930s that singled out victims while most other Germans stood silently by. There was no possibility of appeal and no place to hide. Those who understood early what was happening and who had enough money to buy their way out emigrated to safer places, including Palestine and the United States. But most countries used immigration quotas to block the entry of German and eastern European refugees. Neither Britain nor the United States was willing to deal with a mass influx of European Jews. Jews in the occupied countries and the Axis nations had virtually no chance to escape.

A second reason for the impossibility of effective resistance was the step-by-step nature of the process of extermination, which meant that few understood the final outcome until it was too late. The German authorities deliberately cultivated misunderstanding of what was happening.

Isolated instances of resistance in the camps—rioting at Treblinka, for example—only highlight how impossible rebellion was for physically debilitated people in these heavily guarded centers. In April 1943, in the Warsaw ghetto, Jews organized a resistance movement with a few firearms and some grenades and home-made Molotov cocktails. The uprising did not succeed in blocking the completion of the Final Solution against the Warsaw ghetto the following year, when the SS commandant proclaimed, "The Jewish Quarter of Warsaw is no more!" Polish and Russian Jews accounted for 70 percent of total Jewish deaths.

Who Knew? It is impossible that killing on such a scale could have been kept secret. Along with those who ordered extermination operations, the guards and camp personnel who were involved in carrying out the directives were aware of what was happening. Those who brought internees to the camps, returning always with empty railroad cars, knew it, too. People who saw their neighbors disappearing believed for a time that they were being resettled in the east. But as news filtered back to central and western Europe, it was more difficult to sustain belief in this ruse. People who lived near the camps could not ignore the screams and the fumes of gas and burning bodies that permeated the environs of the camps.

There were some heroes, such as Raoul Wallenberg of Sweden, who interceded for Hungarian Jews and provided food and protection for Jews in the Budapest ghetto. The king of Denmark, when informed that the Nazis had ordered Danish Jews to wear the yellow star, stated that he and his family would also wear the yellow star as a "badge of honor." However, heroic acts were isolated and rare.

Collaborationist governments and occupied nations often cooperated with Nazi extermination policies. The French government at Vichy introduced and implemented a variety of anti-Jewish measures. All of this was done without German orders and without German pressure. By voluntarily identifying and deporting Jews, the Vichy government sent 75,000 men, women, and children to their deaths.

As the war dragged on for years, internees of the camps hoped and prayed for rescue by the Allies. But such help did not come. The U.S. State Department and the British Foreign Office had early and reliable information about the nature and extent of the atrocities. But they did not act.

The Final Solution was a perversion of every value of civilization. The international tribunal for war crimes that met in 1945 in the German city of Nuremberg attempted to mete out justice to the criminals who were responsible for the destruction of 11 million Europeans who had been labeled as demons and racial inferiors. History must record, even if it cannot explain, such inhumanity.

Allied Victory

After a string of German victories between 1939 and 1941, the situation appeared grim for the British and their dominions and the Americans who were assisting them with munitions, money, and food. Hitler had achieved control of a vast land empire covering nearly all of continental Europe in the west, north, south, and center, as well as much of North Africa.

Then, in June 1941, Hitler's troops invaded the Soviet Union, providing the British with an ally. In December, the naval and air forces of Japan attacked U.S. bases in the Pacific, providing the British and the Russians with still another ally. What began as a European war became a world war. This was the war that Hitler did not want and that Germany could not win—a long, total war to the finish against three powers with inexhaustible resources: the British Empire, the Soviet Union, and the United States.

The Soviet Union's Great Patriotic War

Hitler had always considered the Soviet Union Germany's primary enemy. The 1939 Non-Aggression Pact with Stalin was no more than an expedient for Hitler.

Soviet Unpreparedness. On 22 June 1941, when German armies marched into Russia, they found the large Soviet army totally unprepared for war. Stalin's purges in the late 1930s removed 35,000 officers from their posts by dismissal, imprisonment, or execution. Many of the men who replaced them were unseasoned in the responsibilities of leadership. The Russians had not expected the German attack to come so soon, and when the Germans did invade Russian territory, Stalin was so overwhelmed that he fell into a depression and was unable to act for days.

On 3 July 1941, in his first radio address after the attack, Stalin identified his nation with the Allied cause. He accepted offers of support from the United States and Great Britain. With France defeated and Great Britain crippled, the future of the war depended on Soviet fighting power and U.S. supplies.

German Offensive and Reversals. Instead of exclusively targeting Moscow, the capital, the German army concentrated first on destroying Soviet armed forces and capturing Leningrad in the north and the oil-rich Caucasus in the south. In the beginning, the German forces advanced rapidly in a blitzkrieg across western Russia, where they were greeted as liberators in Ukraine. The Germans took 290,000 prisoners of war and massacred tens of thousands of others in their path through the Jewish settlements of western Russia.

Within four months, the German army had advanced to the gates of Moscow, but they concentrated their forces too late. The Red Army rallied to defend Moscow, as thousands of civilian women set to work digging trenches and antitank ditches around the city. The Soviet people answered Stalin's call for a scorched-earth policy by burning everything that might be useful to the advancing German troops. German troops had also burned much in their path, depriving themselves of essential supplies for the winter months ahead. The German advance was stopped, as the best ally of the Red Army—the Russian winter—settled in.

By early December, the German military situation was desperate. The Soviets, benefiting from intelligence information about German plans and an awareness that Japan was about to declare war on the United States, recalled fresh troops from the Siberian frontier and the border with China and Manchuria and launched a powerful counterattack against the poorly outfitted German army outside Moscow. Under the command of General Gyorgi Zhukov (1896–1974), Russian troops pushed the Germans back in retreat across the snow-covered expanses. By February, 200,000 German troops had been killed, 46,000 were missing in action, and 835,000 were casualties of battle and the weather. Thus the campaign cost the German army over one million casualties. It probably cost the Soviets twice that number of wounded, missing, captured, and dead soldiers. At the end of the Soviet counterattack in March, the German army and its satellite forces were in a shambles reminiscent of Napoleon's troops, who had been decimated 130 years earlier in the campaign to capture Moscow. An enraged Hitler dismissed his generals for retreating without his permission, and he himself assumed the position of commander-in-chief of the armed forces.

Hitler was not daunted by the devastating costs of his invasion of Russia. In the summer of 1942, he initiated a second major offensive, this time to take the city of Stalingrad. Constant bombardment gutted the city, and the Soviet army was forced into hand-to-hand combat with the German soldiers. But the German troops failed to capture the city. The Battle of Stalingrad was over in the first days of February 1943. Of the original 300,000 members of the German Sixth Army, fewer than 100,000 survived to be taken prisoner by the Soviets. Of those, only 5,000 returned to Germany in 1955, when German prisoners of war were repatriated.

Soviet Patriotism. The Soviets succeeded by exploiting two great advantages in their war against Germany: the large Soviet population and their knowledge of Russian weather and terrain. There was a third advantage that Hitler ignored: the Soviet people's determination to sacrifice everything for the war effort. In his successive Five-Year Plans, Stalin had mobilized Soviet society with an appeal to fulfill and surpass production quotas. In the summer of 1941, as Hitler's troops threatened Moscow, Stalin used the same rhetoric to appeal to his Soviet "brothers and sisters" to join him in waging "the Great Patriotic War." The Russian people shared a sense of common purpose, sacrifice, and moral commitment in their loyalty to the nation.

The advancing Germans themselves intensified Soviet patriotism by torturing and killing tens of thousands of peasants who might have willingly cooperated against the Stalinist regime. Millions of Soviet peasants joined the Red Army. Young men of high school age were drafted into the armed forces. Three million women became wage earners for the first time as they replaced men in war industries. Women who remained on the land worked to feed the townspeople and the soldiers. Tens of thousands of Russians left their homes in western Russia to work for relocated Soviet industries in the Urals, the Volga region, Siberia, and Central Asia.

More than 20 million Soviet people—soldiers and civilians, men, women, and children—died in the course of World War II. In addition to those who were killed in battle, millions starved as a direct result of the hardships of war. But Soviet resistance did not flag.

The Great Patriotic War had a profound impact on Soviet views of the world and the Soviet Union's place in it. Soviet citizens correctly considered that they had given more than any other country to defeat Hitler. For the Soviet people their suffering in battle made World War II the Soviet Union's war, and their sacrifice made possible the Allied victory.

The United States Enters the War

Victory still eluded the Allies in western Europe, where another nation, the United States, had now entered the fray. Although a neutral power, the United States began extending aid to the Allies after the fall of France in 1940. Since neither Britain nor the Soviet Union could afford to pay the entire cost of defending Europe against Hitler, the U.S. Congress passed the Lend-Lease Act in 1941. This act authorized President Roosevelt to provide armaments to Great Britain and the Soviet Union without payment. America became "the arsenal of democracy."

Tank Production in 1944

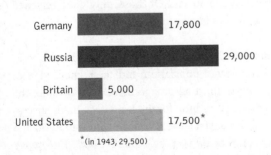

Germany	17,800
Russia	29,000
Britain	5,000
United States	17,500[*]

[*] (in 1943, 29,500)

Japan Attacks. Before the United States entered the war, President Roosevelt and his advisers considered Germany, not Japan, to be America's primary target for a future war. The United States, aware that Japan wanted to expand its control over China and Southeast Asia, initially opposed this expansion through economic embargoes. The presence of the Soviet Union pressing eastward across Asia, coupled with the colonial presences in Asia of Great Britain, France, and the United States, severely constrained Japan's capacity to expand its frontiers and ensure its security. The war in western Europe and the German invasion of the Soviet Union in June 1941 meant that the Japanese could concentrate their attention farther south in China, Indochina, and Thailand. Japan's limited reserves of foreign currency and raw materials drew its attention to the oil and raw materials in Southeast Asia.

In September 1940, Japan joined forces with the Axis Powers of Germany and Italy in the Tripartite Pact, in which the signatories, promising mutual support against aggression, acknowledged the legitimacy of each other's expansionist efforts in Europe and Asia. Japanese-American relations deteriorated after the Japanese invasion of southern Indochina in July 1941. The United States insisted that Japan vacate China and Indochina and reestablish the open door for trade in Asia. However, the United States knew that it was only a matter of time until Japan attacked U.S. interests but was uncertain about where that attack would take place.

On Sunday morning, 7 December 1941, Japan struck at the heart of the U.S. Pacific Fleet, which was stationed at Pearl Harbor, Hawaii. The attack crippled U.S. naval power in the Pacific as the U.S. Navy suffered its worst loss in history in a single engagement. The attack on Pearl Harbor led the United States immediately to declare war on Japan. In President Roosevelt's words, 7 December 1941 was "a date which will live in infamy."

In the next three months, Japan captured Hong Kong, Malaya, and the important naval base at Singapore from the British, taking 60,000 prisoners. In December 1941, the Japanese landed in Thailand and secured immediate agreement for Japanese occupation of strategic spots in the country. They then turned to the Malay peninsula, decisively defeating the British fleet off Malaya and pushing on the ground toward Singapore, which they conquered in February 1942. They conquered British Borneo in January, drove the Dutch from all of Indonesia but New Guinea, pushed U.S. forces in the Philippines into the Bataan peninsula, occupied Burma, and inflicted severe defeats on British, Dutch, and U.S. naval power in East Asia. U.S. General Douglas MacArthur (1880–1964) surrendered the Philippines to the Japanese on 2 January 1942 with the promise to return. With the armies of Germany deep in Russian territory, Australia faced the threat of a Japanese invasion.

Germany Declares War on the United States. Germany, with its armies retreating from Moscow, nevertheless declared war on the United States on

11 December 1941. Within days the United States, a nation with an army smaller than Belgium's, had gone from neutrality to a war in two theaters. Although militarily weak, the United States was an economic giant, commanding a vast industrial capacity and access to resources. The United States grew even stronger under the stimulus of war, increasing its production by 400 percent in two years. It now devoted itself to the demands of a total war and the unconditional surrender of Germany and then Japan.

Winning the War in Europe

The Allies did not always have the same strategies or concerns. President Roosevelt and Prime Minister Churchill had already discussed common goals in the summer of 1941 before U.S. entry into the war. The United States embraced the priority of the European war and the postponement of war in the Pacific. Stalin pleaded for the British and the Americans to open up a second front against Germany in western Europe to give his troops some relief and save Soviet lives. Anglo-American resources were committed to the Pacific to stop the Japanese advance, and the Americans and the British disagreed as to where a second front in Europe might be opened.

The second front came not in western Europe but in the Mediterranean. After the defeat of France in 1940 and the neutralization of the French navy in the Mediterranean, Italy saw a chance to extend its empire in North Africa. With a large army stationed in Libya, Ethiopia, Eritrea, and Italian Somaliland, Mussolini ordered a series of offensives against the Sudan, Kenya, British Somaliland, and Egypt. Most of the Italian advances had been reversed by the British, and 420,000 Italian troops, including African soldiers, were listed as casualties, compared to 3,100 British troops. Germany, however, having succeeded in invading Greece and Yugoslavia, turned its attention to aiding its Axis partner in trouble. In February 1941, Hitler sent General Erwin Rommel (1891–1944), a master strategist of tank warfare, to help the Italians take control of the Suez Canal by launching a counteroffensive in the North African war. Rommel's Axis troops succeeded in entering Egypt and driving the British east of the Egyptian border, thereby dealing the British a serious setback.

The British were simultaneously securing territories in Syria, Palestine, and Iraq to guarantee the oil pipelines of the Persian Gulf for the Allies. Between November 1941 and July 1942, the pendulum swung back and forth between Allied and Axis forces in the Desert War, as the North African campaign came to be known. In August 1942 the Allied forces, now under the command of Bernard Montgomery (1887–1976), launched a carefully planned offensive at El Alamein, and Rommel was forced to retreat to Tunisia.

Now a joint U.S.-British initiative, the first of the war, landed troops in French Morocco and Algeria and advanced into Tunisia, attacking Rommel's Afrika Korps

A United States Army unit joins Allied forces at the beachheads of Normandy during Operation Overlord in 1944. The invasion began the opening of the second front that Stalin had been urging on the Allies since the German armies thrust into Russia in 1941.

from behind. About 250,000 German and Italian soldiers were taken prisoner, as the Axis Powers were decisively defeated in May 1943.

Because of British interests in the Mediterranean, Churchill insisted on a move from North Africa into Sicily and Italy. This strategy was put into effect in 1942. The Italian government withdrew from the war in September, but German troops carried on the fight in Italy. The Anglo-American invasion of Italy did little to alleviate Russian losses, and the Soviet Union absorbed almost the entire force of German military power until 1944. Stalin's distrust of his allies increased. Churchill, Roosevelt, and Stalin met for the first time in late November 1943 in Teheran, Iran. Roosevelt and Churchill made a commitment to Stalin to open a second front in France within six months. Stalin, in turn, promised to attack Japan to aid the United States in the Pacific. The great showdown of the global war was at hand.

On 6 June 1944, Allied troops under the command of the U.S. General Dwight D. Eisenhower (1890–1969) came ashore on the beaches of Normandy in the largest amphibious landing in history. In a daring operation identified by the code name Operation Overlord, 2.2 million U.S., British, and Free French forces, 450,000 vehicles, and 4 million tons of supplies poured into northern France. Allied forces broke through German lines to liberate Paris in late August. The Germans launched a last-ditch counterattack in late December 1944 in Luxembourg and Belgium. This Battle of the Bulge only slowed the Allied advance; in March 1945, U.S. forces crossed the Rhine into Germany. The final German defeat came in April 1945, when the Russians stormed the German capital of Berlin. Hitler, living in an underground bunker near the Chancellery building, committed suicide on 30 April 1945.

Japanese War Aims and Assumptions

Japan and the United States entered the Pacific war with very different understandings of what was at stake. Initially, the Japanese appealed to Southeast Asian leaders as the liberators of Asian peoples from Western colonialism and imperialism.

Japanese Hegemony in Asia. The approach struck a responsive chord as the Japanese established what they called the Greater East Asia Co-Prosperity Sphere. The Greater East Asia Co-Prosperity Sphere began in 1940 and lasted until the summer of 1945. This reorganization of east and southeast Asia under Japanese hegemony constituted a redefinition of world geography with Japan at the center. The Japanese fashioned a romanticized vision of the family living in harmony, all members knowing their places and enjoying the complementary division of responsibilities and reciprocities that made family life work smoothly. Behind this pleasant image lurked the reality of a brutal power structure forcing subject peoples to accept massively inferior positions in a world fashioned exclusively to satisfy Japanese desires and needs. The Japanese viewed southeast Asia principally as a market for Japanese manufactured goods, a source of raw materials, and a source of profits for Japanese capital invested in mining, rubber, and raw cotton. Plans were made for hydroelectric power and aluminum-refining facilities.

Wartime Japanese nakedly displayed their disdain for the people they conquered in southeast Asia. All subject peoples were to bow on meeting a Japanese, while at public assemblies a ritual bow in the direction of the Japanese emperor was required. Japanese holidays, such as the emperor's birthday, were enforced as Co-Prosperity Sphere holidays, and the calendar was reset to the mythical founding of the Japanese state in 660 B.C.E.

The Japanese were less brazen toward the Chinese in their rhetoric, in part because so much of Japanese, and indeed East Asian, civilization had its roots in China. However, Japanese aggression against the Chinese included one of the worst periods of destruction in modern warfare. When the Japanese took over the Nationalist capital of Nanjing in December 1937, 20,000 women were raped, 30,000 soldiers were killed, and another 12,000 civilians died in the more than six weeks of wanton terror inflicted by Japanese soldiers.

Japan's View of the West. With regard to Westerners, Japanese propaganda avoided labeling them as inferior. In part, this reflected Japan's economic and political emulation of the West since the late nineteenth century. Rather than denigrating Western people, the Japanese chose to elevate themselves as a people descended from divine origins. Stressing their unique mythical history gave the Japanese a strong sense of moral superiority, which perhaps led them to misread Westerners. For example, some Japanese mistakenly assumed that individual selfishness and egoism would make Americans and Europeans incapable of mobilizing for a long fight.

WORLD WAR II IN THE PACIFIC, 1941–1945

Japan extended control throughout east and southeast Asia until the Japanese Empire reached its pinnacle in August 1942. Note the direction of major Allied offensives and the necessity of coordinated land, sea, and air offensives. Why were Hiroshima and Nagasaki chosen as atomic bomb targets?

Winning the War in the Pacific

The tide in the Pacific war began to turn when the planned Japanese invasion of Australia was thwarted. Fighting in the jungles of New Guinea, Australian and U.S. troops under the command of General Douglas MacArthur turned back the Japanese army. U.S. Marines did likewise with a bold landing at Guadalcanal and months of bloody fighting in the Solomon Islands. In June 1942, within six months of the attack on Pearl Harbor, U.S. naval forces commanded by Admiral Chester Nimitz (1885–1966) inflicted a defeat on the Japanese navy from which it could not recover. In the Battle of Midway, Japan lost four aircraft carriers, a heavy cruiser, over 300 airplanes, and 5,000 men. Midway was the Pacific equivalent of the Battle of Stalingrad.

In the summer of 1943, as the Soviet Union launched the offensive that was to defeat Germany, the United States began to move across the Pacific toward Japan. Nimitz and MacArthur conceived a brilliant plan in which U.S. land, sea, and air forces fought in a coordinated effort. With a series of amphibious landings, they hopped from island to island. Some Japanese island fortresses such as Tarawa were taken; others such as Truk were bypassed and cut off from Japanese home bases. With the conquest of Saipan in November 1944 and Iwo Jima in March 1945, the U.S. forces acquired bases from which B-29 bombers could strike at the Japanese home islands. In the summer of 1945, in the greatest air offensive in history, U.S. planes destroyed what remained of the Japanese navy, crippled Japanese industry, and mercilessly firebombed major population centers. The attack ended with the dropping of atomic bombs on the cities of Hiroshima and Nagasaki. The Japanese government accepted U.S. terms for peace and surrendered unconditionally on 2 September 1945 on the battleship *Missouri* in Tokyo Bay. Four months after the defeat of Germany, the war in Asia was over.

The Fate of Allied Cooperation: 1945

The costs of World War II in terms of death and destruction were the highest in history. An estimated 50 million lives had been lost, including those of 6 million Jews. Most of the dead were Europeans, and most of them were Russians and Poles. An unusually high incidence of civilian deaths distinguished the Second World War from previous wars: Well over 50 percent of the dead were noncombatants. Deliberate military targeting of cities explains this phenomenon only in part. The majority of civilian deaths were the result of starvation, enslavement, massacre, and deliberate extermination.

Civilian Populations. The psychological devastation of continual violence, deprivation, injury, and rape of survivors cannot be measured. Terrorizing citizens became an established means of warfare in the modern age. Another phenomenon not matched in the First World War emerged in 1945: mass rape. The Soviet officer corps encouraged the advancing Russian army to use sexual violence against German women and girls. The Russians, treated brutally by Hitler's army, returned the savagery in their advance through eastern and central Europe. Rape became a means of direct retaliation. The Great Patriotic War reached its nadir in central Europe with collective rape as a form of war against civilians. In East Asia, victorious Japanese soldiers raped Chinese women as part of the spoils of war. Japanese military commanders also organized camps of "comfort women," unwilling young women who had been abducted from Korea, the Philippines, and other occupied areas to service the sexual "needs" of Japanese soldiers. Regardless of the country that was involved, victorious armies practiced rape against civilian populations as one of the unspoken aspects of conquest.

Material destruction was also great. Axis and Allied cities, centers of civilization and culture, were turned into wastelands by aerial bombing. The Germans bombed Rotterdam and Coventry. The British engineered the firebombing of Dresden. The German army destroyed Warsaw and Stalingrad. The United States leveled Hiroshima and Nagasaki. The nations of Europe were weakened after World War I; after World War II, they were crippled. Europe was completely displaced from the position of world dominance it had held for centuries. The United States alone was undamaged and stronger after the war than before, its industrial capacity and production greatly improved by the war.

The Big Three. What would be the future of Europe? The leaders of the United States, Great Britain, and the Soviet Union—the **Big Three**, as they were called—met three times between 1943 and 1945: first at Teheran; then in February 1945 at Yalta, a Russian Black Sea resort; and finally in July and August 1945 at Potsdam, a suburb of Berlin. They coordinated their attack on Germany and Japan and discussed their plans for postwar Europe. After Allied victory, the governments of both Germany and Japan would be totally abolished and completely reconstructed. No deals would be made with Hitler or his successors; no peace would be negotiated with the enemy; surrender would be unconditional. Germany would be disarmed and de-Nazified, and its leaders would be tried as war criminals. The armies of the Big Three would occupy Germany, each with a separate zone, but the country would be governed as a single economic unit. The Soviet Union, it was agreed, could collect reparations from Germany. With Germany and Japan defeated, a United Nations organization would provide the structure for a lasting peace in the world.

Stalin expected that the Soviet Union would decide the future of the territories of eastern Europe that the Soviet army had liberated from Germany. This area was vital to the security of the war-devastated Soviet Union; Stalin saw it as a protective barrier against another attack from the west. The Big Three agreed that Romania, Bulgaria, Hungary, Czechoslovakia, and Poland would have pro-Soviet governments. Since Soviet troops occupied these countries in 1945, there was little that the British and the Americans could do to prevent Russian control unless they wanted to go to war against the Soviet Union. Churchill realistically accepted this situation. But for Americans who took seriously the proclamations of President Roosevelt that their country had fought to restore freedom and self-determination to peoples oppressed by tyranny, Soviet power in eastern Europe was a bitter disappointment.

WORLD WAR II

1937	Japan begins undeclared war on China
March 1938	Germany annexes Austria to the German Reich
29 September 1938	Chamberlain, Daladier, Mussolini, and Hitler meet at Munich conference
May 1939	Pact of Steel: military alliance between Italy and Germany
1939	Non-Aggression Pact between Germany and the Soviet Union
1 September 1939	Germany attacks Poland
3 September 1939	Great Britain and France declare war on Germany
April 1940	Germany attacks Denmark and Norway
May 1940	Germany invades the Netherlands, Belgium, Luxembourg, and then France
June 1940	Italy enters the war on the side of Germany
17 June 1940	French Marshal Pétain petitions Germany for an armistice and creates a collaborationist government at Vichy
September 1940	Japan, Germany, and Italy sign Tripartite Pact
September–November 1940	The Battle of Britain
22 June 1941	Germany invades the Soviet Union
1941	First extermination camp created in Chelmno, Poland
7 December 1941	Japan attacks Pearl Harbor; the following day, the United States declares war on Japan
11 December 1941	Germany declares war on the United States
January 1942	Wannsee Conference, where the Final Solution is planned
June 1942	Battle of Midway
September 1942	Italian government withdraws from the war
April 1943	Unsuccessful uprising in the Warsaw ghetto
November 1943	Churchill, Roosevelt, and Stalin meet at Teheran conference
6 June 1944	Allied forces land in northern France—D-Day
February 1945	Churchill, Roosevelt, and Stalin meet at Yalta
March 1945	American forces march into Germany
30 April 1945	Hitler commits suicide
July and August 1945	Churchill, Truman, and Stalin meet at Potsdam
6 August 1945	United States drops atomic bomb on Hiroshima
2 September 1945	Japan surrenders

SUMMARY

Aggression and Conquest   Hitler saw a war with the Soviet Union for living space as inevitable. The French and British misunderstood Hitler's intentions and pursued a policy of appeasement in the Czechoslovakia crisis of 1938. Hitler and Stalin stunned the world with the Non-Aggression Pact of 1939. The invasion of Poland by Germany and the Soviet Union triggered general war in Europe. France fell in June 1940 under the pressure of the German *blitzkrieg*. British resistance made the Battle of Britain a failure for Germany. The Germans had more success in the Balkans. Collaboration and resistance to the Nazis took a variety of forms and sprung from a variety of motives.

Racism and Destruction   In both Europe and Asia, claims of racial superiority were used to support the war effort. The Nazis moved quickly to translate their racial theories into law and policy. All groups deemed inferior were subject to sterilization, imprisonment, and death. Nazi racial policies were cloaked in pseudoscience. The anti-Semitic policies of the Third Reich evolved incrementally in the 1930s and 1940s. From 1941, Germany pursued the Final Solution, a policy of systematic extermination of the Jews as a people. Effective Jewish resistance was an impossibility given the totality of the German effort and the unwillingness of other nations, including the United States, to accept Jewish refugees. It is also impossible that the mass killings were kept a secret from the rest of Europe's population or from the Allies.

Allied Victory   By the summer of 1941, Hitler had acquired a vast European Empire. Hitler's invasion of the Soviet Union in June 1941 would prove a fatal mistake. After the Japanese attacked Pearl Harbor in December 1941, the United States formally entered the war. A number of factors including American resources, the harsh Russian winter, and the profound sacrifices of the Soviet people helped the Soviets turn back the German assault. At first, the Japanese made rapid progress in southeast Asia. The United States used its vast economic resources to quickly assemble a powerful military force. The United States and its allies made victory in Europe their first priority. Allied victories in North Africa led to the invasion of Italy. In June 1944, Allied troops invaded France. The final German defeat came in April 1945. The Japanese aimed to dominate east and southeast Asia through their Greater East Asia Co-Prosperity Sphere. The tide in the Pacific war began to turn when the planned Japanese invasion of Australia was thwarted. Allied victories at Midway and elsewhere made Japanese defeat inevitable. Air attacks on Japan culminated with the dropping of atomic bombs on Hiroshima and Nagasaki in August 1945. World War II was a conflict of unprecedented brutality. The United States, Great Britain, and the Soviet Union met in Teheran, Yalta, and Potsdam to plan military strategy and to plan for the postwar world.

QUESTIONS FOR REVIEW

1. What factors made possible Hitler's diplomatic and military successes between 1933 and 1941?
2. Why did the Nazi regime believe that it needed to destroy the Jews, gypsies, and other outsiders, and how did it attempt to justify that policy?
3. How did Hitler's invasion of the Soviet Union and the entry of the United States into the war transform the military situation?
4. How did the Allies coordinate their efforts, and what factors strained relations between them?
5. How did the three Allied victors envision the future of Europe, and what steps did they take to ensure the peace?

CHAPTER 29

The Cold War and Postwar Economic Recovery: 1945–1970

The Origins of the Cold War

For victors and vanquished alike, the situation in Europe at the end of the Second World War was dire. Economies geared totally toward war efforts were incapable of the kind of reorientation needed to reconstruct markets and eliminate economic distress. Governments faced political crises as they attempted to restore or establish democratic principles. Moreover, Europe did not have the capital necessary to begin the process of rebuilding. Political disorganization reigned in Berlin, which was divided into sectors, in Germany, which was divided into zones, and in the former European empires, which were in the process of being dismantled.

Cold War conflict initially developed because of differing Russian and American notions regarding the economic reconstruction of Europe. The Soviet Union realized that American aid to Europe was not primarily a humanitarian program; it was part of an economic offensive in Europe that would contribute to the dominance of American capital in world markets. The United States recognized that the Soviet Union hoped to achieve its own recovery through outright control of eastern Europe.

The World in Two Blocs

The Soviets understood that they ran a sorry second to American military superiority—the United States was alone in possessing the atomic bomb—and to American wealth, which, measured in Gross National Product (GNP), was 400 percent greater than that of the Soviet Union. Stalin, nevertheless, committed the Soviet Union to an arms race in which he refused to accept American dominance. War had made the two superpowers wary allies; peace promised to make them once again active foes.

The Cold War was rooted in the ideological opposition between communism and capitalist democracies, dominated by the two superpowers, the Soviet Union and the United States. It affected the entire world. Drawing on three decades of distrust between the East and the West, the Cold War was related to the economic and foreign policy goals of both superpowers.

The Division of Germany. In central Europe, Cold War tensions first surfaced over the question of how to treat Germany. In fostering economic reconstruction in Europe, the United States counted on a German economy transfused with American funds that would be self-supporting and stable. To the contrary, the Soviet Union, blaming Germany for its extreme destruction, was explicit in its demands: German resources must be siphoned off for Soviet reconstruction.

With Germany's defeat, its territory had been divided into four zones, occupied by American, Soviet, British, and French troops. An Allied Control Commission consisting of representatives of the four powers was to govern Germany as a whole in keeping with the decisions made at Yalta before the end of the war. As Soviet and American antagonisms over Germany's future deepened, however, Allied rule polarized between the East and the West, with the internal politics of each area determined by the ideological conflicts between communism and capitalist free enterprise.

Allied attempts to administer Germany as a whole faltered and failed in 1948 over a question of economic policy. The zones of the Western occupying forces (the United States, Great Britain, and France), now administered as a single unit, issued a uniform and stable currency that the Russians accurately saw as a threat to their own economic policies in Germany. The Soviets blockaded the city of Berlin, which, though behind the frontier of the Russian sector, was being administered in

MAP DISCOVERY

American zone

British zone

French zone

Soviet zone

Berlin airlift
1948–1949

DENMARK

Baltic
Sea

North
Sea

Hamburg

POLAND

Hanover

Berlin

NETH.

Bonn

BELG.

Frankfurt

CZECHOSLOVAKIA

Paris

LUX.

FRANCE

AUSTRIA

French
zone

SWITZ.

British
zone

Berlin Wall

East
Berlin

West
Berlin

ITALY

YUGOSLAVIA

EAST GERMANY

0   20 Miles

0   20 Kilometers

0   200 Miles

0   200 Kilometers

THE DIVISION OF GERMANY

Examine the division of Germany after World War II. Why did the four victor nations divide Germany into zones at the end of the war? How did Berlin come to be divided into two zones? What was the Soviet goal in blockading West Berlin, and why did the blockade fail?

sectors by the four powers and whose western sector promised to become a successful enclave of Western capitalism. With the support of the people of West Berlin, the Allies responded by airlifting food and supplies into West Berlin for almost a year, defending it as an outpost that had to be preserved from the advance of communism. The Russians were forced to withdraw the blockade in the spring

The Berlin airlift of 1948–1949 broke through the Soviet blockade of the city. Called "Operation Vittles," the airlift provided food and fuel for the beleaguered West Berliners. Here, children wait for the candy American pilots dropped in tiny parachute handkerchiefs. The Soviets ended the blockade in the spring of 1949.

of 1949. The Berlin blockade hardened the commitment on both sides to two Germanys. The two new states, the Federal Republic of Germany (West Germany) and the German Democratic Republic (East Germany) came into existence in 1949.

Eastern Europe and the Soviet Bloc. With the support of local Communist parties, Soviet-dominated governments were established in Poland, Hungary, Bulgaria, and Romania in 1947. The following year, Czechoslovakia was pulled into the Soviet orbit. Czechoslovakia served as a significant marker in the development of Cold War confrontation. The tactics of the Communists in Czechoslovakia taught the West that coalition governments were unacceptable and undoubtedly hardened the resolve of U.S. policy makers in support of two Germanys. Needing the stability of peace, the Soviets saw in eastern Europe, hostile as the area may have been to forced integration, a necessary buffer against Western competition.

NATO and Other Treaty Alliances. With the aim of containing the USSR under a policy known as **containment,** the United States entered into a series of military alliances around the world. In order to provide mutual assistance should any member be attacked, the United States joined with Belgium, Canada, Denmark, France, Iceland, Italy, Luxembourg, the Netherlands, Norway, Portugal, and the United Kingdom in 1949 to form the **North Atlantic Treaty Organization (NATO).** Greece and Turkey became members in 1952, West Germany in 1955, and Spain in 1982. By 2009, NATO included 28 member countries embracing former Soviet Bloc countries in the Balkans and Eastern Europe.

A challenge to Cold War power politics came from within the NATO alliance. General Charles de Gaulle, as president of the French Fifth Republic, rejected the straitjacket of American dominance in Western Europe and asserted his country's independent status by exploding the first French atomic bomb in 1960. Refusing to place the

Soviet Union in 1939

Lands gained by the Soviet Union

Iron Curtain

0   300 Miles

0   300 Kilometers

FINLAND

KARELIA

NORWAY

SWEDEN

ESTONIA

North Sea

DENMARK

LATVIA

LITHUANIA

SOVIET
UNION

Baltic Sea

GREAT
BRITAIN   NETH.   Berlin

EAST PRUSSIA

EAST
GERMANY   POLAND

BYELORUSSIA

BELG.

LUX.   WEST
GERMANY

CZECHOSLOVAKIA

RUTHENIA

FRANCE

SWITZ.   AUSTRIA   HUNGARY

BESSARABIA

ROMANIA

Black Sea

YUGOSLAVIA

ITALY

SPAIN

BULGARIA

ALB.

GREECE

TURKEY

THE SOVIET UNION AND THE SOVIET BLOC

Notice the boundary of the Soviet Union before 1939 and the territory it gained after
World War II. Which countries in eastern Europe did the Soviet Union annex after the
war and why? In other countries of eastern Europe the Soviet Union established
economic and political control without annexation. Which countries constituted the
Soviet bloc?

French military under an American general who served as Supreme Allied Commander for NATO, de Gaulle completely withdrew France from participation in NATO in 1966.

The Southeast Asia Treaty Organization (SEATO) in 1954 and the Baghdad Pact of 1955 (known as the Central Treaty Organization after 1959) followed. The United States strengthened its military presence throughout the period by acquiring 1,400 military bases in foreign countries for its own forces.

In 1955, Albania, Bulgaria, Romania, Czechoslovakia, Hungary, Poland, and East Germany joined with the Soviet Union to form a defensive alliance organization known as the **Warsaw Pact.** The USSR intended its Eastern European allies to serve as a strategic buffer zone against the NATO forces.

The Nuclear Club

Stalin understood the political significance of nuclear weapons and committed the Soviet Union to a breakneck program of development following the war. The USSR ended the American monopoly and tested its first atomic bomb in 1949. Both countries developed the hydrogen bomb almost simultaneously in 1953. Space exploration by satellite was also deemed important in terms of the detection and deployment of bombs, and the Soviets pulled ahead in this area with the launching of the first satellite, *Sputnik I,* in 1957. Intercontinental ballistic missiles (ICBMs) followed, further accelerating the pace of nuclear armament.

The atomic bomb and thermonuclear weapons contributed greatly to the shape of Cold War politics. Both the United States and the Soviet Union, the first two members of the **nuclear club,** knew that they had the capability of obliterating their enemy, but not before the enemy could retaliate. They also knew that the technology necessary for nuclear arms was available to any industrial power. By 1974, the nuclear club included Great Britain, France, the People's Republic of China, and India.

The first hydrogen bomb test, on November 1, 1952, destroyed an entire island in the Pacific.

The Nuclear Test Ban Treaty of 1963, the first of its kind, banned tests in the atmosphere and inaugurated a period of lessening tensions between the Eastern and Western blocs. Arms limitation and nonproliferation were the subjects of a series of conferences between the United States and the Soviet Union in the late 1960s and pointed the way to limitations eventually agreed on in the next decade. The United Nations (UN), an organization created by the Allies immediately following World War II to take the place of the defunct League of Nations, established international agencies for the purpose of harnessing nuclear power for peaceful uses. By the early 1970s, both the United States and the Soviet Union recognized the importance of closer relations between the superpowers. On the whole, however, the arms race persisted as a continuing threat in Cold War politics. The race required the dedication of huge national resources to maintain a competitive stance. Conventional forces, too, were expanded to protect Eastern and Western bloc interests.

Decolonization and the Cold War

No part of the globe escaped the tensions generated by the Cold War. By the end of the Second World War, European colonial empires had been weakened or destroyed by the ravages of battle, occupation, and neglect. Nationalist movements had been growing in power in the 1930s, and many nationalist leaders saw the war as a catalyst for independence. Former colonies were no longer directly controlled but, as newly independent countries, they had to contend with Cold War pressures to belong in one or the other superpower camp. Hence, **decolonization** often meant continued dependence.

Former colonies played an important new role in the Cold War strategies with the accession to power of Nikita Khrushchev (1894–1971) in the mid-1950s. The Soviet Union abandoned its previous caution and assumed a global role in offering "friendship treaties," military advice, trade credits, and general support for attempts at national liberation in Asia, Africa, and Latin America. Both East and West took advantage of tribalism and regionalism, which worked against the establishment of strong central governments. Military rule and fragmentation often resulted. Instability and acute poverty continued to characterize former colonies after emancipation, regardless of whether the new leaders joined the communist or democratic camps.

Asia. Great Britain knew that it no longer commanded the resources to control India, historically its richest colony, which under the leadership of Mohandas Gandhi (1869–1948) had been agitating for independence since 1920. Given the title of "Mahatma," or "great-souled," by his people, Gandhi advocated passive resistance to achieve independence. The British granted self-government to India in 1946 with the proviso that if the bitter conflict between Hindus and Muslims was not settled by mutual agreement, Great Britain would decide on the division of power. As a result, Muslim and Hindu representatives agreed to the division of British India into the independent states of India and Pakistan in 1947.

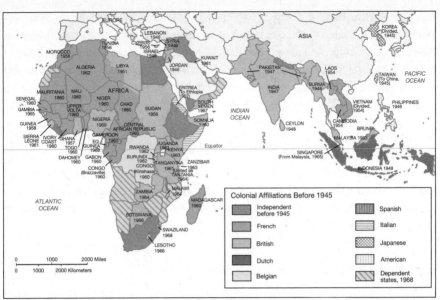

DECOLONIZATION. Few nations in Africa and south and southeast Asia were independent before 1945. Few remained dependent after 1968.

In its march through Asia during the war, Japan had smashed colonial empires. Japan's defeat created a power vacuum that nationalist leaders were eager to fill. Civil wars erupted in China, Burma, Korea, and Indochina. In 1950, the United States and the United Nations intervened when North Korea attacked South Korea. Korea, formerly controlled by Japan, had been divided following the war as a result of the presence of Russian and American troops. Communist-dominated North Korea refused to accept the artificial boundary between it and Western-dominated South Korea. China, a Communist state following the victory of Mao Zedong (1893–1976) in 1949, intervened in the Korean conflict when American troops advanced on Chinese frontiers in October 1950. After three years of military stalemate, Korea was partitioned on the 38th parallel in 1953.

The United States was heavily committed as a military presence in Southeast Asia after the French withdrawal from Indochina following the French defeat at Dien Bien Phu in 1954. The North Vietnamese state was established under the French-educated leader Ho Chi Minh. South Vietnam was declared a republic, and the United States sponsored a regime that was considered favorable to Western interests. Arguing the domino theory—that one Southeast Asian country after another would fall like a row of dominoes to Communist takeover—the United States also intervened in Laos and Cambodia. Between 1961 and 1973, the United States committed American troops to a full-scale war—though officially termed only a military action—against Communist guerrilla forces throughout the region. After almost two decades of escalating involvement, in 1973 American troops were finally withdrawn from a war in Vietnam that they could not win.

Africa. In Africa, a new generation of leaders, many of them educated in European institutions, had moved from cooperation with home rule to demands for independence by the early 1960s. In 1960, Patrice Lumumba (1925–1961) became the first prime minister of the Republic of the Congo (present-day Democratic Republic of the Congo). White European rule continued in Rhodesia (now Zimbabwe) and South Africa, despite continued world pressure. African leader Kwame Nkrumah (1909–1972) of Ghana denounced the situation of African dependence as "neocolonialism" and called for a united Africa as the only means of resistance. He led Ghana in a policy of nonalignment in the Cold War. With Jomo Kenyatta (1894–1978) of Kenya, Nkrumah founded the Pan-African Federation, which promoted African nationalism.

France's problems in Algeria began in earnest in 1954 when Muslims seeking independence and self-rule revolted. Although the Algerian rebels successfully employed terrorist and guerrilla tactics, European settlers and the French army in Algeria refused to accept defeat. Facing political collapse at home, the French, under the leadership of General Charles de Gaulle, ended the war and agreed to Algeria's independence, which was achieved in 1962.

The Middle East. The United States and the Soviet Union used aid to win support of "client" states in the Middle East. The withdrawal, sometimes under duress, of British and French rule in the Middle East and North Africa and the creation of the state of Israel in 1948 destabilized the area and created opportunities for new alliances. Egypt and Syria, for example, sought Soviet support against the new Israeli state, which had been formed out of the part of Palestine under British mandate since 1920 and which was dependent on U.S. aid.

In 1951, a nationalist Iranian government sought to evict Westerners by nationalizing the oil fields. The British blockaded Iranian trade in the Persian Gulf, and the newly formed American espionage organization, the Central Intelligence Agency (CIA), subverted the nationalist government and placed in power the shah of Iran, a leader favorable to American interests.

In 1956, a crisis came in Egypt. Egyptian President Gamal Abdel Nasser (1918–1970), a nationalist in power by virtue of a military coup d'état in 1952, oversaw the nationalization of the Suez Canal. British and French military forces attacked and were forced to withdraw by pressure from both the Soviet Union and the United States, which cooperated in seeking to avert a disaster. The Middle East, however, remained a Cold War powder keg, with Israeli and Arab nationalist interests and Soviet and American aid running on a collision course. The expansion of the Israeli state at the expense of its Arab neighbors further exacerbated tensions.

Latin America. The United States was also experiencing Cold War problems closer to home. In 1954, the CIA plotted the overthrow of Guatemala's leftist regime to keep Soviet influence out of the Western Hemisphere. In 1959, a revolution in Cuba, an island nation only 90 miles off the American coast, resulted in the ejection of

U.S. interests and the establishment of a Communist regime under the leadership of a young lawyer, Fidel Castro. In 1962, a direct and frightening confrontation occurred between the United States and the USSR over Soviet missile installations in Cuba. Following the Russian withdrawal from the island, both U.S. President John F. Kennedy and Soviet leader Nikita Khrushchev pursued a policy of peaceful coexistence, intent on averting nuclear confrontation. Both sides recognized how close they had come to mutual annihilation in the showdown over Cuba.

Postwar Economic Recovery in Europe, Japan, and the Soviet Union

As the chief producer and supplier for the Allied war effort, even before its entry into the conflict, the United States had benefited from the conflict in Europe and actually expanded its economic productivity during the war. In 1945, the United States was producing a full 50 percent of the world's GNP. However, the United States knew that it lacked one important guarantee to secure its growth and its future prosperity: adequate international markets for its goods. Both Europe and Japan were recognized as potential buyers for American goods, but both areas parried with protectionism to foster their own postdepression recovery.

The Economic Challenge

Economists judged that Europe would need at least 25 years to regain its prewar economic capacity. The worst was also feared: that Europe would never recover as a world economic power. Large-scale population movements made matters worse. Displaced persons by the millions moved across Europe.

European industrial production in 1945 was one-third of its level in 1938. Housing shortages existed everywhere. The transportation infrastructure was severely damaged: Railways, roads, and bridges were in shambles all over Europe. Communications networks were in disarray.

Agriculture, too, suffered severe reversals in wartime economies and was unable to resume prewar production in 1945. In general, European agriculture was producing at 50 percent of its prewar capacity. The scarcity of goods converged with ballooning inflation. Black markets with astronomical prices for necessities flourished, while currency rates plummeted. Everywhere the outlook was bleak. Yet in less than a decade, the situation was reversed. The solution came from outside of Europe.

The Economic Solution: The Marshall Plan

On 5 June 1947, U.S. Secretary of State George C. Marshall (1880–1959) delivered the commencement address at Harvard University. In his speech, Marshall introduced the European Recovery Act, popularly known as the **Marshall Plan,** through which billions of dollars in aid would be made available to European states, both in the east and in the west, provided that two conditions were met: (1) the recipient states had to cooperate with one another in aligning national economic policies and improving the international monetary system, and (2) they had to work toward breaking down trade barriers.

Participating countries included Austria, Belgium, Denmark, France, West Germany, Great Britain, Greece, Iceland, Italy, Luxembourg, the Netherlands, Norway, Sweden, Switzerland, and Turkey. The Soviet Union and eastern European countries were also eligible for aid under the original formulation. But the Soviets opposed the plan from the first, wary of U.S. intentions to extend the influence of Western capitalism.

The amount of U.S. aid to Europe was massive. More than $23 billion was pumped into western Europe between 1947 and 1952. By every measure, the Marshall Plan was judged a success in the West. American foreign aid restored western European trade and production while at the same time controlling inflation.

Western European Economic Integration

As significant as the gift of funds to European states undoubtedly was, no less important was the whole administrative apparatus that American aid brought in its wake. In order to expend available monies most effectively and comply with stipulations for cooperation and regulation, the states of western Europe resorted to intensified planning and limited nationalization.

Planning for Recovery. Regulation and state intervention dominated the formulation of economic policy. Special attention was given to workers' welfare through unemployment insurance, retirement benefits, public health, and housing policies. European states recognized the need to provide a safety net for their citizens in order to avoid reexperiencing the disastrous depression and stagnation of the 1930s while attempting to rebuild their shattered economies.

European Economic Cooperation. U.S. foreign aid contributed mightily to the extension of central planning and the growth of the welfare state throughout western Europe. But money alone could not have accomplished the recovery that took place. The chief mechanism for administering Marshall Plan aid was the Office of European Economic Cooperation (OEEC). That master coordinating agency made the requirements for recovery clear. European states had to stabilize their own economies. Cooperation between the public and private sectors was intended to free market forces, modernize production, and raise productivity. The modernization of economies through centrally coordinated planning made Europe once again a major contender in the international economic arena.

The major exception to the establishment of central planning agencies and the nationalization of key industries was West Germany. Deciding against the British and French models of planned growth, the West Germans endorsed a free market policy that encouraged private enterprise while providing state insurance for all workers. What has been described as "a free enterprise economy with a social conscience" produced the richest economy in western Europe by the mid-1950s.

Realizing that Europe as a region needed the cooperation of its member states if it was to contend in world markets, associations dedicated to integration began to emerge alongside economic planning mechanisms.

Belgium, the Netherlands, and Luxembourg were the first European states to establish themselves as an economic unit—Benelux. Internal customs duties among the three states were removed, and a common external tariff barrier was erected. The Schuman Plan joined France and West Germany in economic cooperation by pooling all coal and steel resources, beginning in 1950. In 1951, the Netherlands, Belgium, Luxembourg, France, Italy, and West Germany formed the European Coal and Steel Community (ECSC). In 1957, the same six members created the **European Economic Community (EEC)** and committed themselves to broadening the integration of markets. It was the beginning of what became known as the Common Market.

The Common Market aimed to establish among its member states a free movement of labor and capital, the elimination of restrictions on trade, common investment practices, and coordinated social welfare programs. National agricultural interests were to be protected. Great Britain was initially a vocal opponent of the Common Market and continued to defend its own trading relationship with its Commonwealth countries, eventually founding its own free trade association in 1959. In 1973, Great Britain became a member of the Common Market and joined with other European nations in defining common economic policies.

European union was a phenomenon of exclusion as much as inclusion. It sharpened antagonisms between the West and the East by its very success. While promoting prosperity, European economic unification favored concentration and the emergence of large corporations. Vast individual fortunes flourished under state sponsorship and the rule of the experts. National parliaments were sometimes eclipsed by new economic decision-making organizations that aimed to make western Europe into a single free trade area.

Japan's Recovery

Japanese economic challenges in the postwar era were similar to those of western Europe. As a defeated and occupied nation in 1945, Japan faced a grim future. U.S. aims for Asia were similar to those for Europe: American policy makers sought to create a multilateral system of world trade and preserve America's sphere of influence against Communist encroachment. The American general Douglas MacArthur was appointed the Supreme Commander for the Allied Powers and the head of occupation forces in Japan. His mission in Japan was to impose rapid economic change from above.

Japan turned its wartime devastation into an advantage by replacing destroyed factories with the latest technology, obtained by license from foreign firms. Through a combination of bureaucracy and patronage devoted to planned growth, Japan's GNP reached prewar levels by 1956. By 1968, Japan had turned defeat into triumph and stood as the third largest industrial nation in the world.

Postwar demilitarization freed Japan of the financial exigencies of the arms race. Funds formerly used for arms now flowed into investment and new technology. Slowed population growth after 1948 and an increased volume of foreign trade contributed to Japanese prosperity.

The Soviet Path to Economic Recovery

The Soviet Union countered economic integration in the West with its own alliances and organizations. In 1949, the USSR established the Council for Mutual Economic Assistance, or **Comecon,** with bilateral agreements between the Soviet Union and eastern European states. Comecon was Stalin's response to the U.S. Marshall Plan in western Europe. Rather than providing aid, however, Comecon benefited the Soviet Union at the expense of its partners, seeking to integrate and control the economies of eastern Europe for Soviet gain. The Soviet Union implemented an expansion of its territorial boundaries as a way of reversing some of its drastic losses in the war. Above all, it wanted a protective ring of satellite states as security from attack from the West.

Under Stalin's direction, the Soviet Union concentrated all its efforts on reconstructing its devastated economy and, to that end, sought integration with eastern European states, whose technology and resources were needed for the rebuilding of the Soviet state. In the years before his death in 1953, Joseph Stalin succeeded in making the Soviet Union a vital industrial giant second only to the United States. The Soviet economy experienced dramatic recovery after 1945, in spite of the severe damage inflicted on it during the war. The production of steel, coal, and crude oil skyrocketed under state planning. Heavy industry was the top priority of Soviet recovery, in keeping with prewar commitments to rapid modernization. In addition, the postwar Soviet economy assumed the new burdens of the development of a nuclear arsenal and an expensive program for the exploration of space. Stalin maintained the Soviet Union on the footing of a war economy, restricting occupational mobility and continuing to rely on forced-labor camps.

De-Stalinization. In 1953, Stalin, who had ruled the Soviet Union for almost three decades, died. The vacuum that he left provoked a struggle for power among the Communist party leadership. It also initiated almost immediately a process of **de-Stalinization** and the beginnings of a thaw in censorship and repression. A growing urban and professional class expected improvements in the quality of life and greater freedoms after years of war and hardship. In 1956, at the Twentieth Party Congress, Nikita Khrushchev (1894–1971), as head of the Communist party, denounced Stalin as incompetent and cruel. After five years of jockeying for power among Stalin's former lieutenants, Khrushchev emerged victorious and assumed the office of premier in 1958.

De-Stalinization also took place in eastern Europe. Discontent over collectivization, low wages, and the lack of consumer goods fueled a latent nationalism among eastern European populations resentful of Soviet control and influence. Violence erupted in 1953 in East Berlin as workers revolted over conditions in the workplace, but it was quickly and effectively suppressed. Demands for reforms and liberalization in Poland also produced riots and changes in Communist party leadership.

Hungarians followed suit with their demands for the withdrawal of Hungary from the Warsaw Pact. On 23 October 1956, inspired by the events in Poland, Hungarians rose up in anger against their old-guard Stalinist rulers. Imre Nagy (1896–1958), a liberal Communist, took control of the government, attempted to introduce democratic reforms, and relaxed economic controls. The Soviets, however, were unwilling to lose control of their sphere of influence in Eastern Bloc nations and to jeopardize their system of defense in the Warsaw Pact. Moscow responded to liberal experimentation in Hungary by sending tanks and troops into Budapest. Brutal repression and purges followed.

The Soviet Standard of Living. The Soviet Union's standard of living remained relatively low in the years when western Europe was undergoing a consumer revolution. Soviet consumption was necessarily stagnant, since profits were plowed back as investments in future heavy industrial expansion. In the Soviet Union and throughout the Eastern Bloc countries, women's full participation in the labor force was essential for recovery. In spite of their presence in large numbers in highly skilled sectors such as medicine, Soviet and Eastern Bloc women remained poorly paid, as did women in the West.

The Soviet population was growing rapidly, from 170 million in 1939 to 234 million in 1967. Nikita Khrushchev promised the people lower prices and a shorter workweek, but in 1964, when he fell from power, Soviets were paying higher prices for their food than before.

Eastern Bloc Economies and Dissent. The nature of planned Soviet growth exacted heavy costs in the Eastern Bloc countries. Adhering to the Soviet pattern of heavy industrial expansion at the expense of agriculture and consumer goods, East Germany, Czechoslovakia, Bulgaria, Romania, and Yugoslavia all reported significant industrial growth in this period. Yet dislocations caused by collectivization and heavy defense expenditures stirred up social unrest in East Germany, Czechoslovakia, Poland, and Hungary. The Soviet Union responded with some economic concessions but on the whole stressed common industrial and defense pursuits, employing ideological persuasion and military pressure to keep its reluctant partners in line.

East Berlin in the late 1950s and early 1960s posed a particular problem for Communist rule. Unable to compete successfully in wages and standard of living with the capitalist western sector of the city, East Berlin saw increasing numbers of its population, especially the educated and professional classes, crossing the line to a more prosperous life. In 1961, the Soviet Union responded to the problem by building a wall that cordoned off the part of the city that it controlled. The **Berlin Wall** eventually stretched for 103 miles.

In 1968 the policy of de-Stalinization reached a critical juncture in Czechoslovakia. Early in 1968, Alexander Dubcek, Czech party secretary and a member of the educated younger generation of technocrats, had supported liberal reforms in Czechoslovakia. He acted on popular desire for nationalism, the end of censorship, and better working conditions. Above all, he called for democratic reforms in the political process that would restore rule to the people. Moscow sent in thousands of tanks and hundreds of thousands of Warsaw Pact troops to Prague and other Czech cities to reestablish control. The Czechs responded with passive resistance in what became known as the **Prague Spring** uprising. The Soviet invasion made clear that popular nationalism was intolerable in an Eastern Bloc nation.

The slowed growth of the 1960s, the delay in development of consumer durables, and the inadequacy of basic foodstuffs, housing, and clothing were the costs that Eastern Bloc citizens paid for their inefficient and rigid planned economies dedicated to the development of heavy industry. In eastern Europe and the Soviet Union, however, poverty was virtually eliminated as the state subsidized housing, health care, and higher education, which were available to all.

Soviet tanks rumbled through Prague as troops from the Warsaw Pact countries invaded the Czechoslovakian capital in 1968, bringing an end to Alexander Dubcek's reform movement. Dubcek was rehabilitated in the liberalization of 1989 and elected chairman of the parliament.

COLD WAR AND ECONOMIC RECOVERY

1947	Marshall Plan starts U.S. aid to European countries; pro-Soviet governments established in Poland, Hungary, Bulgaria, and Romania
1948	Pro-Soviet government established in Czechoslovakia
1949	European states and United States form North Atlantic Treaty Organization (NATO); Federal Republic of Germany and German Democratic Republic established; Soviet Union creates Council for Mutual Economic Assistance (Comecon); Soviet Union tests its first atomic bomb
1950–1953	Korean War, ending with the partition of Korea
1953	United States and Soviet Union develop hydrogen bombs
1955	Formation of Warsaw Pact
1956	Hungarian uprising and subsequent repression by Soviet military forces
1957	The Netherlands, Belgium, Luxembourg, France, Italy, and West Germany form the European Economic Community (EEC), also called the Common Market; Soviet Union launches first satellite, *Sputnik I*
1961	Berlin Wall built
1961–1973	U.S. troops engaged in Vietnam
1962	Cuban missile crisis
1963	Soviet Union and United States sign Nuclear Test Ban Treaty
1968	Prague Spring uprising in Czechoslovakia, quelled by Soviet Union

The Welfare State and Social Transformation

The **welfare state,** a creation of the post–World War II era throughout Europe, grew out of the social welfare policies of the interwar period and out of the war itself. Welfare programs aimed to protect citizens through the establishment of a decent standard of living available for everyone. Across Europe, the welfare state developed a related set of social programs and policies whereby the state intervened in the cycles of individual lives to provide economic support for the challenges of birth, sickness, old age, and unemployment.

Prosperity and Consumption in the West

Despite the different paths toward reconstruction following World War II, every western European nation experienced dramatic increases in total wealth. Prosperity encouraged new patterns of spending based on confidence in the economy. That new consumerism, in turn, was essential to economic growth and future productivity.

The New Consumption. The social programs of the welfare state played an important role in promoting postwar consumption. In the mid-1950s, all over western Europe, people began to spend their earnings, knowing that accidents, disasters, and sicknesses would be taken care of by the state. Western Europeans began to buy on credit, spending money they had not yet earned. That, too, was an innovation in postwar markets.

Welfare programs could be sustained only in an era of prosperity and economic growth, since they depended on taxation of income for their funds. Such taxation did not, however, result in a redistribution of wealth. Wealth remained in the hands of a few and became even more concentrated as a result of phenomenal postwar economic growth.

Women's Wages. Just as the welfare state did not redistribute wealth, it did not provide equal pay for equal work. The skills associated with occupations performed by women were downgraded, as were their salaries. Women earned two-thirds or less of what men earned throughout western Europe. Welfare state revenues were a direct result of pay-scale inequities. Lower salaries for women meant higher profits and helped make economic recovery possible.

Family Strategies

The pressures on European women and their families in 1945 were often greater than in wartime. Severe scarcity of food, clothes, and housing required careful management. Women who during the war held jobs in industry and munitions plants earned their own money and established their own independence. After the war, in victorious and defeated nations alike, women were moved out of the work force to make room for returning men. Changing social policies affected women's lives in the home and in the workplace and contributed to the politicization of women within the context of the welfare state.

Demography and Birth Control. Prewar concerns with a declining birthrate intensified after World War II. In some European countries, the birthrate climbed in the years immediately following the war. Nearly everywhere throughout Europe, however, the rise in the birthrate was momentary, with the United States standing alone in experiencing a genuine and sustained "baby boom" until about 1960.

Technology had expanded the range of choices in family planning. In the early 1960s, the birth control pill became available on the European and American markets, primarily to middle-class women. The condom, invented a century earlier, was now sold to a mass market. Information about their reproductive lives became more accessible to young women. Illegal abortions continued to be an alternative for women. Abortion was probably the primary form of birth control in the Soviet Union in the years following the war.

The Family and Welfare. Women and men throughout western Europe and the United States embraced the centrality of the family to society, even if they did not opt for large families. Expectations for improved family life placed new demands on welfare state programs. They also placed increased demands on mothers, whose presence in the home was now seen as all-important for the proper development of the child.

European states implemented official programs to encourage women to have more children and to be better mothers. **Pronatalism,** as the policy was known, resulted from an official concern over low birthrates and a decline in family size. It is unlikely that pronatalism was caused by a fear of a decline in the labor force, since the influx of foreign workers, refugees from eastern Europe, and migrant laborers from poorer southern European nations provided an expanding labor pool. Other considerations about racial dominance and women's proper role seem to have affected the development of policies.

Welfare state programs differed from country to country as the result of a series of different expectations of women as workers and women as mothers. For example, in Great Britain the welfare system was built on the ideal of the mother at home with her children. Family allowances determined by the number of children were tied to men's participation in the work force; women were defined according to their husbands' status. The state welfare system strengthened the financial dependence of English wives on their husbands.

The French system of *sécurité sociale* defined all women, whether married or single, as equal to men; unlike English women, all French women had the same rights of access to welfare programs as men. Family allowances, pre- and post-natal care, maternity benefits, and child care were provided on the assumption that working mothers were a fact of life. French payments were intended to encourage large families and focused primarily on the needs of children. More and more women entered the paid labor force after 1945, and they were less financially dependent on their husbands than were their British counterparts.

Both forms of welfare state—the British that emphasized women's role as mothers and the French that accepted women's role as workers—were based on different attitudes about the nature of gender difference and equality. Women's political consciousness developed in both societies. The women's liberation movements of the late sixties and early seventies found their roots in the contradictions of differing welfare policies.

The Beginnings of Women's Protest. The 1960s were a period of protest in Western countries as people demonstrated for civil rights and free expression. Women participated in all of the movements, and by the end of the 1960s had begun to question their own place in organizations that did not acknowledge their claims to equal rights, equal pay, and liberation from the oppression of male society. A new critique began to form within the welfare state that indicated there were cracks in the facade.

The Second Sex (1949), written by Simone de Beauvoir (1908–1986), a leading French intellectual, analyzed women's place in the context of Western culture. By examining the assumptions of political theories, including Marxism, in the light of philosophy, biology, history, and psychoanalysis, de Beauvoir uncovered the myths governing the creation of the female self. By showing how the male is the center of culture and the female is "other," de Beauvoir urged women to be independent and to resist male definitions. *The Second Sex* became the handbook of the women's movement in the 1960s.

A very different work, *The Feminine Mystique*, appeared in 1963. In that book, author Betty Friedan voiced the grievances of a previously politically quiescent group of women. After World War II, women were expected to find personal fulfillment in the domestic sphere. Instead, Friedan found women suffering from the "sickness with no name" and the "nameless desperation" of a profound crisis in identity.

A new politics centering on women's needs and women's rights slowly took root. The feminist critique did not emerge as a mass movement until the 1970s. Youth culture and dissent among the young further influenced growing feminist discontent. But the agenda of protest in the sixties, reinforced by social policies, accepted gender differences as normal and natural.

Youth Culture and Dissent

Youth culture was created by outside forces as much as it was self-created. Socialized together in an expanding educational system from primary school through high school, the young came to see themselves as a social force. They were also socialized by marketing efforts that appealed to their particular interests as a group.

The young people of the 1960s were the first generation to come of age after World War II. Although they had no memory themselves of the destruction of that war, they were reminded daily of the imminence of nuclear destruction in their own lives. The combination of the security of affluence and the insecurity of Cold War politics created a widening gap between the world of decision-making adults and the idealistic universe of the young.

New styles of dress and grooming were a rejection of middle-class culture in Europe and the United States. Anthropologists and sociologists in the 1960s began studying youth as if they were a foreign tribe. The "**generation gap**" appeared as the subject of hundreds of specialized studies. When the stable base of economic prosperity began to erode as a result of slowed growth and inflation in the second half of the sixties—first in western Europe and then in the United States—frustrated expectations and shrinking opportunities for the young served as a further impetus for political action.

The Sexual Revolution. Increased emphasis on fulfillment through sexual pleasure was one consequence of the technological revolution in birth control devices, and it led to what has been called a revolution in sexual values in Western societies in the 1960s. Women's bodies were displayed more explicitly than ever before in mass advertising in order to sell products from automobiles to soap.

Sex magazines, sex shops, and movies were part of an explosion in the marketing of male sexual fantasies in the 1960s.

Sweden experienced the most far-reaching reforms of sexual mores in the 1960s. Sex education became part of every school's curriculum, contraceptive information was widely available, and homosexuality was decriminalized. Technology allowed women and men to separate pleasure from reproduction but did not alter men's and women's domestic roles. Pleasure was also separated from familial responsibilities, yet the domestic ideal of the woman in the home remained. Some women were beginning to question their exploitation in the sexual revolution. In the early 1970s, that issue became part of mass feminist protest.

The Anti-War Movement and Social Protest. Student protest, which began at the University of California at Berkeley in 1964 as the Free Speech movement, by the spring of 1968 had become an international phenomenon that had spread to other American campuses and throughout Europe and Japan. A common denominator of protest, whether in New York, London, or Tokyo, was opposition to the war in Vietnam.

Student protesters shared other concerns in addition to opposition to the war in southeast Asia. The growing activism on American campuses was aimed at social reform, student self-governance, and a recognition of the responsibilities of the university in the wider community. In West Germany, highly politicized radical activists, a conspicuous minority among the students at the Free University of Berlin, directed protest out into the wider society. Student demonstrations met with brutal police repression and violence, and rioting was common.

For the most part, student protest was primarily a middle-class phenomenon. In France, for example, only 4 percent of university students came from below the middle class. Higher education had been developed after World War II to serve the increased needs of a technocratic society. Instead of altering the social structure, which politically committed student protesters thought it should do, mass education served as a certifying mechanism for bureaucratic and technical institutions.

Isle of Wight Festival, England, 1969. Open-air music festivals were a popular feature of the sixties—the era of pacifism, when young people experimented with sexual liberation, the drug culture, and Eastern mysticism.

Protest and the Economy. Student dissent reflected the changing economy of the late 1960s. Inflation, which earlier in the decade had spurred prosperity, was spiraling out of control in the late sixties. In the advanced industrial countries of western Europe and later in the United States, the growth of the postwar period was slowing down. The dawning awareness of shrinking opportunities in the workplace for students who had attained their degrees and been properly certified further aggravated student frustration and dissent.

By the late sixties, universities and colleges provided the students a forum for expressing their discontent with advanced industrial societies. In their protests, student activists rejected the values of consumer society. The programs and politics of the student protesters aimed to transform the world in which they lived. The spirit of protest was expressed in the graffiti and posters that seemed to appear overnight on the walls of Paris.

In May 1968, French protest spread beyond the university when workers and managers joined students in paralyzing the French economy and threatening to topple the Fifth Republic. Between 7 and 10 million people went on strike in support of worker and student demands. White-collar employees and technicians joined blue-collar factory workers in the strike. Student demands, based on a thoroughgoing critique of the whole society, proved to be incompatible with the wage and consumption issues of workers. But the unusual, if short-lived, alliance of students and workers shocked those in power and induced reforms.

SUMMARY

The Origins of the Cold War Tensions between the United States and the Soviet Union initially surfaced over differing positions on the economic reconstruction of Europe. The Cold War was rooted in an ideological split between communism and capitalist democracies. Cold War tensions resulted in the split of Germany into two countries. The Soviet Union dominated its satellites in eastern Europe. The United States supported its policy of containment with a series of treaty alliances, including the North American Treaty Organization (NATO). The Soviet Union responded with the formation of the Warsaw Pact. The Soviet Union and the United States competed in a nuclear arms race and a number of new nations joined the nuclear club. Decolonization did not mean an end to dependence for many former European colonies in Africa, Asia, and Latin America. The Cold War shaped the destinies of emerging nations around the globe.

Postwar Economic Recovery in Europe, Japan, and the Soviet Union The United States responded to the challenge of reconstructing war-torn Europe with the Marshall Plan. Recipients of American aid were pledged to economic cooperation and reductions in trade barriers. Regulation and state intervention dominated the formulation of economic policy. Central planning agencies played a key role in economic recovery everywhere except West Germany. European nations moved steadily toward economic integration. With American assistance, Japan staged a remarkable economic recovery. The Soviet Union tried to counter economic integration in the West with its own alliances and organizations. The Soviet Union benefited from these arrangements at the expense of its allies. After Stalin's death, many in the Soviet bloc hoped for improvements in their quality of life and for greater freedom. The Soviets took repressive steps when de-Stalinization in eastern Europe threatened their hegemony. The standard of living in the Soviet Union remained low. The costs of supporting Soviet industrialization produced tensions in eastern Europe.

The Welfare State and Social Transformation   The welfare state aimed to protect citizens through the establishment of a decent standard of living available for everyone. Every western European nation experienced increases in total wealth which, in turn, stimulated increased consumption. Social welfare programs stimulated consumption by removing economic anxiety. The welfare state did not redistribute wealth and did not address income disparities between men and women. Welfare policies reflected beliefs about gender roles and the family. Western European governments moved to counter declining birthrates. The 1960s saw the emergence of a new women's rights movement. Youth culture was created by outside forces as much as it was self-created. There was a widening gap between young and old in this period. Birth control contributed to the sexual revolution. Young people were at the center of the anti-war movement and other efforts at social protest. Student protest reflected the diminished economic opportunities of the late 1960s.

QUESTIONS FOR REVIEW

1. What did it mean for postwar European politics that the Continent was divided into two blocs?
2. What factors encouraged decolonization in the decades after World War II?
3. Why did western Europe's economy recover so rapidly, and how did that contribute to a gradual process of European economic integration?
4. How did the Soviet Union's strategy for recovery differ from that of western Europe?
5. What is the welfare state, and how did it transform the lives of ordinary Europeans?
6. What were some of the concerns that provoked protests from women, students, and others in the 1960s?

The End of the Cold War and New Global Challenges, 1970 to the Present

The End of the Cold War and the Emergence of a New Europe

The Cold War, while it lasted from the post-1945 period to the late 1980s, provided a way of ordering the world. Yet chinks in the facade of Communist unity were already present by the mid-1960s, as we have seen in the previous chapter. As the Soviets faced growing discontent within the Soviet bloc, and as the nuclear threat made cooperation necessary, the bipolar security of the Cold War began to crumble.

The Brezhnev Doctrine and Détente

The use of military intervention to resolve the Czech crisis (Chapter 29) opened a new era governed by what came to be known as the **Brezhnev Doctrine.** Leonid Brezhnev (1906–1982), general secretary of the Communist party and head of the Soviet Union from 1966 to 1982, established a policy whereby the Soviet Union claimed the right to interfere in the internal affairs of its allies in order to prevent counterrevolution. After 1968, rigidity and stagnation characterized the Soviet, East German, and Czechoslovakian governments, as well as Communist party rule in other eastern European states.

In the international arena, the Soviet Union had achieved nuclear parity. Now, from positions of equality, both sides expressed a willingness to negotiate. The 1970s became the decade of **détente,** a period of cooperation between the two superpowers. The Strategic Arms Limitation Treaty, known as SALT I, signed in Moscow in 1972, limited defensive antiballistic missile systems.

East–West relations after 1983 were characterized by less confrontation and more attempts at cooperation between the Soviet Union and the United States. The world political system itself appeared to have stabilized, with a diminution of conflict in the three main arenas of superpower competition—the third world, China, and western Europe.

The New Direction in Soviet Politics

By the mid-1980s, Soviet leaders were weighing the costs of increasing conflict within the Soviet bloc, which the Brezhnev Doctrine failed to control, and the promise of benefits from improved relations with the West.

Typical of the new generation of political leaders was Mikhail Gorbachev, who was, above all, a technocrat, someone who could apply specialized technical knowledge to the problems of a stagnant Soviet economy. In 1985, the accession to power of Mikhail Gorbachev as general secretary ushered in a new age of openness.

As the youngest Soviet leader since Stalin, Gorbachev set in motion in 1985 bold plans for increased openness, which he called *glasnost,* and a program of political and economic restructuring, which he dubbed *perestroika.* The economic challenges that Gorbachev faced were enormous. Soviet citizens were better fed, better educated, and in better health than their parents and grandparents had been. Yet while economic growth continued throughout the postwar years, the rate of growth was slowing down in the 1970s. Soviet citizens were increasingly aware of the sacrifices and suffering that economic development had cost them in the twentieth century and of the disparities in the standards of living between the capitalist and communist worlds.

Gorbachev's programs between 1985 and 1988 promised more than they delivered. The promises were part of the problem since they created unmet expectations. Modest increases in output were achieved, but people's demands for food and consumer goods were rising faster than they could be met. The Soviet Union did not increase imports of consumer durables or food to meet the demand, nor did the quality of Soviet goods improve appreciably.

Although his economic reforms broke sharply with the centralized economy established by Stalin in the 1930s, Gorbachev candidly warned that he would not implement a consumption revolution in the near future. Many critics, including fellow communist Boris Yeltsin, believed that Gorbachev did not go far or fast enough with his economic reforms. Yet by 1989, many observers inside and outside the Soviet Union believed that a new age was at hand as the Soviet leader loosened censorship, denounced Stalin, and held the first free elections in the Soviet Union since 1917.

Reform in Eastern Europe

The Soviet example of restructuring and Gorbachev's calls for reforms and openness gave the lead to eastern Europe.

Poland and Grassroots Protest. Throughout the 1970s, the Polish government, based on one-party rule, drew loans from abroad for investment in technology and industrial expansion. The government increased its foreign indebtedness rather than raise prices at home. In 1976, however, price increases were again decreed. A new wave of spontaneous strikes erupted, forcing the government to rescind the increases.

Poland's indebtedness to the West rose from $2.5 billion in 1973 to $17 billion in 1980. At the beginning of July 1980, the government was forced yet again to raise food prices. Shipyard workers in Gdansk were ready, solidly organized in a new noncommunist labor union called **Solidarity** under the leadership of a politically astute electrician named Lech Walesa. The union staged a sit-down strike that paralyzed the shipyards. Union committees coordinated their activities from one factory to the next and succeeded in shutting down the entire economy. The government agreed to a series of union-backed reforms known as the Gdansk

Strike leader Lech Walesa addresses shipyard workers in Gdansk, Poland, on 30 August 1980.

Accords, which, among other measures, increased civil liberties and acknowledged Solidarity's right to exist.

General Wojciech Jaruzelski became prime minister in February 1981, but the situation of shortages did not change appreciably. Jaruzelski attempted to curb the union's demands for democratic government and participation in management by harsh measures: He declared martial law on 13 December 1981. Jaruzelski was trying to save the Polish Communist party by using the Polish military to crack down on the dissidents. The Soviet response was to do nothing. Poland, as a result, was left to Polish rule.

Martial law in Poland produced military repression. Solidarity was outlawed and Walesa was jailed. The West did not lose sight of him: In 1983, the union leader was awarded the Nobel Peace Prize for his efforts. After years of negotiations and intermittent strikes, Solidarity was legalized once again in 1989. The economy was in dire straits, and Jaruzelski knew that he needed Solidarity's cooperation: He agreed to open elections. At the polls, Solidarity candidates soundly defeated the Communist party. Poland was the first country anywhere to turn a Communist regime out of office peacefully.

The great challenge before the Solidarity government, as for the Communist regime that preceded it, was economic recovery. Inflation drove food prices up at the rate of 50 percent a month. In the mid-1990s, Poland continued its pursuit of a free market economy by attracting Western companies and corporations to open subsidiaries and to do business within its borders, as inflation slowed to a still high 20 to 30 percent, and a prosperous management class began emerging.

1. **Poland.** Solidarity party sweeps elections, June 1989.

2. **Czechoslovakia.** Communist leadership ousted, Nov. 1989; Vaclav Havel named president, Dec. 1989.

3. **Germany.** Berlin Wall breached, Nov 1989. Reunification of East and West Germany, Oct. 1990.

4. **Yugoslavia.** Government decides to hold free elections, Dec. 1989.

5. **Romania.** Communist dictator Ceauşescu overthrown and executed, Dec. 1989; Salvation Front led by dissident former Communists wins elections, May 1990.

6. **Albania.** Communist party still retains Leninist orientation, Jan. 1990. Parliament backs liberal reforms, May 1990.

7. **Bulgaria.** Government disavows "dominant role" for Communist party; pledges free elections and new constitution in 1990.

8. **Lithuania** declares independence, March 1990; Moscow calls move illegal.

9. **Hungary.** Free election sweeps non-Communists into power, April 1990.

10. **Latvia and Estonia** begin process of separation from Soviet Union, April 1990.

EVENTS IN EASTERN EUROPE, 1989–1990. The events of 1989 and 1990 seemed to indicate that peaceful democratic change through free elections and liberal reforms would fill the void left by the collapse of communist rule.

Hungary, Czechoslovakia, and Romania. In the same period as the Polish free elections, Hungary dismantled the barbed-wire fences on its Austrian border; all of its borders to the West were opened in September 1989. Unlike other eastern European countries, Hungary had begun experimenting cautiously with free markets and private control as early as the 1970s. As a result, Hungary was best positioned to engage in serious trade with western Europe and made the most prosperous adjustment to democratic autonomy.

Czechoslovakia's revolution began with angry university students. Singing Czech versions of protest songs such as "We Shall Overcome," student protesters were reminiscent of the student activists of 1968. They tried to give flowers to police, who responded by bludgeoning the protesters. That spark touched off a mass movement that within days drove out the Czech Communist party. The dissident playwright Václav Havel, released from jail just before the demonstrations began, emerged as the leader of the democratic opposition and was elected president of the new government. All of the countries underwent what were considered "velvet revolutions," characterized by a lack of violence and an apparently smooth passage to a new order and the achievement of independence.

The year 1989 did not end, however, without bloody upheaval. In December 1989, the Romanian dictator Nicolea Ceaucescu ordered his troops to fire on demonstrators. Thousands of men, women, and children were killed and buried unceremoniously in mass graves. The slaughter set off a revolution in which Ceaucescu and his wife and co-ruler, Elena, were captured, tried, and executed by a firing squad.

Chronology

THE VELVET REVOLUTIONS

1989	Free elections in Poland lead to the ouster of the Communist regime
September 1989	Hungary opens its borders to the West
November 1989	German Democratic Republic lifts travel restrictions between East and West Germany; the Berlin Wall comes down
December 1989	Václav Havel elected president of Czechoslovakia
July 1990	Havel reelected as president of the Czech and Slovak Federated Republic
1990	Boris Yeltsin elected president of the Russian Republic
1990	Gorbachev ends the Communist party's monopoly of power
1990	Lech Walesa elected president of Poland
October 1990	Federal Republic of Germany and German Democratic Republic reunited
December 1991	Eleven former Soviet republics form Commonwealth of Independent States (CIS); Mikhail Gorbachev resigns, and the Soviet Union is dissolved

The Unification of Germany

The crumbling facade of Communist unity within the Soviet bloc was nowhere more evident than in East Germany. The German Democratic Republic (East Germany) and the German Federal Republic (West Germany), divided by the victorious Allies following World War II, continued to develop after 1968 as two separate countries with different social, economic, and political institutions.

Citizens in East Germany were lured by the greater prosperity of the West. The lure proved too great in the 1980s and East Germany increasingly allowed its citizens to emigrate. The dismantling of the Berlin Wall in 1989 was symbolic of a greater opening of borders as greater numbers of East Germans chose the West.

An East Germany with open borders could no longer survive as its citizens poured into the promised land of the West in record numbers. The West German government intervened to assist East Germany in shoring up its badly faltering economy; the West German deutsche mark was substituted for the East German currency. Monetary union prefigured political unification. In October 1990, Germany became a single, united nation once again.

Russia and the New Republics

As eastern and central European nations were choosing self-rule and greater independence from the Soviet Union, the Soviet Union's own Communist party faced a dilemma. How could party rule and centralization be coordinated with the demands for freedom and autonomy that Gorbachev's own reforms fostered?

Aware of his precarious political position, Gorbachev appeared to retrench by increasing control over the media and by attempting to consolidate his base of power. As a result of the attempts, many believed that the regime was becoming authoritarian.

Boris Yeltsin in Power. The shocking end to the Gorbachev experiment came in August 1991. A quasi-military council of Communist hard-liners seized power in order to restore Communist rule and reverse democratic reforms. Gorbachev was taken prisoner in his vacation home in the Crimea. Soviet citizens from the Baltic republics to Siberia protested the takeover, and tens of thousands of Muscovites poured into the streets to defy the tanks and troops of the rebel government.

Boris Yeltsin became a hero overnight, publicly defying the plotters, rallying popular support behind him, and helping convince Soviet army troops to disobey orders to attack the White House, as the parliament building in Moscow is called. After only two days, the coup d'état failed; Gorbachev returned to Moscow and banned the Communist party. Although Gorbachev retained his title of Soviet president, his prestige had been seriously damaged by the coup and by the challenge of Yeltsin's new dominance as a popular hero. In the national elections for the Congress of People's Deputies that followed, Boris Yeltsin garnered 89 percent of the popular vote.

The Big Mac comes to Moscow. McDonald's opened its first Soviet fast-food outlet in 1990, just a few blocks from the Kremlin. Muscovites stood in long lines for milkshakes, fries, and the "Bolshoi Mak."

Economic Challenges. Embarking on a drive toward westernization and playing catch-up with capitalist nations, liberal reformers in Russia pressed after August 1991 for privatization of industry and the lifting of price controls. There was hope inside and outside Russia that the new state would easily enter the capitalist marketplace. The long lines in front of stores disappeared. But inflation ominously galloped to new heights, wiping out savings and pensions overnight. The black market, always in the shadows even in the most repressed of times, emerged boldly as a corrupt "mafia," and its people became the new business leaders of Russia. The combined crises of inflation and rule by a gangster elite weakened the barely emergent market economy and undermined the Russian ruble, whose value crashed in October 1994. While a new wealthy class was emerging, as many as 30 percent of the population had become indigent and lived below the poverty line.

The Nationalities Problem. A crucial element in understanding the end of the Soviet Union was the **nationalities problem** within its borders—the claim to self-determination made by Soviet minorities. The Soviet Union listed 102 separate nationalities in its 1979 census. Twenty-two of those nationalities had populations of one million or more people. That very diversity contributed to the disintegration of the Soviet Union from within. As Gorbachev supported the demands for self-determination in eastern Europe, he faced similar claims to autonomy in a growing number of Soviet republics. The nationalities problem proved to be even more challenging to Gorbachev's regime than the free market economy. In fact, the demands for more freedom in the marketplace went hand in hand with demands for greater cultural self-expression and political autonomy among minority nationalities.

Ethnic minorities, especially in the Soviet Baltic republics of Latvia, Lithuania, and Estonia, threatened the dominance of party rule in favor of immediate self-determination. Large-scale riots erupted in Lithuania over demands for nationalist rights. In 1988, Estonians demanded the right of veto over any law passed in Moscow. The Russian minority in Estonia protested attacks and prejudicial treatment in the Estonian republic. In the same year, outright violence erupted in

MAP DISCOVERY

Legend		
Slavic	Uralian	Caucasian
Baltic	Romance	Iranian
Turkic	Armenian	Other languages or sparsely populated areas

Republics
1 Russian S.F.S.R. 9 Armenia
2 Estonia 10 Azerbaijan
3 Latvia 11 Kazakhstan
4 Lithuania 12 Turkmenia
5 Byelorussia 13 Uzbekistan
6 Ukraine 14 Tajikistan
7 Moldavia 15 Kirghizia
8 Georgia

REPUBLICS OF THE SOVIET UNION

The Soviet Union broke up into 15 independent nations, which embraced a variety of ethnic groups. Note the correspondence between ethnicity/language and independent nation status. What new republics have only one language? In the nation of Uzbekistan, how many ethnicities and languages are there? How many different ethnic groups remained in the new Russian state?

Azerbaijan as tens of thousands of Armenians took to the streets to demand the return of the Armenian enclave of Nagorno-Karabakh, incorporated into Azerbaijan in 1921. In the Azerbaijan capital of Baku, the center of Russia's oil-producing region, demonstrators demanded greater autonomy for their republic and the accountability of their deputies in Moscow.

The Breakaway Republics Lead the Way. One by one, all 15 of the Soviet republics proclaimed their independence, following the lead of the breakaway Baltic republics of Estonia, Lithuania, and Latvia. Rejecting all Soviet authority, Russia, Belarus, and Ukraine joined together in December 1991 to form the Commonwealth of Independent States (CIS). Eight other republics followed their lead. The Soviet Union thereby came to its end on 21 December 1991 with the resignation of Mikhail Gorbachev, who had become a man without a state to rule.

Many issues remained unresolved. The new political organization did not address the endemic problems of economic hardship and left unanswered the questions of who would control the former Soviet Union's vast military machine, including its nuclear arsenal, and how trade networks and a stable monetary policy would be determined. Just as there were millions of Russians living beyond the borders of the Russian state with the rise of independent republics, there continued to be ethnic minorities within Russia who sought independence. Russia, on a smaller scale than its Soviet predecessor, was a federation of different ethnic minorities and a Russian majority population with no clear policy for autonomy or self-rule.

Ethnic Conflict and Nationalism

Freedom was not the only force unleashed with the collapse of communism. Ugly battles based on long-standing grievances erupted. Groups intent on autonomy and independence vied with each other over territories and borders. Chechnya struggled to be free of Russian rule. The Balkans, where borders had been imposed at the end of World War I, erupted into genocidal strife that shocked the world.

The Chechen Challenge

In December 1994, Russia committed itself to a war with another of its ethnic minorities, the secessionist Chechens, who had declared themselves independent of Russia in 1991. By the summer of 1996, Russia appeared to have lost the war and agreed to a truce.

In the summer of 1999, conflict again escalated into open warfare because of terrorist bombings in Moscow attributed to Chechen rebels. Affected by arguments of self-defense against terrorists, Russian popular opinion now turned in favor of repressing the Chechen bid for independence. Russia also had important economic motives for subduing the runaway republic, as Chechnya's location was central to the oil pipeline routes near the Caspian Sea. Several former Soviet states had begun building a new pipeline in the 1990s in order to circumvent the Russian supply and to sell directly to Western buyers.

In 2001, Russian president Vladimir Putin declared the war in Chechnya over. Yet violence continued. Following terrorist attacks in the United States on 11 September 2001, the Russians escalated their war against terrorism in Chechnya. The Chechen insurgents launched terrorist attacks within the Russian state. Putin responded to these terrorist attacks by limiting democracy and civil liberties, a move that unleashed popular discontent within Russia and criticism around the world. With Russian victory in this second phase of the war, the Chechen Republic, part of the Russian Federation, undertook rebuilding of the destroyed capital of Grozny with Russian investment. Concerns for civil liberties and security prevailed in a region that remained barely stable, as insurgency and ethnic hostilities went underground.

War in the Balkans

Yugoslavia was a federation of six people's republics, with Serbia, Croatia, and Bosnia and Herzegovina the three largest in descending order. In 1991, festering differences erupted in civil war between Serbs and Croats, as Serbian nationalists overran multiethnic Bosnia and Herzegovina in a bid for territorial aggrandizement of Serbia. Serbia and Croatia were more than long-standing rival enemies with a history of hostility that had been masked by their federated status in the Yugoslav state.

The History of Ethnic Differences. The divide between the Serbs and Croats was partly identified with religious differences—the Croats were historically Catholic, the Serbs Orthodox—but for the most part, their enmity was based on the competing claims over the South Slavic lands, Bosnia and Herzegovina, that were part of the former Ottoman and Austro-Hungarian Empires.

Conflicting territorial claims of the Serbs and Croatians were considerably exacerbated by two facts. First, a large number of Serbs lived in Croatia, and, of course, Croatians were present in the Serbian-claimed lands of Bosnia. Second, another group, neither Catholic nor Orthodox but Muslim, amounting to 9 percent of the population of the former Yugoslavia and a majority of the Bosnian population, got caught in the crossfire of the war between Serbs and Croats and became a target for massacre and atrocities by the Serbs.

In 1992, the Serbian army evicted 750,000 Muslim civilians from their homes in Bosnia. Serb forces also continued to bomb civilians in the Bosnian capital of Sarajevo. It later came to light that in 1992 Serb leaders had authorized a policy of **ethnic cleansing**—including concentration camps, rape, and starvation—against Muslims. In 1995, the Serb military was also responsible for the mass killings of Muslims from Srebrenica. Such barbarity contributed heavily to forging a strong sense of national identity among Bosnian Muslims, who controlled the Bosnian army and the presidency.

The United Nations placed forces in Bosnia on a peace-keeping mission, which allowed it to take neither side in the war. NATO intervened against the Serbian attempt to overrun Bosnia after the outbreak of hostilities, and in September 1995 NATO stepped up the bombing of Bosnian Serb military installations and Serbian-held positions in Bosnia with the policy of avoiding civilian targets.

The Dayton Peace Accords brokered by the United States brought Muslim, Croat, and Serb leaders together in Ohio in November and December 1995. As part of the commitment to the accord, the Clinton administration sent 20,000 U.S. troops to join the 60,000 NATO troops already present to help enforce the peace. The aim of the accords was to create a unified country in Bosnia while recognizing ethnic interests. The settlement called for a shared three-person presidency chosen by free elections.

Kosovo and the Ongoing Conflict in Eastern Europe. Yet another arena of bloodshed opened up in 1998. Kosovo, one of the six former Yugoslav republics, had been known as the "autonomous province" of Serbia. Checking attempts at Kosovo independence, Serbia proceeded to strip it of its autonomous status after 1990. In addition, there was overwhelming evidence that the Serb state intended to drive more than one million Kosovo Albanians from the province. The Kosovo Liberation Army responded with guerrilla actions against the Serbs.

Civil rights abuses and atrocities against Kosovo Albanians by Kosovo Serbs shocked the world into action in 1998. On the night of 24 March 1999, NATO forces began attacking Serbian targets in Kosovo in a massive military campaign of air strikes that lasted for almost 11 weeks. The war, a first in NATO's history, marked a failure in its policy of deterrence. As the lead partner, the United States justified an unpopular war at home by promising not to commit ground troops in battle. The air war succeeded, and United Nations peace-keeping forces, including U.S. troops, entered Kosovo in June 1999. The Serbs were probably responsible for the deaths of at least 10,000 and the expulsion of 800,000 Kosovo Albanians. With the defeat of Serb forces, Kosovo Albanians took the place of their Serb oppressors and committed new atrocities, now under the nose of peace-keeping forces, with the aim of driving non-Albanians out of the province. Intolerance and the desire for revenge boded ill for the future of peace in the region.

Other eastern European states also were riddled with ethnic troubles—including those between Czechs and Slovaks, the Hungarians and Romanians over the border region of Transylvania, and the Bulgarians and Turks in Bulgaria—but none of those disputes involved the degree of violence that had occurred in the Balkans.

The West in the Global Community

The phenomenal growth and prosperity of western Europe came up against a new set of harsh realities in the 1970s with skyrocketing oil prices, inflation, and recession. With the goal of reviving the economy in the 1980s, the 12 member states of the European Economic Community devoted themselves to making western Europe competitive as a bloc in world markets. They hoped that by uniting they could serve as a counterweight to American economic hegemony in the West. At the same time that Russian satellites in eastern Europe were breaking free of Soviet control and attempting to strike out on their own, the nations of western Europe were negotiating a new unity based on a single market and centralized policy making.

Yet social and economic problems persisted, the costs of the welfare state rose, terrorism tyrannized democratic societies, and a new nationalism vied with cooperation across borders. The rosy vision of the West in a global community that many foresaw in 1990 seemed to have a cloudy future as the West faced the new century.

European Union and the American Superpower

The European Community (EC) had been created in 1967 by merging the three transnational European bodies—the European Coal and Steel Community, the European Economic Community, and the European Atomic Energy Community. It operated with its own commission, parliament, and council of ministers, though it had little real power over the operations of member states. Almost since its inception, the European Community was committed to European integration.

The Politics of Oil. The oil crisis of the 1970s encouraged isolationism among the members of the EC and eroded foreign markets, causing growing dependence on national suppliers and thereby undercutting the goals of the Common Market. As the crisis abated, competition and efficiency reemerged as priorities within the EC. Europeans were well aware that the United States and Japan had surged ahead after the 1973 crisis. Western European leaders realized that integration was the only defense against the permanent loss of markets and dwindling profits.

Toward a Single Europe. In 1985, the EC negotiated the Single European Act, which by 1987 had been ratified by the parliamentary bodies of all the member nations. Final steps were initiated to establish a fully integrated market by 31 December 1992. The 12 members of the EC intended to eliminate internal barriers and to create a huge open market among the member states with common external tariff policies. In addition, the elimination of internal frontier controls with a single-format passport was intended to make travel easier and to avoid shipping delays at frontiers, thereby lowering costs. An international labor market based on standardized requirements for certification and interchangeable job qualifications would result. The easier movement of capital to areas where profitability was greatest was encouraged. All aspects of trade and communication, down to electrical plugs and sockets, had to be standardized. The goal behind the planning was to make the EC think and act as a single country.

Plans for European economic integration moved dramatically forward in October 1991 when the 12-nation European Community and the 7 nations of the European Free Trade Association (EFTA) joined forces to form a new common market to be known as the European Economic Area. The EFTA countries that joined forces with the EC included Austria, Finland, Iceland, Liechtenstein, Norway, Sweden, and Switzerland. Several of the EFTA nations announced plans to join the EC as well.

The European Union. Meeting in Maastricht, the Netherlands, in December 1991, the heads of the 12 EC countries ratified a treaty momentous for the European Union. They agreed that a common currency, the **euro,** would replace the national currencies of eligible nations, and that a single central banking system, known as the European Monetary Institute, would guide member.nations in reducing inflation rates and budget deficits. Economic union would be reinforced by political union, with member states sharing a common European defense system and common social policies regulating immigration and labor practices. In that sense, the new **European Union (EU)** was intended as something more than the European Community (EC), which had been primarily an economic entity to promote free trade.

EUROPEAN UNION. The most stable and prosperous European nations formed the 12 original member states of the European Union in 1992, soon joined by three additional members. These members agreed to share a common currency, economic and social policies, and planning. In 2004, 10 new nations joined the EU.

On 1 January 2002, Europeans in 12 of 15 member nations began using the new euro. Hailed as the European Union's boldest achievement, the new currency was intended to solidify the basis of integrated European markets and be competitive in international markets against the dollar. Within two months of the introduction of the euro, at the end of February 2002, the member nations of the European Union held a convention for the purpose of considering the creation of a Europe-wide constitution.

Many worried, however, that the long histories, traditions, and national identifications of the individual member states would stand in the way of a fully integrated and politically united Europe. Britain was the most reluctant of the member states at the prospect of European integration. British negotiators strongly resisted plans for monetary union because they feared losing national sovereignty rights. In addition to resisting monetary union, British public opinion polls reflected cynicism over the 1991 Maastricht negotiations and a social policy affecting working hours, minimum wages, and conditions of employment throughout Europe.

The biggest expansion in the European Union came on 1 May 2004 when 10 new states, all from eastern Europe, became members of the EU. By 2009 the European Union included 27 member states, representing 498 million citizens. Three other countries—Croatia, Turkey, and the former Yugoslav republic of Macedonia—were accepted as candidates for membership, and a fourth, Iceland, asked to be considered as a candidate in summer 2009. Of the 27 member states, 16 shared the euro as a common currency with other members to follow as their national economies were ready.

The three criteria for membership—a democratic political system, a market economy, and the administrative capacity to function as a member—were linked to the shared goals of raising the standard of living throughout Europe, and of creating frontier-free trade and travel, a common currency, environmental protections, and a competition-driven single market. Yet the challenges were great in the face of a worldwide economic recession that began at the end of 2007 connected to a banking crisis and increased unemployment. As the official Website of the EU stated in 2009: "The EU is not perfect—it is an evolving project and constantly has to be improved."

Originally intended to offset American dominance in European markets, in the 1990s the EU offered the opportunity of a closer economic relationship with the United States. The EU became the largest customer for American products and many American companies entered into partnerships and joint ventures with EU firms. The possibility of the emergence of a truly global marketplace seemed, paradoxically, more likely with the creation of the EU and other regional associations throughout the world.

A New Working Class: Foreign Workers

Foreign workers played an important role in the industrial expansion of western Europe beginning in the 1950s. Migrant employment was by definition poorly paid, unskilled, or semiskilled manual work. Foreign male workers found employment on construction sites all over western Europe. Foreign women worked in domestic service, personal care, and factories. Commonly, married men migrated without their families, with the goal of earning cash to send home to those left behind.

Working Conditions and Rights. The lot of foreign workers was difficult and sometimes dangerous. Onerous and demanding labor was common. Foreign workers were often herded together in crowded living quarters, socially marginalized, and identified with the degrading work they performed. Foreign workers were frequently denied the rights of citizenship and subjected to the vagaries of legislation.

In economic downturns they were the first to be laid off. Yet the obligations of foreign workers to send money back home to aged parents, spouses, children, and siblings persisted. Children who resided in the host country with their foreign-worker parents suffered from severe identity problems, experiencing discrimination in schools in the countries in which they were born and with which they identified.

Women endured special problems within the foreign workforce. Between 1964 and 1974, the majority of Portuguese immigrants to France came with families, but there were few social services to support them on their arrival. Dependable child care was either too expensive or unavailable to female workers with children. Increasing numbers of single women began migrating to western Europe independently of their households. Like men, they worked in order to send money back home.

Opposition and Restrictions. Opposition to the presence of foreign workers was often expressed in ultranationalist rhetoric and usually flared up in periods of economic reversals. In 1986 in France, the xenophobic National Front campaigned on a platform of "France for the French" and captured 10 percent of the vote in national elections. Racism was out in the open in Western countries that had depended on a foreign labor force for their prosperity. Arab and black African workers in France resorted to work stoppages to protest police discrimination and identity controls that they likened to the yellow Stars of David that Jews had been required to wear in Nazi Germany. In 1996, the French government chartered planes to return undocumented Africans to Africa. Riots in Great Britain in 1980 and 1981, particularly in the London ghetto of Brixton, were motivated by racial discrimination against blacks, severe cuts in social welfare spending, and deteriorating working conditions.

The presence of foreign workers in European Union countries heightened racism and overt antagonism from a resurgent extreme Right. In the late 1980s, when movements for democratic freedom and human rights were being endorsed in eastern Europe, the problem of permanent resident "aliens" was without a solution in western Europe. Yet the need for cheap labor made the preservation of such a labor pool likely.

The issue of immigration became a prominent one in electoral campaigns throughout Europe in the 1990s. Opposition to the presence of foreign workers and concerns about protecting small business interests fueled ballot-box victories for the far right in Austria, the Netherlands, and France.

French Laws on Secularity. The presence of populations from north Africa and southern and eastern Europe in western Europe resulted in a clash of cultures, values, and religious beliefs. In France, Muslim girls began wearing veils and head scarves in school in growing numbers beginning in the late 1980s. Citing French laws on the separation of church and state, authorities ultimately banned all accessories and clothing that indicated religious affiliation, including crosses and yarmulkes. An amendment to

Indian immigrants in France sewing in a sweatshop. Immigrant workers in European countries took low-paying, menial jobs. They faced resentment from xenophobic native Europeans.

the law in 2004 raised enforcement to the national level. The public debate about assimilation and citizenship reinforced the idea that citizenship required adherence to a common code and common cultural values.

Women's Changing Lives

During the last quarter of the twentieth century, the lives of Western women reflected dramatic social changes. In that period of increased educational and work opportunities, an international women's movement emerged. Issues such as fertility and sexuality were at the center of the new politics of the women's movement.

Reforms and Political Action. In Italy, political action by women yielded a new law in 1970 that allowed divorce under very restricted circumstances. Italian feminists used the legal system as a public forum. In France, the sale of contraceptives was legalized in 1968. French feminists, like their Italian counterparts, worked through the courts to make abortion legal: They achieved their goal in 1975. With the increasing integration of Europe in the 1990s, differing national practices in child care, health care, and gender parity were reviewed by the deliberative bodies of the European Union. Yet national differences of women's social and family roles still prevailed among European countries, including differences in education, health care, and reproductive rights.

The feminist movement created a new feminist scholarship that sought to incorporate women's experiences and perspectives into the disciplines of the humanities and the social sciences. Women's studies courses, which emphasized the history of women and their contributions to civilization, became part of university and college curricula throughout Europe and the United States. Reformers also attempted to transform language, which, they argued, had served as a tool of oppression.

In addition to promoting political action throughout Europe, issues of domestic violence, incest, and sexual orientation entered the political arena. In 1970, Western feminism was discovering that "socialism was not enough," and that women had to address problems of discrimination in terms of gender as much as class.

Terrorism: The "New Kind of War"

The history of contemporary terrorism began after World War II. The creation of the state of Israel in part of the land of Palestine in 1948 led to conflict between the Israelis and the Palestinian Arabs, who refused to accept the new Jewish state. Israel's Arab neighbors went to war to support the Palestinians but were defeated by Israel in late 1948. Hundreds of thousands of Palestinians became refugees in neighboring Arab states, and Palestinian guerrillas decided that the best way to attack Israel and its protectors was with a global strategy of terrorist violence.

Another influence figured prominently in terrorism of the late twentieth century: Islamic fundamentalism. Muslim militants intent on waging a "holy war" for the oppressed could be found throughout the world in areas as different as Algeria, Bosnia and Herzegovina, France, and the Philippines. Muslim radicals in those and other countries shared a truly global commitment and were often heavily influenced by their formative volunteer experiences in the Afghan war of the 1980s. Conceiving of their mission as a holy one, they were able to form a series of loose connections with Muslims from other countries for the purposes of recruitment, training, and deployment of dedicated fighters.

Terrorists came from many nations and religious backgrounds. Peace-loving Muslims were maligned in Europe and the United States because of fundamentalists' actions. Following the 1995 bombing of the federal building in Oklahoma City, Arabs and Muslims across the United States were singled out for reprisals and intimidation until it was discovered that the Oklahoma City bombing was the act of domestic terrorists protesting U.S. government policies. The Oklahoma City attack, which terrorized the nation, fit the essential definition of the new terrorism as a violent act against innocent civilians for the purpose of undermining the power of the government.

Terrorism in the Last Quarter of the Twentieth Century. By the late 1970s, a strategy of terrorist violence appealed to European revolutionaries intent on advancing a variety of political causes. Political killings became a tactic of choice for terrorists throughout the world. Although motivated by different political agendas, terrorist groups often formed cooperative networks on an international basis, sharing training, weapons, and information.

Western Europe served as an important arena for terrorist acts by non-European groups. To succeed—that is, to terrify mass populations—terrorists needed publicity. Terrorists relied on media exposure and claimed responsibility for acts only after they had been successfully completed. In September 1972, members of the Palestinian Black September movement kidnapped 11 Israeli athletes at the Olympic Games in Munich. An estimated 500 million people watched their televisions in horror as all 11 were slaughtered during an American sports broadcast. In 1979, 52 Americans were kidnapped from the American Embassy in Teheran and were held hostage for 444 days by a group of young Iranian revolutionaries who claimed to be battling against the "great Satan." A recurrent pattern of terrorism prevailed throughout the 1980s with Israel and the United States often the targets of attacks.

Terrorist activities against the United States escalated following the U.S. military action against Iraq in 1991 known as the Persian Gulf War. In February 1993, the explosion of a bomb planted in a small truck parked in the basement garage of the World Trade Center in New York killed six people, wounded a thousand, and did limited damage to the structure. Two terrorist attacks in Saudi Arabia in 1995 and 1996 killed 24 Americans. In August 1998, two major assaults against American embassies, one in Tanzania and the other in Kenya, killed 224 people and injured hundreds of others. In October 2000, a suicide attack against the USS *Cole* in the port of Aden took the lives of 17 sailors.

All of these attacks were attributed to the network of a single man, Osama bin Laden, a Saudi Arabian millionaire, who had been trained by the U.S. Central Intelligence Agency and who, between 1980 and 1989, had fought against the Russians in Afghanistan. In June 2001, bin Laden called on the Muslims of the world to mobilize themselves into a general **jihad,** or holy war, against their enemies. Three months after this call to arms, terrorists dealt their most extreme blow against the United States.

11 September 2001: A Turning Point. On 11 September 2001, four U.S. passenger planes were hijacked and used as flying bombs in a coordinated action that targeted the World Trade Center in New York City and the Pentagon just outside of Washington, DC. Two of the four hijacked planes slammed into the twin towers of the World Trade Center, and a third plane hit its mark by diving into the Pentagon. The fourth plane crashed in a field in Pennsylvania, its suicide attack foiled by passengers who opposed their captors. More than 3,000 people were killed, thousands more were wounded, and the loss of property was unprecedented in the worst terrorist attack in history. The events horrified people around the world who understood that two symbols of American global financial and military dominance had been singled out in a carefully planned and executed mission of destruction. Once again, Osama bin Laden was identified as the mastermind of terrorist devastation. President George W. Bush declared, in the wake of the terrorist attacks, that the United States was entering "a new kind of war," one not waged between nations but one whose stateless enemy would be sought out and hunted down. The event marked a turning point in the struggle against terrorism and a new focus in state security measures of Western governments. It also marked the beginning of a new war.

In October 2001, less than a month after the attacks, the United States and Great Britain undertook war in Afghanistan in pursuit of bin Laden, who was believed to have been harbored there by the Taliban, a fundamentalist Muslim ruling group. Though bin Laden was not captured, the Taliban was removed from power. In the fall of 2004, free elections for the nation's first elected president were conducted throughout Afghanistan under the eyes of military observers. Hamid Karzai was elected president. The resurgent Taliban threatened to block the next round of presidential elections held in August 2009 and to undermine the Karzai government that it characterized as supporting "invading Americans." Growing insurgency in Afghanistan coupled with weak government and with increased casualty rates, especially among British soldiers, weakened European support for the ongoing war at the moment that U.S. president Barack Obama was increasing the American civilian and military presence in the country.

After September 11, the Americans and their allies in Europe and throughout the world joined forces in pledging to eradicate terrorism. Stringent security measures in airports and public places were instituted worldwide as nations faced harsh new political realities, including incidents of bioterrorism—germ warfare against civilians—in the months following the September terrorist attacks. When the European Union and the United States passed new laws and directives to combat terrorism, critics feared the curtailment of civil liberties. Racist incidents against Muslims and Arabs mounted, even as European and American leaders stressed that bin Laden and his network were a nonrepresentative and fanatical fringe within the Muslim world.

Throughout the post–September 11 era, Iraq and its leader Saddam Hussein continued to be singled out by the U.S. government as sympathetic to the terrorist cause and committed to developing "weapons of mass destruction." As a consequence of a United Nations' resolution, UN inspection teams entered Iraq in mid-November 2002 in a search for such weapons. None was found. In further pursuit of such weapons and with the intention of removing Hussein from power, President George W. Bush ordered U.S. troops in coalition with British forces to lead an attack against Iraq in March 2003. Saddam Hussein was captured and executed by the Iraqi government, but insurgent forces resisted the military occupation. Terrorist actions continued to take American and Iraqi lives as the American government attempted to rebuild the Iraqi economy during the peace. American involvement in this war was greatly unpopular and resulted in undermining Western alliances and increasing criticism of American foreign policy throughout the world. At the beginning of 2009, under popular pressure at home and abroad, U.S. President Obama announced the withdrawal of combat forces from Iraq by 2011. But the future of American foreign policy in the region remained uncertain as the question of an independent Palestinian state continued unresolved, and Iran threatened to acquire nuclear capability.

Terrorism and Counterterrorism. Terrorism in the last quarter of the twentieth century was not promoted by a single movement but a wide variety of groups and organizations on both the left and right. Some organizations were Marxist; some were nationalist; some were Islamic fundamentalists. Industrial nations, especially the United States, Israel, and their allies, were common targets of terrorist attacks. Terrorists all shared a vision of the world based on the commonly held belief that destruction of the existing order was the only way to bring about a more equitable system.

This photograph captures the massive explosion caused when a second hijacked plane crashed into the World Trade Center in New York on 11 September 2001. The landmark twin towers were destroyed in the attack, and thousands of people were killed.

Terrorists justified their violent actions in terms of the legitimacy of their cause. Terrorists argued that just as resistance fighters in World War II had used bombs and assassinations as their means of fighting a more powerful enemy, they themselves were engaged in wars of liberation, revolution, and resistance and were using the only weapons at their disposal to fight great imperialist powers.

By the mid-1990s, it was clear that terrorism was an effective challenge to the tranquility of industrial nations. Modern terrorists were often able to evade policing and detection. Surveillance had not prevented terrorists from striking at airplanes and cruise ships.

West European governments often refused on principle to bargain with terrorists. Yet at times, European nations and the United States have been willing to negotiate for the release of kidnapped citizens. They have also been willing to use violence themselves against terrorists. The greatest mobilization in counterterrorist efforts came with U.S. leadership following the events of 11 September 2001. The goal of the "counterterrorism" was to undermine support for terrorists among their own people; its tactics and ends opened counterterrorism to the criticism that it was very similar to the terrorism it was opposing. In fact, torture of prisoners and interrogations in violation of the Geneva conventions at the hands of American soldiers and civilian personnel came to light in an Iraqi prison in the summer of 2004. American policies in the military prison of Guantanamo Bay at the southeastern tip of Cuba also came under international scrutiny, as concerns about detaining foreign terrorist suspects without due process of law mounted. In 2009 the new Obama administration pledged to close the prison and reinstate prisoners' rights to a fair trial.

In spite of tactics of meeting violence with violence, the advanced industrial states of western Europe and the United States remained vulnerable to an invisible terrorist enemy. That elusive enemy could terrorize populations and incapacitate the smooth functioning of the modern industrial state. Into the new century, terrorism continued to threaten peace and paralyze security, at the very moment when people all over the globe celebrated the hope for a better world. After the large-scale terrorist attacks of 2001, the promise of a new and better world seemed, for many, to move further out of reach.

Global Recession

By the end of 2007 global stability was threatened by a problem that soon eclipsed terrorism in affecting people's daily lives. Declining productivity triggered by a banking crisis in the United States affected the whole world. A global recession caused national stock markets to plummet, available credit to shrink, consumption to contract, and unemployment to increase dramatically first in the industrialized countries of the United States, Europe, and Japan. Described as the worst financial crisis since the Great Depression of 1929, this period of economic contraction saw the reemergence of government regulation of the financial sector as a solution to economies in free fall. The United States helped define governmental response by introducing massive government bailouts in billions of dollars to the banking sector and key industries.

A notable example of government intervention was in the U.S. auto industry. Facing bankruptcy, General Motors and Chrysler were forced to restructure to qualify for government loans and to make themselves viable. By 2009 it was unclear if global economies had yet hit bottom in this period of decline. It was clear, however, that Western nations were forced to face new realities of contraction, hardship, and poverty, and that their national economies were deeply interdependent.

SUMMARY

The End of the Cold War and the Emergence of a New Europe   Rigidity and stagnation characterized eastern Europe after the promulgation of the Brezhnev Doctrine. Détente in the 1970s was followed by additional efforts at cooperation between East and West in the 1980s. Mikhail Gorbachev pursued policies of political liberalization and economic reform. His model stimulated reform movements in eastern Europe. In 1989 the Soviet Union's eastern satellites broke free and declared their independence. East and West Germany were unified. The disintegration of the Soviet Union soon followed. The claims to self-determination by Soviet minorities hastened the end of the Soviet Union.

Ethnic Conflict and Nationalism   In 1994 Russia launched a war against secessionist Chechens. Despite the agreement to a truce in 1996, the war escalated again in 1999. Russian President Vladimir Putin declared victory in 2001, but violence on both sides continued. Ethnic and nationalist tensions rose to the surface in Yugoslavia at the end of the Cold War. Religion, ethnicity, and history complicated the ensuing conflicts. Bosnian Muslims were a particular target for massacre and atrocities by the Serbs. Serb leaders engaged in a policy of "ethnic cleansing". United Nations and NATO forces attempted to keep the peace. The United States brokered the Dayton Peace Accords. Kosovo remained a site of ongoing conflict, prompting further NATO intervention.

The West in the Global Community   The formation of the new European Union (EU) and the introduction of a common currency were key moments in the movement toward European economic integration. By 2009, there were 27 member countries committed to economic cooperation. Foreign workers played key roles in the economy, but were the focus of increasing economic and social anxieties within Europe. New educational and economic opportunities for women were accompanied by a new women's rights movement. The history of contemporary terrorism began after World War II. The essential ingredient for the success of a terrorist act was publicity. Terrorist activities against the United States escalated following the 1991 Persian Gulf War. A series of terrorist acts perpetrated by Osama bin Laden and his organization culminated in the attacks of September 11, 2001. Allied forces launched a war against the Taliban in Afghanistan, who were believed to be harboring bin Laden. Intensified security measures brought concerns about curtailment of civil rights. In 2003 President George W. Bush linked a new war against Iraq with the fight against terrorism. Counterterrorism efforts failed to remove the threat of new terrorist attacks. In 2009, President Obama committed the United States to timed withdrawal from Iraq, while renewing the military and civilian presence in Afghanistan. At the end of the first decade of the twenty-first century, the economy and global recession posed the greatest challenges to Western nations.

QUESTIONS FOR REVIEW

1. What caused the end of the Cold War?
2. How did the ideas of *glasnost* and *perestroika* help bring about the end of the Soviet Union?
3. How did the collapse of communist regimes in Russia and eastern Europe promote national and ethnic conflict?
4. What social, economic, and political forces contributed to German reunification?
5. How did the treaty signed by the nations of the European Community at Maastricht in 1991 create both hopes and fears of European unity?
6. How have democracy and nationalism come into conflict since 1989?
7. What nations and populations experienced terrorism in the late twentieth and early twenty-first centuries? What were the causes of terrorism and from what did terrorism derive its power?

absolutism   Government in which power was consolidated in the hands of a divinely ordained monarch; typified by reverence for the monarch, weakening of representative institutions, and expansion of military.

agricultural revolution   Changes in the traditional agricultural system during the eighteenth century that included enclosure, introduction of fodder crops, intensified animal husbandry, and commercial market orientation.

alchemy   Study of metals in an effort to find their essence through purification. Medieval alchemists attempted to find precious metals such as silver and gold as the essence of base metals such as lead and iron.

Allies   In World War I, the United States, Great Britain, France, and Russia—the alliance that opposed and defeated the Central Powers of Germany and Austria-Hungary and their allies.

Anabaptists   Part of the radical Reformation, Protestant groups that varied in belief but agreed on the principle of adult baptism.

anarchism   A political movement based on rejection of extant political systems; most prominent in less-industrialized Western nations.

anti-Semitism   Hostility toward and discrimination against Jews.

appeasement   British policy of making concessions to Germany in the 1930s in order to avoid war. It allowed Hitler to militarize the Sudetenland and eventually take all of Czechoslovakia.

April Theses   Lenin's promise to the Russian people and challenge to the Provisional Government to provide peace, land, and bread. These three issues became the rallying cries for the second Russian revolution and for the withdrawal of Soviet Russia from World War I.

Arians   During the early Christological controversies, followers of the Alexandrine theologian, Arius, who believed that Jesus was not equal to God the Father.

Axis Powers   In World War II, the alliance of Germany, Italy, and later Japan.

balance of power   Distribution of power among nations in alliances so that any one nation is prevented from dominating the others.

Balfour Declaration   The commitment by the British government issued in 1917 to support a Jewish homeland in Palestine.

Berlin Wall   Barrier built by East Germany in 1961 to halt an exodus of skilled professionals to the West; opened in 1989 as a prelude to the reunification of East and West Germany.

Big Three   The British, Soviet, and U.S. leaders who coordinated defeat of Germany and Japan in World War II and negotiated postwar settlements. Referred to Churchill, Stalin, and Roosevelt until 1945; Attlee, Stalin, and Truman by summer 1945.

Black Death   The virulent combination of bubonic, septicemic, and pneumonic plagues that destroyed between one third and one half of the population of Europe between 1347 and 1352.

blitzkrieg   "Lightning war"; the rapid advance accompanied by armored vehicles that typified the German military during World War II.

Bolsheviks   Radical faction of Marxist Social Democrats following a political theory based on necessity of violent revolution. The Bolsheviks came to power with Lenin in November 1917.

bourgeoisie   A French term referring to the commercial classes of Europe after the seventeenth century; primarily an urban class.

Brezhnev Doctrine   Policy of Soviet leader Leonid Brezhnev that approved the use of military intervention in the internal affairs of Soviet allies to prevent counterrevolution.

cahiers de doléances   Lists of grievances sent with representatives to the French Estates-General in 1789; demonstrated the existence of a widespread public political culture in France.

caliph   The successors of Muhammad who served as political and religious leaders of the Islamic world (see Umma).

capitularies   The written instructions for the implementation of royal directives at the local level produced by the clerics of the Carolingian court.

caravels   Small Portuguese ships developed in the fifteenth century that were ideal for ocean travel.

Carnival   One of the traditional sixteenth-century festivals, the feasts and carousing of which preceded the onset of Lent.

Carolingian Renaissance   The cultural revival of classical learning sponsored by the emperor Charlemagne. New schools and the copying of manuscripts were among its important achievements.

cartels   Combinations of firms in a given industry to fix prices and establish production quotas.

Cartesianism   Philosophy of René Descartes that rested on the dual existence of mind and matter, a principle that enabled the use of skepticism to create certainty.

Central Powers   Germany and Austria-Hungary during World War I.

chartism   An English working-class reform movement that flourished in the 1830s and 1840s and that demanded universal male suffrage (right to vote), payment for parliamentary service, equal electoral districts, and secret ballots.

chivalry   The ideals of knighthood, most notably fighting, that spread from northern France across Europe in the High Middle Ages.

Christian humanism   The application of the principles of humanistic education, particularly philology, to the documents of Christianity. It resulted in a program of reform through better education.

Christological controversies   The debate about the Christian Trinity (Father, Son, and Holy Spirit) and the relationship between humanity and divinity within it. It caused great division and conflict in the Church and society from the third to the fifth centuries.

city-states   Self-governing political units centered upon an urban area. During the fifteenth and sixteenth centuries, city-states took on various forms of government, including republics such as Venice and oligarchies such as Milan.

civic humanism   The use of humanistic training and education in the service of the state. Many humanists became advisers to princes or republican governments, holding high office and helping to establish policy.

Cold War   The diplomatic and ideological confrontation between the Soviet Union and the United States that began in the aftermath of World War II, dividing the world into two armed camps.

collectivization   Soviet plan under Stalin to create large communal state farms to replace private farms owned by peasants.

coloni   Tenant farmers who worked on the estates of wealthy landowners in the Roman Empire.

colonization   Process by which colonies, or new settlements with links to a parent state, are established.

Columbian Exchange   The transfer of microbes, animals, and plants in the encounters between Europeans and Native Americans during the age of exploration.

Comecon   The Council for Mutual Economic Assistance established in 1949 with bilateral agreements between the Soviet Union and eastern European states. Comecon was Stalin's response to the U.S. Marshall Plan in western Europe, but rather than providing aid it sought to integrate and control the economies of eastern Europe for Soviet gain.

The Communist Manifesto A call to arms written in 1848 by Karl Marx and Frederich Engels in which they defined in general terms the class struggle in industrializing Europe.

conciliarism The movement proposed by church lawyers in which only a general council of bishops could end the Great Schism.

condottiere A mercenary military leader who sold his services and that of his private army to the highest bidder; used in the wars between the Italian city-states.

Congress of Vienna A meeting of European powers after the Napoleonic wars in 1815; established a balance of power to preserve the status quo in post-revolutionary Europe.

conscription Compulsory service of citizens in the army. France was the first modern state to enforce conscription. The ability to draft all able-bodied men was a key component in the Revolutionary and Napoleonic wars.

conservatism Nineteenth-century ideology that favored tradition and stability and only gradual, or "organic," growth and change.

containment Cold War policy of resisting the spread of Soviet communism.

Continental System The economic boycott of England by Napoleon during the wars beginning in 1803.

Counter-Reformation Catholic response to repel Protestantism.

Crusades Religious wars of conquest directed against non-Christians and heretics in the eleventh through the thirteenth centuries.

Crystal Palace Exhibition This international exhibition, held in London in 1851 in a specially built see-through exhibition hall, featured the greatest technological advances of the day and served as a spur for further industrialization.

culture Those shared beliefs, values, customs, and practices that humans transmit from generation to generation through learning.

cuneiform A form of writing from Mesopotamia characterized by wedge-shaped symbols pressed into wet clay tablets to record words.

Cynics Followers of a Hellenistic Greek philosophy that rejected the world as the source of evil and unhappiness and advocated the reduction of possessions, connections, and pleasures to the absolute minimum.

Declaratory Act A statute enacted in England in 1766 that stated that Parliament held sovereign jurisdiction over the North American colonies.

decolonization Withdrawal of Western nations from colonies in Africa and Asia after World War II.

decurions Members of the city councils in the Roman Empire. Initially, they were the backbone of the provincial elite but by the third and fourth centuries were crippled by their personal responsibility for provincial taxes.

deists Those who believed that God created the universe but then did not intervene in its operation.

Delian League League of Greek cities formed to drive out the Persian invaders. Its leader, Athens, turned it into its own empire.

demesne Land kept by a medieval lord for his direct profit and worked a specified number of days each week by his peasants.

democracy Form of government in which the citizens choose their leaders; began in Athens, Greece, in the fifth century B.C.E.

de-Stalinization Process initiated by Nikita Khrushchev beginning in 1956 that reversed many of Stalin's repressive policies in the Soviet Union.

détente From the French word meaning a relaxation in tension, cooperation between the two superpowers, the Soviet Union and the United States. This policy was characterized by improved U.S.-Soviet diplomatic relationships in the 1970s to lessen the possibility of nuclear war.

dictator In the Roman Republic, an official who was granted unlimited power to rule the state for a period up to six months in a time of emergency. Sulla and Caesar both used the dictatorship for political ends.

diplomas The records of royal grants and decisions produced by clerics in medieval courts.

divine rights of kings Political theory that held that the institution of monarchy had divine origin and that the monarch functioned as God's representative on earth.

doge Chief magistrate of the Venetian Republic who served for life.

Eastern Question The question posed by the Great Powers about the future of the Ottoman territories.

Edict of Nantes The proclamation by Henry IV of France granting limited toleration to Huguenots.

ekklesia The assembly of all free male Athenian citizens.

emirs Local military commanders who took control of provincial administration in the Islamic world at the expense of the caliphs by the tenth century.

empiricism The philosophy propounded by Aristotle which rejected Plato's idea of abstract Forms in favor of practical observation and explanation, building general theories from particular data.

enclosure In the eighteenth century, the closing off of common and public land within the open field system to foster private landholding.

Enlightenment Philosophical and intellectual movement that began in Europe during the eighteenth century. The movement was characterized by a wave of new learning, especially in the sciences and mathematics, and the application of reason to solve society's problems.

entrepôt A place where goods were brought for storage before being exchanged; a commercial concept originated by the Dutch.

Epicureans Those who adhered to a Hellenistic Greek philosophy that the world was a random collection of atoms (atheistic and materialistic), and that one must pursue pleasure, but only in moderation as excess causes pain.

equestrians In the early Roman Republic, the equestrians were one of the richest classes in the Roman army, those who could afford to maintain a horse. By the late republic, their role expanded into banking and commerce.

Estates-General An official body assembled periodically by the medieval French state, consisting of representatives from three separate groups or "estates": those who prayed (the Church), those who fought (the aristocracy), and those who worked (commoners). Long in disuse by the monarch, it was convened by Louis XVI in 1789.

ethnic cleansing Term introduced in the Balkan war of the 1990s to describe the systematic killing and forcible removal of one ethnic group by another.

ethnos Large rural territorial units in the Dark Age and Archaic Greece focused around a central religious sanctuary and dominated by a local oligarchy, such as in Aetolia.

Etruscans Peoples native to Italy who influenced the formation of the Roman state.

eunomia The good order and obedience to the law which was the ideal of Sparta's militaristic society.

euro Common currency of the European Union; accepted as common currency by all members of the European Union except the United Kingdom.

European Economic Community (EEC) Formed in 1957 by Belgium, the Netherlands, Luxembourg, Italy, France, and West Germany to provide a single, integrated European market. Also known as the Common Market.

European Union (EU) Formed in 1992 to succeed the European Community in terms of economic integration; members share defensive, social, and economic policies as well.

extraterritoriality Exempted all foreigners in China from Chinese legal jurisdiction; practiced within foreign "spheres of influence" in China.

Factory Act (1833)   British Parliamentary legislation that prohibited factory work by children under age nine, provided two hours of daily education for factory children, and limited labor for adults to twelve hours each day.

fascism   Rooted in mass politics of the late-nineteenth century, a totalitarian political system that glorifies the state and subordinates the individual to the state's needs. First emerging in Italy after World War I, fascism appeared in virtually all European countries, but particularly Germany.

feudalism   Anachronistic term used by early modern lawyers to describe medieval relations of vassalage.

fief   A parcel of productive land along with the serfs and privileges attached to it granted by a lord to a knightly follower (vassal) in return for loyalty and military service.

Final Solution   The term used by the Third Reich to refer to the extermination of all people deemed unfit; resulted in the execution of 11 million men, women, and children, 6 million of them Jews.

First Triumvirate   Political alliance among Pompey, Crassus, and Caesar to share power in the Roman Republic.

fodder crops   Crops that were grown not for human consumption but to improve the nutrients in the soil. Some, such as turnips, were also used as animal feed.

Forms   In Plato's philosophy, the perfect ideal that underlies all worldly objects. In recollecting them from one's previous existence one communes with all that is good, true, and beautiful.

Fourteen Points   U.S. President Woodrow Wilson's idealistic set of guidelines drawn up as part of the peace process whose goal was to create a lasting peace after World War I.

French wars of religion   Violent clashes between French Catholics and Calvinists (Huguenots) from 1562–1598.

Fronde   An aristocratic revolution in France beginning in 1648 during the minority of Louis XIV, which was initiated by the tax policies of the minority government under Cardinal Mazarin.

futurists   Artists and intellectuals of the late nineteenth and early twentieth century who wanted to create a new culture free from traditional Western civilization. Futurists lionized technology, the masses, violence, and upheaval.

generation gap   The baby boom following World War II resulted in a generation that came of age in the 1960s. The gap refers to the divergence in values between a large cohort of adolescents and young adults and their parents that resulted in more liberal values and socio-cultural mores.

geopolitics   Politics of geography; based on recognition that certain areas of the world are valuable for political reasons.

Girondins   French revolutionary faction that was more moderate than the Jacobins.

glasnost   A Russian term meaning openness; one of the programs of reform initiated by Mikhail Gorbachev in the 1980s.

Glorious Revolution   Change of government in England in 1688–1689 when the Catholic monarch James II was replaced by the Dutch ruler William of Orange. Called "glorious" because it supposedly was accomplished without bloodshed.

Gnostics   An early Christian group that interpreted scripture as gnosis, or secret wisdom, and believed that Jesus had no human element. They were opposed by many bishops.

Golden Bull   The edict of emperor Charles IV in 1356 recognizing that German princes and kings were autonomous rulers.

Great Chain of Being   A hierarchic model of social organization common in the fifteenth and sixteenth centuries in which all parts of creation held a specific place in a divinely ordered universe.

Great Depression   Devastation of the global economy that began in 1929 with the U.S. stock market crash and lasted through the 1930s.

Great Purge   A series of executions between 1934 and 1938 in the Soviet Union that removed Joseph Stalin's political enemies.

Great Reform Bill of 1832   An extension of the right to vote in England to men of the middle class that resulted in a 50 percent increase in those eligible to vote.

Great Schism   The conflict (1378–1415) between two sets of rival popes based in Rome and Avignon that divided the loyalties of states and individuals across Europe.

guilds   Professional associations of merchants or artisans that offered protection of members and regulation of a particular trade or craft.

hadith   The written form of the Sunnah, practices established by the prophet Muhammad that guide the interpretation of the Qur'an.

Hanseatic League   A commercial and political alliance of northern German towns established in the late fourteenth century to monopolize the grain and fish trade of the Baltic Sea.

Hijra   In early Islam, the journey undertaken by Muhammad from Mecca to Medina in 622 in order to govern Medina and calm its internal political dissension.

Holocaust   During World War II, mass extermination of Jews by the Nazis under Adolph Hitler.

Holy Alliance   Prussia, Austria, and Russia, under the leadership of Tsar Alexander I, agreed to protect the peace and the Christian religion following the Congress of Vienna.

honestiores   The privileged classes of the later Roman Empire: senators, municipal gentry, and the military.

hoplites   In Archaic Greece, armed infantry soldiers.

Huguenots   French Calvinists led by Henry of Navarre. Huguenots were victims of the St. Bartholomew's Day Massacre, a slaughter of numerous Protestants in Paris in 1572 during the French wars of religion.

humanists   Scholars who studied and taught the humanities, the skills of disciplines such as philology—the art of language—and rhetoric—the art of expression; concentrated on ancient texts.

humiliores   The lower classes of the later Roman Empire whose status declined from the period of the *Pax Romana* and who suffered disproportionately from the tax increases of the period.

Hundred Years' War   A series of military engagements between England and France (1337–1452) over territorial and dynastic rivalries.

Hussites   Followers of Jan Hus who attacked the sale of indulgences and German political dominance in the kingdom of Bohemia. After his execution, they led a partially successful revolt.

iconoclasts   Breakers of icons; opponents of the mediating use of icons (religious images) in worship. Most emperors supported this faction in eighth- and early ninth-century Byzantium.

iconodules   Venerators of icons; the ecclesiastical faction that resisted the iconoclasts. Most of the people and lesser clergy were iconodules.

icons   Sacred images.

imperium   The powers conferred on magistrates by the Roman people: the supreme power to command, to execute the law, and to impose the death penalty.

indulgences   Remission of temporal punishment in Purgatory due to one's sins. Originally granted for performing pious acts, but later acquired through a grant to the church treasury. In the sixteenth century, indulgences were sold to raise money for the papacy; a critical issue in the Lutheran reform.

industrialization   Process by which production becomes mechanized.

Industrial Revolution   Sustained period of economic growth and change brought on by technological innovations in the process of manufacturing; began in Britain in the mid-eighteenth century.

intendants   Officials appointed by the central government in France to oversee the local administration of the regional aristocracy; a critical component of the centralization of the French state.

iron curtain   The term coined by former British Prime Minister Winston Churchill to describe the ideological divide between western and eastern Europe after World War II.

Jacobins   One of the political factions of the French National Convention that seized the initiative provided by the sans-culottes to take control of the radical revolution in the late eighteenth century; led by Maximilien Robespierre.

Jacquerie   The revolt of French peasants against the aristocracy and crown in 1358. It was part of the struggle for rights caused by the labor shortage after the Black Death.

jihads   Holy wars waged by Muslims against their religious enemies.

jingoism   Use of public opinion to stir support for one's own nation and hatred for another nation; used extensively by political leaders to justify imperial expansion.

joint-stock companies   Business enterprises that raise capital by selling shares to individuals who receive dividends on their investments.

kouros   Nude statues of young men that were a common subject in Archaic art. The stiff posture demonstrates the influence of Egyptian sculpture.

Kristallnacht   "Crystal night" in German; refers to the night of 9 November 1938 when mobs directed by the Nazis destroyed the homes, businesses, and synagogues of German Jews.

laissez-faire   An economic theory that required government to cease interference with private economic activity; Adam Smith and the physiocrats were its leading proponents.

lay investiture   The practice by which kings and emperors appointed bishops and invested them with the symbols of their office. It led to conflict between the papacy and the emperors in the eleventh century.

Lebensraum   "Living room"; one of Hitler's foreign policy objectives to extend the borders of Germany in eastern and central Europe.

liberalism   A political philosophy based on freedom of the individual and the corruptibility of authority; associated with constitutional reform in the first half of the nineteenth century.

Linear B   A syllabic form of writing from the late Greek Bronze Age which preserves the earliest known form of Greek. It was used by Mycenaean elites almost entirely for record keeping.

linear perspective   A technique developed in painting to give a flat surface the appearance of depth and dimension.

Long Parliament   An English Parliament that officially met from 1640 to 1653. It forced reforms under Charles I, defeated the royal armies during the English Civil War, and tried and executed the king.

maat   In Egyptian thought, the ideal state of the universe and of society which the pharaoh was supposed to uphold.

Magna Carta   The "great charter" limiting royal power that King John was forced to sign in 1215.

manses   Farms worked by slaves, serfs, and freemen in the Middle Ages.

Marchfield   The assembly of all free warriors in the early Germanic kingdoms in which the king's authority was all-powerful.

Marshall Plan   The U.S. economic aid program for European countries after World War II; intended to establish U.S. economic influence in European markets.

mercantilism   A popular state economy of the seventeenth century; involved bullionism, protective tariffs, and monopolies.

metics   The non-Athenian residents of Athens who comprised about half of the free population of the city. They were active in commerce and banking.

Minoan civilization   The culture of Crete in the Middle Bronze Age (2000–1550 B.C.E.) in which elites based at great palaces, such as Knossos, dominated the island politically, economically, and religiously.

minuscule   New style of handwriting developed in the Carolingian Renaissance to preserve texts; later adopted as standard script.

Mishnah   In Jewish law, the oral interpretation of the Torah (scripture) that was developed by the Pharisees and later developed into an extensive written body of legal interpretation.

missi dominici   Teams of counts and bishops that examined the state of each county in the Carolingian Empire on behalf of the king.

monasticism   The life of monks devoted to God, from the fourth century onward, either as part of communal organization or in solitary life. Monasticism began in Egypt as a rejection of the worldliness of civilization.

monopoly   Exclusive control of a market or industry; a form of economic regulation in which special privileges are granted in return for financial considerations and an agreement to abide by the rules set out by the state.

Mycenaean   Late Greek Bronze Age civilization that arose ca. 1600 B.C.E. at Mycenae and that encompassed the Greek mainland and parts of Asia Minor. Myceneans developed the Linear B script.

mystery cults   Religions that promised immediate, personal contact with a deity that would bring immortality.

Napoleonic Code   The recodification of French law carried out during Napoleon's reign.

nationalities problem   The existence of numerous ethnic minorities within the borders of the Soviet Union leading to demands for self-determination and political independence.

natural selection   A theory advanced by Charles Darwin that accounted for evolution of species; a realist scientific approach.

Navigation Acts   English economic legislation providing that colonial goods could only be shipped in English ships.

Nazism   National Socialism; German variant of fascism.

Neolithic era   The New Stone Age (8000–6500 B.C.E.) in which modern man developed agriculture and the first villages.

New Economic Policy (NEP)   A state-planned economic policy in the Soviet Union between 1921 and 1928; based on agricultural productivity, it required set payments from peasants; surpluses could be sold on the free market.

new imperialism   Imperialism practiced by European countries after 1870 that was, in essence, the domination by industrial powers over the nonindustrial world. Distinguished from the earlier acquisition of territory, new imperialism took a variety of forms including territorial occupations, colonization, exploitation of labor and raw materials, and development of economic spheres of influence.

New Monarchies   The more centralized European governments of western Europe created in the fifteenth and sixteenth centuries.

New Piety   An aspect of the Roman Catholic reform movement; originated among the Brethren of the Common Life with an emphasis on simplicity and more personalized religious practice.

nominalism   The doctrine of William of Ockham that argued that abstract terms or universals do not represent real existing things and that thus human reason could not aspire to certain truth.

North Atlantic Treaty Organization (NATO)   An organization founded in 1949 the members of which signed a defense pact to protect those countries bordering the North Atlantic.

nuclear club   The group of nations in possession of atomic weapons, originally consisting of the United States and the Soviet Union. By 1974, the nuclear club included Great Britain, France, the People's Republic of China, and India.

Old Regime   The old order; political and social system of France in the eighteenth century before the French Revolution.

oligarchy   Government by an elite few.

optimates   The traditionalist Roman political faction that succeeded the Gracchi and sought to preserve the senatorial oligarchy against the populares.

Orthodox Christianity   The official "right-teaching" faith of Constantinople as opposed to the heterodox peoples on the margins of the Byzantine Empire.

ostracism   A practice in Athenian democracy by which anyone deemed to threaten the constitution could, by popular vote, be exiled for ten years without the loss of property.

Paleolithic era   The Old Stone Age (600,000–10,000 B.C.E.) in which advanced primates developed into Neanderthals and also modern man. They hunted food or collected it by gathering.

Paris Commune   Created in 1871 in the aftermath of the Franco-Prussian War; crushed by the national army after a brief struggle; symbol of revolution for radical politicians, including Marxists.

parties   A form of political organization in which members of the British parliament divided into groups with identifiable interests. Whigs and Tories were the first political parties.

Patent of Toleration   An edict of Joseph II of Austria in 1781 that granted freedom of worship to Protestants and members of the Greek Orthodox Church, in addition to Roman Catholics.

paterfamilias   The male head of household in the Roman family. His power was absolute, including the power of life and death.

patricians   Leaders of the gentes, or clans, in early Roman society.

Pax Romana   The two centuries of peace and stability in the early Roman Empire inaugurated by the emperor Augustus.

perestroika   A Russian term meaning restructuring; part of Mikhail Gorbachev's attempts to reform the Soviet government and economy in the 1980s.

Peterloo Massacre   In August 1819, the English army troops policing a political crowd gathered near Manchester, England, lost control resulting in the deaths of 11 and the injury of hundreds of others.

phalanx   A tightly ordered and well-disciplined body of elite Greek warriors in heavy armor that attacked in close formation with long spears.

philology   The art of language; one of the most important aspects of humanist studies, based on models of ancient texts.

philosophes   A French term for the intellectuals of the eighteenth-century Enlightenment. Voltaire, Diderot, and Condorcet were leading philosophes.

physiocrats   A group of French thinkers who subscribed to the view that land was wealth and thus argued that improvements in agricultural activity should take first priority in state reforms.

pictograms   The earliest form of writing in Mesopotamia, ca. 3500 B.C.E., in which pictures represented particular objects, such as animals.

Pietà   A painting or sculpture of Mary mourning the dead Jesus. The most famous was carved by Michelangelo and is in St. Peter's Basilica.

plebs   Families not organized into gentes, or clans, in early Roman society. The lower classes.

pogroms   State-organized massacres of Jews.

polis   The city-state of Archaic and Classical Greece, particularly found on the shores of the Aegean. A city formed the center of government (tyranny, oligarchy, or democracy) and of religious life with temples on its citadel (acropolis).

politiques   During the sixteenth-century French wars of religion, a group of Catholics who joined with Huguenots to demand a practical settlement of the wars.

populares The Roman political faction that succeeded the Gracchi whose leaders appealed to the masses as a source of power.

Popular Front Socialist governments established in both France and Spain in the 1930s; the French version failed to solve the Great Depression and was voted out of office; the creation of a socialist republic in Spain initiated a civil war.

Pragmatic Sanction The document that attempted to secure the recognition of Maria Theresa as heiress to the Habsburg possessions of Charles VI.

Prague Spring Popular uprising and reform movement in 1968 Czechoslovakia, ended by Soviet invasion in August 1968.

predestination A fundamental principle of Calvin's theology: the belief that all Christians are predestined to either heaven or hell from the act of creation.

presbyters The priests of the early Christian tradition who were subordinated to bishops as hierarchy developed in the Church.

Price Revolution The dramatic price inflation of the fifteenth and sixteenth centuries; caused by monetary debasement and the influx of bullion from the New World.

princeps "First citizen"; the title assumed by the emperor Augustus to reassure public opinion by preserving the traditional constitutional forms.

Proclamation of the German Empire The creation in 1871 of the nation-state of Germany by uniting the 38 German states into a single national entity.

proletariat The industrial working class.

pronatalism State programs implemented after the Second World War to encourage women to have larger families.

Puritans English Protestants who sought to purify the Church of England of all traces of Catholicism.

putting-out system Mobilization of the rural labor force for commercial production of large quantities of manufactured goods; raw materials put out to homes of workers where manufacture took place.

Quadruple Alliance Pact signed in 1815 by the four powers who defeated Napoleon—Great Britain, Austria, Russia, and Prussia—for the purpose of protecting Europe against future French aggression.

Quintuple Alliance The Quadruple Alliance plus France, which joined the pact in 1818.

quinine An important nineteenth-century medical advance derived from cinchona that was an effective treatment for malaria; it permitted large numbers of Europeans to travel without risking death and disease.

realism An artistic and literary style that criticized industrialized society and rejected bourgeois concepts of morality.

realpolitik Pragmatic political theory advanced by Otto von Bismarck; ruthless pursuit by any means, including illegal and violent ones, in the interests of the state.

reconquista The Christian reconquest of the Iberian peninsula from the Spanish Muslims or Moors; completed in 1492 under Ferdinand and Isabella.

Reformation A movement to reform and purify the Catholic Church that resulted in the creation of new religious denominations in Europe collectively known as Protestants.

Reichstag The national legislative body of the German Empire; elected by universal male suffrage.

Reign of Terror The period from 1793 to 1794 when Maximilien Robespierre assumed leadership of the Committee of Public Safety and oversaw the revolutionary tribunals that sentenced about 40,000 people to execution.

Renaissance A "rebirth" of classical learning and emphasis on humanity that characterized the period between 1350 and 1550.

rhetoric   The art of expression and persuasion.

Risorgimento   The nineteenth-century movement to reunite Italy.

romanticism   An artistic and literary tradition based on emotions rather than the intellect; rejection of classical traditions in favor of "nature"; often associated with nationalism.

salons   Informal social gatherings during the Enlightenment, frequently organized by women, in which topics of intellectual interest were discussed.

sans-culottes   Literally "those without knee-breeches"; working-class revolutionaries who initiated the radical stage of the French revolution in 1792.

Schlieffen Plan   The strategy of the German high command at the outset of World War I, predicated on knocking France out of the war.

Scholastic method   The combination of legal analysis from the new university at Bologna with Aristotelian logic established by Peter Abelard in the twelfth century to create the primary method of study in medieval universities.

scientific revolution   In the sixteenth and seventeenth centuries, a period of new scientific inquiry, experimentation, and discovery that resulted in a new understanding of the universe based on mathematical principles and led to the creation of the modern sciences, particularly astronomy and physics.

scramble for Africa   The colonization of Africa as part of the new imperialism. This domination of Africa by Germany, Britain, and France ended with the crisis at Fashoda.

Second Triumvirate   Alliance of Octavian, Mark Anthony, and Lepidus following the assassination of Julius Caesar to defeat the assassins and control the Roman Empire.

seigneur   Manor lord responsible for maintaining order, administering justice, and arbitrating disputes among tenants.

serfs   Peasants of degraded status and very limited legal rights who were dependent on the lords in the High Middle Ages. They formed the great bulk of the population.

Shi'ites   Muslims who follow the tradition that legitimate leadership of Islam can only come through the descendants of 'Ali, whom they regard as the last orthodox caliph.

sola fide   A fundamental principle of Luther's theology: justification of Christians by faith alone.

sola scriptura   By the Word alone; emphasis on scriptural authority in preference to the canons of the Church, a fundamental element of Luther's theology.

Solidarity   A non-communist Polish labor organization founded by Lech Walesa in the Gdansk shipbuilding yards; legalized in 1989 as a political movement, it won a victory in the first Polish democratic elections.

sophists   Professional teachers in fifth-century Greece who traveled from city to city instructing students, for a fee, in rhetoric, the art of persuasion.

soviets   Councils of workers in Russia formed after 1905 that became one center of power after the overthrow of the tsar; source of power for Lenin and the Bolsheviks.

Spanish Armada   The Spanish fleet sent in 1588 to transport troops from the Low Countries for an invasion of England; defeated by the English fleets of Elizabeth I.

Spanish Inquisition   An ecclesiastical tribunal utilized to combat heresy and non-Christians; used by Ferdinand and Isabella against the conversos, or converted Jews of Spain.

spheres of influence   Diplomatic term used to connote territorial influence or control of weaker nations not necessarily occupied by the more powerful ones. The term was first used to explain one kind of control of western European powers in the 1800s during African imperialism, and was later used to describe European and Japanese territorial control and influence over markets in China at the end of the nineteenth century.

Stoics   Followers of the Hellenistic Greek philosophy propounded by Zeno, which teaches that orderliness is proper to the universe and that happiness derives from embracing one's divinely ordained role and unhappiness from rejecting it.

strategoi   Generals, the military commanders of themes in the Byzantine Empire. They were responsible for civil and military administration.

sunnah   In Islamic theology, the practices established by the prophet Muhammad. They were initially preserved by oral tradition.

Sunnis   The majority tradition of Islam that accepts that political succession should be based on consensus, the existing political order, and a leader's merits.

synod   A meeting of bishops called to debate Church policy, such as that at Whitby in 664, which established the customs of the Roman Church among Angles and Saxons.

Table of Ranks   Official state hierarchy in Russia under Peter the Great that established the social position or rank of individuals according to categories of military service, civil service, and ownership of landed estates.

tetrarchy   Rule by four; Diocletian's attempt to regulate the suggestion of the Roman Empire by dividing the empire into eastern and western parts, with both an augustus and a junior emperor, or caesar, ruling each part.

Thermidorian Reaction   Revolt beginning in July 1794 (the month of Thermidor) against the radicalism of the French Revolution, leading to the downfall and execution of Robespierre and the end of the Reign of Terror.

Third Estate   Branch of the French Estates-General consisting of the bourgeoisie and the working classes; separated from the other estates to form the National Assembly in 1789.

Third Reich   "The Third Empire"; Hitler's government, established after 1933.

third world   The former colonies of European and Asian imperialism; sought to separate themselves from European economic control after independence; operated in the United Nations as a nonaligned bloc.

Thirty Years' War   War lasting from 1618–1648.

three-field system   An efficient agricultural system in which one-third of the land was planted in autumn with wheat or rye, one-third remained fallow, and one-third was planted in spring with a crop that added nutrients to the soil.

Time of Troubles   The period of disruption within Russia following the death of Ivan the Terrible; only ended with the Polish invasion of Russia.

Torah   The body of law in Hebrew scripture.

Tories   Members of a political party in England that in the seventeenth century defended the principle of hereditary succession to the crown; in opposition to the Whigs. The Tories sought to preserve the traditional political structure and supported the authority of the Anglican church.

total war   War that requires mobilization of the civilian population in addition to the military; typified by centralized governments with limits on economy and civil rights.

Treaty of Brest-Litovsk   The Treaty between Russia and Germany signed in March 1918 whereby Soviet Russia withdrew from World War I.

Treaty of Tordesillas   A 1494 agreement that recognized Portugal's claims to Brazil, but gave all of the remainder of the New World to Spain.

Treaty of Versailles   Peace settlement with Germany at the end of World War I; included the War Guilt Clause fixing blame on Germany for the war and requiring massive reparations.

triangular trade   A three-way trade system during the seventeenth century involving the shipment, for example, of calicoes to Africa for slaves who were transported to the East Indies in exchange for sugar, which was shipped to Europe.

Triple Alliance   An alliance founded in 1882 between Germany, Austria-Hungary, and Italy at Germany's instigation for the purpose of securing mutual support on the European continent.

Triple Entente   Alliance founded in 1907 between France, Britain, and Russia. With the defection of Russia from the Three Emperors' League, it hemmed in Germany on both eastern and western borders.

tyrants   Rulers who had seized power illegally. Tyrannies replaced oligarchies in many *poleis* in Archaic Greece, such as at Corinth and Athens. The term did not have the negative connotations it does today, as many tyrants were popular leaders welcomed by their subjects.

Umma   The community of all believers in the Islamic faith. Initially, it was both a political and religious supertribe of Arabs.

universitas   The guilds of students that formed the first true universities from the twelfth century onward.

utilitarianism   Jeremy Bentham's philosophical plan to ensure social harmony through measurement of pleasure and pain or the greatest happiness of the greatest number; a liberal philosophy.

vassals   Knights sworn to fealty or loyalty to a lord; in return the lord granted the vassal a means of support, or fief.

Villanovans   Peoples of the first Iron Age culture in Italy (1000–800 B.C.E.), which was based in the north. They made iron tools and weapons and placed the ashes of their dead in large urns.

Warsaw Pact   Defensive alliance organization formed in 1955 by Albania, Bulgaria, Romania, Czechoslovakia, Hungary, Poland, East Germany, and the Soviet Union. The alliance served as a strategic buffer zone against NATO forces.

Weimar Republic   German government founded at the end of the First World War; used by German general staff as scapegoat for German defeat and harsh peace terms; overthrown in 1933.

welfare state   The tendency of post–World War II states to establish safety nets for citizens in areas of birth, sickness, old age, and unemployment.

wergeld   In Germanic society, the payment in reparation for crimes in place of blood vengeance. Tribal leaders used it to reduce internal hostilities.

Whigs   Members of a political party in England that in the seventeenth century supported the Protestant succession and a broad-based Protestantism and advocated a constitutional monarchy that limited royal power; in opposition to the Tories. The Whigs were later identified with social and parliamentary reform.

zemstvos   Local elected assemblies in Russia during the reign of Alexander II; representatives elected by landowners, townspeople, and peasants.

ziggurat   Babylonian tiered towers (or step-pyramids) from ca. 2000 B.C.E. that were dedicated to gods and stood near temples. They were among the most important buildings of Babylonian cities.

Zionism   A program initiated by Theodor Herzl to establish an independent Jewish state in Palestine.

Zollverein   A unified trading zone created by Prussia in which member states adopted the liberal Prussian customs regulations; an attempt to overcome the fragmented nature of the German economy.

CHAPTER 1

General Reading

Cambridge Ancient History, vol. 1 (Cambridge: Cambridge University Press, 1990). Contains essays on every aspect of ancient civilizations.

Barry Cunliffe, *Europe Between the Oceans 9000 BC–1000* (New Haven: Yale University Press, 2008). A broad survey of western Eurasia by an archaeologist.

Brian Fagan, 2007. *World Prehistory: A Brief Introduction*, 7th ed. (New York: Prentice-Hall, 2007). Excellent introduction to prehistory.

Barbara S. Lesko, ed. *Women's Earliest Records from Ancient Egypt and Western Asia: Proceedings of the Conference on Women in the Ancient Near East* (Atlanta: Scholars Press, 1989). Important collection of essays on all aspects of women in ancient societies.

Before Civilization

Barry Cunliffe, *Prehistoric Europe: An Illustrated History* (Oxford: Oxford University Press, 1997). An engaging introduction to early Europe.

Brian M. Fagan, *People of the Earth: An Introduction to World Prehistory*, 7th ed. (New York: Prentice Hall, 2007). Excellent introduction to the prehistory of Europe and Asia.

Daniel Lord Smail, *On Deep History and the Brain* (Berkeley: University of California Press, 2008). An historian's challenging argument on the importance of the Paleolithic.

Colin Renfrew, *Prehistory: The Making of the Human Mind* (New York: Modern Library 2008). A classic introduction to prehistory.

Mesopotamia: Between the Two Rivers

Guillermo Algaze, *Ancient Mesopotamia at the Dawn of Civilization: The Evolution of an Urban Landscape* (Chicago: University of Chicago Press, 2008). The relationship between ecology and civilization between the Tigris and Euphrates rivers.

Jean Bottero, *Everyday Life in Ancient Mesopotamia* (Baltimore: Johns Hopkins University Press, 2001). Social history of Mesopotamia by a leading expert.

Gwendolyn Leick, *The Babylonians, An Introduction* (New York: Routledge, 2003). General introduction to Babylonian history.

Marc Van de Mieroop, *A history of the ancient Near East, ca. 3000–323 BC*, 2nd ed. (Malden, Mass.: Blackwell Pub., 2007). An excellent survey on Near Eastern history.

The Gift of the Nile

Cyril Aldred, *The Egyptians*, 3rd rev. ed. (New York: Thames & Hudson, 1998). Readable general history of ancient Egypt focusing on culture.

Barbara Mertz, *Red Land, Black Land: Daily Life in Ancient Egypt*, 2nd ed. (New York: William Morrow, 2008). A readable account of daily life.

Ian Shaw, ed. *The Oxford History of Ancient Egypt* (Oxford: Oxford University Press, 2000). Comprehensive collaborative survey of ancient Egypt.

Between Two Worlds

John Curtis, *Ancient Persia* (Cambridge, MA: Harvard University Press, 1990). Brief overview of ancient Iran.

Lester L. Grabbe, *Ancient Israel: What Do We Know and How Do We Know It?* (London; New York: T & T Clark, 2007). Reliable introduction to the history and archaeology of ancient Israel.

Henry Jackson Flanders, Robert Wilson Crapps, and David Anthony Smith, *People of the Covenant: An Introduction to the Hebrew Bible*, 4th ed. (New York: Oxford University Press, 1996). A balanced introduction to Hebrew and Jewish history that draws on both Jewish and Christian scholarship.

A. T. Olmstead, *History of Assyria* (Chicago: University of Chicago Press, 1975). The fundamental survey of the Assyrian Empire.

CHAPTER 2

General Reading

S. B. Pomeroy, et. al. *Ancient Greece: A Political, Social, and Cultural History* (Oxford: Oxford University Press, 1998). An important introduction to Greek society and culture.

Greece in the Bronze Age to 700 B.C.E.

M. I. Finley, *Early Greece: The Bronze and Archaic Ages*, 2d ed. (New York: W. W. Norton, 1982). A very readable overview by a leading Greek historian.

Eliezer D. Oren, ed. *The Sea Peoples and Their World: A Reassessment* (Philadelphia, Pa.: University Museum, University of Pennsylvania, 2000). Essays on the debates concerning the Sea Peoples..

Cynthia W. Shelmerdine, ed. *The Cambridge Companion to the Aegean Bronze Age* (Cambridge; New York: Cambridge University Press, 2008). Up to date survey of early Aegean civilizations.

William Taylour, *The Mycenaeans* (London: Thames & Hudson, 1990). General overview of Mycenaean civilization and daily life based on archaeology.

Archaic Greece, 700–500 B.C.E.

John Boardman, *The Greeks Overseas* (New York: Thames & Hudson, 1982). A description of varieties of Greek involvement abroad and their effects on Greece by a distinguished archaeologist.

————, *Greek Sculpture: Archaic Period* (New York: Thames & Hudson, 1985). A well-illustrated survey of early Greek sculpture.

Anne L. Klinck, *Women's Songs in Ancient Greece* (McGill-Queen's University Press: Montreal and Kingston, 2008). An anthology of texts presenting women's performance in Greek poetry.

Catherine Morgan, *Early Greek States beyond the Polis* (New York: Routledge, 2003). A reevaluation of the relationship between ethne and polis in the Archaic period.

H. A. Shapiro, ed. *The Cambridge companion to archaic Greece* (Cambridge; New York: Cambridge University Press, 2007). Comprehensive survey of the archaic period.

Anthony Snodgrass, *Archaic Greece: The Age of Experiment* (Totowa, NJ: Biblio Distribution Center, 1980). An excellent survey of the creative achievements of the Archaic period.

Mark Stansbury-O'Donnell, *Vase Painting, Gender, and Social Identity in Archaic Athens* (New York, NY: Cambridge University Press, 2006). A study of how images on archaic vases can inform concerning social order, gender, ritual and myth.

Christopher Tadgell, *Hellenic Classicism: The Ordering of Form in the Ancient Greek World.* (New York: Whitney Library of Design, 1998). A survey of Greek art and architecture to the construction of Athens' Acropolis.

A Tale of Three Cities

Paul Cartledge, *Sparta and Lakonia: A Regional History 1300–362 B.C.* 2nd ed. (New York: Routledge, Chapman & Hall, 2002). The best survey of Spartan history.

J. B. Salmon, *Wealthy Corinth: A History of the City to 338 B.C.* (New York: Oxford University Press, 1984). A comprehensive history of early Corinth.

David Whitehead, *The Demes of Attica (ca. 508–250 B.C.)* (Princeton, NJ: Princeton University Press, 1986). An excellent study of Athenian politics and society.

CHAPTER 3
General Reading

Cambridge Ancient History, 2d ed., vols. 5 (1989) and 7 (1984). Contains essays on most aspects of Greek history.

Pierre Vidal-Naquet, *The Black Hunter: Forms of Thought and Forms of Society in the Greek World* (Baltimore: The Johns Hopkins University Press, 1998). A brilliant exploration of Greek society and politics approached through its margins, its contradictions, and its oppositions.

War and Politics in the Fifth Century B.C.E.

Lindsay Allen, *The Persian Empire* (Chicago: University of Chicago Press, 2005). Up to date comprehensive survey of ancient Persia.

Sue Blundell, *Women in Ancient Greece* (Cambridge, MA: Harvard University Press, 1995). A good place to start for an understanding of women in classical Greece.

Charles W. Fornara and Loren J. Samons II, *Athens from Cleisthenes to Pericles* (Berkeley: University of California Press, 1991). Detailed survey of the development of Athenian democracy and empire.

Yvon Garlan, *Slavery in Ancient Greece* (Ithaca, NY: Cornell University Press, 1988). A basic study of Greek slavery.

Victor Davis Hanson, *A War Like No Other. How the Athenians and Spartans Fought the Peloponnesian War* (New York: Random House, 2005). An account of the war that emphasizes its novelty and carnage..

Nigel M. Kennell, *The Gymnasium of Virtue: Education and Culture in Ancient Sparta* (Chapel Hill: University of North Carolina Press, 1995). An investigation of Spartan culture.

Helen King, *Hippocrates' Woman: Reading the Female Body in Ancient Greece* (New York: Routledge, 1998). A study of Greek medical theory concerning women and women's bodies.

Josiah Ober, *Mass and Elite in Democratic Athens: Rhetoric, Ideology, and the Power of the People* (Princeton, N.J.: Princeton University Press, 1989). An important investigation into the working of Athenian democracy.

P. J. Rhodes, *Ancient Democracy and Modern Ideology* (London: Duckworth Academic, 2003). An essay from a prominient Greek historian exploring the modern uses of Athenian democracy.

Athenian Culture in the Hellenic Age

J. Boardman, *Greek Art*, 3d ed. (New York: Thames & Hudson, 1985). A handbook introduction by period.

W. Burkert, *Greek Religion* (Cambridge, MA: Harvard University Press, 1985). General survey of the topic.

Mark Golden, *Greek Sport and Social Status* (Austin: University of Texas Press, 2008). A study of the intersection of Greek sport and culture and society.

Simon Goldhill, *Reading Greek Tragedy* (New York: Cambridge University Press, 1986). A general introduction to Athenian tragedy.

David Roochnik, *Retrieving the Ancients: an Introduction to Greek Philosophy* (Malden, MA: Blackwell Pub., 2004). A fresh introduction to Greek philosophers.

C. J. Rowe, *Plato* (New York: St. Martin's, 1984). A good survey of the philosopher's thought.

From City-States to Macedonian Empire, 404–323 B.C.E.

A. B. Bosworth, *Conquest and Empire* (New York: Cambridge University Press, 1988). A scholarly but readable account of Alexander the Great.

Waldemar Heckel and Lawrence A. Tritle, eds. *Alexander the Great: A New History* (Chichester, U.K.; Malden, MA: Wiley-Blackwell, 2009). A fresh collective history of Alexander by international experts.

The Hellenistic World

J. Barnes et al., *Science and Speculation* (New York: Cambridge University Press, 1982). A collection of papers on Hellenistic science.

Peter Green, *Alexander to Actium: The Historical Evolution of the Hellenistic Age* (Berkeley: University of California Press, 1990). A broad examination of the Hellenistic period.

Peter Green, ed., *Hellenistic History and Culture* (Berkeley: University of California Press, 1993). A stimulating series of articles and debates on Hellenistic civilization.

Sarah B. Pomeroy, *Families in Classical and Hellenistic Greece: Representations and Realities* (Oxford: Clarendon Press; New York: Oxford University Press, 1998). Greek society, gender, and sexuality based on written, archaeological, and iconographic sources.

CHAPTER 4

Primary Sources

Many of the works of Polybius, Livy, Cato, Caesar, Cicero, and other Roman authors are available in English translation from Penguin Books. The first volume—*Roman Civilization, Selected Readings, Vol. I: The Republic* (1951), by Naphtali Lewis and Meyer Reinhold—contains a wide selection of documents with useful introductions. An excellent selection of Roman historical writing can be found in Ronald Mellor, *The Roman Historians* (New York: Routledge, 1999).

The Western Mediterranean to 509 B.C.E.

Graeme Barker and Tom Rasmussen, *The Etruscans* (Oxford: Blackwell Publishers, 2000). An introduction to Etruscan studies and history.

Serge Lancel, *Carthage: A History* (Oxford: Blackwell Publishers, 1997). A basic introduction.

From City to Empire, 509–146 B.C.E.

Nigel Bagnall, *The Punic Wars* (London: Hutchinson, 1990). Survey of the wars between Rome and Carthage.

Mary Beard and Michael Crawford, *Rome in the Late Republic* (Ithaca, NY: Cornell University Press, 1985). A short interpretive essay on the crisis of the late republic.

John Boardman, Jasper Griffin, and Oswyn Murray, *The Oxford History of the Roman World* (New York: Oxford University Press, 2001). A balanced collection of essays on all aspects of Roman history and civilization.

K. R. Bradley, *Slavery and Society at Rome* (New York: Cambridge University Press, 1994). The place of slavery in the Roman world.

Klaus Bringmann, *A History of the Roman Republic* (Cambridge, UK; Malden, MA: Polity, 2007). A clear narrative of the Republic by a distinguished European scholar.

Tim Cornell, *The Beginnings of Rome, 1000–264 B.C.* (New York: Routledge, 1995). A new look at the origins of Rome.

Gary Forsythe, *A Critical History of Early Rome: from Prehistory to the First Punic War* (Berkeley: University of California Press, 2005). A fresh reappraisal of the early history of Rome.

Republican Civilization

Geza Alfoldy, *The Social History of Rome* (Berlin: Walter de Gruyter, 1988). A survey of Rome that emphasizes the relationship between social structure and politics.

Erich S. Gruen, *Culture and National Identity in Republican Rome* (Ithaca, NY: Cornell University Press, 1992). Important lectures by a major figure in the field.

Erich S. Gruen, *The Hellenistic World and the Coming of Rome*, 2 vols. (Berkeley: University of California Press, 1984). A detailed history of the Hellenistic world, presenting Rome's gradual and unintended rise to dominance in it.

Sarah B. Pomeroy, ed., *Women's History and Ancient History* (Chapel Hill: University of North Carolina Press, 1991). The place to begin for the history of women in antiquity.

The Crisis of Roman Virtue

Alan E. Astin, *Cato the Censor* (New York: Oxford University Press, 1978). An excellent biography of Cato that also analyzes his writings.

Pat Southern, *Pompey the Great* (Stroud, England: Tempus Publishing Ltd., 2002). The most recent biography of the triumvir.

CHAPTER 5

Primary Sources

Major selections of the works of Caesar, Cicero, Tacitus, Plutarch, Suetonius, and Marcus Aurelius are available in English translation from Penguin Books. The second volume by Naphtali Lewis and Meyer Reinhold, *Roman Civilization Selected Readings, Vol. II: The Empire* (1951), contains a wide selection of documents with useful introductions.

The Price of Empire

E. Badian, *Roman Imperialism in the Late Republic* (Ithaca, NY: Cornell University Press, 1968). A study of the contradictory forces leading to the development of the empire.

Mary Beard and Michael Crawford, *Rome in the Late Republic* (Ithaca, NY: Cornell University Press, 1985). An analysis of the political processes of the late republic as part of the development of Roman society, not simply the decay of the republic.

Henrik Mouritsen, *Plebs and Politics in the Late Roman Republic* (Cambridge: Cambridge University Press, 2001). A study of the political role of the masses in the last years of the republic.

The End of the Republic

Robert Gurval, *Actium and Augustus: the Politics and Emotions of Civil War* (Ann Arbor: University of Michigan Press, 1998). Important study of the end of the republic.

A. J. Langguth, *A Noise of War: Caesar, Pompey, Octavian, and the Struggle for Rome* (New York: Simon & Schuster, 1994). The era of the civil wars and the end of the republic.

Elizabeth Rawson, *Cicero: A Portrait* (Ithaca, N.Y. Cornell University Press, 1983). A sensitive biography of the great orator.

Ronald Syme, *The Roman Revolution* (Oxford, U.K.; New York: Oxford University Press, 2002). A classic study of the fall of the republic and the rise of Augustus.

The Augustan Age and the *Pax Romana*

J. B. Campbell, *The Emperor and the Roman Army* (New York: Oxford University Press, 1984). Essential for understanding the military's role in the Roman Empire.

Eve D'Ambra, *Roman Women* (Cambridge; New York: Cambridge University Press, 2007). An analysis of the daily lives of Roman women examined through material and written sources.

Albrecht Dihle, *Greek and Latin Literature of the Roman Empire: From Augustus to Justinian* (New York: Routledge, 1994). A survey of classical literature.

Catharine Edwards and Greg Woolf, ed., *Rome the Cosmopolis* (New York: Cambridge University Press, 2003). An innovative collection of essays examining the relationship between Rome and its empire.

Karl Galinsky, *Augustan Culture* (Princeton, NJ: Princeton University Press, 1998). An important study of the cultural world of Augustus.

J. E. Lendon, *Empire of Honour: The Art of Government in the Roman World* (Oxford: Oxford University Press, 2001). A provocative study of Roman despotism and the support it enjoyed from the ruling classes of the provinces.

Fergus Millar, *The Emperor in the Roman World* (Ithaca, NY: Cornell University Press, 1992). A study of emperors, stressing their essential passivity by responding to initiatives from below.

D. A. West and A. J. Woodman, *Poetry and Politics in the Age of Augustus* (New York: Cambridge University Press, 1984). The cultural program of Augustus.

Religions from the East

Clifford Ando, *The Matter of the Gods: Religion and the Roman Empire* (Berkeley: University of California Press, 2008). A fresh examination of the role of reason and tradition in Roman religion.
Schuyler Brown, *The Origins of Christianity: A Historical Introduction of the New Testament*, rev. ed. (Oxford: Oxford University Press, 1993). A balanced and comprehensive introduction to early Christianity.

Ekkehard W. Stegemann and Wolfgang Stegemann, *The Jesus Movement: A Social History of Its First Century* (Minneapolis: Fortress Press, 1999). A new survey of the first century of Christianity.

The Culture of Antonine Rome

Jane F. Gardner, *Women in Roman Law and Society* (Bloomington: Indiana University Press, 1986). A study of the extent of freedom and power over property enjoyed by Roman women.

Peter Garnsey and Richard Saller, *The Roman Empire: Economy, Society, and Culture* (Berkeley: University of California Press, 1987). A topical study of imperial administration, economy, religion, and society, arguing the coercive and exploitative nature of Roman civilization in relation to the agricultural societies of the Mediterranean world.

Fergus Millar, *Rome, the Greek World, and the East: The Roman Republic and the Augustan Revolution* (Chapel Hill: University of North Carolina Press, 2000). A collection of essays by a leading historian surveying Rome's rise to empire.

Paul Veyne, *The Roman Empire* (Cambridge, Mass.: Belknap Press of Harvard University Press, 1997). A compelling account of private life in imperial Rome.

CHAPTER 6
The Crisis of the Third Century

G. W. Bowersock, Peter Brown, and Oleg Grabar, eds, *Late Antiquity: a Guide to the Postclassical World* (Cambridge, Mass.: Belknap Press of Harvard University Press, 1999). A comprehensive introduction to Late Antiquity.

Peter Brown, *The World of Late Antiquity, A.D. 150–750* (New York: Harcourt Brace Jovanovich, 1971). A brilliant essay on the cultural transformation of the ancient world.

Averil Cameron, *The Later Roman Empire, A.D. 284–430* (Cambridge, MA: Harvard University Press, 1993). An important survey by an authority.

Hans-Werner Goetz, Jorg Jarnut and Walter Pohl, eds., *Regna and Gentes: The Relationship between Late Antique and Early Medieval Peoples and Kingdoms in the Transformation of the Roman World* (Leiden, The Netherlands: Brill, 2003). A series of essays on the transformation of the Classical world.

Malcolm Todd, *The Early Germans* (Oxford: Blackwell Publishers, 1992). A general introduction to pre-Roman Germanic society.

The Empire Restored

T. D. Barnes, *The New Empire of Diocletian and Constantine* (Cambridge, MA: Harvard University Press, 1982). A current examination of the transformations brought about under the two great emperors.

Ramsay MacMullen, *Paganism in the Roman Empire* (New Haven, CT: Yale University Press, 1981). A sensible introduction to the varieties of Roman religion in the imperial period.

Imperial Christianity

G. W. Bowersock, *Martyrdom and Rome* (New York: Cambridge University Press, 1995). A new look at Christian martyrdom in antiquity.

Peter Brown, *Authority and the Sacred: Aspects of the Christianisation of the Roman* (Cambridge: Cambridge University Press, 1995). A highly readable account of the emergence of Christianity in the Roman world by the leading historian of late antiquity.

W. H. C. Fend, *The Rise of Christianity* (London: Darton, Longman and Todd, 1984). A panoramic survey of Christianity from its origins to the seventh century.

Ramsay MacMullen, *Christianizing the Roman Empire (100–400)* (New Haven, CT: Yale University Press, 1984). A view of Christianity's spread from the perspective of Roman history.

A Parting of the Ways

Peter Brown, *The Rise of Western Christendom* (Cambridge, MA: Blackwell, 2003). A survey of late antiquity by a master scholar and stylist.

Patrick J. Geary, *The Myth of Nations: The Medieval Origins of Europe* (Princeton, NJ: Princeton University Press, 2001). An essay examining the relationship between modern nationalism and ethnic groups in late antiquity.

Judith Herrin, *The Formation of Christendom* (Princeton, NJ: Princeton University Press, 1987). A history of the transformed Mediterranean world, east and west, to 800 from the perspective of a noted Byzantinist.

Brian Ward-Perkins, *The Fall of Rome and the End of Civilization* (Oxford: Oxford University Press, 2005). An archaeologist's argument against seeing the end of Antiquity as a period of peaceful transition. An account of the decline in material culture at the end of Antiquity.

Herwig Wolfram, *The Roman Empire and Its Germanic Peoples* (Berkeley: University of California Press, 1997). Important general survey of the place of the barbarians in the Roman world.

CHAPTER 7

The Byzantines

Jonathan Harris, *Byzantium and the Crusades* (London and New York: Hambledon and London, 2003). A new treatment of relations between Byzantium and Western Europe.

Judith Herrin, *Byzantium: The Surprising Life of a Medieval Empire* (London Penguin, 2008). Brief and lively new synthesis by a leading Byzantinist.

Alexander P. Kazhdan, ed., *The Oxford Dictionary of Byzantium* (New York: Oxford University Press, 1991). Standard reference for Byzantine history and culture.

Michael Maas, ed. *The Cambridge companion to the Age of Justinian* (Cambridge; New York: Cambridge University Press, 2005). Collaborative guide to the sixth century Empire.

Cyril Mango, *Byzantium: The Empire of New Rome* (New York: Scribner's, 1980). An imaginative and provocative reevaluation of the Byzantine world.

John Moorhead, *Justinian* (New York: Macmillan, 1994). A readable biography of the great emperor.

Dimitri Obolensky, *Byzantium and the Slavs* (Crestwood, NY: St. Vladimir's Seminary Press, 1994). A survey of the Byzantine Empire's relations with eastern Europe.

The Rise of Islam

Aziz Al-Azmeh, *Arabic Thought and Islamic Societies* (London: Routledge, Chapman & Hall, 1986). A demanding but valuable introduction to Islamic intellectual history.

Albert Hourani, *A History of the Arab Peoples* (New York: Warner Books, 1992). A clear, thoughtful survey of Arab history for nonspecialists.

Robert G. Hoyland, *Arabia and the Arabs: From the Bronze Age to the Coming of Islam* (New York: Routledge, 2001). A comprehensive survey of the early history of Arabia.

Hugh Kennedy, *The Prophet and the Age of the Caliphates* (White Plains, NY: Longman, 1986). A valuable summary of the early political history of Islam.

Nasser D. Khalili, *Islamic art and culture: a Visual History* (Woodstock; New York: Overlook Press, 2006). A broad introduction to Islamic art through the centuries.

Bernard Lewis, *Islam in History: Ideas, People, and Events in the Middle East* (Chicago: Open Court, 1993). Broad synthesis of Islam.

Bernard Lewis, *The Muslim Discovery of Europe* (New York: W. W. Norton, 1985). Views of the West by Muslim travelers.

Fatima Mernissi, *Women and Islam: An Historical and Theological Enquiry* (Oxford: Basil Blackwell, 1991). Sympathetic study of women in Islam.

Roy P. Mottahedeh, *The Mantle of the Prophet: Religion and Politics in Iran* (New York: Simon and Schuster, 1985). An important introduction to the social values and structures of western Iran and southern Iraq in the tenth and eleventh centuries.

Seyyed Hossein Nasr, *Islam: Religion, History, and Civilization* (San Francisco: HarperSanFrancisco, 2003). A brief and balanced introduction to Islam in historical perspective.

The Byzantine Apogee and Decline, 1000–1453

Michael Angold, *The Byzantine Empire, 1025–1204* (White Plains, NY: Longman, 1997). A solid survey of the Byzantine Empire prior to the capture of Constantinople by the Latins.

P. M. Holt, *The Age of the Crusades: The Near East from the Eleventh Century to 1517* (White Plains, NY: Longman, 1986). An excellent survey of the political history of the Near East in the later Middle Ages.

CHAPTER 8

The Making of the Barbarian Kingdoms, 500–750

Paul M. Barford, *The Early Slavs: Culture and Society in Early Medieval Eastern Europe* (Ithaca, NY: Cornell University Press, 2001). An introduction to eastern Europe in the early Middle Ages.

James Campbell, ed., *The Anglo-Saxons* (Oxford: Phaidon, 1982). A collection of essays on Anglo-Saxon England by an outstanding group of archaeologists and historians.

Roger Collins, *Visigothic Spain, 409–711* (Malden, MA: Blackwell Pub., 2004). A survey of early medieval Spain to the Islamic conquest.

Florin Curta, *The Making of the Slavs: History and Archaeology of the Lower Danube Region, Ca. 500–700* (Cambridge [England]; New York: Cambridge University Press, 2001). A challenging account of Slavic ethnogenesis based on texts and archaeology.

F. Donald Logan, *The Vikings in History* (New York: HarperCollins, 1991). General introduction to the Vikings.

Rosamond McKitterick, ed. *The Early Middle Ages: Europe 400–1000* (New York: Oxford University Press, 2001). A collective introduction to early medieval history.

Walter Pohl, ed., with Helmut Reimitz, *Strategies of Distinction: The Construction of Ethnic Communities, 300–800* (Leiden, The Netherlands: Brill, 1998). An important collection devoted to early medieval ethnicity.

Chris Wickham, *The Inheritance of Rome: A History of Europe from 400 to 1000* (London: Allen Lane; New York: Penguin Group, 2009). A dense but rewarding synthesis by one of the leading specialists of our time.

Ian Wood, *The Merovingian Kingdoms 450–751* (London: Longman, 1994). Excellent survey of early Frankish history with an emphasis on government.

Living in the New Europe

Lisa M. Bitel, *Women in Early Medieval Europe, 400–1100* (Cambridge: Cambridge University Press, 2002). A valuable survey of women in the early Middle Ages.

Bonnie Effros, *Creating Community with Food and Drink in Merovingian Gaul* (New York: Palgrave Macmillan, 2002). An examination of an early medieval society through their social practices.

Yitzhak Hen, *Roman Barbarians: The Royal Court and Culture in the Early Medieval West* (Basingstoke; New York: Palgrave Macmillan, 2007). A comprehensive survey of cultural production at the barbarian courts..

The Carolingian Achievement

Paul Fouracre, *The Age of Charles Martel* (New York: Longman, 2000). An exploration of the Frankish world in the early eighth century.

Valerie L. Garver, *Women and Aristocratic Culture in the Carolingian World* (Ithaca: Cornell University Press, 2009). An examination of elite women in the Frankish world.

Rosamond McKitterick, *The Frankish Kingdoms Under the Carolingians, 751–987* (New York: Longman, 1983). A very detailed study of Carolingian history with an emphasis on intellectual developments.

Rosamond McKitterick, ed., *The New Cambridge Medieval History, c. 700–c. 900, vol. II* (Cambridge: Cambridge University Press, 1995). An excellent collective history of all aspects of Europe in the eighth and ninth centuries.

Janet L. Nelson, *The Frankish World, 750–900* (London: Hambledon Press, 1996). An excellent and balanced survey.

After the Carolingians: From Empire to Lordships

Georges Duby, *The Early Growth of the European Economy: Warriors and Peasants from the Seventh to the Twelfth Century* (Ithaca, NY: Cornell University Press, 1974). An imaginative survey of the economic and social forces forming in Europe in the early Middle Ages.

Heinrich Fichtenau, *Living in the Tenth Century: Studies in Mentalities and Social Orders* (Chicago: University of Chicago Press, 1990). A brilliant evocation of the quest for order on the Continent following the dissolution of the Carolingian Empire.

Timothy Reuter, *Germany in the Early Middle Ages, 800–1056* (New York: Longman, 1991). A readable, original survey of early German history by a British scholar thoroughly knowledgeable about current German scholarship.

CHAPTER 9

The Countryside

Robert Bartlett, *The Making of Europe: Conquest, Colonization, and Cultural Change, 950–1350* (Princeton, NJ: Princeton University Press, 1993). A challenging study of European expansion.

Frederic Cheyette, *Ermengard of Narbonne* (Ithaca, NY: Cornell University Press, 2001). An evocative account of Provençal society in the eleventh and twelfth centuries.

Georges Duby, *The Chivalrous Society* (Berkeley: University of California Press, 1978). Essays on the French aristocracy by the leading medieval historian.

Georges Duby, *The Knight, the Lady, and the Priest: The Making of Modern Marriage in Medieval France* (New York: Pantheon Books, 1984). A short study of the conflict between lay and religious social values in medieval France.

John France, *Western Warfare in the Age of the Crusades, 1000–1300* (Ithaca, NY: Cornell University Press, 1999). Warfare in the High Middle Ages.

Richard W. Kauper, *Chivalry and Violence in Medieval Europe* (Oxford: Oxford University Press, 2001). A comprehensive look at the relationship between chivalry and medieval violence.

Jonathan Riley-Smith, *The Crusades, Christianity, and Islam* (New York: Columbia University Press, 2008). A brief summation by one of the great authorities on the meanings and motivations of the crusades.

Medieval Towns

Hilde De Ridder-Symoens, ed., *A History of the University in Europe, Vol. 1: Universities in the Middle Ages* (Cambridge: Cambridge University Press, 1991). A multi-authored comprehensive history of medieval universities to 1500.

P. J. Jones, *The Italian City-State: From Commune to Signoria* (Oxford, NY: Clarendon Press, 1997). Major survey of Italian urban history.

Robert S. Lopez, *The Commercial Revolution of the Middle Ages, 950–1350* (New York: Cambridge University Press, 1971). An excellent survey of medieval commercial history.

Joseph H. Lynch, *The Medieval Church: A Brief History* (London and New York: Longman, 1992). A short introduction to medieval Church history.

David Nicholas, *The Growth of the Medieval City* (New York: Addison-Wesley Longman, 1997). A survey of the diversity of medieval urban development from late antiquity to the 1330s.

Norman Pounds, *The medieval City* (Westport, Conn.: Greenwood Press, 2005). A modern introduction to medieval urban history.

The Invention of the State

Robert Bartlett, *England under the Norman and Angevin Kings, 1075–1225* (Oxford: Oxford University Press, 2000). A survey of England from the eleventh to thirteenth centuries.

Thomas N. Bisson, *The Crisis of the Twelfth Century: Power, Lordship, and the Origins of European Government* (Princeton, N.J.: Princeton University Press, 2009). An important argument for the rise of centralized government.

Jean Dunbabin, *France in the Making, 843–1180* (New York: Oxford University Press, 1985). Good overview of the formation of France.

Horst Fuhrmann, *Germany in the High Middle Ages, c. 1050–1200* (New York: Cambridge University Press, 1986). A fresh synthesis of German history by a leading German historian.

William Chester Jordan, *Europe in the High Middle Ages* (New York: Viking, 2003). A comprehensive survey.

Bernard F. Reilly, *The Medieval Spains* (Cambridge: Cambridge University Press, 1993). Comprehensive survey of the social, political, and cultural history of the medieval Iberian peninsula.

Teofilo F. Ruiz, *From Heaven to Earth: The Reordering of Castilian Society, 1150–1350* (Princeton, NJ: Princeton University Press, 2004). An intelligent examination of the relationship between language and social and political change in Spain.

Joseph R. Strayer, *On the Medieval Origins of the Modern State* (Princeton, NJ: Princeton University Press, 1970). A very brief but imaginative account of medieval statecraft by a leading historian of French institutions.

CHAPTER 10

General Reading

Johan Huizinga, *The Autumn of the Middle Ages,* trans. Rodney J. Payton and Ulrich Mammitzsch (Chicago: University of Chicago Press, 1996). An important translation of the classic interpretation of culture and society in the Burgundian court in the Later Middle Ages.

Daniel Waley, *Later Medieval Europe: From Saint Louis to Luther* (London: Longman, 1985). A brief introduction with a focus on Italy.

Politics as a Family Affair

Richard W. Kaeuper, *Chivalry and Violence in Medieval Europe* (Oxford: Oxford University Press, 1999). A fine analysis of the complex relationship between chivalric ethos and the violence of aristocratic society in the Middle Ages.

Joachim Leuschner, *Germany in the Late Middle Ages* (Amsterdam: Elsevier, 1980). An introduction to late medieval German history.

Jean W. Sedlar, *East Central Europe in the Middle Ages, 1000–1500* (Seattle: University of Washington Press, 1994). A thematic introduction to the medieval history of the region that today comprises Poland, the Czech Republic, Slovakia, Hungary, Romania, Bulgaria, Albania, and the former Yugoslavia.

Life and Death in the Later Middle Ages

Bronislaw Geremek, *The Margins of Society in Late Medieval Paris,* trans. Jean Birrell (Cambridge: Cambridge University Press, 1987). A landmark study of the urban poor in the Later Middle Ages.

John Kelly, *The Great Mortality: An Intimate History of the Black Death* (London: Fourth Estate, 2005). A popular, well-written account of the great fourteenth-century plague.

James M. Murray, *Bruges, Cradle of Capitalism, 1280–1390* (Cambridge; New York: Cambridge University Press, 2005). A history of the most important commercial city in northern Europe.

David Nicholas, *The Growth of the Medieval City: From Late Antiquity to the Early Fourteenth Century* (London, New York: Longman, 1997). A comprehensive survey of medieval towns.

Teofilo F. Ruiz, *Spanish Society 1400–1600* (Harlow: Longman, 2001). A sensitive and original survey of Spanish society at the end of the Middle Ages.

Daniel Waley, *Later Medieval Europe, 1250–1520,* 3rd ed. rev. by Peter Denley. (New York: Longman, 2001). A brief, revised introduction focusing on western Europe.

The Spirit of the Later Middle Ages

Renate Blumenfeld-Kosinski, ed., trans. Kevin Brownlee, *The Selected Writings of Christine De Pizan: New Translations, Criticism* (New York: Norton, 1997). A selection of de Pizan's works and of scholarship on her. The place to start for learning about her.

Caroline Walker Bynum, *Holy Feast and Holy Fast: The Religious Significance of Food to Medieval Women* (Berkeley: University of California Press, 1987). An imaginative and scholarly examination of the role of food in the spirituality of medieval women.

Eamon Duffy, *The Stripping of the Altars: Traditional Religion in England, 1400–1580* (New Haven: Yale University Press, 1992). A revisionist study of local religion at the end of the Middle Ages.

David A. Fein, *François Villon Reconsidered* (New York: Macmillan, 1997). Villon's poetry and his life examined by an authority.

Malcolm Lambert, *Medieval Heresy: Popular Movements from the Gregorian Reform to the Reformation,* 2nd ed. (Oxford: Blackwell, 1992). A comprehensive survey of heretical movements from the eleventh to the sixteenth centuries.

Scott L. Waugh and Peter D. Diehl, eds., *Christendom and Its Discontents: Exclusion, Persecution, and Rebellion, 1000–1500* (New York: Cambridge University Press, 1995). Important collection of essays on heresy and dissent in western Europe.

CHAPTER 11

General Reading

P. Burke, *Culture and Society in Renaissance Italy* (Princeton, NJ: Princeton University Press, 1999). A good introduction to social and intellectual developments.

Paul Grendler, ed., *Encyclopedia of the Renaissance* (New York: Scribners, 1999). A valuable reference work for all aspects of the Renaissance.

Denys Hay, *The Italian Renaissance* (Cambridge, England: Cambridge University Press, 1977). The best first book to read, an elegant interpretive essay.

John Jeffries Martin, *The Renaissance World* (London, Routledge, 2007). An accessible and wide ranging survey of the entire period labeled the Renaissance.

Renaissance Society

Carlo Cipolla, *Before the Industrial Revolution: European Society and Economy, 1000–1700*, 3rd ed. (New York: W. W. Norton, 1994). A sweeping survey of social and economic developments across the centuries.

Richard Goldthwaite, *The Economy of Renaissance Florence* (Baltimore, MD: Johns Hopkins University Press, 2009). The leading economic historian of the period examines the complex workings of the Florentine economy from banking, trade, and the commercialization of art.

J. R. Hale, *Renaissance Europe: The Individual and Society* (Berkeley: University of California Press, 1978). A lively study that places the great figures of the Renaissance in their social context.

D. Herlihy and C. Klapisch-Zuber, *Tuscans and Their Families* (New Haven, CT: Yale University Press, 1985). A difficult but rewarding study of the social and demographic history of Florence and its environs.

Margaret L. King, *Women of the Renaissance* (Chicago: University of Chicago Press, 1991). A study by a leading women's historian.

Renaissance Art

Michael Baxandall, *Painting and Experience in Fifteenth-Century Italy* (Oxford, England: Oxford University Press, 1972). A study of the relationship between painters and their patrons and of how and why art was produced.

Samuel Edgerton, *The mirror, the window, and the telescope: how Renaissance linear perspective changed our vision of the universe* (Ithaca, NY: Cornell University Press, 2009). An arresting study that amalgamates art and science through the study of masters of perspective like Brunelleschi and Massacio.

Anthony Grafton, *Leon Battista Alberti: Master Builder of the Italian Renaissance* (New York: Hill and Wang, 2000). A lucid biographical study of a truly renaissance man.

Frederick Hartt, *History of Italian Renaissance Art* (Englewood Cliffs, NJ: Prentice-Hall, 1974). The most comprehensive survey, with hundreds of plates.

Howard Hibbard, *Michelangelo* (New York: Harper & Row, 1974). A compelling biography of an obsessed genius.

Lisa Jardine and Jerry Brotton, *Global Interests: Renaissance Art Between East and West* (Ithaca, NY: Cornell University Press, 2000). A bold argument about Renaissance art and its relation to Ottoman culture.

Michael Levey, *Early Renaissance* (London: Penguin, 1967). A concise survey of art, clearly written and authoritative.

Linda Murray, *High Renaissance and Mannerism* (London: Thames & Hudson, 1985). The best introduction to late Renaissance art.

Renaissance Ideals

Hans Baron, *The Crisis of the Early Italian Renaissance* (Princeton, NJ: Princeton University Press, 1966). One of the most influential intellectual histories of the period.

James Hankins, *Renaissance civic humanism: reappraisals and reflections* (New York: Cambridge University Press, 2000). Leading scholars reflect on the nature of civic humanism, the obligations of the citizen, and the Platonic ideal of the philosopher king.

George Holmes, *The Florentine Enlightenment*, 2nd ed. (Oxford: Clarendon Press, 1992). A new edition of the best study of intellectual developments in Florence.

Quentin Skinner, *Machiavelli* (Oxford: Oxford University Press, 1981). A brief but brilliant biography.

The Politics of the Italian City-States

Gene Brucker, *Florence, The Golden Age 1138–1737* (Berkeley: University of California Press, 1998). The best single-volume introduction to Florentine history with excellent illustrations.

J. R. Hale, *Florence and the Medici* (London: Thames & Hudson, 1977). A compelling account of the relationship between a city and its most powerful citizens.

F. W. Kent, *Lorenzo de' Medici and the art of magnificence* (Baltimore, MD: Johns Hopkins University Press, 2004). A reevaluation of the role Lorenzo the Magnificent played in Florentine politics and art.

Frederic C. Lane, *Venice: A Maritime Republic* (Baltimore, MD: Johns Hopkins University Press, 1973). A complete history of Venice that stresses its naval and mercantile developments.

Lauro Martines, *Power and Imagination: City-States in Renaissance Italy* (New York: Alfred A. Knopf, 1979). An important interpretation of the politics of the Italian powers.

Eugene F. Rice, Jr., *The Foundations of Early Modern Europe, 1460–1559*, 2nd ed. (New York: W. W. Norton, 1994). The best short synthetic work.

Charles Stinger, *The Renaissance in Rome* (Bloomington, IN: University of Indiana Press, 1998). A thorough account of one of the great ages in the history of Rome.

CHAPTER 12

General Reading

David Nicholas, *The Transformation of Europe 1300–1600* (New York: Oxford University Press, 1999). A comprehensive survey that emphasizes continuities between the sixteenth century and the preceding period.

Eugene Rice, *The Foundations of Early Modern Europe, 1460–1559*, 2nd ed. (New York: Norton, 1994). An outstanding synthesis.

Merry Wiesner-Hanks, *Early Modern Europe, 1450–1789* (New York: Cambridge University Press, 2006). An outstanding synthesis of the early modern world.

European Encounters

C. R. Boxer, *The Portuguese Seaborne Empire, 1415–1825* (London: Hutchinson, 1968). The best history of the first of the explorer nations.

J. H. Elliott, *The Old World and the New, 1492–1650* (Cambridge: Cambridge University Press, 1970). A brilliant look at the reception of knowledge about the New World by Europeans.

John H. Elliott, *Spain, Europe and the Wider World 1500–1800* (New Haven, CT: Yale University Press, 2009). The leading historian of early modern Spain rethinks its imperial age.

Felipe Fernandez-Armesto, *Columbus* (Oxford: Oxford University Press, 1991). The best of the recent studies. Reliable, stimulating, and up-to-date.

Anthony Pagden, *Lords of All the World: Ideologies of Empire in Spain, Britain and France, c. 1500–c. 1800* (New Haven, CT: Yale University Press, 1995). A fresh look at the ideas behind the European encounter with the New World.

Martin W. Sandler and Dennis Reinhartz, *Atlantic Ocean: The Illustrated History of the Ocean That Changed the World* (New York: Sterling, 2008). The experience of sailors and sailing in the first great age of discovery.

Hugh Thomas, *Rivers of Gold: The Rise of the Spanish Empire* (London: Widenfeld & Nicholson, 2004). A breathtaking retelling of Spain's New World Empire.

The Formation of States

S. B. Chrimes, *Henry VII* (Berkeley: University of California Press, 1972). A traditional biography of the first Tudor.

James Collins, *The State in Early Modern France* (New York: Cambridge University Press, 1995). A study of the unification of France and development of its political institutions.

Robert O. Crummey, *The Formation of Muscovy, 1304–1613* (London: Longman, 1987). The best one-volume history.

Sean Cunningham, *Henry VII* (London: Routledge, 2007). The most recent biography of England's state builder.

Norman Davies, *God's Playground: A History of Poland, Vol. 1, The Origins to 1795* (New York: Columbia University Press, 1982). The best treatment in English of a complex history.

Bernard Guenée, *States and Rulers in Later Medieval Europe* (London: Basil Blackwell, 1985). An engaging argument about the forces that helped shape the state system in Europe.

Henry Kamen, *The Spanish Inquisition: A Historical Revision* (New Haven, CT: Yale University Press, 1998). The best recent assessment of the power and activities of the Inquisition.

Paul M. Kendall, *Louis XI: The Universal Spider* (New York: Norton, 1971). A highly entertaining account of an unusual monarch.

John Lynch, *Spain, 1516–1598: From Nation State to World Empire* (Cambridge, MA: Blackwell, 1994). A valuable and expert survey.

Jaroslav Miller, *Urban societies in East-Central Europe: 1500–1700* (London, Ashgate, 2008). Urbanization in the forgotten states of Europe.

Helen Rawlings, *The Spanish Inquisition* (London: Wiley-Blackwell, 2006). An attempt to view the Inquisition in a broad social context.

J. H. Shennan, *The Origins of the Modern European State, 1450–1725* (London: Hutchinson, 1974). An analytic account of the rise of the state.

The Dynastic Struggles

Jeremy Black, *European warfare, 1494–1660* (London: Routledge, 2002). A valuable account of an age of unrelenting warfare.

J. R. Hale, *War and Society in Renaissance Europe* (Stroud, England: Sutton, 1998). Assesses the impact of war on the political and social history of early modern Europe.

William Maltby, *The Reign of Charles V* (New York: Palgrave, 2002). The most recent study of one of Europe's great emperors.

David Potter, *A History of France, 1460–1560* (London: Macmillan, 1995). A reliable survey that connects medieval and early modern developments.

Julius R. Ruff, *Violence in Early Modern Europe 1500–1800* (New York: Cambridge University Press, 2001). A social contextualization of European warfare.

J. J. Scarisbrick, *Henry VIII* (New Haven: Yale University Press, 1997). The definitive biography.

CHAPTER 13

General Reading

Owen Chadwick, *The Reformation* (London: Penguin Books, 1972). An elegant and disarmingly simple history of religious change.

Patrick Collinson, *The Reformation: a history* (New York: Random House, 2004). A brief account by England's leading historian of religion.

Diarmaid MacCulloch, *The Reformation* (London: Viking, 2003). A vastly impressive survey of the Reformation from a leading scholar.

Steven Ozment, *The Age of Reform, 1250–1550* (New Haven, CT: Yale University Press, 1980). An important interpretation of an epoch of religious change.

Ulinka Rublack, *Reformation Europe* (New York: Cambridge University Press, 2005). A cultural history of religious change.

Hubert J. Smith, *God's Hundred Years: A Brief History of the Reformation* (Cambridge, Lutterworth Press, 2007). An accessible study of the origins and development of Protestantism.

James D. Tracy, *Europe's Reformations, 1450–1650: Doctrine, Politics, And Community* (London, Rowman & Littlefield, 2nd ed., 2006). The long reformation that dominated European politics for two centuries.

The Intellectual Reformation

E. Eisenstein, *The Printing Revolution in Early Modern Europe* (Cambridge: Cambridge University Press, 1983). An abridged edition of a larger work that examines the impact of printing upon European society.

Jean François Gilmont and Karin Maag (eds.), *The Reformation and the Book* (London, Ashgate, 1998). The significance of printing and the book trade in speading ideas of Protestantism.

Adrian Johns, *The Nature of the Book: Print and Knowledge in the Making* (Chicago: University of Chicago Press, 1998). A major synthesis with an unusual interpretation.

Andrew Pettegree, *The French Book and the European Book* World (New York: Brill, 2007). The explosion of printing in Paris and the role of booksellers in the sixteenth century.

R. W. Scribner, *For the Sake of Simple Folk* (Cambridge: Cambridge University Press, 1994). A study of the impact of the Reformation on common people. Especially good on the iconography of reform.

James Tracy, *Erasmus of the Low Countries* (Berkeley, CA:, 1996). A brief biography of the great Dutch humanist.

The Lutheran Reformation

Roland H. Bainton, *Here I Stand: A Life of Martin Luther* (Peabody, MA: Hendrickson, 2009 Publishers). The single most compelling biography of Luther.

Robert Kolb, *Martin Luther: Confessor of the Faith* (New York: Oxford University Press, 2009). Luther's thought set within the context of German politics.

Bernd Moeller, *Imperial Cities and the Reformation* (Durham, NC: Labyrinth Press, 1982). A central work that defines the connection between Protestantism and urban reform.

Heiko Oberman, *Luther: Man Between God and the Devil* (New York: Doubleday, 1992). English translation of one of the best German biographies of Luther. Sets Luther within the context of late medieval spirituality.

G. R. Potter, *Huldrych Zwingli* (New York: St. Martin's Press, 1984). A difficult but important study of the great Swiss reformer.

Lyndal Roper, *The Holy Household: Women and Morals in Reformation Augsburg* (Oxford: Oxford University Press, 1991). The best work to show the impact of the Reformation on family life and women.

R. W. Scribner, *The German Reformation* (Atlantic Highlands, NJ: Humanities Press, 1986). An excellent introduction, especially to the social history of the Reformation.

The Protestant Reformation

William Bousma, *John Calvin* (Oxford: Oxford University Press, 1988). A study that places Calvin within the context of the social and intellectual movements of the sixteenth century.

Claus-Peter Clasen, *Anabaptism, A Social History, 1525–1618* (Ithaca, NY: Cornell University Press, 1972). An important study of the Anabaptist movement.

A. G. Dickens, *The English Reformation*, 2nd ed. (London: Batsford, 1989). The classic study of reform in England.

R. Po-chia Hsia, *The world of Catholic renewal, 1540–1770* (New York: Cambridge University Press, 2nd. ed., 2005). Catholicism resurgent in the early modern world.

Heiko Augustinus Oberman and Donald Weinstein, *The two Reformations: the journey from the last days to the new world* (New Haven, CT: Yale University Press, 2003). Reflections on the age of religious transformation by one of the most important historians of the Reformation.

J. J. Scarisbrick, *Henry VIII* (Berkeley: University of California Press, 1968). The classic biography of the larger-than-life monarch.

Kirsi Stjerna, *Women and the Reformation* (London, Blackwell Pub, 2008). The role of women in spreading new religious ideas.

The Catholic Reformation

Jean Delumeau, *Catholicism Between Luther and Voltaire* (Philadelphia: Westminster Press, 1977). An important reinterpretation of the Counter-Reformation.

Carlos Eire, *From Madrid to Purgatory* (Cambridge: Cambridge University Press, 1995). A brilliant study of the Spanish culture of death during the Counter-Reformation.

W. W. Meissner, *Ignatius of Loyola: The Psychology of a Saint* (New Haven, CT: Yale University Press, 1994). A searching study of the founding spirit of the Counter-Reformation.

John W. O'Malley, *Trent and All That: Renaming Catholicism in the Early Modern Era* (Cambridge, MA: Harvard University Press, 2000). A re-examination of Catholicism in the century surrounding the Council of Trent.

A. D. Wright, *The Counter-Reformation* (New York: St. Martin's Press, 1984). A comprehensive survey.

CHAPTER 14

General Reading

M. S. Anderson, *The Origins of the Modern European State System, 1494–1618* (London: Longman, 1998). A survey of developments stressing war and diplomacy across all of Europe.

Jan de Vries, *The European Economy in an Age of Crisis* (Cambridge: Cambridge University Press, 1976). A comprehensive study of economic development, including long-distance trade and commercial change.

J. H. Elliott, *Europe Divided, 1559–1598* (New York: Harper & Row, 1968). An outstanding synthesis of European politics in the second half of the sixteenth century.

Mark W. Konnert, *Early Modern Europe: The Age of Religious War, 1559–1715* (Orchard Park, NY: Broadview Press, 2006). The most recent survey.

Geoffrey Parker, *Europe in Crisis, 1598–1648* (London: William Collins and Sons, 1979). Compelling study of European states in the early seventeenth century.

The Crises of the Western States

Susan Brigden, *New Worlds, Lost Worlds: The Rule of the Tudors, 1485–1603* (New York: Viking, 2001). The latest volume in the Penguin History of Britain series.

Graham Darby, *The origins and development of the Dutch revolt* (London, Routledge, 2001). A recent collection of essays by leading historians presents the latest findings from a variety of perspectives.

Barbara Diefendorf, *The St. Bartholomew's Day Massacre* (New York: Bedford/St. Martins, 2008). A valuable introduction with a selection of primary documents.

Michael A. R. Graves, *Henry VIII: a study in kingship* (London: Pearson Longman, 2003). An accessible biography of one of England's most powerful monarchs.

J. A. Guy, *Tudor England* (Oxford: Oxford University Press, 1988). A magisterial survey by the leading scholar of Tudor England.

Mack P. Holt, *The French wars of religion, 1562–1629* (New York: Cambridge University Press, 2nd ed., 2005). The best account of civil war, assassination, and ultimate stability.

Henry Kamen, *The Duke of Alba* (New Haven CT: Yale University Press, 2004). A biography of one of the great military figures of the age.

Henry Kamen, *Spain, 1469–1714* (London: Longman, 1983). A thorough survey with valuable interpretations.

Robert Kingdon, *Myths about the St. Bartholomew's Day Massacres, 1572–76* (Cambridge, MA: Harvard University Press, 1988). A study of the impact of a central event in the history of France.

R. J. Knecht, *The French Civil Wars, 1562–1598* (New York: Pearson Education, 2000). A compact survey of the religious, social, and political dimensions of the conflicts that raged in France through the second half of the sixteenth century.

D. M. Loades, *Elizabeth I* (London: Continuum International, 2003.) A compelling biography of the last of the Tudors.

John Lynch, *Spain, 1516–1598: From Nation State to World Empire* (Cambridge, MA: Blackwell, 1994). An expert survey.

Garrett Mattingly, *The Armada* (Boston: Houghton Mifflin, 1959). Still the classic account, despite recent reinterpretations.

Geoffrey Parker, *The Dutch Revolt* (London: Penguin Books, 1977). An outstanding account of the tangle of events that comprised the revolts of the Netherlands.

Geoffrey Parker, *Philip II* (Boston: Little, Brown, 1978). The best introduction.

Richard Rex, *The Tudors* (London: Tempus, 2005). A brief introduction to England's golden age.

Michael Roberts, *Gustavus Adolphus and the Rise of Sweden* (London: English Universities Press, 1973). A highly readable account of Sweden's rise to power.

Robert Tittler and Norman Jones (eds.), *A companion to Tudor Britain* (London: Wiley-Blackwell, 2004). Essays by leading scholars on every aspect of the Tudor world.

C. V. Wedgwood, *William the Silent, William of Nassau, Prince of Orange, 1533–1584* (New York: Norton, 1968). A stylish biography.

Alison Weir, *Elizabeth the Queen* (London: J. Cape, 1998). A lively biography of the great queen.

The Struggles in Eastern Europe

David Kirby, *Northern Europe in the Early Modern Period: The Baltic World, 1492–1772* (London: Longman, 1990). The best single volume on Baltic politics.

S. F. Platonov, *The Time of Troubles* (Lawrence: University Press of Kansas, 1970). A good narrative of the disintegration of the Muscovite state.

Michael Roberts, *The Swedish Imperial Experience* (Cambridge: Cambridge University Press, 1979). Reflections on Swedish history by the preeminent historian of early modern Sweden.

The Thirty Years' War

Ronald G. Asch, *The Thirty Years War: The Holy Roman Empire and Europe, 1618–1648* (New York: Macmillan, 1997). A rich account of the destruction the war caused in the Empire.

Graham Darby, *The Thirty Years' War* (London, 2001). A brief introduction and narrative of a complex war.

J. H. Elliott, *Richelieu and Olivares* (Cambridge: Cambridge University Press, 1984). A comparison of statesmen and statesmanship in the early seventeenth century.

Peter Limm, *The Thirty Years' War* (London: Longman, 1984). An excellent brief survey with documents.

Geoffrey Parker, ed., *The Thirty Years' War*, 2nd ed. (London: Routledge, 1997). A revised edition of the standard survey of the conflict.

Boris F. Porshnev, *Muscovy and Sweden in the Thirty Years' War, 1630–1635* (New York: Cambridge University Press, 1995). The great Russian historian's account of the Thirty Year's War in the east.

CHAPTER 15

General Reading

Peter Burke, *Popular Culture in Early Modern Europe* (New York: Harper & Row, 1978). A lively survey of cultural activities among the European populace.

Henry Kamen, *European Society, 1500–1700* (London: Hutchinson, 2000). A general survey of European social history.

Peter Laslett, *The World We Have Lost: Further Explored* (New York: Scribners, 1984). One of the pioneering works on the family and population history of England.

Economic Life

Judith Bennett, *Ale, Beer, and Brewsters: Women's Work in a Changing World* (Oxford: Oxford University Press, 1996). An important study of the role of women in one of the most traditional trades.

Fernand Braudel, *Civilization and Capitalism: The Structures of Everyday Life* (New York: Harper & Row, 1981). Part of a larger work filled with fascinating detail about the social behavior of humankind during the early modern period.

Emmanuel Le Roy Ladurie, *The French Peasantry, 1450–1660* (London: Scholar Press, 1987). A complex study of the lives of the French peasantry.

Peter Musgrave, *The Early Modern European Economy* (New York: St. Martin's Press, 1999). A multidimensional survey of economic life.

Patrick O'Brien and Derek Keene (eds), *Urban achievement in early modern Europe: golden ages in Antwerp, Amsterdam, and London* (New York: Cambridge University Press, 2001). Essays by leading economic historians from a comparative perspective.

Social Life

Yves-Marie Bercé, *Revolt and Revolution in Early Modern Europe* (New York: St. Martin's Press, 1987). A study of the structure of uprisings throughout Europe by a leading French historian.

Edward Bever, *The Realities of Witchcraft and Popular Magic in Early Modern Europe: Culture, Cognition and Everyday Life* (London: Palgrave Macmillan, 2008). A brief introduction to the relationship between magic and culture.

Jonathan Dewald, *The European Nobility 1400–1800* (Cambridge: Cambridge University Press, 1996). An outstanding survey based on a wide range of sources.

Cissie C. Fairchilds, *Women in early modern Europe, 1500–1700* (London: Pearson/Longman, 2007). An argument for female agency in a patriarchal world.

Kaspar von Geyretz, *Religion and Culture in Early Modern Europe, 1500–1800* (Oxford: Oxford University Press, 2008). How ideas influenced social practices.

Barbara J. Harris, *English aristocratic women, 1450–1550: marriage and family, property and careers* (Oxford: Oxford University Press, 2002). A study of elite women and their role in lineage.

Roger B. Manning, *Hunters and Poachers: A Social and Cultural History of Unlawful Hunting in England, 1485–1640* (Oxford: Oxford University Press, 1993). Crime, cultural conflict, and social disorder intersect in the history of poaching.

Edward Muir, *Ritual in Early Modern Europe* (Cambridge: Cambridge University Press, 1997). A fascinating account of the transformations in concepts of time and the body in early modern Europe.

Barry Reay, *Popular Cultures in England, 1550–1750* (New York: Addison Wesley Longman, 1998). A sound and insightful thematic survey.

E. M. W. Tillyard, *The Elizabethan World Picture* (New York: Harper & Row, 1960). The classic account of the social constructs of English society.

Natalie Zemon Davis, *Women on the Margins: Three Seventeenth-Century Lives* (Cambridge, MA: Harvard University Press, 1995). Three short and stimulating biographies of early modern European women by a leading historian of popular culture.

Private and Community Life

Richard Adair, *Courtship, illegitimacy, and marriage in early modern England* (Manchester: Manchester University Press, 1996). A study of the dynamics of love both inside and outside of wedlock.

Helen Berry and Elizabeth A. Foyster (eds.), *The Family in Early Modern England* (New York: Cambridge University Press, 2007). A collection of essays by the leading historians of family life in England.

Roger Chartier, ed., *A History of Private Life, Vol. 3, Passions of the Renaissance* (Cambridge, MA: Harvard University Press, 1989). A lavishly illustrated study of the habits, mores, and structures of private life from the fifteenth to the eighteenth centuries.

Stuart Clark, *Thinking with Demons: The Idea of Witchcraft in Early Modern Europe* (Oxford: Oxford University Press, 1997). A sensitive reading of the sources for the study of witchcraft.

Beatrice Gottlieb, *The Family in the Western World from the Black Death to the Industrial Age* (Oxford: Oxford University Press, 1994). An outstanding introduction to the transformations in the lives of families.

R. A. Houston, *Literacy in Early Modern Europe* (London: Longman, 1988). How literacy and education became part of popular culture from 1500 to 1800.

Brian Levack, *The Witch-Hunt in Early Modern Europe* (London: Longman, 1987). A study of the causes and meaning of the persecution of European witches in the sixteenth and seventeenth centuries.

R. Muchembled, *Popular Culture and Elite Culture in France, 1400–1750* (Baton Rouge: Louisiana State University Press, 1985). A detailed treatment of the practices of two conflicting cultures.

Steven Ozment, *Ancestors: The Loving Family in Old Europe* (Cambridge, MA: Harvard University Press, 2001). A brief and accessible survey by a leading historian, making a spirited defense of early modern family life against historians who have portrayed the premodern family in grim terms.

D. Underdown, *Revel, Riot, and Rebellion* (Oxford: Oxford University Press, 1985). An engaging study of popular culture and its relationship to social and economic structures in England.

Merry E. Wiesner, *Women and Gender in Early Modern Europe* (Cambridge: Cambridge University Press, 1993). The best introduction to European women's history.

CHAPTER 16

General Reading

Perry Anderson, *Lineages of the Absolutist State* (London: NLB Books, 1974). A sociological study of the role of absolutism in the development of the Western world.

Euan Cameron, ed., *Early Modern Europe: An Oxford History* (Oxford, New York: Oxford University Press, 1999). Valuable essays by leading historians with well-chosen topics and illustrations.

Thomas Munck, *Seventeenth-Century Europe, 1598–1700* (New York: St. Martin's Press, 2005). A comprehensive survey.

David Sturdy, *Fractured Europe 1600–1721* (Oxford: Blackwell, 2002). A thorough survey of the complex military and political events of the long seventeenth century.

The Rise of the Royal State

Yves-Marie Bercé, *The Birth of Absolutism* (London: Macmillan, 1996). A history of France from the reign of Louis XIV to the eve of the Revolution by a leading historian of France.

Philip Edwards, *The Making of the Modern English State, 1460–1660* (London: Palgrave, 2001). A survey of how the medieval monarchy became modern.

J. H. Elliott, *Richelieu and Olivares* (Cambridge: Cambridge University Press, 1984). A brilliant dual portrait.

J. H. Elliott and Jonathan Brown, *A Palace for a King* (New Haven, CT: Yale University Press, 1980). An outstanding work on the building and decorating of a Spanish palace.

Alan James, *The origins of French absolutism, 1598–1661* (London: Pearson Longman, 2006). A study of kingship and the expansion of the bureaucracy.

Graham Parry, *The Golden Age Restor'd* (New York: St. Martin's Press, 1981). A study of English court culture in the reigns of James I and Charles I.

The Crises of the Royal State

Jacqueline Broad and Karen Green, *A history of women's political thought in Europe, 1400–1700* (Cambridge: Cambridge University Press, 2009). Includes chapters on women's writings about the Fronde and the Revolution of 1688.

Barbara Donagan, *War in England 1642–1649* (Oxford: Oxford University Press, 2008). A study of the nature of early modern warfare.

Tim Harris, *Revolution: The Great Crisis of the British Monarchy, 1685–1720* (London: Allen Lane, 2006). The Revolution of 1688 told from the perspective of the British archipelago.

Jonathan Israel, ed., *The Anglo-Dutch Moment* (Cambridge: Cambridge University Press, 1991). Essays by an international team of scholars on the European dimensions of the Revolution of 1688.

M. A. Kishlansky, *A Monarchy Transformed* (London: Penguin Books, 1996). A narrative survey of a remarkable era.

G. Parker and L. Smith, eds., *The General Crisis of the Seventeenth Century* (London: Routledge & Kegan Paul, 1978). A collection of essays on the problem of the general crisis.

Quentin Skinner, *The Foundations of Modern Political Thought*, 2 vols. (Cambridge: Cambridge University Press, 1978). A seminal work on the history of ideas from Machiavelli to Calvin.

W. A. Speck, *The Revolution of 1688* (Oxford: Oxford University Press, 1988). The best single volume on the event that transformed England into a global power.

Lawrence Stone, *The Causes of the English Revolution* (New York: Harper & Row, 1972). A vigorously argued explanation of why England experienced a revolution in the mid-seventeenth century.

The Zenith of the Royal State

Joseph Bergin, *The Rise of Richelieu* (New Haven, CT: Yale University Press, 1991). A fascinating portrait of a consummate politician.

Peter Burke, *The Fabrication of Louis XIV* (New Haven, CT: Yale University Press, 1992). A compelling account of a man and a myth.

Paul Dukes, *The Making of Russian Absolutism* (London: Longman, 1982). A thorough survey of Russian history in the seventeenth and eighteenth centuries.

Nicholas Henshall, *The Myth of Absolutism: Change and Continuity in Early Modern European Monarchy* (London: Longman, 1992). A searching examination of the problem of absolutism in the western European states.

Vasili Klyuchevsky, *Peter the Great* (London: Random House, 1958). A classic work, still the best study of Peter.

H. W. Koch, *A History of Prussia* (London: Longman, 1978). A comprehensive study of Prussian history, with an excellent chapter on the Great Elector.

Geoffrey Parker, *The Military Revolution* (Cambridge: Cambridge University Press, 1988). A lucid discussion of how power was organized and deployed in the early modern state.

John Wolf, *Louis XIV* (New York: Norton, 1968). An outstanding biography of the Sun King.

CHAPTER 17

General Reading

Jeremy Black, *The Rise of the European Powers, 1679–1793* (New York: Edward Arnold, 1990). A look at diplomatic history from an English point of view.

Jan de Vries, *The European Economy in an Age of Crisis* (Cambridge: Cambridge University Press, 1976). A comprehensive study of economic development, including long-distance trade and commercial change.

K. H. D. Haley, *The Dutch in the Seventeenth Century* (London: Thames and Hudson, 1972). A well-written and well-illustrated history of the golden age of Holland.

A. Rupert Hall, *The Revolution in Science, 1500–1750* (London: Longman, 1983). The best introduction to the varieties of scientific thought in the early modern period. Detailed and complex.

John Henry, *The Scientific Revolution and the Origins of Modern Science* (New York: Palgrave, 3rd ed., 2008). A brief introduction of the main discoveries of the early modern period and their long term impact.

Derek McKay and H. M. Scott, *The Rise of the Great Powers, 1648–1815* (London: Longman, 1983). An outstanding survey of diplomacy and warfare.

SUGGESTIONS FOR FURTHER READING

R-28

The New Science

H. F. Cohen, *The Scientific Revolution* (Chicago: University of Chicago Press, 1994). The history of the idea of the scientific revolution and of the events that comprised it.

Stillman Drake, *Galileo* (New York: Hill and Wang, 1980). A short but engaging study of the great Italian scientist.

Deborah E. Harkness, *The Jewel house: Elizabethan London and the scientific revolution* (New Haven, CT: Yale University Press, 2007). The contributions of ordinary Londoners to the advancement of the study and understanding of nature.

Marcus Hellyer, *The Scientific Revolution: The Essential Readings* (London: Blackwell, 2003). The best writings by historians of science on an array of subjects from astronomy to chemistry.

Margaret C. Jacob, *The Cultural Meaning of the Scientific Revolution* (New York: Alfred A. Knopf, 1988). Scientific thought portrayed in its social context.

Lisa Jardine, *Ingenious Pursuits: Building the Scientific Revolution* (New York: Anchor Books, 1999). A study emphasizing the technical contexts of the scientific revolution and interactions between its major figures.

Eileen A. Reeves, *Galileo's glassworks: the telescope and the mirror* (Cambridge, MA: Harvard University Press, 2008). A history of the Dutch invention put to use by the Italian scientist.

Londa Schiebinger, *The Mind Has No Sex? Women in the Origins of Modern Science* (Cambridge, MA: Harvard University Press, 1990). The role of women in the scientific revolution.

Steven Shapin, *The Scientific Revolution* (Chicago: University of Chicago Press, 1996). An excellent brief introduction.

Pamela H. Smith, *The body of the artisan: art and experience in the scientific revolution* (Chicago: University of Chicago Press, 2004). A study of the impact of art and craft on the new science.

Richard Westfall, *The Construction of Modern Science: Mechanisms and Mechanics* (Cambridge: Cambridge University Press, 1977). A survey of scientific developments from Kepler to Newton. A good introduction to both mechanics and mathematics.

Richard Westfall, *The Life of Isaac Newton* (Cambridge: Cambridge University Press, 1993). The best short biography.

Empires of Goods

J. N. Ball, *Merchants and Merchandise: The Expansion of Trade in Europe* (London: Croom Helm, 1977). A good overview of European overseas economies.

K. N. Chaudhuri, *The Trading World of Asia and the English East India Company* (Cambridge: Cambridge University Press, 1978). A brilliant account of the impact of the Indian trade on both Europeans and Asians.

Linda Colley, *Captives: Britain, Empire, and the World, 1600–1850* (New York: Anchor Books, 2004). The interrelationship between the emerging British empire and the people it held captives.

Philip Curtin, *The Atlantic Slave Trade* (Madison: University of Wisconsin Press, 1969). A study of the importation of African slaves into the New World, with the best estimates of the numbers of slaves and their destinations.

Ralph Davis, *The Rise of the Atlantic Economies* (Ithaca, NY: Cornell University Press, 1973). A nation-by-nation survey of the colonial powers.

Douglas R. Egerton and Jane G. Landers (eds.), *The Atlantic World: A History, 1400–1888* (New York: Harlan Davidson, 2007). A collection of essays on the slave trade and its impact on the international economy.

Jonathan Israel, *Dutch Primacy in World Trade, 1585–1740* (Oxford: Oxford University Press, 1989). The triumph of Dutch traders and techniques, written by the leading authority.

D. M. Loades, *England's Maritime Empire: seapower, commerce, and policy, 1490–1690* (London: Longman, 2000). An accessible account of Britain's rise to power.

Victor H. Mair, *The True History of Tea* (London: Thames & Hudson, 2009). The complete history of the commodity that changed diet and culture in Europe.

Joseph Miller, *Way of Death: Merchant Capitalism and the Angolan Slave Trade, 1730–1830* (Madison: University of Wisconsin Press, 1988). An illuminating portrait of the eighteenth-century slave trade, with an unforgettable account of the slave voyages.

Sidney Mintz, *Sweetness and Power* (New York: Viking Press, 1985). An anthropologist explores the lure of sugar and its impact on Western society.

Maarten R. Prak, *The Dutch Republic in the seventeenth century: the golden age* (New York: Cambridge University Press, 2005). A survey of the connection between political power and mercantile expansion.

Simon Schama, *The Embarrassment of Riches* (New York: Alfred A. Knopf, 1987). A social history of the Dutch Republic that explores the meaning of commerce in Dutch society.

The Wars of Commerce

Jeremy Black, *A System of Ambition? British Foreign Policy, 1660–1793* (London: Longman, 1991). The best survey of Britain's international relations during the long eighteenth century.

A. C. Carter, *Neutrality or Commitment: The Evolution of Dutch Foreign Policy, 1667–1795* (London: Edward Arnold, 1975). A tightly written study of the objectives and course of Dutch diplomacy.

Paul Langford, *The Eighteenth Century, 1688–1815* (New York: St. Martin's Press, 1976). A reliable guide to the growth of British power.

Virginia W. Lunsford, *Piracy and Privateering in the Golden Age Netherlands* (London: Palgrave Macmillan, 2005). An account of official and unofficial warfare on the high seas.

J. A. Lynn, *The Wars of Louis XIV, 1667–1714* (London: Longman, 1999). A comprehensive study by a leading military historian of France.

David Ormrod, *The rise of commercial empires: England and the Netherlands in the age of mercantilism, 1650–1770* (New York: Cambridge University Press, 2003). The best scholarly account of the clash of empires.

Richard Pares, *War and Trade in the West Indies, 1739–1763* (Oxford: Oxford University Press, 1936). A blow-by-blow account of the struggle for colonial supremacy in the sugar islands.

CHAPTER 18

General Reading

M. S. Anderson, *Europe in the Eighteenth Century, 1713–1783*, 3d ed. (London: Longman, 1987). A country-by-country survey of political developments.

Thomas Benjamin, *The Atlantic World: Europeans, Africans, Indians and Their Shared History, 1400–1900* (New York: Cambridge University Press, 2009). A wide ranging look at the peopling of the British Atlantic.

Jeremy Black, *Europe and the World 1650–1830* (New York: Routledge, 2002). An intelligent survey of Europe in a wider perspective.

David Kirby, *Northern Europe in the Early Modern Period* (London: Longman, 1991). Political history from a Baltic perspective, with excellent chapters on Sweden and Russia.

Nicholas Riasanovsky, *A History of Russia* (New York: Oxford University Press, 1993). The best one-volume history of Russia.

Michael Schaich, *Monarchy and Religion: The Transformation of Royal Culture in Eighteenth-century Europe* (Oxford: Oxford University Press, 2007). Essays that include studies of Russia and eastern Europe. Four essays on royal funerals present a comparative perspective.

Hamish M. Scott and Brendan Simms (eds.), *Cultures of power in Europe during the long eighteenth century* (New York: Cambridge University Press, 2007). A collection of essays by leading scholars on the connections between politics and culture in Prussia, France and Britain.

The Rise of Russia

John T. Alexander, *Catherine the Great: Life and Legend* (Oxford: Oxford University Press, 1989). A lively account of the public and private life of the Russian Empress.

M. S. Anderson, *Peter the Great* (London: Thames and Hudson, 1978). A well-constructed, comprehensive biography.

Simon Dixon, *Catherine the Great* (Profile Books, 2009). The latest biography emphasizes Catherine's iron will and struggle to bring Russia into modern Europe.

Paul Dukes, *The Making of Russian Absolutism, 1613–1801* (London: Longman, 1982). An extensive survey of the Russian monarchy in its greatest period.

Lindsey Hughes (ed.), *Peter the Great and the West* (London: Palgrave, 2001). Essays by leading scholars on the occasion of the 300th anniversary of Peter's visit to London.

Lindsey Hughes, *Russia in the Age of Peter the Great* (New Haven: Yale University Press, 1998). A detailed, thematically organized reappraisal of Russia in the era of Peter's reign.

Isabel de Maderiaga, *Russia in the Age of Catherine the Great* (London: Phoenix, 2002). A complete history of politics, culture and society from the leading scholar of the period.

The Two Germanies

Reed S. Browning, *The War of the Austrian Succession* (London: Macmillan, 1995). A comprehensive history of a complicated event.

David Fraser, *Frederick the Great: King of Prussia* (New York: Allen Lane, 2001). The latest biography.

J. Gagliardo, *Germany Under the Old Regime* (London: Longman, 1991). The best single-volume history.

H. W. Koch, *A History of Prussia* (London: Longman, 1978). A study of the factors that led to Prussian dominance of Germany.

C. A. Macartney, *Maria Theresa and the House of Austria* (Mystic, CT: Verry Inc., 1969). Still the best introductory study.

Theodor Schieder, *Frederick the Great* (London: Longman, 2000). An abridged translation of the work of Germany's leading historian of the age.

Dennis E. Showalter, *The wars of Frederick the Great* (London: Longman, 1996). A study of Frederick's military innovations and triumphs.

The Greatness of Great Britain

Bernard Bailyn, *The Ideological Origins of the American Revolution* (Cambridge, MA: Harvard University Press, 1967). A brilliant interpretation of the underlying causes of the break between Britain and the North American colonies.

Jeremy Black, *Britain as a Military Power* (London: UCL Press, 1999). A reliable survey of military developments in Britain.

Jeremy Black, *Eighteenth Century Britain* (New York: Palgrave, 2nd ed., 2008). A brief and accessible survey.

John Brewer, *The Sinews of Power: War, Money, and the English State, 1688–1783* (Cambridge, MA: Harvard University Press, 1990). An influential and clearly written book on the fiscal and military innovations that underwrote English power in the eighteenth century.

J. C. D. Clark, *English Society, 1688–1832* (Cambridge: Cambridge University Press, 1985). A bold reinterpretation of the most important features of English society.

Linda Colley, *Britons* (New Haven, CT: Yale University Press, 1992). A lively account of how a nation was forged from Welsh, Scots, and English and how unity and diversity intermixed.

Stephen Conway, *War, state, and society in mid-eighteenth-century Britain and Ireland* (Oxford: Oxford University Press, 2006). An accomplished history of the impact of war on British society.

Paul Langford, *A Polite and Commercial People: England 1727–1783* (Oxford: Oxford University Press, 1989). The standard survey in the Oxford history series.

Jim Smyth, *The Making of the United Kingdom, 1660–1800: State, Religion and Identity in Britain and Ireland* (London: Longman, 2001). A readable account of the relationships between England, Ireland and Scotland in the forging of its union.

Gordon Wood, *The Radicalism of the American Revolution* (New York: Alfred A. Knopf, 1992). How the ideals of the American Revolution shaped an emerging nation.

CHAPTER 19

General Reading

T. C. W. Blanning, *The Culture of Power and the Power of Culture: Old Regime Europe 1660–1789* (New York: Oxford University Press, 2002). An outstanding example of the new cultural history.

William Doyle, *The Old European Order, 1660–1800*, 2d ed. (Oxford: Oxford University Press, 1992). An important essay on the structure of European societies and the ways in which they held together.

Gertrude Himmelfarb, *The Roads to Modernity: The British, French, and American Enlightenments* (New York: Random House, 2004). A bold argument about the impact and importance of the other enlightenments.

Henry Kamen, *Early Modern European Society* (New York: Routledge, 2000). A concise social history by a leading historian.

Thomas Munck, *The Enlightenment: A Comparative Social History 1721–1794* (London: Arnold, 2000.) Lives of ordinary people in Paris, London, and Hamburg.

Eighteenth-Century Culture

A. J. Ayer, *Voltaire* (New York: Random House, 1986). A brief and vibrant study.

Alexander Broadie, *The Cambridge Companion to the Scottish Enlightenment* (New York: Cambridge University Press, 2003). Valuable essays on the Scottish contribution to advanced ideas in the eighteenth century.

Nicholas Cronk, *The Cambridge Companion to Voltaire* (New York: Cambridge University Press, 2009). Essays on all aspects of Voltaire's massive achievement.

Robert Darnton, *The Forbidden Best-Sellers of Pre-Revolutionary France* (New York: W. W. Norton, 1995). A look at the underbelly of the Enlightenment that both provides gripping reading and makes us think about the Enlightenment in new ways.

John G. Gagliardo, *Enlightened Despotism* (New York: Thomas Y. Crowell, 1967). A sound exploration of the impact of Enlightenment ideas on the rulers of Europe, with emphasis on the east.

Norman Hampson, *The Enlightenment* (London: Penguin Books, 1982). The best one-volume survey.

Patrick Mauries, *Cabinets of Curiosities* (London: Thames and Hudson 2002). A fascinating account of collectors and collecting.

Daniel Roche, *France in the Enlightenment* (Cambridge, MA: Harvard University Press, 1998). A wide-ranging survey of everything from politics to popular culture.

Judith Sklar, *Montesquieu* (Oxford: Oxford University Press, 1987). A concise, readable study of the man and his work.

Robert Zaretsky and John T. Scott, *The Philosophers' Quarrel: Rousseau, Hume, and the Limits of Human Understanding* (New Haven, CT: Yale University Press, 2009). A fascinating look at the brief and tempestuous relationship between two giants of enlightened thought.

Eighteenth-Century Society: The Nobility

Jonathan Dewald, *The European Nobility, 1400–1800* (Cambridge: Cambridge University Press, 1996). An insightful survey.

William Doyle, *Aristocracy and Its Enemies in the Age of Revolution* (Oxford: Oxford University Press, 2009). A study of the roots of anti-aristocratic ideology in France.

Jerzy Lukowski, *The European Nobility in the Eighteenth Century* (New York: Palgrave MacMillan, 2003). Especially valuable for its treatment of eastern Europe.

Eighteenth-Century Society: The Bourgeoisie

Maxine Berg, *Luxury and pleasure in eighteenth-century Britain* (Oxford: Oxford University Press, 2005). A lively study of the consumer revolution and its effects on British society.

John Brewer, *The Pleasures of the Imagination: English Culture in the Eighteenth Century* (London: HarperCollins, 1997). A fascinating study of the making of high culture in England.

Robert Darnton, *George Washington's false teeth: an unconventional guide to the eighteenth century* (New York: W. W. Norton & Company, 2003). An engaging collection of essays by the leading American historian of French cultural history.

Peter Earle, *The Making of the English Middle Class* (London: Methuen, 1989). The manners, mores, and mindset of the group that would come to dominate nineteenth-century Britain.

Jean-Louis Flandrin, *Families in Former Times* (Cambridge: Cambridge University Press, 1979). Strong on family and household organization.

Olwen Hufton, *The Prospect Before Her: A History of Women in Western Europe* (New York: Alfred Knopf, 1996). A survey of women's history that is particularly strong on the eighteenth century.

James Melton, *The rise of the public in Enlightenment Europe* (New York: Cambridge University Press, 2001). The emergence of the public sphere where culture and politics intersected.

Simon Shama, *The Embarrassment of Riches* (Berkeley: University of California Press, 1987). The social life of Dutch burghers, richly portrayed.

Lawrence Stone, *The Family, Sex and Marriage in England, 1500–1800* (New York: Harper & Row, 1979). A controversial but extremely important argument about the changing nature of family life.

Eighteenth-Century Society: The Masses

Peter Burke, *Popular Culture in Early Modern Europe* (New York: Harper & Row, 1978). A wide survey of practices throughout the Continent.

Olwen Hufton, *The Poor in Eighteenth-Century France* (Oxford: Oxford University Press, 1974). A compelling study of the life of the poor.

Karen O'Brien, *Women and Enlightenment in eighteenth-century Britain* (New York: Cambridge University Press, 2009). A survey of the contribution made to enlightenment thought by both English and Scottish women.

Kristina Straub, *Domestic Affairs: Intimacy, Eroticism, and Violence Between Servants and Masters in Eighteenth-Century Britain* (Baltimore, MD: Johns Hopkins University Press, 2008.) A study of the vulnerability of servants drawing on classic literary texts.

E. A. Wrigley and R. S. Schofield, *The Population History of England* (Cambridge, MA: Harvard University Press, 1981). The most important reconstruction of a national population, by a team of researchers.

CHAPTER 20

The French Revolution and the Fall of the Monarchy

Keith Michael Baker, *Inventing the French Revolution* (Cambridge: Cambridge University Press, 1992). The author views the French Revolution as a basically political event that can only be understood in the context of the changing political culture of the eighteenth century, with special attention to the use of language and the role of public opinion as a political invention.

Roger Chartier, *The Cultural Origins of the French Revolution*, tr. Lydia G. Cochrane (Durham, NC: Duke University Press, 1991). Argues for the importance of the rise of critical modes of thinking in the public sphere in the eighteenth century and of long-term de-Christianization in shaping the desire for change in French society and politics.

François Furet, *The French Revolution 1770–1840* (Oxford: Blackwell, 2006). One of the great historians of the French Revolution examines the tensions between the two revolutionary movements—egalitarianism and authoritarianism—within the French Revolution.

Peter McPhee, *The French Revolution, 1789–1799* (New York: Oxford University Press, 2002). An excellent short history of the Revolution and overview of recent scholarship are provided with particular strengths in the examination of rural life and women's experiences.

Michael Sonenscher, *Before the Deluge: Public Debt, Inequality, and the Intellectual Origins of the French Revolution* (Princeton: Princeton University Press, 2007). The author demonstrates how attitudes about the public debt in France provide new insights into the intellectual origins of the French Revolution.

Timothy Tackett, *Becoming a Revolutionary: The Deputies of the French National Assembly and the Emergence of a Revolutionary Culture* (Princeton: Princeton University Press, 1996). This collective biography of the cohort of deputies to the National Assembly demonstrates that their practical experience was distinct from that of the nobility.

Experimenting with Democracy, 1792–1799

Jack Censer and Lynn Hunt, *Liberty, Equality, Fraternity: Exploring the French Revolution* (University Park: Pennsylvania State University Press, 2001). This book is accompanied by a CD-ROM and provides a unique multimedia introduction to the French Revolution.

Lisa Di Caprio, *The Origins of the Welfare State: Women, Work, and the French Revolution* (Urbana: University of Illinois Press, 2007). The author argues that a new concept of the state emerged in the French Revolution by focusing on the relationship between old-regime charity and revolutionary welfare with special attention to the role played by sans-culottes women.

Dominique Godineau, *The Women of Paris and Their French Revolution* (Berkeley: University of California Press, 1998). A compelling account on the lives of women revolutionaries. Godineau presents women's protests as a mass movement within the revolution.

Michael L. Kennedy, *The Jacobin Clubs in the French Revolution, 1793–1795* (New York: Berghahn Books, 2000). The final volume of Kennedy's three-volume history of the Jacobin Club focusing on the period between May 1793 and August 1795.

Sara E. Melzer and Leslie Rabine, eds., *Rebel Daughters: Women and the French Revolution* (New York: Oxford University Press, 1992). Contributors from a variety of disciplines examine the importance of women in the French Revolution, with special attention to the exclusion of women from the new politics.

Peter McPhee, *Living the French Revolution, 1789–1799* (New York: Palgrave Macmillan, 2006). McPhee brings the Revolution to life through the experiences of peasants and town-dwellers.

John Shovlin, *The Political Economy of Virtue: Luxury, Patriotism, and the Origins of the French Revolution* (Ithaca: Cornell University Press, 2007). The author contends that ideas about a declining economy and about the financial abuses of courtiers and financiers contributed to the origins of the French Revolution by making economic actors into potential citizens, and making public virtue a revolutionary cause.

Michael Sonenscher, *Sans-Culottes: An Eighteenth-Century Emblem in the French Revolution* (Princeton: Princeton University Press, 2008). A new history of the sans-culottes and the role they played in the French Revolution.

G. Charles Walton, *Policing Public Opinion in the French Revolution: The Culture of Calumny and the Problem of Free* (New York: Oxford University Press, 2009). This study finds the cultural and political roots of the Reign of Terror in the Old Regime by coupling the history of public opinion with the new problems of free speech.

The Reign of Napoleon, 1799–1815

Louis Bergeron, *France Under Napoleon* (Princeton, NJ: Princeton University Press, 1981). An analysis of the structure of Napoleon's regime, its social bases of support, and its opponents.

Philip G. Dwyer and Peter McPhee, *The French Revolution and Napoleon: A Sourcebook* (London: Routledge, 2002). The authors have selected key primary texts that illuminate the period from 1787 to 1815.

Jean Tulard, *Napoleon: The Myth of the Saviour* (London: Weidenfeld and Nicolson, 1984). In this biography of Napoleon, the Napoleonic Empire is presented as a creation of the bourgeoisie, who desired to end the revolution and consolidate their gains and control over the lower classes.

Isser Woloch, *Napoleon and His Collaborators: The Making of a Dictatorship* (New York: Norton, 2001). Woloch explains the success of Napoleon's regime in terms of the support of his civilian collaborators.

Isser Woloch, *The New Regime: Transformations of the French Civic Order* (New York: Norton, 1994). Woloch's study emphasizes the break of the new regime from the old, placing the institutions created or revamped after 1789 in the context of a new civic order and citizenship.

CHAPTER 21

General Reading

Robert Allen, *A Global History of the British Industrial Revolution* (New York: Cambridge University Press, 2008). An explanation of European industrialization that places it in the context of the world economy.

T. S. Ashton, *The Industrial Revolution* (Oxford: Oxford University Press, 1997). A compelling brief account of the traditional view of industrialization.

Niall Ferguson, *The Cash Nexus: Money and Power in the Modern World, 1700–2000* (New York: Basic Books, 2001). A transnational history of the role of finance in the making of the modern world.

Jordan Goodman and Katrina Honeyman, *Gainful Pursuits: The Making of Industrial Europe, 1600–1914* (London: Edward Arnold, 1988). A brief overview of the entire process of industrialization.

David Landes, *The unbound Prometheus* (New York: Cambridge University Press, 2003). A brilliant synthesis of the impact of industrialization on European development.

The Traditional Economy

Richard Brown, *Society and Economy in Modern Britain, 1700–1850* (London: Routledge, 1991). A comprehensive survey.

J. D. Chambers and G. E. Mingay, *The Agricultural Revolution* (London: Batsford, 1966). The classic survey of the changes in British agriculture.

Thomas Crump, *A Brief History of the Age of Steam: From the First Engine to the Boats and Railways* (New York: Carroll & Graf, 2007). Power before coal, the precondition of industrialization.

Mark Overton, *Agricultural Revolution in England* (New York: Cambridge University Press, 1996). A brief survey by a leading historian of agricultural practices.

The Industrial Revolution in Britain

Joyce Burnette, *Gender, Work and Wages in Industrial Revolution Britain* (New York: Cambridge University Press, 2008). Explores the contributions of women to industrial development.

N. F. R. Crafts, *British Economic Growth During the Industrial Revolution* (Oxford: Oxford University Press, 1986). A highly quantitative study by a new economic historian arguing the case that economic growth was slow in the early nineteenth century.

François Crouzet, *The First Industrialists* (Cambridge: Cambridge University Press, 1985). An analysis of the social background of the first generation of British entrepreneurs.

Martin Daunton, *Progress and Poverty: An Economic and Social History of Britain, 1700–1850* (Oxford: Oxford University Press, 1995). The best single-volume survey on the Industrial Revolution and its effects on British society.

Phyllis Deane, *The First Industrial Revolution*, 2d ed. (Cambridge: Cambridge University Press, 1979). The best introduction to the technological changes in Britain.

Leandro Prados de la Escosura (ed.), *Exceptionalism and industrialisation: Britain and its European rivals, 1688–1815* (New York: Cambridge University Press, 2004). Leading economic historians debate the question of why Britain led the industrial transformation.

Richard Price, *British Society, 1680–1880: Dynamism, Containment, and Change* (New York: Cambridge University Press, 1999). A new argument about the nature of British society in the age of the Industrial Revolution.

John Rule, *The Vital Century: England's Developing Economy, 1714–1815* (London: Longman, 1992). A comprehensive survey of the British economy.

David Sunderland, *Social capital, trust and the industrial revolution 1780–1880* (London: Routledge, 2007). The role that family and community ties played in underwriting industrialization.

E. P. Thompson, *The Making of the English Working Class* (New York: Random House, 1966). A brilliant and passionate study of the ways laborers responded to the changes brought about by the industrial economy.

The Industrialization of the Continent

Iván Berend, *History derailed: Central and Eastern Europe in the long nineteenth century* (Berkeley, CA: University of California Press, 2003). The parts of Europe that industrialization passed by.

Lenard R. Berlanstein, *The Industrial Revolution and Work in Nineteenth-Century Europe* (London: Routledge, 1992). The impact of industrialization upon the European working class.

W. O. Henderson, *The Rise of German Industrial Power* (Berkeley: University of California Press, 1975). A chronological study of German industrialization that centers on Prussia.

Tom Kemp, *Industrialization in Nineteenth-Century Europe*, 2d ed. (London: Longman, 1985). Survey of the process of industrialization in the major European states.

Sidney Pollard, *Peaceful Conquest* (Oxford: Oxford University Press, 1981). Argues the regional nature of industrialization throughout western Europe.

Roger Price, *The Economic Transformation of France* (London: Croom Helm, 1975). A study of French society before and during the process of industrialization.

Wolfgang Schivelbusch, *The Railway Journey* (Berkeley: University of California Press, 1986). A social history of the impact of railways, drawn from French and German sources.

Clive Trebilcock, *The Industrialization of the Continental Powers, 1780–1914* (London: Longman, 1981). A complex study of Germany, France, and Russia.

CHAPTER 22

The New Ideologies

Jonathan Beecher, *Charles Fourier: The Visionary and His World* (Berkeley: University of California Press, 1986). An intellectual biography that traces the development of Fourier's theoretical perspective and roots it firmly in the social context of nineteenth-century France.

Craig Calhoun, *The Question of Class Struggle: Social Foundations of Popular Radicalism During the Industrial Revolution* (Chicago: University of Chicago Press, 1982). Presents popular protest of eighteenth- and early nineteenth-century England as the reaction of communities of artisans defending their traditions against encroaching industrialization.

Gareth Stedman Jones, *Languages of Class: Studies in English Working Class History, 1832–1982* (Cambridge: Cambridge University Press, 1983). A series of essays, on topics such as working-class culture and Chartism, that examine the development of class consciousness.

William H. Sewell, Jr., *Work and Revolution in France: The Language of Labor from the Old Regime to 1848* (Cambridge: Cambridge University Press, 1980). Traces nineteenth-century working-class socialism to the corporate culture of Old Regime guilds through traditional values, norms, language, and artisan organizations.

Denis Mack Smith, *Mazzini* (New Haven, CT: Yale University Press, 1994). Mazzini is presented as an important force in legitimizing Italian nationalism by associating it with republicanism and the interests of humanity.

Edward P. Thompson, *The Making of the English Working Class* (New York: Pantheon Books, 1963). A classic in social history that spans the late eighteenth to mid-nineteenth centuries in examining the social, political, and cultural contexts in which workers created their own identity and put forward their own demands.

Protest and Revolution

Maurice Agulhon, *The Republican Experiment, 1848–1852* (Cambridge: Cambridge University Press, 1983). Traces the Revolution of 1848 from its roots to its ultimate failure in 1852 through an analysis of the republican ideologies of workers, peasants, and the bourgeoisie.

Clive Church, *Europe in 1830: Revolution and Political Change* (London: Allen & Unwin, 1983). Considers the origins of the 1830 revolutions within a wider European crisis through a comparative analysis of European regions.

R. J. W. Evans and Hartmut Pogge von Strandmann, eds., *The Revolutions in Europe, 1848–1849: From Reform to Reaction* (Oxford: Oxford University Press, 2000). A focused collection of articles on the mid-nineteenth-century collapse of authority across Europe.

Alan J. Kidd, *State, Society, and the Poor in Nineteenth-Century England* (New York: St. Martin's Press, 1999). This volume is part of the *Social History in Perspective* series; it provides an overview of poverty in industrializing England, the role of the poor laws, public welfare, and charitable organizations in the nineteenth century.

Catherine J. Kudlick, *Cholera in Post-Revolutionary Paris: A Cultural History* (Berkeley: University of California Press, 1996). Examines the cultural values of ruling elites and demonstrates the role disease played in shaping political life and class identity in nineteenth-century France.

Patricia O'Brien, *The Promise of Punishment: Prisons in Nineteenth-Century France* (Princeton: Princeton University Press, 1982). An overview of the creation of the penitentiary system in nineteenth-century France and the rise of the new science of punishment, criminology, and the eventual appearance of alternatives to the penitentiary system.

Redcliffe N. Salaman, *The History and Social Influence of the Potato*, revised impression edited by J. G. Hawkes (Cambridge: Cambridge University Press, 1985). The classic study of the potato. A major portion of the work is devoted to the potato famine.

Jonathan Sperber, *Revolutionary Europe, 1780–1850* (New York: Longman, 2000). Considers the revolutions of 1848 within the context of economic and social changes rooted in Old Regime politics and society and from the perspective of the twenty-first century.

CHAPTER 23

Building Nations: The Politics of Unification

Derek Beales, *The Risorgimento and the Unification of Italy* (London: Allen & Unwin, 1982). Drawing a distinction between unification and national revival, Beales situates the period of unification within the larger process of cultural and political revival.

David Blackbourn, *The Long Nineteenth Century: A History of Germany, 1780–1918* (New York: Oxford University Press, 1998). This book examines the emergence of Germany from the late eighteenth century through the First World War in terms of politics, economics, and culture.

John A. Davis, ed., *Italy in the Nineteenth Century, 1796–1900* (New York: Oxford University Press, 2000). The essays of nine specialists provide an historical analysis of Italian society, politics, and culture.

Dieter Langewiesche, *Liberalism in Germany* (Princeton, NJ: Princeton University Press, 2000). This study traces the roots of German liberalism to the late eighteenth century and emphasizes the role of individual German states, with a special chapter on the local influences on the formation of the nation-state between 1815 and 1860.

Lucy Riall, *The Italian Risorgimento: State, Society, and National Unification* (New York: Routledge, 1999). Riall examines the historiography of Italian unification and presents the turbulent period of "resurgence" as a turning point in Italian history.

Denis Mack Smith, *Cavour* (London: Weidenfeld and Nicolson, 1985). Smith contrasts Cavour and his policies with those of Garibaldi and Mazzini and considers the challenge of regionalism to the unification process.

Reforming European Society

Jane Burbank and David Ransel, eds., *Imperial Russia: New Histories for the Empire* (Bloomington: Indiana University Press, 1998). A collection of essays using new methodologies for understanding Russian history in the eighteenth and nineteenth centuries.

Judith Flanders, *Inside the Victorian Home: A Portrait of Domestic Life in Victorian England* (New York: W.W. Norton & Co., 2004). This examination of the daily lives of ordinary people reconstructs the drudgery of Victorian domesticity and "the different mental world" of that era.

Catherine Hall, Keith McClelland, and Jane Rendall, *Defining the Victorian Nation: Class, Race, Gender and the British Reform Act of 1867* (Cambridge: Cambridge University Press, 2000). This study presents a cultural, social, and gender history of the extension of the vote in 1867, accompanied by strong bibliographic aids.

Sudhir Hazareesingh, *From Subject to Citizen: The Second Empire and the Emergence of Modern French Democracy* (Princeton, NJ: Princeton University Press, 1998). In showing the relationship between the local and the national, the author provides a reevaluation of the emergence of republican citizenship in the Second Empire.

Margaret Homans, *Royal Representations: Queen Victoria and British Culture, 1837–1876* (Chicago: University of Chicago Press, 1998). Victoria is examined as a monarch, a symbol, and a wife and mother as a key to British culture.

Alain Plessis, *The Rise and Fall of the Second Empire, 1852–1871*, tr. Jonathan Mandelbaum (Cambridge: Cambridge University Press, 1985). Discusses the Second Empire as an important transitional period in French history, when the conflict was between traditional and modern values in political, economic, and social transformations.

Changing Values and the Force of New Ideas

Jenni Calder, *The Victorian Home* (London: B. T. Batsford, 1977). A cultural and social history of Victorian domestic life in which the author describes both bourgeois and working-class domestic environments.

Bonnie G. Smith, *Ladies of the Leisure Class: The Bourgeoises of Northern France in the Nineteenth Century* (Princeton, NJ: Princeton University Press, 1981). Explores the impact of industrialization on the lives of bourgeois women in northern France and demonstrates how the cult of domesticity emerged in a particular community.

Robert Tombs, *The Paris Commune, 1871* (London: Longman, 1999). A synthetic overview of the events of the commune and their impact on the course of French and European history.

Martha Vicinus, *Independent Women: Work and Community for Single Women, 1850–1920* (Chicago: University of Chicago Press, 1985). Chronicles the choices that Victorian women made to live outside the norms of marriage and domesticity in various women's communities, including sisterhoods, nursing communities, colleges, boarding schools, and settlement houses.

CHAPTER 24

European Economy and the Politics of Mass Society

Edward Arnold, ed., *The Development of the Radical Right in France: From Boulanger to Le Pen* (New York: St. Martin's Press, 2000). Part I examines Boulangism, Socialism, anti-Semitism, right-wing working-class politics, and roots of right-wing radicalism.

Martin P. Johnson, *The Dreyfus Affair* (New York: St. Martin's Press, 1999). A concise and comprehensive overview of the Affair as a defining event in French history.

Kevin Repp, *Reformers, Critics, and the Paths of German Modernity, 1890–1914* (Cambridge, MA: Harvard University Press, 2000). The author looks at the reformers, intellectuals, and activists who shaped the modernist movement in Germany.

Outsiders in Mass Politics

June Purvis and Sandra Stanley Holton, eds., *Votes for Women* (New York: Routledge, 2000). The editors have brought together a collection of essays that reappraise the history of British suffragism by examining the activities of various women's groups and individuals from the nineteenth century to the interwar period.

Richard Stites, *The Women's Liberation Movement in Russia: Feminism, Nihilism, and Bolshevism, 1860–1930* (Princeton, NJ: Princeton University Press, 1978). Situates the Russian women's movement within the contexts of both nineteenth-century European feminism and twentieth-century communist ideology and traces its development from the early feminists through the rise of the Bolsheviks to power. Includes a discussion of the Russian Revolution's impact on the status of women.

Sophia A. van Wingerden, *The Women's Suffrage Movement in Britain, 1866–1928* (New York: St. Martin's Press, 1999). A chronological overview of the history of the British suffrage movement.

Shaping the New Consciousness

Geoffrey Crossick and Serge Jaumain, eds., *Cathedrals of Consumption: The European Department Store, 1850–1939* (Aldershot, England: Ashgate Publishing, 1999). A collection of articles about the creation of department stores in different European countries from the perspectives of culture, consumption, gender, and urban life.

Theodore M. Porter, *The Rise of Statistical Thinking, 1820–1900* (Princeton, NJ: Princeton University Press, 1986). This work traces the origins of modern statistical innovation of the early 1900s and shows the interdependence of the natural and social sciences.

Vanessa Schwartz, *Spectacular Realities: Early Mass Culture in Fin-de-Siécle Paris* (Berkeley: University of California Press, 1998). This work examines the formation and emergence of mass urban culture in late nineteenth-century Paris.

John Tosh, *A Man's Place: Masculinity and the Middle-Class Home in Victorian England* (New Haven, CT: Yale University Press, 1999). This work examines the roles of men in the private world of the domestic sphere and argues that Victorian masculinity was constructed not only in terms of work and male associations but also in terms of the home.

CHAPTER 25

The European Balance of Power, 1870–1914

Norman Rich, *Great Power Diplomacy, 1814–1914* (New York: McGraw-Hill Higher Education, 1992). This work surveys diplomatic activities from the end of the Napoleonic Wars to the eve of World War I.

Alan Sked, *The Decline and Fall of the Habsburg Empire, 1815–1918* (London: Longman, 1989). An overview of the Habsburg Empire's history from Metternich to World War I. The author interprets the various historiographical debates over the collapse of Habsburg rule. Rather than treating the late empire as a case of inevitable decline, the book examines the monarchy as a viable institution within a multinational state.

The New Imperialism

Antoinette Burton, ed., *After the Imperial Turn: Thinking With and Through the Nation* (Durham, NC: Duke University Press, 2003). This collection provides a critical cultural analysis of nationalism and imperialism by showing the inadequacies of the nation as an analytic category.

David Cannadine, *Ornamentalism: How the British Saw Their Empire* (New York: Oxford University Press, 2001). The author approaches the history of the British Empire as interconnected with the history of the British nation and considers this "entire interactive system" in terms of a social construction and social perceptions.

Michael W. Doyle, *Empires* (Ithaca, NY: Cornell University Press, 1986). Nineteenth-century imperialism is placed in a broad historical context that emphasizes a comparative perspective of the European imperial experience.

Richard Drayton, *Nature's Government: Science, Imperial Britain, and the "Improvement" of the World* (New Haven, CT: Yale University Press, 2000). A fascinating examination of the role scientists, and especially botanists, played as partners with bureaucratic government in British imperial expansion.

Daniel R. Headrick, *The Tentacles of Progress: Technology Transfer in the Age of Imperialism, 1850–1940* (New York: Oxford University Press, 1988). Argues that the transfer of technology to Africa and Asia by the Western imperial powers produced colonial underdevelopment.

Robert H. MacDonald, *The Language of Empire: Myths and Metaphors of Popular Imperialism, 1880–1918* (Manchester, England: Manchester University Press, 1994).

In studying the new metaphors of imperialism, the author examines the role of mythmakers, such as Rudyard Kipling, and popular fiction in shaping imperial perceptions and experiences. The author argues that the very shaping of language about non-European lands and peoples helped determine the form empire took in Great Britain.

The Search for Territory and Markets

Winfried Baumgart, *Imperialism: The Idea and Reality of British and French Colonial Expansion, 1880–1914* (New York: Oxford University Press, 1982). Principally concerned with the motives that led to imperial expansion, the author argues that the motives were many and that each action must be studied in its specific social, political, and economic context.

Raymond F. Betts, *The False Dawn: European Imperialism in the Nineteenth Century* (Oxford: Oxford University Press, 1976). Explores the ideology of empire and the process of cultural transmission through colonial institutions.

Eric Hobsbawm, *The Age of Empire, 1875–1914* (New York: Pantheon, 1987). A wide-ranging interpretive history of the late nineteenth century that spans economic, social, political, and cultural developments.

Thomas Pakenham, *The Scramble for Africa* (New York: Random House, 1991). A narrative history of how Europeans subdivided Africa among themselves.

Results of a European-Dominated World

Tony Ballantyne, *Orientalism and Race: Aryanism in the British Empire* (New York: Palgrave, 2002). Ballantyne traces how the idea of an Aryan race became an important feature of British imperial culture in the nineteenth century.

Johannes Fabian, *Language and Colonial Power: The Appropriation of Swahili in the Former Belgian Congo* (Cambridge: Cambridge University Press, 1986). Demonstrates how colonial power was exercised in the Belgian Congo through the study of the growth of Swahili as a lingua franca. The author pays particular attention to the uses of Swahili in industrial and other work situations.

Leila Tarazi Fawaz and C. A. Bayly, eds., *Modernity and Culture: From the Mediterranean to the Indian Ocean* (New York: Columbia University Press, 2002). This collection of essays demonstrates how cities in this vast region were increasingly cosmopolitan loci for a new kind of modernity that responded to political, economic, social, and cultural change.

Anne McClintock, *Imperial Leather: Race, Gender, and Sexuality in the Colonial Contest* (New York: Routledge, 1995). By using novels, diaries, advertisements, and other sources, the author demonstrates the relationship between images of domestic life and an ideology of imperial domination and focuses on the role of women in the colonial experience.

Paul B. Rich, *Race and Empire in British Politics* (Cambridge: Cambridge University Press, 1986). An intellectual history of ideas about race in the imperial tradition. Focusing on the years between 1890 and 1970, the author examines the political dimensions of race and race ideology in British society.

CHAPTER 26

The War Europe Expected

Keith Robbins, *The First World War* (Oxford: Oxford University Press, 1984). The author explores the major cultural, political, military, and social developments between 1914 and 1918, including the course of the land war and modes of warfare.

Jeffrey Verhey, *The Spirit of 1914: Militarism, Myth, and Mobilization in Germany* (Cambridge: Cambridge University Press, 2000). The author captures the fervor and patriotism that surrounded the August experiences and the declaration of war and chronicles the survival of the memory of the "spirit of 1914" in the postwar period.

A New Kind of Warfare

Roger Chickering, *Imperial Germany and the Great War, 1914–1918* (Cambridge: Cambridge University Press, 1998). The author offers a synthetic treatment of the history of the war and its impact on German society.

Frans Coetzee and Marilyn Shevin-Coetzee, eds., *Authority, Identity and the Social History of the Great War* (Providence: Berghahn Books, 1995). Recognizing that 1914 marks the beginning of the twentieth century, contributors examine the variety of national responses involved in waging total war and stress the interrelatedness of the home fronts and the battlefronts in affecting individual lives and identities.

Mark Cornwall, *The Undermining of Austria-Hungary: The Battle for Hearts and Minds* (New York: St. Martin's Press, 2000). This study presents extensive research on how propaganda was used by and against Austria-Hungary as a weapon of war.

Paul Fussell, *The Great War and Modern Memory* (New York: Oxford University Press, 2000). This twenty-fifth anniversary edition is a cultural history of World War I that treats the patterns and tendencies in war literature within the framework of a literary tradition.

John Keegan, *The First World War* (New York: Alfred A. Knopf, Inc., 1998). Keegan offers the definitive military history of the war based on diaries, letters, and reports, and in so doing illuminates the origins and progress of the war and the experience of the combatants.

Hew Strachan, ed., *The Oxford Illustrated History of the First World War* (Oxford: Oxford University Press, 1998). This extensively illustrated volume contains 23 chapters on key themes in the history of the Great War covering military issues, the home front, and the role of propaganda.

Adjusting to the Unexpected: Total War

Roger Chickering and Stig Förster, eds., *Great War, Total War: Combat and Mobilization on the Western Front, 1914–1918* (Cambridge: Cambridge University Press, 2000). In a collection of specialist essays, the authors consider the nineteenth-century origins of total industrialized warfare in search of a consensus on what constitutes total war.

Claire A. Culleton, *Working-Class Culture, Women, and Britain, 1914–1921* (New York: St. Martin's Press, 1999). A cultural and social history of British working-class women's experiences.

Belinda J. Davis, *Home Fires Burning: Food, Politics, and Everyday Life in World War I Berlin* (Chapel Hill: University of North Carolina Press, 2000). This thorough study examines the actions of women, especially poorer women, in Berlin during the war and the impact they had on politics and policy.

Patrick Fridenson, ed., *The French Home Front, 1914–1918* (Providence: Berg Publishers, 1992). The collection of articles demonstrates that unity on the home front concealed deep divisions, which led to open resistance and a redefined political universe at the end of the war.

Susan R. Grayzel, *Women's Identities at War: Gender, Motherhood, and Politics in Britain and France During the First World War* (Chapel Hill: University of North Carolina Press, 1999). A carefully documented cultural history of women's roles in World War I on the French and British home fronts.

Aviel Roshwald and Richard Stites, eds., *European Culture in the Great War: The Arts, Entertainment, and Propaganda, 1914–1918* (Cambridge: Cambridge University Press, 1999). This volume encompasses Europe to include western and eastern Europe and the South Slavic lands and examines the relationship between culture and politics during the war.

Jay Winter, Geoffrey Parker, and Mary Habeck, eds., *The Great War and the Twentieth Century* (New Haven, CT: Yale University Press, 2000). This volume of essays by leading scholars contributes to a comparative history of total war in the twentieth century.

The Russian Revolution and Allied Victory

Jane Burbank, *Intelligentsia and Revolution: Russian Views of Bolshevism, 1917–1922* (New York: Oxford University Press, 1982). The author examines the thinking of Russian intellectuals from the beginnings of revolution to the consolidation of Bolshevik power.

Sheila Fitzpatrick, *The Russian Revolution, 1917–1932* (Oxford: Oxford University Press, 1982). An analysis of the October Revolution of 1917 from the perspective of Stalinist society. The February and October revolutions of 1917, the civil war, and the economic policies of the 1920s are treated as various aspects of a single revolutionary movement.

Jane McDermid and Anna Hillyar, *Midwives of the Revolution: Female Bolsheviks and Women Workers in 1917* (Athens, OH: Ohio University Press, 1999). This work provides a good overview of the importance of women's actions in the Russian Revolution.

Settling the Peace

Manfred E. Boemeke, Gerald D. Feldman, Elisabeth Glaser, eds., *The Treaty of Versailles: A Reassessment After 75 Years* (Cambridge: Cambridge University Press, 1998). The volume is a synthetic reappraisal of the peace treaty, divergent peace aims, and postwar context in which it was developed.

David Stevenson, *The First World War and International Politics* (Oxford: Oxford University Press, 1988). A study of the global ramifications of World War I, this work traces the development of war aims on both sides, the reasons peace negotiations failed, and why compromise proved elusive.

CHAPTER 27

Crisis and Collapse in a World Economy

Gerald Feldman, *The Great Disorder: Politics, Economy, and Society in the German Inflation, 1914–1924* (New York: Oxford University Press, 1993). Feldman's monumental study of the German inflation provides a detailed historical account of the economic conditions and monetary policy in Germany during and after the war.

The Soviet Union's Separate Path

Stephen F. Cohen, *Bukharin and the Bolshevik Revolution: A Political Biography, 1888–1938* (Oxford: Oxford University Press, 1980). This milestone work is a general history of the period, as well as a political and intellectual biography of Bukharin, "the last Bolshevik," who supported an evolutionary road to modernization and socialism and whose policies were an alternative to Stalinism.

Sheila Fitzpatrick, *Everyday Stalinism—Ordinary Life in Extraordinary Times: Soviet Russia in the 1930s* (New York: Oxford University Press, 1999). The author explores the rituals, family life, and institutions of the Stalinist era, what the author calls the "distinctive Stalinist habitat" of Russian urban life in the 1930s.

Arch Getty and Roberta Manning, *Stalinist Terror: New Perspectives* (Cambridge: Cambridge University Press, 1994). Leading revisionist scholars of the Stalinist period provide a reassessment of the regime.

Robert C. Tucker, *Stalin in Power: The Revolution from Above, 1928–1941* (New York: W.W. Norton & Company, 1992). The author portrays how Stalin deliberately chose terror, mass murder, forced resettlement, and prison camps as a means of enforcing "revolution from above."

Chris Ward, ed., *The Stalinist Dictatorship* (New York: Oxford University Press, 1998). A collection of leading Soviet scholars examine Stalin's character, his role within the Soviet Union, and how Stalinism was a lived experience.

The Rise of Fascist Dictatorship in Italy

MacGregor Knox, *Dictatorship, Foreign Policy, and War in Fascist Italy and Nazi Germany* (London: Cambridge University Press, 2000). Expanding on his earlier work on Mussolini's foreign policy, the author offers a comparative perspective of Italy's and Germany's moves from unification to militant dictatorships, the similar forces that shaped their creation, and the differences in expansionist zeal, military traditions, and fighting power.

Zeev Sternhell with Mario Sznajder and Maia Asheri, *The Birth of Fascist Ideology: From Cultural Rebellion to Political Revolution* (Princeton, NJ: Princeton University Press, 1994). Approaches fascism as an ideology rather than a social movement and argues that it was already fully formed before World War I.

Hitler and the Third Reich

Ian Kershaw, *Hitler, 1889–1936: Hubris* (New York: W.W. Norton & Company, 1998); and *Hitler, 1936–1945: Nemesis* (New York: W.W. Norton & Company, 2000). The definitive two-volume biography provides a history of Germany society through Hitler's extraordinary political domination.

Dieter Langewiesche, *Liberalism in Germany*. Translated by Christiane Banerji. (Princeton, NJ: Princeton University Press, 2000). This work traces the history of German liberalism from the early nineteenth century to post-1945 politics in West Germany as it was embodied in political movements, organizations, and values.

Bernd Widdig, *Culture and Inflation in Weimar Germany* (Berkeley: University of California Press, 2001). Through literary and filmic sources, the author provides a cultural analysis of a defining economic event in German history.

Democracies in Crisis

Ivan T. Berend, *Decades of Crisis: Central and Eastern Europe Before World War II* (Berkeley: University of California Press, 1998). The author offers a comprehensive overview of central and eastern Europe in the first half of the twentieth century and argues that the region "embarked on a historical 'detour'" in rejecting the parliamentary system and turning to nationalist authoritarian regimes.

John Hiden and Patrick Salmon, *The Baltic Nations and Europe: Estonia, Latvia, and Lithuania in the Twentieth Century* (London and New York: Longman, 1991). Surveys the development of the Baltic states in the twentieth century, discussing Baltic independence, the period between the wars, and the states' incorporation into the Soviet Union, as well as renewed efforts toward independence in the Gorbachev era.

Julian Jackson, *The Popular Front in France: Defending Democracy, 1934–1938* (Cambridge: Cambridge University Press, 1988). An in-depth study of Léon Blum's government, with a special emphasis on cultural transformation and the legacy of the Popular Front.

Michael Jackson, *Fallen Sparrows: The International Brigades in the Spanish Civil War* (Philadelphia: American Philosophical Society, 1994). A careful description of the members and activities of the International Brigades, which were organized under the direction of the Comintern to save the Spanish Republic.

Stanley G. Payne, *Fascism in Spain, 1923–1977* (Madison: The University of Wisconsin Press, 1999). The author presents a comprehensive history of Spanish fascism from its origins to the death of Franco.

Michael Richards, *A Time of Silence: Civil War and the Culture of Repression in Franco's Spain, 1936–1945* (Cambridge: Cambridge University Press, 1998). This work examines Spanish society during and after the Spanish Civil War in relation to Franco's policy of "moral and economic reconstruction" based on self-sufficiency.

CHAPTER 28

Aggression and Conquest

Paul Kennedy, *The Realities Behind Diplomacy: Background Influences on British External Policy, 1865–1980* (London: Allen & Unwin, 1981). Essays dealing with the continuity of appeasement in British foreign policy across two centuries.

Ian Kershaw, *The Nazi Dictatorship* (London: Edward Arnold, 1985). A fine synthesis of key problems of interpretation regarding the Third Reich. Special attention is paid to the interdependence of domestic and foreign policy and the inevitability of war in Hitler's ideology.

Donald Cameron Watt, *How War Came: The Immediate Origins of the Second World War* (London: Heinemann, 1989). An international historian chronicles the events leading to the outbreak of the war.

Racism and Destruction

Renate Bridenthal, Atina Grossmann, and Marion Kaplan, eds., *When Biology Became Destiny: Women in Weimar and Nazi Germany* (New York: Monthly Review Press, 1984). A volume of essays pursuing common themes on the relation between sexism and racism in interwar and wartime Germany.

Raul Hilberg, *The Destruction of the European Jews*, 3 vols. (New York: Holmes and Meier, 1985). An exhaustive study of the annihilation of European Jews beginning with cultural precedents and antecedents. Examines step-by-step developments that led to extermination policies and contains valuable appendixes on statistics and a discussion of sources.

Charles S. Maier, *The Unmasterable Past: History, Holocaust, and German National Identity* (Cambridge, MA: Harvard University Press, 1988). A thoughtful discussion of the historical debate over the Holocaust and the comparative dimensions of the event. Especially valuable in placing the Holocaust within German history.

Michael R. Marrus, *The Holocaust in History* (New York: New American Library, 1987). A comprehensive survey of all aspects of the Holocaust, including the policies of the Third Reich, the living conditions in the camps, and the prospects for resistance and opposition.

Allied Victory

John Campbell, ed., *The Experience of World War II* (New York: Oxford University Press, 1989). This richly illustrated work provides an overview of the Second World War in both the Asian and European theaters in terms of origins, events, and consequences.

Akira Iriye, *The Origins of the Second World War in Asia and the Pacific* (London: Longman, 1987). Examines the events of the 1930s leading up to hostilities in the Pacific theater, with a special focus on Japanese isolation and aggression.

John Keegan, *The Second World War* (New York: Viking, 1990). Provides a panoramic sweep of "the largest single event in human history," with special attention to warfare in all its forms and the importance of leadership.

Gerhard L. Weinberg, *A World at Arms: A Global History of World War II* (New York: Cambridge University Press, 1994). An overview of the interactions among Germany, the Soviet Union, and Japan, which provides an integrated history of World War II with a helpful bibliographic essay.

CHAPTER 29

The Origins of the Cold War

Franz Ansprenger, *The Dissolution of the Colonial Empires* (London: Routledge, 1989). An analysis of Europe's withdrawal from Asia and Africa following the Second World War, beginning with an examination of post–World War I imperialism.

Edward H. Judge and John W. Langdon, eds., *The Cold War: A History Through Documents* (New York: Prentice-Hall, 1998). Includes about 130 edited documents covering the period from 1945 to 1991.

Charles S. Maier, *In Search of Stability: Explorations in Historical Political Economy* (Cambridge: Cambridge University Press, 1987). Covers a wide variety of issues affecting twentieth-century Europe, including the foundation of American international economic policy after World War II and the conditions for stability in western Europe after 1945.

Bruce D. Porter, *The USSR in Third World Conflicts: Soviet Arms and Diplomacy in Local Wars, 1945–1980* (Cambridge: Cambridge University Press, 1984). A case study approach to the Soviet Union's changing postwar policies toward the third world that centers on local wars in Africa and the Middle East.

Postwar Economic Recovery in Europe, Japan, and the Soviet Union

Eric Hobsbawm, *The Age of Extremes: A History of the World, 1914–1991* (New York: Vintage Books, 1996). This volume covers what the author calls "the short twentieth century" from the outbreak of World War I to the fall of the Soviet Union. Of particular interest is the section on the 30 years following World War II, which the author sees as a "golden age" of extraordinary economic growth and social transformation.

Michael J. Hogan, *The Marshall Plan: America, Britain, and the Reconstruction of Western Europe* (Cambridge: Cambridge University Press, 1987). A thoroughly researched argument on the continuity of U.S. economic policy in the twentieth century. Hogan counters the belief that the Marshall Plan was merely a response to the Cold War.

Derek W. Urwin, *Western Europe Since 1945: A Political History*, 4th ed. (London: Longman, 1989). An updated general survey of postwar politics, with a special focus on the problems of reconstruction and the role of the resistance after 1945.

The Welfare State and Social Transformation

Simone de Beauvoir, *The Second Sex* (New York: Knopf, 1963). The author, one of France's leading intellectuals in the twentieth century, describes the situation of women's lives in the postwar West by placing them within the context of the history and myths governing Western culture.

David Caute, *The Year of the Barricades: A Journey Through 1968* (New York: Harper & Row, 1988). More than its title suggests, this work is an overview of postwar youth culture on three continents. The politics of 1968 is featured, although other topics regarding the counterculture, lifestyles, and cultural ramifications are considered.

John R. Gillis, *Youth and History: Tradition and Change in European Age Relations, 1770–Present* (New York: Academic Press, 1981). Connects the history of European youth to broad trends in economic and demographic modernization over the past 200 years.

Jane Jenson, "Both Friend and Foe: Women and State Welfare," *Becoming Visible: Women in European History*, ed. Renate Bridenthal, Claudia Koonz, and Susan Stuard (Boston: Houghton Mifflin, 1987). This essay illuminates the mixed blessing of the welfare state for women after 1945 by focusing on the experiences of women in Great Britain and France.

Walter Laqueur, *Europe Since Hitler: The Rebirth of Europe* (New York: Penguin Books, 1982). Surveys politics, economy, society, and culture in order to explain Europe's postwar resurgence.

Margaret Mead, *Culture and Commitment: The New Relationships Between the Generations in the 1970s* (New York: Columbia University Press, 1978). This series of essays, written by one of America's premier anthropologists, explores the origins and consequences of the generation gap, with special attention to Cold War politics, historical conditions, and technological transformations.

Susan Pederson, *Family, Dependence, and the Origins of the Welfare State: Britain and France, 1914–1945* (Cambridge: Cambridge University Press, 1994). Although this work covers the earlier period, the comparative approach to differing attitudes and policies provides an essential background to understanding family policy in postwar Europe.

Denise Riley, *War in the Nursery: Theories of the Child and Mother* (London: Virago Press, 1983). Treats social policies of postwar pronatalism within the context of the popularization of developmental and child psychologies in Europe, with special attention to Britain and the United States and an emphasis on the postwar period as a turning point in attitudes toward women and the family.

Mary Ruggie, *The State and Working Women: A Comparative Study of Britain and Sweden* (Princeton, NJ: Princeton University Press, 1984). A sociological study comparing the economic status of women in two European welfare states.

CHAPTER 30

The End of the Cold War and the Emergence of a New Europe

Timothy Garton Ash, *In Europe's Name: Germany and the Divided Continent* (London: Jonathan Cape, 1993). An original and complex thesis that looks at German reunification from its origins in the 1970s.

Archie Brown, *The Gorbachev Factor* (New York: Oxford University Press, 1996). Traces Gorbachev's career and examines in detail his attempts to convert the Soviet Union into a social democratic variant of socialism.

Geoffrey Hosking, *The Awakening of the Soviet Union* (Cambridge, MA: Harvard University Press, 1990). Published in the midst of the dramatic changes taking place in the Soviet Union, this study emphasizes the social bases of reform and the challenges to Soviet leadership.

Michael Ignatieff, *Blood and Belonging: Journeys into the New Nationalism* (Toronto: Viking Press, 1993). A companion to a BBC television series, the volume provides a sophisticated exploration of expressions of nationalism throughout Europe.

Walter Laqueur, *The Dream That Failed: Reflections on the Soviet Union* (New York: Oxford University Press, 1994). This work recognizes the tenuous hold of capitalism in Russia and the possibility of a Communist party return.

Martin Malia, *The Soviet Tragedy: A History of Socialism in Russia, 1917–1991* (New York: Maxwell Macmillan International, 1994). A reevaluation by a leading Russian historian of the failure of communism.

Adam Michnik, *Letters from Freedom: Post–Cold War Realities and Perspectives* (Berkeley: University of California Press, 1998). Michnik, a journalist, politician, and writer imprisoned for his political views in the 1980s, is widely regarded as a hero in Poland today. This volume includes his articles, speeches, and interviews with leading European political figures and addresses the political realities of Europe after the end of the Cold War.

Joseph Rothschild, *Return to Diversity: A Political History of East Central Europe* (New York: Oxford University Press, 1989). A historical and analytical survey of Poland, Czechoslovakia, Hungary, Yugoslavia, Romania, Bulgaria, and Albania that appeared just before the great changes that swept through eastern Europe in 1989. Rothschild highlights the tensions between nationalist aspirations and Communist rule.

Henry Ashby Turner, Jr., *The Two Germanies Since 1945* (New Haven, CT: Yale University Press, 1987). A political history of the postwar division of Germany until 1987 that bridges a period the author contends was one of increasing involvement and underlying mutual interests between the two nations.

Ethnic Conflict and Nationalism

Richard Holbrooke, *To End a War* (New York: The Modern Library, 1998). The author offers a firsthand account of the intense diplomatic negotiations surrounding the Dayton Accords and a clear understanding of the problems plaguing Bosnia.

Tim Judah, *Kosovo: War and Revenge* (New Haven, CT: Yale University Press, 2000). Based on careful research, the author analyzes "the last great European war of the twentieth century."

Noel Malcolm, *Kosovo: A Short History* (New York: Harper Collins, 1999). The author is a historian who traces Kosovo's history to medieval times and challenges myths and debates about national origins.

Julie A. Mertus, *Kosovo: How Myths and Truths Started a War* (Berkeley: University of California Press, 1999). Having spent two years in Kosovo interviewing people affected by the conflict, the author offers an understanding of events from the perspective of the victims.

Michael A. Sells, *The Bridge Betrayed* (Berkeley: The University of California Press, 1996). The author stresses the role of religious nationalists, Serbian Orthodox and Croatian Roman Catholic, in waging a holy war resulting in genocide and destruction.

Susan L. Woodward, *Balkan Tragedy: Chaos and Dissolution After the Cold War* (Washington, DC: The Brookings Institution, 1995). This important study explains, in terms of the breakdown of political and civil order, why Yugoslavia disintegrated into ethnic hatreds so rapidly after 1989.

The West in the Global Community

Michael Emerson et al., *The Economics of 1992: The E.C. Commission's Assessment of the Economic Effects of Completing the Internal Market* (Oxford: Oxford University

Press, 1988). A work replete with empirical data that give a comprehensive assessment of the potential impact of establishing a single internal market in the European Economic Community.

Mark Juergensmeyer, *The New Cold War? Religious Nationalism Confronts the Secular State* (Berkeley: The University of California Press, 1994). The author examines the growing significance of religious nationalism from a global perspective.

Geir Lundestad, *"Empire" by Integration* (New York: Oxford University Press, 1998). Provides a comprehensive overview of U.S. policy toward European integration.

Wolfgang Mommsen and Gerhard Hirschfeld, eds., *Social Protest, Violence and Terror in Nineteenth- and Twentieth-Century Europe* (London: Macmillan, 1982). Places terrorism within a historical context in Europe over a century and a half in a series of articles that takes a national case-history approach.

Richard E. Rubinstein, *Alchemists of Revolution: Terrorism in the Modern World* (New York: Basic Books, 1987). Examines the local root causes of terrorism in historical perspective and argues that terrorism is the social and moral crisis of a disaffected intelligentsia.

discovering western civilization online

CHAPTER 1

You can obtain more information about the first civilizations at the Websites listed below. See also the Companion Website that accompanies this text, *www.pearsonhighered. com/kishlansky*, which contains an online study guide and additional resources.

Before Civilization

Origins of Humankind
www.pbs.org/wgbh/evolution/humans/humankind/
Educational information on prehistory of humanity.

Rock Art Links—Petroglyphs and Pictographs
www.electronics-ee.com/Art/Art_History/Rock_Art.htm
Online database of links to prehistoric rock art throughout the world.

Prehistoric Cultures
www.d.umn.edu/cla/faculty/troufs/anth1602/
A course Website at the University of Minnesota–Duluth that links to materials on prehistoric cultures around the world.

Mesopotamia

ABZU: Guide to Resources for the Study of the Ancient Near East Available on the Internet
www.etana.org/abzu/
A major site for all aspects of Ancient Mesopotamia and Egypt maintained by the Oriental Institute of the University of Chicago.

Egypt

NM's Creative Impulse: Egypt
http://eawc.evansville.edu/egpage.htm
Award-winning site for Egyptian history.

Survey of Ancient Egypt
www.cofc.edu/~piccione/hist270/index.html
Excellent class Web page on Ancient Egypt.

Egyptian Kings
touregypt.net/kings.htm
A site that provides information on all of the pharaohs.

Giza Plateau Computer Model
www.oi.uchicago.edu/OI/DEPT/COMP/GIZ/MODEL/Giza_Model.html
A site devoted to Giza with a computer model of its pyramids and other monuments.

Israel

The Hebrews: A Learning Module
www.wsu.edu/~dee/HEBREWS/HEBREWS.HTM
An excellent course site devoted entirely to the ancient Hebrews.

The Israel Museum, Jerusalem: Archaeology
http://www.english.imjnet.org.il/htmls/article_15.aspx?co=13013&bsp=12940
Site on early Israel archaeology.

Nineveh and Babylon

Babylon
http://www.livius.org/ba-bd/babylon.html
A brief history of Babylon with further links.

CHAPTER 2

You can obtain more information about early Greece at the Websites listed below. See also the Companion Website that accompanies this text, *www.pearsonhighered. com/kishlansky*, which contains an online study guide and additional resources.

General Websites

The Perseus Digital Project
www.perseus.tufts.edu/
A digital library dedicated to all aspects of ancient Greek civilization.

Thomas R. Martin, An Overview of Classical Greek History
www.perseus.tufts.edu/cgi-bin/ptext?doc=1999.04.0009
This page of The Perseus Digital Project includes an extremely detailed outline of Greek history up to the death of Alexander, with wonderful links to other sources.

Greece in the Bronze Age

Palace of Knossos in Minoan Crete
www.dilos.com/region/crete/kn_01.html
A site devoted to the city of Knossos.

Bureaucrats and Barbarians
www.wsu.edu/~dee/MINOA/CONTENTS.HTM
A site devoted to Minoan and Mycenean civilizations.

Archaic Greece

The British Museum Compass
www.thebritishmuseum.ac.uk/compass/
Search the British Museum Collection, which includes Greek antiquities.

Educated Women in Ancient Society
www.domz.org/Society/People/Women/History/Ancient
A site devoted to elite women in Greece and their education.

Classical Myth: The Ancient Sources
http://web.uvic.ca/grs/department_files/classical_myth/index.html
A site devoted to classical mythology with iconography of Greek mythical figures.

A Tale of Three Cities

Everything Spartan, Lakonian, and Messenian
www.geocities.com/Athens/Aegean/7849
A site dedicated to Sparta.

The Coming of Persia

Internet Ancient History Sourcebook: Persia
www.fordham.edu/halsall/ancient/asbook05.html
A site devoted to sources of ancient Persian history.

CHAPTER 3

You can obtain more information about classical and Hellenistic Greece at the Websites listed below. See also the Companion Website that accompanies this text: *www.pearsonhighered.com/kishlansky*, which contains an online study guide and additional resources.

War and Politics in the Fifth Century B.C.E.

Articles on Ancient Persia
www.livius.org/persia.html
Links to articles on many aspects of ancient Persian history.

The Greeks: Crucible of Civilization
www.pbs.org/empires/thegreeks/
A Public Broadcasting System site devoted to ancient Greece.

The Peloponnesian War
www.multimania.com/sdelille/gdpa.html
A site developed by Sven Delille on the Peloponnesian War.

Diotima: Women and Gender in the Ancient World
www.stoa.org/diotima/
A site devoted to women and gender in antiquity.

Alexander the Great
history.boisestate.edu/westciv/alexander/
Dr. Ellis L. Knox's page devoted to Alexander the Great.

The Hellenistic World

A Brief History of Clocks: From Thales to Ptolemy
www.perseus.tufts.edu/GreekScience/Students/Jesse/CLOCK1A.html
A history of clocks in the Hellenistic world.

Archimedes
www.mcs.drexel.edu/~crorres/Archimedes/contents.html
A site devoted to Archimedes and Hellenistic science.

CHAPTER 4

You can obtain more information about early Rome at the Websites listed below. See also the Companion Website that accompanies this text, *www.pearsonhighered. com/kishlansky*, which contains an online study guide and additional resources.

General Websites

Carthage (Tunsinia)
www.archaelogy.about.com/od/cterms/g/carthage.htm
A site with links to information on Carthage archaeology.

From City to Empire

Frank E. Smitha's World History: The Rise of Ancient Rome
fsmitha.com/h1/ch15.htm
An outline by Frank Smitha of early Roman history beginning with the legendary accounts of Rome's foundation.

The Forum Romanum: History and Religion
http://intranet.grundel.nl/thinkquest/homehis.html
A Thinkquest site on Roman history and religion including links to Roman archaeology.

Republican Civilization

Women's Life in Greece and Rome
www.stoa.org/diotima/anthology/wlgr/
A site devoted to women in Rome and Greece.

Republican Roman Government
www.utexas.edu/depts/classics/faculty/Riggsby/RepGov.html
A detailed explanation of the republican constitution of Rome.

CHAPTER 5

You can obtain more information about imperial Rome at the Websites listed below. See also the Companion Website that accompanies this text, *www.pearsonhighered.com/kishlansky*, which contains an online study guide and additional resources.

General Websites

Ancient/Classical History with N. S. Gill: The Gracchi
ancienthistory.about.com/od/gracchi/
An introduction to the Gracchi with links to other sites.

Pompeii Forum Project

www.iath.virginia.edu/pompeii/page-1.html
A great site devoted to the Roman city of Pompeii, which was destroyed by Mount Vesuvius in 79 C.E.

The End of the Republic

History & Literature of the Roman Revolution
johara.web.wesleyan.edu/CCIV274links.html
Dr. Jim O'Hara's Web page devoted to the end of the Roman Republic.

The Cicero Home Page
www.utexas.edu/depts/classics/documents/Cic.html
A site dedicated to Cicero, including texts of his orations and a bibliography.

The Vergil Project
Vergil.classics.upenn.edu/
A site dedicated to providing resources and teaching materials on Virgil.

The Augustan Age and the *Pax Romana*

Augustus and the Foundation of the Empire
www.carthage.edu/outis/augustus.html
A Web page devoted to the Emperor Augustus with links to archaeology and art of the Augustan age.

Reborn Rome
www.romereborn.virginia.edu
A site that provides a virtual tour of the Roman Forum.

The Corinth Computer Project
http://corinth.sas.upenn.edu/
A computer reconstruction of Roman Corinth.

The Dinur Center for Research in Jewish History: Second Temple and Talmudic Era
http://jewishhistory.huji.ac.il/Internetresources/historyresources/second_temple_and_talmudic_era.htm/
A site at The Hebrew University of Jerusalem with links to many other sites concerning Judaism and early Christianity.

CHAPTER 6

You can obtain more information about the transforming Roman world at the Websites listed below. See also the Companion Website that accompanies this text, *www.pearsonhighered.com/kishlansky*, which contains an online study guide and additional resources.

General Websites

ORB Online Encyclopedia: Late Antiquity in the Mediterranean
www.nipissingu.ca/department/history/MUHLBERGER/ORB/LT-ATEST.HTM
A guide to late antiquity in the Mediterranean.

The Crisis of the Third Century

Worlds of Late Antiquity
www.georgetown.edu/faculty/jod/wola.html
A comprehensive site dedicated to late antiquity created by Professor James O'Donnell.

The Empire Restored

Diocletian's Palace
www.st.carnet.hr/split/diokl.html
A site devoted to Emperor Diocletian's palace in modern Split.

Imperial Christianity

Resources for Constantine the Great
shsu.edu/~eng_wpf/con-hist.html
Links connecting to sites concerning Constantine.

A Parting of the Ways

A Visual Tour Through Late Antiquity
www.nipissingu.ca/department/history/muhlberger/4505/show.htm
Images of people and places of late antiquity.

CHAPTER 7

You can obtain more information about the classical legacy in the East at the Websites listed below. See also the Companion Website that accompanies this text, *www.pearson-highered.com/kishlansky*, which contains an online study guide and additional resources.

The Byzantines

Byzantium: Byzantine Studies on the Internet
www.fordham.edu/halsall/Byzantium/
A major site with links to every aspect of Byzantine civilization maintained by Paul Halsall.

Medieval Sourcebook: The Institutes of Justinian, 535 C.E.
www.fordham.edu/halsall/basis/535institutes.html
www.fordham.edu/halsall/source/corpus1.html
Extensive selections from the *Institutes,* a digest of laws and legal opinions designed for law students. The *Institutes,* the *Codex Justinianus,* and the *Digest* were part of the *Corpus Iurus Civilis* (Body of Civil Law) issued under Justinian. This codification of Roman law stands as a great monument of Western jurisprudence.

The Rise of Islam

IslamiCity.com—Education
www.islamicity.com/education/islamiceducation
A site for Islamic history maintained by IslamiCity, dedicated to advancing Islamic information, fostering community, and educating people about Islam.

Internet Islamic History Sourcebook
www.fordham.edu/halsall/islam/islamsbook.html
Paul Halsall's site dedicated to sources on Islamic history and culture.

About Islam and Muslims
www.ummah.org.uk/what-is-islam/index.html
A site devoted to explaining Islam maintained by the UNN Islamic Society.

Welcome to Isfahan!
www.isfahan.org.uk/
A site devoted to eleventh-century Isfahan, capital of medieval Persia.

The Metropolitan Museum of Art: Islamic Art
metmuseum.org/collections/department.asp?dep=14
A guide to New York's Metropolitan Museum Islamic collection.

The Byzantine Apogee and Decline

The Glory of Byzantium
metmuseum.org/explore/Byzantium/byzhome.html
A site dedicated to Byzantine art and history at the Metropolitan Museum of Art.

Church History with a Focus on Orthodoxy
aggreen.net/church_history/c_histry.html
A site dedicated to Orthodox Christianity with links to Byzantine history and culture.

CHAPTER 8

You can obtain more information about the West in the early Middle Ages at the Websites listed below. See also the Companion Website that accompanies this text, *www.pearsonhighered.com/kishlansky,* which contains an online study guide and additional resources.

General Websites

The Labyrinth: Resources for Medieval Studies
www.georgetown.edu/labyrinth/labyrinth-home.html
Labyrinth is the central Website for all medieval studies.

The Making of the Barbarian Kingdoms

Medieval Art at the Metropolitan Museum
metmuseum.org/collections/view50.asp?dep=17
A look at some of the Metropolitan Museum's collection of medieval art, including migration-period jewelry.

Living in the New Europe

Wharram Percy: The Lost Medieval Village
loki.stockton.edu/~ken/wharram/wharram.htm
A site devoted to exploring a lost medieval village from Roman times to the High Middle Ages.

The Carolingian Achievement

St. Gall Monastary Plan
stgallplan.org
A site devoted to Carolingian material and textual culture.

After the Carolingians

Viking Archaeology
bubl.ac.uk/link/v/vikingarchaeology.htm
A site devoted to Viking society and archaeology.

CHAPTER 9

You can obtain more information about the High Middle Ages at the Websites listed below. See also the Companion Website that accompanies this text, *www.pearsonhighered.com/kishlansky*, which contains an online study guide and additional resources.

General Websites

Medieval Women
http://labyrinth.georgetown.edu
Links to resources on medieval women.

Byzantine and Medieval Studies Links
www.fordham.edu/halsall/medweb/
Professor Paul Halsall's links to the medieval world.

The Countryside

Castles on the Web
www.castlesontheweb.com/
An entire Website dedicated to castles, abbeys, and medieval churches.

Medieval Towns

Durham Cathedral and Castle
www.dur.ac.uk/~dlaowww/c_tour/tour.html
A virtual tour of Durham's cathedral.

Paris at the Time of Philippe Auguste
www.philippe-auguste.com/uk/index.html
Medieval Paris at the end of the twelfth century.

Medieval Toledo
geocities.com/Athens/Academy/8636/Toledo.html
A site devoted to the city of Toledo in the Middle Ages with an emphasis on its Jewish history links to other related Spanish sites.

The Invention of the State

Les Capetiens-Les Croisades (Capetians to the Crusades)
philae.sas.upenn.edu/French/caroly.html
. A hypertext site devoted to Capetian France (in French).

Medieval England
http://labyrinth.georgetown.edu/
The Labyrinth site with links to every aspect of medieval England.

Magna Carta
www.medieval sources.co.uk/portal_magna.htm
A site devoted to the Magna Carta, with links to images of the manuscripts.

Ebstorf World Map
http://weblab.uni-lueneburg.de/kulturinformatik/projekte/ebskart/content/start.html
An interactive reproduction of a thirteenth century world map.

CHAPTER 10

You can obtain more information about the Later Middle Ages at the Websites listed below. See also the Companion Website that accompanies this text, *www.pearsonhighered. com/kishlansky*, which contains an online study guide and additional resources.

Politics as a Family Affair

Web Gallery of Art: Bohemian School
www.wga.hu/index.html
Overview of art and architecture in Bohemia under the patronage of Charles IV.

Life and Death in the Later Middle Ages

Internet Resources on the Black Death
www.historyguide.org/ancient/death.html
An annotated list of Web links to sites about the Great Plague of the fourteenth century.

CHAPTER 11

You can obtain more information about the Italian Renaissance at the Websites listed below. See also the Companion Website that accompanies this text, *www.pearsonhighered.com/kishlansky*, which contains an online study guide and additional resources.

Renaissance Society

NM's Creative Impulse: Renaissance
www.history.evansville.net/renaissa.html#Resources
A site of links to a wide array of subjects relating to the era of the Renaissance. A good starting point.

The Florentine Republic
www.mega.it/eng/egui/epo/secrepu.htm
The history of the Florentine Republic with links to major tourist attractions and buildings. Brief biographies of important Florentine citizens can also be found.

Renaissance Art

Renaissance Art
www.anu.edu.au/ArtHistory/renart/pics.art/index_1.html
A pictorial guide to the major artists of the Italian Renaissance and their works. Thumbnail representations lead to links on specific pieces.

Leon Battista Alberti—Great Buildings Online
www.greatbuildings.com/architects/Leon_Battista_Alberti.html
A page devoted to Alberti's architecture with a brief biography and links to pictures.

Michelangelo Buonarroti
www.mega.it/eng/egui/pers/micbuon.htm
A Website devoted to Michelangelo with a variety of links to text and images of Renaissance Florence.

WebMuseum: The Italian Renaissance (1420–1600)
www.ibiblio.org/wm/paint/tl/it-ren/
Reproductions of Renaissance art, with accompanying text.

CHAPTER 12

You can obtain more information about the European empires at the Websites listed below. See also the Companion Website that accompanies this text, *www.pearsonhighered.com/kishlansky*, which contains an online study guide and additional resources.

European Encounters

Discoverers Web
www.win.tue.nl/cs/fm/engels/discovery/
A site devoted to all ages of discovery with maps, short biographies, and time lines. There are links to the writings of Columbus, Cortés, and others of the early voyagers.

The Columbus Navigation Homepage
www.minn.net/~keithp/
Everything you ever wanted to know about Christopher Columbus.

1492: An Ongoing Voyage
www.loc.gov/exhibits/1492
A Library of Congress online exhibit on the causes and consequences of European exploration and expansion.

Christopher Columbus—A Culinary History
www.castellobanfi.com/features/story_3.html
A site devoted to the food and drink associated with a long ocean voyage in the fifteenth century.

Medieval Sourcebook: Exploration and Expansion
www.fordham.edu/halsall/sbook1z.html
Dozens of primary sources relating to the voyages of discovery.

The Formation of States

Henry VIII: Intrigue in the Tudor Court
www.archsoc.com/games/Henry.html
A board game that teaches both history and strategy.

CHAPTER 13

You can obtain more information about the reform of religion at the Websites listed below. See also the Companion Website that accompanies this text, *www.pearsonhighered.com/kishlansky*, which contains an online study guide and additional resources.

The Lutheran Reformation

Lutherstadt Wittenberg, Martin Luther
www.wittenberg.de/e/seiten/personen/luther.html
A site devoted to Martin Luther and the city of Wittenberg. Texts of the famous Ninety-five Theses and other of Luther's writings as well as pictures of locations associated with the Lutheran reformation.

The Protestant Reformation

The Reformation Guide
www.educ.msu.edu/homepages/laurence/reformation/index.htm
The Reformation guide is the best starting place for information about all aspects of the Protestant Reformation. Dozens of links to follow.

Discovery and Reformation
www.wsu.edu/~dee/REFORM/REFORM.HTM
A primarily text-based site created by Washington State University, with profiles of key individuals and explanations of the issues at stake.

Project Wittenberg
www.iclnet.org/pub/resources/text/wittenberg/wittenberg-home.html
The home page of Project Wittenberg, containing a large number of texts (including hymns) by Luther and other reformers.

Tudor History
tudorhistory.org/
A site with links to a variety of subjects relating to England under the Tudors. Biographies of the kings and queens, bibliographies, maps, and documents.

Reformation Picture Gallery
www.mun.ca/rels/hrollmann/reform/pics/pics.html
Contemporary pictures of leading reformers and the places associated with the Protestant Reformation. Excellent reproductions, especially from woodcuts.

Internet Modern History Sourcebook: Reformation Europe
www.fordham.edu/halsall/mod/modsbook02.html
Sources for both the Reformation and Counter-Reformation with links to other valuable sites.

CHAPTER 14

You can obtain more information about Europe at war at the Websites listed below. See also the Companion Website that accompanies this text, *www.pearsonhighered. com/kishlansky*, which contains an online study guide and additional resources.

The Crises of the Western States

Internet Modern History Sourcebook: Early Modern West
www.fordham.edu/halsall/mod/modsbook1.html#Conflict
Links to documents on the French wars of religion, the invasion of the Spanish Armada, and the Thirty Years' War.

WebMuseum: The Northern Renaissance (1500–1615)
www.ibiblio.org/wm/paint/tl/north-ren/
Links to pictures and portraits from the late sixteenth and early seventeenth centuries.

Pieter Brueghel the Elder: *The Triumph of Death*
www.ibiblio.org/wm/paint/auth/bruegel/death.jpg
A Web page depicting Peter Brueghel's *Triumph of Death*, one of the most evocative paintings of the destruction wrought by warfare in early modern Europe.

The Thirty Years' War, 1618–1648

The Avalon Project: Treaty of Westphalia
www.yale.edu/lawweb/avalon/westphal.htm
The full text of the Treaty of Westphalia that ended the Thirty Years' War.

CHAPTER 15

You can obtain more information about life in early modern Europe at the Websites listed below. See also the Companion Website that accompanies this text, *www. pearsonhighered.com/kishlansky*, which contains an online study guide and additional resources.

Social Life

Internet Modern History Sourcebook: Everyday Life in Premodern Europe
www.fordham.edu/halsall/mod/modsbook04.html
A site with links to sources, pictures, and accounts of everyday life in early modern Europe. A good place to start.

Modern History Sourcebook: Social Conditions in 17th Century France
www.fordham.edu/halsall/mod/17france-soc.html
Documents illustrating social conditions in early modern France.

Private Life

Witchcraft
www.kenyon.edu/projects/margin/witch.htm
A site with links to sources concerning European witchcraft. Also includes suggestions for further reading and a brief overview of the subject.

Witches and Witchcraft
Womenshistory.about.com/cs/witches
This site offers historical information about witches and witchcraft in Europe and America and includes links to related sites.

Life in Tudor England
englishhistory.net/tudor/tudorlife.html
Part of a comprehensive site on Tudor England, this section on life in Tudor England offers information on topics including food and drink, pastimes and entertainment, and mental illness.

CHAPTER 16

You can obtain more information about the royal state in the seventeenth century at the Websites listed below. See also the Companion Website that accompanies this text, *www.pearsonhighered.com/kishlansky*, which contains an online study guide and additional resources.

The Crises of the Royal State

Internet Modern History Sourcebook: Constitutional States
www.fordham.edu/halsall/mod/modsbook06.html
Links to sources relating to the reign of Charles I and the revolution against him.

The Execution of Charles I
www.baylor.edu/BIC/WCIII/Essays/charles.1.html
Excerpts from primary sources describing the execution of Charles I.

The Zenith of the Royal State

Baroque Living History Society: L'Age d'Or & Kirke's Lambs
www.kipar.org/

A site on the Golden Age of France in the seventeenth century but with extensive links to English and Dutch materials on a variety of subjects.

Chateau de Versailles
www.chateauversailles.fr/en
The Website of Versailles, with views of the gardens and rooms inside the palace. (Version of site in English.)

Creating French Culture
www.loc.gov/exhibits/bnf/bnf0005.html
The Library of Congress's exhibition on the Age of Absolutism shows manuscripts, medals, and portraits of leading figures at the French court.

CHAPTER 17

You can obtain more information about science and commerce in early modern Europe at the Websites listed below. See also the Companion Website that accompanies this text, *www.pearsonhighered.com/kishlansky*, which contains an online study guide and additional resources.

The New Science

Internet Modern History Sourcebook: Scientific Revolution
www.fordham.edu/halsall/mod/modsbook09.html
Links to sources and other sites dealing with the scientific revolution.

The Art of Renaissance Science
www.crs4.it/Ars/arshtml/arstoc.html
An interesting site dealing with the relations between Renaissance art and early modern science.

Sir Isaac Newton
www-gap.dcs.st-and.ac.uk/~history/Mathematicians/Newton.html
A miscellany of material on Sir Isaac Newton.

The Galileo Project
es.rice.edu/ES/humsoc/Galileo/
A site devoted to Galileo that contains pictures of his instruments and guides to his experiments.

Empires of Goods

Trade Products in Early Modern History
www.bell.lib.umn.edu/Products/Products.html
A site describing the new products introduced to Europe during the period of global expansion.

Holland Museums
www.hollandmuseums.nl/
An online gallery of Dutch art, with text available in English.

History House: Tulipomania
www.historyhouse.com/in_history/tulip/
The story of tulip mania in seventeenth-century Holland.

CHAPTER 18

You can obtain more information about the balance of power in eighteenth-century Europe at the Websites listed below. See also the Companion Website that accompanies this text, *www.pearsonhighered.com/kishlansky*, which contains an online study guide and additional resources.

The Rise of Russia

Russia
www.english.upenn.edu/~jlynch/FrankenDemo/Places/russia.html
A site detailing the history of Russia from the time of Peter the Great. Links to the building of St. Petersburg.

Modern History Sourcebook: Catherine the Great
www.fordham.edu/halsall/mod/18catherine.html
Sources from the reign of Catherine the Great.

The Two Germanies

Friedrich II, the Great (1712–1786)
www.hfac.uh.edu/gbrown/philosophers/leibniz/FriedrichGreat/FriedrichGreat.html
A hyper-linked biographical essay on Frederick the Great of Prussia.

The Greatness of Great Britain

The American Revolution
www.revolution.h-net.msu.edu/
A site with extensive links to all aspects of the American Revolution.

Declaring Independence: Drafting the Documents
www.loc.gov/exhibits/declara/declara1.html
An online exhibit at the Library of Congress on the drafting of the Declaration of Independence.

CHAPTER 19

You can obtain more information about culture and society in eighteenth-century Europe at the Websites listed below. See also the Companion Website that accompanies this text, *www.pearsonhighered.com/kishlansky*, which contains an online study guide and additional resources.

Eighteenth-Century Culture

NM's Creative Impulse: Enlightenment
www.history.evansville.net/enlighte.html
The best starting point for the culture and history of the age of Enlightenment.

Eighteenth-Century Resources
andromeda.rutgers.edu/~jlynch/18th/
A gateway to a wealth of sources on many different aspects of eighteenth-century culture.

Eighteenth-Century Studies
eserver.org/18th/
A list of links to a wide range of material relating to eighteenth-century literature and culture.

Internet Modern History Sourcebook: The Enlightenment
www.fordham.edu/halsall/mod/modsbook10.html
An outstanding collection of texts of Enlightenment writers.

Eighteenth-Century Society

The New Child: British Art and the Origins of Modern Childhood
www.bampfa.berkeley.edu/exhibits/newchild/
A site devoted to the nature of childhood in eighteenth-century Britain.

Voice of the Shuttle: Restoration and 18th Century
vos.ucsb.edu/browse.asp?id=2738
An inclusive page of links and resources for the study of English literature in the eighteenth century.

CHAPTER 20

You can obtain more information about the French Revolution and the Napoleonic Era at the Websites listed below. See also the Companion Website that accompanies this text, *www.pearsonhighered.com/kishlansky*, which contains an online study guide and additional resources.

The French Revolution and the Fall of the Monarchy

Creating French Culture
www.loc.gov/exhibits/bnf/bnf0001.html
Different aspects of French culture as a form of elite power from Charlemagne to Charles de Gaulle are presented by the Library of Congress. Most of the material is from the collections of the Bibliothèque Nationale de France.

Liberty, Equality, Fraternity: Explaining the French Revolution
Chnm.gmu.edu/revolution/
This site contains an extraordinary archive of key images, maps, songs, timelines, and texts from the French Revolution. The site is authored by Professors Lynn Hunt and Jack Censer, leading scholars in the field of French revolutionary history.

Chateau de Versailles
www.chateauversailles.fr/en/
Devoted to the history and images of Versailles, this site provides brief essays about the people and events significant to court culture during the seventeenth and eighteenth centuries. It also explores the role of Versailles in French culture after the French Revolution.

Experimenting with Democracy, 1789–1792

St. Just
history.hanover.edu/texts/stjust.html
Texts by St. Just, a close colleague of Robespierre and a member of the Committee of Public Safety, which orchestrated the Reign of Terror.

Modern History Sourcebook: Robespierre: The Supreme Being
www.fordham.edu/halsall/mod/robespierre-supreme.html
This site contains Robespierre's words on The Cult of the Supreme Being and links to other sites.

The Reign of Napoleon, 1799–1815

Internet Modern History Sourcebook: French Revolution
www.fordham.edu/halsall/mod/modsbook13.html
This site directs students to the Modern History Sourcebook section of documents on the French Revolution, Napoleon, and the Napoleonic Wars.

Napoleon
www.napoleon.org/en/home.asp
Sponsored by the Foundation Napoleon for "the furtherance of study and research into the civil and military achievements of the First and Second Empires," this site is aimed at a nonacademic audience and provides chronologies, essays, images and videos, and links to other sites on Napoleon.

CHAPTER 21

You can obtain more information about industrial Europe at the Websites listed below. See also the Companion Website that accompanies this text, *www.pearsonhighered.com/kishlansky*, which contains an online study guide and additional resources.

The Industrial Revolution in Britain

Reminiscences of James Watt
www.history.rochester.edu/steam/hart/
A nineteenth-century account of the life of James Watt and his role as inventor of the steam engine with links to the history of the steam engine.

Women in World History Curriculum: Industrial Revolution
www.womeninworldhistory.com/lesson7.html
Sponsored by Women in World History Curriculum, this site details the plight of working women in industrial England.

Child Labour in the 19th Century
www.spartacus.schoolnet.co.uk/IRchild.main.htm
This site chronicles child labor in Britain, including life in the factory and first-hand experiences.

The Industrialization of the Continent

Modern History Sourcebook: Tables Illustrating the Spread of Industrialization
www.fordham.edu/halsall/mod/indrevtabs1.html
Charts and statistics about industrialization in Europe.

Internet Modern History Sourcebook: Industrial Revolution
www.fordham.edu/halsall/mod/modsbook14.html
An outstanding collection of documents on the Industrial Age with links.

CHAPTER 22

You can obtain more information about political upheavals and social transformations between 1815 and 1850 at the Websites listed below. See also the Companion Website that accompanies this text, *www.pearsonhighered.com/kishlansky*, which contains an online study guide and additional resources.

Geographical Tour: Europe in 1815

Internet Modern History Sourcebook: Conservative Order
www.fordham.edu/halsall/mod/modsbook16.html
The site provides documents, discussions, and bibliographics on the Congress of Vienna and charts the development of conservative thought.

The New Ideologies

McMaster University Archive for the History of Economic Thought
socserv.mcmaster.ca/econ/ugcm/3113
A site for texts in modern economic theory.

Internet Modern History Sourcebook: Liberalism
www.fordham.edu/halsall/mod/modsbook18.html
A collection of links to primary documents and bibliographies on liberalism.

Internet Modern History Sourcebook: Nationalism
www.fordham.edu/halsall/mod/modsbook17.html

The Nationalism Project
www.nationalismproject.org/
These sites provide links to primary documents and bibliographies of nationalism.

Internet Modern History Sourcebook: Romanticism
www.fordham.edu/halsall/mod/modsbook15.html
This site provides links to primary texts on romantic philosophy and literature.

Voice of the Shuttle
vos.ucsb.edu/index.asp
This comprehensive database for humanities research provides links to general resources, criticism, and primary texts. Type "Romantics" into the search function for resources on romantic philosophy and literature.

Marxist Internet Archive: Marxist Writers
www.marxists.org/archive/index.htm
The site provides translated texts of Marx and Engels as well as other prominent Social Democrats and Communists.

Protest and Revolution

Child Labour in the 19th Century
www.spartacus.schoolnet.co.uk/IRchild.htm
A collection of biographies of reformers and promoters of child labor laws, electronic texts of major child labor legislation, and excerpts from primary sources concerning child labor in nineteenth-century Britain.

The Emancipation of Women: 1750–1920
www.spartacus.schoolnet.co.uk/women.htm
The site contains links to biographies of major figures, essays on the major organizations and societies, and electronic texts of the women's movement in Britain.

Internet Modern History Sourcebook: 1848
www.fordham.edu/halsall/mod/modsbook19.html
The site provides documents, discussions, bibliographies, and other links on the revolutions of 1848.

CHAPTER 23

You can obtain more information about state building and social change in Europe between 1850 and 1871 at the Websites listed below. See also the Companion Website that accompanies this text, *www.pearsonhighered.com/kishlansky*, which contains an online study guide and additional resources.

Building Nations: The Politics of Unification

The Crimean War (1853–1856)
www.loc.gov/rr/print/coll/251_fen.html
Mid-19th century photographs by Roger Fenton provide one of the earliest photographic records of war. This is a Library of Congress site.

Internet Modern History Sourcebook: 19th Century Italy
www.fordham.edu/halsall/mod/modsbook23.html
This site focuses on documents relating to the unification of Italy and the Risorgimento.

Modern History Sourcebook: Documents of German Unification, 1848–1871
www.fordham.edu/halsall/mod/germanunification.html
This site provides translations of major primary documents concerning the unification of Germany.

Reforming European Society

The Victorian Web
www.victorianweb.org
A comprehensive collection of links to Victorian England.

Internet Modern History Sourcebook: Russian Revolution
www.fordham.edu/halsall/mod/modsbook39.html
This site, a repository for links to the Russian Revolution, provides links to documents on nineteenth-century tsarist Russia.

Changing Values and the Force of New Ideas

Florence Nightingale
www.spartacus.schoolnet.co.uk/REnightingale.htm
A brief biography of Florence Nightingale with links to related sites.

The Eighteenth Brumaire of Louis Napoleon
www.marxists.org/archive/marx/works/1852/18th-brumaire/index.htm
Electronic text of Karl Marx's famous work.

1851 Project: The Great Exhibition
www.victorianweb.org/history/1851/index.html
An overview with links to exhibits.

Charles Darwin
www.darwin-literature.com/
This site contains the complete works of Charles Darwin.

Paris Commune Archive
dwardmac.pitzer.edu/Anarchist_Archives/pariscommune/Pariscommunearchive.html
A Pitzer College political studies site providing summaries of the major players and events of the Paris Commune as well as an extensive bibliography.

Internet Women's History Sourcebook
www.fordham.edu/halsall/women/womensbook.html
This section of the Modern History Sourcebook focuses on women's history from antiquity to the present. The subchapter on modern European women's history provides links to texts on the structure of working women's lives as well as texts on feminism and the suffrage movement.

CHAPTER 24

You can obtain more information about the crisis of European culture between 1871 and 1914 at the Websites listed below. See also the Companion Website that accompanies this text, *www.pearsonhighered.com/kishlansky*, which contains an online study guide and additional resources.

European Economy and the Politics of Mass Society

Encyclopaedia of British History: Socialism
www.spartacus.schoolnet.co.uk/socialism.htm
This is a fairly comprehensive site on the English labor movement, including texts, biographies of major figures, and other links.

Habsburg Source Texts Archive

www2.h-net.msu.edu/~habsweb/sourcetexts
Sponsored by the H-Net Discussion list HABSBURG, this site provides electronic texts relating to the creation of the Dual Monarchy.

Outsiders in Mass Politics

The Emancipation of Women: 1750–1920
www.spartacus.schoolnet.co.uk/women.htm
This site contains links to biographies of major figures, essays on the major organizations and societies, and electronic texts of the women's movement in Britain.

The Genesis Project
www.londonmet.ac.uk/genesis/
This mapping project on women's history research sources is provided by the Women's Library of London and the Research Support Libraries Programme.

Shaping the New Consciousness

Sigmund Freud and the Freud Archives
users.rcn.com/brill/freudarc.html
An exhaustive collection of links to archives, electronic texts, bibliographies, and other resources on Freud and the history of psychoanalysis.

Internet History of Science Sourcebook
www.fordham.edu/halsall/science/sciencesbook.html
A comprehensive collection of links to primary source materials, Websites, and bibliographies on major scientists, discoveries, and theories in the nineteenth century.

Art History Resources: 19th-Century Art & 20th-Century Art
witcombe.sbc.edu/ARTHLinks5.html
witcombe.sbc.edu/ARTH2othcentury.html
The first Web page contains numerous links on the artists, styles, and schools of art in the nineteenth century, including impressionism, post-impressionism, and symbolism. The second page includes links to resources on art and artists of the twentieth century.

CHAPTER 25

You can obtain more information about Europe and the world between 1870 and 1914 at the Websites listed below. See also the Companion Website that accompanies this text, *www.pearsonhighered.com/kishlansky*, which contains an online study guide and additional resources.

The European Balance of Power, 1870–1914

Internet Modern History Sourcebook: World War I
www.fordham.edu/halsall/mod/modsbook38.html
This site is part of a larger site on World War I primary and secondary sources, but it contains a section on the developments among the Great Powers from the 1870s to 1914.

The European Search for Territory and Markets

Francophone Africa: Bibliographies
www.hum.port.ac.uk/slas/francophone/bibliographies.htm
A collection of bibliographies on the partition of Africa and the impact of colonization in Africa.

The Boer Wars
www.spartacus.schoolnet.co.uk/WARboer.htm
A site that gives the history, context and related links for the two Boer wars.

China: A Traveling Exhibit, 1903–1904
www.chinaexhibit.org
A virtual museum exhibit of photographs taken in 1903 of the Chinese countryside after the Boxer Rebellion.

CHAPTER 26

You can obtain more information about war and revolution between 1914 and 1920 at the Websites listed below. See also the Companion Website that accompanies this text, *www.pearsonhighered.com/kishlansky*, which contains an online study guide and additional resources.

The War Europe Expected

The Heritage of the Great War
www.greatwar.nl
This site includes photographs, political cartoons, poetry, prose, and documents from the Great War.

A New Kind of Warfare

World War I (Document Archive)
wwi.lib.byu.edu/index.php/Main_Page
This archive contains primary documents and has an international perspective on the Great War.

Adjusting to the Unexpected: Total War

World War I: Trenches on the Web
www.worldwar1.com/
This site on World War I is sponsored by the History Channel.

The First World War Poetry Digital Archive
www.hcu.ox.ac.uk/jtap/warpoems.htm
This site contains works from major poets of the period including Wilfred Owen, Isaac Rosenberg, and Robert Graves.

The Russian Revolution and Allied Victory

Russian Revolution Resources
www.historyguide.org/europe/rusrev_links.html
This site provides electronic texts in English of Lenin and Trotsky and several other links to sites on the Russian Revolution.

Settling the Peace

The Versailles Treaty
www.state.gov/r/pa/ho/time/wwi/89875.htm
This site by the U.S. Department of State provides an analysis of the treaty that ended world War I.

CHAPTER 27

You can obtain more information about the European search for stability between 1920 and 1939 at the Websites listed below. See also the Companion Website that accompanies this text, *www.pearsonhighered.com/kishlansky*, which contains an online study guide and additional resources.

Crisis and Collapse in a World Economy

Internet Modern History Sourcebook: The Depression
www.fordham.edu/halsall/mod/modsbook41.html

Comprehensive collection of primary sources and links to materials on the Great Depression in Europe and the United States.

The Soviet Union's Separate Path

Soviet History Archive
www.marxists.org/history/ussr/
For a Marxist perspective of the founding of the Soviet Union, consult this site.

Revelations from the Russian Archives
www.loc.gov/exhibits/archives
A virtual exhibit by the Library of Congress on material from the secret archives of the Central Committee of the Communist Party of the USSR.

The Rise of Fascist Dictatorship in Italy

Internet Modern History Sourcebook: Fascism in Europe
www.fordham.edu/halsall/mod/modsbook42.html
This site refers to fascism in general, but it focuses on a speech of Mussolini and Spanish Civil War materials.

Hitler and the Third Reich

The National Socialist Era, 1933–1945
www.h-net.msu.edu/~german/gtext/nazi/index.html
This is a small collection of electronic texts relating to the rise of the Nazis, the creation of the Third Reich, and World War II.

Internet Modern History Sourcebook: Nazism
www.fordham.edu/halsall/mod/modsbook43.html
A collection of primary documents and links on the Weimar Republic and the rise of Nazism.

Third Reich Stamps
www.geocities.com/WallStreet/Exchange/5456/third.html
A Website of stamps issued during the Third Reich with brief descriptions depicting the cultural values propagated by the Nazis.

Democracies in Crisis

Spanish Civil War Archive
dwardmac.pitzer.edu/anarchist_archives/spancivwar/Spanishcivilwar.html
This site was created by a political studies professor at Pitzer College (see link for Paris Commune in Chapter 23) and contains essays, bibliography, and photographs.

CHAPTER 28

You can obtain more information about World War II at the Websites listed below. See also the Companion Website that accompanies this text, *www.pearsonhighered. com/kishlansky*, which contains an online study guide and additional resources.

Aggression and Conquest

The Avalon Project: Munich Pact 9/29/38
avalon.law.yale.edu/imt/munich1.asp
Electronic text of the Munich agreements.

The Avalon Project: World War II Documents
avalon.law.yale.edu/subject_menus/wwii.asp
An important collection of documents from the prewar years, the war years, and the subsequent peace settlements.

Racism and Destruction

United States Holocaust Memorial Museum
www.ushmm.org
Home page of the United States Holocaust Museum. The site contains a searchable online catalog of both documentary and photographic sources.

Simon Wiesenthal Center
www.wiesenthal.com
Home page of the Simon Wiesenthal Center and the Museum of Tolerance. It has an extensive collection of materials related to the Holocaust and anti-Semitism.

The Vidal Sassoon International Center for the Study of Antisemitism (SICSA)
sicsa.huji.ac.il/

This site contains an extensive bibliography on the Holocaust.

Allied Victory

Internet Modern History Sourcebook: World War II
www.fordham.edu/halsall/mod/modsbook45.html
A collection of primary source documents and links to materials on World War II.

World War II
www.archives.gov/digital_classroom/teaching_with_documents.html#great_depression
War documents from the U.S. National Archives and Research Administration.

Soviet War Photography
www.schicklerart.com/exhibitions/soviet_war/index.html
Images of World War II from the Soviet perspective.

Women Come to the Front
www.loc.gov/exhibits/wcf/wcf0001.html
A virtual exhibit by the Library of Congress on women journalists, photographers, and broadcasters during World War II.

CHAPTER 29

You can obtain more information about the Cold War and postwar economic recovery at the Websites listed below. See also the Companion Website that accompanies this text, *www.pearsonhighered.com/kishlansky*, which contains an online study guide and additional resources.

The Origins of the Cold War

The Berlin Airlift: Documents, Images, History
www.trumanlibrary.org/whistlestop/study_collection/berlin_airlift/large/
A virtual exhibit with electronic texts on the Berlin Airlift as presented by the Harry S Truman Library and Museum.

Internet Modern History Sourcebook: A Bipolar World
www.fordham.edu/halsall/mod/modsbook46.html
A collection of primary source documents and links to the creation of the United Nations and the outbreak of the Cold War.

Cold War International History Project
www.wilsoncenter.org/index.cfm?fuseaction=topics.home&topic_id=1409
This site, sponsored by the Woodrow Wilson International Center for Scholars, provides a comprehensive list of primary documents and images, secondary sources, bibliographies, and working paper series on all aspects of the Cold War.

Soviet Archives Exhibit
www.ibiblio.org/expo/soviet.exhibit/entrance.html
A Soviet archive exhibit on the Cold War with images and electronic texts by the Library of Congress.

Postwar Economic Recovery in Europe, Japan, and the Soviet Union

Internet Modern History Sourcebook: Eastern Europe Since 1945
www.fordham.edu/halsall/mod/modsbook50.html
Two collections of links to primary sources and other sites on postwar western and eastern Europe.

For European Recovery: The Fiftieth Anniversary of the Marshall Plan
www.loc.gov/exhibits/marshall
A virtual museum exhibit with images and electronic primary and secondary texts on the Marshall Plan.

The Welfare State and Social Transformation

Internet Modern History Sourcebook: Modern Social Movements
www.fordham.edu/halsall/mod/modsbook56.html
A collection of primary source documents and links to sites on modern social movements including feminism, black power, and gay and lesbian rights.

The Sixties Project Home Page
lists.village.virginia.edu/sixties/
Web site of the Sixties Project, which brings together discussion lists, primary documents, bibliographies, museum exhibits, and personal testimonies about the 1960s and the Vietnam War from an exclusively American perspective.

Paris May 1968
www.iisg.nl/collections/may68/images.php
A collection of posters of the 1968 protest movement in Paris provided by the International Institute of Social History.

You can obtain more information about the end of the Cold War and new global challenges at the Websites listed below. See also the Companion Website that accompanies this text, *www.pearsonhighered.com/kishlansky*, which contains an online study guide and additional resources.

The End of the Cold War and the Emergence of a New Europe

Mikhail Sergeyevich Gorbachev
www.almaz.com/nobel/peace/1990a.html
A biography of Mikhail Gorbachev with electronic texts compiled by the Nobel Prize Internet Archive.

Russian and Soviet History Resources
facstaff.bloomu.edu/hickey/Russian%20and%20Soviet%20History%20Resource%20 20Page.htm
A research guide to Soviet history sponsored by the University of North Carolina libraries.

Boris Yeltsin
www.acs.brockport.edu/~dgusev/Russian/bybio.html
A chronology of Yeltsin's presidency with links to further materials on key events and personalities.

The Fall of the Berlin Wall 1989
www.remote.org/frederik/culture/berlin
A photo tour of the fall of the Berlin Wall supplemented by text from several German newspapers (in English).

Ethnic Conflict and Nationalism

International Helsinki Federation for Human Rights
www.ihf-hr.org/
Official Website of the International Helsinki Federation for Human Rights, a nonprofit organization. This site is useful as a resource for the latest developments in Chechnya, Belarus, and Central Asia from a human rights activist perspective.

Physicians for Human Rights: Chechnya Resources
physiciansforhumanrights.org/
The Physicians for Human Rights official Web page with links devoted to global hotspots that violate human rights, including current newspaper and journal articles.

U.S. Institute of Peace
www.usip.org/
The United States Institute of Peace provides links to Web resources on current international conflicts in order to promote stability and mediation and professionalize the field of peacebuilding.

The West in the Global Community

Europa: Gateway to the European Union
http://europa.eu/index_en.htm
This is the official website of the European Union with up-to-date information on members, activities, institutions, and services.

The Council on Foreign Relations: Terrorism
www.cfr.org/issue/135/
The U.S. Council on Foreign Relations provides a topical approach and current information on terrorism around the world.

index

A

'Abbasid Revolution, 166–167
'Abd ar-Rahman III (caliph), 167
Abdul Hamid II (sultan), 562
Abelard, Peter, 212, 213, 240
Abortion, 616, 623
Abraham, 23, 162
Absolutism: in east, 379–380; French,
380–384; royal state and, 380–382;
Russian, 379–380
Acropolis (high citadel), 39
Adam, 124, 258, 260
Adamson, Robert, 533
*Address to the Christian Nobility of the
German Nation* (Luther), 303
Adoption, 99
Adowa, battle of, 571–572
Aegean Sea, 22, 31, 32, 46, 60, 61, 66, 71
Aegina, 64
Aeneas, 87
Aeolians, 36
Aerial bombs, 627
Aeschylus, 69, 70
Afghanistan, 74
Africa, 119, 275; cave paintings in, 6–7;
chronology of new imperialism in Asia
and, 576; Cold War, decolonization and,
663; drive for markets and profits in,
569–570; Ethiopia as exception in, 571–572;
Europe, diplomacy, conflict and scramble
for, 569–572; first humanlike creatures in,
4; map of 1914, 574; muslims and North,
288; nationalism in, 663; passage to India,
Prince Henry and, 274; slaves from,
278–279, 395, 397; South, 572–573, 663
Afrikaners, 572–573
Afterlife, ancient Egypt and democratization
of, 19–20
Agamemnon, 37
Agincourt, battle of, 232
Agoge (state education system), 49
Agora (marketplace), 39, 40

Agriculture: changes in, 354–355–356; early
modern Europe and reliance on, 344–346;
eighteenth-century improvements to,
443–444; enclosures and, 354–355, 474;
feeding pyramid laborers and, 18; first
civilizations and, 6–7; fodder crops and,
444; Germany's, 491; innovations in,
474–475; Mesopotamian, 8; peasants and
innovations in, 201–202; revolution in
industrial Europe, 471, 474–475; subsis-
tence, 251; water supplies and, 10
Ahmose (king), 20
Akhenaten (king), 21
Akkadian empire, 13–14, 27, 29
Alaric II (king), 147, 177
Alba (duke), 328, 329
Alban League, 87–88
Albania, Warsaw Pact and, 660
Albert, Charles, 512
Alberti, Leon Battista, 256, 257, 261
Albinus, Spurius Postumius, 100
d'Albret, Jeanne, 322
Alchemists, 360
Alcibiades, 66
Alcmaeonid clan of Athens, 50, 52
Alcuin of York, 190, 191
Alemannic barbarians, 132, 135
Alexander I (tsar), 468, 528
Alexander II (tsar), 549; emancipation
of Russian serfs and, 528–529; Great
Reforms and, 529; populist movement
and, 529
Alexander the Great, 76, 78, 81; empire of,
73–75; map of conquered lands, 74
Alexandra (tsarina), 596
Alexandria, 77, 154
Alexis (prince), 408
Alexius (emperor), 172
Alfonso I (king), 261, 265
Alfred (king), 221
Algebra, 168. *See also* Mathematics
Algeria, 663

I-1

ages and life in, 183–188; governing, 187–188; kings and aristocrats governing, 186; peasantry in, 183–184; royal administration and, 187; royal justice in, 186–187; rural households in, 184–185

Europe, search for stability (1920-1939): chronology of international politics, 611; crisis and collapse in world economy and, 607–611; democracies in crisis and, 624–627; dependence on American economy and, 609–610; fascist dictatorship in Italy and, 617–619; Great Depression and, 609–610; Great Depression's political repercussions on, 610; Hitler's Third Reich and, 619–624; international loans, trade barriers and, 608–609; Soviet Union's separate path and, 611–617

Europe, social change (1850-1871): building nations, politics of unification and, 516–524; changing values and force of new ideas in, 530–537; Darwin, new science and, 533–534; Marx, science of society and, 534–535; new revolution?, 535–537; politics of homemaking and, 530–531; realism in art and, 531–533; reforming society in, 524–530; state building in, 516–538

Europe, western: EU, American superpower and, 687–688; EU and, 688–690; in global community, 687–697; politics of oil and, 688; toward single, 688

Europe, world and (1870-1914): balance of power in, 559–564; critiquing capitalism and, 580; engineering empire and, 565; Franco-German tensions and, 561–562; gold, empire building, Boer War and, 572–573; imperialism, ecology and, 579–580; imperialism in Asia, 573–576; imperialism in U.S. and, 576–577; instability of alliance system and, 561–563; medical advances and, 565; motives for empire and, 566–568; new imperialism and, 564–568; Ottoman empire and, 560–561; race, culture and, 579; results of world dominated by, 577–580; Russian aspirations, congress of Berlin and, 562–563; scramble for Africa, diplomacy, conflict and, 569–572; search for territory, markets and, 568–577; technology of empire and, 564–565; three emperors' league and, 560, 563

European Atomic Energy Community, 687

European Coal and Steel Community (ECSC), 666, 687

European Community (EC), 687

European Economic Community (EEC), 666, 687

European empires, 295; Africa, passage to India and, 274; Asian trade and, 275; chronology, 281; Columbian exchange and, 279–280; Columbus and, 275–277; dynastic struggles of, 290–294; encounters of, 273–281; formation of states and, 282–290; gold, God, glory and, 279; Italian wars and, 291–294; legacy of encounters, 278–281; Magellan and, 277; *mundus novus* and, 275–277; Portuguese explorations and, 276; power and glory in, 291; Prince Henry's explorations and, 274; reflections of, 280–281; slave trade beginnings and, 274–275; Spain and Portugal's claims to overseas, 280; Spanish conquests and, 277–278

European Free Trade Association (EFTA), 688

European Recovery Act, 664

European Union (EU), American superpower and, 687–690

Evans, Mary Ann, 532. *See also* Eliot, George

Eve, 124, 258, 260

Everard of Friuli (count), 191

Excommunication, 172, 303

Exodus, 23–24

Exorcisms, 139

Exploration, European encounters and, 273–281

Expression, art of, 259

Extraterritoriality, 575

Ezra, 26

F

Factory Act: of 1833, 484, 502; of 1875, 527

Fairfax, Thomas (sir), 375

Falange party, 627

Families: beginnings of women's protest and, 672–673; bourgeoisie, 439–440; Byzantine villages and, 158; demography, birth control and, 671; early modern Europe, 356–358; early modern Europe, rural life and, 344–346; Italian Renaissance, marriage and, 253–254; late middle ages, politics and, 226–233; role of men in, 358; Roman, 98–99, 102,

rebellion in, 372, 382, 386; genealogy of successions in England and, 229; Great Powers and, 504–505, 517; Huguenots or Calvinists in, 322–323; impact of revolution on, 489; industrial revolution in, 488–490; intendants and, 366; international loans, trade barriers and, 608–609; Joan of Arc and salvation of, 233; Maginot Line and, 633; Marshall Plan and, 665; Napoleon III and, 525; Napoleonic era and revolution in, 449–470; nation-states of England and, 219–223; political scandals and mass politics in, 544–545; Popular Front and, 624–625; population data, 369; rebuilding Paris, 525; revolutionary, 454, 509–510; salt tax, *nu-pieds* revolt and, 369; second empire in, 524–526; slow population growth in, 489; spheres of influence and, 575; stages of industrial progress in, 489–490; unification of states in, 286–288; vernacular literature and, 247; war with Spain, 339; wars of religion and, 321–323; WWI and Plan XVII, 585–586; WWII and fall of, 634

Francis I (king), 291, 292, 293–294, 304, 307, 309; courtiers employed by, 365

Francis II (king), 321, 322, 519, 520

Francis of Assisi, 214–215, 219

Francis of Lorraine, 418

Franciscans, 313; poverty and, 214–215; William of Ockham and, 244–245

Franco, Francisco (general), 627

Franconia, 215

Frankincense, 20

Franks, 132, 135, 160; aristocracy, 185–187; Clovis of, 148, 177, 179, 182, 183, 185, 188; collapse of, 195; eastern kingdoms, 215; legacy of, 182–183; Martel and, 188–189; Pippin III of, 189; Salian, 182

Franz Josef I (king), 512

Frederick I Barbarossa, 218

Frederick I Barbarossa (emperor), 206

Frederick II "the Great," 218, 414, 415, 418, 445

Frederick III of Saxony (prince), 303

Frederick III "the Wise" (king), 301

Frederick V "the Winter King" (king), Thirty Years' War and, 336–337, 340

Frederick William I "the Great Elector," 379, 414–415

Frederick William IV (king), 510–511

Free Speech movement, 674

Free will, 311

Freedom: peasants negotiating, 202; political upheaval, intellectuals, artists and, 497–498

Freemen, 51, 183–184; miles, knights and, 202–203; serfs and, 200–202. *See also* Peasants

Free-standing statues, 256–257

French Revolution (1789-1815), 503–504; chronology, 464; civil liberties and, 458; convening estates-general and, 451–453; counterrevolution and, 459; declaring political rights and, 457–458; end of, 463; experimenting with democracy and, 460–463; fall of monarchy and, 449–460; fiscal crisis and, 459–460; Jacobin ascendancy, 461–462; Napoleonic era and, 449–470; Napoleon's reign and, 464–469; outbreak of revolutionary action in 1789 and, 453–457; peasant fear of aristocratic plot and, 455–456; peasant revolt and, 456; people's revolution and, 460–461; political/fiscal crisis in eighteenth century and, 450–451; Robespierre, reign of terror and, 462; storming of Bastille and, 454; terror and, 461–463; Thermidorian reaction and, 463; trials of constitutional monarchy and, 458–460; women excluded and, 462–463; women marching and, 456–457; women's rights and, 458

French wars of religion: Calvinism, religious division and, 321–322; civil war and, 322; Saint Bartholomew's Day massacre and, 322–323, 324

Freud, Sigmund, 555

Friedan, Betty, 673

Frisians, 180

Funeral masks, 37

G

Gaius. *See* Caligula

Galapagos Islands, 534

Galen, 261, 262, 388

Galerian, 136, 138

Galileo Galilei, 387, 388, 389, 390

Galli, Jacopo, 258

Galton, Francis, 579

Gandhi, Mohandas, 661

Garibaldi, Giuseppe, 518, 519, 520

Gas, poison, 619, 638

Goddesses, 32, 43; Athena, 44, 45; Minoan Crete's mother, 34; Venus, 100. *See also specific goddesses*

Godwinson, Harold (earl), 221

Goebbels, Joseph, 623, 624

Gold, 11, 578; Aztec, 278; coins, 50, 177; empire building, Boer War, territory and, 572–573; European empires, God, glory and, 279; foreign-owned, 610; Great Depression and standard of, 610, 625; as liquid assets, 353; new world, 290; shortage, 273

Golden Bull edict, 228–229

Gondebaud (king), 177

Gorbachev, Mikhail, 678–679, 682, 684

Gorgias, 67

Göring, Hermann (general), 635

Gothic architecture, 256

Goths, 147, 148; confederation of, 135; conversion to Christianity by, 149

Gouges, Olympe de, 462

Government: Carolingian, 192–193; communal, 209; decline of royal, 217–218; England's Instrument of, 376; English, 365–368, 376; Europe and, 187–188; French, 366; Imperial Rome and crisis in, 109–110; Islam and, 165–166; military and rise of Roman, 131–132; Polish Diet, 331–332, 334; royal state and drive to centralize, 365–366; rule of four and, 136; Spanish, 366–367; Sweden's Rad and, 333; Weimar Republic and, 619–620; WWI and controls of, 593–594

Gracchus, Gaius, 108–109, 127

Gracchus, Tiberius, 108, 109, 116, 127

Grandes, 435

Great Britain: America's revolt and, 424–426; appeasement policy and, 632; banking collapse in, 610; Big Five and, 559; Big Three and, 651; chartist movement and, 506–507; Constitution of, 421; cotton factories and, 481; domestic industries and, 479–480; early coal mining in, 478–479; economic infrastructure in, 477–478; eighteenth-century Europe, power and greatness of, 420–426; entrepreneurs, managers and, 482–484; family and welfare in, 672; first railways in, 481; Gladstone, Disraeli and, 526–528; from goods to passengers and, 482; Great Powers and, 504–505, 517; Hitler and battle of, 634–636; industrial revolution in, 476–487; international loans, trade barriers and, 608–609; iron horse and, 481–482; king cotton and, 479–481; Marshall Plan and, 665; minerals, metals and, 478–479; muddling through, 625–626; Owens' mills and, 484; Parliamentary reform and, 526, 542–543; parties and ministers of, 422–423; reform in, 505–507; rule of land in, 506; slow recovery and, 625; social costs and, 486; spheres of influence and, 575; steam engine and, 479; Tories, 422; Victorian compromise and, 526–528; wages of progress and, 484–486; war in South Africa, 572–573; water and coal in, 477; wealth expansion and, 485; Wedgwood's pottery and, 483–484; Whigs, 422. *See also* England

Great Chain of Being, 350–351, 386

Great Council, 266

Great Elector. *See* Frederick William I "the Great Elector"

Great Khan, 208. *See also* Kublai Khan

Great Powers, 504–505, 517

Great Purge, 616

Great Rebellion, 238

Great Reform Bill of 1832, 506

Great Reforms, 529

Great Schism, 241, 245, 265

Great Trek, 572

Great War. *See* World War I

Greater East Asia Co-Prosperity Sphere, 648

Great Depression, 620, 697; dependence on U.S. economy and, 609–610; gold standard and, 610, 625; political repercussions and, 610

Greece: Archaic, 38–54; Bronze Age, 31–37; classical and Hellenistic, 57–81; democracy in, 71; early, 31–56; koine dialect of, 76; Marshall Plan and, 665; Mycenaen, 34–36; philosophy and polis in, 71–72; sexuality in, 42; temples and, 42; terrain of, 31; trade collapse in, 36. *See also* Athens

Greece, Archaic (700-500 B.C.E.): art and individuals in, 44–45; Athens in, 50–54; chronology, 43; colonists and tyrants, 40–41; coming of Persia and end of, 54; Corinth in, 45–47; ethnos and polis in, 39, 40, 43; gender and power in, 41–42;

Ionia, 54, 58, 59
Ionian Sea, 31
Ionians, 36, 57
Iran, 28, 164, 167; first civilizations and, 6
Iraq, 164, 167; first civilizations and, 6
Ireland, 594; Christianity, conversion and, 180–181; famine in, 502; Irish home rule and, 543
Irene (queen), 193
Iron, 15, 36, 83, 564
Iron horse, 481–482
Irrigation systems, 167
Isabella of Castile (queen), 229, 230, 275; *reconquista* and, 288–289; tapestry of, 290
Ishtar, 11
Isidorus of Miletus, 154, 155
Isis (goddess), 122
Islam: 'Abbasid revolution and, 166–167; Arabia before prophet and, 160–161; Arabian faith and, 163; authority and government in, 165–166; Bedouin society and, 161; Christian invasion and, 169; civilization, 167–169; classical legacy of Byzantium and, 153–175; conversion to, 163; division, revolt and, 167; harams and, 161; Hijra and, 162; Judaism, Christianity and, 162; last orthodox caliphs and, 165–166; marriage contracts and, 163; Muhammad and, 161–162; philosophy and, 169; preaching, 162; return to Mecca and, 163; rise of, 160–169; science, faith and, 168–169; Shi'a, 166; spread of, 163–164; triumph of, 162–163; Turks and, 167; Umayyad caliphate and, 166; Umma and, 165; women in early, 163
Isle of Wight Festival, 674
Israel, 23, 663; establishment of kingdom of, 25–26; map of, 25; slaves and, 25; Yahweh as god of, 24, 26. *See also* Hebrew society
Israelites, 22, 29. *See also* Israel
Istanbul, 155
Italian city-states: decline of, 269–270; end of hegemony and, 269–270; five powers, 263, 265–266; Florence as banking and wool center, 267–269; political and military unrest in, 269; politics of, 263–270; Venice as seaborne empire, 266–267
Italian Renaissance, 271–272; architect, sculptor, painter and, 256–258; art, 255–259; artistic style, 256–258; childhood

and, 252–253; church and, 254–255; cities, countryside and, 250–251; civic humanism and, 261; decline, 269–270; end of hegemony and, 269–270; experience of life in, 252–254; five political powers and, 263, 265–266; Florence and, 267–269; humanists, liberal arts and, 256–258, 259–261; ideals, 259–262; Machiavelli, politics and, 262; marriage and family in, 253–254; Michelangelo and, 258–259; philology, Valla and, 261; political and military unrest during, 269; politics of city-states, 263–270; population decline and, 252; production and consumption in, 251–252; quality of life in, 254–255; science, 261–262; society, 249–255; studying classical world and, 260–261; Venice and, 266–267
Italian wars, European empires and, 291–294
Italy, 36, 46, 82; Cavour's political realism and, 518–520; chronology of politics in, 270; cities in medieval, 208–209; communal government in medieval, 209; early republic and, 90; ECSC and, 666; EEC and, 666; first civilization of Etruscans in, 85–86; incorporating conquered peoples and, 92; king for unified, 520–521; Lombard conquest of, 179; map of, 264; map of medieval trade networks and, 210; Marshall Plan and, 665; medieval towns in, 208–215; merchants and capitalists in medieval, 208–209; Mussolini's, 617–619; Northern towns in medieval, 209–211; Ostrogoth and Lombard barbarians in, 177–179; patricians, plebians and public law in, 90–91; pirates and, 92; political expansion and, 91–92; population data, 369; renaissance, 249–272; revolutions and nationalism in, 512; rise of fascist dictatorship in, 617–619; Rome and, 90–92; slave revolts in, 107; unification map, 519; unifying, 518–521; vernacular literature and, 246; Villanovans in, 83; wars of, 270. *See also* Rome
Ivan III "the Great," 283, 331
Ivan IV "the Terrible," 283–284, 331, 332
Ivory, 274

J

"J'accuse!", 545
Jacobins, 461–462, 503

Order of Friars Minor, 214. *See also* Franciscans

Oresteia (Aeschylus), 69

Origen of Alexandria: Christianity and, 142, 143, 169; western thinkers and philosophy of, 213

Orlando, Vittorio Emanuele, 602

Orléans, 233, 287

Osiris (god), 16

Ostracism, 58

Ostrogoths, 155, 157, 183; Italy, Lombards to, 177–179; kingdom of, 177–179; Theodoric of, 148, 177

Oswy of Northumbria (king), 181

Otto I. *See* Otto the Great (emperor)

Otto the Great (emperor), 197, 215; imperial church as cornerstone to empire and, 215–216

Ottoman empire, 317, 504, 517; Central Powers and, 587, 588, 594; Europe, world and, 560–561; map of, 173; Suleiman the Magnificent and, 293; Turks, 269; WWI and, 592

Ovid, 118

Owen, Robert, 483, 484

Owls, as symbol of Athena, 52

P

Pachomius, 144

Pacification of Ghent, 329

Pacific: WWII and winning in, 650; WWII map of, 649

Padua medical school, 262

Paganism, 147; Bedouins and, 161; Christian missionaries and Anglo-Saxon, 180–182; disestablishment of, 139; solar symbols and, 138; torture used against, 139

Paintings: cave, 6, 7; as cultural record, 6, 7

Pakistan, 74

Palace(s): as city center, 13; complexes, 32; Linear B writing in Mycenaean, 34

Palaeologus, Michael, 173

Paleolithic era (Old Stone Age), 5, 29

Palermo, 369

Palestine, 23, 54, 111, 155, 167, 169, 206, 663; Jews in, 120, 122, 549, 551

Palestinian Black September movement, 693

Pan-African Federation, 663

Panama Canal, 577

Pan-Hellenic cult centers, 42

Pankhurst, Christabel (daughter), 547

Pankhurst, Emmeline, 547

Pankhurst, Sylvia (daughter), 547

Papacy: abuses of, 316; Avignon, 240–241; benefices and, 241; chronology of Carolingians and, 194; college of cardinals and, 240; conciliarism and, 241–242; curia and, 240–241; Donation of Constantine and, 261; excommunications by, 172, 303; Fourth Lateran Council and, 219; Great Schism and, 241, 245, 265; indulgences and, 241, 300–301; pinnacle of power by, 219; Pisan and Avignon popes and, 241–242; power and, 193; prominent popes and religious figures of high middle ages and, 219; revenue sources for, 240–241; Roman Question and, 618; spirituality and crisis of, 240–242; spread of, 197–198; universal authority claimed by, 216, 218; universal states, empire and, 215–219. *See also specific popes*

Paracelsus, 388

Parallel Lives (Plutarch), 126

Paris, 364; as center of educational movement, 212–213; commune, 536–537; peace of, 404, 517; rebuilding, 525; siege of, 535; University of, 213, 227; uprisings, 237

Parliament, 282; bill of 1911, 542; Civil War and long, 374, 375; House of Commons, 366, , 378; extraparliamentary protest and, 526–543; Germany's, 543–544; House of Commons, 368, 379, 422, 542; House of Lords, 368, 542; laws passed by, 286; reform of, 526, 542–543; religion legislated through, 310

Passchendaele, 591

Pasteur, Louis, 553

Patent of Toleration, 434

Paterfamilias (male head of household), 88, 98, 102

Patricians (descendants of fathers), 88, 90–91, 95, 176

Patronage, Roman poetry and, 118

Paul (saint), 302

Paul III (pope), 314

Paul of Tarsus, 124–125, 128

Pavia, 292, 293

Pavlov, Ivan, 555

Pax Romana (Peace of Rome), Augustus and, 115–121, 127

influenced by, 134–135; Constantine and, 138–139; crisis of third century in, 130–135; Diocletian and, 130, 136–138, 152; economic disaster in, 131, 132; empire restored in, 136–139; external threats and, 132–133; fiscal reform and, 137–138; imperial Christianity and, 140–146; militarized society and, 136–137; parting of ways and, 147–151; rise of military government in, 131–132; slaves in, 133; tetrarchy and, 136; transformation of, 130–152; triumph of Christianity in, 139

Rome, Early (800-146 B.C.E.): adoption in, 99; chronology, 97; from city to empire, 509-146 B.C.E., 87–96; crisis of virtue in, 101–103; equestrian order and, 98; families in, 98–99, 102; farmers and soldier in, 98; religion in, 100; republican civilization in, 97–101; republican letters in, 101; Roman republic and, 82–104; slaves in, 99; social effects of expansion and, 99; treatment of children in, 99; western Mediterranean to 509 B.C.E., 82–86

Rome, Imperial (146 B.C.E.-192 C.E.): Augustan age and *Pax Romana* in, 115–121, 127; Caesar and, 110, 111, 112; civil wars in, 110; crisis in government and, 109–110; culture of Antonine, 126–127; end of republic in, 109–114; *equites* or equestrians in, 106, 110; Jugurtha and, 109; oligarchy's optimates in, 105–108, 110, 128; philosophy and, 113–114; price of empire in, 105–109; provincial revolts in, 107; religions from east and, 121–126; Republican crisis in, 110–111; slave revolts in, 107; triumverates and, 111–113, 128; war's influence on winners and losers in, 105–107

Rommell, Erwin (general), 647

Romulus, 87

Roosevelt, Franklin D., 636, 644, 645; winning WWII and, 646–648

Rothschild, Baron de, 551

Rousseau, Henri, 556

Rousseau, Jean-Jacques, 432, 462–463, 498

Rousseau Henri, 556

Royal power: Akhenaten's consolidation of religion and, 21; counts, counties, ealdormen, shires and, 188; decline of Egyptian, 19; demise of, 530; marriage alliances and, 227, 293; royal administration and, 188; royal councils and, 367; "rulers of foreign lands" and assumption of, 19–20; taxation and, 287–288. *See also* Kings; Monarchy

Royal state: absolutism in east and, 379–380; court and courtiers in, 365; crisis of, 368–378; divine kings and, 364–365; drive to centralize government and, 365–366; English civil war and, 372–375; English revolutions and, 375–377; Louis le Grand and, 382–384; nature of absolute monarchy and, 379; need to resist and, 368–369; origins of French absolutism and, 380–382; right to resist and, 370–372; rise of, 363–368; in seventeenth century, 363–384; taxing demands of war and, 367–368; zenith of, 377–384

Rubens, Peter Paul, 314, 364

Russia: absolutism and, 379–380; Alexander II and emancipation of serfs in, 528–529; Big Five and, 559, 560; Bonaparte, Battle of Nations and invasion of, 468–469; breakaway republics lead the way and, 684–685; Cold War, new republics and, 682–685; dual power and, 596–597; economic challenges, 683; eighteenth-century Europe, power and rise of, 408–413; enlightened Empress Catherine and rise of, 412–413; expansion of, 381; Great Powers and, 504–505, 517; great reforms in, 529; last tear and, 595–596; Lenin, opposition to WWI and, 597–598; life in rural, 411–412; mafia in, 683; nationalities problem and, 683–684; October revolution and, 598–599, 613; Peter the Great's reforms and, 409–411; population data, 369; populist movement in, 529; reforming, 528–529; serf-holding nation of, 528; treaty of Brest-Litovsk, 599–600; war with Japanese and, 576; WWI allied victory and revolution in, 595–601; WWI mobilization plan and, 585–586; Yeltsin in power in, 682. *See also* Soviet Union

Russo-Japanese War, 576

Rutherford, Ernest, 553

S

Sahara Desert, 16, 18

Saint Bartholomew's Day Massacre, 322–323, 324

Crusades; Revolutions; World War I; World War II

War Guilt Clause, 604

Warfare, 13; chariots, 20; chief officers selected by lot for, 58; da Vinci's sketches for, 262; germ, 695; gunpowder and, 282; hoplites in, 40, 41; Hundred Years' War, chivalry and, 230–231; longbows and, 231; phalange in, 40; scorched-earth policy and, 189; technology of, 39–40; trench, 587; WWI and new kind of, 587–592. *See also* the Military; Sparta

Warrior(s): aristocracy, heiresses and, 202–205; graves, 34; monks and bishops as spiritual, 206. *See also* Knighthood; Knights

Warrior bands. *See* Comitatus

Wars of Liberation, 496

Wars of the Roses, 233, 285

Warsaw Confederation, Poland-Lithuania and, 331

Warsaw Pact, 660, 668

Water: aqueducts and, 116; canals and, 11, 13, 89; coal and, 477; hydraulic systems and, 86; irrigation systems and, 167; supplies, 11

Waterloo, 469, 496

Watt, James, 479

The Way of Perfection (Saint Teresa), 313

Wealth: Corinth's, 45; Great Britain's expansion of, 485; monasteries, power and, 205–206

Weapons: bombs, 627, 658, 660; flamethrowers and barbed wire, 588; gunpowder, 282; ICBMs, 660; longbows, 231; machine guns, 570–571, 588; metal and alloy, 11; nuclear, 660–661; poison gas, 588, 619, 638; tank production in 1944, 627, 644; WWI and new, 587–588

Weddings, 359–360. *See also* Marriage contracts

Wedgwood, Joshua, 483–484

Weimar Republic, 619–620

Welfare state: Cold War, social transformation and, 670–675; family strategies and, 671–673; prosperity, consumption in west and, 670–671; youth culture, dissent and, 673–675

Wenceslas IV (king), 244

West Germany, 658; ECSC and, 666; EEC and, 666; Marshall Plan and, 665; unification of Germany and, 682

Western civilization: concept/idea of "west" in, 1; idea of, 1–3; legacies, 2

Westinghouse, George, 553

What Is Enlightenment (Kant), 429

What Is Property (Proudhon), 500

Whigs, 422

White Mountain, battle of, 336, 337

Wilkinson, John, 479

William III (king), 377, 401–402

William of Normandy, 220, 221

William of Ockham, 244–245

William of Orange (king), 328, 336, 376, 377, 400

William the Conqueror (king), 221–222

Wilson, Woodrow, 600; fourteen points and, 602–603

Winged Victory (*Nike*), 78

Witches: craze, 361–362; discerning spirit of God, witchcraft and, 242; early modern Europe and persecution of, 360–361; magical practices and, 360–361

Witches' Hammer, 242

Wittelsbachs, 226–227

Wittenberg, Germany, 301, 302

Wizards, 360

Wladislaw II, 284

Woden (war god), 135

Women: aristocratic society's influence on, 186–187; Athenian, 61–62; Bible's portrayal of, 305; biology and destiny of, 555–556; changing lives, 692; Christian humanism and education for, 298; Christianity and, 125–126; convents and, 313; countryside living and, 201–202; courtly love and, 204; deities, 34; domestic violence and, 692; in early Islam, 163; Easter Bloc wages for, 668; equality of men and, 77; Etruscan's elevated status of, 86; familial power and Roman, 98–99; families and beginnings of protest by, 672–673; family roles and, 357, 358; fertility, religion and, 7; French Revolution and exclusion of, 462–463; gender, power, ancient Egypt's bureaucracy and, 18; Hammurabi's code protecting childen and, 14; as head of households, 184; Hellenistic kingdoms and public lives of, 76–77; Hitler targeting

637–642; enforcing Nazi racial policies in, 637; Europe in, 632–633; fall of France in, 634; fate of allied cooperation and, 650–651; final solution and, 638–640; German declares war on U.S. in, 645–646; Hitler's foreign policy and appeasement in, 631–632; Hitler's war and, 632–636; Japanese attacks in, 645; Japanese war aims and assumptions in, 648; Jews' death in, 641–642; map of Europe, 634; map of Pacific in, 649; racism and destruction in, 636–642; resisting destruction and, 640–641; Soviet Union's great patriotic war and, 642–644; tank production in 1944 for, 644; U.S. enters, 644–646; winning in Europe, 646–647; winning in Pacific, 650

Writers: Dhuoda, 191; Hellenistic, 78; Herodotus, 68; Thucydides, 69. *See also* Playwrights; Poets

Writing: Caroline miniscule and, 191; cuneiform and, 11; disappearance of, 36; Linear A, 32; Mesopotamia's technology and, 10–11; Phoenician technology of, 39–40; pictograms and, 11, 19

WSPU. *See* Women's Social and Political Union

Wundr, Wilhelm, 555

Wycliffe, John, 243

X

Xavier, Francis, 315

Xenophobia, 568

Xerxes (king), 58, 59, 60, 85

X-rays, 553

Y

Yahweh (god), 24, 26, 140

"Year of the Four Emperors," 119, 121

Yeltsin, Boris, 679; in power, 682

Yemen, 160

Young Plan, 609

Youth: Hitler, 620, 623; state terrorism by Sparta's, 48

Youth culture: anti-war movement, social protest and, 674; Cold War, dissent and, 673–675; protest, economy and, 675; sexual revolution and, 673–674

Yugoslavia, 685–686

Z

Zacharias (pope), 189

Zagros Mountains, 14, 22

Zealots, 122

Zemsky Sobor, 332

Zeno (emperor), 79, 148, 153

Zeus (god), 42, 100

Zhukov, Gyorgi (general), 643

Ziggurats, 12

Zimmermann, Arthur, 600

Zionism: anti-Semitism and, 548–549; map of Jewish migration and, 550; mass politics, Jewish question and, 548–551

Zola, Émile, 545

Zollverein, 491–492

Zoroastrians, 165

Zwingli, Huldrych, 308, 311, 318; doctrinal issues between Luther and, 317; mass and, 306, 312

Additional Titles of Interest

Note to Instructors: These selected titles can be packaged with this book at a significant discount. Contact your local Pearson sales representative for details on how to create a Penguin Value Package.

Anonymous, *The Epic of Gilgamesh*
Homer, *The Iliad*
Homer, *The Odyssey*
Herodotus, *The Histories*
Plato, *The Republic*
St. Augustine, *The Confession of St. Augustine*
Procopius, *The Secret History*
Einhard, *Two Lives of Charlemagne*
Anonymous, *The Song of Roland*
Abelard, *The Letters of Abelard & Heloise*
Alighieri, *The Divine Comedy*
De Pizan, *Treasure of the City of Ladies*
Machiavelli, *The Prince*
More, *Utopia*
De Cervantes, *Don Quixote*
Rousseau, *The Social Contract*
Shelly, *Frankenstein*
Mill, *On Liberty*
Von Clausewitz, *On War*
Marx, *The Communist Manifesto*
Orwell, *1984*
Solzhenitsyn, *One Day in the Life of Ivan Denisovich*

For a complete list of titles, go to: *http://www.pearsonhighered.com/historyvaluepacks/*